Community Treatment for Youth

Evidence-Based Interventions for Severe
Emotional and Behavioral Disorders

Barbara J. Burns
Duke University Medical Center

Kimberly Hoagwood
National Institute of Mental Health

New York   Oxford
Oxford University Press
2002

Oxford University Press

Oxford   New York
Athens Auckland Bangkok Bogotá Buenos Aires Cape Town
Chennai Dar es Salaam Delhi Florence Hong Kong Istanbul Karachi
Kolkata Kuala Lumpur Madrid Melbourne Mexico City Mumbai Nairobi
Paris São Paulo Shanghai Singapore Taipei Tokyo Toronto Warsaw

and associated companies in
Berlin Ibadan

Published by Oxford University Press, Inc.
198 Madison Avenue, New York, New York 10016
http://www.oup-usa.org

Oxford is a registered trademark of Oxford University Press

Library of Congress Cataloging-in-Publication Data

Burns, Barbara J.
  Community treatment for youth : evidence-based interventions for severe emotional
and behavioral disorders / Barbara J. Burns, Kimberly Hoagwood.
     p. cm. — (Innovations in practice and service delivery with vulnerable populations)
  Includes bibliographical references and index.
  ISBN 0-19-513457-5 (alk. paper)
    1. Youth—Mental health services. 2. Community mental health services. 3. Adolescent
psychiatry. 4. Evidence-based medicine. I. Haogwood, Kimberly. II. Title. III. Series.

RJ503 .B87 2002
362.2'083—dc21

2001054571

Printing number: 9 8 7 6 5 4 3

Printed in the United States of America
on acid-free paper

To my eight nieces and nephews, for sharing lessons learned in mastering childhood, and who are now applying those lessons as parents to my eleven great-nieces and great-nephews.

—B.J.B.

To my daughter, Hilary, from whom I have learned the value of questioning adult assumptions about children.

—K.H.

Innovations in Practice and Service Delivery with Vulnerable Populations

Series Editors:

David E. Biegel, Ph.D.
Arthur Blum, D.S.W.
Case Western Reserve University

Volume 1: *Innovations in Practice and Service Delivery Across the Lifespan*, David E. Biegel and Arthur Blum

Volume 2: *Community Treatment for Youth: Evidence-Based Interventions for Severe Emotional and Behavioral Disorders*, Barbara J. Burns and Kimberly Hoagwood

This series is sponsored by the Mandel School of Applied Social Sciences, Case Western Reserve University.

Contents

WITHDRAWN

Part I. Context

Part II. Comprehensive Interventions

Foreword

It is a genuine pleasure for me to introduce to readers this remarkable volume by Burns and Hoagwood. Why? Simply stated, the book reflects the convergence of the growing evidence base for child mental health treatment. This is reflected even by the identities of the editors themselves, who to my mind represent the finest leadership, thinking, and research in children's mental health services and intervention, as well as the activities of the federal components with the major investments in this area.

Synthesizing current theory, evidence, and implementation approaches, the editors have brought together an outstanding group of authors, all leaders in their own right. This volume assembles the growing scientific evidence for specific interventions inside the "black box" of mental health services; the research data describing the impact of *how* these interventions are assembled, provided, and coordinated; *and* the merits of the *values* underpinning newer forms of service delivery. Extended discussion of the presumably polar opposites of "efficacy versus effectiveness" studies is refreshlying absent, since the current need of the child mental services research community is to fuse these historically discrete approaches, building efficacious treatment interventions within effective, compassionate, and competent systems of care.

The various chapters not only define the values implicit in our newer systems of care, but also describe the research studies that have operationalized and tested these values- and research-based interventions with these systems of care approaches. Terms that too easily can become jargon, such as "wraparound," "culturally competent," "family centered," "system of care," and even "case management," are defined by leaders in the field, and the studies describing the implementation of these constructs are reviewed. A remarkable bonus of the volume is the comprehensive annotated review of the evidence base for psychosocial and psychopharmacological interventions for children with various mental disorders—the most informative and up-to-date review that I have seen anywhere.

Moving us beyond the status quo, the volume closes with an elegant summary of what remains to be done, not just in terms of specific types of studies, but also in terms of the necessary further integration of empirical methods with the values that place responsibility and control of mental health services delivery with the families and communities these programs are intended to benefit.

Peter S. Jensen, M.D.
Ruane Professor for the Implementation of
    Science in Children's Mental Health, and
Director, Center for the Advancement of
    Children's Mental Health,
College of Physicians and Surgeons
Columbia University

Preface

The historical context for this book arises from a tradition of placing youth with severe emotional and behavioral disorders in institutional care away from their homes and communities. At the present time, this continues to occur despite evidence of negative outcomes and fiscal and personal expense. A belief among caregivers and families that institutional placement is in the best interest of these youth perpetuates this phenomena. However, several fairly recent bodies of evidence have made it possible to reassess this approach to care. Controlled studies of institutional care have found no evidence of benefit (e.g., a lack of positive outcomes) in such settings as psychiatric hospitals, residential treatment centers, and detention centers. As long as placement was the only option to protect youth from themselves and/or to protect society, a shift in this pattern of care remained unlikely. The current availability of evidence for effective home- and community-based interventions makes it possible for communities to redirect their approach to care—and many are beginning to do so.

This book was inspired primarily by a wish to bring together in one volume the available information about evidence-based interventions for youth with severe emotional and behavioral disorders. The comprehensive interventions described in detail in part II are intensive services that are based in the home or community. Targeted psychosocial and psychopharmacological treatments are subsequently identified in part III. These diagnostic-specific approaches can be used either in conjunction with or following the former set of interventions. We also present these interventions in the context of system of care concepts, policy implications, training requirements, and research directions.

The editors recognize that revolutionary change is necessary to improve outcomes for youth. Many answers to the questions of what works and for whom are still unknown. Nevertheless, the significant growth in the research base over the past two decades is sufficiently robust to suggest that new findings be incorporated into standard clinical care. As these new approaches become the standards for clinical care, the research base will also concurrently

---

AUTHORS' NOTE: The material in the Preface is in the public domain and may be reproduced without the permission of the authors or the publisher.

continue to expand with a similar level of diligence, commitment, and good science.

This book was created through close collaboration between the editors and the chapter authors. Michael English, J.D., Director, Division of Knowledge Development and Systems Change, Center for Mental Health Services, assisted us initially with identifying the interventions and the authors who could address them from the perspectives of theory, practice, and research. We are most grateful to the chapter authors and coauthors for their willingness to follow a uniform outline and to be responsive to feedback over several iterations. Support from the National Institute of Mental Health, Duke University Medical Center, and the Center for Mental Health Services was critical. We are especially appreciative to two Duke staff members: Linda Maultsby, who conscientiously and creatively oversaw the publication process from beginning to end, and Elizabeth Potter, for her diligent assistance and attention to detail. We are grateful to David Beigel, Ph.D., Case Western Reserve University, for his initiative to include this book in the Oxford University Press Series "Innovations in Practice and Service Delivery with Vulnerable Populations," for which he and Arthur Blum, DSW, are coeditors. We would also like to thank our editors at Oxford University Press, Jeffrey Broesche and Lisa Grzan, whose steady and gentle encouragement helped move the book to fruition.

In conclusion, making innovative therapeutic interventions available to high-risk youth and their families, as well as pursuing a clearly delineated research agenda, will require the efforts of many groups of people. These include practitioners in child-serving agencies and organizations (mental health, education, juvenile justice, child welfare, substance abuse, and primary health care), educators and students, administrators and policymakers, scientists, and children and families. This book is devoted to the concerns of these groups. We encourage them to apply their diverse capabilities to implementing state-of-the-art care and linking science to service delivery.

Through such linkages, the editors and chapter authors hope that the movement which has already begun to bring effective community-based care *home* to youth and families will become a permanent hallmark of mental health care for this country.

Barbara J. Burns
Kimberly Hoagwood

Part I

Context

1

Reasons for Hope for Children and Families: A Perspective and Overview

BARBARA J. BURNS

There are many reasons for hope in the field of child mental health. When the focus is effective treatment for youth with severe emotional and behavioral disorders, what is a relatively young field has come of age in the past decade. In stark contrast to a history of placing such youth far away from their homes, most often with poor results, the potential for children and their families to receive evidence-based care in their own communities now exists (see U.S. DHHS Surgeon General's Report, 1999). Whether this potential will be further realized relies upon multiple stakeholders accepting the challenge to implement evidence-based interventions for youth with severe emotional and behavioral problems.

A doubting parent, clinician, educator, administrator, or policymaker might well question the basis for hope for improved treatment and better outcomes for youth. Children and adolescents at risk for emotional and behavioral problems are likely to have experienced: (1) significant early traumas, such as loss of major people in their lives or exposure to violence; (2) impaired functioning at home, in school, and or in the neighborhood; (3) a negative concept of self; (4) co-occurring disorders (i.e., combinations of behavioral, attention-deficit/ hyperactivity, anxiety, depressive, and substance-abuse disorders); and (5) being bounced from one service system to another, including education, health, child welfare, juvenile justice, and mental health. Such children do come to the attention of the various authorities who are responsible for their welfare; their parents and siblings also feel challenged and uncertain about what to do. What happens for these youth and their families beyond the recognition of their emotional or behavioral problems is critical both to their own future and to society, which requires the competence of children expressed in productive living and working.

The target population for interventions presented in this book typify the characteristics described in the preceding paragraph. Youth with a severe emotional or behavioral disorder represent 9–13% of youth across the United States, where the rate is dependent upon the socioeconomic graphic characteristics of

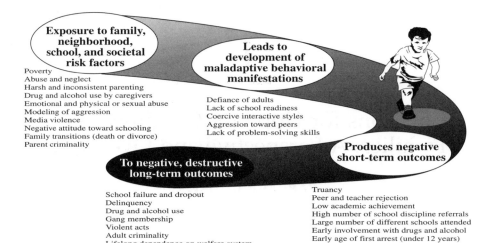

Exposure to family, neighborhood, school, and societal risk factors

Poverty
Abuse and neglect
Harsh and inconsistent parenting
Drug and alcohol use by caregivers
Emotional and physical or sexual abuse
Modeling of aggression
Media violence
Negative attitude toward schooling
Family transitions (death or divorce)
Parent criminality

Leads to development of maladaptive behavioral manifestations

Defiance of adults
Lack of school readiness
Coercive interactive styles
Aggression toward peers
Lack of problem-solving skills

Produces negative short-term outcomes

To negative, destructive long-term outcomes

School failure and dropout
Delinquency
Drug and alcohol use
Gang membership
Violent acts
Adult criminality
Lifelong dependence on welfare system
Higher death and injury rate

Truancy
Peer and teacher rejection
Low academic achievement
High number of school discipline referrals
Large number of different schools attended
Early involvement with drugs and alcohol
Early age of first arrest (under 12 years)

FIGURE 1.1 The Path to Long-Term Negative Outcomes for At-Risk Children and Youth *Source:* Walker & Sprague, (1999).

a given state (Friedman, Katz-Leavy, Manderscheid, & Sondheimer, 1996). These youth typically begin life with multiple risk factors and, depending upon when intervention occurs in their development, are at risk for negative outcomes, which are quite apparent by adolescence. Figure 1.1 graphically displays the increasingly severe sequence of risks and resultant emotional and behavioral problems, if left unattended.

For most childhood disorders, the emergence of symptoms varies with a child's developmental stage. Disorders such as conduct problems or attention-deficit/hyperactivity disorder are likely to appear at quite young ages, while for others (e.g., depression and childhood schizophrenia) the onset is more likely to occur in adolescence. Ideally, intervention would occur at the earliest point in time. There is evidence that preventive interventions with parents during early infancy (U.S. DHHS Surgeon General's Report, 1999) can impact expected negative outcomes during adolescence. While infancy may clearly be the most important time to initiate intervention, the possibility that more high-risk youth will be identified than necessary raises a question of cost for the policymaker. Intervening with high-risk children in early childhood (preschool) is another option, as is beginning to work with them during elementary school or early adolescence. As the evidence base becomes more clearly delineated by developmental stage, it will be more possible to prevent long-term impairment. The evidence base as it stands in the present suggests very early intervention during infancy (Olds et al., 1997); diagnostic-specific interventions during elementary school; and then, as necessary, more intensive home- and community-based interventions for adolescents usually with multiple co-occurring disorders.

The provision of effective treatment in the community depends first upon evidence of benefits and second upon demonstration of the feasibility of dissemination into a usual care treatment setting. The four factors listed below provide the basis for hope and the rationale for taking action to implement care in community instead of institutional settings. They include:

- significant growth in the evidence documenting positive outcomes for community-based interventions;
- increased understanding about how to change clinical practice;
- the availability of tools and training approaches to improve clinical practice; and
- policy to facilitate and support implementation of selected community-based interventions.

Each of these points, as they relate to the content of this book, are developed subsequently.

The Evidence Base

A discussion of the evidence base needs to begin with some understanding of what is meant by evidence. Briefly, the development of scientific knowledge in the health field has relied on controlled studies (randomized clinical trials [RCTs], quasi-experimental designs, or a series of single-case designs) that typically compare the benefits of a new treatment with usual care or with another established treatment. Requirements for considering an intervention to be "well-established" or "probably efficacious" were recently established by the Society of Clinical Psychology (Lonigan, Elbert, & Johnson, 1998). At least two well-conducted group-design studies or a large series of single-case design studies conducted by at least two investigators are required to meet the "well-established" criteria, whereas an intervention tested by a single investigator qualifies as "probably efficacious." In addition, the use of a treatment manual is preferred and sample characteristics must be clearly specified. Additional criteria include: (1) evidence of uniform therapist training and of therapist adherence to planned procedures, (2) clinical samples of youth who clearly would have been candidates for treatment, (3) tests of clinical significance of outcomes, (4) inclusion of functioning outcomes in addition to symptoms, and (5) assessment of long-term outcomes well beyond treatment termination (Chambless et al., 1996).

These criteria have also been applied to psychosocial interventions for five categories of childhood mental disorders: disruptive behavior (Brestan & Eyberg, 1998), anxiety (Ollendick & King, 1998), autism (Rogers, 1998), attention-deficit/hyperactivity (Pelham, Wheeler, & Chronis, 1998), and depression (Kaslow & Thompson, 1998). These reviews revealed multiple "well-established" or "probably efficacious" interventions for all conditions except autism. However, since the major focus of this book is on alternatives to institutional

Table 1.1   The Evidence Base for Comprehensive Interventions

Intervention Type	Controlled Studies
Case Management (see chapter 3): An approach to assessing, planning, and coordinating treatment, linking to formal or informal services; may be done by single case manager or team. A small caseload and greater intensity of services differentiates intensive case management from case management.	2 randomized clinical trials (RCTs), 1 quasi-experimental design
Wraparound (see chapter 4): A team approach to case management and treatment provision distinguished by no time limits, flexible funds, and other specified requirements.	2 RCTs 2 quasi-experimental designs
Multisystemic Therapy (see chapter 5): Associated with family preservation: A clinician works with parents in the home and neighborhood around the management of child problems on a daily basis if necessary, but for a limited period of time (3–5 months).	7 RCTs, 1 quasi-experimental design
Treatment Foster Care (see chapter 6): Foster parents with professional training are supervised to work with children who live in their homes.	4 RCTs
Mentoring (see chapter 7): A nonprofessional with good child relationship skills helps children increase their engagement in school or in the community after school, up to 5 days a week.	1 RCT
Family Education and Support (see chapter 8): Often a parent-led group designed to increase understanding of childhood disorders and offer peer (parent) support to decrease the stress of other parents.	2 RCTs (including 1 underway)

placement, the use of single diagnosis-specific interventions identified in the above reviews probably would not be sufficient for the target population of this book; those interventions receive only brief attention in chapter 11. This same limitation also applies to psychopharmacology (see chapters 11 and 12 for consideration of diagnosis-specific psychosocial and psychopharmacological interventions which can be utilized in conjunction with interventions described in earlier chapters). Several examples of interventions designed for specialized settings—that is, special education and trauma with co-occuring substance abuse—are described in chapters 9 and 10.

The preceeding criteria provide a context for considering the evidence for the interventions presented in chapters 3 to 8. A brief definition of each intervention is given in Table 1.1 followed by the number of controlled studies supporting the intervention.

Although the evidence in Table 1.1 is not summarized (except for design), this research offers noteworthy documentation in the relevant chapters, very strong in some cases and emerging in others, and sufficient to encourage dissemination. However, the above intervention types do not include the full set of interventions that are needed and may be effective—for example, respite care and crisis services—because of a lack of published controlled studies (with the exception of one very recent study of respite care; Bruns & Burchard, 2000). As delineated in the final chapter of this book, the development of the knowledge base is a lengthy and complex process that will further benefit the preceding interventions as well as others for which controlled research has not yet been either conducted or published.

The feasibility of disseminating the interventions described—particularly those in parts two, three, and four of this book—will depend on increased understanding of the organizational factors, training, and policy requirements necessary for successful adoption. These alternatives to institutional care (chapters 3 to 8) are quite different from usual outpatient or institutional treatment, which lack evidence of effectiveness. Creating ways to treat children at home may enhance acceptability to families, while also creating challenges for clinicians accustomed to traditional approaches to practice and to administrative personnel who are comfortable with the accountability afforded when services are provided on site (for example, in clinics or hospitals, where clinician behavior is more observable). The research evidence provides a rationale for moving ahead with implementation. Because these interventions represent a significant diversion from usual care, major educational efforts will be necessary to achieve acceptance of these newer approaches which are likely to yield better outcomes. The shared characteristics of the interventions presented in this book offer some clues both about the merits of these approaches and also about the risks vis-à-vis acceptability.

- They function as service components in a system of care and adhere to system of care values (e.g., individualized, family-centered, strengths-based [not pathology-oriented], and culturally competent).
- They are provided in the community—homes, schools, and neighborhoods—not in an office.
- With the exception of multisystemic therapy and sometimes case management, the direct-care providers are not formally clinically trained. They are parents, volunteers, and counselors, although training and supervision are provided by traditionally trained mental health professionals.
- These interventions may operate under the auspices of any of the human service sectors (i.e., education, child welfare, or juvenile justice), not just mental health.
- Their external validity is greatly enhanced because they were developed and studied in the field with real-world child and family clients, in contrast to volunteers in university-based studies.
- When the full continuum of care in the community is in place, they are less expensive to provide than institutional care.

Practice Change

Following the availability of an evidence base, the second reason for hope is based on considerable theory and empirical evidence that can be invoked about changing behavior. While behavioral health providers are experts in changing the behavior of others, in this instance the tables are turned. The focus here is on changing their clinical practice, creating a threat to their status quo which risks chaos for them involving a sense of their work being devalued, doubts about new directions, and their ability to integrate new interventions into practice.

For practitioners to function differently, corresponding responses by educators, administrators, and policymakers are required. At the macro level, sanctions by professional and governmental organizations are needed, followed by curriculum changes in professional graduate programs for the mental health disciplines, as well as undergraduate human services programs. Other stakeholders, such as consumer groups, regulatory agencies, payers, and finally society, all play significant roles in determining whether change will occur. These groups represent external challenges to service organizations, and may either facilitate or inhibit change.

At the local organizational level, a study of dissemination and adoption of psychosocial interventions (Backer, Liberman, & Kuehnel, 1986) identified a number of factors necessary to embed new interventions in service organizations. They include interpersonal contact, outside consultation, organizational support, persistent championship of the intervention, adaptability of the intervention, and availability of credible evidence of success. These factions are relevant to implementation and sustainability within an organization. The change process may begin with practitioners learning new approaches to care; however, successfully embedding new interventions into service organizations so that they can be sustained depends on multiple factors supporting change.

The major approaches to change range from motivational to educational, behavioral, and environmental, and all will be required to implement and sustain the massive reform necessary to make evidence-based interventions for high-risk youth truly available. Each is introduced briefly below.

MOTIVATION

The readiness-to-change model developed by Prochaska and DiClemente (1983) presents change as a process—precommitment, commitment, action, maintenance, and relapse prevention. New behavior is not expected until stage three, when action is actually initiated, versus the earlier stages which are involved with thinking and decision-making. It has been applied to substance-abuse treatment (see chapter 10) and is probably broadly applicable to adopting any new behavior. Other theorists of behavioral change articulated the following eight concepts through an NIMH conference (Fishbein et al., 1992). They might be usefully considered by clinicians preparing to alter their own practice.

- The person forms a strong positive intention, or makes a commitment to perform the behavior.
- There are no environmental constraints that make it impossible for the behavior to occur.

- The person possesses the skills necessary to perform the behavior.
- The person believes that the advantages (benefits, anticipated positive outcomes) of performing the behavior outweigh the disadvantages (costs, anticipated negative outcomes). In other words, the person has a positive attitude toward performing the behavior.
- The person perceives more normative pressure to perform the behavior than to not perform the behavior.
- The person perceives that performance of the behavior is more consistent than inconsistent with his or her self-image, or that it does not violate personal standards.
- The person's emotional reaction to performing the behavior is more positive than negative.
- The person perceives that he or she has the capabilities to perform the behavior under a number of different circumstances. In other words, the person has self-efficacy with respect to executing the behavior in question.

EDUCATION

Most typically, education provided through formal course work or in-service training is the path providers take to learn new treatment approaches. Unfortunately, the message from the research on continuing medical education is that brief courses or lectures are not sufficient to alter clinical practice (Davis, Thomson, Oxman, & Haynes, 1995; Oxman, Thomson, Davis, & Haynes, 1995). Such change requires incorporating new knowledge and skills, requiring understanding and considerable practice. Thus, the message from other research (Katon et al., 1996) is that even when results are achieved through on-site training, consultation, and supervision, such efforts must be ongoing for change to be sustained. This principle is clearly demonstrated in the adoption process for multisystemic therapy—although at some cost, ongoing training, supervision, and monitoring the fidelity of implementation of multisystemic therapy is essential to achieving positive outcomes on a long-term basis (see chapter 5).

In addition to educating providers, another approach is to educate consumers (families and children) about the types of treatments available and the advantages and disadvantages of each. This can place them in the position of being informed to request and then negotiate for what might be best for their child and family.

BEHAVIORAL

A behavioral perspective offers at least three major approaches to practice change. Modeling, through which much of child behavior is originally learned by a child copying a parent's behavior (Bandura, 1971), has been utilized very successfully in the drug industry (viz., the familiar drug detailer) and has recently been adapted to *academic detailing,* whereby a respected leader in the health community promotes an intervention that needs to be adopted by providers. Behavioral feedback to clinicians about the specific interventions they provide offers another way to shape behavior. Feedback that one's clinical practice is deviant (usually through a comparison between a single clinician and the provider group or national standards) offers one way to alter practice before more punitive measures are taken. Also, incentives contribute to positive behavioral change. The old adage that "money matters" is not lost on clinical providers. As certainty increases that evidence-based interventions produce better outcomes, linking reimbursement to the provision of evidence-based interventions could be an option. Finally, environmental factors influence whether new clinical practices are adopted. Sanctions created by professional organizations or local leadership will have an impact, but only if constraints around issues, such as limited time for training to learn new approaches, are removed (Fishbein & Ajzen, 1975).

There is a great deal to learn about effective implementation of innovative interventions. To alter clinical practice for the interventions specified in this book (comprehensive and diagnostic-specific), both for the student and the practicing clinician, priorities will need to be established, support provided, and user-friendly educational approaches and tools developed.

TOOLS AND TRAINING APPROACHES TO GUIDE PRACTICE

In the movement toward implementing evidence-based interventions and outcome-driven practice, tools have been developed by professional organizations, clinicians, policymakers, and investigators to promote appropriate and high-quality care while also emphasizing accountability. Tools for achieving more relevant and consistent clinical practice vary in their development, specificity, and practical applicability to clinical practice.

Six approaches to deriving and implementing quality are described briefly as follows.

1. *Best practices* tend to set out fairly general statements about clinical practice. They may be consumer- or provider-developed, based on consensus, and may or may not be specific either to diagnosis or to specific interventions. An example is "Promising Practices in Wraparound for Children with Serious Emotional Disturbance and Their Families" (Burns & Goldman, 1999).

2. *Practice guidelines* for diagnosis-specific interventions are evidence-based and may be consensus-based as well. They are developed by clinicians and researchers to guide treatment for specific disorders. Those that have been developed for childhood disorders are identified as practice parameters and include attention-deficit/hyperactivity disorder (AACAP, 1991), conduct disorders (AACAP, 1992), anxiety disorders (AACAP, 1993), schizophrenia (McClellan & Werry, 1994), substance-use disorders (AACAP, 1997b), bipolar disorder (AACAP, 1997a), and mental retardation and comorbid mental disorders (AACAP, 1999).

3. *Clinical protocols/manuals* were historically designed to assure adherence to highly specific types of treatment. Previously, rigid adherence to a verbal script was the approach taken, but manuals of today are more likely to expand on principles for implementing a specific intervention (e.g., Henggeler, Schoenwald, Borduin, Rowland, & Cunningham, 1998b, for MST; and VanDenBerg & Grealish, 1998, for wraparound).

4. *Quality monitoring,* usually developed by clinicians to monitor clinical practice, consists of general indicators to assess treatment, such as criteria for admission, treatment continuation, or termination by level of care. They may also include performance indicators that are population-based, such as rates of access to care. In the future we can expect to see quality indicators derived from practice guidelines for specific disorders; for example, the prescription of a selective serotonin reuptake inhibitor, instead of a tricyclic antidepressant, for the treatment of adolescent depression. The American Psychiatric Association Task Force on Quality Indicators for Children will soon release a comprehensive set of quality indicators (mostly evidence-based) for children and adolescents across multiple clinical conditions.

5. *Fidelity/adherence* measures assess the extent to which a given intervention is provided as intended. Developed in research settings, to date these measures have been utilized in controlled and uncontrolled research but not in clinical practice. Among the interventions for youth with severe emotional and behavior disorders, three have reasonably well-developed methods for assessing fidelity: multisystemic therapy (Henggeler et al., 1998b), treatment foster care (Foster Family-Based Treatment Association, 1995; Farmer, Burns, Chamberlain, & Dubs, 2001); and wraparound (Epstein et al., 1998).

6. *Regulations* are specified largely for licensure, accreditation, or reimbursement by regulatory agencies. They may include criteria for client eligibility for level of care, structural quality criteria (staff qualifications and institutional capability), and occasionally practice parameters (e.g., frequency of contact, availability, intensity, duration of care, and caseload ratios).

The six preceding approaches have been applied only to a limited extent to interventions for youth who are comorbid, highly impaired, or in need of services from multiple service sectors. However, most of these tools do exist for multisystemic therapy, wraparound, case management, and treatment foster care. Diagnostic-specific interventions, both psychosocial and psychopharmalogical, receive attention in practice guidelines, however, the full range of childhood psychiatric disorders has not yet been addressed.

While the above tools may be helpful in justifying and directing clinical practice, a further need is strategies for combining the multiple approaches with formal training, supervision, and consultation, also provided on a sustained basis. The idea of developing a toolkit that combines the preceding tools and training approaches has been promulgated for a set of interventions for adults with schizophrenia (this will actually include six toolkits—see Torrey et al., 2001). Also integral to this toolkit effort will be long-distance learning involving training and consultation utilizing the Internet. The latter effort is being supported by the Robert Wood Johnson Foundation and the Center for Mental Health Services Substance Abuse and Mental Health Services Administration. Similar efforts could be initiated for childhood disorders and interventions.

POLICY FOR COMMUNITY-BASED INTERVENTIONS

Policy support for the interventions presented in this book are derived from multiple sources of federal and state legislation. Mandates that can encourage the provision of and/or help to reimburse costs for these interventions derive from legislation affecting multiple human service sectors, especially health, education, child welfare, and to some extent juvenile justice. They are fully discussed in chapters 2 and 14, and thus are not repeated here.

It is critically important to recognize that the legislation already exists to cover needed mental health services. The pivotal question is whether the necessary fiscal appropriations follow. Much of this decision-making is under the control of states, where there is great variability in fiscal authorization, reflected (expectedly) in variation in the rates of access to care, type of treatment, and the intensity of services provided. Managed care, with considerable control and ability to ration both public and private insurance dollars, and limited change in service provision since the federal parity legislation for mental health benefits in 1999, has only begun to reimburse the intensive alternatives (described in chapters 3 through 8) to institutional care.

While considerable barriers have historically prevented movement of public and private dollars into the community, there are some powerful events that offer promise for expansion in the future. The Child and Adolescent Service System Program (CASSP) was initiated in the early 1980s by the National Institute of Mental Health (NIMH) and has subsequently been administered by the Center for Mental Health Services (CMHS). Small capacity-building grants were funded in the early years; by 1999, there were 67 large demonstration grants in U.S. communities. Through CASSP, both the concept and policy necessary to support alternatives to institutional care have been adopted by all 50 states. However, obtaining support for these community services beyond the CMHS demonstrations has required other federal legislation, including waivers from the Centers for Medicare and Medicaid Services. A prime example of the latter is the increased availability of case management (including wraparound) when it became possible to pay for case management with Medicaid funds under HCFA waivers from the Health Care Financing Administration.

A second success for community-based interventions is the story of multisystemic therapy. As information about positive outcomes for youth in the juvenile justice, child welfare, and (more recently) mental health sectors has become available, states and counties have created ways to pay for this intervention because it was clearly more beneficial to youth than usual care provided in their public institutions. A similar phenomena is beginning to occur for treatment foster care in all three child service sectors.

Leslie Rose

The most critical question for the future is, what will it take to convince payers, public and private, to support the interventions that are backed up by evidence about improved outcomes? Assuming that the pool of dollars available for mental health treatment may not increase, it will be necessary to shift resources away from institutional care (which lacks evidence of effectiveness) toward community alternatives. This will require reductions in funds allocated to institutional care, where a significant portion of the child mental health money is still being spent. The solution is not as easy as it might seem because time will be necessary to establish evidence-based community alternatives. This may require double-funding for several years—a policy that legislators tend to be aversive to. The latter funding strategy is critical to prevent the disaster of deinstitutionalization observed for adults with severe mental disorders since the 1960s. They were released from psychiatric hospitals before community services were available and have never received treatment; others still live on the streets as homeless persons.

The recently published *Mental Health: A Report of the Surgeon General* (1999) included a significant section on children, and the "Surgeon General's Conference on Children's Mental Health: Developing a National Agenda" (September 18–19, 2000, in Washington, D.C.) is expected, among other initiatives, to facilitate the implementation of evidence-based interventions in the community for children. Recommendations also include encouragement for training dedicated to insuring that mental health providers (new and practicing) develop new skills for the effective treatment of high-risk youth (U.S. PHS, 2000).

Aims of the Book

Since the primary purpose of this chapter is to introduce this book, it is reasonable to communicate something about its aims, its intended audience, and the structure of the book and its chapters. In light of the preceding reasons for hope for improved outcomes for youth with severe emotional and behavioral disorders, the major aim of the book is to begin to close a series of gaps. These include gaps between the evidence base, training, policy, and clinical practice. In order to close the most critical gap—between evidence and practice—training and policy will have to become available first. Figure 1.2 offers a visual representation of this process, whereby the evidence base acts as a stimulus for new policy and training. This sequence is a prerequisite to the ultimate goal: better outcomes for children and families.

Consistent with the goal to reduce the above gaps, this book is designed to facilitate implementation of evidence-based interventions in communities for youth with severe emotional and behavioral disorders. The target audience is the people who can close the above gaps: families, educators, students, mental health practitioners, administrators, policymakers, and investigators. It is hoped that the material provided in these chapters will be responsive to the interests and needs of the preceding groups of people. For some it may function as a text, for others as a guide for decision-making, and others will use it as a link to other training resources.

The book is organized in four parts. Part I, including this chapter and

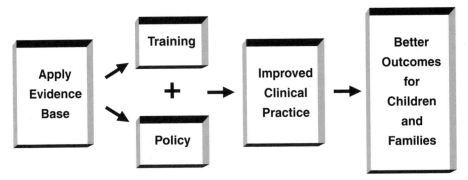

Figure 1.2 Closing the Gap between Evidence, Practice, and Outcomes

chapter 2, introduces the context for changing the provision of services for youth with severe emotional and behavioral disorders. The role of the evidence base, training, and policy are emphasized in relation to the feasibility of incorporating evidence-based interventions into systems of care.

The second part presents comprehensive community-based interventions, including case management, wraparound, multisystemic therapy, treatment foster care, mentoring, and family support and education. The description of the preceding interventions, as well as those in chapters 9 (focused on early intervention in schools) and 10 (on co-occuring conditions), follow a common format. Each of those chapters covers the following topics for a specific intervention:

- theory of change, essential elements, active ingredients, and major principles
- target population(s) and intended outcomes
- intervention parameters (i.e., specific clinical practices; service sites; frequency, intensity, and duration of the intervention; and other adjunctive clinical interventions)
- role of the family perspective and cultural competence
- program development aspects: staffing (qualifications, client ratios), training materials (curriculum, videos, training time, and supervision), quality monitoring (practice guidelines, standards, manuals, fidelity measures), and resource requirements (office space, transportation, and costs per episode of care)
- the evidence base: target populations studied, research design, sample size, comparison condition, follow-up periods, outcomes assessed and findings, assessment of adequacy, and future research directions

Part III presents selected targeted interventions that are more likely to be provided in schools or clinics than the part II interventions, which are more likely to be home-based. First Step to Success (chapter 9) is a preventive intervention for young school-age children at risk for severe emotional or behavioral disorders. Chapter 10 provides an example of an integrated treatment for youth who have experienced trauma (characteristic of so many of this target population) and also substance abuse. This intervention does not require seeking care in two agencies, as typically would occur for youth with multiple problems, and may offer a model for developing other interventions for other co-occurring conditions. The last two chapters in part III (11 and 12) introduce psychosocial and psychopharmacological interventions that are diagnostic-specific. They are likely to be provided in mental health clinics, schools, or primary health care, and may be utilized as adjunctive interventions to those described in part II for youth with severe emotional and behavioral disorders.

To conclude, part IV reviews and addresses the central themes of this book. Policy implications, critical to implementation of evidence-based interventions in communities, are addressed in chapter 13. In addition to summarizing recent research developments, chapter 14 offers a model for treatment development research with a real-world orientation.

In concluding, my coeditor, Kimberly Hoagwood, and I, along with the authors of these chapters, offer three major challenges to the child mental health field. The first one is to continue to assess the emerging evidence base to identify both comprehensive and diagnostic-specific interventions that are ready for dissemination to high-risk youth and their families in systems of care. Second is to include in future research the factors that help sustain these interventions in communities; for example, it is critical to increase our understanding of how training and policy influence the quality of evidence-based practice. Third, as evidence becomes the criterion for reimbursement (Garber, 2001), to conduct efficacy studies for interventions that are practiced without a strong evidence base (e.g., some of the family therapies), or risk the loss of potentially beneficial interventions. In the interim, it is our hope that this book will serve as a resource to move selected interventions with evidence into the community and to children and families who can benefit.

2

Community-Based Interventions in a System of Care and Outcomes Framework

ALBERT J. DUCHNOWSKI

KRISTA KUTASH

ROBERT M. FRIEDMAN

The mental health system's response to troubled youth and their families, with roots that extend back to psychodynamic theory and the dominance of the medical model of treatment, is in a period of transition, and a shift in both the conceptualization of what constitutes effective intervention and in how services are delivered is now in progress. The course of this shift can be described as episodic and uneven, with more change apparent in the last few years than previously. The purpose of this chapter is to describe and document the initiatives and research findings that have been the impetus for these changes within a system of care and outcomes framework.

In the past, intensive services for children with severe emotional disorders were almost exclusively located either in the office of a mental health professional or in a residential institution. A major characteristic of the emerging service delivery system that is taking shape in this country is the change in location of intensive treatment from office and institution to home and community settings. A second important characteristic of the shift is the change in attitude toward the families, from that of a dysfunctional cause of the child's psychopathology to an effective partner with professionals. A third characteristic is the reconceptualization of services in terms of support for the families and the child in a culturally and ethnically relevant manner.

The subsequent chapters in this text can be considered as illustrations of how these changes are taking place through the development of effective community-based interventions that are family centered and culturally competent. For example, chapters 4, 5, and 6 demonstrate the feasibility of locating intensive services and support in the home with the family as an integral partner in implementing the intervention. Even if an out-of-home placement is deemed necessary, the treatment foster care model is proposed as an effective intervention based on the concept of the family unit as the primary caregiver. Chapters 3 to 8 contain descriptions of very specific community-based approaches that have demonstrated effectiveness with children who display severe levels of emotional disorders. The wraparound process and multisystemic therapy both share a value base that accepts and honors families as equal decision-making partners in the development of treatment plans. Further, these interventions are aimed at the broad goal of empowering families so that they may be in control of their lives and achieve the highest quality of life for themselves and their children. Supports such as an effective mentor can even assist families of children who are extremely aggressive and often resistant to traditional psychotherapeutic interventions. It is most encouraging to find community-based interventions that are effective with aggressive children and substance-abusing youth who were formerly viewed as candidates for institutionalization.

Youth who have severe emotional disorders can often present symptoms and behaviors that are clearly dangerous to themselves or others. Advances in psychopharmacology (chapters 11 and 12) have significantly improved the quality of life for these children and enabled them to remain in the community in the least restrictive and most natural living arrangement possible. Effective medication often is a critical component of community-based treatment and may even make the difference in avoiding a restrictive placement. As youth with more and more severe disorders are effectively treated in their own communities, local schools find themselves challenged with designing effective programs that will meet the academic and social needs of these students. In chapter 9, best practices in the special education community are presented. The inclusion of a chapter on special education in this text is critical in order to truly describe the total community in which the youths of concern reside and the total array of integrated services needed to bring about the best possible outcomes.

In this chapter we have attempted to integrate exemplary community-based services into the system of care framework. The chapter traces the history of children's mental health services to the present, and concludes with our forecast for future developments.

Overview of the History of Public Policy in Children's Mental Health

In 1969, the Joint Commission on Mental Health of Children conducted an extensive study of the quality of the children's mental health system. The commission concluded that services for children were seriously inadequate. This was true across the socioeconomic spectrum for children rich or poor, rural or urban. The finding that only a fraction of children in need were being served was of particular concern (Joint Commission on Mental Health of Children, 1969). At that time, the mental health system functioned primarily within the framework of the medical model. A significant amount of human resources were expended on the diagnostic process, which was based on the current version of the Diagnostic and Statistical Manual of Mental Disorders (DSM) of the American Psychiatric Association. Treatment consisted of office-based psychotherapy or play therapy, and if that failed, residential placement was prescribed. The treatment continuum consisted of end points that varied greatly in terms of restrictiveness and intensity, with few services in between.

Also during this time, an ironic twist occurred for children with emotional and behavioral problems with the passage of the Education for all Handicapped Children Act (P.L. 94-142) in 1975. When this law passed, it was assumed by the mental health establishment that the special education system would take care of troubled children. The capacity to work with children and youth actually was reduced in mental health centers and the community mental health system focused its limited resources on adults with chronic mental illness. The child welfare and special education system were to become the main players in supplying mental health services to children. However, neither system had the resources or the expertise to meet the needs adequately. For example, the federal share of excess costs for mandated special education was promised to reach 40%, yet it never has exceeded 10%.

This was the situation that Knitzer encountered in her investigation of the lack of public responsibility for children in need of mental health services in the early 1980s (Knitzer, 1982). State mental health agencies placed a very low priority on services for children. Less than half of the states had a staff member assigned to direct children's mental health services. Only a fraction of the children in need were served, and many were ineffectively served in restrictive settings. Very little had changed since the report of the Joint Commission in 1969.

Current Policy on Community-Based, Integrated Systems of Care

The public-sector mental health response to children is divided between several authorities, including state and local departments of mental health, juvenile justice, child welfare, and special education (among others), and children and adolescents with the most severe disorders often have needs that required services from two or more these authorities. This multiple-agency involvement was a major factor contributing to the development of the Child and Adolescent Service System Program (CASSP), funded in 1984 by the services component of the National Institute of Mental Health, currently the Center for Mental Health Services. CASSP recognized the need for public-sector programs to become more integrated in their attempts to more fully and efficiently meet the needs of the population of children with severe emotional disorders and their families. The concept of a system of care for this population, as delineated by Stroul and Friedman in 1986, grew out of CASSP. The influence of CASSP on the mental health delivery system for children has been substantial and greater than anticipated, even by those who developed the initiative, and a new vision of service provision for children and adolescents and their families has emerged (Day & Roberts, 1991; Duchnowski & Friedman, 1990).

CASSP provided the conceptual framework for other initiatives aimed at providing an integrated system of care for children. These include the Robert

Wood Johnson Foundation's Mental Health Services Program for Youth (MHSPY) and the Annie E. Casey Foundation's Urban Mental Health Initiative, supporting the development of local interagency models for meeting this population's needs. These private foundation programs were followed by the largest federal program to date for child mental health services, the Comprehensive Community Mental Health Services for Children and Their Families Program, authorized by Congress in 1992. This federal program provides grants to states, communities, territories, and Indian tribes and tribal organizations to improve and expand systems of care to meet the needs of the ever-growing population of children and adolescents with emotional and behavioral problems and their families.

This federal program builds on the principles of CASSP and promotes the development of service delivery systems through a system of care approach. The system of care approach embraced by this program is defined as a comprehensive spectrum of mental health and other services and supports organized into a coordinated network to meet the diverse and changing needs of children and adolescents with severe emotional disorders and their families (Stroul & Friedman, 1986). The system of care is based upon three main elements: (1) The mental health service system efforts are driven by the needs and the preferences of the child and family and are addressed through a strengths-based approach; (2) the locus and management of services occur within a multiagency collaborative environment and are grounded in a strong community base; and (3) the services offered, the agencies participating, and programs generated are responsive to cultural context and characteristics.

Defining and Counting the Population within a System of Care Framework

Little consensus has been achieved in defining emotional and mental disorders in children. This problem has been the focus of attention of advocacy groups as well as researchers. To some degree, the problem of definition was settled by a request from Congress to the then newly created federal Center for Mental Health Services. This agency was required to develop standardized definitions and methodologies for states to use in determining prevalence and incidence rates of severe emotional disorder in children and adolescents. The following definition was published in the Federal Register on May 20, 1993.

> Children with serious emotional disturbance are persons from birth to age 18 who currently, or at any time during the past year have had a diagnosable mental, behavioral, or emotional disorder of sufficient duration to meet diagnostic criteria specified within DSM-III-R, that resulted in functional impairment that substantially interferes with or limits the child's role or functioning in family, school, or community activities. *(Federal Register, 1993)*

While no national epidemiological study has been conducted to document the number of children and adolescents with mental health needs, estimates have been recently established (Friedman, Katz-Leavy, Manderscheid, & Sondheimer, 1996). These estimates indicate that 5–9% of the child and adolescent population has a severe emotional disorder with extreme functional impairment, 9–13% of all youth have a severe emotional disorder with substantial functional impairment, and 20% of youth meet established criteria for a diagnosable disorder. These estimates have been supported by two recent studies and are helpful in understanding service utilization in relation to need for services. Leaf and his colleagues (1996) reported on the use of services in the Methods for the Epidemiology of Child and Adolescent Mental Disorders (MECA) study. Their sample of 1,285 youth between the ages of 9 and 17 were recruited from New Haven, Connecticut; Atlanta, Georgia; West Chester, New York; and Puerto Rico. They report that while the prevalence rate of a diagnosable disorder was 32.2%, within twelve months prior to the study only 14.9% of the sample had received mental health services. Further analysis of the data revealed that 8.1% received services in the specialty mental health sector, 8.1% received services in the schools, 2.9% received services in the medical sector, 1.2% received services from clergy, 1.6% received services from a social service agency, and .7% received services from other sources. This indicates that a high percentage of youth with a diagnosable disorder did not receive any mental health services at all during the preceding 12 months, and that the schools are an especially important part of the caregiving system.

Costello and her colleagues (1996) reported on a community epidemiological study conducted in western North Carolina, the Great Smoky Mountains Study of Youth (GSMS), that oversampled youth with externalizing disorders. Their sample consisted of 1,007 youth who were 9, 11, or 13 years old when data collection began. Interviews at the beginning of the study revealed that 20% of the sample met criteria for a psychiatric diagnosis. During the first year of the GSMS, 21.1% of the sample received some type of service to address their mental health problems, and most of these (68.1%) reported prior use of services during their lifetime (Farmer, Stangl, Burns, Costello, & Angold, 1999).

During the first 12 months of the study, services from the educational sector were the most commonly reported, with 12% of the sample reporting receiving services, most from a school counselor. Nearly 8% received services from the mental health sector and 4% receiving services from the general medical community. Overall, 66% of children who used services during the year received them from only one service system. Slightly more than half (53.3%) of children who used only one sector received their services through the education sector. Children who received services from two service sectors were more likely to receive services from specialty mental health. Again, for youth who received services from two service sectors, over half (57.7%) received them from education. These findings led Burns and colleagues (1997) to conclude that the major player in the de facto system of care was the education sector.

CHARACTERISTICS OF THE POPULATION OF CONCERN

Two recent reviews of findings from studies that have examined the characteristics of children with severe emotional disorders who are served in public systems have resulted in similar findings (Friedman, Kutash, & Duchnowski, 1996; Quinn & Epstein, 1998). Friedman and colleagues (1996) conclude, based on a review of six prior studies, that the youth served in public systems have problems in many life domains—school, community, and home relationships, for example. While this obviously includes emotional and behavioral functioning, it also includes intellectual and educational performance and social and adaptive behavior. In addition, they report that "Diagnoses are varied and often multiple and show a high prevalence of both mood disorders and disruptive behavior disorders" (p. 86).

Quinn and Epstein (1998) indicate that while young people of varying ages are served in the public system, adolescents are the most highly represented group. They also report a consistent finding of an overrepresentation of males among those receiving services, and deficits in educational functioning. Scores on standardized tests of intellectual functioning tend to cluster between the normal and low-normal range, revealing mild deficits. In describing the relationship between emotional/behavioral functioning and academic performance, they indicate that "the solution to the reciprocal interaction of learning and behavior problems in the classroom and school remains a critical but apparently elusive aspect of the total treatment effort" (p. 104). They also indicate that the children and their families had frequent contact with many systems other than the mental health system, a finding that is consistent with other studies (Duchnowski et al., 1998; Greenbaum et al., 1998; Landrum, Singh, Nemil, Ellis, & Best, 1995). The most prominent of these systems are special education, child welfare, and juvenile justice.

The relationship between racial and ethnic characteristics, and service use is less clear. McCabe and colleagues (1999) explored service use for youth with severe emotional disorders in San Diego County, California, within the public mental health, child welfare, juvenile justice, substance abuse, and public school systems, by race and ethnicity. After controlling for socioeconomic status, they found that African Americans were overrepresented in four of the five public sectors examined, with the only exception being substance abuse programs. White Americans were overrepresented in all five sectors of care, Latino Americans were served at lower than expected rates in all five service sectors, and Asian/Pacific Islander Americans were represented at the expected rate in the substance abuse and juvenile justice systems and at a lower than expected rate in the other three service systems.

Empirical Base and Outcomes Framework for a System of Care Approach

Since the early 1980s, the children's metal health field has emphasized the development of comprehensive, interagency, community-based systems of care in which professionals and parents work together collaboratively to serve children with severe emotional disorders and their families. Currently, a key task is to determine the effectiveness of such systems in relation to more traditional systems. A related question has to do with the desired outcomes of interventions. Several models have been presented as ways of conceptualizing the different types of outcomes that might be intended and assessed. Hoagwood, Jensen, Petti, and Burns (1996) offer "five outcome domains that represent significant areas in which to look for evidence of impact" (p.1059). These five domains, which are hierarchically organized to reflect widening spheres of influence, are: symptoms and diagnoses, functioning (i.e., capacity to adapt to the demands of home, school, and community), consumer perspectives (e.g., quality of life, satisfaction with care, family strain or burden), environments (i.e., stability of child's primary environment), and systems (i.e., change in use of services, restrictiveness of services, organizational relationships, and costs). Rosenblatt and Attkisson (1993) offered four types of treatment outcomes: clinical status, functional status, life satisfaction and fulfillment, and safety and welfare. Clearly, there are multiple levels at which outcomes of interventions can be examined, ranging from system outcomes (e.g., costs of services and utilization of restrictive residential services) to outcomes for children (e.g., symtomology and functioning). There are many challenges in conducting evaluations of complex, community-wide systems of care, and these have been discussed by numerous researchers (e.g., Bickman & Heflinger, 1995; Burchard & Bruns, 1998; Burns; 1994; Friedman, 1997; Rosenblatt, 1998). One of the challenges is the difficulty in identifying appropriate comparison groups for evaluation of community-wide systems of care. Implementing a research design utilizing random assignment in a community-wide effort is difficult if not impossible. Creating a reasonable and convincing counter-factual explanation (what would have happened in the absence of the program) also remains a major challenge (Hollister & Hill, 1995). Additional challenges include presenting clear program theories—that is, providing models of how the intervention is supposed to work in adequate detail so that it can be measured—and then measuring the degree to which the intervention has been implemented as it was intended or modeled (Bickman & Heflinger, 1995; Friedman & Burns, 1996; Morrissey, Johnsen, & Calloway, 1998).

Given the multiple levels of outcomes that can be assessed, along with the inherent challenges in conducting community-based research, several reviews of studies on the effectiveness of systems of care have been conducted in recent years (Bruns, Burchard, & Yoe, 1995; Rosenblatt, 1998). Overall, as all of the authors indicate, the results are encouraging. Bruns and colleagues (1995) reviewed findings from the demonstration project of the Robert Wood Johnson Foundation, their own work in Vermont, research conducted in California and Alaska, and early findings from the Fort Bragg evaluation, and conclude that, "Initial findings are encouraging, especially with the history of disappointing results of outcome studies for child and adolescent services" (p. 325).

In their own evaluation of the system of care in Vermont, Bruns and colleagues (1995) compared their outcomes with data from a longitudinal study of 812 youth who received "traditional services" (Greenbaum et al., 1998). This comparison indicated that while the youth served in Vermont appear to have had problems at least as serious as those studied in the longitudinal project, they fared better on system outcomes such as the rates of reinstitutionalization after discharge from a residential facility. Within the first 12 months after discharge, 11% of the Vermont youth were readmitted to a residential facility, compared to 32% in the national longitudinal study. Recent findings from the evaluation of the system of care in Vermont have led to the conclusions that, "the rate of out-of-state placement was reduced, individualized care was found to be cost-effective, and local interagency teams experienced an increased level of self-reported collaboration" (Santarcangelo, Bruns, & Yoe, 1998, p. 129). In addition, youth receiving community-based individualized care reported high service and life satisfaction compared to those participating in more traditional residential delivery systems. Such improvements in life satisfaction have been demonstrated by the Vermont team to be related to decreases in negative behaviors. Similarly, an evaluation in Kentucky of a system of care approach found substantial evidence of clinical gains in areas such as behavior problems, greater placement stability, stronger family support and consumer satisfaction, and large reductions in the psychiatric hospitalization of children (Illback, Nelson, & Sanders, 1998).

In an evaluation of the effectiveness of community-based systems of care in three California counties, Attkisson and colleagues (1997) compared outcomes for children in system of care services with outcomes for children in other California counties that had more traditional services. On system indicators, such as cost and use of restrictive placements, they found more positive outcomes for the children served in the system of care counties. They found lower per capita rate of group home placements, and decreased foster home expenditures. They conclude, based on a comparison of the system of care counties with non-system of care counties, that, for the six years that the system of care had been in operation, the state of California could have saved a total of $1.1 billion in group home cost if the state had followed the trend of the system of care counties instead of the existing trend (Attkisson et al., 1997).

Rosenblatt (1998) examined the results of 20 community-based system of care studies. He found that the majority of studies focused on system outcomes, such as reductions in cost or in utilization of restrictive service options, while less than half of the studies presented results on clinical or functional status, and fewer than 20% of the studies assessed direct indicators of safety and welfare of children and families. Notwithstanding these shortcomings, Rosenblatt found that these studies showed that youth who were served within community-based systems of care consistently showed improvements across a range of outcome domains. For example, there was improvement in eight of the nine studies in which clinical status was assessed, and in ten of the eleven studies in which functional status was assessed. In 17 of the 18 studies in which cost or utilization was assessed, there were either decreased costs or decreased use of restrictive placements after the system of care was implemented.

Rosenblatt's major concern, however, is that the most frequently used evaluation design was a pre-post design, although times series were used and three studies used non-equivalent group comparison designs. Overall, however, there is a shortage of studies with comparison groups, making it more difficult to infer that the improved outcomes were causally linked to the interventions.

Rosenblatt is further concerned that the results from the evaluation of the Fort Bragg demonstration project, a large-scale study that used a quasi-experimental design involving a comparison group, are less favorable.

The Fort Bragg study, conducted by Bickman and colleagues (Bickman, 1996a; Bickman, Gruthrie, & Foster, 1995) merits further discussion. The Fort Bragg study was an evaluation of a large-scale system change project initiated in 1990 by the State of North Carolina and the Department of Defense. This project was designed to determine the systemic, clinical, and functional outcomes that could be achieved if a wide range of individualized and family-centered services were provided without any barriers to their availability. It involved replacing the traditional health care benefit for children who were military dependents in the Fort Bragg area with a continuum of care that included a broad range of services, a single point of entry, comprehensive assessments, and no co-payment or benefit limit. The impact of this change on children served in Fort Bragg was compared to two other military communities in the Southeast where the traditional health benefit package was in effect. The health benefit package for the two comparison communities restricted services to outpatient treatment, placement in a residential treatment center, or treatment in an inpatient hospital setting with regular co-payments and benefit limits in effect.

Over a three-year period, the evaluators collected service use, cost, satisfaction, clinical, and functional data for 984 youth served either at Fort Bragg ($n = 574$), or at the comparison communities ($n = 410$). Overall, there were a number of favorable findings for the demonstration program at Fort Bragg. The demonstration site at Fort Bragg increased access for children in need of help, and parents and adolescents were more satisfied with the services they received than parents and adolescents at the comparison sites. Children received services sooner, care was provided in less restrictive environments, and there was heavy use of intermediate-level services; there were fewer clients who received only one session of outpatient treatment, children overall stayed in treatment longer (while the length of stay was shorter in hospitals and residential treatment centers), and there were fewer disruptions in services (Bickman, 1996a). Bickman concluded, however, that despite these positive indicators and despite the fact that the intervention was well implemented, there were no differences between sites in clinical outcomes, and the cost was considerably greater at Fort Bragg.

The interpretation of these results has generated much discussion and controversy in the children's mental health field, both in support of and challenging the conclusions (Behar, 1997; Feldman, 1997; Friedman & Burns, 1996; Hoagwood, 1997; Saxe & Cross, 1997; Sechrest & Walsh, 1997; Weisz, Han, & Valeri, 1997). Several commentators have pointed out that children both at Fort Bragg and in the comparison sites showed improvements on clinical and functional measures (Hoagwood, 1997; Saxe & Cross, 1997). Other have pointed out that when the evaluation results were examined specifically for youth with severe emotional disorders (the population for whom the system of care approach was developed), the results were more positive (Friedman & Burns, 1996). On three of the seven key independent outcome measures, there were significant differences in favor of the demonstration site at 12 months after entry when the analysis was restricted to children with severe emotional disorders. For the only two measures for which data were still available after 18 months, there were still significant differences in favor of the Fort Bragg site (Hammer, Lambert, & Bickman, 1997). It also has been pointed out that without specific information on the services that were actually provided, it is difficult to interpret the results (Friedman & Burns, 1996; Weisz, Han, & Valeri, 1997).

Overall, despite the controversy that has surrounded it, the Fort Bragg evaluation has served several important purposes for the field. On one hand, it has reinforced the positive findings of other studies on such issues as satisfaction with services and use of restrictive services. It has provided encouraging findings on increasing access to services and decreasing dropping out of services. It has challenged the field to examine the theory of change that links changes at the system level with changes at the practice level and, ultimately, with improved outcomes for children and families, and it has stimulated an increased focus on practice-level issues.

The lack of focus on practice-level issues is further reinforced by results from another study conducted by Bickman and his colleagues (Bickman, Summerfelt, & Noser, 1997; Bickman, Noser, & Summerfelt, 1999) on children with emotional disorders who were served in Stark County, Ohio. This study focused on children served within the public mental health system, rather than military dependents (as in Fort Bragg), and on a multi-agency system of care rather than a mental health funded and operated continuum of care (also as in Fort Bragg). Children and families who consented to participate in the study were randomly assigned to one of two groups. The first group was immediately eligible to receive services within the existing community-based system of care in Stark County. Families in the second group were required to seek services on their own rather than to receive them within the system of care. The major differences in services provided were that significantly more children and families in the system of care group received case management and home visits than those in the comparison group. Findings indicate that children and families who were served within the system of care were served sooner; however, no differences between the two groups were found in clinical or functional status 18 months after intake. The results from this study again underscore the importance of understanding the differences in the services that are actually provided within a system of care compared to a more traditional approach. This includes being clearer about concepts that are important within a system of care approach, such as individualized treatment, family-centered care, cultural competence, and strengths-based interventions. As the children's mental health field gets clearer about the definitions and characteristics of these concepts of the theory of change, it will become more possible to train practitioners to implement them, to measure the implementation, and to test the impact of systems of care.

Inherent in the system of care framework, as with other community-based intervention models, is the use of multidimensional components or principles in guiding care. As these models are implemented in a variety of community-based settings, naturally occurring field experiments are possible. These studies traditionally have been limited to pre-post descriptive studies, many without the benefit of a fully explicated intervention model. By attending to the underlying theory of change of an intervention model, the field can move beyond description and produce generalizable knowledge (Leginski, Randolph, & Rog, 1999). Weiss (1995) has underscored the importance of explicating the proposed intervention before implementation. These theories of change or logic models specify the intervention's intended outcomes, the activities it expects to implement to achieve those outcomes, and the contextual factors that may have an effect on implementation of activities and their potential to bring about desired change (Connell & Kubisch, 1998). This description of the intervention or model directs the measurement that is to occur during implementation. These models of change also facilitate the monitoring of the intervention during implementation (i.e., fidelity to the model). Ultimately, however, the importance of specifying the theory of change is in documenting the role and impact of each component in a multidimensional care model, in linking these components to outcomes, and in being able to provide a documented conceptual framework that can facilitate generalization of findings among a variety of community settings.

Role of Families

It is not an exaggeration to state that families hold a primary position in terms of factors that influence and are associated with community-based interventions for children who have emotional disorders. In the almost decade and a half since Stroul and Friedman first presented their conceptualization of a comprehensive community-based system of care (Stroul & Friedman, 1986), families have participated in a passage that has taken them from the role of "cause" of the psychopathology of their child to that of equal decision-making partners in the development of treatment interventions for their children as well as in the evaluation of the system of care that delivers the services (Friesen & Stephens, 1998). While it is true that progress in this passage has been difficult and uneven, it is also true that families have access to community-based services in more communities today than at any previous time in the history of children's mental health services. However, there is still a long way to go, and the challenge of moving from a few demonstration projects to a significant level of capacity continues to test policymakers and planners, and to frustrate families.

The need for an integrated and coordinated system of care to serve as the framework for community-based interventions is very clear when the perspective of the family is considered. The natural challenges of raising a child who has an emotional disorder are significant in and of themselves. Such factors as disrupted sleep, increased social isolation, and heightened family stress are often par for the course (Friesen & Koroloff, 1990). A fragmented and uncoordinated service delivery system can serve as an additional unnatural source of stress for the very families who are the intended recipients of assistance. For example, because children who have severe emotional disorders are a complex group of youth with multiple needs, they and their families need help from many sources (Friedman, Kutash, & Duchnowski, 1996). In a fragmented service system, families will encounter conflicting regulations and requirements; different expectations and attitudes in the various staff they meet; and even contradictory opinions, advice, and messages as they travel from office to office in their quest for help.

For the relatively small group of providers, policymakers, and researchers who are on the cutting edge of innovative service delivery systems, the issues stated above are not new. After fifteen years of CASSP and the system of care, the changing roles of families and the need for a coordinated system of care have become frequent themes in services demonstration projects and the services research programs funded by various federal agencies and private foundations. The problem is that, "The movement to expand family roles, decision-making, and control, however, has outstripped professional training and practice. The necessary research base for this practice is also underdeveloped" (Friesen & Stephens, 1998, p. 231). Consequently, the message needs to be restated, disseminated in new ways, and continually presented until a critical mass of professionals are trained in the underlying value system and a convincing research base is produced to demonstrate the effectiveness of family-centered interventions.

Family-centered interventions have characteristics that set them apart from program-centered interventions (Friesen & Huff, 1996). Family-centered practitioners must understand that the simplistic view of families as the cause of the problems of their children is no longer tenable, and that the evidence against this view has been available for some time (see, for example, Schopler, 1971; Schriebman, 1988; Thomas & Chess, 1984). Another important guiding principle is that families should be full participants in all aspects of the planning and treatment of their children. This value is central to both the system of care model (Stroul & Friedman, 1986) and the wraparound approach (VanDenBerg & Grealish, 1996). When families operate in their role as equal decision-making partners, they may request an array of support services such as respite care, employment counseling, and homemaker assistance. These are supports that may be central to the needs of a family but are very different from outpatient therapy or a day treatment program, which are more representative of the services of the typical community mental health program.

A further indication of the changing roles of families is the increasing evidence of family members as service providers (Koroloff, Stuntzner-Gibson, & Friesen, 1990). Several research demonstration projects have involved family members in such service provision roles as case managers, support group facilitators, respite providers and trainers, and outreach workers (Ignelzi & Dague, 1995; Koroloff, Elliot, Koren, & Friesen, 1990; Tannen, 1996). As more and more family members become involved in direct service provision, it is reasonable to expect that the relationship between type of service provider (family versus professional) and outcomes will be examined. If the spirit of collaboration and partnership continues, we can hope for increased effectiveness

of services as opposed to a developing rivalry between families and professionals. Given the tremendous discrepancy between need and available services in this country, there is certainly room for an increase in capacity.

The inclusion of family members in all phases of research and evaluation
is increasing in the children's mental health services field. Family members and
youth are playing an increasing role in the design of services, the development
of related research designs, and the implementation of the research (Kutash &
Rivera, 1996). This role in research and evaluation for families is being advanced
by several federal agencies that actively encourage their grantees to employ
participatory methods that include family members and consumers as participants in all phases of the research (Friesen & Stephens, 1998). While this role
for families is still emerging, there already is a measurable record of progress
in terms of the number of family members co-presenting with researchers at
annual research conferences (e.g., Willis, Liberton, Kutash, & Friedman, 1999)
and family members as coauthors of peer-reviewed journal articles (e.g., Vander Stoep, Williams, Jones, Green, & Trupin, 1999).

Advocacy has traditionally been considered to be an important family activity, and even this role is undergoing change and expansion. In the past, the
scope of parent advocacy was limited to case advocacy for their own child or
perhaps for that of the child of a friend. Today, families are active in systems-
level advocacy, training other family advocates, and proposing and responding to policy initiatives (Hunter, 1993; McManus, Reilly, Rinkin, & Wrigley,
1993). Leadership for these activities is provided by two major national organizations, the National Alliance for the Mentally Ill and the Federation of
Families for Children's Mental Health. These are two family-run organizations
that have been successful in supporting families as well as influencing policy
affecting children who have emotional disorders. Family members participate
in policy formation through membership on state boards that implement the
comprehensive mental health plan (P.L. 99-660) and the Individuals with Disabilities Education Act, and through recent legislation in several states that requires family participation in planning and decision-making about resource
distribution (Koroloff, McManus, Pfohl, & Sturtevant, 1996).

Practitioners who work with children who have emotional disorders need
to be prepared and competent to develop a partnership with the families of
these children that will encompass all aspects of all interventions: planning,
treatment strategies, outcome determination, and effectiveness evaluation.
Clinicians will find that more and more families will be sophisticated in terms
of best practices, that families will expect to be treated as equal decision-making partners, and that they may be part of a governing body that controls resources for the very agency that employs the practitioner. These new roles for
families are bringing about a whole new dynamic in the field and, hopefully,
increased effectiveness of services for children and families in need.

Cultural Competency

Current population and immigration trends in the United States emphasize the
need to consider the role of culture in the design of children's mental health

services and in the training of mental health professionals. Strikingly, while people of color taken together represent 21% of the United States' population, they comprise 40% of the public school population (Hoberman, 1992). It is currently estimated that approximately 31% of the United States' adolescent population is from racial or ethnic groups that are not White (Glover & Pumariega, 1998). By 2020, this percentage is expected to increase to 40%.

According to Hernandez and colleagues (1998b), the role of cultural influences and the manner in which diverse children and families approach and utilize mental health services must be understood if effective treatments are to be created and delivered. For example, what may be seen as a helpful service in one culture may be seen as inappropriate or even disrespectful in another. Uncovering these differences in order to change how services are defined and delivered should be the goal of mental health services in the quest to become culturally competent in planning and delivering services to diverse children and families.

Research findings underscore the important relationship between culture and seeking professional help. For example, Briones and colleagues (1990) and Hoberman (1992) report that minority parents are more likely to seek input regarding their problems from family and community contacts than are nonminority parents. In Hispanic families, for example, important decisions related to health and mental health are often made by the entire family network rather than by individuals (Council of Scientific Affairs, 1991). Further, McMiller and Weisz (1996) found that two thirds of parents of minority children did not seek help from professionals and agencies as their first choice. According to Ruiz (1993), health care settings that are not modified to work with Hispanic family networks will find that their clients will not comply with medical advice and that as a result, their health status can be compromised. Evidence also exists to show that specialized programs and supports linked with the culture of the community being served are successful at promoting favorable patterns of service utilization (Snowen & Hu, 1997). Mental health programs designed to be linked to community culture find that the children and families served are less likely to drop out of treatment compared to similar people in mainstream programs (Takeuchi, Sue, & Yeh, 1995).

Cultural competence is one approach to helping mental health service systems and professionals create better services and to ensure their adequate utilization by diverse populations (Cross, Bazron, Dennis, & Isaacs, 1989). Cultural competence is defined as a set of congruent behaviors, attitudes, and policies that come together in a system, agency, or among professionals and enable that system, agency, or group of professionals to work effectively in cross-cultural situations (Cross et al., 1989). Action is implied by the term "competence." The implication is that any provider or agency, regardless of their own cultural orientation, is capable of becoming culturally competent. This notion is especially important because most mental health providers are not people of color (Hernandez et al., 1998b). Using the term "competence" places the responsibility on all employees of an organization and challenges all to become part of a process of providing culturally appropriate services. Culturally competent mental health providers are characterized by acceptance of and respect for difference, continuous self-assessment regarding culture, careful attention to the dynamics of difference, continuous expansion of cultural knowledge and resources, and adaptation of service models in order to better meet the needs of diverse communities. This approach emphasizes understanding the importance of culture and building service systems that recognize, incorporate, and value cultural diversity.

Place of Interventions and the Role of Schools

A major goal of the system of care model is to increase the availability of intensive treatment interventions in community-based settings, in contrast to being limited to restrictive residential centers as the only option for such treatment. The ensuing chapters in this text contain presentations of state-of-the-art implementation of major components, concepts, and program requirements of community-based interventions that may be incorporated in a system of care model. Interventions such as treatment foster care, family-centered case management, and multisystemic therapy, for example, are very intensive in terms of the level and comprehensiveness of services provided as well as in terms of the high level of emotional disorder present in the children being served by these interventions. Through the growing body of research on these and other community-based interventions, it is becoming more and more evident that children who have severe emotional disorders can be effectively treated in their home communities (Epstein, Kutash, & Duchnowski, 1998). A major challenge, as stated above, is to bring the capacity of the system of care up to scale in more of the communities of the country.

Increasing capacity of the system of care involves increased resources, staff who are trained to effectively implement innovative treatment interventions, and a widespread commitment to the values and principles of the system of care by the providers in the community. This is a tall order for most communities and may imply that it is impractical to expect the widespread adoption of the system of care approach as a model of service delivery. However, there are strategies that are being used to increase community-based services in all parts of the country, and there are additional approaches that remain to be fully utilized. One of the most frequently used tactics by community planners is the concept of the reinvestment of resources from expensive restrictive placements to more cost-effective community-based services. For most of the history of publically funded children's mental health services, expenditures have been out of balance with as much as 70% of total funding supporting residential services (Knitzer, 1993). This is no longer acceptable in view of the increasing number of evaluations of the system of care that demonstrate that more children can be served at less cost in community-based settings (Rosenblatt, 1998). It is time for policy and practice to reflect this paradigm shift. The task for community planners and advocates is to keep the money following the children and not allow it to be diverted to some other budgetary area.

In the category of underutilized strategies, the effective collaboration between the school and the mental health system is perhaps the most dramatic example of a process that has the potential for significant positive impact on children and families but has not been sufficiently implemented to realize meaningful change (Adelman et al., 1999). There are several levels at which the lack of effective school/mental health collaboration exhibits a negative impact on the overall reform process. First, the concept of an integrated service delivery system requires effective collaboration between all of the child care-giving agencies that constitute the system of care. While all agencies need to be active collaborators, the schools have a crucial role because of their scope of influence on the lives of children (Kutash & Duchnowski, 1997). Consequently, without the active participation of the education community, system reform has been marginalized. Second, the concept of mental health services in the schools remains controversial, ill defined, and poorly implemented. When the Education for All Handicapped Children Act (P.L. 94-142) was passed in 1975, the implementation of related mental health services for children with severe emotional disorders faced immediate barriers that continue into the present under the Individuals with Disabilities Education Act (IDEA), the current version of the federal special education law (Kutash & Duchnowski, 1997). These barriers included inadequate funding and a lack of effective program models, and led school administrators to be very wary of recommendations for mental health services on the Individual Educational Plans (IEP) of children who had disabilities. When Jane Knitzer conducted her study of the child care-giving agencies (Knitzer, 1982), she found an atmosphere of mistrust between agencies that contributed to a "turf" mentality in which the schools viewed mental health as the responsibility of social service agencies. The result of this situation has been a lost opportunity to more adequately meet the mental health needs of children who are identified as having severe emotional disorders, to develop schoolwide programs that could help children who are at risk for more severe disorders, and even to realize an effective prevention initiative in schools across the country.

While much time has been lost in the campaign to establish effective school/mental health collaboration, there are several signs of recent developments that may improve this situation. These include the publication of results of research demonstration projects that examined school-based mental health programs (see, for example, Eber, Osuch, & Redditt, 1996; Catron, Harris, & Weiss, 1998) and a federal initiative entitled Mental Health of School-Age Children and Youth, funded by the Bureau of Maternal and Child Health (Adelman et al., 1999). In addition, the increasing incidence of violence in the schools—and particularly the tragic events in Littleton, Colorado, in the spring of 1999—have served as a flashpoint to bring the issue of meeting the mental health needs of America's school-age children to the fore of popular discourse. A very important new federal initiative is the Safe Schools/Healthy Students Initiative funded by U.S. Departments of Education, Health and Human Services, and Justice. This collaboration will provide students, schools, and communities the benefit of enhanced comprehensive educational, mental health, social service, law enforcement, and, as appropriate, juvenile justice system services that can promote healthy childhood development and prevent violence and drug and alcohol abuse.

MENTAL HEALTH SERVICES IN THE SCHOOLS

It is clear that the education community has had a long history of addressing the needs of children who have emotional and behavioral disorders (Peacock Hill Working Group, 1991). For the most part, these efforts have focused on improving on-task behavior, increasing prosocial skills, and reducing inappropriate behavior. The use of behavioral techniques may be the dominant strategy employed, but every theoretical approach from psychoanalysis to cognitive training has been used to develop classroom interventions (Dane & Schneider, 1998). Clearly, there are many interventions that are available to help children with emotional and behavioral challenges (Hoagwood & Erwin, 1997). The dilemma for the field has been the continued poor outcomes for these children in spite of an extensive practice base that has a strong foundation of empirical support (Peacock Hill Working Group, 1991). A major explanation for this situation has been the observation that there is a serious gap between the research base and the actual level of practice in the field (Malouf & Schiller, 1995).

Advocates of a system of care have proposed that the path to improved outcomes for these children may lie in the implementation of an integrated, collaborative service delivery system that would be holistic and ecological, addressing the multiple domains of the child's life that affect his or her level of functioning (Duchnowski, 1994). Two examples of this type of service delivery system are the "Re-ED" model and school-based wraparound.

Project Re-ED

Over three decades ago, Nicholas Hobbs (1964) proposed a framework for a school-based mental health initiative that has served as the basis for many innovative models of service delivery that have followed. Hobbs (1964) anticipated and understood many of the issues that challenge the field today. Aware of the lack of resources for children's mental health services, the human resource needs, and the lack of cooperation between the mental health and education communities, he proposed a model based on state-of-the-art knowledge in psychology and psychiatry and implemented through specially trained educators called teacher-counselors. Guided by social learning theory, he characterized the model as psychoeducational and proposed that children who had emotional disorders needed to relearn how to function, hence the term re-education or "Re-ED." Hobbs was also guided by ecological theory, and the Re-ED model employed holistic strategies that addressed multiple domains of the child's life. This was facilitated by the interdisciplinary training that the staff received. The teacher-counselors did not view dealing with the child's emotional symptoms as a conflict with their role as academic instructor. They understood the interrelationship between these behaviors and developed broad interventions to improve total functioning. Fortunately, some of Hobbs's original students from the first days of Re-ED at Peabody College in Nashville have kept the model alive and there are indications of Re-ED emerging in concert with the framework of CASSP and the system of care. Today, Re-ED programs can be found in 26 different location across the country (Epanchin, 1998).

School-Based Wraparound

The LaGrange Area Department of Special Education (LADSE) in La Grange, Illinois, has demonstrated the feasibility of the school system serving as the lead agency in a coordinated community system of care (Eber, Osuch, & Redditt, 1996). Using wraparound as the approach to deliver services, Eber and her colleagues at LADSE demonstrated that a school system could play a major role in developing mental health services for children who have emotional disabilities, as well as services for their families. In LADSE, the decision was made to go beyond operating just one component of a system of care and to develop an integrated system with a range of services delivered within the principles and philosophy of individualized care (wraparound). A coalition of family members and public and private providers from the fields of education, mental health, child welfare, and juvenile justice came together to establish a coordinating council that served as the umbrella agency for school-based wraparound teams. Among the broad array of services offered were family support groups, crisis service, respite care, tutoring, traditional mental health services, and teacher support services. These services were integrated with the classroom-based strategies typical in special education programs and were carried out in self-contained classes, resource rooms, and regular education classes, depending on individual student needs. Though the evaluation component of the project is weak, in a report of initial results (Eber, Osuch, & Redditt, 1996), students served in LADSE had a significant reduction in restrictive out-of-school and out-of-home placements. The primary importance of this demonstration project is the fact that it was implemented, the capacity of community-based services was significantly increased, and the program mechanisms are specific enough to have led to a statewide initiative in which the LADSE model is now being adopted in other communities throughout Illinois. The field looks forward to a rigorous evaluation of this statewide initiative.

School-Based Counseling

An example of a different type of strategy to increase community-based interventions is the Vanderbilt School-Based Counseling Program (SBC) (Catron, Harris, & Weiss, 1998). While this program is technically not an initiative to establish a system of care service delivery model, some of the results of the project are so encouraging that it warrants mention in this section. The SBC is a demonstration program that employs one component of a system of care—that is, psychotherapy or counseling. The question examined in the project was whether or not access and utilization of outpatient therapy could be increased for children if the services were delivered in school during school hours. Community-based clinics have long reported the poor attendance of children at therapy appointments and the high rate of failure that families exhibit in following through on the referral process. By placing traditional therapy services in the school, the SBC could evaluate effects on utilization. In a well-designed study, all factors were carefully controlled, allowing for a direct test of the importance of place of service. Of the children and families who were offered services in school during school hours, 96% began services compared to 13% of the children in the community mental health center group, a statistically significant and socially relevant result. While parents of children who received treatment expressed greater levels of satisfaction with services than parents of children in the tutoring group, an additional finding indicated no differences in the clinical outcomes for the children in the therapy groups compared to those in an academic tutoring control group (Weiss, Catron, Harris, & Phung, 1999). While this dampens the excitement over the results of the study, increased access to services supports our contention that the school must be considered to be an important place to locate community-based mental health services for children.

Training for Collaboration

The system of care has been anecdotally characterized as an innovative program model that is driven by the field as opposed to academia. When the CASSP initiative was being implemented in the late 1980s, the observation was frequently made at annual meetings of project directors that provider agencies were patiently waiting for the universities to catch up. Agency directors would point out that they had to allocate some of their scarce resources to train newly hired staff who were recent graduates of university professional training programs but were deficient in the skills and values of community-based system of care service models. An additional burden resulted from the need for agencies to retrain existing staff when new treatment interventions were developed and adopted. In many ways the situation is still the same. An objective measure of this is the sizable amount of the budget for the CMHS Children's Services Grant Program that is devoted to training.

In the last decade, as family-centered collaborative systems of care have assumed more of a presence in the services field, more attention has been focused on training. The Research and Training Center on Family Support at Portland State University conducted a national survey of training programs that incorporated the CASSP values and emphasized family-centered, community-based interventions (Jivanjee, Moore, Schultze, & Friesen, 1995). They identified 51 programs, mostly university based, that met their criteria for inclusion in the survey. Their descriptions of each program indicate that there is consensus on curricular issues, there is a lack of training materials available, resulting in a good number of locally produced manuals and monographs, and there are frequently reported administrative barriers inhibiting multidisciplinary training across traditional university departments. These 51 programs are attempting to overcome the barriers to multidisciplinary training and to increase the number of professionals who understand the importance of families' perspectives as they develop multidisciplinary courses. One example of such a program is the Parent in Residence Model operating in East Carolina University, where parents are paid to co-teach university courses (Osher, de-Fur, Nava, Spencer, & Toth-Dennis, 1999).

There are two themes that emerge as being important in system of care training. The first is as much the incorporation of a value as a skill. Practitioners in the system of care model need to respect parents as equal decision-making partners in all aspects of intervention as well as have familiarity with all the data concerning the relationship between family characteristics and child psychopathology. Second, practitioners need to learn how to collaborate. With only an emerging research base to support the system of care, the concepts and mechanisms that drive the system fluctuate between skills, values, and beliefs. Fortunately, the field has several creative leaders who have been able to make sense of this situation and clearly articulate what needs to be done to help children and their families. The authors of the intervention chapters in this text are representative of this creative leadership. As the number of demonstration projects grows and the research and evaluation base develops, training for the system of care will reach a level of clarity and effectiveness that will contribute to the challenge of bringing these services to the majority of America's communities.

Future

Proposing what should be done next in a social change initiative is different from predicting what will actually happen, but the two processes are certainly related. There have been several texts recently published on the topic of children's mental health and the system of care (e.g., Epstein, Kutash & Duchnowski, 1998; Kutash & Rivera, 1996; Stroul, 1996). The closing chapters (or the designated "future" chapter) of these texts reveal a growing consensus in the field as to the future. Briefly stated, the consensus is that we know what to do, the question is, will we do it? Burns, Hoagwood, and Maultsby (1998) have produced an excellent chapter that focuses on future directions for children's mental health services. They have cast their discussion in the context of improving outcomes and have produced a strategic model to bring about positive change. The model begins with a call to fully implement existing policy that guides children's mental health services, and concludes with the implementation of quality standards. The strategy proposed is heavily dependent on expanded research and affords ample opportunity for the participation of all stakeholders, including families. Burns and colleagues, and the other authors who recently have charted a path for the future, have given the field an excellent set of directions. If the proposed plans are followed, we are very confident in predicting a better future for children who have emotional disorders and their families. That is the easy part. The perplexing part is to attempt to predict how the most current and potentially important processes will play out, in both the short and long term, and impact the system of care. We have identified two such factors and conclude this chapter with a brief discussion of each.

The first is *managed care*. Even though national health care reform has not been actualized in this country, the rapid increase of managed care programs has had a significant effect on all aspects of health care, including mental health. The concept of a pre-paid plan, for a specified group of participants, with an overall goal to contain costs, is a dramatic contrast to the traditional fee-for-service (FFS) mechanism that has been the foundation of health care delivery in the United States. By 1995, it was reported that 43 of the states were actively involved in health care reform efforts that included children's mental health care, and managed care was the focus of this reform for most of the states (Stroul et al., 1997). Managed care has expanded so rapidly that extensive rigorous evaluation has yet to be accomplished. However, researchers who are concerned with children's mental health services are well aware of the need for such evaluation data, especially as it relates to the system of care (Scholle & Kelleher, 1998). In their review of the effects of managed care on children's mental health services, Scholle and Kelleher concluded that ". . . it is unclear whether managed care's continued evolution will shape it to a system that is more comprehensive, coordinated, child centered, and community-based, or less so" (p. 679). In this state-of-the-art review, they reported conflicting data from studies comparing FFS with managed care programs. However, the overall tone of their review may be interpreted as being cautiously optimistic. There are several instances in which they point out that managed care goals are similar to those of CASSP and the Stroul and Friedman model of the system of care. For example, both approaches are a response to a fragmented service delivery system, both espouse the use of community-based services as opposed to restrictive residential placements, and both advocate the use of information management systems that will enhance the coordination of care. The caveat comes from the financial incentives that prompt managed care to restrict overall service utilization as a mechanism to contain costs. There are controls or solutions available for the prevention of deep cuts in services for managed care participants. Foremost among these, at least in the public sector, is the establishment of oversight panels that have strong consumer representation and a legal mandate to monitor managed care operations. Such panels are becoming more prevalent across the country (the structure of Pennsylvania's current managed care contract guidelines is a good example of efforts to protect consumers). Thus, the stage is set for managed care to play out its impact on the system of care model for community-based interventions. We can expect short-term impact to be assessed in the near future.

The second critical factor is *school reform*. The nation continues to wrestle with the need to bring about systemic change in schools in order to improve outcomes (Kutash & Duchnowski, 1997). Demands for accountability, rising standards, and alternative educational experiences offered at public expense through vouchers are a few of the multitude of strategies that are being promoted to bring about systemic reform and improved outcomes. The role of special education in this reform movement has the potential to significantly impact children who have emotional disorders. As stated above, there is a growing base of evidence that removing the psychosocial barriers to learning will result in improved learning outcomes for children as well as improvement in overall quality of life (Adelman et al., 1999). It is this kind of evidence that will get the attention of reformers and hopefully result in improved mental health services for all children in our nations schools. There is an advantage to incorporating the school mental health initiative into the broader school reform process because of the systemic nature of the national school reform movement.

The activities encompassed in school reform go beyond curriculum and instruction and include factors such as methods of participatory governance; changing roles of teachers and support personnel; and an emphasis on multiple outcomes, including such topics as citizenship and adjustment to adult life. These are certainly issues that are compatible with system of care values and principles and indicative of the critical need for the schools and community service agencies to collaborate effectively. An obvious area of compatibility is the emphasis on family involvement in both school reform and the system of care. The education community perceives families as being estranged from the schools, and this is viewed as negatively impacting the education of children. The system of care offers a model of families as equal partners, an ideal antidote for the mistrust, disapproval, and criticism that currently exists between school personnel and families. In a previous section of this chapter, we proposed that families have a central role in the system of care. It also is not an exaggeration to state that families probably have the crucial role in determining what happens to our nation's schools and the children who attend them. Whether or not families will understand their power and join the reform movement remains to be seen. However, more and more educators are beginning to understand the need to "do whatever it takes" (to borrow from the wraparound lexicon) to forge effective collaboration with families.

Part II

Comprehensive Interventions

3

What Is Case Management?

MARY E. EVANS

MARY I. ARMSTRONG

Case management is one of the most common interventions employed when children are using services from several child-serving sectors. This does not mean, however, that case management is the same everywhere it is used; in fact, it is quite variable and requires exploration of its definitions, common components, and diverse models before examining the evidence base for this intervention. In the literature on interventions for children with emotional and behavioral problems, a commonly cited definition of case management is that developed by Austin (1983). This definition states that case management is a mechanism for linking and coordinating segments of a service-delivery system within a single agency or involving several providers, to ensure the most comprehensive program for meeting an individual client's needs for care. A second commonly used definition is Solomon's (1992), which states that case management is a coordinated strategy on behalf of clients to obtain the services they need, when they need them and for as long as they need them. This expands Austin's definition by adding the time dimension and is exemplary in its simplicity. A third similar definition (Intagliata, 1992) proposes that case management is a process or method for ensuring that individuals are provided with whatever services they need. This definition also states that the specific meaning is shaped by the particular characteristics of the system in which the case management will be provided. Other definitions of case management might include information on the target population, primary goal, or intensity of the service. In general, however, as noted by Stroul (1995), definitions of case management have at least two things in common. These definitions tend to refer to a set of common functions and indicate a common purpose, which is to mobilize, coordinate, and maintain an array of services and resources to meet the needs of individuals over time.

Core Functions

Many authors have proposed a set of core functions of case management and Rubin (1992) identifies four common functions: assessment, planning, linking,

Table 3.1   Elements of Case Management that May Influence
Description and Outcomes

Core Functions (What the case manager does most often):
   Assessment: determining the comprehensive needs and strengths of children and families
   Service planning: coordinating the development of an individualized service plan
   Service implementation: ensuring that the individualized service plan is carried out
   Service coordination: linking the various agencies, systems, and persons that may be involved
   with the care and support of the child and family
   Monitoring and evaluation: checking and assessing the appropriateness of services over time
   Advocacy: serving as an advocate for the child and family and for other children and families
   with similar needs

Secondary Functions or Roles (Other things the case manager may do)
   Provision of clinical services: functioning as the child or family's primary therapist
   Financial management: managing a budget for the care of the child and family, overseeing the
   expenditure of flexible funds, or gatekeeping to expensive services
   Role modeling: serving as a role model for parenting skills, activities of daily living skills, or
   advocacy activities
   Case identification and outreach: increasing public awareness of the program and being open to
   the possibility that others may benefit from case management services

Case Management Process (How the case manager does what he or she does)
   Forming and sustaining relationships with the child and family and with care providers in the
   child-serving system.

Organizational or System Elements (Exogenous factors influencing practice)
   Auspices or agency: organization that is responsible for the provision of case management
   Location: whether case management is within the service organization or outside of it
   Agent: whether the case management function is assigned to a team or a single individual
   Status and authority of case manager: the extent to which the case manager has authority
   regarding treatment, placement, and/or financial decisions
   Financing of case management: factors influencing the relationship between financing
   mechanism and service availability or frequency
   Qualifications of case manager: preservice education of case managers that may influence case
   management practice
   Case manager-to-client ratio: the caseload of case managers that may influence case
   management practice
   Intensity, frequency of contact, and duration of service: factors that may be influenced by child,
   family, organizational, and/or financial factors and could be related to outcomes
   Focus of services: how a case is defined (i.e., child, child and family)
   Service availability: time frame in which a service is available
   Service site: location where services are provided
   Client variables: factors such as eligibility, crisis status, etc.

---

and monitoring. The core functions of case management as noted by Stroul
(1995) are assessment, service planning, service implementation, service coordination, monitoring and evaluation and advocacy. These core functions and
other salient elements describing case management practice or influencing its
outcomes are described in Table 3.1.

     Assessment refers to determining the comprehensive needs of children and
families as well as their current and potential strengths, which can be the foun-

dation for the intervention process. The case manager often is the only person in the provider system who is aware of all the needs and strengths of the child and family. An important aspect of assessment is assisting the child and family in articulating their immediate and long-term goals. Assessment should not be a one-time effort, but should continue over the course of the case management relationship. This aspect of assessment is further addressed under monitoring and evaluation.

Service planning is coordinating the development of an individualized service plan to address the needs identified during assessment. This function is viewed by many as the core responsibility of the case manager, and requires a comprehensive knowledge of community resources and informal supports. In keeping with the system of care principles and values, service planning should include assisting families in becoming involved in the service-planning process. Some might argue that empowering families to become their own advocates is perhaps the most valuable outcome of case management, as it decreases their dependence on a case manager or others.

Service implementation ensures that the individualized service plan is carried out as planned. It involves linking the child and family to appropriate providers, service agencies, and formal and informal resources. A particular challenge about which little is known is identifying, mobilizing, and sustaining informal resources to support families. This tests the creativity of the case manager to use indigenous resources so that when case management services have terminated, there are sufficient informal supports to sustain the positive gains made during the case management intervention. Anecdotally, case managers have reported that it takes longer to identify, develop, and/or link to informal resources than to formal resources and, in at least one study, case managers were not as satisfied with their performance in the area of linking to informal resources as they were to other aspects of their performance (Evans, Boothroyd, & Armstrong, 1997).

Service coordination involves linking the various agencies, systems, and persons who may be involved with the care or support of the child and family. This is perhaps the heart of many case management interventions and tests the leadership, communication, and persistence qualities of the case manager. When done well, service coordination can introduce efficiencies into a system of care and decrease levels of frustration among providers and children and families.

Monitoring and evaluation includes ensuring the adequacy and appropriateness of services over time. That is, it represents an ongoing assessment of needs, effectiveness of interventions, and changes in family status, including empowerment. Adjustments in service plans and interventions should be made in response to the changing circumstances of the child and family and new information about needs, services available, and child and family response to interventions. An important aspect of evaluation is determining the concordance between the child and family's goals for the intervention and the outcomes they perceive, including their satisfaction with services.

Advocacy has several components. Initially it may mean serving as an advocate or voice for the child and family in overcoming barriers to their receiving services. It may also include empowering families with skills and knowledge so that they can begin to advocate successfully for themselves. Finally, advocacy may extend beyond an individual child and family to encompass children and families with similar needs, and result in changes to the service-delivery system that will benefit a larger group of individuals. An example of this broad type of advocacy is when a case manager notes a deficit in the child-serving system, such as the lack of an after-school program for a child with special needs, and begins to work with service providers to develop such a community resource, which will benefit not only one individual child and family but other families outside that caseload.

ALTERNATE OR SECONDARY ROLES

Beyond these roles, Stroul (1995) notes "newer roles." At this time, these roles perhaps should be called optional, alternate, secondary, or subsidiary roles, as they represent roles that may be salient in some case management interventions but not in others. The provision of clinical services is one example of an additional role that case managers may be expected to fulfill. The case manager may actually be the child or family's primary therapist and be expected to act also as the case manager in securing resources and coordinating services. In such therapeutic or clinical case management arrangements, the therapist/case manager may provide individual, group, or family therapy; teach parenting or living skills; and/or provide crisis intervention. The advantage is that the therapist/case manager often has had a prolonged and intensive relationship with the child and family and is familiar with their changing needs and strengths. The development of a trusting relationship may also be important in working effectively with the family. The disadvantages are that time constraints, organizational characteristics and constraints, and perhaps personal interest and the skills of the therapist/case manager may result in greater attention to one of these roles, with less attention to the other.

A second alternate role, which often becomes a primary role of the case manager, is financial management. Some case managers may be required to develop and manage a budget for the care of individual children and their families, and/or they may oversee the expenditure of flexible service funds. In addition, given the current concerns about health care costs and managed care, some case managers have the responsibility to act as gatekeepers to the most expensive services, such as inpatient care and residential placements. This function may increase in its saliency as public mental health systems more frequently contract for services and special needs plans with managed care organizations.

A third alternate role, which may be most important when other parents serve as case manager or a part of the case management team for a family, is role modeling. Role modeling may involve parenting skills, activities of daily living skills, or advocacy activities. In some team approaches to case management, the professional case manager is primarily responsible for the core functions noted above while the parent case manager or family advocate is responsible for supportive care and role-modeling activities related to the child's parent.

A fourth alternate or secondary role is case identification and outreach. This likely involves two efforts on the part of the case manager. The first is letting the public know that case management services are available for a given population. This may occur through advertisements or speaking engagements. It may also occur through informal contacts with community members such as teachers, religious leaders, and civic groups during the case manager's work on behalf of a family or target group of children and families. The second effort is for case managers, during their daily activities, to be aware of others who could benefit from case management services and to make referrals for these services when indicated.

THE PROCESS OF CASE MANAGEMENT

It is insufficient to describe what a case manager does without describing the process by which he or she accomplishes these functions. The process of case management is accomplished largely through relationships. Case managers form parent-professional relationships to accomplish goals related to enablement, empowerment, and advocacy. They form collaborative relationships with other professionals to accomplish coordinated assessment and evaluation and joint planning and decision-making (Weil, Zipper, & Dedmon, 1995). They frequently form relationships, including therapeutic relationships, with the children they serve. Establishing a therapeutic relationship with a child may be facilitated through spending time with the child in an activity of his or her interest—for example, fishing or visiting a zoo. A therapeutic alliance between the case manager and the child and family may be necessary for maximizing the positive outcomes of the case management intervention, although the field of children's mental health currently lacks research evidence to support this thesis.

In summary, although case management is not a unitary concept or role, there are a number of core functions that define the content of the role. Within these core functions there is a tremendous amount of flexibility regarding who fills the role and how the functions are accomplished. Alternate or secondary functions add to the variability of the case manager's role. The process of case management is accomplished through building relationships between professionals and children and their families. Both the selection and emphasis on particular functions and the case manager's skill in the process of case management introduce variability into describing case management models and evaluating their associated outcomes. This variability will be discussed in greater depth in the section on models of case management.

OTHER VARIABLES RELATED TO DESCRIBING CASE MANAGEMENT

Burns, Gwaltney, and Bishop (1995) identify four organizational or system variables that are important in the description of case management and which need to be considered when planning case management programs or conducting research on case management. The first of these is auspices, or the agency responsible for the provision of case management. The second is location—that is, whether the case management function is within the service organization or outside of it. The third is whether case management is conducted by a team or by an individual, and the fourth relates to the status of case managers and the nature of their authority regarding treatment decisions, placement decisions, and financial decisions. Some authors view these variables as helping to determine whether case management is provider-driven or client-driven. In addition, these variables assist in the description of case management models and may be related to the practice and outcomes of case management. To date, little research has been done to compare models of case management on these variables, although Burns and her colleagues (1996) have conducted one randomized trial comparing two models of case management.

To this list of system variables could be added the financing of case management and the pre-service educational preparation and training for case managers. Financing may affect the number and nature of contacts between the case manager and the child, his or her family, or collaterals such as teachers. It also may affect the length of the intervention. The qualifications of case managers that may be specified by a system of care could have important implications for the practice of case management and perhaps its outcomes. For example, paraprofessionals are less likely to be engaged in therapeutic case management than persons trained in the health professions. Research is needed in both of these areas.

PRACTICE PARAMETERS

Burns and colleagues (1995) identify a number of parameters of practice that are essential in describing case management interventions and also in conducting research. These parameters are the case manager–to–client ratio, the intensity or frequency of contact between case managers and clients, and the duration of service. All of these aspects of case management vary greatly from one setting to another. Caseloads can vary from 1:4 in crisis case management to 1:75 or more. Frequency of contact may be prescribed because of the funding requirements; for example, case management in New York State was reimbursed by Medicaid as long as there were four documented face-to-face contacts with the client during a month. Frequency of contact could also be specified by policies governing the frequency of plan updates or could be based primarily on the needs of the clients. The duration of services is often related to the population being served, with children with severe emotional disorder (SED) receiving services for prolonged periods of time compared to those with more acute and/or fewer multisystem needs, who received services for shorter periods of time. Based on the program evaluation for 199 children with SED receiving intensive case management services in New York State, the mean length of service was 771 days. The length of case management service could

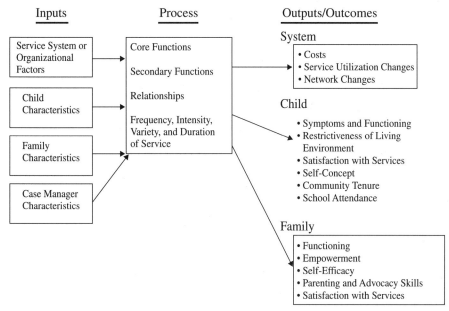

Inputs	Process	Outputs/Outcomes

Figure 3.1   A model for describing and evaluating case management.

be significantly impacted by the availability of step-down or less intensive services.

To this list of variables related to practice, Willenbring, Ridgely, Stinchfield, and Rose (1991) would add additional descriptors or variables such as the focus of services—for example, the definition of the case as the child or the family, the availability of services in hours and days per week, the site where services are provided (office versus a community base), and the amount and nature of client direction in the practice of case management. All of these variables are independent of client variables, and it is important to recognize that the definition of eligibility for case management services, which is often based on client characteristics, may impact the practice and outcomes of case management interventions. A simple heuristic model that may be of use in describing case management and in evaluating the outcomes associated with its practice is found in Figure 3.1. This model links the inputs to the process of case management and then to system, child, and family level outcomes. The elements of case management that were identified in Table 3.1 may be sorted into these various domains to examine the relationships among them. The contents of the domains in this figure are illustrative, and other variables or concepts of interest could be added or substituted.

HISTORY AND DEVELOPMENT OF CASE MANAGEMENT

There is no clear historical record regarding the origins of case management. Weil and Karls (1985) trace its roots to 1863 in the formation of the Massachusetts Board of Charities, early settlement houses, and the Charity Organization Societies. Rose (1992) traces its more recent development to the 1960s, when human service programs in the United States experienced tremendous growth as part of President Johnson's Great Society plan. During this time, the variety of human or social services available and the disparate eligibility requirements for these services made services coordination and accountability priorities. During the early 1970s, the federal government funded a number of services integration demonstration projects that included the case management function (Rubin, 1992). The roots of case management, however, can probably be traced further back into the development of social work and public health nursing before the turn of the 20th century. Regardless of its origins, much of what was known about case management, particularly in the area of mental health, resulted until recently from reports of service coordination for adult clients.

The widespread use of case management for children with emotional and behavioral problems and their families is more recent than for adults, and became more common after the National Institute of Mental Health developed the Child and Adolescent Service System Program (CASSP) in 1984. This program resulted in a concerted state-by-state effort to develop systems of care for this population. The articulation of the principles and values of a system of care for children with severe emotional disorder (Stroul & Friedman, 1986) further accelerated the development of case management for these children and their families. One of the system of care principles, for example, relates to receiving services that are "integrated, with linkages between child-caring agencies and programs and mechanisms for planning, developing and coordinating services" (Stroul & Friedman, 1986, p. 17). This principle emphasizes the importance of system-level coordination. Another principle states that "children with emotional disturbances should be provided with case management or similar mechanisms to ensure that multiple services are delivered in a coordinated and therapeutic manner and that they can move through the system of services in accordance with their changing needs" (Stroul & Friedman, 1986, p. 17). The emphasis here is primarily on a client level ensuring that individual children receive the services they need when they need them.

The federal government has stimulated the growth of case management through legislation. For example, Stroul (1995) reports the Omnibus Health Act (P.L. 99-660), amended by the Alcohol, Drug, and Mental Health Administration Reorganization Act (P.L. 102-321), required states to create plans to develop and deliver community-based services for adults and children with serious mental illness. The legislation mandated the provision of case management services to persons receiving substantial amounts of publicly funded services. Further, P.L. 99-457 (Education of the Handicapped Act Amendments of 1986) required the development of individualized family service plans and the use of case managers who would be responsible for implementing the plan and service coordination activities. More recently, the public law authorizing the Comprehensive Community Mental Health Services for Children and their Families Program, being implemented by the Center for Mental Health Services, requires case management services for all children who receive access to the system of care being developed with these federal grants (Stroul, 1995).

A WORD ABOUT TERMINOLOGY

The most commonly used term to refer to the individual or team that provides services coordination and other core case management functions is case manager. Some people feel that this is not a family-friendly term since it refers to individuals as cases to be managed. In the literature related to children's mental health, a number of other titles have been created to replace case manager. Examples of these include family associate, family partner, service coordinator, family service coordinator, care coordinator, and parent or family advocate. Although the plethora of terms may be confusing, it serves to emphasize that the individual and family perspectives should not be lost in the efforts to obtain and coordinate services. In this chapter the term case manager is retained, as it is probably the most common term used and helps to link developments in the field of children's mental health to those in other areas of human services.

A second, and sometimes challenging, definitional issue is the differentiation of case management from wraparound. Within the mental health field, a strengths model of case management has been implemented and evaluated (Kisthardt & Rapp, 1992). The strengths model includes six principles and functions: a process of engagement between the case manager and consumer, a strengths assessment, personal planning by the consumer and a shared implementation, sustaining client gains, advocacy, and a graduated disengagement process with the goal of empowerment. Clark and Hieneman (1999) have defined the wraparound process as a "strengths-based, family-centered team approach for creating individually tailored supports and services to meet the unique needs of children with difficulties—and those of their families—in two or more life domains" (p. 184). In this process, a resource coordinator conducts the assessment of strengths and needs and facilitates the creation and implementation of a support plan. Using this definition, wraparound could be viewed as the process through which comprehensive case management is accomplished and in which the case manager functions as the resource coordinator. It is certainly true, however, that not all case management interventions or approaches use a wraparound process. For additional information on the wraparound process, see chapter 4.

MODELS OF CASE MANAGEMENT FOR CHILDREN AND THEIR FAMILIES

Weil (1985) identified seven case management models for human services programs for adults or children. These models commonly form the basis for the discussion of models of case management for children with emotional and behavioral problems (Burns et al., 1995). The seven models are the generalist or service broker, primary therapist, interdisciplinary team, comprehensive service center, family as case manager, supportive care, and volunteer as case manager. Each model is outlined briefly below.

Generalist or Service Broker

A common model of case management in which a professional, often a social worker, nurse, or psychologist, carries out the core functions of case management. The emphasis is frequently on linkage, services coordination, and advocacy, both at an individual child level and at the systems level for all children with similar needs.

Primary Therapist

A model in which a mental health professional who has primary responsibility for providing therapy to the child and/or family also functions as the case manager.

Interdisciplinary Team

A model in which multiple child-serving agencies are represented. Commonly, one agency is designated as the lead agency and the team representative of this agency is primarily responsible for carrying out the role of case manager. In another form of the team model, the ultimate responsibility for the case management functions and the child's and family's care rests with the team rather than with one case manager.

Comprehensive Service Center

A "one-stop shopping" multiservice center in which services are co-located. The designated case manager fulfills a number of roles related to the agency's mission and makes linkages to other agencies as needed. This model may include financial management related to individual service plans, and gatekeeping to more expensive services may be an important function of the case manager located in the service center.

Family as Case Manager

A situation in which a parent or other family member is trained to function as the case manager for his/her own family. The family member may be linked with a professional case manager, and the emphasis here is frequently on linkage, advocacy, and family empowerment. In some models, the family member and a professional case manager share case management functions and tasks (Mailick, Seltzer, Ivry, & Litchfield, 1992).

Supportive Care

Provided by ordinary citizens or parents external to the family receiving services as case managers. These individuals are trained and paid to provide services, which are often focused on linkage and role modeling. These citizen or parent case managers are trained by a human service agency that retains legal and programmatic responsibilities for services.

Volunteer as Case Manager

Trained but unpaid citizens do case management. Volunteers are supervised by professional staff who retain legal responsibility for the services that are provided. This model takes advantage of the pool of retired persons or others in communities who wish to provide public service but who do not require financial compensation.

Theory of Change

The theory of change in case management is poorly specified. There are probably several reasons for this, including the paucity of research focused on case management and the inherent variability related to the extant multiple models of case management and the core and secondary functions that may be emphasized within each model. Further, the importance given to individualizing case management services to best meet the needs of the family, and the tailoring of services and approaches to be culturally competent, contribute to the difficulties in viewing case management as a unitary concept with a common underlying theory of change. Therefore, in specifying the theory of change in a case management intervention, particularly for research purposes, it is incumbent on the researcher to clearly describe the model of case management with its component functions, link the intervention approaches to expected outcomes, and provide the theoretical underpinnings regarding why and how the intervention approach is expected to result in a given outcome. Proceeding with these cautions, the section below outlines some theories or theoretical constructs that may be explanatory in understanding the outcomes of interest in case management.

Bronfenbrenner's ecology of human development, Maslow's hierarchy of needs, Bandura's self-efficacy and modeling theories, Ajzen's theory of planned behavior, and Prochaska's stages of change represent five well-developed theories that have relevance for case management. The remaining theoretical constructs described in this section are empowerment, therapeutic alliance, social support, role modeling and socialization, and goal-setting and autonomy. These theoretical constructs may be viewed as examples of potential mediators of change in human interactions, including case management. Because of the atheoretical approach that has been used to design case management interventions and to evaluate their outcomes, it is very likely that additional theories and key constructs may be relevant in understanding change associated with case management.

ECOLOGY OF CASE MANAGEMENT

In general, case management takes place in a child's and family's natural settings—such as home, school, and community—rather than in institutional settings. A relevant theory here is that of Bronfenbrenner (1979). This theory acknowledges the importance and interconnectedness of everyday settings and interactions with peers and family on child and family functioning. Behavior problems can be maintained by transactions within or between one or a combination of these systems or settings. If one of the goals of the case management intervention is to maintain the child at home and to improve functioning of the child in his/her natural environment, then it is essential to conduct the intervention in those natural environments and with the salient individuals found there. In the absence of an ecological approach, the gains experienced in decreasing a child's deviant behavior while hospitalized or in a group home removed from his or her community might not be sustained when that child is discharged to his home community and he renews his association with deviant peers.

HIERARCHY OF NEEDS

In case management there is an underlying assumption that having resource and service needs met is better than the alternative. A relevant theory here is Maslow's (1970) hierarchy of needs, in which lower level needs such as safety and food must be met in order for an individual to make progress in meeting higher order needs such as self-esteem and self-actualization. In keeping with this understanding of the hierarchy of needs, case managers frequently attend to the immediate needs of the family for food, shelter, and peer-appropriate clothing before focusing on other case management functions and assessed needs. Flexible service funds are an important tool in ensuring that basic needs are met while application is being made for services to which the family may be entitled.

SELF-EFFICACY

Bandura (1982) defines self-efficacy as self-reported confidence in making and implementing decisions. Self-efficacy is an important element in effective parenting. In order to increase parental self-efficacy, case management interventions may use formal parenting curricula (Evans et al., 1994) or parent discussion and support groups (Ruffolo, 1994) to increase knowledge, skills, and confidence in behavior-management techniques and child care.

PLANNED BEHAVIOR

Ajzen's (1988) theory of planned behavior represents a modification of Fishbein and Ajzen's (1975) theory of reasoned action. The original theory postulated relationships between a person's attitude toward the behavior and the subjective norm for a particular behavior, which led to a person's intention to carry out some planned behavior. This theory proved valuable in describing behaviors that were mainly under volitional control, but was less valuable in describing or predicting behaviors over which an individual had incomplete control (Godin & Kok, 1996). Ajzen's modification asserts that a person's attitude toward the behavior and the subjective norm for a behavior interact with a person's perceived behavioral control to result in intention to carry out a planned behavior, which in turn leads to enactment of the behavior itself. Perceived behavioral control is closely related to the concept of self-efficacy noted above. The theory of planned behavior could be used as a basis for exploring case management and child and family outcomes, particularly when the case management intervention includes a focus on empowerment or increasing self-efficacy.

STAGES OF CHANGE

This theory or model of behavior change was developed by Prochaska and DiClemente (1982) to facilitate understanding of how people intentionally change their behavior, either with or without treatment. The theory postulates a spiral pattern of how most people move through five stages of change. The stages are: (1) *precontemplation,* or no intention to change behavior in the immediate future, (2) *contemplation,* in which there is awareness of a problem and thinking about overcoming it without a commitment to take action, (3) *preparation,* in which individuals intend to take action in the near future, (4) *action,* in which individuals modify their behavior, experiences, or environment in order to overcome their problem, and (5) *maintenance,* in which people attempt to prevent relapse and consolidate the gains they made during the action stage. Progress through these stages is seldom linear. This theory has been useful in understanding how people change various health-related behaviors (Prochaska, DiClemente, & Norcross, 1992) and could prove useful in designing case management interventions and in facilitating understanding of and prediction of the trajectory of behavioral changes associated with case management interventions.

EMPOWERMENT

Empowerment means promoting the family's ability to utilize its strengths to meet its needs (Dunst, Trivette, & Deal, 1988). A critical element here is the family's identification of its strengths and use of these strengths as a foundation for the case management intervention. McQuaide and Enrenreich (1997) offer a strengths self-assessment instrument that case managers can use with families during the assessment phase. The empowerment perspective within case management has been defined as a commitment to facilitating change in clients from objects known and acted upon to subjects who are knowing and acting (Rose, 1992). Although this is a fairly widely accepted tenet of case management, many individualized service plans are focused primarily on needs and deficits, rather than strengths. Several models of case management stress the importance of families learning how to advocate for themselves. This self-advocacy could be accomplished through role modeling of the case manager's behavior or through joining support or self-help groups. According to Koren, DeChilo, and Friesen (1992), empowerment can occur at three levels: individual, family, and community. Case managers who are interested in empowering families may find their instrument, "Family Empowerment Scale," of value in assessing this outcome.

THERAPEUTIC ALLIANCE

A critical but understudied element in case management for children and families as in other helping and therapeutic relationships is therapeutic alliance, or a positive working relationship between the clinician and the child and family. Conceptually, therapeutic alliance is composed of two dimensions: a bonding or affective dimension and an interactive, collaborative dimension (Horvath, 1995). Therapeutic alliance is viewed as a facilitative condition or process variable that can enhance the effectiveness of a variety of interventions and which is therapeutic in its own right. The mechanisms of establishing, maintaining, and evaluating the outcomes associated with therapeutic alliance in case management interventions are virtually unknown, despite the importance that clinicians give to this aspect of care.

SOCIAL SUPPORT

All but the most socially isolated among us get by with help from our family, friends, and other citizens in our community. In some models of case management, it is of critical importance to identify the existing and potential sources of social support for the family, and an important outcome of case management is to strengthen these informal social supports. This decreases the family's dependence on formal, often governmental, support systems. Having a child with an emotional, behavioral, or mental health problem often has caused strains in or exhausted the informal support system. Case managers may facilitate the referral to self-help or support groups or linkages to the faith community and to neighbors in an attempt to increase and strengthen a family's informal social supports.

ROLE MODELING AND SOCIALIZATION

Socialization involves learning a set of behaviors that comprise a societal role. One of the ways social roles are learned is through role modeling (Bandura, 1971). Some case management interventions use the behavior-management skills of the case manager as an example to teachers and parents of how to intervene in a child's problem behaviors. Other models of case management use a family partner or parent advocate who has raised a child with an emotional, behavioral, or mental health disorder to provide role modeling and socialization to the parental role (Bandura, 1982). The activities of the parent advocate may include playing with the child, setting limits for the child, shopping with the family, cleaning house with the family, developing a family budget, and engaging in other skills of daily living so that family members learn by example and experience.

GOAL-SETTING AND AUTONOMY

Families are more likely to work toward the achievement of goals that they view as relevant to their life situation, and which they have set themselves, than to work toward goals they feel have been imposed upon them. The goals of a case management intervention should be set with the family early in the intervention process and evaluated periodically to determine progress in accomplishing them. Although not a particularly popular technique at this time, goal attainment scaling (Kiresuk, Smith, & Cardillo, 1994) is one means of determining progress in meeting a family's goals, and accomplishment of self-identified or jointly established goals should be positively related to satisfaction with services.

According to Stroul (1995), the value of case management services cannot be established outside the context of a system of care that includes all the essential elements, including an array of service options, mechanisms for system-level coordination, and mechanisms for client-level coordination. If this assertion is true, the theories of change underlying case management for children with emotional, behavioral, and mental health disorders must therefore be consistent with the principles and values of a system of care.

Program Requirements

The establishment and maintenance of a case management program requires consideration of organizational arrangements, identification of the target population, selection, preparation, and support of case managers, and ensuring the resources necessary for supporting the program.

ORGANIZATIONAL ARRANGEMENTS

Friesen and Briggs (1995) identify two major approaches to the organization of case management services, the first focusing on the goals (or outcomes) and content of service coordination and the second on structure and process issues concerned with how service coordination will be carried out. Regarding the first approach, organizations that sponsor case management programs need to be clear about issues related to the goal of the program; accountability to children, families, and the sponsoring organization; the expected duration of case management services; and the model of case management to be supported. Decisions regarding these issues are in turn derived from the mission of the organization, assessment of local need, and beliefs of the key actors about theories of change. There is considerable interest in the field of human services at this time in outcomes driving the services provided. Hernandez, Hodges, and Cascardi (1998a) describe an approach called the ecology of outcomes, which assists organizations in integrating into decision-making information on who is being served, what services have been provided, and what change has been experienced. This type of planning and evaluation is essential to ensure both system and client accountability.

Regarding structural and process issues, research has found that a critical element in the effectiveness of an organization providing human services is its organizational characteristics. Glisson and Hemmelgarn's (1998) study of children's service organizations found that the effects of organizational characteristics, including climate, was the major predictor of positive child outcomes and a significant predictor of service quality. Characteristics of a positive organizational climate were identified as low-conflict, cooperation, role clarity, and personalization within the organization. These factors were found to be more powerful predictors of positive child outcomes than interorganizational coordination. This has important implications for case management programs that are often strongly focused on interorganizational relationships. The message is that sponsoring organizations need to focus greater efforts on their internal climate.

IDENTIFICATION OF THE TARGET POPULATION

Although it may sound simplistic, it is important to consider who will be served in case management interventions. Specialized case management programs have been developed for transitional-age youth aged 16 to 25 years (Armstrong, 1995), children experiencing a psychiatric crisis (Evans, Boothroyd, & Armstrong, 1997), homeless adolescents (Cauce et al., 1994), and other special populations. Policies and procedures need to be developed for the identification and enrollment of the target population. Some case management programs provide services to children requiring services from multiple child-serving systems regardless of where the child is living, while other programs focus on children transitioning from a particular program, such as foster care or inpatient hospitalization.

SELECTION, PREPARATION, AND SUPPORT OF CASE MANAGERS

Unfortunately, very little research has been done to clarify the characteristics of case managers and the training associated with effectiveness in case management. Based on what is known from other human service endeavors, however, there must be a match between the goals of the program and the persons selected to implement case management services. Some of the characteristics that would appear to be important are a genuine liking for children and parents, effective communication skills, an engaging personal style, creativity in problem-solving, leadership skills, ability to instill a sense of hope in family members (Beckstead & Evans, 2000), and an ability to deal with novel and less structured environments than those typically found in human service organizations. No particular level of education guarantees these characteristics.

The level of education required for case managers varies considerably, but typically a bachelor's degree is the minimal educational requirement. Level of education required is an important factor in the status given to case managers in a service system. Given the scope of the case manager's functions, orientation and in-service training are considered essential. Several training curricula have been developed for case management. These focus on how to assess and understand client needs and strengths, the variety of local resources and client entitlements available, record-keeping, problem-solving, crisis intervention, and advocacy (Intagliata, 1992).

To be accepted by families and to be maximally effective, interventions need to be culturally competent. This is a core value of the system of care. The emphasis on individual child and family needs and goals helps to ensure culturally competent care. Training programs must be developed to sensitize case managers about culturally competent care, and supervision and consultation must be made readily available to case managers who are facing challenges in providing care that is respectful and acceptable to families.

Support of case managers involves providing essential resources to do the job, as well as providing supervision, consultation, and emotional support. It is difficult and frustrating for case managers to function in the community without appropriate resources, such as a reliable car, means of accessing flexible service money (e.g., credit or debit card, checkbook), and means of communication (e.g., portable phone). Given today's technology, lightweight laptop computers can provide a portable office, ensuring communication by e-mail and fax and facilitating record-keeping.

Supervision has a long history in social work, nursing, and psychology, and may occur on a group or an individual basis. Supervisors are responsible for ensuring the availability of resources, providing for accountability and monitoring of case manager performance, assisting in problem-solving, providing emotional support, offering continuing education and consultation, and generally facilitating the work of the case managers. The relationship between the case manager and supervisor needs to be comfortable enough that problems experienced in the community are brought up for discussion and problem-solving.

RESOURCE REQUIREMENTS

There are many issues to consider in the development of a budget for a new case management program. On the personnel side, staff requirements include case managers, supervisors, and administrative support staff. Salary levels for case managers depend on the task requirements of the case manager role as well as the educational and experiential requirements for the position. National organizations such as the National Association of Social Workers and the National Case Management Association have developed recommended salary levels for both case managers and supervisors, as well as caseload sizes and supervisor to case manager ratios. The amount of administrative staff required depends on the level of administrative support needed for the case management program. For example, if Medicaid-targeted case management funds will be used, both federal and state guidelines for case recording, documentation, and billing need to be followed. An additional resource consideration is the support for training programs for case managers.

On the non-personnel side, start-up requirements include office space, furniture, phones, and computers. Some case management programs provide laptop computers for case managers and software packages designed for case management case records. Transportation needs of case managers also need to be considered. For liability reasons, most case management programs do not allow case managers to use their own cars for transportation.

Another resource consideration is flexible funds. For case management programs that use a strengths-based individualized approach for case planning, often the child and family identify concrete needs that are typically difficult to fund. For example, a child may need after-school tutoring and assistance with homework, or membership in a youth activities program such as the YMCA, or a parent may identify the need for a fence around the family's yard so that their child can play outdoors without safety concerns. Typically, such requests for flexible funds are not extensive and a small amount of money set aside for flexible purposes is sufficient. If flexible dollars are available, bookkeeping mechanisms need to be developed to track use of funds.

A final resource consideration is funds to develop new services and support options. As case managers work with a particular population in a community, they often identify services that are needed by a large percentage of the children and families, but are not being provided. As these gaps are identified, it is useful to have funds available for service development.

An Example of a Case Management Intervention: Children and Youth Intensive Case Management

In 1988, the New York State Office of Mental Health officially initiated its system of care activities through the development and implementation of three community-based services for children with SED. One of these services was Children and Youth Intensive Case Management (CYICM). The purposes of the case management programs were to offer community-based alternatives to hospitalization and to augment the outpatient clinic services then available as the primary community-based intervention for children with SED and their families. CYICM programs were initiated in several areas of the state and subjected to monitoring and evaluation before being disseminated to the entire state.

CYICM was developed specifically to respond to the individuals whose needs were not being met by the current services available. The programmatic goals were loosely defined and included reduction of inappropriate hospitalization, increased community engagement, and achievement of the child's and family's goals. Given the economic, political, geographic, and cultural differences throughout the state, the decision was made to develop a set of statewide principles, but to permit local autonomy in the development of organizational strategies for service provision. The following principles were established at the state level.

PRINCIPLES

Program Goal

The statewide goal was to enable children to succeed in natural environments, including family, school, and community. Emphasis was placed on providing services in these natural environments and offering supports to parents, siblings, and teachers as well as the rostered child.

Focus

All activities of the case manager should reflect the goals of the person being served, with mutual efforts to create opportunities for treatment, support, and rehabilitation.

Target Population

A number of high-risk populations were identified for enrollment. The child population was defined as youth between the ages of 5 and 18 who had histories of psychiatric hospitalization in the past year, were heavy users of crisis services, or who had failed in a variety of treatment options, such as day treatment or treatment foster care. Enrolled youth were required to have a DSM III-R or IV diagnosis and serious impairments affecting their functioning at home, school, and/or community.

Identification of Cases

A rostering process was developed in which children were nominated locally by those responsible for the mental health system. It was recommended that a local interagency committee nominate individuals since the target children and families often have multiple needs requiring simultaneous intervention by several child-serving systems. Once rostered, a "no eject" policy was established in which no child could be removed from the roster or the program without a major life event, such as a move away from the locality. Rostering was analogous to becoming entitled to a wide array of treatment and support services.

Caseload Size

Caseloads could be no higher than an average of 10 persons per case manager. Local variations, such as a team approach, were permitted.

Location

Case management activities were expected to occur in the community. Case managers were not expected to be in their office except for collateral contacts and completion of paperwork. Every effort was made to ensure that case managers had adequate transportation and communication resources.

Role

The role of case managers was not limited to service coordination, but extended to advocacy, change agent activities, and development of supports. The case manager was also expected to teach, model productive behaviors and problem-solving skills, and assist clients in accessing health and mental health care and social services. Case managers were expected to assist clients in developing permanent, informal supports. This could be accomplished by working to improve relationships or links with friends, family, the faith community, and other community organizations, or through referral to support groups. Case managers were also expected to spend time in schools working with teachers, principals, and guidance counselors. The mandates of P.L. 99-142 were used to advocate for the least restrictive educational setting, and parents were educated on their rights under this law.

Access

Case managers were expected to be available 24 hours a day, seven days a week. This access could be either direct to a family's case manager—for example, by providing a home phone number—or through a rotation system using other local case managers.

Duration

CYICM was not time-limited, but was to be provided for as long as the client and case manager believed it was necessary.

Partnerships

The local interagency team, including family members, was responsible for identifying and developing strategies to remove systemic barriers to service. Case managers used linkages with social services, juvenile justice programs, alcohol and substance abuse programs, health care organizations, and mental health programs to meet the needs of their clients.

FINANCING

Two financing mechanisms were developed to facilitate the accomplishment of the principles described above. First, using the Medicaid-targeted case management option, a capitated financing strategy was selected in order to give case managers the flexibility they needed. The sole billing requirement was that the case manager see each person on their caseload four times each month, with the intent that the intensity of services would vary by client need. Secondly, a pool of flexible funds was made available to localities to meet individual's needs and to fill service gaps, such as respite programs and after-school programs. The expenditure of funds varied locally, with the state requiring that at least 25% of the pool be used for client-specific requests.

EVALUATION

Three primary strategies were used for the evaluation of CYICM. These strategies were the use of (1) a monitoring and quality assurance approach based on data contained in a minimum data set, (2) program evaluation of the outcomes of 199 children and their families, and (3) a matched data analysis of the inpatient utilization of 392 children enrolled in CYICM and 392 eligible children who had not been enrolled in CYICM and who functioned as the comparison group. These evaluation strategies provided evidence that the target population was being served and that children enrolled in CYICM experienced a significant decrease in aggression, suicidal behavior, sexual acting-out, cruelty to animals, fire-setting, and psychotic behavior over the course of the intervention. They also experienced a significant decrease in their needs for education and housing services, while demonstrating a continuing need for social supports, mental health, vocational, medical, dental, and recreational services. Enrolled children showed a decrease in inpatient utilization when compared to their own hospitalization histories over a four-year period (two years before and after enrollment in CYICM) and when compared to a matched sample of non-enrolled children (Evans, Banks, Huz, & McNulty, 1994). These findings supported the conclusion that CYICM was an effective intervention for decreasing more restrictive hospitalizations and was associated with positive child outcomes. Although the evaluation failed to demonstrate any changes in family functioning, this could have been expected, as the CYICM model is focused on the child in the context of his/her family, rather than being truly family-focused.

The Evidence Base

In their 1996 book, *What Works in Children's Mental Health Services: Uncovering Answers to Critical Questions,* Kutash and Rivera reviewed the existing studies related to the effectiveness of case management (at the time there were six studies, some not completed), and concluded that the research base was too limited to allow any definitive conclusion. Recently, Burns (1999) identified case management as a potentially promising intervention whose quality standards have been based largely on regulation, rather than on practice parameters, best practices, quality monitoring, or other approaches to achieving relevant and consistent practice. Since Kutash and Rivera's review, three experimental studies of the effectiveness of various models of case management have been completed. All three have shown positive benefits to children and families when a particular model of case management was used. These studies and their results, as well as other major studies conducted on case management for children and youth with mental disorders, are discussed below and summarized in Table 3.2. This comparison of studies is limited to those using a rigorous experimental design, as this design controls for the greatest number of threats to internal validity and represents a parsimonious way to assess effectiveness of interventions. As noted by Farmer and colleagues (1997), conducting randomized trials in community settings has unique challenges. Because of the nature of case management, however, and in the absence of a widely accepted research model (Burns, 1999), the strongest test of the effectiveness of case management is likely to come from randomized clinical trials in community settings.

Building on a base of monitoring and program evaluation studies related to New York State's model of intensive case management that had been shown to have positive outcomes (Evans, Banks, Huz, & McNulty, 1994), Evans and her colleagues (Evans et al., 1994) conducted a randomized clinical trial com-

Table 3.2 Randomized Clinical Trials of Case Management Studies for Children with Severe Emotional Disorders

Author(s)	Target Population	Sample Size	Comparison	Follow-up	Outcomes	Findings
Burns, Farmer, Angold, Costello & Behar, 1996	Children eligible for the children's initiative: psychiatric diagnosis, functional impairment, out of home or at imminent risk, 8–18 years, no sibling in the study.	82 Experimental 85 Controls	Team with a case manager (Experimental); Team in which the primary therapist also functioned as case manager (Control)		Child	Less use of alcohol for experimental
					Family	More positive assessment with mental health centers System Experimental
					Services	Richer array of services, more in community services for Experimental
					Hospital use	Decreased hospital days for Experimental
					Satisfaction	Greater satisfaction with services for Experimental
Evans, Armstrong et al., 1994; 1998b; 1998c	Children with SED approved for placement in treatment foster care, ages 5–13 years	27 Experimental 15 Controls	Family-centered intensive care management (FCICM) (Experimental); Family-based treatment (FBT) (treatment foster care) (Control)	18 months	Child	Experimental had more favorable outcomes in role performance, behavior, overall functioning, externalizing & internalizing behavior, social problems & thought problems.
					Family	No differences in functioning or self-efficacy
					System	Costs/child/18months $51,965 FBT $18,000 FCICM

Study	Sample	N	Intervention	Follow-up	Outcome	Findings
Ruffolo, 1999	Children 5–17 with SED referred to children and youth intensive case management in two New York counties, ages 5–18 years	56 Experimentals 38 Controls	Support, education, and empowerment (SEE) model (Experimental); Children and youth intensive case management (Control)	18 months	Child	Both groups showed improvement in symptom and problem behavior over time; Experimental group improved more
					Services	Use decreased significantly over time in both groups
					Family	No differences in coping and problem-solving
					System satisfaction	No significant findings

Studies with Special Populations

Study	Sample	N	Intervention	Follow-up	Outcome			
Cauce et al., 1994; 1998	Homeless youth in Seattle	78 Experimentals 72 Controls	Services plus intensive case manager (Experimental); Services as usual with case manager (Control)	1 year	Child	Mental health and social adjustment		
					Homelessness	Both groups had decreased homelessness during last 3 months of study		
Evans, Boothroyd, & Armstrong, 1997	Children 4–18 presenting in crisis at two psychiatric emergency services in the Bronx, NY	90 HBCI 85 HBCI+ 63 CCM	Homebuilders Family Preservation (HBCI); Enhanced Homebuilder's model (HBCI+); Crisis case management (CCM)	Discharge and 6 months post-discharge	At Discharge*	CCM	HBCI	HBCI+
					Family adaptability	+	+	+
					Children's self-confidence	+	+	+
					Parental self-efficacy	+	+	+
					Child social competence	+	+	+
					Family cohesion		+	+

(continued)

Table 3.2 Randomized Clinical Trials of Case Management Studies for Children with Severe Emotional Disorders (*Continued*)

Author(s)	Target Population	Sample Size	Comparison	Follow-up	Outcomes	Findings
						6 Months Post-discharge** CCM HBCI HBCI+
					Social support	+
					Family adaptability	+ + +
					Children's self confidence	+ + +
					Parental self-efficacy	+ + +
					Child social competence	+ + +
					Family cohesion	
					Social support	

* + = Change from baseline to discharge (p < .05)
**+ = Change from baseline to 6 months post-discharge (p < .05)

paring the outcomes of two intensive community-based interventions for children with SED in three rural counties in New York State. These interventions were Family-Centered Intensive Case Management (FCICM), which used a team of case manager and parent advocate to provide care, and Family-Based Treatment (FBT), a treatment foster care program developed by People Places, Inc. (Bryant, 1981). Children 5 to 13 years who had been approved for out-of-home placement by an interdisciplinary team and whose caregivers agreed to participate in the research were randomly assigned to either FCICM (receipt of intensive services at home) or to FBT (treatment of the child out-of-home in a treatment foster care setting). This experimental study was funded by the National Institute of Mental Health and the Center for Mental Health Services. For additional information on the interventions, see Evans and colleagues (1994).

A total of 42 children and their families ($n = 27$ in FCICM and $n = 15$ in FBT) were enrolled in the study. Assessments of child and family functioning, child symptoms, and the restrictiveness of the child's living environment were done every six months for a period of 18 months. Since both FCICM and FBT were intensive family-based interventions, the child outcomes were expected to be similar. Because support activities and behavior-management skills training were offered to families enrolled in FCICM, family outcomes were expected to favor those families in that intervention, while program costs were expected to be within 10% of each other.

The study indicated that the FCICM group experienced more positive outcomes. Children in both groups evidenced a decrease in symptoms and an improvement in functioning over time. The children enrolled in FCICM, however, had more positive outcomes in role performance, behavior, overall functioning, externalizing behavior, internalizing behavior, social problems, and thought problems. The children enrolled in FBT did not show more positive outcomes on any measure. Unfortunately, at the end of the 18-month follow-up, families in neither the experimental nor the control intervention showed statistically significant changes in functioning or parenting skills. Some positive changes evidenced by families in FCICM at earlier assessment periods were not sustained until the 18-month follow-up. (Evans et al., 1998b, 1998c). A cost study was conducted as part of the study (Johnson, 1998; Evans, Armstrong, Kuppinger, Huz, & Johnson, 1998a). For equal mean lengths of stay, the costs for a child enrolled in FBT were nearly three times higher than for children enrolled in FCICM.

A randomized clinical trial was conducted by Burns and colleagues (1996) in North Carolina. This study compared the outcomes of 167 children enrolled in two models of case management. This study was designed in conjunction with the Children's Initiative funded through the Robert Wood Johnson Foundation's Mental Health Services Program for Youth (England & Cole, 1992), although the case management study was separately funded by the National Institute of Mental Health. Youth eligible for the case management study were those who were the target population for the Children's Initiative, were characterized as having a psychiatric diagnosis and displaying substantial functional impairment, and were placed out-of-home or at imminent risk of such placement. In addition, to be eligible for the case management intervention they had to be at least 8 years old and living in one of two most populous counties in which the parent initiative was being conducted. Finally, an enrollee could not be a sibling of another study participant. Children were followed for one year after their entry into the project.

Children were referred to the research study at the time of their entry into the Children's Initiative. Following parental agreement to participate, the research study coordinator randomly assigned the child to either the experimental ($n = 82$) or control group ($n = 85$). The experimental condition was a treatment team with a case manager while the control condition was a treatment team in which the child's primary mental health clinician served as the case manager. The study showed that designating a clinician as a case manager did not increase the amount of time the clinician spent on case management activities (Burns et al., 1996). In regard to child outcomes, the youth in the experimental condition reported less use of alcohol than youth in the control condition. The system outcomes included a longer length of stay in treatment for the children in the experimental condition, with a richer array of services and more community-based services being used by them. The children in the experimental group also used fewer hospital days and they reported greater satisfaction with services than children and families in the control condition.

A recent quasi-experimental study, completed by Ruffolo (1994, 1999), involved a sample of 94 children newly enrolled in Children and Youth Intensive Case Management in two upstate New York counties. This study was funded by the National Institute of Mental Health. The experiment involved assignment to the NYS CYICM expanded broker model of case management (comparison condition) or to a Support, Education and Empowerment (SEE) model of case management (experimental condition). The latter condition was a combination of NYS CYICM service broker model plus a specific therapeutic approach. This therapeutic approach was based on McFarlane's (1990) research on expressed emotions and multiple family groups, which had been conducted with parents of adults who have schizophrenia. The resulting combination of model and therapy resulted in a new model of therapeutic case management. The children enrolled in this study were 11.7 years on average and had been identified as having SED. Data on children and families were collected at baseline, 9 months, and 18 months after assignment to treatment condition. The data from this study are still being analyzed, but it is apparent that both groups showed improvement over time in problem behaviors, with the experimental group (SEE) evidencing a greater amount of improvement. Both groups showed a decrease over time in the number of services used. Again, however, there were no significant findings on the outcome measures for families, except that the experimental group's number of people available to advise them increased over time (Ruffolo, 1999).

There are also two experimental studies of case management models used for different—not necessarily children with SED—target populations. Cauce and her colleagues (1994, 1998) studied homeless youth aged 13 to 21 in Seattle and randomly assigned them to services as usual (YouthCare's Orion Center, $n = 72$) or services enhanced with use of an intensive case manager (Project Passage, the experimental condition, $n = 78$). Caseloads for case managers in the usual-care condition ranged from 20 to 30 active cases, while those in the experimental condition did not exceed 12 youth. The nine key components of Project Passage were assessment, use of treatment teams, individualized treatment plans, linkage, monitoring and tracking, advocacy, crisis services, flexible funds, and development of a therapeutic relationship. Youth were followed for a year, with assessments at baseline and every three months. Preliminary findings at the three-month follow-up noted that youth in both groups demonstrated significant improvements in mental health outcomes and social adjustment. The experimental group youth also showed decreased self-reported aggression and externalizing behavior and increased satisfaction with their quality of life. Findings based on 150 youth followed for one year showed that the mental health and social adjustment of youths in both conditions improved over time and that the amount of time they spent homeless in the preceding three months decreased. There was no indication that youth in Project Passage improved more than those in the regular case management provided by YouthCare's Orion Center.

The second study conducted with a special population was done by Evans, Boothroyd, and Armstrong (1997). These investigators randomly assigned children presenting at psychiatric emergency services in crisis to one of three intensive, in-home services, one of which was Crisis Case Management (CCM). Although the families assigned to CCM experienced positive short-term outcomes, as measured at discharge, they failed to show the same gains in family cohesion and social support as the families enrolled in Enhanced Home-Based Crisis Intervention had shown. At six months post-discharge, however, families in all three models of crisis care showed retention of their gains in family adaptability, children's self-concept, parental self-efficacy, and child social competence. Additionally, CCM was as successful as the other two interventions in keeping the child in crisis at home.

What can be concluded about the effectiveness of case management? Based on the limited number of studies available, it appears that use of a dedicated case manager or case management team is associated with more positive child, family, and system outcomes than not using a case manager or designating the primary mental health clinician as the case manager. This conclusion is tentative, however, as research has not yet dealt adequately with the plethora of factors related to structure (e.g., where case management is based and the qualifications of staff) and process (e.g., how services are provided and paid for), as identified by Burns and colleagues (1995). Nor have there been any published studies examining the effects of case management versus no case management. In addition, only a few models of case management have been tested, and the issue of the embeddedness of case management within systems of care with varying degrees of complexity and maturity has not been researched. For example, research has not investigated the effects of a client-driven model of independent case management versus other case management models. The outcomes associated with managed care's model of care management versus an advocacy/empowerment model have not been examined. The field of children's mental health has not yet mined the research on case management in adult mental health and other service areas, such as physical disabilities, for outcomes and methodologies that can be applied in advancing research in the child field.

It is also critical that research be directed to the practice of case management in order to understand the relationship between therapeutic alliance with clients (both children and their caregivers) and outcomes and to identify the most effective strategies to use in coordinating services across family-serving agencies. Of some concern are the findings in several of the reviewed studies that, although a portion of the intervention was focused on families, significant changes in family functioning or caregiver skills and coping have not been realized as expected. This failure to produce fundamental change in the context in which the child is living may have important implications for the child's long-term functioning and placement and that of his/her siblings.

Finally, it is essential that program developers in the area of case management and evaluators of these interventions focus more on the cultural diversity of the populations served. The cultural identity and level of acculturation of persons receiving services have important implications for the training of case managers. Training programs should identify culture as a salient factor that influences the ways in which case managers can work most effectively with the children and families in their caseloads. All of the currently unstudied or understudied aspects of case management have important implications, not only for current practice and improving child and family outcomes, but also for the training of future case managers.

4

The Wraparound Approach

JOHN D. BURCHARD

ERIC J. BRUNS

SARA N. BURCHARD

Wraparound is an approach to treatment that has evolved over the past 15 years through efforts to help families with the most challenging children function more effectively in the community. More specifically, it is a definable planning process that results in a unique set of community services and natural supports that are individualized for a child and family to achieve a positive set of outcomes (Burns & Goldman, 1999). Wraparound is child and family centered, focused on child and family strengths, community based, culturally relevant, flexible, and coordinated across agencies (VanDenBerg & Grealish, 1998; Burchard, Burchard, Sewell, & VanDenBerg, 1993).

While most of the development of wraparound has focused on families who have children with severe emotional and behavioral problems, the approach has also been used for these problems with "emancipated" adolescents and with families who have family members who are experiencing severe and/or chronic physical illnesses and developmental disabilities. In general, wraparound has been implemented in the mental health, education, child welfare, and juvenile justice sectors.

The philosophy that spawned wraparound is relatively simple: Identify the community services and supports that a family needs and provide them as long as they are needed. As one parent said, "This isn't rocket science, this is common sense." It is a philosophy that developed in response to the realization that traditional services for helping the most challenged children and youth were not working. According to another parent, "It doesn't make much sense to ignore a family that has a child with severe emotional problems and then send the child away for expensive treatment that doesn't work."

While the initial philosophy behind wraparound was relatively simple, the development and implementation of the intervention is complex. In addition, there has been increasing observation that the term "wraparound" has been applied to describe a vast range of interventions, many of which are not consistent with the original approach. In response, through the efforts of many service providers, administrators, family members, advocates, and researchers, an intervention has been developed that has a clear set of values, essential elements, practice principles, training guidelines, and an emerging base of research and evaluation.

One reflection of the efforts toward better definition is the reference to wraparound as an intervention rather than a service. The more common label of a "wraparound service" is often interpreted as a specific service or an array of categorical services. For example, some agencies have declared that they have offered wraparound if they provided respite or individualized services, even though many essential elements of the approach were lacking (e.g., the parents were not involved in the decision-making process). Other agencies have described their intervention as wraparound because they utilized funding from two separate agencies, even though all families received the same array of services. There has also been the misconception that wraparound can be administered outside the community, in residential treatment centers or psychiatric hospitals, even though wraparound was conceived as and is intended to be an alternative to institutionalization. In short, there has not always been the awareness that wraparound is a comprehensive approach that requires a specific set of values, elements, and principles, all of which have to be in place.

Theory

Wraparound was not developed from a formal theory of change, but rather as an alternative to the more medically oriented models of service that have failed to recognize the importance of context and normative roles on behavioral development and adjustment. The wraparound theory of change that has evolved from this grassroots development is that children with severe emotional and behavioral problems will develop a more normal lifestyle if their services and supports are family centered and child focused, strengths based, individualized, community based, interagency coordinated, and culturally competent.

The formulation and application of the principles of wraparound are consistent with several prominent psychosocial theories of child development. Particularly influential was the social-ecological theory of Urie Bronfenbrenner (1979), which sees behavior as developing in the context of multiple reciprocal interactions over time: The child, the family, the neighborhood, the school, and the community interact to affect one another in a continuous fashion. These relationships are critical to the development of both adaptive and maladaptive behaviors within a specific family and cultural milieu. The most important contribution of Bronfenbrenner's theory to the development of wraparound is that the developmental process occurs within the unique ecological environment of each child and family. Therefore, behavior change or adjustment needs to take place within the normative roles, expectations, and opportunities of those settings, and in interaction with those systems or contexts.

Wraparound also incorporates much of the social learning theory of Bandura (1977). While each child brings a unique set of biological characteristics into the environment, behavior is still shaped by the interaction of those biological characteristics and the many reciprocal relationships that occur within the child's environment over time. The key message from Bandura's theory is that maladaptive behavior is learned according to the same principles as adaptive behavior, and the task at hand is to help rearrange the environment so the child can learn to behave in a more adaptive manner. This is why wraparound must be extremely individualized. What will be the most helpful intervention for one family is unlikely to be the most helpful for another. For example, one family may benefit from more informal supports (e.g., respite, a support group, a mentor, or after-school services) while another may benefit most from a more professional intervention (e.g., training in anger management, behavior modification, or marriage or substance-abuse counseling).

Finally, the wraparound process is consistent with the systems theory espoused by Munger (1998). In addition to ecological sensitivity, this theory recognizes that change in one part of a system can influence other parts of the system and that the most effective system is one that maximizes the collaboration and coordination among the multiple parts. As a result, planning and implementation of wraparound must involve representatives of all the important "systems" for a given child (e.g., parents, friends, school, work, and community). Systems theory also guides the need for multidisciplinary training and supervision.

In the latter half of the 1980s, efforts to implement wraparound began to spread as many state and county public services agencies began to explore new ways to provide community-based services to children with severe mental health challenges. By 1990, the wraparound approach had been established as a viable alternative to residential treatment, with many advocates expressing the belief that wraparound was more youth- and family-friendly, less costly, and more effective than traditional services. Since that time there has been a remarkable expansion in the utilization of the wraparound approach. The interest is reflected in an increasingly large attendance at four national wraparound conferences (550 in Pittsburgh in 1991, 850 in Chicago in 1993, 1,150 in Vermont in 1994, and over 2,000 in California in 1996). With respect to utilization, the results of a 1998 survey of the United States and its territories suggests that the current number of youth with their families engaged in wraparound could be as high as 200,000 (Faw, 1999).

Coinciding with the rapid proliferation of wraparound has been concern for more uniform definitions and practice standards. As noted above, an increasing recognition of the multiple and complex mechanisms that can operate within the wraparound approach, combined with concerns about inappropriate application of the term "wraparound," have demanded a more exacting definition of the intervention. The delineation of operationally defined elements and practice standards is also necessary to allow for controlled, replicable studies of wraparound's effectiveness.

In the late spring of 1998, a focus group of wraparound leaders and advocates met at Duke University to address some of these issues. This group identified a set of essential elements and requirements for practice that are neces-

Table 4.1   Essential Elements of Wraparound

1. Wraparound must be based in the community.

2. The wraparound approach must be a team-driven process involving the family, child, natural supports, agencies, and community services working together to develop, implement, and evaluate the individualized plan.

3. Families must be full and active partners in every level of the wraparound process.

4. Services and supports must be individualized, built on strengths, and meet the needs of children and families across life domains to promote success, safety, and permanence in home, school, and community.

5. The process must be culturally competent, building on the unique values, preferences, and strengths of children and families, and their communities.

6. Wraparound child and family teams must have flexible approaches and adequate and flexible funding.

7. Wraparound plans must include a balance of formal services and informal community and family supports.

8. There must be an unconditional commitment to serve children and their families.

9. The plans should be developed and implemented based on an interagency, community-based collaborative process.

10. Outcomes must be determined and measured for the system, for the program, and for the individual child and family.

Source: Goldman, 1998

sary components of wraparound. They are listed in Tables 4.1 and 4.2. A more detailed account of the definitions, values, essential elements, and requirements for practice is provided in Burns and Goldman (1999).

Intervention Parameters

The elements and practice principles listed above provide the framework for the two main components of the wraparound intervention. The first component is a family-centered decision-making process that identifies those services and supports that will help meet the family's needs. The second component is the actual array of services and supports that are implemented. Operating together, these two components provide the primary active ingredients of the wraparound intervention.

While the individualization of wraparound precludes a step-by-step set of algorithms, the elements and practice principles define a measurable decision-making process that can be applied consistently across children and families. For example, the elements of family-centered care and team-driven planning mandate that decisions are made by family members, professionals, and advocates who work together as a team. The elements of individualized and

Table 4.2 Requirements for Practice

1. The community collaborative structure, with broad representation, manages the overall wraparound process and establishes the vision and mission.

2. A lead organization is designated to function under the community collaborative structure and manage the implementation of the wraparound process.

3. A referral mechanism is established to determine the children and families to be included in the wraparound process.

4. Resource coordinators are hired as specialists to facilitate the wraparound process, conducting strengths/needs assessments, facilitating the team-planning process, and managing the implementation of the services/support plan.

5. With the referred child and family, the resource coordinator conducts strengths and needs assessments.

6. The resource coordinator works with the child and family to form a child and family team.

7. The child and family team functions as a team *with* the child and family engaged in an interactive process to develop a collective vision, related goals, and an individualized plan that is family-centered and team-based.

8. The child and family team develops a crisis plan.

9. Within the service/support plan, each goal must have outcomes stated in measurable terms, and the progress on each monitored on a regular basis.

10. The community collaborative structure reviews the plans.

Source: Goldman, 1998

strengths-based planning demand that, for all families, strengths will be identified and utilized to identify services and supports that will meet family goals, and natural supports will be maximized and replace professional services as soon as possible. However, the wraparound principles of flexibility and individualization also demand that there will be a different set of active ingredients for each family, and that the methods used for each family may change dramatically over time.

CASE EXAMPLE

The following example illustrates one application of the 10 principles of the wraparound model, and attempts to demonstrate where definable procedures may be used to achieve them. Though family stories describing wraparound exist elsewhere (e.g., Burchard et al., 1993), the following example details methods employed to achieve the 10 core principles and, where appropriate, describes where alternative processes may have been employed to do so. The names of the youth and family members and some details have been changed to protect the family's identity. This case study is drawn from those described in Kendziora, Bruns, Osher, Pacchiano, and Meija (2001).

Laura, an 8-year-old girl of Caucasian and African American descent, was referred to an interagency project using the wraparound model after a 6-month stay in a residential treatment center (RTC). Laura was originally placed in regular foster care at age 5 when it was determined that her biological mother was not able to provide a safe home for Laura and her sister because of involvement in drugs and street life. Laura reportedly witnessed significant abuse of her mother at the hands of her father and other men, and was herself the victim of emotional and physical abuse. Shortly after placement in foster care, Laura was sexually abused by another foster child in the home, after which she was discharged to the care of Cathy, her maternal grandmother, with services from the local mental health center.

However, Laura's behavior quickly deteriorated. She became physically aggressive, threatening others with knives and other household tools, and also became sexually aggressive toward her sister. She also would occasionally become dissociative, having a blank stare and screaming that her assailant was in the house. These behaviors led to the 6-month residential placement. At the end of this stay, Cathy was adamant that Laura return to her home rather than transition to foster care, a setting in which Laura had been abused previously. However, providers at the residential treatment center staunchly advocated for treatment foster care, because they viewed Cathy, who herself had a history of substance abuse and incarceration, as lacking necessary skills to care for Laura. During this debate, Cathy was referred to the interagency wraparound project by a neighbor, a social worker familiar with the service delivery system.

Element 1: Community Based

In order to facilitate an alternative plan of returning Laura to her grandmother's house, Cathy was aided by the director of the local Federation of Families for Children's Mental Health (FFCMH), which collaborated with the local mental health and social services agencies in administering wraparound. After they found that there was no child protective services order for Laura, FFCMH advocates immediately began attending transition-planning meetings with Cathy and RTC staff to support a community-based placement in the home. As one advocate said to RTC staff, "If you're going to put $4,000 per month into a treatment foster home, why can't we spend the same money and put the 'treatment' into Cathy's home?" As described below, Cathy and her team eventually identified supports the family needed to keep Laura at home, and the project secured these supports through flexible funding mechanisms.

Element 2: Team-Driven

Once the decision to transition Laura home was in place, FFCMH helped Cathy identify the persons in her life she wished to have on the child and family team. The team's first step was to convene for a three-session "training" that actually functioned as initial team meetings. One of the first tasks of this training was to identify what services and supports were needed in order for Laura to remain at home with her grandmother, her sister, and 12-year-old aunt (Cathy's daughter). These included finding a larger house to rent that was closer to providers and in which Laura could have her own room, installing alarms on Laura's bedroom door, and securing formal services such as respite, tutors, parent training, and other in-home supports to assist Cathy in providing caregiving. Flexible funds from the interagency project were used to provide all such formal and informal supports that were identified in these intensive initial planning meetings, including money for a security deposit on the new house, which was rented within 2 weeks of intake into services.

Following these initial meetings, the team convened on an as-needed basis to solve problems faced by the family, to assess progress, to set new goals, or to identify "action opportunities" to meet goals. However, Cathy's methods of accessing team members to help set and accomplish her family's goals were primarily her decision. Often, she would mobilize team members—be they formal service providers or community supports—through informal communications such as phone calls. On other occasions, she and her supports would decide that a full team meeting was necessary. As such, 1–2 months would occasionally pass between full team meetings. An alternative practice would be a more proactive team meeting schedule in which the full team meets monthly or bimonthly; however, in the current example, it could be argued that the principle of "family centered" was considered more primary than that of "team driven."

Element 3: Families are Partners

For the project in the current example, the initial team training emphasized from the outset that the parent (or grandparent, in this case) was an integral part of the team and had ownership of the plan and that the plan was family centered rather than child centered. As described above, team meetings demand that the family members be the focal point in identifying goals and the requirements necessary to meet these goals. In addition, the very construction of the team was driven by Cathy and her daughters and granddaughters. Before the initial training, a team composition exercise was conducted with Cathy and FFCMH advocates. Laura was drawn at the center of a diagram, followed by concentric circles that included immediate family members in the next ring, friends and community supports in the second ring, and professionals and service providers in the most distal ring. Such an exercise encouraged brainstorming about inclusion of team members and also was referred to during service planning as a method of ensuring primacy among the most proximal supports to the family. For example, the initial training included very few formal providers, because primacy was granted to family members, friends, and informal support persons. As another example, the role of the family's case manager (employed by the interagency project) was not to coordinate or dictate services, but rather primarily to ensure that funds required by Cathy and her team were quickly and efficiently mobilized.

Element 4: Individualized and Strengths Based

As noted above, one of the purposes of the initial team meetings was to brainstorm the specific needs of Cathy's family. This included an exercise called a "24-7 chart," in which Laura's entire week was described, hour-by-hour, by family members as a way of ensuring that a full complement of needs was identified. During the course of wraparound, regular meetings were held to assess success toward initial goals, which were broadly defined by Cathy and her support network as (1) "To keep Laura home and provide for safety," and (2) "to move to a bigger house closer to [the center of town]." For each goal, and goals that were identified in subsequent team meetings, specific steps—or "action opportunities"—were delineated. Services and supports changed with each meeting, with family members always taking the lead in identifying goals. As time progressed, formal supports that were required initially, such as intensive in-home professional support to model methods of behavior management, yielded to more informal supports such as karate lessons for the three oldest children in the home.

To ensure that services were strengths based, an intensive exercise was conducted at the initial meeting to identify the strengths of the child, family members, and all other team members. These strengths then were posted on the walls during all team meetings as a way of assisting in identification of "action opportunities" needed to meet goals. For example, Cathy's desire to "build the family and keep it together" was identified as a strength, and as such she became empowered to advocate for necessary services and supports, and was encouraged to work intensively with in-home providers to improve her behavior-modification skills. One professional's strength was that she preferred flexibility in her work hours, which allowed her to be the expert on-call for crisis or respite. Laura's 12-year-old aunt's strengths included enjoying outdoor activities, so she was built into the plan as a "professional playmate" for Laura. Finally, Laura's strengths included an affinity for drawing and coloring, which was built into her Individualized Education Program (IEP) at school, and a desire to learn karate, which was identified as an informal support in which the family could participate.

Another method of reinforcing a strengths-based approach in the team was the completion of a "normalization exercise" during the initial team training. Team members were presented with nine life domains (e.g., family, living situation, social/recreational) and asked to independently write down a number of important "norms" within each domain that were pertinent to Laura and her family. For example, "it is normal for kids . . . to have someone to talk to, to have sleepovers, to have some privacy" and "it is normal for parents . . . to have lives of their own, to be able to work if they want to, to be safe," etc. This exercise was completed before the team defined the family's goals and needs, so that needs were identified that would enable the achievement of norms rather than merely address deficiencies.

Element 5: Culturally Competent

For Cathy and her family, providers and team members, there were two primary levels of cultural awareness. Perhaps foremost, Cathy's need to maintain control of her own family's situation (something she referred to as "driving her own bus") was identified as essential, despite her need for help. Previous providers had been reluctant to give Cathy control over planning and delivery of services, which was viewed as disempowering and detrimental to her ability to care for her children and grandchildren. Thus, providers and team members supported her desire to be at the center of the planning and coordination process, and to keep the children at home. A second cultural issue pertinent to the family was that Cathy was Caucasian, while her daughters and granddaughters were of both Caucasian and African American descent. Providers and team members were diligent to schedule team meetings that would enable Laura's uncles—who were African American—to attend, and to support action opportunities that involved these uncles and other African American team members.

Element 6: Flexible Funding

For Cathy and her family, a key to the achievement of a milieu of individualized and family-centered services and supports was the flexible funding mechanism employed by the interagency wraparound project. The project succeeded in blending funds from the local mental health and social services agencies, augmented the pool with grant money, and sought reimbursement wherever possible. With this pool, the project was able to front money to the team and family to buy whatever was necessary, including security deposits, automobile repairs, and $397 per month for a "relative placement"—aid to Cathy beyond her public-assistance allotment. Project staff dealt with the issues of reimbursement and unbundling of service and support funds at an administrative level. Even with such an array of expenses, total costs for the family fell within two months to below the $4,000 monthly expense that would have been required for a treatment foster care placement.

Element 7: Balance of Formal and Informal Supports

In order to achieve the overarching goal of "to keep Laura home and provide for safety," a number of needs and action opportunities were identified. The team decided that a number of these needs required formal services; however, each service was tied to a subgoal of the overarching goal of keeping Laura at home safely. Formal services included family therapy (to work on how family interactions affected Cathy's caregiving and Laura's behavioral functioning), psychiatric services (to manage Laura's medication), sexual assault services (individual therapy for Laura, which Cathy was allowed to observe in order to better understand Laura's sexual acting-out behaviors), and an in-home worker (to aid Cathy and model behavior management). Wherever possible, however, family needs were met through informal supports. Some of these informal supports required reimbursement, such as respite care (provided by a skilled and trusted neighbor) or karate lessons, while others did not, such as involvement of church members to support Cathy and to help her feel connected to her new neighborhood. Another mechanism employed by the project that encouraged use of informal supports was a rule that at least 50% of all team members be nonprofessionals.

Element 8: Unconditional Commitment

The interagency wraparound project that served Cathy and her family had no exit or termination criteria; the project was committed to serving each family until it voiced that it no longer needed the intensive interagency services. This commitment was extremely important to Cathy and her family, who had previous experiences with providers who had discontinued services before the family was ready for such termination. The care manager's ability to obtain funds for the array of formal and informal supports also contributed to the sense of unconditional commitment. Finally, the team's collaborative creation in the initial team meetings of a 24-hour crisis plan that included responsibilities for both professionals and nonprofessionals reinforced a sense of unconditional commitment to the family. At press time, Cathy's family had been served via the interagency project for approximately one and one-half years. The significant improvement in Laura's behavior and the family's functioning (and the concomitant reduction in overall service expenses) was viewed by the project as evidence of a successful intervention, but not as evidence of the need for termination of services.

Element 9: Collaboration

At the system level, collaboration between the local mental health and social services agencies enabled the project's flexible and blended funding scheme to be realized. The project's arrangement with FFCMH as a training facilitator and resource developer also was essential for the successful intervention scheme for Laura and her family. FFCMH designed the training protocol in which the family's team participated, and FFCMH advocates remained a primary point of contact with Cathy because of her trust in them. At the family level, as described above, team meetings were convened that included all service providers and informal supports as needed, while the care manager arranged for the reimbursement of funds expended.

Element 10: Outcomes Determined and Measured

For Laura's family, outcomes were set at macro and micro levels. One macro-level goal (move to a bigger house) was achieved rather readily, while the other (keep Laura home and provide for safety) required consistent revisiting, with outcomes for smaller intermediate goals set and measured. For example, Cathy and the team identified bedtime as a stressful and difficult time of day for Laura and the family, because of Laura's fears of going to sleep. As a result, the in-home interventionist created a behavior plan specific to bedtime that was monitored as a method of assessing progress, and that was also part of a behavioral reward system. Outcomes also were set around other activities and intermediary goals (e.g., success in tutoring over the summer, creation of a successful crisis plan). When outcomes were not being achieved, the team took that opportunity to reassess the plan that was in place.

The project also maintained an overarching evaluation plan that informed the family's own assessment of outcomes. The project hired family members to independently assess the teams' successes through interviews. Interviews included an assessment across six service and family categories at baseline and at periodic follow-up points, evaluating, for example, the family's level of community supports and the level of normalization of the child's educational and social domains. Such information was translated into easily interpretable pictographs for each family. For Laura's family, results revealed dramatic improvement in child behavior and parental empowerment over the first 6 months. However, the assessment also revealed that, despite the large number of informal resources, Cathy and Laura still had a need for more community supports—Cathy, in the form of neighborhood friends and contacts, and Laura, in the form of playmates and friends at school.

A graphic depiction of the steps and decision points for Laura's family is provided in Figure 4.1. This diagram may represent a typical process for families served through the wraparound model. However, it is also specific to Laura's family's experience and the project that served them. As is demanded in the principles of wraparound, the active ingredients of the intervention were unique to Laura and her family. Key components of the family-centered decision-making process were a grandmother who was committed to having Laura return to the family, and the family members, friends, and professionals who provided guidance and support to help make it happen. Through these efforts, more than a dozen identifiable services and supports were implemented. These included relocating the family to a larger house, installing alarms, and providing security deposits, respite, behavior management training, automobile repairs, family therapy, medication, sexual assault services, and karate lessons. Clearly, these ingredients are unique to this family and differ from what would be appropriate for any other family.

Comparison with Other Approaches

The utilization of multiple active ingredients is not unique to wraparound. Many community-based interventions for challenged children and their families (treatment foster care, case management, multisystemic therapy) emphasize an individualized array of services in which any particular service or combination of services and supports could be responsible for any change that occurs. Nonetheless, principles and practices vary greatly across these models. Major differences include (1) the process for identifying supports or developing service plans; (2) the methods of implementing the arrays of services and supports, including the locus of the therapeutic relationships; (3) target populations; (4) the duration of the intervention; and (5) the nesting of "responsibility" for behavioral change. For example, within multisystemic therapy (MST), the MST therapist works primarily with the parent who administers most of the direct services. If Laura and her family received MST instead of

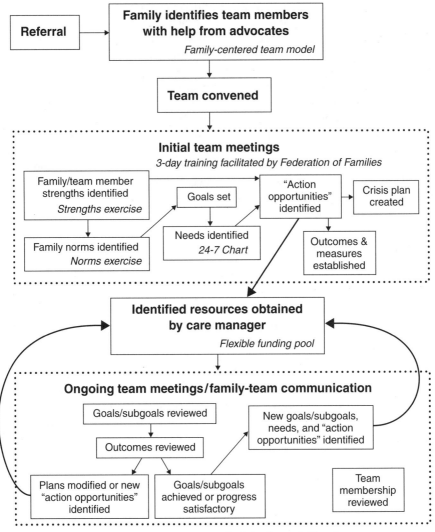

Figure 4.1 The Wraparound Process as Applied for Laura's Family.

wraparound, the locus of therapeutic relationships would primarily have been between the therapist and the grandmother rather than through a complex matrix of supports that included behavior-management training for the grandmother, family therapy, and individual therapy for Laura, and informal supports identified by the child and family team. In addition, had MST been used to assist Laura and her family, the intervention would have been structured, intensive, and short-term. Within wraparound, however, the intervention's intensity and character was guided by Cathy and her supports, and was intended to be available as long as needed by the family. Thus, it is clear that wraparound is a distinct model of intervention for children and their families, with an emerging consensus about principles and standards of practice.

Program Development

Historically, wraparound has been established in communities in different ways (VanDenBerg & Grealish, 1996). In some locations, wraparound initiatives were implemented through a top-down process, with state or county agencies creating polices, blending financial resources, and conducting training programs for service providers, family members, and advocates. In other locations, efforts to establish the wraparound approach were more grassroots, with advocacy for systems change originating with small groups of family members and providers and by case-by-case demonstrations. In most locations, however, it was probably some combination of these approaches that spurred development of wraparound.

An increasingly popular method for developing and implementing wraparound is through the Brief Community Analysis (VanDenBerg & Grealish, 1998). This method employs a qualitative examination conducted by one or more people with recognized experience with the wraparound process, to create a snapshot of current practice in the community. Approximately 30 current child cases from the community are identified, along with at least 40 people (including family members) who have been involved with the delivery of services. Over a 2-day period, experienced wraparound investigators review case files and interview informants. Draft reports are submitted that analyze existing services in the context of wraparound and efforts are made to validate the analysis of the existing services. A final report is then written that details the steps that could be taken to move from the current service-delivery system to the wraparound process. At the line staff level, resource coordinators (also referred to as case managers or resource facilitators) are key players in developing wraparound, responsible for enacting the wraparound principles for each family. The importance of the position is reflected in the following skills and functions:

- assembling a team of people who are key players in the lives of children and families;
- inspiring a strong, nonjudgmental, family-centered approach and performing strengths discoveries;
- helping to develop and implement individualized service and support plans;
- helping to develop crisis plans;
- accessing necessary professional services;
- developing and accessing necessary informal supports;
- initiating necessary training;
- managing flexible funds;

- delivering direct services as needed;
- evaluating the progress of the child and family; and
- preparing transition plans.

Wraparound Training

The diverse skills and functions that are required of the resource coordinator highlight the importance of training. This is especially true given the limitations of most higher education training programs, which stress values, skills, and attitudes that are inconsistent with those associated with the wraparound process. For example, most clinical training programs (e.g., counseling, psychology, psychiatry, social work, nursing, etc.) are based on curricula that are unidisciplinary and guild-driven, focus on deficit discovery, and relate to family members as "clients" rather than "partners."

In response to these limitations, the proponents of wraparound are attempting to meet training needs in three important ways. The first is to establish formal training curricula. Probably the most developed curriculum is the PEN-PAL project implemented in the community mental health site affiliated with East Carolina University in Greenville, North Carolina (Meyers, Kaufman, & Goldman, 1999). The training program, which is primarily provided for agency staff, is based on a comprehensive, seven-chapter manual that begins with an orientation and then guides the staff through the entire wraparound process. There is also a quality-improvement protocol consisting of child and family services and system of care assessments that provides feedback to the PEN-PAL administrators. Similar wraparound training curricula are also being implemented in California, Illinois, and Florida (Faw, Grealish, & Lourie, 1999).

A second training approach involves the creation of a new higher education training program that is based on the core competencies essential to the wraparound process. This approach is exemplified by the Program in Community Mental Health (PCMH) at Trinity College in Vermont. PCMH is a distance-learning, certification, and/or masters-level training program that has been or is being offered to more that 200 students in Vermont, Connecticut, Pennsylvania, Wisconsin, Maryland, and Alaska (Meyers, Kaufman, & Goldman, 1999). The student population is mostly comprised of mid-career human-service providers and administrators as well as family members and consumers.

The most prevalent approach to training, according to a recent wraparound survey, is an expert-driven train-the-trainer model (Faw, 1999). Most of the states that provide formal training report that they have relied on short training programs performed by a small group of wraparound experts. The people who are trained are then involved in training others, with additional consultation being provided as needed. As part of this effort, there is now a comprehensive training manual and videotape presentations on the essential elements of the wraparound process and the development and function of a child and family team (VanDenBerg & Grealish, 1998).

Research on Wraparound

Fifteen studies were identified which attempted to assess the effectiveness of the wraparound approach: two qualitative case studies, nine pre-post studies, two quasi-experimental studies, and two studies involving randomized clinical trials. Fourteen of the studies were reviewed elsewhere (Burns, Goldman, Faw, & Burchard, 1999), while one of the quasi-experimental studies is more recent. The remainder of this section will consist of a brief summary of these studies, followed by a review of their limitations and some suggested areas for further research.

The 15 studies were conducted in 10 different states. In each study, the authors described the wraparound intervention as family centered, community based, culturally relevant, individualized, strengths based, flexible, and coordinated across agencies. This is not meant to imply, however, that the intervention was the same in each study. As will be discussed below, methods for establishing the fidelity of wraparound are currently being developed, and until that occurs the degree of variability in the intervention is unclear. The population targeted by these wraparound initiatives was children with severe emotional or behavioral problems who were either receiving some form of residential treatment or were at risk of residential treatment.

CASE STUDIES

Early research on the wraparound approach featured case study designs and focused on wraparound programs that were developed and implemented under the leadership of John VanDenBerg and Karl Dennis, two of the founders of the wraparound approach. The first was an extensive retrospective analysis that included personal interviews with approximately 75 key informants who were involved with 10 youth who had been receiving wraparound through the Alaska Youth Initiative (Burchard et al., 1993). Included were 3 youth with a primary diagnosis of schizophrenia, 5 diagnosed with conduct disorders, and 2 with diagnoses of borderline personalities. One to two years after entry to wraparound, all the youth were still residing in the community. Five youth were no longer requiring services, 4 youth still receiving services with a stable adjustment, and adjustment of the remaining youth was very unstable.

The other case study consisted of a retrospective analysis of 8 child welfare families that had been receiving the wraparound intervention through the Kaleidoscope program in Chicago for an average of 3 years (Cumblad, 1996). These families entered wraparound with histories of abused and neglected children, poor parenting skills, substance abuse, depression, criminal activity, and unstable housing. During the time that these families received wraparound (mean duration 3 years), there no longer was any evidence of abuse or neglect and none of the children were removed from their parents. At the time the study was conducted, all the children were in more stable family environments. In addition, none of the children were exhibiting the high-risk behaviors that led to their referral for wraparound.

The primary purpose of these two studies was to provide detailed and comprehensive, qualitative information on wraparound, particularly with respect to its use with children at high risk for removal from the community. The studies provide a rich array of information pertaining to how the child and family teams were assembled and how individualized service and support plans were developed and implemented. However, while these studies are descriptive of wraparound and reveal promising outcomes, they do not establish a causal link between wraparound and improved community adjustment of the youth.

PRE-POST STUDIES

The nine pre-post studies provide preliminary evidence that positive outcomes are correlated with wraparound (Bruns, Burchard, & Yoe, 1995; Clarke, Shaefer, Burchard, & Welkowitz, 1992; Eber & Ousch, 1995; Eber, Osuch, & Redditt, 1996; Eber, Osuch, & Rolf, 1996; Hyde, Woodworth, Jordan, & Burchard, 1995; Illback, Neill, Call, & Andis, 1993; Kamradt, 1996; Russell, Rotto, & Matthews, 1999; Yoe, Santarcangelo, Atkins, & Burchard, 1996). While the case studies provide a rich base of subjective information on a few children and families, these nine studies provide data from empirically based measures on hundreds of children and families.

Taken together, the findings of these nine pre-post studies provide evidence that the majority of these children were able to maintain a stable adjustment in the community. The clearest evidence of this is the fact that almost all of the children were living in the community months and sometimes years after they entered wraparound. This alone is a significant finding. Research demonstrates that a large percentage of children with severe emotional and behavioral problems who receive traditional services are eventually placed in more restrictive programs outside their communities. This is evidenced by the findings of the National Adolescent and Child Treatment Study, which found that 32% of the children and adolescents who were "discharged successfully" from 28 different residential treatment centers where either readmitted to a residential program or incarcerated in a correctional facility within 12 months of discharge (Greenbaum et al., 1996). After 6 years, the recidivism rate was 75%.

In terms of specific areas of improvement, these nine studies are more difficult to assess. Although they reported positive change in many areas, the studies tended to employ different outcome measures (Child Behavior Checklist [CBCL], Teacher Report Form, Youth Self Report, Daily and Quarterly Adjustment Indicator Checklist, Child and Adolescent Functional Assessment Scale, etc.) and in many instances measures were employed that had not been standardized. There is some evidence that greater change took place in the home and community than in the school (Clarke et al., 1992; Eber et al., 1996), however, school data was not reported in many of the studies. In general, the nine studies indicate that positive outcomes are associated with wraparound, but without a comparison group it is difficult to say that the change was a result of the wraparound.

QUASI-EXPERIMENTAL STUDIES

The two quasi-experimental studies consist of one study that compared the community adjustment outcomes of different groups of subjects who received wraparound and residential treatment services and one within-subject study that employed a multiple-baseline design. The group study was conducted under the auspices of the Family Preservation Initiative in Baltimore City (Hyde, Burchard, & Woodworth, 1996). The study sample consisted of four groups: group one ($n = 25$) received wraparound upon discharge from residential treatment, group two ($n = 24$) received wraparound as an alternative to residential treatment, group three ($n = 39$) received residential treatment during the time that groups one and two received wraparound, and group four ($n = 18$) received residential services before groups one, two, and three received services. The participants were not randomly assigned to the groups and there was considerable variability across groups in terms of age, gender, and ethnicity.

Community adjustment data were obtained on 92% of the youth who received wraparound either after residential treatment or as an alternative to residential treatment, and on 42% of the youth who received only residential treatment. Fifty-eight percent of the youth who had received only residential treatment could not be located for follow-up.

The primary follow-up measure was a multi-informant, multidomain questionnaire from which each participant's level of community adjustment was classified based on predetermined criteria. To achieve a community adjustment rating of "good," the youth had to meet operationally defined criteria pertaining to the restrictiveness of living environment, participation in school or work, and rate of at-risk behaviors. Approximately two years after the beginning of wraparound, a "good" adjustment rating was obtained by 47% of those who received wraparound and 8% of those who received residential treatment only. Given the rather stringent criteria required for classification in the "good" adjustment category (e.g., 85% school attendance or 35 hours per week of vocational activity), the results are very promising. However, as noted above, only 42% of the group that received residential treatment alone participated in the study.

In the second quasi-experimental study conducted in southwest Michigan rural St. Joseph county, four youths with histories of chronic offending who were receiving services through the wraparound approach were studied using a multiple-baseline research design (Myaard, Crawford, Jackson, & Alessi, 2000). Baseline behaviors consisted of low rates of compliance and appropriate peer interaction in all four participants and high rates of physical aggression, alcohol and drug use, and extreme verbal abuse in three participants. Fidelity to wraparound treatment principles was validated through the on-site analysis of experts. In each case, marked behavioral improvement occurred shortly after the beginning of wraparound. Because the intervention was introduced at different times for each subject, results were interpreted as providing strong evidence that wraparound was responsible for the participants' behavioral change.

RANDOMIZED CLINICAL TRIALS

The research base on wraparound includes two randomized clinical trials, one conducted in New York and a second in Florida. In the New York study (Evans, Armstrong, & Kuppinger, 1996; Evans, Armstrong, Kuppinger, Huz, & Johnson, 1998), 42 children who were referred to out-of-home placements were assigned to either treatment foster care ($n = 15$) or family-centered intensive case management ($n = 27$). The latter condition (FCCM) employed most of the values and elements of the wraparound process, particularly at the family level, where case managers, parents, and parent advocates were part of a treatment team that developed strengths-based, individualized services with a maximum of eight families at a time.

The results of the New York study showed more favorable outcomes for the children that received wraparound. This was evidenced by a greater decline in behavioral symptoms as measured by a client description form, lower overall impairment (as measured by the Child and Adolescent Functional Assessment Scale; Hodges, 1990); and fewer externalizing, social problems, and thought problems (as measured by the Child Behavior Checklist; Achenbach, 1991c). There were no between-group differences in family functioning (as measured by the Family Adaptability Cohesiveness Scale; Olson, Portner, & Lavee, 1985). There were no measures for which children in the treatment foster care condition showed more positive outcomes than children in the FCICM condition.

In the Florida study (Clark et al., 1998), 131 youths in the foster care system were randomly assigned to either wraparound foster care ($n = 54$) or standard foster care ($n = 77$). The wraparound foster care intervention employed family-centered case managers who coordinated strengths-based assessment, life-domain planning, clinical case management, and follow-along supports and services. Each case manager eventually carried 12 active cases and up to 10 maintenance-level cases that were monitored monthly and reactivated when necessary.

One of the major findings of this study was fewer placement changes and fewer days absent from school for the wraparound group. In addition, the boys in the wraparound group showed lower rates of delinquency and better externalizing adjustment than the boys in standard foster care. Also, the older wraparound youths were more likely to achieve a permanent living arrangement in the community (with their parents, relatives, or adoptive parents, or living on their own).

STUDY LIMITATIONS

While findings from the above studies are encouraging, there are several limitations to the research base on wraparound. First, it is not possible to conclude that the wraparound interventions were the same in all studies. While all the interventions involved a process that is consistent with most of the essential elements described above (family centered, community based, culturally relevant, individualized, strengths based, flexible, and coordinated across agencies) the studies present very little data that documents the degree of adherence to these elements. Such documentation is especially important given some of the contextual differences associated with the implementation of wraparound, such as the wide range of settings in which wraparound has been administered. For example, in the nine pre-post studies, four of the wraparound programs were school-based programs, five were mental health–based, and one was an extension of intensive family-based services. While the programs appeared to involve substantial coordination across agencies, vast differences in the degree and nature of agency oversight and collaboration is likely—for example, it is likely that there was greater school involvement in the school-based programs.

Other limitations include variability of data collection instruments and sampling methods utilized across studies. While the CBCL was administered in many of the studies, some studies relied exclusively on restrictiveness of living environment and changes in placement as outcome measures. Others used a variety of measures, some of which were developed just for that study. With respect to sampling, neither of the case studies and few of the pre-post studies appear to have employed random or representative sampling techniques. Studies often included families chosen by researchers or nominated by program staff as being particularly illustrative of success or degree of challenge presented by the family or child. Other studies appear to have selected participants for whom extant data was available or for whom follow-up data could be collected. Although the results are informative, it is unlikely they are based on a representative sample of children with severe emotional and behavioral problems.

An additional limitation of most of the studies is the lack of a control group. While the behavioral changes that are associated with wraparound are impressive, it is not possible to conclude that the changes might not have occurred with another type of intervention. The multiple-baseline study provides more convincing evidence of a causal relationship between wraparound and positive behavior change, but the sample of subjects is small and only included youthful offenders. The two randomized control studies provide the best empirical evidence for the effectiveness of wraparound, however, even with those studies the numbers are relatively small and there is little evidence supporting the fidelity of the approach.

Suggestions for Future Research

The 15 studies described above provide a preliminary research base on the effectiveness of wraparound. However, much work remains to be done, particularly in two priority areas: (1) establishing a reliable, valid, cost-effective method to establish the fidelity of the intervention; and (2) conducting more controlled studies that compare the wraparound intervention with other types of intervention.

With respect to the fidelity of the intervention, there is only limited evidence that wraparound intervention is being implemented consistently, both across studies and across sites. Clearly, there is a need to operationally define and measure adherence to the essential elements of the process in order to ensure that wraparound advocates and evaluators are referring to the same intervention. With respect to service delivery, lack of adherence to key elements and inadequate clinician skills in delivering the intervention can result in a dilution or negation of positive effects (Burns & Goldman, 1999). With respect to research, a crucial step in demonstrating the effectiveness of an intervention is to ensure that it has been adequately described and implemented (Lourie, Stroul, & Friedman, 1998).

There have been at least three studies that have focused on fidelity. In one study (Rosen, Heckman, Carro, & Burchard, 1994), it was determined that the majority of a sample of 20 youths who were receiving "wraparound services" reported that they were involved in the process (e.g., "the members of my treatment team ask for my ideas and opinions"; "I have a choice in the services I receive") and that their care was unconditional (e.g., "I believe my service providers will stick with me no matter what"). While this study validates some of the wraparound elements from the perspective of the youth—that is, youth voice and choice and unconditional care—it does not incorporate the opinions of other key participants, such as parents and case managers, nor does it examine other key features or elements of wraparound.

A second study demonstrated that 20 youths who were receiving wraparound services reported more involvement and had a greater sense of unconditional care than 20 comparable youths who were receiving traditional services (Donnelly, 1994). This study demonstrated that wraparound elements could be quantified and measured through third-party interviews, and that these elements could be differentially observed in a between-group comparison of intervention approaches. In a third study, independent observers were able to validate that many of the critical elements of the wraparound process were occurring at the level of the child and family team (Epstein et al., 1998). While this approach is limited by an observer effect and requires on-site personnel, it can provide useful feedback for training and supervision.

Building on the results of these studies, more cost-effective methods for establishing fidelity are under development. In Florida, a fidelity form is administered to all participants immediately after each child and family team meeting (Burns & Goldman, 1999). The form consists of questions concerning who attended and to what extent the youth, parents, school personnel, community representatives, and other team members were involved, and concludes with ratings of the extent to which some of the elements of the wraparound process were evident during the meeting. Thus far, there are no psychometric properties associated with this instrument. In Vermont, a Wraparound Fidelity Index (WFI) has been developed to measure the presence or absence of wraparound elements through brief third-party telephone interviews with the parent, the youth, and the resource facilitator. A preliminary pilot study assessed the validity of the WFI by comparing WFI scores with ratings from an intensive on-site assessment by a wraparound expert for the same families. Results showed that overall fidelity scores from the WFI correlated significantly with the ratings of the on-site expert. Scores from the majority of individual elements assessed via the WFI also correlated with the expert's ratings (Bruns, Ermold, & Burchard, 2000). Other components of this series of preliminary studies found that (1) test-retest reliability of the WFI was good overall, and that (2) the measure featured limited sensitivity and variance across pilot programs, which will have to be addressed in future revisions.

In addition to assisting in future effectiveness research on the intervention, it is expected that the revised WFI will allow programs to assess their own adherence to the wraparound process, thus facilitating quality assurance and staff training. Initial interest in the newest revision of the WFI (WFI 2.0) among sites nationally is also currently being leveraged to conduct basic research on the wraparound process. Participating sites will be provided the WFI (and technical assistance on its use) for no charge if the programs agree to share data with the national research team (with confidentiality assurances) and participate in additional data collection. Programmatic and administrative data from sites (e.g., years of existence of the program, caseload sizes, degree of pooled funding and interagency collaboration), as well as child- and family-level outcome data will then be associated with fidelity data across a broad sample of sites. Such analyses will allow for better understanding of how agency and programmatic factors affect wraparound fidelity, and how sites' fidelity to different wraparound principles may impact on outcomes.

Despite the potential of the research efforts described above, research that compares the effectiveness of wraparound with other interventions is also needed. The effectiveness studies employing random assignment from New York and Florida provide good support for wraparound; however, the findings are limited with respect to the measurement of the fidelity of the intervention— it is uncertain to what extent the interventions studied mirrored the wraparound process as described in this chapter. While it seems clear that many of the elements of wraparound were in place in both studies, there are indications that critical elements may have been missing. For example, in the New York study, the authors specifically state that their intervention did not simulate a full wraparound model because a state-level interagency team did not exist. This, however, is a standard that was addressed in the 1998 wraparound consensus meeting at Duke. In the Florida study (in which all the youth were in foster care), it is not clear that the biological parents had the "access, voice, and choice" that are critical to the wraparound process.

Conclusion

Although it is difficult to apply a specific algorithm or decision tree to the planning and decision-making process or to the specific services and supports implemented in a wraparound intervention, the key constituent elements have been identified (Burns & Goldman, 1999). In addition, efforts are underway to establish the fidelity of the intervention to the practice elements and principles. These efforts should enable empirical tests of the model's effectiveness through future controlled research designs. Such research should also help differentiate wraparound from other community-based treatments for families, and point to principles and practices that are most effective for specific subpopulations of children.

Wraparound is a model that is receiving considerable interest and has had wide application throughout the United States and Canada. As with any new approach to a problem that is resistant to treatment, it is sometimes adopted widely and uncritically, without care to the critical principles and practice elements. Development of fidelity measures and controlled comparative research of the intervention's effectiveness are essential steps away from the realm of anecdotally supported treatments and toward an understanding of wraparound's status among empirically supported methods for serving children and families.

5

Multisystemic Therapy

SONJA K. SCHOENWALD

MELISA D. ROWLAND

Multisystemic therapy (MST) is a family- and community-based treatment that addresses the multiple determinants of serious clinical problems that place youth at high risk of out-of-home placement (Henggeler, Schoenwald, Borduin, Rowland, & Cunningham, 1998b). Originally developed and empirically validated (Kazdin & Weisz, 1998) for youth engaged in serious antisocial behavior and their families, ongoing research is examining the effects of MST on youth with a variety of severe behavioral and emotional problems.

MST Treatment Theory

MST was conceived in the tradition of psychotherapy research, in which understanding of a specific clinical problem one wishes to ameliorate guides the development of a treatment approach. Conceptualization of clinical problems refers to what can be said about the likely factors leading to the pattern of functioning we wish to change (Kazdin, 1997, p. 117). Such conceptualizations are informed by empirical evidence regarding the correlates and causes of the problem and by theoretical constructs. The problematic pattern of functioning MST originally sought to ameliorate was serious antisocial behavior (i.e., chronic and violent juvenile offending), for which available treatments and services for chronic juvenile offenders had been shown to fail. The MST conceptualization of serious antisocial behavior draws upon causal modeling studies of delinquency and adolescent substance abuse and on social-ecological and systemic models of human behavior.

EMPIRICAL EVIDENCE REGARDING THE ETIOLOGY OF ANTISOCIAL BEHAVIOR

At least 20 research groups have conducted causal modeling studies in an attempt to describe how the multiple factors known to predict serious antisocial behavior interrelate. Findings from the fields of delinquency and substance abuse have been relatively clear and consistent. First, association with deviant peers is virtually always a powerful direct predictor of antisocial behavior. Second, family relations either predict antisocial behavior directly or indirectly (through predicting association with deviant peers). Third, school difficulties predict association with deviant peers. Fourth, neighborhood and community support characteristics have a direct or indirect role in predicting antisocial behavior. Across studies, research has shown that youth antisocial behavior is linked directly or indirectly with key risk and protective factors of youth and of the indigenous systems in which they interact (for reviews see Elliott, 1994; Henggeler, 1997; Huizinga, 1995; Loeber, Keenan, & Zhang, 1997). A summary of these factors appears in Table 5.1.

Recent reviews of the correlates of juvenile sex offending (Becker, 1998) and of problems characterized as severe emotional disorders (SED) indicate that

Table 5.1 Risk and Protective Factors for Serious Antisocial Behavior in Youth

Context	Risk Factors	Protective Factors
Individual	• low verbal skills • favorable attitudes toward antisocial behavior • psychiatric symptomatology • cognitive bias to attribute hostile intentions to others	• intelligence • being firstborn • easy temperament • conventional attitudes • problem-solving skills
Family	• lack of monitoring • ineffective discipline • low warmth • high conflict • parental difficulties (e.g., drug abuse, psychiatric conditions, criminality)	• attachment to parents • supportive family environment • marital harmony
Peer	• association with deviant peers • poor relationship skills • low association with prosocial peers	• bonding with prosocial peers
School	• low achievement • dropout • low commitment to education • school weaknesses such as poor structure or chaotic environment	• commitment to schooling
Neighborhood & Community	• high mobility • low community support (neighbors, church, etc.) • high disorganization • criminal subculture	• ongoing involvement in church activities • strong indigenous support network

they are also multidetermined (see, for example, Evans, Dollard, & McNulty, 1992; Greenbaum, Prange, Friedman, & Silver, 1991; Quinn & Epstein, 1998; Rosenblatt & Attkisson, 1992; Singh, Landrum, Donatelli, Hampton, Ellis, 1994). Indeed, chronic and violent juvenile offenders also generally meet the criteria for SED (Yell & Shriner, 1997) in that they carry one or more diagnoses, experience school failure, suspension, or expulsion at high rates, and are frequently placed in restrictive settings because their behavior is perceived as a threat to the community.

EMPIRICAL EVIDENCE REGARDING THE ETIOLOGY OF PSYCHIATRIC CRISES IN YOUTH

Although research on the predictors of psychiatric hospitalization for youth with SED in changing systems of mental health care remains inconclusive (see Bickman, Foster, & Lambert, 1996), evidence suggests that a number of these youth are hospitalized for emergency mental health services (Gutterman, Markowitz, LoConte, & Beier, 1993). Since 1993, a study examining MST as an alternative to hospitalization for such youth, funded by the National Institute of Mental Health (NIMH), has been underway (Henggeler et al., 1997b; Henggeler et al., 1999; Schoenwald, Ward, Henggeler, Rowland, & Brondino, 2000).

The American Academy of Child and Adolescent Psychiatry's (AACAP) criteria for admission of a youth to an acute inpatient psychiatric hospital indicate that the youth must pose a significant threat of harm to self or others due to suicidal ideation, homicidal ideation, or other emotional or behavioral sequelae related to a psychiatric illness (AACAP, 1996). Youth experiencing psychiatric crises display symptoms that can generally be classified as overt behavioral problems (i.e., impulsivity, runaway behavior) (Kashani & Cantwell, 1983) or as suicidal, homicidal, or psychotic behaviors (Hillard, Slomowitz, & Deddens, 1988). Research on the factors contributing to overt behavioral problems was described previously. Here, the focus is on the correlates of suicidal, homicidal, and psychotic behaviors in youth.

Suicidal Behavior

An abundance of correlational data links suicidal behavior in adolescents with multiple psychosocial variables including poor parent-child affective relationships, exposure to marital conflict, family psychopathology, and discordant relationships with siblings (Kaslow, Deering, & Racusin, 1994; Wagner, 1997). Risk factors for suicidal behavior include physical or sexual abuse, poor family or parent-child communication, loss of a caregiver to separation or death, and psychopathology in first-degree relatives (Wagner, 1997). The availability of firearms in the home is highly correlated with completed youth suicide (Brent et al., 1988), and mounting evidence links the increased availability of firearms in the United States to rising suicide and homicide rates among American youth (Rutter, Giller, & Hagell, 1998). Risk factors for depression in children and adolescents are similar to those for suicidal behavior in that they include parental psychopathology, family conflict, and poor peer support. In general, the family environments of depressed youth are more likely to be characterized by conflict, rejection, and poor communication relative to families of youth who are not depressed (Birmaher et al., 1996).

Homicidal Behavior

The evidence base regarding factors contributing to homicidal behavior in youth is limited to retrospective studies of youth who have completed homicides and descriptive studies comparing these youth with other clinical and nonclinical samples. Youth referred for hospitalization because they are experiencing homicidal ideation generally engage in other types of antisocial behavior and/or experience suicidal, depressive, or psychotic symptoms (Crespi & Rigazio-DiGilio, 1996). Descriptive studies of youth who have committed homicide suggest that they have experienced high levels of family disorganization, conflict, economic insecurity, parental brutality, psychopathology, and substance abuse (Corder, Ball, Haizlip, Rollins, & Beaumont, 1976; Lewis et al., 1988). Yet, in studies comparing violent, homicidal adolescents with other clinical youth samples such as suicide completers (Yates, Beutler, & Crago, 1984) and nonviolent offenders (Cornell, Benedek, & Benedek, 1987), no risk factors specific to homicide unfold.

Psychotic Behavior

A number of psychiatric or medical conditions can give rise to symptoms of psychosis in adolescents. The psychiatric conditions which may include psychotic symptoms are: mood disorders (bipolar affective disorder, depression), substance use disorders, posttraumatic stress disorder, schizoaffective disorder, dissociative disorder, schizophrenia, pervasive developmental disorders, and personality disorders (McClellan & Werry, 1994; Tolbert, 1996; Volkmar, 1996). Hence, the risk factors contributing to psychotic symptoms vary depending upon the underlying etiology. Correlates pertinent to the etiology of depression and substance abuse in youth were identified earlier in this chapter. Emerging data on psychotic symptoms associated with schizophrenia in adolescents (Asarnow & Asarnow, 1996) and a larger database for adults with schizophrenia (Graham & Rutter, 1985) suggest that although genetic and biological factors almost certainly play a role in the development of psychotic symptoms, family patterns of communication and affective expression may contribute to the precipitation of symptoms, and specific types of family intervention programs may help to reduce relapse rates (McClellan & Werry, 1994).

In summary, available research suggests that childhood psychopathology in general—and suicidal, homicidal, depressive, and psychotic behaviors specifically—correlate with characteristics of the individual and the family, peer, school, and community contexts in which the youth is embedded.

SYSTEMS AND SOCIAL ECOLOGICAL THEORIES

General systems theory (von Bertalanffy, 1968) and the theory of social ecology (Bronfenbrenner, 1979) fit closely with the research findings on the correlates and causes of serious behavioral and emotional problems in youth, and serve as the theoretical foundations of MST.

Systems Theory

In contrast with traditional scientific conceptualizations of phenomena as having a mechanistic, linear, A-causes-B focus, systems theory depicts causality in terms of simultaneously occurring, mutually influential, and interrelated phenomena. In this view, the whole is greater that the sum of its parts. The implications of systems theory for human behavior are that a given behavior is seen as having multiple causes, and that behavior makes sense within the reciprocal and circular patterns of interaction that characterize a given system. This shift in perspective precipitated the development of a variety of family therapy approaches (i.e., strategic, structural, and behavioral systems family treatment approaches). A central tenet in these approaches is that the perspectives and feelings of family members regarding identified problems are important in understanding how those problems make sense and, therefore, in how to help solve them (for a review, see P. Minuchin, 1985). The implication of this tenet is that family members and clinicians collaborate to build a mutual understanding of the nature of the identified problems and of possible solutions to those problems.

Social Ecology

The theory of social ecology as explicated by Bronfenbrenner (1979) played an important role in the development of MST. Although this theory shares the same basic tenets of systems theory, social ecology is broader in its scope. The theory of social ecology understands human development as a reciprocal interchange between the individual and "nested concentric structures" that mutually influence one another. The individual is embedded within interconnected systems, which include the family system and extrafamilial systems, such as school, work, peers, and even community and cultural institutions. Individuals are viewed as growing entities that are actively influenced by their environments while actively restructuring those environments. Problem behaviors may arise as a function of difficulty within any of these systems (e.g., parent-child or teacher-child interactions) and/or difficulties that characterize the interfaces between these systems (e.g., family-school relations, family-peer contact, etc.).

IMPLICATIONS FOR THEORY OF CHANGE

The manner in which a particular treatment model achieves change has been referred to as a "treatment theory" (Lipsey, 1988). The treatment theory underlying MST proposes that by addressing the known risk factors and protective factors that directly and indirectly contribute to serious problems in youth (i.e., delinquency, substance abuse, SED), such problems will be reduced. Developments in learning theory and behavioral treatment are also converging on the perspective that complex problems such as these require complex treatment responses (see Henggeler, Schoenwald, & Pickrel, 1995). Consistent with the systemic and social ecological theories underlying MST, many risk and protective factors (e.g., "high family conflict," "effective monitoring") are interpersonal processes. Even a factor such as "cognitive bias to attribute hostile intentions to others," while categorized as an individual risk factor, reflects the cognitive response of an individual to social interactions (Beck, 1995; Kendall & Braswell, 1993).

One implication of systems and social ecological theories is that treatment must be individualized to the characteristics of each individual and his/her particular social ecology. A second implication of these theories, and of the evidence base regarding risk factors and correlates of serious behavioral and emotional problems in youth, is that assessment and intervention should occur in the natural ecology. Thus, MST interventions are delivered in the home, at school, and in the neighborhood and community.

Target Populations

YOUTH WITH SERIOUS ANTISOCIAL BEHAVIOR

The direct impact of serious antisocial behavior on society involves both perpetrators and victims. Chronic and violent juvenile offending are associated with numerous concurrent and long-term difficulties (for reviews, see Elliott, 1994; Schoenwald, Thomas, & Henggeler, 1994), including poor academic performance, substance use and abuse, and precocious sexual activity. Academic difficulties contribute to dropping out of school and to future unemployment. Violent behavior in adolescence is associated with a variety of other health problems, including accidents and suicide. Victim costs are also substantial, as are societal costs including property damage and loss and cost for law enforcement, courts, and corrections.

YOUTH WITH SERIOUS EMOTIONAL DISORDERS EXPERIENCING PSYCHIATRIC CRISES

Studies indicate that youth with SED exhibit impairment in functioning in multiple domains as they enter young adulthood. For example, a national study following 600 youth with SED for a 7-year period (Greenbaum et al., 1998) found continued impairment in adaptive functioning, which declined relative to peers over time; poor educational outcomes, with a 40% dropout rate by 18 years of age; use of multiple services that crossed the mental health, child welfare, school-based special education, vocational rehabilitation, and juvenile justice systems; and substantial involvement with law enforcement. These outcomes are substantiated by other studies describing youth with SED in system of care projects (Quinn & Epstein, 1998; Singh et al., 1994; Rosenblatt & Attkisson, 1992; Evans et al., 1992; Greenbaum et al., 1991). Thus, while difficult to measure, there is a significant cost to society in terms of unmet potential, loss of productivity, and the continued need of special services for these individuals and their families.

INTENDED OUTCOMES OF MST

As originally conceived for the treatment of juvenile offenders and their families, the broad goals of MST were to reduce criminal activity in youth, avoid out-of-home placement, decrease association with deviant peers and increase association with prosocial peers, increase educational/vocational performance, improve caregiver discipline strategies and enhance family relations, empower families and their indigenous support systems to address future problems, and decrease the costs of treating youth engaged in serious antisocial behavior. These outcomes are consistent with the framework for evaluating the effectiveness of care put forward by Hoagwood and colleagues (1996). That is, the intended outcomes of MST subsume youth *symptoms* (aggressive, violent, and other antisocial behaviors); youth *functioning* (attendance and performance at school, positive peer relations, reasonable behavior at home); family, school, and neighborhood *environments* (reductions in *family* conflict, increases in effective discipline, monitoring, and affective relations; less disruption in and outside of class in school; positive school-family, family-neighborhood, and family-community linkages); and *systems* (avoidance of out-of-home placement and accrual of cost savings). As MST evolves to address the problems of youth referred for psychiatric crises, the variety of symptoms to be addressed expands to include depression, suicidal and homicidal behavior, and psychotic symptoms. The functional, environmental, and systems outcomes MST seeks to achieve remain quite similar, however. In addition, measures of consumer satisfaction incorporated into randomized trials and community-based evaluations of MST indicate that families are more satisfied with MST than with other treatment received in their communities.

For each youth and family referred to MST, outcomes are considered positive when the referral problems placing a youth at imminent risk of out-of-home placement have been alleviated or significantly reduced, treatment goals developed by the family and other key stakeholders in the youth's ecology (e.g., extended family, teachers, probation officers) are met, and evidence indicates that the family and its indigenous support system are able to manage future difficulties largely independent of unwanted agency (i.e., juvenile justice, child welfare, mental health) involvement.

MST Intervention Parameters

THE HOME-BASED OR FAMILY PRESERVATION MODEL OF SERVICE DELIVERY

A core feature of MST is its emphasis on changing the social ecology of youths and families in ways that promote positive adjustment and attenuate emotional and behavioral difficulties. Since accomplishing this goal requires a high level of involvement in the natural environments of youths and their families, the home-based or family-preservation model of service delivery is ideally suited for MST. Despite some commonalities among various home-based or family preservation programs (i.e., services are focused on families with children at risk of placement, are time-limited, are flexibly scheduled, are available 24 hours a day and 7 days a week, and are provided in the context of a family's values, beliefs, and culture; see Fraser, Nelson, & Rivard, 1997), they vary considerably in purpose, treatment delivered, and outcomes achieved (Schoenwald & Henggeler, 1997). As applied to MST, the home-based model of service delivery is implemented for 3–5 months per family, depending on the seriousness of the problems and success of interventions. Therapists are available 24 hours a day, 7 days a week, and treatment is delivered at times that are convenient to families, such as evening hours and weekends. Each MST therapist works with 4–5 families at a time. Frequency, duration, and intensity of face-to-face contact varies in accordance with the needs and treatment gains experienced by families. Thus, daily contact is common early during treatment and when periodic setbacks occur, with contact reduced to several times per week as treatment progresses.

THE PRINCIPLES AND PROCESS OF MST

Because MST is individualized, specification of interventions in a step-by-step or session-by-session fashion is not possible. A manual for practitioners (Henggeler, Schoenwald, Borduin, Rowland, & Cunningham, 1998b) does, however, describe the implementation of MST in significant detail. Within the constraints of nine principles for assessment and intervention derived from the systemic, social-ecological, and empirical underpinnings of MST, clinicians tailor treatment techniques to the needs and strengths of each client family. The choice of modality used to address a particular problem is based largely on the empirical literature concerning its efficacy. As such, MST interventions are usually adapted and integrated from pragmatic, problem-focused treatments that have at least some empirical support, but have historically focused on a limited aspect of the youth's social ecology (e.g., the cognitions or problem-solving skills of the youth, the discipline strategies of a parent). These include behavioral parent training (Munger, 1993), cognitive behavior therapies (Kendall & Braswell, 1993), strategic family therapy (Haley, 1976), and structural family therapy (Minuchin, 1974). In addition (and as appropriate), biological contributors to identified problems are identified and psychopharmacological treatment is integrated with psychosocial treatment. In contrast with combined (e.g., Kazdin, 1996; Kazdin, Siegel, & Bass, 1992) and multicomponent approaches to treatment (e.g., Liddle, 1996), however, the different types of interventions are not delivered as separate elements or self-contained modules. Rather, consistent with systemic and social-ecological theory, interventions are strategically selected and integrated in ways thought to maximize synergistic interaction within and between systems.

MST Principles

The purpose of the MST principles is to guide and organize therapists' ongoing case conceptualization and development and prioritization of interventions. The nine principles that guide the MST assessment and intervention process are as follows.

1. The primary purpose of assessment is to understand the fit between the identified problems and their broader systemic context.
2. Therapeutic contacts emphasize the positive and should use systemic strengths as levers for change.
3. Interventions are designed to promote responsible behavior and decrease irresponsible behavior among family members.
4. Interventions are present-focused and action-oriented, targeting specified and well-defined problems.
5. Interventions target sequences of behavior within and between multiple systems that maintain the identified problems.
6. Interventions are developmentally appropriate and fit the developmental needs of the youth.
7. Interventions are designed to require daily or weekly effort by family members.
8. Intervention effectiveness is evaluated continuously from multiple perspectives, with providers assuming accountability for overcoming barriers to successful outcomes.
9. Interventions are designed to promote treatment generalization and long-term maintenance of therapeutic change by empowering caregivers to address family members' needs across multiple systemic contexts (Henggeler et al., 1998b, p 23).

MST Analytic Process

The MST treatment process entails interrelated steps that connect the ongoing assessment of the fit of referral problems with the development and implementation of interventions. Clinicians are encouraged to engage in hypothesis testing when they have hunches, beliefs, or theories about the causes and correlates of particular problems in a family; the reasons that improvements have occurred; and barriers to change. This iterative analytical process, depicted in Figure 5.1, has been dubbed the MST Do Loop. The ongoing MST assessment and intervention process begins with a clear understanding of the *reasons for referral*. The next task is to develop *overarching treatment goals* that address the referral problems and reflect the goals of the family and other key stakeholders in the youth's ecology (e.g., teachers, probation officers). Following the development of overarching treatment goals, a preliminary *multisystemic conceptualization of the fit* of referral problems—of how each referral problem makes sense within the ecology of the youth—is developed with the family. This initial conceptualization of fit encompasses strengths and weaknesses observed in each of the systems in the youth's ecology, and becomes more detailed as the clinician gathers information and observations about interactions within and between each system that directly and indirectly influence the referral behavior. Next, the treatment team and family delineate *intermediary treat-*

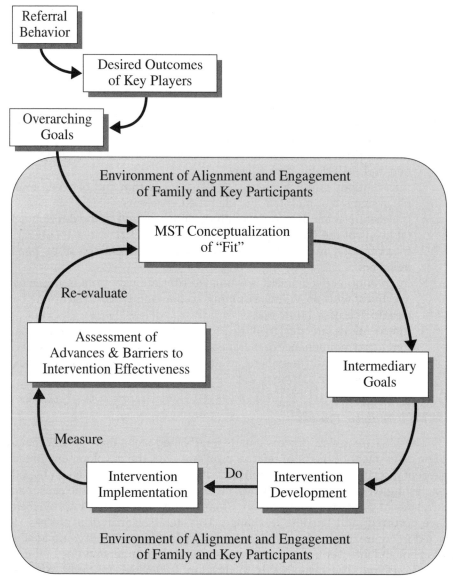

Figure 5.1   The MST Analytical Process (Do Loop). *Source:* Henggeler et al., 1998b, p. 47.

ment goals—goals that are logically linked to overarching goals, reflect steps toward achieving the overarching goals, and are achievable in the short term. With initial intermediary goals defined, the team identifies the range of treatment modalities and techniques that might be effective toward meeting the intermediary goals, and tailors these to the specific strengths and weaknesses of the targeted client system (e.g., marital, parent-child, family-school).

Before interventions are implemented, MST therapists document the anticipated outcomes of each intervention in observable and measurable terms. Interventions are considered successful if they result in observable changes in a target behavior. Thus, for example, decreased association with deviant peers would indicate that interventions designed to increase parental monitoring (establishing and enforcing a curfew, calling the parents of peers) were effective. Interventions that have no effect are discontinued quickly, and the fit of the ineffective strategy is identified. *Barriers* to favorable outcomes may become evident at several levels. For example, at the family level, previously unidentified parental difficulties such as marital problems, parental depression, or parental drug use might emerge. Likewise, clinician limitations (e.g., inexperience in marital therapy, poor repertoire of engagement strategies) may present barriers to change. *Strategies for overcoming the barriers to intervention effectiveness* are developed and implemented. Refinement continues until the desired results are achieved.

EXAMPLES ILLUSTRATING PRINCIPLES AND PROCESS

Extensive case examples illustrating the implementation of MST with youth referred for serious antisocial behavior and their families are available in the MST treatment manual (Henggeler et al., 1998b) and other published book chapters about MST (see, e.g., Henggeler, Rone, Thomas, & Timmons-Mitchell, 1998a; Schoenwald, Borduin, & Henggeler, 1998; Schoenwald, Brown, & Henggeler, 2000). Thus, the current example illustrates the application of the MST principles and analytic process (Do Loop, see Figure 5.1.) to the treatment of a youth referred to the aforementioned study of MST as an alternative to hospitalization. Names and minor details have been changed to protect the identity of the youth and her family.

Jan Hardell, a 15-year-old white female, was referred for admission to the psychiatric hospital by her outpatient mental health counselor due to increasingly aggressive behavior and suicidal ideation. Jan was in the custody of the Department of Social Services (DSS) and had been living with her paternal grandparents for several months. DSS took custody of Jan following several instances of physical aggression between Jan and her father during which police intervened and charges of domestic violence were filed against Jan. Jan's father continued to be involved in parenting and wanted to regain custody. Just prior to the referral, Jan's behavior had become increasingly defiant (breaking rules, violating curfew, arguing) and threatening, and she verbally threatened to harm her grandparents and father. Jan also experienced increased irritability and sleep problems, was frequently truant from school, and was spending increased time with a group of peers who used drugs.

Principle 1: Finding the Fit

The therapist and team identified several factors associated with the aggressive and suicidal behaviors Jan displayed in her grandparents' home and in her father's home. First, Jan had some symptoms of depression (difficulty falling asleep, depressive cognitions, attributional bias) and irritability. Second, her suicidal ideations were always preceded by verbal or physical altercations with family members; Jan did not display violent behavior in school or with her peers. Importantly, the factors that precipitated or exacerbated Jan's violent behavior were different in the two home settings. In the grandparent's home, the grandmother had an authoritarian parenting style (directive and overcontrolling, with little warmth), maturity expectations exceeding Jan's developmental level, and a painful physical disability. Thus, the grandmother issued many directives, had low tolerance for even normative adolescent behavior, and became agitated and emotional when Jan broke rules or acted defiantly. Jan became increasingly verbally aggressive and physically agitated in response, and conflicts escalated rapidly. Jan's father, on the other hand, had a very permissive parenting style (tolerant and low in structure, with high warmth) and poor monitoring skills, and he behaved very impulsively (i.e., said and did things without thinking, moved quickly from one thought and activity to the next, had trouble focusing and following through on tasks). When Jan became defiant and irritable, Mr. Hardell was unable to effectively set limits and responded impulsively, thus escalating a sequence of increasingly impulsive and agitated interactions between the two of them. Jan's depressive symptoms and deviant peer associations promoted oppositional behaviors (truancy, marijuana use) that were possible triggers for violent interactions in both homes.

Principle 2: Positive and Strengths-Focused

Although some interactions in both home environments maintained Jan's problem behaviors, many strengths characterized Jan, her family, and the systems in which they were embedded. Specifically, Jan did not have academic or behavioral problems in school (other than truancy), possessed good social skills, was affectively bonded with her father, and wanted to stop her violent behavior. Jan's social skills ultimately enabled the family to help her find employment in a setting with prosocial peers. Mr. Hardell loved his daughter and wanted very much to regain custody of her. The therapist capitalized on Mr. Hardell's desire to obtain custody of Jan to help him to follow through with interventions when they were difficult for him. Mr. Hardell's parents were supportive of him regaining custody, but unwilling to have the granddaughter in their home on a permanent basis. The therapist leveraged the grandparents' love and concern for their son to engage them in treatment and allow Jan to remain in their home while the therapist worked with Mr. Hardell to create a home environment that would keep Jan safe from self-harm and him and his parents safe from physical harm.

The Analytic Process (aka MST Do Loop, see Figure 5.1)

With an initial assessment of fit and of systemic strengths and weaknesses, the therapist and team embarked upon the ongoing assessment and treatment process. The *overarching goal* of treatment was to enable Jan to live safely with her father; in this instance, the primary threats to safety were self-harm and physical violence to family members. The Hardells identified several *desired outcomes* of treatment consistent with this overarching goal. These included ending violent family conflicts, diminishing Jan's depressive symptoms, reducing Jan's drug use and association with deviant peers, and increasing her school attendance and engagement in prosocial activities.

Mr. Hardell's permissive parenting style and poor monitoring skills were identified as directly contributing to violent interactions with Jan. Thus, an *intermediary goal* was to develop more effective discipline and monitoring practices. Because Mr. Hardell stated that he did not know how to handle Jan's behavior, the therapist hypothesized that he lacked the skills required to implement effective practices. Thus, the therapist initially designed interventions to remedy knowledge and skill deficits. For example, the therapist described the steps involved in setting up a developmentally appropriate behavioral plan, provided practical reading material about such plans (Munger, 1993), and helped Mr. Hardell and Jan to develop rules, set consequences, and track outcomes. As these interventions were implemented, the therapist noticed that Mr. Hardell had difficulty regulating his affect and focusing his thoughts during interactions with Jan in which he tried to set limits, and often said things impulsively that were not part of the limit-setting plan (i.e., "If you don't come in on time, I'll ground you for a month"). Thus, the limit-setting efforts were rarely successful. The therapist tried to understand the possible causes (fit) of Mr. Hardell's impulsive behavior. Initial hypotheses were that he may have adult attention-deficit/hyperactivity disorder (ADHD), be using drugs, or both. To evaluate theses hypotheses, the therapist obtained information (with Mr. Hardell's consent) from multiple sources (family, friends, boss) and asked the MST team psychiatrist to evaluate the symptoms. This information supported the diagnosis of ADHD, but not substance abuse. Thus, the hypothesis that Mr. Hardell did not have the knowledge and skills to effectively discipline and monitor Jan was modified. The new conceptualization was that, although Mr. Hardell did lack some knowledge and skills relevant to parenting a challenging adolescent, ADHD interfered with his ability to implement newly learned skills. Interventions targeting the ADHD symptoms were thus seen as central to changing parenting practices. These interventions included a trial of medication prescribed by the team psychiatrist and modification of previous interventions to accommodate the father's impairments (poor attention span, difficulty understanding written material) and utilize his strengths (high energy, interest in visual materials). For example, although the impulsive symptoms diminished while Mr. Hardell was on medication, he continued to be verbally and physically intrusive (i.e., standing close, putting his face close to his daughter's, loudly repeating his argument) when setting limits. To help Mr. Hardell understand that this behavior was not effective and needed to change, the therapist asked him to audiotape his attempts to set limits with Jan, and then played the tapes back to him in treatment sessions. Mr. Hardell also allowed the therapist to videotape some sessions in which the therapist role-played limit-setting techniques and demonstrated basic parenting skills. Mr. Hardell watched the videotapes at a later time, mastering the material at his own pace.

Principle 3: Increasing Responsibility

Reducing Jan's depressive symptoms, association with deviant peers, and drug use, and increasing her school attendance required, among other things, reductions in family conflict and increases in effective parenting practices. Family conflict, in turn, was precipitated or exacerbated by the impulsive behaviors of all participants (Mr. Hardell, Jan, and her grandmother). Thus, all participants had to decrease impulsive behavior and increase responsible behavior in interactions with one another. Jan also was responsible for helping to manage her depressive cognitions, and Jan and her father shared responsibility for limiting her contact with deviant peers and increasing her prosocial peer network and activities. Obtaining employment was one of the interventions implemented toward this goal.

Principle 4: Present-Focused, Action-Oriented, and Well-Defined

The interventions summarized earlier (developing behavioral plans, setting limits, administering consequences, taking medication) were present-focused and action-oriented, targeting specific and well-defined problems (e.g., Jan's threats of physical violence and impulsive behavior; father's impulsive behavior and poor monitoring skills) that were contributing to the presenting problems (violence, threatening behavior).

Principle 5: Targeting Sequences Between and Within Systems

Within the family system, parent-child and grandparent-grandchild interactions leading to physical altercations and suicidal ideation were addressed using interventions that changed limit-setting techniques, helped individuals to identify language that signaled impending escalation of verbal conflict, and provided alternatives to the escalation, such as taking time-outs from the conversation at hand. Individual and peer factors also contributed to putting Jan at risk for aggressive and suicidal behavior. At the individual level, the irritability associated with Jan's depression, combined with depressive cognitions (e.g., "No one really cares what happens to me") made it more likely that she would become explosive and oppositional when interfacing with her father and grandparents. Interventions within the individual realm included psychopharmacologic treatment of her depressive symptoms and therapist implementation of some cognitive-behavioral techniques to address her depressive cognitions and attributional biases.

Peer interactions, and the lack of family-peer contact, also contributed to Jan's behavior problems. Specifically, being with certain friends correlated highly with marijuana use and truancy, which in turn were the topics of some of the altercations at home. Interventions in the peer system involved teaching Mr. Hardell how to assess and monitor appropriate peer interactions. Mr. Hardell met Jan's peers, gathered information about which peers were involved in truant and drug-using behavior, and limited access to these peers while facilitating involvement with prosocial peers. Interventions to address Jan's marijuana use consisted of obtaining weekly random urine drug screens, with Mr. Hardell providing incentives for negative screens and consequences for positive screens. Jan's urine drug screens were all negative during the last month of treatment.

Principle 6: Developmentally Appropriate

Examples of developmentally appropriate interventions include helping the father to provide incentives and consequences that were age appropriate such as increased use of the telephone, earning trips to the mall with appropriate peers, helping the grandmother to understand that Jan was not yet capable of making adult decisions about her behavior, and having Mr. Hardell meet Jan's peers and inquire about their whereabouts when she went out with them.

Principle 7: Daily or Weekly Effort

The therapist met with the Hardell family daily at the onset of therapy to ensure safety, then several times a week for the next few months, and finally weekly to ensure that progress was being made toward treatment goals. For most of the interventions, the therapist gave homework assignments to be completed before the next meeting (i.e., audiotaping attempts to set limits, meeting peers, administering behavioral plans). The purpose of the homework was to ensure progress toward treatment goals between sessions and obtain feedback so that lack of progress could be identified quickly and new conceptualizations and interventions be developed immediately.

Principle 8: Evaluation and Accountability

The therapist looked for evidence of intervention effectiveness by talking with Jan's grandparents and with teachers and counselors at her school, and by obtaining information from attendance records and urine screen results.

Principle 9: Generalization

Throughout treatment, the therapist tried to ensure that the interventions implemented were ecologically valid and could be carried out by family members after MST ended. For example, the therapist was concerned that Mr. Hardell's effective parenting practices would be compromised if he stopped taking his medication, and if new situations arose with Jan that required new interventions. The therapist had been helping Mr. Hardell to implement effective responses to new situations during the course of treatment. The therapist and father identified three ways of addressing these concerns. First, Mr. Hardell invited a close female friend whom he and Jan had known for many years to several therapeutic meetings. The goal of these meetings was to inform the friend of how the current behavioral system worked and to establish a mutually agreed upon plan in which Mr. Hardell would solicit her advice if changes in the behavior plan were required. The friend also agreed to encourage Mr. Hardell's compliance with medications for ADHD. To back up this plan, arrangements were made for a family advocate from a local community service organization to meet with Mr. Hardell several times a month in his home to serve the same functions. A final safety net consisted of having Jan referred back to her outpatient counselor and psychiatrist for medication management of her depressive symptoms (now greatly improved). Jan's outpatient counselor also agreed to monitor Mr. Hardell's success in continued implementation of the behavioral plan and to promote his continued compliance with medications for ADHD symptoms.

Jan and her family received MST for 16 weeks. Upon discharge from the MST program, Jan was no longer exhibiting violent outbursts at home, and her depressive symptoms (irritability, sleep disorder, suicidal ideation) were improved. Jan was attending school on a regular basis (except for one truant episode), was not using drugs (random urine screens were negative), and was employed at a local county park. Jan's father was taking medication for ADHD and was monitoring Jan's behavior and providing appropriate rewards and consequences. The therapist referred Jan back to her outpatient mental health counselor and psychiatrist for continued management of the medication aspect of treatment of her depressive symptoms.

Program Development

STAFFING REQUIREMENTS

MST is delivered by master's level counselors or social workers, and sometimes highly competent bachelor's level professionals, who receive on-site clinical supervision from doctoral level and sometimes highly experienced and skilled master's level professionals. For programs serving youth referred for serious antisocial behavior, each clinician works with 4–5 families at a time. To assist clinicians in carrying out MST with integrity, therapists are organized into treatment teams. Typically, each MST team consists of three to four clinicians and a part-time clinical supervisor. Teams of this size provide services for about 50 families a year. There are several advantages to using a team format: (1) team members provide instrumental and affective support for each other; (2) team members become familiar with all cases so that therapists can competently cover for one another during vacation and personal time off; and (3) therapists are able to become proficient in MST more quickly because they have the opportunity to learn from each others' successes and mistakes.

Therapists are selected on the basis of their motivation, flexibility, common sense, and street smarts, with the master's degree being viewed more as a sign of motivation than as evidence of a particular type or level of clinical expertise (Henggeler, 1997). Experience suggests that practitioners who are open to peer supervision and learning empirically based treatment models, and who are as excited about working with families as they are about working with individual children, are well suited to MST.

MST AS AN ALTERNATIVE TO PSYCHIATRIC HOSPITALIZATION

An ongoing study examining MST as an alternative to psychiatric hospitalization for youth experiencing psychiatric crises (Henggeler et al., 1997b; Henggeler et al., 1999; Schoenwald, Ward, Henggeler, Rowland, & Brondino, 2000) has required modification of some aspects of service delivery and clinical coverage. Changes in team composition, supervision frequency, and caseload were made for this study (for further details, see Henggeler et al., 1997b). Child psychiatrists receiving training in MST were fully incorporated into the treatment team and were available 24 hours a day, 7 days a week to provide psychiatric evaluations of youth and other family members, to consult with the team, and to prescribe and monitor psychotropic medications. Bachelor's level mental health professionals were hired as crisis caseworkers to provide clinical and administrative support to the therapists and assistance during crisis situations. Clinical supervision was initially provided daily when the project began and three times per week once the team became more seasoned in working with this population. The client caseload was reduced from 4–5 families per therapist to 3–4 families per therapist. The modified version of MST has not yet been replicated, and modifications to the MST training and quality-assurance package needed to support its implementation outside of a research protocol (see subsequent sections of this chapter) have not yet been finalized. Follow-up data regarding the long-term clinical effectiveness and cost-effectiveness of MST as an alternative to psychiatric hospitalization and evidence of successful community-based replication are needed before dissemination of this version of MST is pursued.

MST Training and Quality Assurance: A Multicomponent Approach

In response to community demand for MST programs, a training and quality-assurance package has been developed. The package is designed to optimize therapist adherence to the MST model and provider accountability for meaningful, measurable outcomes. Quality assurance mechanisms include on-site task-oriented supervision, weekly case consultation with an MST expert, use of adherence measures, quarterly booster training, and an introductory 5-day orientation training for all MST staff, plus pre-training site assessment and assistance. In addition, there are manuals describing procedures for supervision (Henggeler & Schoenwald, 1998b) and consultation (Schoenwald, 1998). Technical assistance for program start-up and organizational practices that support MST are made available to providers engaged in the training process.

SITE ASSESSMENT AND PROGRAM START-UP

The extent to which organizational and service system factors influence the implementation of MST is an empirical question, albeit one the original developers of MST at the Medical University of South Carolina Family Services Research Center are planning to investigate (see "Future Directions" section in this chapter). Anecdotal evidence from efforts to disseminate MST to communities in 15 states and Canada suggests, however, that contextual factors do impact program implementation and success. Thus, the MST training and quality-assurance package begins with a site assessment process that allows the potential provider organization and representatives from referring and reimbursement agencies and consumer groups to discuss the extent to which the establishment of an MST program is both desirable and viable. This process is designed to assess the philosophical compatibility of MST with community agency and consumer groups; identify referral and funding incentives and disincentives (i.e., a referring agency pays for MST but not for group home placement) that could impact long-term sustainability of the program; establish the interagency collaboration necessary to allow the MST program and its client families to take the lead in clinical decision-making; and align the structure, procedures, and culture of the organization hosting the MST program to support therapist adherence to MST and provider accountability for engagement and outcomes. The site assessment process also includes technical assistance in outcomes and adherence monitoring.

ORIENTATION AND BOOSTER TRAINING

A 5-day orientation training is provided on-site using essentially the same protocol that has been used in successful clinical trials of MST with violent and chronic juvenile offenders. All staff who can influence treatment (e.g., a consulting psychiatrist, utilization review manager) must be trained in and support MST. The initial training includes didactic and experiential components. Didactic components include (1) instruction in systems theories, social learning theory, and the major psychological and sociological models and research regarding serious emotional disorder in youth; (2) research relevant to problems experienced by targeted youth (e.g., learning disabilities, substance abuse); and (3) research on interventions used in MST (e.g., empirically validated family and marital therapy approaches, behavioral parent training, cognitive behavior therapy, school consultation). Experiential components include role-plays on engagement, assessment, and intervention strategies and exercises designed to stimulate critical thinking about the treatment process (e.g., what evidence therapists use to draw conclusions about the correlates/causes of a problem to determine whether an intervention is effective.)

Quarterly booster training sessions are conducted on-site as therapists gain field experience with MST. The purpose of these 1½-day boosters is to provide additional training in areas identified by therapists and clinical supervisors (e.g., marital interventions, treatment of parental depression in the context of

MST) and to facilitate in-depth examination, enactment, and problem-solving of particularly difficult challenges that arise in working with referred youth and their families.

ON-SITE SUPERVISION[1]

MST supervision sessions are the primary forum in which supervisors obtain evidence of clinicians' development and implementation of the conceptual and behavioral skills required to implement MST effectively. As such, supervision serves three interrelated purposes: (1) development of case-specific recommendations to speed progress toward outcomes for each client family, (2) monitoring of therapist adherence to MST treatment principles in all cases, and (3) advancement of clinicians' developmental trajectories with respect to each aspect of the ongoing MST assessment and intervention process. The supervisor plays a critical role in the developmental process through which clinicians learn to implement MST effectively and consistently. Clinician adherence to the MST principles is linked with favorable outcomes (Henggeler, Pickrel, & Brondino, 2000), and supervisors are primarily responsible for helping clinicians adhere. Thus, just as therapists are encouraged to do whatever it takes to achieve treatment goals with families, supervisors must be prepared to expend considerable effort in promoting clinicians' adherence to the MST protocol.

Assumptions Underlying MST Supervision

Because seasoned clinicians are typically accustomed to practicing independently, compulsory supervision is often perceived as a foreign experience when they begin to work with MST programs. Several assumptions about MST supervision are explicitly discussed to facilitate clinician adaptation to active supervision of their cases.

- Each clinician implementing MST is a hardworking, competent professional who brings unique personal strengths and professional experiences to the treatment process.
- Ongoing clinical supervision is necessary to monitor adherence to MST and to achieve positive, sustainable outcomes with youth presenting serious clinical problems and their families.
- The purpose of clinical supervision is to enable clinicians to adhere to the nine principles of MST in all aspects of treatment—engagement of client families, case conceptualization, intervention design and implementation, and evaluation of outcomes.
- The process of clinical supervision should mirror the process of MST. That is, supervision is present-focused and action-oriented and targets specific and well-defined problems that the clinician appears to be having in (1) conceptualizing the fit of referral problems with the family's ecological con-

---

[1]Information in this section has been excerpted (with permission) from Henggeler, S.W., & Schoenwald, S.K. (1998). *The Multisystemic Therapy supervision manual: Promoting quality assurance at the clinical level.* Charleston, SC: MST Institute.

text, (2) identifying and using strengths as levers for change, (3) designing interventions, (4) implementing interventions adequately, and
(5) overcoming barriers to intervention implementation or success. Supervision should also enable clinicians to sustain MST-like conceptualizations
and intervention skills across cases (generalization).

• Clinicians and clinical supervisors (and the provider organization that
houses the MST program) are accountable for outcomes (Henggeler et al.,
1998b, p. 46–47).

Format and Structure of Supervision

MST supervision typically occurs in a small-group format (i.e., treatment
teams). Group supervision takes place at least once each week, for 1½–2 hours
per session. Supervision sessions may occur two or more times weekly when
clinicians and supervisors are new to MST, with sessions generally decreasing
to once weekly as teams gain more experience and produce evidence of positive treatment outcomes. As noted previously, however, the MST team providing an alternative to psychiatric hospitalization for youth in crises continued to meet three times per week during the course of the study.

Advanced preparation for supervision is required, as clinicians are expected to document treatment developments for each youth and family in terms
of the MST Do Loop (Figure 5.1). Clinicians and supervisors jointly prioritize
the discussion of cases to maximize the effort directed toward addressing barriers to progress and to minimize the time spent discussing cases that are going well. The supervisor bears the responsibility for assuring that supervision
is efficient, effective, and enjoyable; the competencies and procedures required
to fulfill this responsibility are described further in the supervisor's manual
(Henggeler & Schoenwald, 1998) and supported through MST training and consultation activities.

As described earlier, MST treatment teams typically include 3–4 therapists,
and supervisors are responsible for the conduct and outcomes of all supervision sessions. Group supervision provides several advantages. First, team members have the opportunity to learn from each others' successes, mistakes, and
dilemmas. Second, team members have the opportunity to practice (role-play)
clinical interventions, especially those that are difficult to implement, in a safe
setting. Third, the group supervisory process can facilitate the types of collaboration among team members that lead to better outcomes for families. For example, when progress has been slow and barriers to progress are elusive, another team member may attend one or more treatment sessions to attain direct
family contact. This second practitioner often develops new hypotheses about
the barriers to progress as a result of having a fresh perspective. Fourth, MST
programs must be prepared to meet the needs of families in crisis who (1) have
not yet made the necessary ecological changes that will prevent out-of-home
placement, and (2) whose therapist is not available (e.g., is on vacation). If team
members have helped in the conceptualization and development of interventions for that family through group supervision, these individuals will be in a

stronger position to ameliorate crises while covering for their colleague who is unavailable.

Although group supervision is the norm in MST, some circumstances warrant individual supervision sessions. These include the emergence of a case crisis between scheduled supervision sessions, development of a specific clinical competency by a particular clinician, and assessment and remediation of consistently poor adherence to the model by a particular clinician. In addition, all supervisors conduct periodic field supervision and reviews of therapists' audiotaped treatment sessions to ensure that they have continued firsthand experience with clinician performance in the field.

Since few clinicians possess all clinical competencies required to execute MST, on-site supervisors, usually in collaboration with MST consultants, provide training experiences (appropriate reading, role-play exercises, etc.) to assist with the development of needed skills (e.g., marital interventions, cognitive-behavioral treatment for depressed adults). When the requisite skills exist, but evidence from weekly supervision and adherence measures suggests that a particular clinician is not adhering to MST principles and is making little progress in most of her/his cases, individual supervision may be needed to assess the lack of fit between adherence and poor progress. A variety of factors may contribute to poor adherence, including poor understanding of the model, continued allegiance to and practice of treatment orientations antithetical to the model, lack of experience with certain intervention techniques, and personal problems. The supervisor's response to lack of experience has already been discussed. Discussion of allegiance to other treatments or personal problems is generally best facilitated in individual supervision. When a practitioner's personal problems interfere with his or her performance, however, the supervisor does not become the practitioner's "therapist." The supervisor is responsible for treatment adherence and, as such, must take steps to identify, discuss, and conjointly develop strategies to increase therapist effectiveness. The supervisor's role is to evaluate the extent to which a therapist's difficulties impede adherence to the MST protocol. Thus, the supervisor may not meet individually with a therapist who is experiencing personal problems but who can adhere to MST and obtain outcomes, but would meet with a therapist whose personal problems are interfering with adherence and outcomes.

CONSULTATION PRACTICE[2]

MST consultation is designed to support therapist and supervisory fidelity to the MST treatment model on an ongoing basis. For this reason, weekly consultation from an MST expert is a central component of the comprehensive training and quality assurance package developed for use with providers who wish to establish MST programs. Although an adequate understanding of the nature of child and family behaviors and problems is important, the consulta-

[2]Information in this section has been excerpted (with permission) from Schoenwald, S.K. (1998). *Multisystemic therapy consultation manual*. Charleston, SC: MST Institute.

tion process is directed more at the behavior of the clinicians and supervisors than at the behavior of youth and families referred to MST programs.

Objectives of MST Consultation

The overarching objectives of expert MST consultation are:

- to facilitate clinician learning and application of MST principles to cases when both the clinicians and the on-site supervisor are novices at MST;
- to facilitate logical and critical thinking throughout the ongoing assessment and intervention process, as depicted in the MST analytic process (see Figure 5.1);
- to monitor and support clinician and supervisor adherence to the MST treatment principles as teams become more seasoned in MST;
- to coach supervisors in the effective use of the MST supervision protocol (see Henggeler & Schoenwald, 1998) and monitor the consistency of their supervisory practices with this protocol;
- to provide guidelines to clinicians and supervisors for incorporation of specific treatment modalities into MST intervention plans;
- to provide updated information as needed regarding research relevant to MST, empirically supported treatments subsumed within MST, and the etiology of problems experienced by target populations served by MST programs; and
- to identify organizational and service system barriers to the effective implementation of MST, and to assist the team (and the organizational leadership, as needed) to address those barriers.

At this time, fewer than a dozen individuals have served in the consultation role, and these individuals have all been directly trained by faculty involved in the ongoing research and development of MST. In the interest of helping communities develop the capacity to implement MST programs successfully, dissemination projects that involve training therapists to become supervisors and supervisors to become consultants are just beginning. The findings from these projects will illuminate the extent to which the combination of therapist, supervisory, and consultation practices can effectively sustain fidelity to the MST treatment model.

THE MST ADHERENCE SCALE

Therapist adherence to the principles of MST can be measured using the 26-item Likert-format MST Adherence Scale (Henggeler & Borduin, 1995) developed by expert consensus and administered to the caregiver, youth, and therapist at regular intervals during treatment. Factors derived from respondent ratings have been associated with key ultimate outcomes—arrest, incarceration, self-reported criminal activity, and out-of-home placement (Henggeler et al., 1997a). In contrast with the majority of treatment-specific adherence measures developed for clinical trials in the adult, child, and family psychotherapy literatures (Hill, Nutt, & Jackson, 1994; Hogue, Liddle, & Rowe, 1996; Waltz, Addis, Koerner, & Jacobson, 1993), the measure has been implemented in more than one study and with different types of samples (i.e., chronic violent offenders, substance-abusing offenders, youth in psychiatric crisis), and presents a low response burden to the client and clinician. Providers receiving MST training are encouraged to use the MST Adherence Scale as one index of therapist adherence to the treatment model. Therapist adherence scores can be made immediately available to clinical supervisors who are being trained in accordance with a manual describing MST supervision procedures (Henggeler & Schoenwald, 1998).

Evidence Base for MST

COMPLETED STUDIES

Leading child treatment researchers concur that MST is a well-validated treatment model (Kazdin & Weisz, 1998). Multiple randomized clinical trials have been completed, including three with violent and chronic offenders, one with inner-city delinquents, one with substance-abusing and dependent juvenile offenders, one with maltreating families, and one with adolescent sexual offenders. An early quasi-experimental study with inner-city juvenile offenders (Henggeler et al., 1986) and randomized trials with small samples of juvenile sex offenders (Borduin, Henggeler, Blaske, & Stein, 1990) and families in which maltreatment occurred (Brunk, Henggeler, & Whelan, 1987) suggested the promise of MST with these populations. Larger randomized trials with long-term follow-up data have since been conducted to evaluate the clinical effectiveness and cost-effectiveness of MST with youth who engage in serious antisocial behavior (Borduin et al., 1995; Henggeler et al., 1991; Henggeler et al., 1997a; Henggeler, Melton, & Smith, 1992; Henggeler, Melton, Smith, Schoenwald, & Hanley, 1993; Henggeler, Pickrel, & Brondino, 2000). For example, a randomized clinical trial comparing MST with usual services (Henggeler, Melton, & Smith, 1992) in the treatment of serious juvenile offenders at imminent risk of incarceration showed that youths receiving MST had substantially reduced recidivism and out-of-home placement rates at the 59-week follow-up, and substantially reduced rearrest rates at a 24-month follow-up (Henggeler et al., 1993). A randomized trial comparing MST with individual therapy (Borduin et al., 1995) in the treatment of serious juvenile offenders showed decreases in arrest rates, other criminal offenses, and substance-related offenses at a 4-year follow-up. A third randomized trial with violent and chronic juvenile offenders (Henggeler et al., 1997a) demonstrated the effectiveness of MST in reducing out-of-home placements, as well as the importance of therapist adherence to the MST principles in obtaining favorable outcomes.

Evidence also indicates that MST may be more cost-effective than the traditional services provided to youth at risk of imminent placement and their families. A study conducted by the Washington State Institute for Public Policy (1998) identified MST as the most cost-effective intervention for juvenile offenders among 16 programs evaluated. In addition, Schoenwald and colleagues (1996) showed that the incremental costs of providing MST to substance-abusing and substance-dependent juvenile offenders were nearly offset by the savings incurred as a result of reductions in days of out-of-home placement one year following referral for treatment, even with a population not at imminent risk of placement.

MST AS AN ALTERNATIVE TO HOSPITALIZATION

The primary purpose of the NIMH-funded study referred to previously (see p. 107) is to determine whether MST, modified for use with a sample of youth presenting in psychiatric crisis, can serve as a safe, clinically effective, and cost-effective community-based alternative to hospitalization. While data are still being collected in this randomized trial, preliminary outcomes evaluating the first 113 youth are promising. Analyses of post-treatment data (approximately 4 months from intake) show that MST was more effective than emergency hospitalization in reducing youth externalizing symptoms, improving family functioning, and increasing youth school attendance. MST was at least as effective as emergency hospitalization in reducing youth internalizing symptoms, substance use, and psychological distress, and in improving social functioning (Henggeler et al., 1999). Importantly, MST youth experienced a significant reduction in hospitalization and other out-of-home placements relative to youth in the control condition (Schoenwald et al., 2000).

Future Directions

MST-BASED CONTINUA OF CARE

To date, MST has been delivered in a home-based model of service delivery with a time-limited duration. Children and adolescents presenting serious and chronic mental health problems often need continued access to a range of effective services that vary in intensity (i.e., outpatient to home-based to time-limited crisis stabilization). Experience from the study of MST for youth in psychiatric crises also suggests that cultivation of high-quality community services (i.e., shelter, respite, treatment foster care) can be helpful to the crisis stabilization process for youth receiving MST and their families (see Henggeler et al., 1997a). Evidence regarding the services arrays delivered in innovative systems of care has been somewhat disappointing (see Chapter 2). To respond to the need for an effective continuum of services, the Annie E. Casey Foundation and other public sources have funded the development and evaluation of MST-based continua of care in several sites. In the Annie E. Casey project, an MST-based continuum of care will assume responsibility for all treatment needs of a sample of youths who are currently in out-of-home placement for the duration of the project. The evaluation includes an experimental design (randomized assignment).

In a second project, an MST team and prevention interventionists (primary and secondary) have been placed in an inner-city middle school that has a high rate of violence, drug use, and dropout. The MST team provides intensive family-based treatment for youths who have been expelled or have been caught using drugs or perpetrating crimes in school. The prevention personnel are implementing empirically based violence and drug use prevention and consultation techniques. A quasi-experimental design (the comparison is an inner-city middle school with similar demographics and rates of problems) is being used to examine cost-related issues and ultimate outcomes. A third project has developed neighborhood- and school-based services in collaboration with neighborhood residents to address the problems of adolescent drug dealing, drug abuse, prostitution, school expulsion, and suspension. Another quasi-experimental study (the comparison is a neighborhood with similar demographics) is focusing on reductions in the identified problems and cost savings.

EARLY CHILDHOOD INTERVENTION

One recently completed (Pickrel & Henggeler, 1999) and one ongoing study are exploring the use of MST in combination with other empirically validated interventions and/or early childhood education models with families of very young children at risk of abuse, neglect, behavioral problems, or developmental delays. The completed study was conducted in collaboration with local mental health and substance abuse agencies, and funded by the Center for Mental Health Services.

Results of this quasi-experimental study of a small sample of parents experiencing both mental health and substance abuse problems suggest the promise of combining MST with the empirically validated Community Reinforcement Approach (CRA; Budney & Higgins, 1998) for adult substance abuse with this population. Compared with treatment that included a combination of medical, interpersonal, and cognitive behavior models of substance abuse treatment, the MST+CRA package evidenced more favorable child development outcomes, reductions in parenting stress, increases in the time the child spent at home, and increases in consumer satisfaction.

The ongoing study of early childhood education is occurring in the context of a national initiative to evaluate Early Head Start programs. The impact of an early childhood intervention program modeled after MST is being examined relative to Early Head Start programs for teenage mothers.

EXAMINING THE TRANSPORTABILITY OF MST

The success of MST has led to the development of MST programs at approximately 25 sites across the United States and Canada. It remains to be seen, however, whether such programs can be implemented with the fidelity required to achieve the types of positive outcomes observed in previous MST studies.

In recognition of the intensive training and quality assurance mechanisms necessary to enhance therapist adherence to MST, the Office of Juvenile Justice and Delinquency Prevention has funded research aimed at promoting the successful dissemination of MST. In this project, therapist adherence is being measured using caregiver and therapist reports on the MST Adherence Scale, and these scores are being made immediately available to clinical supervisors, who are being trained in accordance with the MST supervision manual (Henggeler & Schoenwald, 1998). A measure of supervision is also being administered throughout the course of this study, thus allowing for examination of the associations among supervision practices, therapist adherence, and child outcomes.

A recently initiated NIMH-funded study includes organizational and extra-organizational factors in an examination of the transportability of MST to real-world practice settings. The study proposes to examine linkages between treatment outcomes, therapist adherence, supervisory practices, organizational variables, and extra-organizational factors (e.g., referral and reimbursement mechanisms, interagency relations).

In conclusion, the original studies of MST documented significant benefit for multiple target populations under conditions of training and close supervision by the MST developers. From studies currently in the field, we hope to increase our understanding of factors associated with the adoption and dissemination of an innovative intervention. The results of these investigations should inform future efforts to make science-based treatment models available in community-based service systems.

6

Treatment Foster Care

PATRICIA CHAMBERLAIN

Treatment foster care (TFC) is a family-based alternative to residential, institutional, and group care for children and adolescents with significant behavioral, emotional, and mental health problems.[1] Kutash and Rivera (1996) defined TFC as a service that provides treatment to troubled children within private homes of trained families. The TFC model was first seen in the United States in the mid-1970s as an alternative to institutional placements and has grown steadily within the child welfare, juvenile justice, and mental health systems. TFC is now one of the most widely used forms of out-of-home placement for children and adolescents with severe emotional and behavioral disorders and is considered to be the least restrictive form of residential care (Kutash & Rivera, 1996; Stroul, 1989). An estimated 1,200 youth in the United States receive TFC at any one time, representing over 6 million "client days" at a cost of one-half billion dollars per year (Farmer, Burns, Chamberlain, & Dubs, 2001).

This chapter will highlight the use of TFC with children and adolescents with antisocial and conduct problems. In terms of prevalence, displays of the more common forms of child antisocial behavior—such as aggression, noncompliance, and stealing—are the most frequent reason that children and adolescents are brought to mental health clinics, accounting for almost half of all referrals (Burns, 1991; Robins & Radcliff, 1980). Using conservative population estimates, the prevalence of children who exhibit clinically extreme forms of antisocial behavior make up approximately 2.6% of the population in the United States, or 1 to 4 million children and adolescents at any given time (Kazdin, 1994).

This chapter will present a brief overview of the developmental progression of antisocial behavior throughout childhood and adolescence, including a description of the antecedents and risk factors at various stages of develop-

---

[1] In the literature, TFC has been variously referred to as therapeutic foster care, specialized foster care, and foster family–based care. All of these terms refer to the same service, which in this chapter will be called treatment foster care (TFC).

ment. This overview is intended to set the stage for discussion of the theory of change in TFC programs dealing with this population. Contributing to this theory will be the identification of the key factors that can be targeted as active ingredients in interventions and an examination of how these factors are expected to act as mediators that predict treatment outcomes.

Next, examples of the use of the TFC model with various populations of children and adolescents with conduct problems will be given, including identification of outcomes that are targeted for change in treatment. The key parameters of the Oregon TFC model developed with my colleagues at the Oregon Social Learning Center (OSLC) will be described, along with data on the relationship between active ingredients or areas of emphasis in the model and outcomes for youth and their families. Practical aspects of running a TFC program will be discussed, such as staffing requirements, training, and supervision considerations and costs. A parent's perspective on participating in TFC will be presented, and finally a brief summary of research that has been conducted on TFC programs will be presented.

Developmental Progression of Antisocial Behavior: Relationships between Risk Factors, Behavioral Continuities, and Adjustment

Over the last three decades, knowledge about the development, maintenance, and escalation of patterns of child antisocial behavior has increased significantly. This has been in large part due to the findings from several carefully conducted longitudinal studies that have focused on the identification of factors that predict and account for variance in the development of antisocial behavior throughout childhood and adolescence (e.g., Dishion & Patterson, 1997; Elliott, Huizinga, & Ageton, 1985; Farrington, 1991; Thornberry & Krohn, 1997). A variety of factors are now known to put young families at risk for beginning and shaping their child's developmental trajectory towards serious forms of antisocial behavior. These include an array of community, economic, biological, family, and child factors.

From a clinical perspective, the variables of most interest are those that are potentially malleable—the ones that can be changed as part of a treatment program or service. For example, economic disadvantage appears to be a good predictor of participation in an antisocial trajectory but it is probably not likely to be directly affected by treatment. However, the impact of economic disadvantage appears to be at least partially mediated by a more malleable set of factors (e.g., consistent and constructive parenting) that could be reasonably targeted in an intervention. Studies have shown that to the extent that parent supervision and engagement can be strengthened, even in the context of economic disadvantage, the child will be at decreased risk for the development of antisocial behaviors and conduct problems (e.g., Sampson & Laub, 1993).

If risk factors accumulate that lead to the eventual development of child and adolescent antisocial behavior, it is well documented that there are cascading sets of circumstances that have the potential to drive the escalation and diversification of antisocial trajectories over time (Farrington, 1983; Loeber, 1982). For example, when the child is a preschooler, inconsistent and harsh parent discipline and child noncompliance and aggressiveness have been shown to set the stage for later child antisocial behavior in the school setting. In school, the child who is noncompliant and aggressive is seen as having poor cooperation skills, and these youngsters tend to engage in coercive interactions with peers and be disliked and rejected by teachers. Problems that develop in elementary school in turn become powerful predictors of many types of conduct problems in middle school, such as school failure, a tendency to associate with delinquent peers, early initiation of substance use, and sexual activity (Patterson, Reid, & Dishion, 1992). These problems are then the key antecedents of adolescent delinquency, drug use, and associated problems. Figure 6.1 depicts a developmental model of child antisocial behavior (from Reid & Eddy, 1997) and identifies key malleable factors that contribute to the development of serious and chronic antisocial behavior. The development of antisocial behavior throughout the life course has been likened to the growth of a weed (Patterson, 1982). Like most weeds, once started, it needs very little to keep it growing, and the longer it grows the stronger it gets. However, because it grows in predictable ways and because major roots lie in family interaction patterns and in other malleable factors (e.g., association with delinquent peers), it is possible to design clinical interventions that combat it or at least stunt its growth.

Such an intervention was designed and tested in Oregon from 1990–1996 for 79 boys who were serious and chronic juvenile offenders. Participating boys had an average of 14 arrests and 4.6 felonies before entering the study. The study examined the relative effectiveness of TFC and group care placements. It was funded by the National Institute of Mental Health (Violence and Traumatic Stress Branch) and not only examined key outcomes but also looked at the role that potentially malleable factors that had been identified in developmental research played in predicting those outcomes. The questions that this study addressed examined not only who improved and who didn't, but also the ingredients in treatment that related to why some boys had more successful outcomes than others.

The Oregon TFC model is theoretically based. That is, in addition to using Social Learning Theory as a specified treatment approach, the targets of the treatment are based on those factors that have been identified by research as relating to the development, maintenance, and escalation of delinquency. The Oregon TFC model has been used with a variety of populations of youngsters and families.

Target Populations and Expected Outcomes

Most of the research on the Oregon TFC model has been done with youth referred from the juvenile justice system. Although the program began with a state contract and no funding for research, we have been committed to examining program outcomes from the beginning. In 1990 (Chamberlain, 1990a) we compared outcomes for the first 16 youth served, with a matched sample of 16

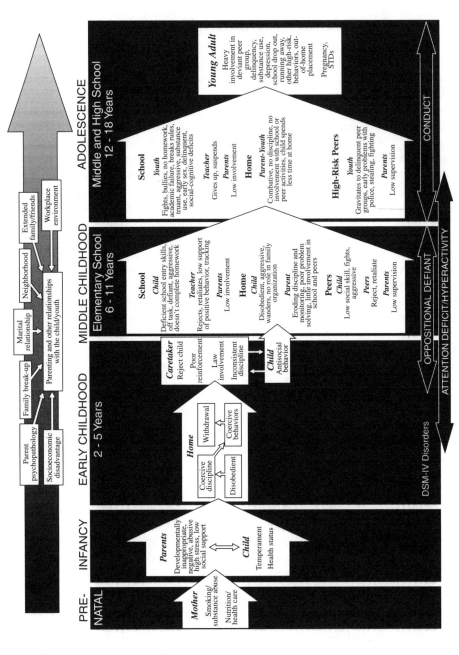

Figure 6.1 Illustrative developmental model of child antisocial behavior. *Source:* Reid and Eddy, 1997

youth served in other residential programs in Oregon. In that pilot study we found that youth in TFC completed their programs more often and spent fewer days incarcerated than those in the comparison group. We have subsequently conducted a larger randomized trial that will be described later, where both outcomes and processes that predicted outcomes were examined. Expected outcomes for juvenile justice–referred youth first and foremost include reduced rates of criminal activity and incarceration. Other important outcomes include decreased alcohol and drug use and positive relationships with parents, at school, and with employers, as well as with future romantic partners.

Over the years we have come to recognize the unique treatment needs of female adolescents who are referred from the juvenile justice system. The Oregon TFC model, like other treatment programs and the major theories on delinquency, was developed based on information about antisocial behavior in boys. Yet there appear to be many differences between girls and boys who find their way into juvenile justice. For example, some of the risk factors for girls and boys referred to our program from juvenile justice are shown in Table 6.1 . As can be seen there, girls appear to come from more chaotic families than their male counterparts, as evidenced by girls having a higher rate of parents who have been convicted of a crime, having more siblings institutionalized, and having higher rates of previous out-of-home placements. Girls also have higher rates of physical and sexual abuse, a fact that relates to their greater number of out-of-home placements. Whereas the majority of the previous out-of-home placements for boys were in delinquency treatment programs, girls' previous placements were in foster care, due to parental abuse and neglect.

Table 6.1 Some Characteristics and Risk Factors for Boys and Girls Referred from Juvenile Justice

	Boys **(n = 79)**	**Girls** **(n = 36)**
Age	14.36	14.8
Adopted	9%	8%
Mother convicted of a crime	10%	36%*
Father convicted of a crime	22%	70%*
At least one parent convicted	22%	72%*
Youth attempted suicide	3%	62%*
Number of prior out-of-home placements	1.33	5.34*
Number previous arrests	14.2	9.8*
Number days in detention in past year	66	131*

*Significant at p < .05 level.

Table 6.2   Percent of Boys and Girls Who Meet
Clinical Cutoffs (T-score >63)

Symptoms	Boys (%)	Girls (%)
Anxiety	11.4	80.0
Depression	7.6	40.0
Somatization	5.1	86.7
Paranoid/Psychotic	10.1	66.7
General Psychopathology	1.3	73.3

Comparing the rates of symptoms for mental health disorders, we also find gender differences. Table 6.2 shows the percentage of youth who are in the clinical (versus the normal) range on the Behavior Symptom Inventory (BSI) scores for boys and girls at the time of referral. On all of the scales measured, girls have significantly higher scores than boys. In addition, we find that although girls have committed fewer crimes at baseline (an average of 10 versus 14 for boys), they have spent approximately twice as many days in detention during the past year than their male counterparts (131 versus 66 days). Also, although it seems to be the belief that girls are far more prone to running away than boys, in our sample there were no significant differences between boys and girls on the percent who had run away at least once (74% for boys, 84% for girls). This information on gender differences in these populations is presented as a means of illustrating that girls and boys may have different treatment needs and that in order to design effective programs for girls, it will probably be necessary to conduct a close analysis of these differences and to modify treatment protocols to fit. We are currently engaged in such an effort, with funding from the National Institute of Mental Health. We are 2 years into a 5-year trial where an adaptation of the Oregon TFC model for girls is being developed and tested.

In 1986, we adapted the TFC model for work with children and adolescents who were referred from the Oregon State Hospital because they were severely emotionally disturbed. Since that time, we have continued to provide TFC services for this population and have expanded the availability of these services to children and adolescents who are in state foster care. During 1997–98 we provided TFC placements and services to 90 such youngsters and their families. Major outcomes expected included: stability of living situation; improved behavioral adjustment at home, at school, and with peers; and moving out of TFC to the least restrictive living situation possible. Results from the State Hospital Study, where children were randomly assigned to TFC or usual community treatment, are presented in detail in Chamberlain and Reid (1991).

As the number of referrals for TFC have increased, we have developed a specialized program model for the younger children that we serve (ages 3–7). The early intervention TFC model emphasizes behavioral outcomes, promoting attachment, remediating developmental delays, and increasing emotional regulation skills. Providing these young children with a stable living environment is of the utmost importance, as is working with their parents, relatives, or other aftercare resource with support and skills. In December 1999 we began a randomized clinical trial to evaluate that model (Fisher, Ellis, & Chamberlain, 1999).

Another population of youngsters who are served using the Oregon TFC model are children and adolescents who are developmentally delayed and who have histories of acting out in sexually inappropriate ways. Beginning in 1998, the State of Oregon Office of Services to Children and Families (child welfare) awarded the Oregon Social Learning Center a contract to provide TFC services to this population. For this group of youngsters there is an intense dual emphasis on supervision and skill building. So far, 30 youth have participated in this version of TFC. The disruption rates are low (two cases) and we have not experienced significant resistance from the community.

Intervention Parameters

DESCRIPTION OF THE CORE ELEMENTS OF THE TFC MODEL

The Oregon TFC model is comprised of a set of interlocking components that, taken together, target coordinated interventions in the key settings in which the youth lives and interacts. Because TFC is individually tailored to meet the needs of each child and family, the specific content of each youth's program varies, and each individual's program changes over time to be relevant to his or her changing level of progress toward treatment goals. For example, the level of supervision that a youth receives is typically titrated over time, beginning with adult supervision during their entire day then gradually moving to having periods of free time in the community. The coordination, specific content, and pace of the interventions is managed by a supervisor or case manager who is the leader of the youth's treatment team. The team also consists of the TFC parents who are the primary caretakers and change agents in the TFC model, the youth's advocate, who can be a therapist or a skill builder depending on the youth's needs, the family therapist, who assists the family of origin or other provider of aftercare resources, and the parole/probation officer or caseworker who is the system agent monitoring the case. In many instances, other team members are recruited, including a psychiatrist to advise on and manage medication and a school liaison who conducts observations and interventions in that setting.

In order to monitor the daily progress and problems for each youth, the TFC parents are telephoned each weekday and asked about the youth's adjustment during the past 24 hours. This contact is conducted by a former TFC parent who then passes the daily data on to the case manager so that he or she has a current view of case status. Table 6.3 summarizes the core components of the model that are delivered to the youth, to their TFC parents, and to their biological, adoptive, or other aftercare placement resource.

Table 6.3   Core Program Components

For the youth:
   Daily structure and support through an individualized point and level system
   Daily school card to monitor attendance, homework completion, and behavior
   Weekly therapy, skill-building, and advocacy
   Close supervision of whereabouts and peer associations
   Consistent teaching-oriented discipline
   Recreational interest development and skill-building
   Family therapy with parents or aftercare placement resource
   Psychiatric consultation, as needed

For the TFC parents:
   Preservice training
   Daily weekday telephone contact from program to collect data and troubleshoot
   Weekly support and training meetings with other TFC parents and staff
   24-hour, 7-day on-call access to program staff
   Crisis intervention services as needed
   Respite

For the youth's parents:
   Weekly family consultation focusing on parent management
   Family therapy with youth
   Frequent home visits with on-call crisis backup from program staff
   Aftercare parent group
   24-hour, 7-day access to program staff

KEY PRINCIPLES OF PRACTICE

Most of the youngsters who participate in the Oregon TFC programs have longstanding patterns of aggressive and antisocial behavior that have caused them problems at home, in school, with peers, and in their communities. For many of these youth, it is not simply a matter of motivating them to act differently; they often do not have the skills required to negotiate successful performance or relationships in the multiple settings in which they interact each day. It is common for a youngster to report that there was a period of time in which he or she tried hard to change—to be more cooperative, comply to adult demands, to avoid delinquent friends. Their experiences of failure during these attempts have convinced them that their choices and strategies for reacting to stress and for dealing with societal demands are limited. The goal of the TFC program is to expand the behavioral repertoires of these youngsters by teaching and having them practice an expanded set of skills that emphasizes building positive relationships and behaving in prosocial ways so they can begin to experience the naturally occurring rewards available to individuals at their developmental stage (e.g., being on sports teams or in clubs, being selected for participation in school or community events). To accomplish this we use three key strategies, described more fully below, that are aimed at helping turn around ingrained negative antisocial patterns:

1. A proactive approach is used for dealing with antisocial behavior and teaching prosocial behavior.
2. Program staff and TFC parent's roles are stratified to create maximum flexibility and impact.
3. A consistent positive environment is created for program youth.

USING A PROACTIVE APPROACH

In the Oregon TFC model, we "sweat the small stuff" in terms of both positive or appropriate youth behaviors and attitudes and negative ones. That is, we keep close tabs on the youth's progress and problems on a daily basis, including his or her behavior in the TFC home, at school, and in other relationships (e.g., with peers, coaches, employers). There are a number of mechanisms through which this is accomplished. The most systematic method is that TFC parents are telephoned every weekday and asked to report on the occurrence or nonoccurrence of a number of behaviors during the past 24-hour time period. They are also asked how stressed or angry they were about specific youth problems, how many minutes the youth spent without adult supervision, and what recreational activities he or she participated in. They also give the day a grade (from A to F) and report on how many points the youth gained and lost during the past 24 hours, and for what specific behaviors. These telephone calls, called Parent Daily Report (PDR) calls, are conducted by a former TFC parent because we have found that foster parents feel more comfortable and less intimidated sharing information with someone who has "been there." The PDR calls form the basis for the ongoing clinical monitoring by the case managers, who receive copies of the PDR data every day. The PDR has been used in numerous studies conducted at OSLC and elsewhere to measure clinical outcomes and to provide monitoring of case progress (e.g., Chamberlain & Reid, 1987).

A second mechanism is frequent contact between the case managers and the TFC parents. During preservice training, TFC parents are told not to hesitate to call their case manager at any time of day or night if they have a concern or question—"If you think about calling," they're told, "*call.*" A common question is whether this doesn't make the job of the case manager difficult or overwhelming. The fact is that almost without exception, when given free access, people are respectful and considerate and do not make unnecessary calls, especially during late evening or nighttime hours.

A point and level system is used in the TFC homes that is designed to recognize and reward positive and appropriate youth behaviors and attitudes on a daily basis. Also, it is a mechanism for noting and providing small but consistent consequences for minor lapses and rule violations. In addition, the point and level system is used to provide consequences for larger transgressions, such as having unsupervised time without permission, lying, or being in possession of something that cannot be accounted for (i.e., suspicion of stealing). The skillful use of the point and level system allows the TFC parents and the program staff to actively shape youth behavior and attitudes towards more positive directions, and specifically to teach youth new skills by breaking such skills down into small steps and reinforcing incremental gains.

STRATIFICATION OF ROLES

An advantage of the TFC model is that there are a number of adults who, when they effectively work together, have the potential to have a strong positive impact on the youth's functioning in multiple domains. The potential exists, however, for the adults to work at cross-purposes, to think that their relationship or point of view is the most important or salient, and to inadvertently undermine each other. For these reasons, we have found that it is important to develop clear role definitions for the adult treatment team members. Additionally, when clear roles exist, the potential to reduce conflict between the youth and relevant others (teachers, TFC parents, their own parents, "the system") is greatly reduced and the capacity to advocate for the youth's point of view is increased.

An advantage of the TFC model is that it has the potential to capitalize on the natural mentoring abilities of the TFC parents and the modeling of positive family living that occurs in their homes. However, if the TFC parents are undermined by treatment agents such as the therapists for the child or the family therapist, or are put in a position where they are having frequent power struggles with the youth, their influence is diminished. For these reasons, in the Oregon programs, we strive to protect and enhance the role of the TFC parent as being a primary advocate and mentor for the youth. To the extent that the youth is noncompliant and has a pattern of rule-breaking in the home, the mentorship role of the TFC parent can be increasingly challenged because it can be difficult to simultaneously set and enforce limits and form alliances, especially with teenagers. In these instances, it is helpful to have the case manager play the role of the "heavy," the individual who articulates the program rules and structure to the youth and (in the presence of the youth) articulates to the TFC parents details on enforcing the structure and rules. These expectations for behavior then become the TFC parent's "job" in working with the program, and subtly remove the TFC parent from being the focus of the youth's power struggles.

This same stratification is used between the case manager and the parole/ probation officer. To the extent that the youth can keep problems and difficulties that he or she has while in the program "in house" rather than having to have parole or probation involved, his or her life will be easier (e.g., the sanctions are likely to be less severe, he or she is less likely to be threatened with removal from the placement). The TFC parent is backed up by the case manager, who in turn is backed up by parole/probation. If this arrangement is well understood by the youth, he or she is less likely to directly challenge the daily authority imposed by the TFC parents, allowing them to focus more on reinforcing and encouraging positive youth skills and development.

CREATING AND MAINTAINING A CONSISTENT ENVIRONMENT FOR YOUTH

Why is it that negative behavior is a lot more salient than positive behavior? A youth who is arguing or swearing is more likely to attract adult attention than one who is quietly complying with adult expectations. In TFC we work intensively with foster parents to notice and reinforce youngsters for behaving appropriately. In addition, we place emphasis on the technique of shaping behavior in areas where the youth's skills are below average. The concept of shaping is well described in the behavioral literature (Galbicka, 1994; Scott, Scott, & Goldwater, 1997) and involves breaking complex chains of behaviors down into small steps and reinforcing successive approximations towards completion or success. Conceptualizing interventions in terms of shaping and reinforcement allows for a focus on strengthening skills and positive support for youth. In this way, the occurrence of problem behaviors can be framed as "teaching opportunities" by the program staff and TFC parents.

In addition to finding and creating opportunities to provide the youth with positive feedback, TFC parents are trained and supported to provide consequences for transgressions and for minor and major rule-breaking. However, in most instances, discipline is conducted with a light touch; that is, youth may lose one or two points for minor (but reoccurring) problems such as arguing or sulking. More serious instances (being late for or cutting class) result in losing one point per minute of unexcused time. Work chores or repetitive tasks are used as consequences for more intractable problems. For law violations, brief stays in detention are available. The constellation of rewards and sanctions, although individualized to be responsive to the needs of each youth and TFC home, are well understood by program youth, and the aim is to have program staff and TFC parents work together to consistently implement these.

MEDIATORS OF OUTCOME AND HOW THEY ARE EMPHASIZED IN PRACTICE

In the randomized clinical trial that was completed in 1996 (Chamberlain & Reid, 1998), we studied what were hypothesized to be key components or active ingredients of treatment. Four factors were examined that, based on the literature on the determinants of antisocial behavior, were expected to predict continued criminal offending. These four factors were (1) the type and amount of supervision the youth received, (2) the consistency and perceived fairness of the discipline the youth received, (3) the presence and quality of the relationship with a mentoring adult, and (4) the youth's association with delinquent peers. These four factors had been identified in a number of longitudinal studies on the development of delinquency (see Farrington, 1997, for a review). In order to collect data on these four factors, after boys had been placed for three months in either the group care (GC) settings or in TFC homes, we interviewed each boy and his primary caretaker during face-to-face visits to the programs and during five telephone interviews (with each boy and each caretaker) over a two-week period. Telephone interviews were conducted to assess boy and caretaker reports of each boy's behavior problems, involvement in discipline situations, and patterns of association with adults and delinquent peers during the past 24 hours. Telephone interviews were arranged so that boys and caretakers could not hear each other.

On average, the caretakers in both the GC and TFC programs reported that boys engaged in about the same rate of problem behaviors (3.7 and 3.6 per day, respectively). However, boys in the two groups differed significantly in their own reports of how many problem behaviors they engaged in. GC boys reported engaging in an average of 6.6 problem behaviors per day while TFC boys reported engaging an average of 3.0 per day. In TFC, the perceptions of boys and their caretakers were more in accord with each other than in GC. On discipline given and received, caretakers in TFC said they gave disciplinary consequences significantly more frequently than those in GC (62% and 34% of the times the boy misbehaved, respectively). Boys in TFC said they were disciplined 37% of the times they misbehaved and those in GC reported being disciplined 15% of the times (also a statistically significant difference).

On the peer and adult contact variables, as could be expected by the fundamental differences in the program structures, boys in GC spent significantly more time with delinquent peers than did those in TFC. In addition, we measured how much time boys spent with delinquent peers living outside their program and how much they felt they were negatively influenced by delinquent peers. In GC, boys reported spending significantly more time with delinquent peers than their caretakers reported. In TFC, the findings were in the opposite direction. Boys reported spending less time with delinquent peers than their caretakers reported. In GC, boys reported that they were significantly more negatively influenced by delinquent peers than boys in TFC. Boys in TFC spent more time with a parent figure or other adult caregiver than those in GC (5 hours per day and 3 hours per day, respectively). Group care boys reported that they spent an average of 79 minutes per day unsupervised, and TFC boys reported an average of 12 minutes per day unsupervised. A full description of these findings can be found in Chamberlain, Ray, and Moore (1996).

In terms of the design of future treatment strategies for highly delinquent youngsters, a most interesting finding was that two of these program variables, association patterns with delinquent peers and discipline consistency *during* placement, predicted both the total number and the seriousness of arrests at one-year follow-up, regardless of treatment condition (TFC or GC). In other words, no matter whether they were placed in GC or TFC, those boys with low rates of association with delinquent peers and who experienced consistent discipline during their placements had fewer arrests during follow-up than boys who had more association with delinquent peers and lax or inconsistent discipline. During placement, association with delinquent peers also predicted an *increase* in the seriousness of offenses committed at follow-up. The results of the analyses that examine the relationship between key mediators and treatment outcomes are described in Eddy and Chamberlain (2000).

These findings suggest that it is easier to supervise and discipline a boy who has severe problems with delinquency when he is not part of a group of peers who have the same type of problems. Boys themselves report that the more they associate with delinquent peers, the more those peers negatively influence them. In a group setting there are greater discrepancies between what boys and their caregivers report is going on than in a family setting. The differences between these two program models are important only if they relate in a lawful way to case outcomes. In our study, how the boy was disciplined and the amount of contact he had with delinquent peers while in treatment predicted later criminal offending, as well as the seriousness of that offending. These findings imply that regardless of the program structure or model, to the extent that treatment programs can successfully provide youngsters with consistent consequences for daily rule breaking and misbehavior, and to the extent that they can help youngsters avoid contact with peers who are engaging in delinquency, they will be successful in preventing or lessening the probability of future criminality.

In TFC we have developed methods and strategies for providing participants with high levels of adult supervision and contact and consistent and fair discipline, we attempt to isolate them from contact with delinquent peers, and after they are stabilized and doing well at home and in school, we encourage contact with prosocial peers. These are the during-program features that appear to be the most important in predicting success. A key factor in follow-up for youth leaving such structured placements is the parent (or other adult caregiver) support that they receive (Hoagwood & Cunningham, 1992). Involvement of parents is a crucial aspect of the Oregon TFC model.

Overview of Stresses and Goals of Family Involvement

Having one's child removed from home by the juvenile authorities after months, or in the case of youngsters with severe antisocial behavior, years of problems most often leaves parents feeling demoralized, hopeless, and sometimes angry at "the system." Many parents have given up thinking that they are able to have any impact or influence on their child. Others fight to protect their child, feeling that the child's needs are not being met, or that they are being punished unfairly. In either case, parents of youth entering TFC through the juvenile justice system usually do not welcome the placement. They are suspicious, resistant to the idea that their child might do well in a family placement, and worried about how they will be treated.

The first task of the program staff is to offer assurances to parents that they will play an important role in the treatment of their child. Prior to the placement, the case manager meets with parent(s) to explain how the program works, and to hear from them what they think are important factors to consider in the development and implementation of their child's treatment plan. Before placement, the plan for reunification begins. What are the barriers that the parents see to having their adolescent return home and not be engaging in criminal activities? Once identified, these are the factors that will be worked on with the youth and the family during the TFC placement. In most instances, youth who are enrolled in TFC have long histories of criminal behavior and when they return home they will require intensified levels of adult supervision. This is often a difficult requirement for parents who work and have other obligations outside of the home that make supervision difficult. Many parents resist the idea of increasing supervision because of their child's age and the idea that the child "should" be able to function more autonomously. A process of negotiation between parents and program staff begins when the child enters the program and continues throughout the placement. To facilitate this, the parents are given their own therapist to advocate for them as well as to convey key elements that, from the program's point of view, their youngster will need in order to be successful when he or she returns home.

Home visits are scheduled regularly throughout the placement. These are not just a time for family get-togethers but opportunities for parents to implement new methods for dealing with their child that are intended to maximize the chances that reunification will be successful and sustainable. During home visits and throughout the placement time, parents are encouraged to telephone the case manager or the therapist if they have concerns or questions. Parents are given pager numbers for all program staff. Keeping open lines of communication is essential if parents and program staff are to work together successfully to change the often intractable problems the youth is having.

The Family Perspective: Comments from One Parent

Mary, whose 15-year-old son Kevin graduated from the program one year ago, commented on her experience.

> On the positive side, Sherrie and Jean [TFC parents] were great. Who the foster parents are makes a huge difference. The fact that they are so well supported was a major advantage. The support that the foster parents have should be the model for support for all parents in the community. They had access to respite that was not punishing. They were not blamed when they were confused about a kid. They had a problem-solving team at their disposal. They got paid so it makes it possible for them to focus on the job of parenting.

> JP [the case manager] was my main support and Aaron [the therapist] was there too. I could call JP. She, I felt, respected me, and my intelligence was never questioned. The connection was human. She might have not known the answer but was there to listen. We laughed a lot. Something about unlimited access was good. That made a huge difference.

> The support setup, the team with somebody for the kid, somebody for the parent, somebody to work the whole thing through, that's a nice model. The consistency of the program and how it built on itself was good. The way that it fit things together was consistent and predictable. For Kevin, the stability and structure and knowing what to expect was important. Living in an out-of-home placement where a man and a woman treated each other so well was wonderful for him, because I cannot give him that model. He was exposed to a relationship that was healthy. Jean [the foster father] was the first man that was not domineering or overpowering with Kevin. Every man up the ladder from the beginning of his difficulty was negative and domineering. They used macho to push kids around, and this modeled behavior that was not what I wanted him to do. [This is] critical for boys if we want to model positive behavior.

> The obvious intention [of the program] was a focus on well-being of kids, not that people don't have selfish interests, but their intention around helping was

clear. Another positive was the willingness to struggle with me. Not [to] force or intimidate me with doing something that did not feel comfortable. The biggest benefit was Kevin's experience of being successful.

On the negative side, respite should be extended to all parents. Knowing that my kid was safe, that there was nothing bad happening to him, at first [I was] not sure about that. Parents need to hear that [the] program is not a way to sever relationships between parents and kids. My parenting did change and at some level practicing using outside resources has allowed me to continue using outside resources. [But] the same shit that was hard before is hard now. I came in feeling like the whole world blames parents. I wanted acknowledgment of my woundedness, of my efforts and my strengths and my lack of resources and all that as a parent I had attempted to do.

Collaborating with Community Partners

Before initiating the TFC programs in Oregon, contacts were made with juvenile court directors, parole and probation officers, and the juvenile court judge. Some of these individuals found the idea that community families could provide effective treatment for tough juvenile offenders hard to accept. In fact, when we first initiated our program in 1983, parole and probation staff were quite dubious about the applicability and feasibility of the model. Now they are our most ardent supporters. The fact is, delinquent youngsters are markedly easier to deal with on an individual basis than they are in group settings, and many times juvenile corrections personnel have only had experience with individual youth in the context of groups.

When implementing a program model like TFC that involves interventions in a number of systems, interagency collaborations that work well and that are flexible enough to respond to the individual needs of youth and families are essential. In our program with juvenile justice–referred youth, key collaborators are parole and probation staff, judges, school personnel, and in some instances case workers from child protective services.

JUVENILE PAROLE/PROBATION STAFF

These team members facilitate placements, serve as backup when youth violate program rules, and provide a "law enforcement" presence. We had several initial meetings with parole/probation staff when we first set up the program in order to understand their priorities and concerns. During a youth's placement in our program, we have regular in-person and telephone contact with parole/probation, providing them with case updates. We also share PDR data with parole/probation staff.

Backup services provided by parole/probation range from routine monthly check-ins with the youth (to monitor progress, reinforce the program rules, and remind the youth of the court presence) to a more active partnership where the parole/probation officer assists in problem situations. For example, it is helpful to have the option to use juvenile detention as a backup if the youth becomes highly noncompliant or aggressive or commits a law violation. Depending on the nature of the infraction, the parole/probation officer can admit the youth to detention for a brief stay. We find that the occasional use of a short detention stays (1 to 2 days) can be helpful for some youth.

JUVENILE COURT JUDGES

In our area, juvenile court judges rotate each year, so we need to acquaint each judge with the goals of the program and with our operating procedures. We have a one-page description of the program that we send prior to meeting with the judge.

SCHOOLS

It is important to have good working relations with the schools. Once school personnel know that program staff can be relied on to provide backup, they are usually more than willing to be cooperative with the program. We use a daily school card that each youth carries to each class and that teachers can fill out quickly and easily. On the card, the youth's behavior in class and homework completion are rated. Future assignments are also noted. We have frequent telephone contact with key teachers to monitor a youth's progress, or if we suspect that school cards are forged.

School personnel are urged to call program staff at the time that they are having a problem with the youth. In critical situations, TFC staff (case manager, therapist, or school liaison) are available to pick up the youth from school. If a youth is suspended or expelled, he or she spends school hours in the TFC offices completing homework assignments or work chores. We have found in these instances that removing the youth from the TFC home during the day is more effective in that the youth is less likely to escalate and become more negative if his or her consequences are supervised at the office rather than at the TFC home.

CHILD PROTECTIVE SERVICES CASEWORKERS

In cases where there has been reported parental abuse or neglect, the child has a CPS worker assigned. Coordination of the family treatment with the goals of CPS is critical.

Program Development

STAFFING PATTERNS AND KEY DUTIES OF STAFF

Program Director

The program director oversees all clinical and management aspects of the program, obtains funding, designs and monitors evaluation activities, and serves as a backup for case managers. The director conducts the weekly clinical meetings, reviews the weekly PDR data, and sets the direction for development of and changes in program policies and practices.

Case Managers

Case managers are familiar with adolescent development and developmental psychopathology and are trained in social learning principles. Levels of formal education vary from bachelors' degree with extensive experience to Ph.D. in psychology or related fields. The case managers' tasks are complex in that they balance the agendas of all of the team members to provide youth with integrated treatment plans. Key characteristics of successful case managers are that they be excellent problem-solvers who are practically oriented and think flexibly. They also have to possess outstanding interpersonal skills. They are the key contact with the TFC parents, provide supervision and direction for the therapists, and are the liaison with individuals in the community (e.g., the juvenile court judge, parole/probation officers, teachers) who have contact with or influence on the child. Case managers have a maximum caseload of 10 and are supervised weekly by the program director.

TFC Parents

These parents are the key front-line implementors of the program. They are selected for their experience and willingness to deal with adolescents with difficult problems, their willingness to work as part of a treatment team, and their nurturing family environment. After participating in a 20-hour preservice training orientation and being certified as foster parents by the state agency, they are supervised by the case managers during daily telephone contacts and in weekly group meetings. Successful TFC parents come from all walks of life. They are flexible, like teenagers, and have good judgment and a sense of humor.

Therapists

Therapists are typically masters' level individuals who have been trained in family and individual therapy with adolescents or in related fields. Therapists are supervised by the case manages and in weekly clinical meetings by the project director.

Foster Parent Recruiter

This person is responsible for advertising, recruitment, and conducting the initial screening and home visit. It is helpful to have a person with some experience in advertising who has good interpersonal skills. The recruiter is the first program person that potential foster parents have contact with, so this person needs to have a complete understanding of the goals and methods of operation of the program, and a good familiarity with the types of youth being served by the program.

PDR Caller

This person contacts the TFC parents on weekdays by telephone and collects information about the youth's behavior during the past 24 hours. It is important that this person is someone in whom TFC parents feel that they can confide. We employ former TFC parents as PDR callers.

TFC Parent Trainer

This individual organizes and conducts the preservice training for potential TFC parents. He or she also assists the case manager in providing continued consultation and support to TFC parents during placements. The TFC trainer needs to have an excellent grasp of how to implement the point and level system, and be familiar with issues related to providing foster care services. We employ a former TFC parent in this role.

TRAINING MANUALS, BOOKS, AND VIDEOS

Preservice Training

All program staff are given a 3-day orientation to the approach, which includes a combination of didactic instruction, role-plays, and case examples. New staff are expected to read available treatment manuals, descriptions, and research publications. In addition, all clinical staff (case managers, therapists) attend the next scheduled TFC parent training session. The TFC parent training involves a manualized program with involvement from current TFC parents. Role-plays and home practice exercises are used as well as more traditional didactic-style instruction.

The TFC program is described in two books: *Family Connections* (Chamberlain, 1994; available from Northwest Media at 541-343-6636 or through Amazon.com) and *Blueprint for Multidimensional Treatment Foster Care* (Chamberlain & Mihalic, 1998; available from the Center for the Study and Prevention of Violence at 303-492-8465). The Oregon TFC model has also been described in a number of journal articles and book chapters that are available on the OSLC website (http:\\www.oslc.org).

MONITORING FIDELITY OF THE INTERVENTION

The consistent and effective daily performance of the TFC parents is seen as a crucial component of the Oregon model. Therefore we use two main mechanisms to monitor and support the TFC parent's implementation of the program. First, they are telephoned each weekday and asked to report on the youth's performance on the point and level system during the past day. This also serves as a check on their implementation of the system. In addition, during that call they are asked how many minutes the youth spent unsupervised (low supervision predicted future arrests after leaving TFC; Eddy & Chamberlain, 1999), and if anything particularly positive or negative happened during the past day. We ask about positive and negative events to gauge if the TFC parent is frustrated or upset by the youth's behavior. Foster parent frustration and feelings of hopelessness are thought to lead to placement disruptions, and a positive relationship with the TFC parent was shown to predict fewer arrests in follow-up (Eddy & Chamberlain, 1999). The second mechanism involves collection of the daily point charts and school cards during the weekly supervision and support meetings conducted with the TFC parents. These are checked against the data collected during the PDR calls and discrepancies are discussed with the TFC parents.

In the Oregon TFC programs, case managers complete weekly adherence ratings where they rate the level of the therapist's adherence to key program activities (e.g., use of contingencies, reinforcement of new or existing prosocial skills, focus on behavior management, focus on increasing supervision and clear limit-setting, and alternatives to delinquent peer association). Family and individual therapists are asked to show videotapes of treatment sessions in weekly supervision meetings.

Program Standards on Treatment Foster Care were published by the National Foster Family–Based Treatment Association in 1995. The purpose of the standards is to "provide an operational definition and guide to quality Treatment Foster Care programming" (FFTA, 1995). The standards are divided into three sections: program, treatment families, and children, youth, and their families. In each section there is a series of practices that are defined by specific activities. A self-rating is available for programs.

As part of a study designed to examine the effectiveness of existing community-based TFC programs in North Carolina, Farmer and colleagues (2001) have constructed an interview that they have given to 42 TFC program providers to determine how well their practices related to the FFTA Program Standards for Treatment Foster Care. The interviews were designed to provide information about agency-level practices and fidelity. They coded each of the 55 FFTA domains as not meeting, partially meeting, or fully meeting the standards. A total score for each agency summed codings for these 55 domains. The potential range of conformity scores was from 0–110 and the observed range for the agencies was 45–85, indicating moderate to good conformity and substantial variation in this overall assessment of conformity. They found no significant differences between conformity to standards among public, private for-profit, or private nonprofit programs.

On some dimensions, they found little variation among TFC programs, while on others there was a great deal of variation. For example, most programs (79%) had a well-developed program statement, developed initial treatment plans within 30 days of placement (90%), and encouraged meetings between a youth and perspective treatment parents prior to placement (93%). Fewer programs had the ratio of supervisors to caseworkers recommended in the standards (67%), less that half of the TFC programs provided weekly support to treatment parents, and only 21% provided at least 24 hours of annual in-service training. These results suggest that real-world TFC programs might pay less attention to supporting and training foster parents than the research-oriented Oregon programs. Farmer's focus on the relationship between conformity to standards and outcomes is essential to an analysis of the effectiveness of TFC in community settings.

COSTS AND RESOURCES REQUIRED

There has been recognition in a number of publications that the cost of TFC is lower than costs for traditional residential treatments that serve comparable populations of youngsters (e.g., Burns & Friedman, 1990; Burns, Hoagwood, & Mrazek, 1999; Kutash & Rivera, 1996). Information on the relative cost/benefit of the TFC model has been available only recently. In a study by the Washington State Institute for Public Policy (Aos, Phipps, Barnoski, & Leib, 1999), the economics of a set of 33 programs designed to reduce crime were evaluated from two perspectives. The first question addressed was from the perspective of the taxpayer. For each taxpayer dollar spent on the program, what monies will be saved in the future? The second question addressed the future costs to crime victims. The Washington study evaluated a range of programs, from those that focused on early childhood to those that focused on adult offenders. Adding together taxpayer benefits and criminal justice (victim) costs saved, the Oregon TFC model was estimated to save $43,661 per participant and to have a benefit-to-dollar cost of $22.58. This was the second highest rated program model reported on of the 33 examined in terms of benefit-to-dollar cost (Aggression Replacement Training was first at $31.40).

The per-youth cost of TFC varies depending on the specific components included in the model (e.g., whether family treatment is provided), geographical location, and specific population being targeted. In general, TFC costs from one third to one half less that congregate group care models.

Overview of the Research on the TFC Model

Over the past two decades in the United States and Canada, a series of studies with varying degrees of experimental rigor have been conducted on the characteristics and efficacy of the TFC service model (reviewed in Meadowcroft, Thomlison, & Chamberlain, 1994). These include descriptive studies with single samples, surveys of TFC programs, comparison studies using quasi-experimental designs, and controlled clinical trials. To summarize, the results from these studies suggest that:

- TFC programs serve children and adolescents who have problems similar to those being served in more restricted forms of residential care. Although the literature on outcomes for youth in TFC is by no means extensive, it is more developed than for any other type of residential care.
- The majority of TFC placements are completed as planned, suggesting that TFC is a viable placement alternative for children and adolescents with severe emotional/behavioral problems.

- While in the TFC placements, most youth improve on behavioral indicators of adjustment, and in several studies, youth in TFC have shown better adjustment at follow-up in terms of post-discharge stability of living situation and restrictiveness of placement setting than youth served in congregate care settings (e.g., Chamberlain & Reid, 1998; Chamberlain & Reid, 1991; Clarke, Hawkins, Murphy, & Sheeber, 1993; Fanshel, Finch, & Grundy, 1990).
- From 60–89% of the children/adolescents are discharged to less restrictive living settings following placement in TFC (Hudson, Nutter, & Galaway, 1990).

In a study on the Oregon TFC model described in this chapter, the effectiveness of TFC was compared to group/residential care for serious adolescent offenders. Adolescents who participated in TFC were involved in significantly (over 50%) less criminal activity at one- and two-year follow-ups according to both official record data and self-reports of criminal activities. In that same study, significantly more TFC youth completed their programs than did youth in group/residential care, and the TFC youth spent 60% fewer days incarcerated in follow-up. Also, more TFC youth returned to live with their families rather than staying in out-of-home care. At two-year follow-up, TFC youth continued to participate in less criminal activity, held more legal jobs, had used hard drugs and marijuana less frequently than GC boys during the past year, and reported that they had more positive relationships with their parents than did GC boys. Boys in TFC also reported that they had refrained from unprotected sex more often than boys in GC.

In another randomized trial testing elements of the TFC model, Chamberlain and colleagues (1994) found that providing weekly support and daily telephone calls to foster parents increased foster parent retention rates and decreased child problem behaviors and placement disruptions. Foster parents in the enhanced services condition were also less likely to drop out of providing care than control families. Clarke and colleagues (1998) conducted a similar study with foster families and children in the child welfare system. They found that adding a family specialist to work with foster parents and youth produced positive results; youth were less likely to run away, spent less time incarcerated, and had greater improvements in behavioral and emotional problems than youth in control group foster families who did not receive such services.

RESEARCH LIMITATIONS AND FUTURE DIRECTIONS

Results from preliminary studies on the efficacy of TFC are promising but there are clear limitations to the evidence that is available. Therefore, the conclusions that can be made about the general effectiveness of the TFC model are limited. For example, it is not known what are the necessary and sufficient components of the TFC model that lead to successful outcomes for the various populations of youngsters being served using this model. How do the positive results demonstrated for the small number of TFC programs that have been studied apply to the large number of other sites and populations of children and adolescents? Program characteristics and practices such as methods for selection and training of TFC parents, availability of staff backup and support, and level of staff expertise could all be reasonably expected to affect outcomes. What neighborhood/community conditions relate to program success/failure? Issues of length of service and intensity also need attention. More well-controlled studies are needed on the critical components of TFC that examine a variety of populations of children and adolescents and post-discharge outcomes, as are large-scale effectiveness trials.

7

Mentoring to Facilitate Resiliency in High-Risk Youth

J. ERIC VANCE

Resilient children and youth appear to be skillful in selecting and identifying with resilient models and sources of support. . . . They did not seek any professional help, but preferred instead a network of informal relationships that included peer friends, older friends, ministers, and some trusted teachers. *(Werner and Smith, 1989)*

Community mentoring is a rapidly expanding movement that seeks to affiliate high-risk youth with healthy adult role models from outside their immediate families. Mentoring has recently gained great popularity as a public service calling for volunteers, as well as a government-sponsored social program. Renowned entertainers and sports figures solicit volunteers on television, even as the federal government dispenses millions of dollars to support mentoring programs within the public school system to improve reading skills among at-risk students. This chapter explores the concept of mentoring, discusses the rationale for this type of intervention, and presents a detailed description of a model of community mentoring designed to enhance psychosocial resiliency in high-risk youth. Finally, the research evidence for the effectiveness of mentoring as a strategy for intervening in the lives of youth with severe emotional disorders is examined.

The concept of "mentor" goes back to Greek mythology, when Odysseus went to war, leaving his son Telemachus to be raised at the hand of his guardian, named Mentor. The word "mentor" means advisor, wise and trusted counselor, or teacher. Many social and intellectual movements were, and still are, propagated by the mentoring process of a teacher or leader providing direction to his or her followers. Apprenticeships in the guilds of the Middle Ages can be viewed as mentoring of the apprentice by the master. In certain Native American cultures, elders of the tribe traditionally served as mentors to the young men as they made their initiation into the rites of manhood. All of these relationships involve the transmission of wisdom and maturity from the mentor to the learner. Successful individuals in many walks of life—including entertainers, professional athletes, academics, and business professionals—can point to troubled childhoods or poverty from which they rose with the help and moral support of a special teacher or coach.

Beyond the historical traditions of mentoring, there are several observations that lead to the idea of community mentoring for youth with severe emotional disorders (SED). First, it has been noted that important adult mentors are nearly always mentioned in life stories of children who were at high risk for SED, but who somehow avoided developing SED (Werner & Smith, 1992). These so-called "resilient" youth are children who have been exposed to many of the known risk factors for SED (see Table 7.1), yet seem to escape significant disability and have relatively stable lives. Detailed longitudinal studies of resilient youth have consistently noted that these particular children possess a variety of protective factors (see Table 7.2) that seem to confer resilience in the face of risk (Rutter, Cox, Tupling, Berger, & Yule, 1975; Rutter, 1978; Rutter, 1979; Rutter, 1985a; Werner & Smith, 1982; Werner, 1989; Werner & Smith, 1992; Sameroff & Seifer, 1983; Garmezy, Masten, & Tellegen, 1984; Masten, 1986; Kaplan, 1996) Very often, an adult mentor outside the immediate family serves as one of the powerful protective factors in the lives of these high-risk youth (Zimrin, 1986; Werner & Smith, 1992). Most often such mentors are teachers, ministers, coaches, neighbors, or extended family members, who develop a special and supportive relationship with the child over an extended period of time. Their advice is welcome, they provide a shoulder to cry on, and the relationship seems to serve as a safe harbor in the otherwise stormy lives of these children.

The second observation that supports the potential utility of community mentoring for youth with SED is the success of various volunteer mentoring programs for high-risk youth. The largest and most established of these is the nationwide Big Brothers Big Sisters of America (BBBSA) program, which matches adult volunteers with youth who have been referred by someone in the community because of a perceived need for a supportive adult or mentor figure. Most of the referred children have been identified as at-risk or have developed minor problems leading up to the referral. As such, they may not be so "naturally" resilient as the youth described above in various longitudinal studies. Nonetheless, a fairly rigorous study of the effectiveness of BBBSA showed a positive impact of the program (Tierney, Grossman, & Resch, 1995). This study, which is described in detail later in this chapter, suggests that mentors may be inserted into the life of a high-risk child and enhance long-term outcomes.

Finally, support for community mentoring of youth with SED comes from anecdotal reports of approaches to community-based services for highly disturbed youth. The Willie M program in North Carolina for youth with serious aggression and emotional disorders is one such program, frequently using trained, professional mentors as an important component of treatment and habilitation. Clinicians and case managers from the Willie M program have observed that clients with mentors seem to benefit from the added social support, improve their social skills, and participate more in community activities. Par-

Table 7.1 Psychosocial Risk Factors

Early Developmental Risk Factors	Family Stress Factors	Parental Factors	Parent-Child Relationship	Trauma and Neglect	Childhood Disorders	Social Drift
Complications of pregnancy, birth, or prematurity	Poverty	Substance abuse	Insecure/poor mother-infant attachment	Witness to violence and conflict	Chronic medical problems	School failure or dropout
Fetal substance exposure	Divorce, separation, single-parent home	Emotional or mental disorder	Long absences of main caregiver in infancy	Physical abuse, harsh punishment	Neurodevelopmental delays and disorders	Delinquent peer group
"Difficult" temperament	Four or more siblings	Criminality	Mostly conflicted parent-child relationship	Sexual abuse	Mental retardation, IQ < 70	Teen pregnancy
Shy/anxious temperament	Frequent family moves			Substantiated child neglect	Behavioral or emotional disorder	
Siblings born within 2 years				Removal from home by public agency	Drug or alcohol use	
					Delinquency	
					Pattern of aggressive behavior	

Table 7.2 Psychosocial Protective Factors

Temperamental Characteristics of the Child	Social Skills of the Child	Child Competencies	Protective Perceptions	Aspects of the Home Environment	Parent-Child Relationship	Social Support Network
Easy temperament type	Seen as likeable	Above average intelligence	Child perceived competency	Firstborn child	Secure mother-infant attachment	Adult mentor outside of the home
Independent, outgoing toddler	Gets along with peers	Good problem-solving abilities	Internal locus of control	Parent with high school education or better	Child perception that parent cares	Peer support
	Gets along with adults	Good reading abilities	Realistic hopes and expectations for the future	Parent consistently employed	Warm and positive relationship with a parent	Church group
	Has a good sense of humor	Good school student	Independent-mindedness	Alternate caretakers available to the family		Inner spiritual faith
	Demonstrates empathy and nurturance	Extracurricular/ vocational involvement		Regular church involvement		
				Rules, routines, curfews, and rituals		
				Discipline with discussion and fair punishment		

ents of the mentored youth have sometimes judged the mentoring to have been the most valuable component in serving their child's many needs. The Willie M program has embraced a model of intervention based on attempting to build protective factors into the lives of youth with SED. As such, mentors are viewed both as a protective factor and a vector to promote other protective factors. Support for this approach is provided by longitudinal outcome studies of Willie M youth indicating that relatively high levels of initial protective factors predict improved behavioral functioning a year later (Bowen, 1999).

During the course of healthy social development in functional families, a child is likely to be immersed in a loving and supportive relationship with a parent or parents, who attend to the child's needs and serve as role models. Unfortunately, the lives of high-risk or children with emotional or behavioral disorders often include parents who are stressed, suffer from mental illness, have substance abuse problems, or are absent. It is these children, from stressed families, who might be lucky enough to enter into a mentored relationship and thereby gain some buffering from the turmoil in their other relationships. Even children from highly functioning and nurturing families often reach a point in adolescence when they turn away from their parents and seek advice and support from adults and peers outside the family. This natural process of finding mentors outside the family can be crucial or even life-saving for high-risk youth.

It is on the strength of success stories in which they appear in the lives of resilient youth, and through some research, that mentors have emerged as a potentially useful psychosocial intervention for children with SED. From the perspective of service provision, mentoring programs are also relatively inexpensive when compared to traditional mental health interventions. It has also been suggested that clients and their families are more often willing to engage with mentor services than with traditional clinic-based therapies. Mentoring is done in the community with a provider who looks more like an adult friend than a professional, but who can be trained, clinically supervised, and offer therapeutic benefits. As such, professional mentoring has a high degree of "ecological validity," in the sense that it is an intervention that can take place in the natural environment of the child and family. Even in cases where a child's family is extremely resistant, or absent, an intensive mentor relationship can still be used to enhance a child's level of functioning.

Theory

It is easy to intuitively understand how mentoring would benefit a high-risk youth, who might have a disorder that alienates him in relationships, or who comes from a stressful home environment where overwhelmed or disabled adults have little positive energy to spend on him. Beyond the intuitive understanding, however, it is not precisely known how mentoring affects positive change. This section will discuss potential explanatory frameworks from various schools of psychotherapy, as well as mentoring as a form of social support, and some of the beneficial neurobiological effects of close relationships.

PSYCHOTHERAPY AND THE RELATIONSHIP

Psychotherapy has long been used as a treatment for emotional and be-havioral disorders, and involves the development of a talking relationship between a patient and a therapist. It might be assumed that the therapist then becomes a mentor of sorts. However, the tradition of psychoanalysis influenced many generations of therapists to assume an interpersonal position of profes-sional objectivity and relative passivity, and to provide little advice or self-disclosure. This type of relationship bears little resemblance to the nurturing guidance that emerges from a mentoring relationship. In breaking from this tradition, therapists began to advocate for a more active and nurturing role, to engage in teaching, problem-solving, and even loving the patient (Fromm, 1956; Glasser, 1965). These more interpersonal and supportive forms of psychother-apy rely on the strength of the relationship and may derive their benefits from the formation of what amounts in essence to a mentoring relationship. This school of thought eventually led to the assertion that a sort of "mentor-psychotherapist" approach might be the most effective mode of treatment for adolescents with emotional disturbance or at extremely high risk (Bratter, Cameron, & Radda, 1987). Certainly anyone who has provided psychotherapy to troubled adolescents knows that success rides on forming a positive rela-tionship, which begs the question of whether it is the "relationship" or the "therapy" that works.

MENTORING AS SOCIAL SUPPORT

Beyond mentoring as a "therapy," it can also be seen as a source of social support. Seen within a context of resiliency theory, warm and positive rela-tionships that increase social support networks serve as protective factors and in turn promote resiliency. It should be noted how many of the different psy-chosocial protective factors (see Table 7.2) can be enhanced from within a men-tor relationship. For example, mentors are often acquired in relation to some competency building activity, such as special teachers promoting academic achievement, or coaches in athletic activities. These mentors not only serve as an important relationship, but also link the youth to extracurricular involve-ment and encourage the development of tangible skills which enhance the per-ceived competency of the child. Some mentors of high-risk youth discover a special talent in the youth that can be nurtured into a source of self-confidence, which may allow the youth to rise above adversity. Even youth with problems of aggression and SED who might not be particularly gifted in academic tasks have demonstrated educational progress that is related to the presence of a spe-cial mentor at school (Vance, Fernandez, & Biber, 1998).

In addition to competencies, other protective factors such as social skills are enhanced in the context of a mentor relationship. The process of establish-ing a strong relationship, especially with a youth who has SED, always involves passing on lessons about how to get along with others, how to be sensitive to the feelings of others (empathy), and how to resolve interpersonal conflicts. Most of us learn these lessons (protective factors) in the context of caring relationships with family or friends. Likewise, youth with SED might learn these most easily in the context of a warm and forgiving relationship with a mentor. Many mentors have observed that even the most disruptive youth seem to practice their very best social skills when around their mentor, in deference to this valued relationship. It has also been found that social skills acquired in the mentor relationship generalize to other relationships, unlike the social skills acquired in context-bound, formal social skills groups (Chamberlain, 1990a; Tierney, Grossman, & Resch, 1995). Finally, for youth with troubled relationships, it is possible that being "liked" for the first time in a mentor relationship might enable them to feel, and be, more "likeable."

NEUROBIOLOGY OF RELATIONSHIPS

Thus it seems that the potential benefits of a mentor relationship might operate by enhancing any or all of several important psychosocial protective factors. That still leaves the question of how the mentor relationship might be acting on the neurobiology of high-risk or youth with SED to enhance psychosocial functioning. Some clues have emerged from recent neurophysiological and endocrine findings.

For example, social contact and social support have been shown to diminish secretion of cortisol, the body's chief stress hormone (Hofer, 1984; Gunnar, 1992). Positive social interactions also serve as powerful releasers of the brain neuropeptide called oxytocin (OT), which has been shown to play a major role in maternal or nurturing behaviors, the formation of social bonds, and countering the effects of stress on the nervous system (Carter, 1998; Insel, 1997). A variety of social sensory stimuli that commonly occur in the context of close relationships—such as light touch, massage, and even sharing a meal—are thought to release OT in the central nervous system (Uvnas-Moberg, 1997). In turn, OT release in the brain and periphery has profound psychophysiological effects, including decreasing the tone of the body's autonomic "fight or flight" system and promoting the relaxation response and behavioral calm.

Oxytocin is also known to enhance the activity of the autonomic parasympathetic nervous system (PNS), as reflected in measured levels of "vagal tone." Recent theories of the autonomic nervous system have described how the PNS not only serves as a sort of antistress system, but also ties into the neurological machinery responsible for reading and expressing emotional facial responses (Porges, 1997). This may someday explain how behavioral features of a warm social relationship work through the nervous system to relieve stress and enhance socioemotional regulation.

It is no surprise, therefore, to note that massage has been shown to reduce anxiety and lower cortisol levels in humans, and that the quality of touch during childhood correlates with adolescent mental health (Field et al., 1992; Gonzalez et al., 1994; Pearce, Martin, & Wood, 1995). The action of OT in certain parts of the brain that are responsible for long-term emotional memory storage may explain why OT-mediated social bonds (i.e., mother-infant attachments, monogamous bonds) are highly specific relationships to particular individuals over a long course time. Among high-risk youth who have bonded to mentors, it has been noted that they benefit most from stable relationships with particular caring individuals, which endure over time (Zimrin, 1986). Through this sort of relationship, high-risk youth not only gain psychosocial protective factors, but also likely neurophysiological buffering.

Target Population

This chapter presents the application of community mentoring to youth with severe emotional disorders. However, it has been shown that mentors have also been used successfully with high-risk youth, who by virtue of possessing a number of psychosocial risk factors are known to be at increased risk for the development of emotional disorders. This raises the distinction between using community mentors for purposes of treatment versus prevention of emotional disorders. This distinction may be moot, since recent studies have pointed out that impairment in psychosocial functioning may be a better indicator of psychiatric needs than presence of a defined psychiatric disorder (Angold, Costello, Farmer, Burns, & Erkanli, 1999). An understanding of the implications of resiliency theory would suggest that providing mentors for either population should result in the benefits of improved psychosocial functioning as well as the acquisition of protective factors.

The majority of children and youth who are referred to mental health services are subsequently diagnosed with emotional or behavioral disorders, including oppositional defiant disorder, conduct disorder, attention-deficit/hyperactivity disorder, or anxiety disorders. The remainder are diagnosed with internalizing disorders, including posttraumatic stress disorder, depression, and, more rarely, bipolar disorder, psychotic illnesses, or severe developmental disorders. Any child with severe emotional disorder may benefit from a mentor. In fact, some of those with the most difficulty in forming healthy relationships may benefit most from having a determined mentor.

In a world with limited financial and human resources, it is important to determine which youth with SED might benefit most from the services of a professional mentor. Some youth with SED are particularly difficult to engage in traditional mental health services. For example, many youth with conduct disorder or a history of psychosocial trauma are mistrustful in relationships, and especially with doctors, therapists, and other obvious members of "the system." They are notoriously resistant in psychotherapy, and often fail to stay involved in outpatient programs. In contrast, these youth are often more open to spending time with a mentor and ironically may frequently begin sharing intimate details of their lives with the mentor, details that might have been long hidden from other professionals.

Another way to think about targeting mentors is to identify youth whose families are resistant to treatment. It is clear from the research on effective interventions that certain treatments targeting families are very helpful, even with severely impaired youth (Henggeler & Borduin, 1995; Patterson, Dishion, & Chamberlain, 1993). However, even with the best efforts, some families remain resistant, disabled, or even absent from the child's life. In these cases, using mentors may be particularly helpful in building social competencies and social support outside the family system. Werner and Smith (1992) have suggested that resilient youth often use the warmth and support of mentor relationships outside the family to offset the turmoil within the family. Finally, it has been observed that older youth seem to benefit less from family-targeted interventions, and developmentally may be more ready to bond with adult role models outside the family system (Patterson, Dishion, & Chamberlain, 1993).

Active Intervention Elements

LESSONS OF THE RELATIONSHIP

From the first meeting of a mentor with a youth, a bond must be forged with warmth and active engagement. This may mean long talks, drives, outings, or eating together as the groundwork for the alliance is laid. The mentor must be prepared to take advantage of the inevitable "lessons of the relationship." Some youth with SED will disappoint, disrespect, or vehemently test the developing affiliation. These incidents must be processed with interpersonal problem-solving skills to move the relationship forward. Sharing personal feelings with the child in the context of conflict resolution helps to build empathy, and mutual commitment to preventing future interpersonal problems teaches the child how to get along with others. The art of apology is taught, and the use of humor is encouraged. It has been our experience that these social skills, which serve as protective factors, are best learned and generalized from the context of such a real and meaningful association.

Professional mentors are also trained and encouraged to be involved in helping the youth to work through any of the many conflicts that arise in the community, school, and family, if permitted. This is *not* to say that the mentor should be called to settle each crisis, since such a role can drag a mentor into conflicts and severely interfere with the developing relationship. However, as an adult who is at least somewhat trusted by the child, the mentor should be involved in the aftermath of crises to assist the child in the process of problem-solving, perspective-taking, and making amends. This role assists the child in building social skills in meaningful contexts, and helps to maintain or strengthen his or her ties to important social support systems.

Monitoring of an evolving mentor relationship involves assessing the quality of interpersonal interaction. Signs of a successful bond include a child's stated desire to spend time with the mentor, the two-way sharing of personal information, the successful passage through interpersonal conflicts, and modeling or mirroring of the mentor's personality by the child. In the context of a trusting relationship, many topics of relevance to building resilience are fair game, including discussions of hopes for the future, the evolution of personal beliefs, and perceptions of family relationships. These are all very important areas where the well-trained and clinically supervised mentor can guide a high-risk youth in a positive direction.

Mentors and their partners are encouraged to develop a scrapbook together that includes photographs, souvenirs, and short narratives written by the child, to document the shared experiences. This serves several important functions.

First, it is kept by the child as tangible evidence of the ongoing relationship—reassuring for children with SED, who often have shaky confidence in the strength of their interpersonal relationships. Also, the personal narratives may serve as an opportunity to compose and write about meaningful events outside the classroom setting. Finally, the scrapbook can serve as a lasting memento of a relationship that was an important part of a child's life.

Most formal programs that serve SED or high-risk youth are time-limited and naturally must move client cases through the system. However, the type of professional mentoring program described here is designed not to "terminate" with the client, but rather to transition the relationship towards what resembles a lifelong friendship, as one might have with a distant relative or high school friend. This leaves open the expectation of a lifelong relationship between the mentor and client, which will of course decrease in intensity over time. As most of us call on our social supports in times of crisis, the formerly mentored youth can be expected to call on a mentor intermittently through time. The conventional process of termination does not seem well suited to the population of children with SED, who might easily be left with the question of whether an abruptly terminated mentor relationship was "real," or simply another impersonal product of "the system."

ACTIVITIES OF THE RELATIONSHIP

Beyond the relationship, mentoring is based on sharing activities with the child. This immediately gives the child a sense of choice and control over his or her chosen activities, encouraging an internal locus of control. Together, the child and mentor then pursue the chosen activities over time, and several crucial elements of building self-esteem are fostered. First, by repeatedly practicing an activity (such as a sport), some skill and competency is acquired, giving the child a sense of mastery. As the child receives praise from the mentor and other meaningful people related to his or her emerging skills, pride emerges. Finally, if the activity takes place in a social context, other healthy children and adults might become available for the youth to develop friendships with and practice social skills. Taken together, this process persuades the youth that positive growth is possible, and may connect him or her to organizations in the community for further social support.

A number of known protective factors are built through this process. First, the mentor is involved with the child in identifying interests and competencies, and encouraging the child to choose an activity where skills can be built. The process of choosing and pursuing activities together fosters a number of other protective factors. Mentors are encouraged to sit down with the child and actively plan activities, building the skills of planning and realistic goal-setting. By pursuing not only a single skill-building activity, but also outings that expose the child to a wide range of experiences, the mentor expands the worldview of children who often come from disadvantaged backgrounds. Exposures to experiences such as museums, fancy restaurants, backwoods hiking, or college campuses may be highly novel situations for the child. Novelty is known to provoke anxiety in some youth with SED, but also enhances learning and promotes bonding to the person sharing the experience. Children with trusted mentors may be more likely to follow through on anxiety-provoking but necessary tasks and activities as they prepare for the transition to adulthood. For the older child, outings with the mentor might focus on job-hunting; identifying adult educational resources, visiting rental properties, banks, and utility companies, and preparing for the autonomy of adulthood. From the range of activities and skill-building shared with the mentor, the child with SED can form some realistic hopes and expectations for the future.

One of the primary goals of the professional mentor relationship is to identify and link the client with other mentors in the "natural" social environment. This process is invariably made easier for the youth by the experience of being in a relationship with a professional mentor. The mentored youth develops social skills in the relationship that lower the threshold for engaging in healthy relationships with others. As mentors taper down the intensity of involvement with a given child, they actively promote other bonds and social connections with people in the child's family and community. Even as the professional mentor helps the child to bond to natural sources of support, the original relationship should continue. True mentors understand that their impact on the life of a child never ends entirely, though the frequency of contact naturally diminishes over time as the child improves and the mentor takes on new cases. In fact, it has been observed that the most meaningful mentor relationships are marked not by their intensity, but by the duration of the relationship (Zimrin, 1986).

A final and crucial role of the mentor is to facilitate the connection of the child to services in the mental health system. Most children with SED have clinical needs that will require at least the intermittent services of psychotherapists or psychiatric evaluation. It is frequently the case that high-risk youth are resistant to this treatment, or have difficulty making it to appointments. Missed appointments are a great waste of clinical resources and may slow down the progress of therapy. In these cases, the mentor can provide outreach, persuasion, and facilitation for the child's involvement. In some cases, the mentor can be included in therapy sessions and provide valuable information to the clinician, based on experience with the youth.

Recruitment, Training, and Supervision of Mentors

Certain basic components are required in order to develop an effective community mentoring program for youth with severe emotional disorders. Regular administrative and clinical supervision and oversight of a pool of carefully recruited, trained, and committed mentors is the essential foundation. Financing and billing for such services within a system of care often requires creativity and advocacy for the effectiveness of the intervention.

RECRUITMENT

Careful recruitment of prospective mentors is crucial to serving youth with severe behavioral and emotional disorders. Experience in working with tough children requires a thick skin, but a soft heart is equally as necessary to be an effective mentor. Within a pool of providers for children with SED, it is often well known which particular adults consistently and easily form working relationships with the most difficult clients. From this standpoint, it is preferable to handpick mentors from people known to the system. In general, mentor qualifications have little correlation with the type of education possessed, and more to do with being able to relate to, tolerate, and accept children.

In recruiting for professional mentors in the Willie M program, it was noted that "high-risk children grown up" can make some of the best mentors. This is similar to the tradition of assigning recovering alcoholic "sponsors" as mentors and supports for newly sober alcoholics with the Alcoholics Anonymous program. Sometimes, these are adults who may have been through hard times themselves but possess the protective factors that made them resilient. On the other hand, some individuals whose lives have not been filled with trauma have a special gift for forming relationships with even the toughest youth. In any case, good mentors have good social skills, networks of friendships and social support in the community, and are involved in hobbies and activities outside of work. These are features that can be shared with and modeled for the child. Recruitment for professional mentors should target local mental health or juvenile justice organizations and special education providers, who are not likely to shy away from challenging children. Many recruits from such institutions are grateful for the opportunity to work in a more personal relationship with SED youth in a community setting, to satisfy some of the motivations that originally brought them to work with SED youth.

TRAINING

Training a group of qualified mentor recruits can be like preaching to the choir. These may be people who are already competent at developing relationships with SED children. Nonetheless, certain techniques for initial meetings with the child, role definition, and activities for early trust-building are reviewed. Training of mentors in a resiliency-building framework also requires reviewing key elements of resiliency theory, such as the impact of a child's risk factors, and which protective factors the mentor intervention can expect to target. A general review of types of psychopathology and the specific problems they pose is also helpful. The majority of training focuses on aspects of the interpersonal relationship with mentors, and the shared activities of the relationship that are most likely to establish enduring psychosocial protective factors for the child.

SUPERVISION

Beyond recruitment and training of professional mentors, it is essential to provide ongoing, weekly clinical and administrative supervision. As with other intervention activities, careful documentation of work on specific treatment goals must be completed to support billing and financial necessities. Caseloads must be adjusted and maintained relative to the intensity of clinical and organizational needs. Obstacles within the treatment system or community to the effective implementation of the mentor program must be identified and addressed. Supervisors need to allow flexibility in work schedules and be able to think creatively about how to minimize turnover and maximize longevity in mentor relationships.

High-quality clinical supervision is essential to foster a good understanding of the particular aspects of psychopathology posed by the various children on a mentor's caseload. Work with children with SED is emotionally difficult, and it has repeatedly been shown that regular support and supervision serves to revitalize workers and decrease staff turnover. This is especially crucial in the mentor intervention, where a long-term, stable relationship is the active ingredient. Individually shaping a mentor relationship to the particular needs of the child with SED involves accounting for the child's age, developmental stage, and clinical features. The activities and interactions with a younger child might involve more concrete discussions and activities focused on building basic competencies for self-esteem. In contrast, mentored activities with adolescents will naturally include discussions of evolving belief systems and plans for the future, and should include outings to prospective job sites, educational options, and housing resources to prepare the youth for adulthood. Collaboration between a mentor and a good clinical supervisor can accomplish treatment goals that neither alone could attain.

Finally, it is important to provide supervision that maintains the fidelity of the mentor intervention. This involves assessing the interpersonal quality of the evolving relationship and directing mentors to maximize the teaching opportunities from the "lessons of the relationship." Within a resiliency-building framework, the supervisor should insure that efforts are focused squarely on building protective factors (such as social and problem-solving skills and competencies for school, recreation, or vocation) and on connecting to prospective sources of social support. Supervision may also be directed to prevent the mentor from falling into the role of a therapist, self-righteous preacher, substitute parent, or crisis interventionist for the child. Such roles may jeopardize the developing friendship and prevent much of the potential to build resiliency.

Effectiveness Research on Community Mentoring

One of the most enduring community mentoring programs in the country is Big Brothers Big Sisters of America (BBBSA). This is a nationwide organization that matches volunteer adult mentors with moderate- to high-risk children who are referred by concerned parents or agencies (see www.bbbsa.org). The intervention consists of sharing recreational activities three times per month for a few hours, over a year or more. Several years ago, a controlled study was done to gauge the intervention's effectiveness (Tierney, Grossman, & Resch, 1995). The results of this study are particularly important to review, since it was the largest well-designed study to assess the impact of mentoring on the outcomes of high-risk youth.

The BBBSA study examined functional outcomes among 959 youth from eight major cities across the United States. The study youth were randomly assigned to a treatment group that was matched with a Big Brother or Big Sister

($n = 378$) or to a control group that remained on a waiting list for the duration of the study. At baseline and after 18 months, the status of each child was assessed in the areas of school performance and behavior, relationships with family, relationships with friends, self-concept, social and cultural enrichment, and antisocial activities.

The study sample consisted of 60% boys, over half of which were minority youth. The ages ranged from 10 to 16 years old and almost all were from single-parent homes. Many were from low-income households, and a number of families had histories of family violence or substance abuse. An effort was made to match adult volunteer mentors based on background, preferences, and geographic proximity.

After analysis of the outcomes using multivariate techniques, the researchers found some noteworthy differences between those youth who had been mentored and those who had remained on the waiting list. Mentored youth were only half as likely to initiate drug use in comparison to controls. Little Brothers and Little Sisters were 27% less likely than controls to initiate alcohol use. This protection against the initiation of substance abuse was even stronger for the minority youth in the mentored group. The mentored youth skipped half as many school days as the controls, felt more competent in school, and had modest gains in grade point averages. Overall, the mentored group improved the quality of relationships with both parents and peers, and Little Brothers and Little Sisters were almost one third less likely than controls to hit someone. These positive impacts of the BBBSA program were calculated to cost $1,000 per child per year.

In spite of the success of the BBBSA program for at-risk youth, the question remains whether community mentoring is an effective intervention for children with SED. Many community-based mental health programs have used professional and paraprofessional staff as mentors. These programs, exemplified by the Willie M program in North Carolina, seek to serve even the most difficult or aggressive youth with SED in community-based settings. The Willie M program is a state-run program for aggressive children with SED, developed from a class-action suit caused by exclusion of such youth from available mental health or special education resources in their community. The State of North Carolina created a multidisciplinary system of care for such children, which includes group homes, treatment foster care homes, and in-home interventions, with the frequent use of paraprofessional or professional behavioral aides and mentors to support treatment in the least restrictive setting. The functional and clinical outcomes of Willie M youth are assessed annually, allowing for assessment of the effectiveness of various interventions.

A recent longitudinal outcome study in the Willie M program followed 337 teenaged youth from the time of their entry into the program until one year later. It was found that those who attained a high level of behavioral stability after a year were more likely to have initially had good reading and problem-solving skills, family support, associations with prosocial peers, and had engaged in extracurricular activities (Bowen, 1999). The presence of these protective factors significantly predicted positive future outcomes. Many of the mentor interventions in the Willie M program are specifically designed to increase extracurricular activities, expose youth with SED to normative peers, and enhance interpersonal problem-solving skills by using mentors to help teach the youths to verbally process interpersonal conflicts. It is thought that the anecdotal successes of mentors in the Willie M program arise from building these protective factors, which in turn improves the long-term behavioral outcomes of the youths served.

One particular mentor program, the Blue Ridge Mentor Program, located in Asheville, North Carolina, specifically targeted building reading skills in addition to other activities in the mentor relationship. It was noted that the youths who participated were able to maintain their grade level of reading skills, while a comparison group of Willie M youth fell progressively behind (State of North Carolina, 1999). An informal parent and client survey of families from the Blue Ridge Mentor Program revealed a high level of satisfaction with the intervention. All of the youth served reported very positive feelings and attachment to the relationship with their mentor. Parents of the youth uniformly felt that the service had helped their children, and even enhanced their own relationship with their children. A majority reported that this particular intervention had been the most valuable service provided within the broad array of mental health services for their SED children. These findings support the ecological validity of the intervention, and suggest that mentoring may be met with minimal resistance and a high level of treatment compliance.

Conclusion

The concept of intensive community mentoring as an intervention strategy for youth with SED has grown out of a long history of mentoring as a natural means for an experienced adult to encourage the psychological growth of a young person through friendship and teaching. Research on the development of high-risk youth has revealed that a frequent source of psychosocial resilience can be found in an enduring relationship with a supportive adult outside the immediate family. Natural mentors have been found to confer protection against problems of anxiety and depression, and offset the stress of relationship problems (Rhodes, Contreras, & Mangelsdorf, 1994). Designing an intervention using trained, supervised, professional mentors for children with SED takes advantage of a very natural process to enhance the resilience of such youth by consciously building protective factors into their lives. Preliminary studies on the effectiveness of this type of intervention for even the most severely disabled youth are encouraging.

8

Family Support and Education

HENRY T. IREYS

KATHERINE A. DEVET

DIANE SAKWA

Family support programs involve systematic efforts to bolster psychological and social resources of family members as they respond over time to a continuing stressor. Most family support interventions serve to complement or extend services offered by mental health professionals. These programs often involve "experienced peers," "veteran parents," or "support partners" who develop relationships with target parents on the basis of having coped themselves with the specific stressor and its consequences.

Limited work to date suggests that family support programs enhance positive outcomes for children with serious emotional and behavioral problems (Friesen & Koroloff, 1990; Patterson, Reid, & Dishion, 1992) and have beneficial effects for parents. Some of these benefits include increased self-esteem and awareness of the child's normalcy (Lutzer, 1987), a sense of competence in managing child behavior (Dreir & Lewis, 1991), and effective advocacy skills (Fine & Borden, 1992). As noted in a recent overview (Burns, Hoagwood, & Mrazek, 1999), family support programs have infrequently received systematic evaluation or conceptual analysis.

In this chapter, we focus on community-based support programs for families of children with serious emotional disorders. We first describe selected concepts that can form a theoretical foundation for family support interventions and then discuss a variety of issues and parameters affecting the development, implementation, and evaluation of our family support program, Parent Connections.

Theoretical Foundations for Family Support Programs

Family support programs are typically based on concepts drawn from several domains of theory and research. In developing Parent Connections, we have drawn from five conceptual areas commonly used to inform the development of parent support programs.

EFFECTS OF SOCIAL SUPPORT

We define social support as information leading people to believe they are esteemed and valued and that they belong to a network of mutual obligations (Cobb, 1976). Previous work (e.g., Dunst, Trivette, & Deal, 1988, 1994) has suggested that the provision of social support (especially affirmational support) can contribute to improvements in maternal mental health. Furthermore, several investigators have highlighted the importance of using family-oriented interventions to meet the nonmedical needs of families with a chronically ill child (e.g., Miller & Diao, 1987). One well-known means of providing such services effectively is the use of neighborhood lay counselors who combine home visits with telephone contact. These workers are able to make a unique contribution because of their neighborhood affiliation and nonprofessional status (Halpern & Larner, 1988; Larner & Halpern, 1987). In addition, Stein and Jessop (1984) showed that home visits, together with consistent telephone follow-up, can be powerful agents for creating a relationship within which support can be offered to families with children who have chronic illnesses.

In many family support programs, veteran parents, mentors, or support partners are available to parents who have children with emotional disorders. In theory, these experienced individuals bring new resources (information, genuine empathy, a new or renewed sense of community, and practical connections to services) into the parents' interpersonal networks (Gottlieb, 1988; Thoits, 1986).

THE VALUE OF "WEAK TIES" IN SOCIAL NETWORKS

Small social groups or networks, composed of a few acquaintances or close friends, can themselves be linked by an acquaintance relationship to different social groups. These relationships, referred to as "weak ties," function as bridges or links between discrete social groups or institutions (Granovetter, 1973). Wellman (1981) notes that weak ties "are the source of novel news." Consequently, weak ties can provide unique channels to new, diverse sources of information, and if sustained over time can become effective links to knowledge about upcoming events, unfamiliar institutions, or the rules and procedures within a service system.

The concept of weak ties is integral to understanding the role of the experienced peer or support partner. Parents of children with severe emotional or behavioral disorders report many unmet needs when working with traditional service providers. In some instances, a support partner may function as a weak tie by developing only an acquaintance relationship; yet within this relationship, the partner may link a parent to community resources, people, or institutions and thus serve as a relationship or social network bridge-builder.

EMOTIONAL REACTIONS TO OFFERS OF HELP

Many intervention programs focus on persons who may be struggling to cope with burdens in life but who have not utilized professional help or formal mental health services to the maximum extent possible for the problems or stresses they are encountering. The intervention program typically offers the target population some type of help—usually without considering how its members might react to such offers. In many instances, persons reject what appear to be reasonable efforts for assistance (Greenberg, 1980) or experience mixed feelings about accepting offers of help (Fisher & Nadler, 1974).

The literature on recipient reactions to aid (e.g., Fisher, Nadler, & Whitcher-Alagna, 1983) provides numerous clues regarding the conditions that can shape a target population's reaction to offers of assistance. For example, accepting help can lead to feelings of indebtedness or inequity—an aversive state that motivates a person to restore equity either by reciprocating the help in some fashion, by minimizing the importance of the help, or by derogating the person who provided the help (Greenberg, 1980). Because of this phenomena, family support programs emphasize opportunities for reciprocity in order to help parents avoid feelings of indebtedness. For example, support partners observe frequently that "we are all in this together and we have to help each other with ideas and suggestions."

Altruistic acts are often viewed with suspicion: "Why does this person want to help me?" The answer to this question depends on two factors. The first factor is the recipient's attributions regarding the intention and motives of the donor. If these attributions are positive, reactions to offers of aid are likely to be positive (Fisher, Nadler, & Whitcher-Alagna, 1983). The second factor is the recipient's belief about the implicit message contained within the offer of help: Does it mean that the recipient is incompetent or helpless (an attribution of internal difficulties) or that current stresses are especially difficult (an external attribution)? The intervention that we designed (described below), includes a rationale that convincingly focuses on (1) external reasons (such as obstacles in the mental health or education system) that may explain why persons need extra assistance, and (2) the benefits of reciprocal assistance within a group of parents facing similar issues.

SOCIAL COMPARISON PROCESSES

In their discussions of social comparison theory, Festinger (1954) and Schachter (1959) describe the processes through which persons compare themselves to others. Studies investigating this theory have shown that comparing oneself with others appears to be a universal tendency that has significant consequences for mental health status (Suls & Miller, 1977). Persons tend to feel better when they compare themselves favorably with others in similar situations, in part because they can validate their reactions and observe the consequences of others' behaviors under similar conditions (Cottrell & Epley, 1977). For example, one of the participants in our program told her support partner that she felt "terrible" because it had taken her 4 months to find the right school placement for her 12-year-old son. The support partner replied, "Sister, you worked hard. Many of us, we pushed and pushed for a year before we got what we wanted. It's tough. You did good on this one." In this way, the support partner provides information that allows the mother to draw a more favorable evaluation of her efforts in comparison to the efforts of others.

Social comparison processes can also lead to unintended, negative consequences unless they are carefully monitored. A participating parent may feel that she could never become as competent as a veteran peer or support partner, and contact with these persons may leave her feeling hopeless. Because of these considerations, it is important for the peer to acknowledge that (1) he or she has been through a similar experience, (2) every person's experience is unique, and (3) his or her own efforts may have yielded success only after a long time. In this way, peers combine both aspects of the social comparison process: Because of similar experiences, they can understand what the target person is going through, but they also avoid the potential negative consequences of threatening comparisons.

This theoretical orientation has special relevance for parent support programs because it suggests ways in which social comparisons can be deliberately fostered to promote mental health functioning in a target population. For example, social comparison can help explain the psychological effects derived from talking to someone who has been through a similar stressful experience (Gottlieb, 1988). Thus, a person with experiential expertise (Borkman, 1976) may be effective because he or she can (1) encourage hope by being an example of a survivor of the stressful experience; (2) communicate an understanding of the stressful event by virtue of "having been there"; or (3) offer programmatic, experience-based advice in dealing with day-to-day demands associated with the stressful event (Rogers, Bauman, & Metzger, 1985).

EMPOWERMENT

The concept of empowerment includes both a sense of choice and an active participation in one's life circumstances. Empowerment theory moves away from the idea of a professional as the sole expert and instead suggests that change results from collaborations between professionals and community members (Rappaport, 1981, 1987). The concept is related to a sense of efficacy (Lazarus & Folkman, 1984) and implies that persons who may have felt little power to affect change recognize their *potential* to do so. This potential can be realized when circumstances are supportive (Rappaport, 1981). The empowered person not only understands the need for support but can actually choose to establish his or her own support network if no useful one is available. For example, a parent may discover that natural supports, such as immediate family, are inadequate because they lack relevant experience and understanding. As a result, "veteran" parents who have weathered similar challenges may be more useful.

Most parent support programs aim to generate opportunities for parents to realize their capacity to make and sustain changes. Studies of programs that are designed to enhance empowerment in their participants have found increased sense of personal control (Trivette, Dunst, & Hamby, 1996), increased participation in community organizations (Schulz, Israel, Zimmerman, & Checkoway, 1995; Zimmerman, Israel, Schulz, & Checkoway, 1992), and positive adjustment (Cowan, 1994).

A sense of efficacy in parenting is an important psychological resource for parents. For our purposes, this construct is defined as the perception that challenges in caring for a child can be met in an increasingly successful manner (Gecas, 1989). Efficacy is an important resource because parents with low efficacy may be vulnerable to anxiety, depression, and distress (Donovan, Leavitt, & Walsh, 1990; Lazarus & Folkman, 1984; Silver, Ireys, Bauman, & Stein, 1997).

Program Theory: A Practical Guide to Program Implementation

Good theory must drive both program design *and* implementation. As demonstrated by studies focused on the implementation of interventions (e.g., Bickman, 1990; Conrad & Conrad, 1994; Rossi & Freeman, 1993), articulating the specific links between conceptual frameworks and actual program activities is important for program evaluation and development. Consequently, for Parent Connections, we developed both an overarching evaluative framework (Figure 8.1.) and an implementation model (Table 8.1). The framework provides the "big picture" for both our intervention and its evaluation; it shows that the intervention is designed to enhance parental resources, which in turn will have effects on child mental health. The implementation model illustrates the links between the desired outcome of the intervention (i.e., enhanced parental resources), the program's operating principles (drawn from Figure 8.1 and discussed further in subsequent sections), the program's specific objectives, and the actual activities of the persons in the field. These nested levels of specification provide the means for addressing the twin challenges of making theory come alive in "real-life" intervention activities while simultaneously assuring that these activities are supported by a theoretical scaffold (see Bauman, Stein, & Ireys, 1991). Parent Connections has been developed, implemented, and evaluated in the context of a working partnership between psychologists and parents who became involved with the mental health system on behalf of their own children, who were suffering with serious emotional or behavioral disorders. As a group, we are convinced that the process of program planning, implementation, and evaluation has to be based on the kind of family-professional collaboration that the program is designed to foster.

The collaborative nature of our team is based on an understanding of a partnership as a relationship in which two or more persons have different responsibilities, equal voice, and a common purpose. This perspective has given us the opportunity to integrate a diversity of thoughts, observations, and experiences to develop a program that remains grounded in the reality of a family's day-to-day life. In particular, successful implementation of a family support program depends on understanding intimately the "culture" of families who have limited resources and who are struggling with the challenges of raising a child with a serious emotional disorder.

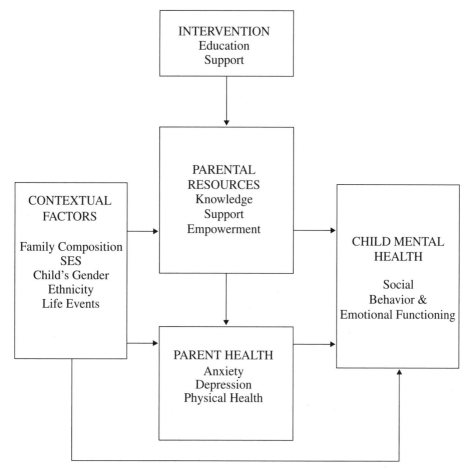

Figure 8.1   Conceptual framework for Family Connections.

Two interrelated aspects of this culture are especially salient. The first aspect involves a sense of isolation, one of the greatest enemies to effective parenting. Parents need to know they are not alone in their challenges or in their world. They require affirmation and assurance. They also need a safe sounding board that will allow them to vent and release whatever comes into their mind, no matter how terrible it may sound for a brief moment. They also long to be with someone who does not have to like or respect them, but does. This basic human need is often denied to parents of children with serious emotional disorders because of their inability to overcome the stigma of parenting children with socially undesirable behaviors. Also, they frequently neglect themselves and their own needs because they mistakenly believe that they must sacrifice their own social connections to be available to their children. What many parents fail to recognize is the relief that they gain from socialization—in fact, socialization can give them the physical and emotional energy they require to

Table 8.1 Implementation Model for Parent Connections

Parental Resources	Operating Principles	Objectives	Activities
Increase knowledge about the system	Create and maintain the relationship through regular engagement	Story-swapping	Phone calls
Increase amount of support for mother	Model behavior	Identifying and nurturing positive thoughts	Visits
Increase sense of empowerment	Affirm mother's competencies	Listening when mother needs to talk	Notes and cards
	Identify opportunities for enlarging network	Expressing care and concern when mother is stressed	Participating in educational workshops
	Encourage people to help each other	Offering suggestions regarding specific problems	
	Provide follow-up coaching	Recognizing mother's and child's strengths	Making referrals to services
		Encouraging learning and application of new skills	
		Reinforcing and expanding existing skills	

face the daily challenges their children present. Once they begin to understand the advantages of regular conversations with persons who have gone through or are going through similar experiences, participating parents may be more open to learning about other opportunities that could assist them in establishing a "personhood" that could support their sense of "parenthood."

The second important cultural characteristic is a sense of powerlessness: a feeling that nothing matters, that action brings no results, and that even survival is in jeopardy. From a parent's perspective, it is easy to lose faith in oneself and the so-called helping community when one is faced with a situation that appears too gigantic to tackle and a system that is too rigid to change. When a parent's dream of a happy, loving child is shattered by the reality of an aggressive, self-destructive, or unresponsive youngster, he or she may slowly lose the ability to conjure up hope within him- or herself. The outside world's response to the child's behaviors and its expectations of the parent's responsibilities attach unanticipated pressure and animosity to the shame, guilt, and disappointment he or she may already feel. Add to this mix the indelible scar of the parent's own childhood, where the origins of his or her fears and pain may lie, and you will find a recipe for impotence.

Both support and knowledge are needed to counter feelings of isolation and impotence. In particular, experience has underscored parents' need and desire for a foundation of knowledge in at least three areas (see also Friesen, 1996). First, a sound knowledge base regarding service opportunities and the rights of parents within the service system will enhance parents' confidence in their ability to find and negotiate appropriate services. Second, parents need skills to collaborate with professionals in treatment planning and implementation in order to make effective use of existing services and assure that their children remain in treatment or move to a more appropriate level of treatment (see Tarico, Low, Trupin, & Forsyth-Stephens, 1989; Wandersman, 1987). Third, in order to implement effective parenting strategies at home, parents need to have a foundation of knowledge about causes and consequences of behavior within a developmental and strengths-based framework.

Few community mental health service systems have programs designed specifically to enhance these resources (Elliot, Koroloff, Koren, & Friesen, 1998). Despite an emerging consensus that parents should be involved in treatment discussions, few mental health facilities routinely consider parents to be an essential part of the team that manages the child's care. This situation perpetuates the assumption that parents do not have the resources to be active partners with clinicians in the treatment of their own children (see Helfinger & Bickman, 1996).

From our perspective, this assumption is misplaced. In general, parents know their children well and want to be positive agents of change for them, including those who have serious emotional and behavioral disorders. The stigma associated with the child's mental illness does not obscure the fact that parents have dreams for their children and families. They also have ideas about how to realize those dreams, even though they may lack the resources needed to translate their ideas into actions. In many cases, parents of these children are passive recipients of mental health services delivered by "high status" professionals, especially during the years immediately following a diagnosis. The absence of sufficient support and knowledge hobbles them in initiating active collaboration with mental health professionals or, more broadly, in organizing the mental health services needed by their children.

Based on both a review of the literature and direct experience, we concluded that a combination of support and education would be more useful than either intervention alone (Koroloff & Friesen, 1991), and that any parent-focused program had to be implemented in a way that preserved and enhanced parents' sense of efficacy in their role as parents. Consequently, we designed an intervention that provides both education and support in a manner that acknowledges (1) the critical role parents play in caring for their children, and (2) the value of the parents' experience and knowledge of their own children.

Intervention Parameters

Parent Connections is a 15-month family support and education program designed to promote psychological and social functioning of children aged 9–14 years who are in treatment for serious emotional or behavioral disorders. The specific goals of the program are to (1) enhance parental recognition that specific types of social support are available; (2) promote knowledge of practical, appropriate, and relevant parenting strategies, and knowledge of the causes and consequences of their child's behavior; (3) enhance parents' ability to collaborate with professionals; and (4) strengthen parenting efficacy. Parent Connections integrates two mutually reinforcing components into a comprehensive program. The first component is referred to as the social support component; the second is referred to as the educational component. These components are described further in a manual available from the lead author.

SOCIAL SUPPORT COMPONENT

In the social support component, selected and trained support partners (mothers who have raised children with serious emotional or behavioral disorders into their late teens or beyond) are linked with participating mothers of children 9–14 years old who are in treatment for serious emotional disorders. Through regular telephone calls and occasional face-to-face meetings, the partners establish and maintain a supportive relationship with assigned mothers during the 15 months of the program. Partners each work with up to eight families and are paid an hourly rate.

The types of social support that the partners seek to enhance include informational or practical support, affirmational support, and emotional support.

- Informational support is provided by sharing information about child behavior, developmental transitions, parenting, and coping strategies. The support partners assist mothers to identify difficulties, issues, or unmet needs and to clarify alternative solutions to resolving these issues or meeting these needs. By encouraging mothers to discuss and negotiate desired outcomes regarding their child's care with mental health and education professionals, the partners help to increase the mother's access to relevant information, knowledgeable advice-givers, and needed services.

- Affirmational support is provided by enhancing a mother's confidence in parenting and by reassuring her that her concerns and issues are appropriate and important. Specifically, the partners (1) recognize and create opportunities on a continuing basis to praise the mother's parenting, and (2) identify the mother's special competencies and provide feedback about those skills that contribute to positive self-evaluations.

- Emotional support is provided by partners being available to listen to a mother's concerns, by demonstrating a continued interest in the mother's viewpoints and experiences, and by effectively communicating an understanding and appreciation of the mother's feelings and concerns. There can be a fine line between providing emotional support and encouraging dependency, and the program addresses this distinction in several ways. For example, participating mothers know from the start that the program is time-limited, and partners start preparing for termination several months before the ending date.

The social support component of Parent Connections consists of "story-swapping," conversations between two parents of children with severe emotional and behavioral disorders. In these conversations, both persons learn about each other by sharing information and experiences. At all times, however, the conversations are guided by the partner's knowledge of programmatic objectives and his or her communication of a genuine interest in the mother's welfare.

EDUCATIONAL COMPONENT

The educational component involves three workshops, each of which includes six meetings (one 3-hour meeting a week for 6 weeks). This component of Parent Connections aims to increase participants' knowledge and support networks; provide opportunities for families to gather in a social atmosphere to exchange stories, ideas, and experiences; and allow for partners and their assigned families to meet with each other in person and share experiences and insights.

Two experienced mental health professionals and the director of the sponsoring organization (Families Involved Together, or FIT) facilitate the workshops, with partners playing a key role. Active participation by the families is an important component of all the sessions. Participating mothers are encouraged to bring support people to the workshops, such as partners, friends, or other family members who help with child-rearing. Support partners play an active role in the educational workshops by encouraging parents to attend, welcoming and sitting with their assigned mothers, and helping to facilitate a portion of the small break-out groups. Workshops are held in the community and begin with a meal for all participants. Child care and transportation are provided as needed. In the course of subsequent contacts with assigned families, support partners discuss what was covered in the workshops and encourage mothers to apply new concepts and abilities to actual situations in their families.

In each workshop, the facilitators focus on enhancing knowledge related to the causes of children's mental health problems, collaborating with mental health professionals, and managing behavioral problems at home. Each successive workshop aims to build upon skills learned in previous sessions by challenging participants to grow in their understanding of the material. Certain cross-cutting themes are covered throughout the sessions, including (1) knowing your own strengths and limitations; (2) staying cool under stress; (3) knowing how to advocate for your child in a positive, assertive manner, (4) the importance of respite and support, (5) listening skills, and; (6) "giving back" to others when possible.

PROGRAM PROCEDURES

Potential participants are identified by therapists or teachers in mental health clinics, special schools, and school mental health programs. The clinicians and teachers give parents an information packet and ask them to sign a release form, which allows a Parent Connections recruiter to contact the parents, explain the program, and invite them to join. The recruiter is a parent of a child with serious emotional disorder.

The recruiter explains the two components of the program and how they work together. If the parent joins Parent Connections, a support partner is assigned. This person makes contact with participants by telephone and establishes a relationship based on our parent-to-parent support model. They explain further about the workshops and clarify the parameters of the program (e.g., the role of the support partners and the 15-month duration).

Assignment Procedures

Assignments are made on the basis of which partner is next on the list to receive a family. Letters are sent to participating families welcoming them to the program and noting the name of their assigned partner. Within a week after the welcome letters are mailed, a partner contacts the parent or parents by telephone to introduce him- or herself, explain the program, and start the relationship-building process. We considered various strategies for "matching" partners to families (e.g., by diagnosis, geographical proximity, etc.). The lack of a convincing rationale for any particular matching procedure and the practical realities of balancing assignments led us to a simple rotating procedure.

Practical Strategies for Establishing the Relationship

The first few telephone contacts and the initial workshops are guided by the perspective that the participants have important experiences to share. The underlying guidelines for the initial telephone conversations are:

- using self-disclosure to establish a foundation for the relationship;
- communicating the idea that mothers have valuable experiences in raising a child with special needs and that mothers will benefit from sharing their experiences;
- generating a sense that Parent Connections is an exciting, worthwhile program and that other mothers have enjoyed and benefitted from being active members;
- emphasizing that the partners have experience with many mothers and will share how different mothers respond to varying challenges; and
- clarifying for mothers the scope, duration, and general purpose of the program.

To assist in the initial conversations, the partners usually ask a set of specific open-ended questions. These questions are designed to elicit discussion of broad topics and are meant to be asked in a natural way with pertinent follow-up questions. Most outreach in Parent Connections is done by telephone because this is the most expedient way to establish contact, given time and scheduling constraints. We elected not to encourage home visiting to avoid the stress of having a visitor come to the home, suspicions that the support partner works for a welfare agency, and potential liability issues. Occasionally, face-to-face visits in a school or nearby coffee shop are useful for consolidating a relationship that is slow to warm up.

Much of the power of Parent Connections resides in the similarity between the partners and the mothers assigned to them. An early emphasis on this aspect of the program tends to create a foundation on which a relationship can be built. We encourage the partners to share with the mothers the relevant aspects of their own history and to tell the mothers something about their own children and experiences. A significant portion of the training of support partners covers the strengths of self-disclosure and the development of good judgment about the timing and extent of self-disclosure. In general, the partners have noted that talking about their own child during the first few contacts tends to enhance the "legitimacy" of the program and substantially strengthens the relationship. Mothers may mention their need for specific services and may be uncertain about how to obtain them. The partners assist mothers in locating appropriate services, but this happens only when the mothers themselves identify or acknowledge the need.

Maintaining the Relationships

Sometimes, the new relationships created by Parent Connections between the support partners and their assigned parents quickly yield strong bonds. In other instances, a relationship is slow to emerge. A great deal of energy is sometimes needed to maintain a "grafted" relationship over a 15-month period. Partners may become discouraged because mothers are sometimes too busy to speak with them. Mothers may appear uninterested in the program, or have telephones that become disconnected. We use a number of strategies to assist the partner in maintaining the relationship under these circumstances. For example, we hold weekly group meetings with all partners to stabilize morale and generate solutions to particular problems. Because virtually all of the partners have had this experience of working with hard-to-reach mothers, the group can offer collective support for hanging in with the family despite few signs of response. In addition, in previous programs, many parents who seemed to connect little with the partners nonetheless said during the post-program evaluation interview how important it was to know that the partner was there, even if the actual amount of contact time was small. Reading comments gathered from the evaluations of prior programs also helps to maintain morale.

SUPPORT PARTNERS' OPERATING PRINCIPLES

Overall, five operating principles serve to guide the nature and content of the interactions between support partners and participating mothers:

1. *Listen effectively.* During their own training period, support partners strengthen their skills in listening and communication, identifying appropriate and useful parenting strategies, and setting limits. As relationships evolve between the support partner and the participating mother, there are many opportunities for assisting the mother by using active listening skills. This principle is the foundation for all of the program activities.

2. *Affirm mother's "expertness" and competencies.* Previous field experience with similar partnering programs (e.g., Walsh, Ireys, & Sills, 1996) has shown that placing the mother in the role of an "expert"—i.e., someone with considerable experience and knowledge in raising a child with a serious emotional disorder—serves several functions: (1) it helps to establish a positive relationship in which the parent can discuss a variety of experiences; (2) it serves to counteract the usual role in which the parent and child are typically passive recipients of services from mental health experts; and (3) it creates an opportunity for parents to feel positively about themselves and the possible contributions they can make to other parents. This approach may also contribute to a sense of empowerment and have direct, positive effects on maternal confidence.

3. *Encourage reciprocal assistance.* By emphasizing that Parent Connections is composed of many mothers in similar situations, support partners can underscore the utility of mutual assistance. Consequently, when a partner discusses one topic with a mother, she often notes that other mothers respond in a particular way or that other mothers find it helpful to use a particular service. New ideas can be introduced and discussed in a nonthreatening fashion. Furthermore, the mothers know that some of the things that worked for them will be relayed to other mothers facing a similar difficulty.

4. *Create and maintain relationship through regular engagement.* Program activities are designed to be consistent with stages in the evolution of relationships between two parents who share certain experiences. We conceptualize four stages: initial contact, rapport-building, maintenance of interest, and termination. Specific activities must be linked to each stage for the relationship to achieve its goals.

5. *Provide follow-up coaching.* Concepts and ideas discussed in the workshops can evaporate quickly when the mother returns home to meet an enduring source of aggravation. A few workshops are not likely to transform years and even generations of ineffective parenting strategies. In the workshops, parents may begin to recognize that their expectations and the rules that they established for their children may be unrealistic. Away from home, they may start to understand that enforcement of their old rules is inappropriate and counterproductive. But when confronted with their children in actual and emotional conflict, extra support may be needed in order to make changes. We refer to this extra support as "coaching." It involves assisting the participating parent to apply ideas from the workshops to actual situations in day-to-day life. This may mean extra telephone calls that deal specifically with how mothers can translate concepts into practice within the reality of their own abilities and life constraints.

Case Study

Carol is the mother of two daughters, Rebecca and Cindy. Both girls exhibited severely inappropriate behaviors at home and school. In fact, Rebecca, at the age of 16, had already dropped out of school and had brought her boyfriend to live in her mother's home. The younger girl, Cindy (age 10), created havoc in the home, classroom, and neighborhood. She was uncooperative and abusive toward her mother and made racist remarks to would-be playmates as well as adults. As a Caucasian girl living in a predominantly African American community, her actions were not appreciated by anyone she met.

Carol is a diminutive Caucasian woman in her early 30s. When she first became involved with Parent Connections, her hair was long, stringy, and a dull shade of brown. Her face was pale and drawn. She looked about 10 years older than her actual age. She had few friends or family members she could turn to for support.

When Carol was first contacted by her support partner, Joyce, she was reluctant to return phone calls and to become involved with the program. She appeared reluctant to accept the involvement of a stranger in her business. Joyce had to make numerous phone calls before she could engage Carol in a meaningful conversation. Finally, Carol stayed on the phone long enough to talk about her children and herself. At this point, something important seemed to happened. Carol began to realize what she had been missing: talking to another adult who knew what she was going through because Joyce had gone through it too. Soon, Carol was not only taking advantage of Joyce's calls, she was making calls of her own in return.

Joyce succeeded in convincing Carol to come to the workshops. She apparently learned a great deal from them. She took the lessons home with her and put them into practice, often consulting Joyce when things didn't work as she expected. Before long, a series of changes in Carol became apparent. First, based on information she learned about from another parent in one of the workshops, she managed to transfer Cindy from a public school program into a private, special-education school, where Cindy began to improve. Not only did Carol begin to act differently, her looks changed as well. She began to dress in a more stylish way; she had her hair cut, styled, and dyed red. She spoke about "taking back her life." By the end of the program, she seemed prepared to pursue and fight for a more stable future for herself and her children.

Program Development

LEADERSHIP AND COMMUNITY CONTEXT

Parent Connections and its evaluation were designed over a period of several years by two of the authors (Ireys and Sakwa), who met periodically to work out both the program's basic principles and its operational details. At the present time, staff from Families Involved Together identify, hire, and monitor the support partners and are responsible for all of the activities related to the educational workshops. One of the authors (Sakwa) is the director of FIT. Staff from the School of Public Health at Johns Hopkins University (Ireys, DeVet, and others) are responsible for the evaluation activities. However, all decisions that affect program or evaluation design are made in the context of biweekly meetings of both FIT and university staff. The project is supported by a research grant from the National Institute of Mental Health.

Families Involved Together was formed in 1991 to provide peer support to families of children with severe emotional disabilities. Established as a program of the Family Preservation Initiative of Baltimore City, FIT became an independent, private, nonprofit organization in 1997. It is staffed entirely by parents of children with special needs and has continued to expand its community-based outreach, education, mentoring, and support efforts in areas of special education, kinship care, and juvenile justice. FIT has established partnerships with numerous agencies in Baltimore and is also well known as an effective and credible family advocacy organization.

SUPPORT PARTNER SELECTION AND TRAINING

Like most programs in human services, the fate of Parent Connections depends on selecting the appropriate individuals, strengthening their skills, and providing the support necessary for them to perform effectively in their role. Recruitment of partners begins by contacting parents who have been involved with FIT as active members of previous educational workshops, who are known to the FIT staff through their community contacts, or who respond to special outreach efforts. Potentially suitable parents with affected children in their teens or early twenties are identified. More parents are identified than are needed in the program. These parents are enrolled in the first phase of the training program and paid at an hourly rate.

The potential partners participate in an initial training program that continues for 4 weeks, 5 hours a week (two meetings each week, lasting two and one-half hours each). The program directors share responsibilities for conducting the training programs, building on experience in previous programs.

The training focuses on enhancing listening and communication skills through role-plays, interactive activities, and in-class practice session.

In addition to practicing active listening skills, a significant amount of time is spent on the nature and timing of self-disclosure. Self-disclosure is the basis for the legitimacy of the partner, helps establish a mutual, trusting relationship, and is a way for the partner to model desirable behaviors or make suggestions without telling the mother what to do. However, because self-disclosure can be inappropriate at times, we encourage partners to think about when it is and is not advisable. Additional details regarding the training program are in our program manual, which can be obtained from the lead author.

Efforts with similar programs (see Ireys, Sills, Kolodner, & Walsh, 1996; Silver, Ireys, Bauman, & Stein, 1997; Walsh, Ireys, & Sills, 1996) have taught us that not all parents are suited to be support partners, often because of other events and challenges in their own lives. Therefore, we train more parents than needed in order to assure that we can select those who demonstrate the best capacity to function effectively in the role of support partner. In preparation for Parent Connections, numerous programs that used similar "parent mentoring" models were reviewed. Characteristics of warmth and empathy were mentioned by virtually every account that described selection criteria—a pattern that is consistent with research showing that these attributes may be necessary for any helping relationship. Other characteristics include (1) an active interest in new ideas and a capacity to learn; (2) a tendency to engage other people that is driven by curiosity and a desire to make connections; (3) an ability to communicate that "one has been there, and understands" in a nonjudgmental fashion; (4) an ability not to become enmeshed in other persons' lives; (5) emotional maturity derived from real-life experiences in raising children with serious ongoing mental health problems; (6) relative freedom from stress or strain in one's current personal life; and (7) general likeability. At the end of the training period, the facilitators use a standard form to evaluate participants on these characteristics and the ratings are used in making the final determination of whom we invite to be support partners in Parent Connections.

After the initial training, the selected partners participate in advanced training. They meet for an additional 5 hours a week for 4 weeks to practice initial contacts, learn about their role in the educational workshops, and review procedures for documenting contacts with assigned families. In addition, the intensive training seeks to enhance partners' skills in identifying unmet needs, serving as a supportive link to resources, and responding to crises.

QUALITY MONITORING

Meeting Weekly with Partner Group

Program directors meet with support partners for 2 hours each week in order to review their issues and concerns and to review their contacts with assigned families. Supporting the partners is an extremely important aspect of the program as a whole, and these weekly meetings are in fact the key to whether Parent Connections is implemented successfully. In some instances, partners have questions about finding appropriate resources or handling a specific problem with a mother. In other instances, they discuss their emotional reactions to their conversations or visits with families. On many occasions, a discussion of issues raised by one partner is relevant to others as well.

The partner role is complex. Its boundaries are not easily defined, and it contains inherent tensions that may strain emotional resources. Moreover, the parents who become partners do not have advanced degrees or professional training in mental health, education, or social work. Yet, the role of being a partner requires professionalism because it involves maintaining some emotional distance from assigned families. In some instances, the assigned families initially view the partner as a social worker. In other instances, families are facing difficulties or situations that closely resemble issues with which the partner had struggled herself. It is critical to appreciate the initial discomfort that partners may feel in the early stages, discomfort that can reoccur throughout the program.

Overall, weekly meetings and special retreats provide a forum for informal "process evaluation" of the program and serve to generate a sense of mutual support among the partners. The meetings are designed to keep morale high during periods when successes may be few and, over time, contribute to unity of purpose and method.

Monitoring the Fieldwork

Like all service programs, Parent Connections has to document the activities of the staff. We have two forms that assist us in this process[1]:

- *The Contact Log* is a running account of all contacts, attempted contacts, letters sent, educational workshops attended, and other pertinent activities for each family. From this log it is possible to compute on a monthly basis the total number of contacts, total time spent in contact, and total number of attempted contacts for each family.
- *The Contact Checklist* consists of two parts, a checklist of topic areas discussed and a checklist of actual activities (e.g., telephone attempts, telephone contacts, face-to-face visits, workshop attendance) undertaken during the contact. This form is completed for every face-to-face contact and telephone call of 5 minutes or longer.

The partners also find it useful to keep their own notes about conversations with parents. This is not a requirement of the program, and the partners may use various formats that they find most useful to remember what they discuss with assigned mothers.

ORGANIZING EDUCATIONAL WORKSHOPS

Substantial planning and organization are needed to make the workshops a success. Partners play an important role in encouraging families to attend the

---

[1]Available from the author.

workshops through phone calls and personal invitations. Flyers are sent to pique the interest of families and remind them of the dates and times of the workshops. Transportation is facilitated through providing cabs or bus fares, as needed. The workshops begin with a hot meal that is shared by the families, the partners, and the facilitators. After the meal, the children are watched by child-care providers while the mothers participate in the educational session. Door prizes or other small incentives are used to increase participation in the workshops.

FAMILIES AND CHILDREN IN CRISIS

Although most mothers in the program are not in crisis at the beginning of the program, many mothers face a crisis with their child at some point during the program. The partners are encouraged to increase contact with families during these periods of crisis. The support derived from simply "being there" frequently deepens an existing relationship, and at times even encourages a hesitant or marginally participating mother to become actively involved with the program regardless of when in the intervention the crisis occurred.

ASSURING SAFE TERMINATION

Adding a supportive person may influence the mother's use of her existing support network by (1) suppressing support-seeking from others by substituting the support derived from the partner, or (2) enhancing help-seeking by providing a model of how to use help offered and by demonstrating the positive effect of using support. To assure that termination of contacts with the partner is not a threat to the mother's mental health status, the partner does several things. Throughout the intervention, she seeks to identify underutilized sources of support and information within the mother's own network and within the mental health and education systems. As the intervention draws to an end, these efforts are intensified. In addition, links among participating mothers are made during educational workshops. Finally, as the intervention draws to a close, the partner actively discusses with the mother the importance of finding and using other supports.

The Evidence Base

Despite the widespread application of family support programs, systematic evaluations of their effectiveness have been rare. Randomized clinical trials of community-based family support programs for parents of children with chronic illnesses have demonstrated some success in reducing symptoms of depression and anxiety in mothers (e.g., Ireys et al., 1996; Silver et al, 1997). A program that used an education and support model for parents of children receiving mental health services led to significant improvements in parents' knowledge of mental health services and in their perceptions of self-efficacy (Bickman, Heflinger, Northrup, Sonnichsen, & Schilling, 1998).

We developed a project to assess the effectiveness of Parent Connections through a randomized, repeated-measures, controlled clinical trial design with

250 families enrolled at baseline. We will sample from all families of children aged 9–14 who live in Baltimore and are in treatment for serious emotional disorders at one of 15 treatment sites. The primary goals of the intervention are to improve children's emotional and behavioral functioning and to decrease maternal symptoms of depression and anxiety. We hypothesize that the intervention will achieve its goals by enhancing parents' psychological and social resources, including (1) knowledge of the causes of children's mental health problems and key strategies for both managing behavioral problems and collaborating with mental health professionals, (2) perceived availability of specific types of social support, and (3) sense of efficacy.

We will assign families to either Parent Connections or a low-dose control group. The low-dose control group receives informational packets three times a year. Assignments will be stratified by treatment site using permuted blocks. This procedure serves to maintain a balance between the experimental and control groups across recruitment sites.

Data are being collected through face-to-face interviews at enrollment and at 2, 12, and 20 months postenrollment, and through telephone interviews at 8 and 16 months postenrollment. Interviews include measures of the child's functioning (e.g., the Child and Adolescent Functional Assessment Scale), maternal mental health (e.g., the Psychiatric Symptom Index) and sense of parenting efficacy (e.g., the Vanderbilt Mental Health Services Efficacy Scale), child and maternal perceptions of the availability of social support, use of health and mental health services, and indices of socioeconomic and family status.

Participants randomized to the experimental group will participate in Parent Connections. We will monitor closely (1) the frequency, duration, and nature of contacts between parents and mentors; and (2) the amount of time that parents actually participate in the educational seminars. Measures of participation in the overall program (i.e., the "dose" of the intervention that is actually delivered) will be incorporated into analyses of program effects. Based on previous work (e.g., Ireys et al., 1996; Silver et al., 1997), we anticipate that at least two thirds of the experimental group will participate actively.

ASSESSING INTERVENTION EFFECTS

After initial data review and reduction, we will compare the experimental to the control group using dependent measures collected at Time 2 (T2, the end of the intervention) in an intent-to-treat analysis. In a follow-up, we will use regression models to control for baseline covariates (e.g., socioeconomic status). The independent variables will include a variable that identifies the group (experimental or control) and covariates measured at baseline if the two groups are found to be different at baseline on key covariates (e.g., maternal age or child's gender). Longitudinal data analyses will be performed to account for the longitudinal structure of the data. Random effects models will be used to account for subject specific effects (Laird & Ware, 1982). Also, models will be fit that allow the effect of the intervention to change with time in order to show when the intervention begins to have an effect and whether the effect changes over time. This will be accomplished by including interaction terms between group and time using data from T1–T3 (Diggle, Liang, & Zeger, 1994).

As indicated in Figure 8.1, the intervention is hypothesized to have its effects by increasing parents' resources, defined as knowledge, social support, and empowerment. Therefore, if the intervention is found to have positive effects, we will conduct additional analyses using random effects models to examine whether the intervention's effects occurred via this postulated route. Essentially, this step adds a time-varying covariate (i.e., resource variables) to the random effects model that represents the mechanism by which the intervention is presumed to have its effect.

An important aim of the study is to assess the intervention's success in reaching its specific objectives of enhancing informational and social resources (i.e., knowledge of key issues and availability of social support). Specifically, we hypothesize that at Time 2 (at end of intervention), controlling for scores at Time 1, parents in the experimental group, compared to parents in the control group, will report (1) greater knowledge of the service system, causes and consequences of children's behavior, and practical strategies for managing behavioral problems; and (2) enhanced availability of social support. Therefore, we will compare the experimental to the control group using resource measures (e.g., social support) collected at T2, controlling for baseline independent variables. The independent variables will include a variable that indicates the group (experimental or control) and covariates measured at baseline. These covariates will include T1 scores and other factors (e.g., socioeconomic status), depending on results of bivariate analyses.

Another important question for this study is, which parents benefit the most from the intervention? A series of exploratory analyses will be conducted. These analyses will focus only on data from the experimental group. Differential effects will be analyzed using change scores in resource variables from T1 to T2. First, using analyses of variance, differential effects of the intervention will be explored as a function of level of resources at T1. Second, differential effects of the intervention will be examined in relation to different subgroups defined by condition-related variables (e.g., severity of illness) and by contextual factors (e.g., socioeconomic status). Third, differential effects will be examined in relation to interactions between key variables (e.g., child's functioning and family composition).

ASSESSING INTERVENTION COSTS

We will draw from our program implementation and outcome data to complete analyses of both cost-effectiveness and cost benefit using the cost-procedure-process-outcome analysis model developed by Yates (1995, 1996). Costs will be based on time spent by key personnel and actual dollar resources for materials, mailings, space, and other supplies. Process data pertain to the different goal functions noted in Table 8.1. Procedure data involve the specific activities between support partners and assigned parents, as indicated in the activity column of Table 8.1.

IMPLEMENTATION RESULTS TO DATE

At the time of this writing, recruitment for the first cohort has been completed and we are about one third of the way into the second cohort. Of the 66 families recruited in the first cohort, 40% of the mothers did not complete high school, about 30% graduated from high school, and the remaining 30% had at least some college. Seventy-seven percent of the families are African American and 42% are currently receiving public assistance. Almost half of the families are headed by a mother or grandmother alone; 28% of the families have two adults present in the home; and 12% have two biological parents. The children have a wide range of mental health disorders, including attention-deficit/hyperactivity disorder, conduct disorder, depression, and anxiety disorder. Many children have multiple diagnoses and co-occurring problems, including vision or hearing problems, speech or communication problems, and learning disabilities.

Conclusion

Although we are awaiting the results of the randomized trial to determine whether Parent Connections is accomplishing its objectives, we have heard numerous testimonials to the program's impact. Participating parents have expressed many times—both personally to their support partners and more generally in the educational workshops—that the program is different, meaningful, and of great benefit to them and their children. The directors of the program who participate in the workshops observe parents being welcomed by their support partners and entering into a group of people who go out of their way to be nurturing, respectful, and informative. Presentations in the educational workshops are understandable and relevant to the participating parents, and are often accompanied by the type of restorative humor that only survivors can share among themselves. Participating parents feel part of something comfortable and worthwhile. Some have expressed amazement that the program actually changed the way they parent their children and the way their children respond to them; some have told us that they have begun to have hope again.

Parent Connections is essentially about promoting hope, empowerment, and efficacy in a culture where survival itself is sometimes questioned. In this program, support partners can meet participating mothers with respect, emotional nourishment, and genuine empathy. They can do so in part because they have seen their children grow up despite a mental health disorder and in part because the program is designed to support them in their role as "hope-givers," mentors, and coaches. Support partners can offer parents not only words of encouragement for success but also the recognition that failure is also inevitable. In the throes of enormous stress, survival becomes more desirable than success. Knowing that others have failed or stumbled or felt unsure or been intimidated *and still survived* can be powerful knowledge for parents of children with serious emotional disorders. It can be so encouraging that they may begin to understand that if they can survive the failures, they can devote themselves, with dignity, to capturing the successes, no matter how small. This understanding itself is a true signal of hope and a beginning step to empowerment.

Acknowledgments

Support for this chapter was provided, in part, by a grant from the National Institute of Mental Health (MH 56995; Henry Ireys, Principal Investigator). We learned much about implementation from the women who served as support partners for Parent Connections, and we thank them for teaching us. Angela Lloyd and Robert Blue also have been important in shaping our understanding of how to make programs work; they were an extremely important part of Parent Connections and earned our affection, love, and respect. Laurence Jackson and Shawan Gregory provided exceptional guidance in the educational seminars and contributed much insight into what worked, what didn't, and why.

Part III

Targeted Interventions in Education, Substance Abuse, and Mental Health

9

Special Education: Best Practices and First Step to Success

MICHAEL H. EPSTEIN

HILL M. WALKER

Approximately 400,000 students each year receive special education and related services in our nation's schools because they have been identified as students having severe emotional or behavioral disorders (EBD; U.S. Department of Education, 1998). Perhaps no other area of education presents more challenges to parents, school administrators, teachers, and policymakers than this school population. Although controversy and debate continue regarding the processes and outcomes of special education for students with EBD, a sufficient knowledge base has evolved that documents the availability of successful strategies and programs. In this chapter we first provide a brief overview of the basis for special education services; that is, who are the students being served and what are the types of educational settings in which they are served? Next, we identify the strategies that have been found to be successful with these students. Finally, we describe the development, implementation, and research evidence on a relatively new early intervention program called First Step to Success, based on these strategies.

The Context of Special Education

Today, special education for students with disabilities generally and for students with EBD in particular has been shaped by a diverse array of contributing factors. Perhaps one of the most influential of these factors has been the complex legal developments and judicial rulings that have clarified and extended the educational and related rights of students with disabilities. The access of students with disabilities to public education has been developed through a process called the "litigation-legislation-litigation cycle" (Bateman & Herr, 1981). The process starts with court cases in which specific issues are articulated and certain rulings are made that establish legal precedents. Next, these court decisions are codified into law through legislation. Then, additional court cases are brought forth that clarify and define the intent of the law.

LITIGATION AND LEGISLATION

The earliest court cases dealing with the rights of students with disabilities to a public education occurred in the early 1970s. These court cases called into question the practices of excluding students with disabilities from public education and the discriminatory assessment and identification processes used to place students into restrictive special education settings. At the center of these court cases were two basic constitutional principles: equal protection of individuals under the law and due process. In almost all of these cases, the courts ruled in favor of the plaintiffs and set in motion the passage of legislation guaranteeing the educational rights of all students with disabilities.

Passed in 1975, the Education for All Handicapped Children Act (P.L. 94-142) became known as the educational Bill of Rights for students with disabilities. The act contained some key provisions, as follows:

- All children with disabilities, aged 3–21, have a right to a free, appropriate public education. This includes special education and related services (e.g., counseling, occupational therapy) at no cost to the family.
- All children with disabilities must be educated as much as possible in the least restrictive environment. This requires that to the maximum extent possible, students with disabilities are to be educated with their nondisabled peers.
- Assessment and evaluation procedures must be conducted in a nondiscriminatory manner. This requires that (1) tests be nondiscriminatory and given in the child's native language, (2) eligibility into a program is decided on the basis of information from several sources, (3) evaluations must be conducted by a multidisciplinary team, and (4) parents must have the right to request an independent evaluation.
- An individualized educational program (IEP) must be written for each student. The IEP includes a statement of the child's present level of functioning, annual goals and short-term objectives, the extent to which the child will participate in general education, the services to be provided, when they will commence and their duration, and how services will be evaluated.
- Due process must be provided to the child and family. Specifically, if a parent or student disagrees with the school regarding assessment procedures, eligibility, services, or any provision of the plan, no changes can be made in the student's educational program until the issue has been resolved through an impartial hearing or court decision.

In 1990, the law was amended and its name changed to the Individuals with Disabilities Education Act (IDEA). Amended again in 1997, IDEA continues to guide the provision of educational services for U.S. students with disabilities, including children and adolescents with EBD. The 1997 amendment addresses such issues as eligibility, individual education programs, placement, and assessment of students. Of particular interest to the education of students with EBD were the provisions on discipline with students with disabilities. These provisions focused on such issues as suspensions, behavior intervention plans, change of school placement, and alternative education placement. For a detailed discussion of these issues, the reader is referred to Yell and Shriner (1997). Since passage of P.L. 94-142 and IDEA, numerous lawsuits have been filed seeking to clarify how the law is to be implemented. Litigation issues specific to students with EBD have included suspension and expulsion, placement in the least restrictive setting, and disciplinary practices.

TARGET POPULATION FOR SPECIAL EDUCATION

There is no consensus definition of "emotional and behavioral disorders" (Kauffman, 1997). Indeed, there is significant disagreement on such basic issues as the very existence of EBD as well as the assessment and diagnosis of the condition. Unambiguous definitions of EBD are important for several reasons. First, a definition reflects how a person, group, or organization views EBD which in turn influences how a special education program for students with EBD is communicated to consumers and staff. Second, because a definition describes the conditions that students must satisfy to receive services, a definition influences the estimates of prevalence for EBD. Third, decisions of policymakers, administrators, and advocacy groups on such issues as services, research, funding, and so forth are influenced by the definition of the condition. Finally, communication about EBD issues within and across disciplines is mediated and shaped by the definition used.

Numerous types of definitions of EBD exist (Epstein & Cullinan, 1998). Perhaps this is the case because definitions of EBD can serve a variety of purposes. A research definition is designed to clarify the nature of the students having EBD who are involved in a study. It assists readers of the study in determining whether the results are applicable to other children not involved in that particular study. An authoritative definition is offered by an expert and reflects that individual's personal philosophy, experience, and professional training. These definitions are offered to promulgate a theory of EBD or to structure a discussion of its nature and parameters. An administrative definition, as found in rules, regulations, and laws, is intended to guide the identification of children eligible for specialized services. One important administrative definition is the U.S. Department of Education's definition of EBD. The definition of EBD, as stated in IDEA, is presented in Table 9.1.

Because of the difficulty in measuring the various components and conditions of the definition, it has been severely criticized by professionals in the field (see, for example, Kauffman, 1997). Based on this definition, the reported prevalence of children receiving educational services for EBD is about 1% of the school-age population. Many professionals believe this is a significant un-

Table 9.1   Federal Definition of Emotional Disturbance

(i) The term means a condition exhibiting one or more of the following characteristics over a long period of time and to a marked degree, which adversely affects educational performance:

    (a) an inability to learn that cannot be explained by intellectual, sensory, or health factors;
    (b) an inability to build or maintain satisfactory relationships with peers and teachers;
    (c) inappropriate types of behaviors or feelings under normal circumstances;
    (d) a general pervasive mood of unhappiness or depression; or
    (e) a tendency to develop physical symptoms or fears associated with personal or school problems.

(ii) The term includes children who are schizophrenic. The term does not include children who are socially maladjusted, unless it is determined that they are seriously emotionally disturbed.

Source: Federal Register, 1977, 1981.

derestimate of the actual prevalence. Recent efforts by Epstein and Cullinan (1998) have led to the development of a psychometrically sound instrument for use in operationalizing the federal definition of EBD as presented in IDEA.

EDUCATIONAL PLACEMENTS

As we have previously stated, P.L. 94-142 and IDEA mandated that students with disabilities be provided a full continuum of educational and related services. A full continuum should include placement in the regular classroom with supports, modified regular classroom placement with consultation services, resource room services, self-contained special classes in regular school buildings, alternative schools, day treatment settings, residential centers, and homebound instruction. However, the wording of the federal legislation has suggested that, to the extent possible, the preferred least restrictive placement for students with disabilities is to be placed with students not having disabilities. Thus, considerable debate exists about inclusion of students with disabilities in general education settings—specifically, which students should be included, and for how much of the school day?

The inclusion debate for students with EBD has been particularly controversial (Kauffman, Lloyd, Baker, & Reidel, 1995). Advocates for full inclusion argue that it is a basic human right to attend a neighborhood school and be educated with peers (Friend & Bursuck, 1999). They believe that with support, all children having disabilities can be educated in a general education classroom. In sharp contrast, proponents of a full continuum argue that to place all students with disabilities in inclusive classrooms ignores the individual characteristics and needs of the student with disabilities. They believe that many classrooms and regular education teachers are ill prepared and lack the necessary supports to meet the needs of substantial numbers of students with disabilities. MacMillan, Gresham, and Forness (1996), in a now classic article on empirical perspectives regarding full inclusion, make a compelling case that the full-inclusion model lacks scientific support for its efficacy, despite its advocates' claims to the contrary.

Our view is that the inclusion debate has been instrumental in moving numerous children from restrictive to more inclusive education settings and that certainly some, but perhaps not all, have likely benefitted from this change in placement. It seems clear that not all children have the behavioral, cognitive, and psychosocial attributes necessary to derive adequate benefit(s) from an inclusive setting, with its associated demands; thus, we are strongly supportive of a full continuum of placement services and options to meet the needs of the complete range of students with disabilities. Even more important than placement (i.e., where a child is educated) are the principles of instruction and educational strategies provided the child. How children develop, what they are taught, and that which they learn and master are of substantially greater import than who they sit beside or associate with and whether they spend all day in a regular, mainstream classroom setting. In the section to follow, we describe the strategies and best practices that have proven successful in our field for students with EBD.

SERVICES FOR STUDENTS WITH EBD

Students with EBD present significant challenges to schools, and there is the increasing recognition that the traditional continuum of services in the public schools is not adequate to meet the broad range of challenging medical, psychological, social, and academic-related behaviors that students with EBD often present (Knitzer, Steinberg, & Fleisch, 1990). Students with EBD may have serious attention problems that require medication and counseling in addition to a school-based behavior-management program (Kauffman, 1997). Students with EBD may also exhibit a range of social adjustment problems including withdrawal, aggression, depression, peer rejection/isolation, and substance abuse, many of which may require the additional support of health, welfare, mental health, or law enforcement agencies. Some may have serious health problems requiring careful medical monitoring and interventions. Finally, the state of poverty itself, within which a sizable number of students with EBD are likely to be, will necessitate additional health and social services.

Unfortunately, the typical service delivery system available to many students with EBD is often unable to respond in a timely, coordinated, and comprehensive fashion to the multiple and interconnected needs of students and their families (Nelson & Pearson, 1991). This is because, traditionally, schools have worked largely in isolation, without systematically involving parents and community agencies as necessary supports to meet student needs (Knitzer, Steinberg, & Fleisch, 1990). Indeed, in the past, mental health, child welfare, and schools were involved in a largely hit-or-miss fashion, and rarely coordinated services to the child and family. Moreover, parents were more often viewed as the source of the problem, and therefore their wants or needs regarding treatment goals, plans, or interventions were not sought or were ignored (Friesen & Koroloff, 1990). It is clear that if the challenging behaviors of students with EBD are to be adequately met, school, parent, and public and private provider efforts must be directed toward a comprehensive, coordinated system of care.

A comprehensive system of care refers to "a spectrum of mental health and other necessary services which are organized into a coordinated network to meet the multiple and changing needs of severely disturbed children and adolescents" (Stroul & Friedman, 1986, p. iv). The development of a system of care thus requires collaboration and coordination across agencies and among professionals. Along with mental health, child welfare, juvenile justice, vocational rehabilitation, health, and recreational services, education—and particularly special education—needs to play a significant role in a system of care. Excellent descriptions of system of care programs that include education services have been published elsewhere (e.g., Epstein, Kutash, & Duchnowski, 1998). More importantly, the education strategies and practices and the model program described later in this chapter fit well within a system of care approach.

EFFECTIVE SCHOOL-BASED INTERVENTION STRATEGIES AND PRACTICES

Over the past three decades, a substantial body of applied research has developed on strategies and practices for working with students having emotional or behavioral disorders in the context of schooling. Reviews of this knowledge base have yielded mixed results (see Dunlap & Childs, 1996; Hoagwood & Erwin, 1997; Knitzer, Steinberg, & Fleisch, 1990; Peacock Hill Working Group, 1991; Steinberg & Knitzer, 1992). Mental health services generally, as delivered in school settings, have had weak to minimal effects in addressing the challenges of students with mental health problems and needs (See Dunlap & Childs, 1996; Hoagwood & Erwin, 1997; Knitzer, Steinberg, & Fleisch, 1990; Steinberg & Knitzer, 1992). On the other hand, reviews of the school-based literature on interventions for students with EBD, where the interventions are derived from a behavioral or social learning paradigm, show quite different results (See Peacock Hill Working Group, 1991; Walker et al., 1998a). These interventions, if implemented with reasonable fidelity, tend to show acceptable treatment outcomes within the context of schooling (see, as examples, recent experimental and longitudinal studies reported by Eddy, Reid, & Fetrow, 2000; Trembly, Pagani-Kurtz, Masse, Vitaro, & Pihl, 1995; Walker et al., 1998b). These school-based intervention approaches have been determined effective with the broad range of children and youth having EBD; further, their effects have generally been replicated across the full age-grade range (i.e., preschool, elementary, and secondary school settings [Peacock Hill Working Group, 1991; Walker, et al., 1998a]). Gottfredson found similar effects as reported in a comprehensive review on what works and does not work in school crime prevention (1997). That is, intervention approaches with a strong behavioral focus tended to be substantially more effective in producing positive empirical outcomes in this regard than did other intervention approaches.

The strategies and practices described above have been evaluated using multiple, methodological approaches involving case study, single-subject, and experimental research designs that include randomized assignment to treatment and control groups of students as well as longitudinal follow-up assessments and monitoring. Additionally, meta-analyses have also documented the beneficial effectiveness of many of these strategies (Carlberg & Kavale, 1980). Described below, they include continuous assessment and monitoring of progress, provision for practice of new skills, treatment matched to problem, multicomponent treatment, programming for transfer and maintenance, commitment to sustained intervention, and family involvement (Peacock Hill Working Group, 1991). The First Step to Success program for addressing the aggressive, destructive behavioral characteristics of at-risk children at the point of school entry, as described in the next section, incorporates many of these strategies and practices.

CONTINUOUS ASSESSMENT AND MONITORING OF PROGRESS

Central to the systematic and high-fidelity application of interventions is the strategy of continuous assessment and monitoring of the resulting behavioral and academic outcomes. Attention is directed to designing sensitive assessment tools that measure observable behavior on a regular basis. Direct, daily measurement of target behavior(s) using curriculum-based measurement procedures is an example of measurement approaches that orchestrate success (see Deno, 1985).

PROVISION FOR PRACTICE OF NEW SKILLS

Students with EBD need many opportunities to practice before they acquire a skill. Emotional and behavioral competencies that are being taught need to be practiced quite frequently and in their natural settings. Verbal and overt rehearsal, guided practice, and corrective feedback are required for students with EBD when important complex behaviors are being taught (Kerr & Nelson, 1989; Morgan & Jenson, 1988).

OBSERVATIONAL LEARNING AND BEHAVIOR

Children acquire much of their behavior by observing and imitating the behavior of others (Bandura, 1977) and learn many prosocial and socially skilled behaviors by attempting to reproduce or model the behavior of others. In school settings, students observe and imitate the behavior of teachers and peers, particularly those peers who are perceived as popular and having high status. Peer tutoring, peer mentoring, and vicarious learning are successful strategies that are all based on observational learning.

TREATMENT MATCHED TO PROBLEM

Successful strategies focus on the presenting emotional and behavioral problems of the student and are applied at the level of intensity and duration necessary to achieve success. For example, students with EBD who have difficulty interacting with their peers may receive intensive social skills instruction 4–5 days per week for as long as is required to develop socially competent forms of peer-related behavior. Or students who fail to complete homework on a regular basis may be required to have a daily note signed by their parents until the problem of homework completion is corrected.

MULTICOMPONENT TREATMENT

Because the onset of most emotional and behavioral disorders of children are multifactored and complex, it is reasonable to assume that multicomponent treatments will be required to successfully address them. This may involve the use of combinations of intervention strategies within and across settings. For example, the use of direct instruction procedures, peer mentoring, and social skills training may be combined for an EBD student within one or more classroom settings. Or it may require the use of several strategies across the child's important social environs, such as home, school, and neighborhood. The essential factor is to match the treatments to the specific, identified needs of the student and monitor the additive effects of these treatments across both intervention and nonintervention settings.

PROGRAMMING FOR TRANSFER AND MAINTENANCE

Behavioral changes and improvements that occur in special education or clinical settings do not, as a matter of course, generalize to natural settings. In order for these changes to occur in a student's general-education classroom, home, or neighborhood, generalization strategies to facilitate transfer of achieved gains must be planned and implemented in these settings. For example, in order for a student to generalize recently acquired social skills, he or she may need to be instructed in and practice these skills with peers in a general education classroom or playground situation.

COMMITMENT TO SUSTAINED INTERVENTION

Given the complex needs of children and adolescents with EBD, it is unrealistic to think their problems are amenable to short-term solutions. This is particularly true for adolescent students with EBD. There are no "quick fix" cures available for this population. Strategies that are successful require implementation over a significant period of time, perhaps even several years, and also provide for subsequent periodic "booster sessions."

ENLIST PARENT INVOLVEMENT AND SUPPORT

The origins of many of the behavior problems of students with EBD are associated with the home and family situation. Because of this relationship, most professionals agree that students with EBD have the best chance to be successfully educated when the school and home work together (Walker, Colvin, & Ramsey, 1995). Therefore, whenever possible, parents of students with EBD need to be involved in the planning and delivery of school-based educational services. Parent involvement may include having parents help create the goals and objectives of educational services, monitor and assess the child's behavior, implement interventions in the home setting, and enhance home-school communication.

First Step

THEORY OF BEHAVIOR CHANGE

The First Step intervention program was developed through a 4-year federal grant that provided the necessary resources to cover its development and short-term follow-up evaluation. The program's development involved a collaborative partnership between the Eugene School District 4J, the Oregon Social Learning Center, the Oregon Research Institute, and the Institute on Violence and Destructive Behavior at the University of Oregon. Investigators and professionals from each of these organizations made important contributions to the First Step program's development. This collaboration also represents an important partnership between the fields of psychology and education and joint funding and support by the U.S. Office of Special Education Programs and the National Institute of Mental Health.

The three modules of the First Step program are based upon a foundation of over 25 years of research in the areas of screening and early detection, school intervention, and parent training contributed by investigators in the fields of psychology and education (Walker, Colvin, & Ramsey, 1995). Four years of research and development were initially invested in the program's development, including its initial construction, testing, refinement, and evaluation. Two cohorts of at-risk kindergartners were identified respectively in the school years 1993/94 and 1994/95 for participation in the program. Cohort 1 consisted of 24 kindergartners and cohort 2 had 22 participants. Target students in these cohorts have recently completed their fifth and fourth grades in school. They have been followed up through the fourth and third grades respectively following their exposure to the First Step program in their kindergarten year.

The First Step program is based upon a social learning model of the development, prevention, and treatment of antisocial behavior patterns as described by Patterson and his colleagues (see Patterson, Reid, & Dishion, 1992). They outlined an eight-step, sequential process that governs the development of this unfortunate behavior pattern, which usually originates in the family context and results in a host of negative developmental outcomes by adolescence and beyond. This sequential model has been verified though multiple longitudinal studies conducted by Patterson and his colleagues and replicated by others (Loeber & Farrington, 1998). The model is illustrated in Figure 9.1.

The eight-step process functions as follows. First, the family experiences severe stressors caused by exposure to a host of risk factors such as poverty, unemployment, family upheaval, neglect, abuse, substance use, and so forth. These stressors have the effect of disrupting normal parenting practices, which in turn prompts high rates of negative interactions among family members.

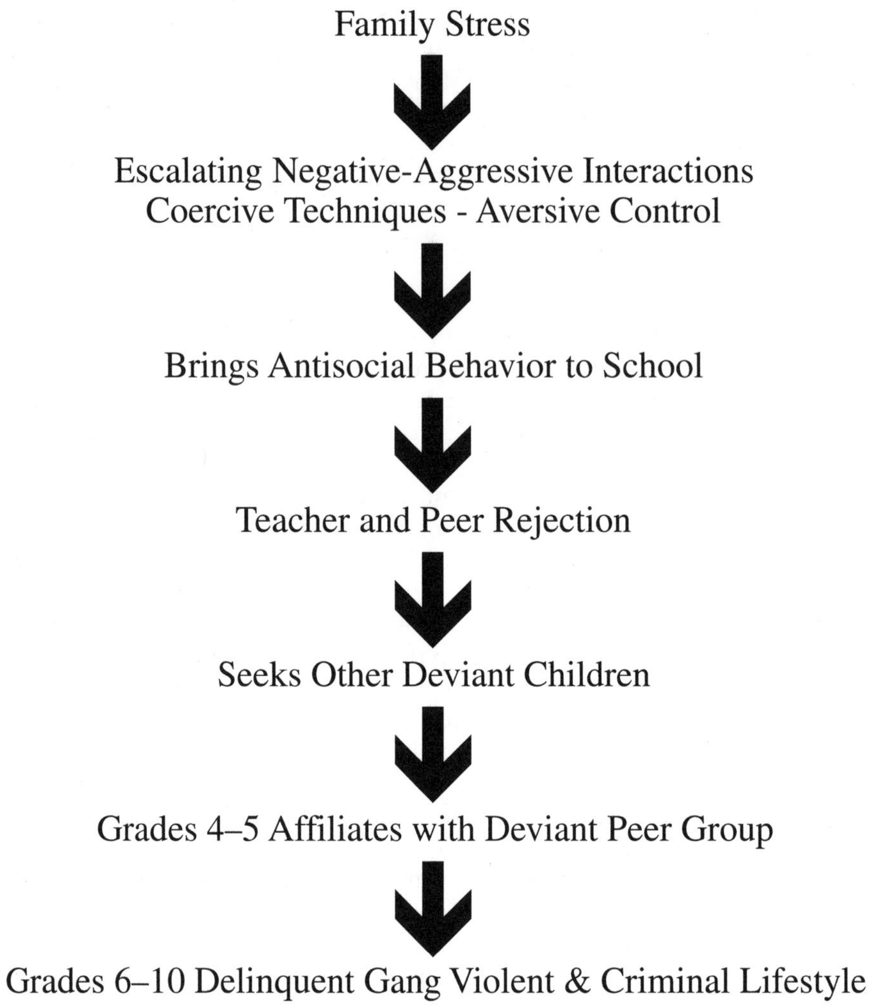

Family Stress

Escalating Negative-Aggressive Interactions
Coercive Techniques - Aversive Control

Brings Antisocial Behavior to School

Teacher and Peer Rejection

Seeks Other Deviant Children

Grades 4–5 Affiliates with Deviant Peer Group

Grades 6–10 Delinquent Gang Violent & Criminal Lifestyle

Figure 9.1   Casual events for antisocial behavior. *Source:* Patterson, Reid, & Dishion (1992)

These negative interactions can eventually develop into coercive processes and aversive control strategies used both to control others' behavior and to escape or avoid certain situations/tasks (Patterson, Reid, & Dishion, 1992). This set of social contingencies provides a powerful context for inadvertently teaching antisocial behavior patterns that are highly resistant to change.

At-risk children who bring this behavior pattern to school are very likely to experience peer and teacher rejection, to affiliate with deviant peers, to fail and drop out of school, and to adopt a delinquent, sometimes violent lifestyle in adolescence. The First Step program has the overall goal of diverting children from this path or trajectory at the point of school entry by (1) teaching school success and friendship-making skills; (2) discouraging aggressive, destructive, and challenging forms of behavior and replacing them with a positive, adaptive behavior pattern; and (3) changing the ways in which parents and teachers react to and interact with the at-risk child. Children with whom the First Step program is successful have a far better chance to get off this destructive path and to have productive, rewarding school careers. It is not possible at this point to claim that the First Step program has any impact on delinquency in adolescence, as the necessary long-term studies have not been conducted as yet.

PARAMETERS OF THE INTERVENTION
AND THEORY OF BEHAVIOR CHANGE

Essential features of the First Step to Success program are described below (Walker, 1998; Walker, Stiller, & Golly, 1998). First Step was designed as an early intervention for kindergartners who are showing the early signs of antisocial behavior. If not addressed early on in its initial stages, this pattern of behavior can sometimes develop into conduct disorder (Kazdin, 1987). First Step is designed to achieve secondary prevention goals for at-risk children at the point of school entry by focusing on developing their school readiness and teaching them social and academic skills in both home and school contexts.

The First Step to Success program was developed through a 4-year federal grant to the second author from the U.S. Office of Special Education Programs (see Walker et al., 1998b; Walker et al., 1997). The important features of the First Step intervention program are as follows.

- First Step to Success requires approximately 3 months for implementation from start to finish and is applied within regular kindergarten and home settings. During this period, only small amounts of teacher and parent time are required daily in the implementation process. (The per case cost of each program application ranges from approximately $500 to $800, including materials and consultant time invested.)
- The program is implemented by a professional who can serve kindergarten teachers in a consultative capacity (i.e., early interventionist, early childhood educator, behavior specialist, school psychologist, counselor, social worker, and others). This person will invest approximately 50–60 hours total per child and family during the program's implementation. Teachers can operate the program as part of their regular teaching and management duties.
- First Step to Success consists of three interrelated modules: (1) proactive, universal screening of all kindergartners to identify those at risk; (2) a school intervention component involving teachers, peers, and parents that teaches the child an adaptive behavior pattern for school; and (3) a parent-training component that assists parents in teaching their child skills that contribute to school success (e.g., cooperation, accepting limits, self-esteem, sharing in school, and so forth).

- During its development and testing, the First Step to Success intervention program was applied successfully to 46 kindergartners and their families divided into two cohorts of 24 and 22 kindergartners respectively. The program has also been replicated, to date, in numerous intervention sites in Oregon, in 10 other states, and in three Canadian provinces.
- The First Step to Success intervention produces very powerful behavior changes in the following areas, as indicated by teacher ratings and direct observations: adaptive behavior, aggressive behavior, maladaptive behavior, and the amount of time spent appropriately engaged in teacher-assigned tasks.
- Follow-up studies show that First Step to Success intervention effects persist well beyond the end of the intervention period and into subsequent school years.
- First Step to Success participants (children, parents, peers, and teachers) consistently report high levels of consumer satisfaction with the program (Walker, Stiller, & Golly, 1998).

The 1999 session of the Oregon legislature approved approximately $500,000 for the Institute on Violence and Destructive Behavior at the University of Oregon to begin the process of making First Step available statewide to all schools and districts that wish to adopt it. An independent evaluation of the program and its effects, relative to untreated control students, will be conducted as part of this effort.

PROGRAM MODULES

A description of the program's three modules is provided in this section. The early-detection module of the program uses a universal screening procedure so that every child in the class has an equal chance to be evaluated and identified for participation in the intervention. There are four options built into the screening module. The screening options range from simple teacher nominations to use of a three-stage multiple gating process that combines teacher nominations and rank ordering, teacher ratings, and direct observations in structured and unstructured school settings (Walker, Severson, & Feil, 1995). In screening stage one, teachers nominate 5 students each on externalizing and internalizing behavioral dimensions. The students are then rank-ordered on how well their characteristic behavior patterns correspond with descriptions and examples of these behavioral dimensions. High-ranked students are then rated on a series of brief checklists and teacher rating scales in screening stage two. These instruments measure aggression, social interaction(s) with peers, adaptive classroom behavior, maladaptive classroom behavior, and a critical events index that defines high-intensity behavioral occurrences (e.g., physically attacking an adult, inappropriate sexual behavior, extreme cruelty, and so forth). Those students who exceed normative cutoff points on these measures are then observed in screening stage three using *in vivo* coding procedures that assess academic engagement and free-play social interactions in terms of their duration and quality (+ or −). At-risk children who emerge through this screening process generally have severe behavioral adjustment problems and are nearly always found to be in need of early intervention through a program such as First Step.

The school intervention component of First Step consists of an adapted version of the *CLASS* (Contingencies for Learning Academic and Social Skills) Program for Acting Out Children (Hops & Walker, 1988). The school intervention begins with two 20-minute periods daily and is gradually extended to the whole school day, or half-day as the case may be, over a 2- to 3-month period. The first phase of the school intervention lasts for 5 days and is operated by the program consultant. During the two daily 20-minute periods of this phase, the consultant sits close to the target child and monitors his or her behavior closely using a green/red card that serves three purposes: (1) to signal the child as to the appropriateness or inappropriateness of his or her behavior, (2) to record points, and (3) also to record praise and bonus points. If most of the available points are awarded on the green side of the card, the child earns a brief group activity or privilege (e.g., Simon Says, 7-Up game) for him- or herself and the rest of the class at the end of the period. If the activity or privilege is earned for both periods, the child can also earn a home privilege prearranged with parents. By the end of the 5-day consultant phase, the child can earn one point for each 5-minute block of the daily period(s). The teacher phase of the program lasts for 15 days and begins on program day 6 when the classroom teacher assumes control of the program. The teacher operates the green/red card and awards praise and points during regular teaching and classroom management routines. The program consultant serves the teacher in a support role during this phase. The final phase of the program—maintenance—begins on program day 21 and goes to program day 30. During this phase, the child's improved behavior is maintained for the full day and supported primarily by teacher, consultant, and parental praise.

The home intervention module of First Step, called "homeBase," begins on program day 10 of the school intervention and lasts for 6 weeks. In this module, the child's parents are enlisted as partners with the teacher and program consultant in helping the child get off to the best possible start in school. Parents are taught how to help their child master six key skills that are essential to school success: (1) communication and sharing at school, (2) cooperation, (3) limit-setting, (4) problem-solving, (5) friendship-making, and (6) developing confidence. The First Step program consultant is responsible for implementing this component; as a rule, one skill is taught to the parents each week during an hourlong session, which is held in the parents' home. Parents are given a handbook of essential materials and a box of games and activities for use in practicing the skills with their child. The homeBase goals for parents, children, and teachers are as follows.

- *Parents:* Learn the skill, provide daily practice, reward daily practice;
- *Child:* Learn the skill, practice the skill;
- *Teachers:* Know the skill, praise use of the skill, give feedback to parents.

The ultimate goal of homeBase is to get educators and parents/caregivers to work collaboratively in helping vulnerable young children experience early school success. Having the target child, parents, and teacher(s) all working on and communicating about the same school success skills is a powerful tool for strengthening the child's school performance. In addition, participation in the First Step program seems to indirectly teach parents some essential parenting skills, such as daily debriefing, monitoring, how to provide feedback consistently, and how to praise the child's school achievements systematically. Home-Base has proven to be a very popular component of the First Step program with the professionals and parents/caregivers who have participated in it.

ROLE OF THE FAMILY AND CULTURAL COMPETENCE

Families have a very important role to play in the First Step intervention program. First, they must consent to have their child participate after having the program (along with their role in its implementation) explained to them. In the first two weeks of the intervention, they are asked to support their child's First Step participation, to monitor and praise their child's school performance at home, and to communicate frequently with the program consultant and the child's teacher(s), by phone and in person, if needed. After the first two weeks, the child's parents are approached regarding their participation in the home-Base part of the First Step program. Rather than blaming them for their child's school problems, parents are asked if they would like to work with the consultant and teacher in helping their child get off to a good start in school. If they agree to do so, their role in the homeBase part of the program is explained to them, along with its demands on their time and effort. As a general rule, a majority of parents agree to participate in homeBase.

Most parents prefer to receive the weekly one-hour training session in their home. The First Step program contains well-sequenced and user-friendly parent-training and homeBase implementation materials. It also contains a set of cards describing activities that are easy to do at home and can be used to help the child practice the newly learned homeBase skills.

The First Step program attempts to respect parents as important contributors to its successful implementation and to treat them as coequal partners with the program consultant and teacher. Parents' voices are heard, listened to, and acted upon by all that are associated with the First Step implementation process. To date, First Step has been applied successfully by a diverse array of parents representing differing economic, social, and ethnic backgrounds. The First Step program has recently been translated into Spanish for effective use with Latino children and families for whom English is not the first language. However, to date, the program has not been formally or systematically tested with underrepresented groups of children and their families.

IMPLEMENTING PROGRAM FIDELITY

A number of processes and measures have been incorporated into the First Step program to address fidelity issues. First, the program consultant must be a knowledgeable professional (school counselor, psychologist, early interventionist, behavioral specialist, etc.) who is skilled in working with teachers in a consultative, supportive capacity and who can invest the necessary time and effort to set the program up, operate it initially, and monitor and supervise its implementation over time. First Step consultants are carefully trained to correctly implement the program and to monitor, supervise, and manage it after the teacher assumes control, during an intensive two-day in-service training session. Participating teachers are enrolled in the first half of this training regimen, where the focus is on daily management of the intervention and the respective roles of the teacher and consultant. Each training participant also receives a First Step training guide, which is used as a study guide during the training and as a resource for implementation following training. This training guide is available through the publisher, Sopris West, Inc. (see Golly, Stiller, & Walker, 1997).

The program consultant also has the responsibility for carefully monitoring the First Step program's implementation and the child's, teacher's, and parents' responses to it. As part of this process, the consultant keeps a log that records the following: (1) the total number of red and green points earned daily, (2) the number of activity time-outs used, (3) the consultant and teacher's praise rates, (4) the number and types of school-home privileges earned, and (5) the number of times the target child has to repeat a program day. These records provide an ongoing measure of how well the child is progressing through the program as well as whether participating teachers and parents are adhering to their assigned roles in the program.

Evidence Base

The First Step to Success program has been evaluated using traditional group designs with wait-list controls and by single-subject methodology, in which single cases are studied intensively. The development and initial evaluation of the program and its effects have been described by Walker and colleagues (1998b). The program has since been replicated in a study reported by Golly, Stiller, and Walker (1998). Finally, a study involving the single-case analysis and evaluation of 4 kindergartners using multiple baseline designs is reported in Golly, Sprague, Walker, Beard, and Gorham (2000).

In the above studies, a combination of teacher ratings and direct observations has been used to evaluate effects of the First Step intervention. Teacher rating measures include the following: (1) the Adaptive and Maladaptive Rating Scales from the Early Screening Procedure developed by Walker, Severson and Feil (1995); and (2) the Aggression and Withdrawn subscales of the Teacher Rating Form of the Child Behavior Checklist (Achenbach, 1991a). Direct observational measures of Academic Engaged Time, from the Systematic Screening for Behavior Disorders Screening Procedure (Walker & Severson, 1990) were used to record the target participants' classroom behavior in pre- and postintervention and follow-up assessments. Normative data and scores are available for each of these measures in national standardization samples that allow normative comparisons across school years.

Evaluations of the First Step program indicate that it produces relatively powerful effects. Across the five measures used to evaluate pre- and postintervention effects in a randomized control trial conducted by Walker and colleagues (1998b), the average effect size was .86 across four teacher ratings and one direct observational measure. Table 9.2 presents raw scores for teacher ratings and direct observation measures on the following dimensions: (1) pre and post assessments for cohort 1 and 2 participants; (2) normative averages for the five evaluation measures used in these assessments, derived from national standardization data; and (3) 4-year follow-up results for cohort-1 participants and 3-year follow-up results for cohort-2 participants.

The data and results in Table 9.2 indicate that exposure to the First Step program produced substantial initial treatment gains on four of the five evaluation measures from pre- to postintervention time points (approximately 3 months). Further, these gains tended to persist during follow-up assessments on these same measures across subsequent school years. It should be noted that the Withdrawn Subscale of the Child Behavior Checklist Teacher Rating Form was not sensitive to the intervention; this is not unexpected, given the focus of the program on reducing antisocial forms of behavior and replacing them with adaptive behavior. A further limitation is the absence of a control group during follow-up assessments, since the Walker and colleagues (1998b) study design involved a wait-list control group that also received the First Step intervention subsequent to the exposure of cohort 1. In spite of these limitations, these results are promising and indicate the First Step program is worthy of further study involving longitudinal study designs in which control groups are used and procedures are implemented to reduce participant attrition across years.

Conclusions

As the burgeoning population of at-risk children and youth put increasing pressures on our school systems for effective management and accommodation, calls are being made for the expansion of special education programs and services to larger and larger numbers of students who are failing in school and experiencing mental health problems. However, others view the special education option for addressing this population's needs with skepticism due to legal-judicial, fiscal, philosophical, and programmatic concerns. Special education is costly in terms of its financial demands, legal mandates, and procedural regulations and processes. Many school administrators are wary of the potential costs of special education eligibility and concerned about its protections as guaranteed to students and family members under the auspices of IDEA. Thus, special education is not broadly perceived by regular educators as a viable response to the increasing numbers of children entering the schoolhouse door who are not ready for school and may also exhibit disruptive and/or aggressive behavior problems. The need has never been greater for cost-effective short-term interventions that can produce powerful and sustained effects on at-risk children's challenging behavior. Special education eligibility cannot and should not be a precondition for accessing such best practices solutions to this growing problem.

In the past 25 years, millions of dollars have been invested in programs for early childhood interventions by a range of federal and state educational agencies. In spite of this considerable investment, there are almost no preschool programs in the early childhood education field currently available that are *specifically* designed to address the challenging forms of child behavior that are often associated with negative long-term developmental outcomes, including school failure, dropout, and delinquency. This dearth is even more apparent at the kindergarten and first-grade levels, where the stage is set for a child's school career and future development.

However, there are some very promising mental health interventions that can be used to address this need. Recent reviews by Brestan and Eyberg (1998); Greenberg, Domitrovich, and Bumbarger (1999); and Kashani, Jones, Bumby, and Thomas (1999) have identified and profiled effective early intervention programs that address the risk factors and behavioral precursors of conduct disorder, school failure, and later delinquency. These promising interventions should be incorporated into the practice of special education and early childhood education.

The First Step to Success program was developed to address the problems experienced by at-risk children at the point of school entry. School entry is the point at which there is the best chance to get at-risk children off of a destructive path through collaborative school and family partnerships that focus on building school success. Zigler, Taussig, and Black (1992) have argued persuasively that early intervention approaches involving school and family collaborations are one of the best options we have for preventing future delinquency. Currently, there are literally thousands of at-risk children who are on a clear path or trajectory that too often leads to a host of later problems, beginning with rejection by peers and teachers and sometimes by parents and caregivers. If implemented with integrity, the First Step to Success program has the potential to improve the chances of school success for these children.

Table 9.2 Raw Score Intervention and Follow-up Results: Means and Standard Deviations by Cohort (1993/94 and 1994/95)

Measures Teacher Ratings	Normal Range	Kindergarten		1st Grade (N = 21)	2nd Grade (N = 18)	3rd Grade (N = 17)	4th Grade (N = 10)
		Pre- (N = 24)	Post- (N = 23)				
				Evaluation Time Points' Mean (SD) 1993/94 Cohort 1			
ESP Adaptive[1]	(35.9)	21.96 (4.57)	28.83 (6.25)	25.43 (4.70)	26.72 (5.66)	30.60 (5.60)	29.43 (8.36)
ESP Maladaptive[2]	(13.5)	32.58 (7.61)	22.26 (8.86)	23.48 (6.50)	23.83 (9.37)	19.40 (5.58)	18.14 (12.50)
CBC Aggression[3]	(7.0)	20.33 (11.10)	11.04 (8.31)	14.19 (10.06)	14.55 (11.79)	8.60 (7.22)	7.00 (11.25)
CBC Withdrawn[4]	(0–1)	7.04 (4.87)	4.50 (4.41)	4.62 (4.05)	6.11 (4.08)	4.90 (3.07)	5.29 (4.89)
AET Observations[5]	(75.19%)	(N = 24) 62.54% (16.35)	(N = 24) 79.83% (22.16)	(N = 20) 90.65% (10.62)	(N = 17) 83.67% (14.02)	(N = 17) 78.68% (12.90)	(N = 10) 90. 40% (5.52)

(continued)

Table 9.2 Raw Score Intervention and Follow-up Results: Means and Standard Deviations by Cohort (1993/94 and 1994/95) (*Continued*)

		1994/95 Cohort 2					
		Kindergarten					
Teacher Ratings	Normal Range	Pre- (N = 22)	Post- (N = 22)	1st Grade (N = 15)	2nd Grade (N = 12)	3rd Grade (N = 8)	4th Grade
ESP Adaptive[1]	(35.9)	21.73 (5.26)	26.68 (4.86)	26.47 (5.78)	28.33 (3.05)	29.63 (9.12)	—
ESP Maladaptive[2]	(13.5)	31.45 (6.97)	26.27 (8.04)	23.67 (6.95)	21.33 (7.50)	23.00 (10.11)	—
CBC Aggression[3]	(7.0)	24.82 (10.41)	16.77 (10.56)	17.27 (9.17)	16.00 (7.00)	16.88 (12.33)	—
CBC Withdrawn[4]	(0–1)	4.00 (3.49)	2.64 (3.40)	1.20 (1.90)	0.33 (.58)	2.88 (4.73)	—
AET Observations[5]	(75.19%)	(N = 22) 59.64% (14.41)	(N = 22) 90.77% (6.71)	(N = 13) 81.85% (10.31)	(N = 12) 89.85% (9.63)	(N = 8) 75.00% (20.25)	—
Evaluation Time Points' Mean (SD)							
		(6.71)	(10.31)	(9.63)	(20.25)		

[1]ESP Adaptive: Early Screening Project, Adaptive Behavior Rating Scale
[2]ESP Maladaptive: Early Screening Project, Maladaptive Behavior Rating Scale
[3]CBC Aggression: Child Behavior Checklist, Aggressive Subscale
[4]CBC Withdrawn: Child Behavior Checklist, Withdrawn Subscale
[5]AET Observations: Academic Engaged Time

10

Integrated Cognitive-Behavior Therapy
for Traumatic Stress Symptoms
and Substance Abuse

JOHN A. FAIRBANK

SHARON R. BOOTH

JOHN F. CURRY

Many adolescents with substance-use disorder (SUD) have a history of trauma and symptoms of posttraumatic stress disorder (PTSD; Clark & Neighbors, 1996; Deykin & Buka, 1997). The negative effects of PTSD among individuals with SUD are substantial in terms of poorer functioning and response to substance-abuse treatment, shorter times to relapse, and greater use of treatment services (Brown & Ouimette, 1999; Ouimette, Moos, & Finney, 2000; Triffleman, Carroll, & Kellogg, 1999). Kilpatrick and colleagues (2000) hypothesize that substance use represents an effective but maladaptive strategy to cope with the negative emotional, cognitive, physiological, and social/interpersonal reactions produced by traumatic experiences. To the extent that substance abuse among some adolescents is a response to negative PTSD symptoms produced by traumatic events, issues related to PTSD symptoms should be addressed in interventions for substance abuse.

Integrated cognitive-behavior therapy (CBT) for co-occurring PTSD and SUD in adolescents is a phased approach to intervention in which the same clinician or team of clinicians provides treatment for both disorders at the same time (see Mueser, Drake, & Noordsy, 1998, model for adults with severe co-occurring psychiatric and substance abuse disorders). Integrated CBT for PTSD and SUD may include any of the following components: education about PTSD and substance abuse and their interactive effects; coping skills training for both SUD and PTSD; stress innoculation training (SIT) and relapse prevention; and exposure therapy for PTSD (Abueg & Fairbank, 1992; Najavits, Weiss, Shaw, & Muenz, 1998; Triffleman, Carroll, & Kellogg, 1999). Although integrated CBT for adolescents with co-occurring SUD and PTSD has yet to be evaluated empirically, findings from a controlled trial of integrated CBT for adolescents diagnosed with SUD and a heterogeneous array of psychiatric disorders are promising (Kaminer, Burleson, Blitz, Sussman, & Rounsaville, 1998).

Psychosocial Conceptual Models of the Etiology of PTSD and the Role of Substance Abuse

LEARNING THEORY: CLASSICAL AND INSTRUMENTAL CONDITIONING

Early behavioral conceptual models of stress-related illnesses such as PTSD were largely based on the two-factor learning theory of psychopathology originally proposed by Mowrer (Keane, Zimering, & Caddell, 1985). As applied to PTSD, two-factor conditioning models posit that fear and other aversive emotions are learned through association via mechanisms of classical conditioning (Fairbank & Nicholson, 1987). Such fear conditioning is the first factor in the acquisition of aversive emotions characteristic of PTSD. The second factor involves principles of instrumental conditioning in that persons with PTSD will learn to escape from and to avoid cues that stimulate aversive emotions. Through the process of fear conditioning, neutral cues associated with a traumatic (or otherwise aversive) events acquire the capacity subsequently to evoke a conditioned emotional (fearful) response in the absence of the aversive stimulus. First described by Pavlov and associates, this psychological mechanism is posited to preserve information about exposure to previous threats to promote future survival.

INFORMATION PROCESSING THEORY

More recent conceptual models have emphasized the role of cognitive factors in the development and maintenance of PTSD symptoms (Brewin, Dalgleish, & Joseph, 1996; Chemtob, Roitblatt, Hamada, Carlson, & Twentyman, 1988; Foa, Steketee, & Rothbaum, 1989; Lang, 1977a; Resick & Schnicke, 1993). Information-processing theory has been proposed as an explanation of the ways in which information associated with traumatic experiences is encoded and recalled in memory (Foa & Kozak, 1986; Foa, Rothbaum, & Molnar, 1995; Foa, Steketee, & Rothbaum, 1989). Foa and colleagues (1989), for example, have offered a model based upon the concept of a fear structure, which they describe as a network in memory that includes three types of information: (1) information about the feared stimulus situation; (2) information about verbal, physiological, and overt behavioral responses; and (3) interpretive information about the meaning of the stimulus and the response elements of the structure (Foa et al., 1989, p. 166). Foa and colleagues propose that during periods of extreme distress, information processing is interrupted, and consequently, traumatic memories are fragmented and disorganized. Nevertheless, persons with PTSD are assumed to have an attentional bias toward threat cues, which is hypothesized to account for the reexperiencing phenomenon of PTSD. Foa and colleagues (1995) have proposed that treatment should be based upon activation and correction of information in fear structures, accomplished through prolonged exposure to traumatic stimuli and cognitive restructuring, respectively.

According to Foa and colleagues, exposure within and across treatment sessions provides an opportunity to integrate traumatic memories with the individual's existing conceptualization of safety versus dangerousness. Foa and colleagues further hypothesize that this exposure can result in the organization of trauma memory. The information-processing model has yielded a productive theoretically grounded approach to research on the efficacy of CBT for PTSD.

SOCIAL-COGNITIVE MODELS

A number of authors have proposed social-cognitive models that emphasize that traumatic experiences challenge people's preexisting core beliefs and assumptions about themselves and others, fostering negative emotions and maladaptive belief structures that produce and maintain the array of signs, symptoms, and disorders characteristic of stress-related illnesses. Although empirical studies of the social-cognitive model are still rare, some supporting research evidence has been reported. Dalgleish (1993) examined maladaptive belief structures in survivors of a disaster involving the sinking of a ferry and found that survivors with PTSD were more likely to believe that a range of negative events would occur in the future than survivors without a traumatic stress disorder. Using a semistructured interview procedure, Newman, Riggs, and Roth (1997) examined an array of cognitive (e.g., ideas and expectations that the world is malevolent) and emotional (e.g., emotional self-reproach) issues in individuals with and without traumatic stress disorders. These investigators found that PTSD symptom severity and the level of interpersonal violence associated with the traumatic events was associated with deficits in the processing of cognitive and emotional material.

SOCIAL SUPPORT MODELS

A vast body of research on acute and chronic stress has demonstrated that social support influences the development of stress-related illnesses and affects physical and mental health (e.g., Cohen & Wills, 1985; Holahan & Moos, 1981; Norris & Murrell, 1990). Research on the readjustment of trauma survivors has also documented the importance of the quality and quantity of social support to well-being and recovery from stressful life events.

Research also indicates that posttrauma outcomes may not be solely the product of a single precipitating event (e.g., Green, 1994; Resnick, Kilpatrick, & Lipovsky, 1991). Rather, what is observed as a stress reaction may be the consequence of a series of highly stressful events, extending back into one's personal history prior to a focal traumatic experience or forward in time to the present. Current findings suggest that adverse life events have a strong negative relationship with social support. Stressful life events appear, therefore, to deplete social resources, which in turn exacerbates stress-related illnesses. Not only may stressful life events deplete social resources by placing an excess demand upon them, but many stressful life events in and of themselves are the loss of important interpersonal support resources (e.g., the loss of a parent through death [King, King, Fairbank, Keane, & Adams, 1998]).

COPING THEORY OF SUBSTANCE USE

Several investigators have suggested that traumatic experiences play an important role in substance abuse for some adolescents and adults (Clark & Neighbors, 1996; Giaconia et al., 2000; Kilpatrick et al., 2000). Hypothetically, substance use represents a strategy to cope with the negative emotional, cognitive, physiological, and social/interpersonal reactions produced by the traumatic experience (Abueg & Fairbank, 1992; Kilpatrick et al., 2000; Penk, Peck, Robinowitz, Bell, & Little, 1988). Brinson and Treanor (1988), for example, suggest that individuals with PTSD abuse alcohol to dampen adverse emotional reactivity, cope with sleep disturbance, and escape intrusive PTSD reexperiencing phenomena. Classical and instrumental conditioning, information-processing, social-cognitive, and social support models have all been influential in the development of such conceptualizations.

The coping theory of substance use presupposes that emotional, cognitive, and physiological distress produced by traumatic experiences elicits behaviors, such as substance use, aimed at reducing such distress (Kilpatrick et al., 1997). Specifically, the use or abuse of substances following a traumatic event may be an effective, albeit maladaptive, strategy to diminish the negative symptoms of PTSD. Support for this model is provided by studies that show that (1) exposure to interpersonal violence and other trauma enhances risk for problem substance use in youth (Kilpatrick et al., 2000), (2) traumatized youth begin using substances at an earlier age than nontraumatized youth (Kilpatrick et al., 2000), (3) onset of PTSD symptoms predates or co-occurs with the onset of substance use or abuse for some youth (Giaconia et al., 2000), and (4) youth with PTSD are at greater risk for using and abusing marijuana and hard drugs than youth exposed to traumatic violence who do not develop PTSD (Kilpatrick et al., 2000).

The complexity of the human response to traumatic events suggests the need for continued efforts to develop, refine, and test models of stress-related illnesses and substance use, abuse, and dependence that take into account the complexity of person/environment/outcome interactions. Promising work in this direction includes the dual-representation theory proposed by Brewin and colleagues (1996). However, the conceptual models reviewed here are not particularly rigorous with respect to accounting for human developmental factors that are likely to influence trauma/substance-use outcomes in adolescents. Given a growing body of research that shows that traumatic exposures are age and gender related, conceptual models must be more sensitive to developmental factors to improve their practical relevance to research and treatment delivery efforts (Cole & Putnam, 1992; Costello, Erkanli, Fairbank, & Angold in press; Maercker, Schutzwohl, & Solomon, 1999).

INTEGRATED CBT FOR PTSD AND SUBSTANCE-USE DISORDERS

Theoretical, practical, empirical, and more speculative treatment considerations suggest the need for an integrated approach to interventions for adolescents with co-occurring substance abuse and PTSD. As noted by Mueser and colleagues (1998) in their review of models for integrated mental health and substance-abuse treatment for adults with severe psychiatric disorders, "attempts to treat one disorder before attending to the other are invariably doomed to failure" (p. 131).

Theory of Change

The basic principles of learning theory that have served as reliable guideposts for the development of behavioral and cognitive-behavioral interventions for adolescents with (1) substance-abuse disorders (Hawkins, Catalano, Gillmore, & Wells, 1989; Winters, Latimer, & Stinchfield, 1999), (2) PTSD (Deblinger, Lippman, & Steer, 1996; Goenjian et al., 1997; March, Amaya-Jackson, Murray, & Schulte, 1998a; Perrin, Smith, & Yule, 2000), and (3) comorbid SUD and mixed psychiatric disorders (Kaminer et al., 1998) are relevant for the development of integrated interventions for coexistiing PTSD and SUD. Since we were unable to identify published descriptions of any integrated interventions for adolescents with co-occurring PTSD and SUD, it appears that descriptions of integrated interventions developed for adults are relevant (Najavits, 1999; Najavits et al., 1998; Triffleman et al., 1999). Finally, we reviewed the more extensive CBT efficacy literature for adults who have either PTSD (Friedman, 2000) or SUD (Kadden, 1999; Kadden et al., 1992; Project MATCH Research Group, 1997) to identify components potentially applicable to the concurrent treatment of both disorders in adolescents with co-occurring SUD and PTSD.

In principle, new behaviors for coping with PTSD are acquired in the presence of appropriate reinforcement, are practiced over time, are generalized across settings, and become maintained in those settings (Abueg & Fairbank, 1992). Integrated cognitive-behavioral interventions for PTSD and SUD can be viewed as an ongoing process of differential reinforcement, counterconditioning, and other types of social learning within an interpersonal context, with the aim of producing more adaptive strategies or skills in living.

Target Population: Youth with Co-Occurring PTSD and SUD

The target population is youth with co-occurring PTSD and SUD. The significance of addressing PTSD in adolescents with SUD follows from elevated risk for poorer outcomes (Brown, Stout, & Mueller, 1999; Ouimette, Moos, & Finney, 2000).

SUBSTANCE USE, ABUSE, AND DEPENDENCE AMONG ADOLESCENTS

Substance abuse among adolescents is a major public health problem in the United States. Among adolescents, SUD is associated with multiple negative outcomes, including causes of death (fatal accidents and suicide), drug-related violence, sexual behavior that increases risk of HIV infection, academic failure, and neuropsychological dysfunction (Blum, 1987; Rhodes & Jason, 1990; Hawkins, Catalano, & Miller, 1992; Hernandez & DiClemente, 1992; McCaffrey & Fomeris, 1997; O'Malley, Johnston, & Bachman, 1999). Substance-use disorders are one of the three most common psychiatric disorders in adolescents, have a peak period of onset between ages 14 and 17, and have a high relapse rate (Lewinsohn, Hops, Roberts, Seely, & Andrews, 1993; Giaconia, Reinherz, Silverman, Pakiz, Frost, & Cohen, 1994).

During the period from the late 1970s to the early 1990s, there was improvement in the rates of substance use among American adolescents, but in 1992 rates began to rise (O'Malley, Johnston, & Bachman, 1999). Recent findings from the Monitoring the Future Study (Johnston, O'Malley, & Bachman, 1999) showed that use of any illicit substances by 12th graders in the past year increased from 41.4% in 1998 to 42.1% in 1999, continuing on an upward trend from 27.1% in 1992. A 1995 national household study (Kilpatrick et al., 2000) of adolescents aged 12–17 years found that 7% met DSM-IV criteria (American Psychiatric Association, 1994) for past-year abuse of or dependence on any substance, including alcohol (4%), marijuana (4%), and other illicit drugs (1%). Although most adolescents who use drugs do not go on to abuse them, use alone can raise the risk of motor vehicle accidents, exposure to traumatic events, including interpersonal violence; and high-risk sexual behavior (McFarlane, 1998; Weinberg, Rahdert, Colliver, & Glantz, 1998).

TRAUMATIC EXPERIENCES AND PTSD IN YOUTH

Epidemiologic studies have examined the prevalence of exposure to potentially traumatic events among adolescents, with the majority of studies assessing physical victimization, sexual victimization, or exposure to community violence (Fairbank, Ebert, & Costello, 2000). A telephone survey of a nationally representative sample of 2,000 10- to 16-year-old children found that over 40% reported at least one experience that could be categorized as violent victimization (Boney-McCoy & Finkelhor, 1995). Consistent with these findings, Kilpatrick, Saunders, and Resnick (1998) estimated the lifetime prevalence of exposure to sexual assault, physical assault, and witnessing violence as 8%, 17%, and 39%, respectively, in a national sample of 12- to 17-year-old adolescents. In addition, a number of school surveys have evaluated rates of exposure to community violence. In one sample of over 500 African American elementary and middle school students in Chicago, 30% said they had witnessed a stabbing and 26% reported that they had seen someone being shot (Bell & Jenkins, 1993). Another survey of 2,248 students in the 6th to 8th and 10th grades in an urban public school system found that 41% reported witnessing a stabbing or shooting in the past year (Schwab-Stone et al., 1995).

Another survey of 3,735 high school students in six schools in Ohio and Colorado found relatively high rates of exposure to violence within the past year that varied by size and location of the school (Singer, Anglin, Song, & Lunghofer, 1995b). Among male adolescents, 3% to 22% reported being beaten or mugged in their own neighborhoods, 3% to 33% reported being shot at or shot, and 6% to 16% reported being attacked with a knife. Reported rates of most types of victimization were lower for adolescent females than males; however, more females reported sexual abuse or assault. Indeed, studies of adolescents in Germany (Perkonnig & Wittchen, 1999) and the United States (Costello et al., in press; Kilpatrick et al., 2000) have identified gender as a risk factor for exposure to type of traumatic event. For example, a community survey in Munich found that sexual abuse as a child was reported by young women as compared to young men at a ratio over ten to one (Perkonnig & Wittchen, 1999).

PTSD is an anxiety disorder that occurs in some individuals who have been exposed to traumatic events. Traumatic events are defined in the DSM-IV as experiences that (1) "involve actual or threatened death or serious injury, or a threat to the physical integrity of oneself or others" and (2) produce feelings of "intense fear, helplessness, or horror" (American Psychiatric Association, 1994, pp. 427–428). PTSD is characterized by three kinds of symptoms: reexperiencing symptoms, avoidance and numbing symptoms, and symptoms of increased arousal. The best available estimates suggest a current PTSD prevalence of 5% among adolescents in the general population of the United States (Kilpatrick et al., 2000). As noted above, epidemiologic studies in the United States indicate that 40–50% of adolescents are likely to be exposed to a potentially traumatic victimization event at some time before reaching their 19th birthday (Boney-McCoy & Finkelhor, 1995; Kilpatrick et al., 2000). Taken together, these findings suggest that most youth exposed to a potentially traumatic event will not develop PTSD. Thus, researchers have attempted to identify risk factors that affect the likelihood of developing PTSD following exposure to such events (e.g., Breslau et al., 1998; Bromet, Sonnega, & Kessler, 1998).

PTSD AMONG ADOLESCENTS WITH SUD

Clinical, school, and general-population studies consistently find that the experience of exposure to trauma and PTSD is common among youth with SUD. Deykin and Buka (1997) reported a nearly 30% lifetime prevalence of PTSD in a sample of adolescents in residential treatment for substance abuse. Giaconia and colleagues (2000) found a lifetime PTSD prevalence of nearly 11% among 18-year-old high school students who met diagnostic criteria for SUD, compared to a roughly 4% PTSD prevalence for their counterparts without SUD. A general-population study of risk factors for adolescent substance abuse reported that PTSD was associated with increased risk of marijuana and hard drug abuse or dependence (Kilpatrick et al., 2000). Among youth that met diagnostic criteria for PTSD, 13% met criteria for alcohol abuse/dependence, 16% met criteria for marijuana abuse/dependence, and 6% met criteria for abuse of or dependence on "hard drugs" (e.g., cocaine, opiates, inhalants). For youth without PTSD, 4% met criteria for alcohol abuse/dependence, 3% for marijuana abuse/dependence, and 1% for abuse of hard drugs. Therefore, adolescents with SUD appear two to six times more likely to be at risk for PTSD than their counterparts without SUD in the general population (11–30% PTSD prevalence versus 4–5%, respectively).

At present, we can only conclude that there is a strong association between PTSD and SUD among adolescents. The extent to which PTSD is a determinant of adolescent substance use and vice-verse is as yet unknown. From the perspective of functional behavioral analysis, however, it seems clear that the negative emotional and physiologic reactivity characteristic of PTSD elicits substance use in some individuals. Adolescents' use of substances as a way of coping with PTSD may increase risk for cumulative exposure to other trauma and revictimization, exacerbating both PTSD and SUD.

INTENDED OUTCOMES OF INTEGRATED CBT FOR CO-OCCURRING PTSD AND SUD

Common goals of integrated treatment programs are (1) the reduction of substance use and PTSD symptoms, (2) the development of positive coping skills and improved functioning, and (3) an increase in sense of control through increased understanding of the functional relationship of substance use and PTSD symptoms (Abueg & Fairbank, 1992; Deas & Thomas, 2001; Perrin, Smith, & Yule, 2000). CBT often involves teaching the adolescent to recognize triggers for substance abuse and PTSD symptoms and giving the adolescent effective ways to manage trauma- and PTSD-related antecedents and consequences in order to break their connection with substance use.

CBT Intervention Parameters for Integrated PTSD and SUD Treatment Programs: Basic Principles for Integrated Treatment Programs

In 1998, Mueser, Drake, and Noordsy published an influential paper that described the common components of integrated mental health and substance-abuse treatment programs for adults with severe psychiatric disorders. They outlined a set of general and fundamental principles for developing integrated programs for treatment of dual disorders in adults that appear applicable to the development of programs for adolescents with PTSD and SUD: comprehensiveness, long-term perspective, shared decision-making, and stages of treatment.

Comprehensiveness means that integrated mental health and SUD treatment programs address a broad range of clients' needs. Shared decision-making among the clients, his or her family, and the treating clinician is a core value of integrated treatment that recognizes the critical role that an array of stakeholders play in the lives of adolescents. Collaborative decision-making requires that clients and their families have as much information as possible about SUD and PTSD and treatments to enhance their decision-making. Long-term commitment to the integrated provision of services is required because treatment programs for the dually diagnosed do not usually produce dramatic changes in most clients over brief periods of time. More commonly, clients improve gradually.

The provision of treatment in stages is a basic characteristic of integrated programs (Abueg & Fairbank, 1992; Mueser, Drake, & Noordsy, 1998; Triffleman, Carroll, & Kellogg, 1999). Prochaska and DiClemente (1983) significantly influenced the field of substance-abuse treatment through their conceptualization of the naturalistic stages of change in which substance users attempt to achieve abstinence. They classified the strategies naturalistically employed by substance users into five stages: (1) precommitment, (2) commitment, (3) action, (4) maintenance, and (5) relapse. The first stage, precommitment, involves the contemplation of stopping the substance use and considering the options, risks, and consequences. The second stage, commitment, involves a resolution or formal decision to quit using substances, with strong intentions to engage in behaviors that will reduce the behavior. Some experimentation with ways to decrease or cease substance use occurs at this stage. The third stage, the action stage, is marked by strong efforts at behavior change and abstinence. At this stage, persons with SUD may intuitively adopt many traditional behavior-change techniques, such as stimulus control, thought-stopping, delays to use, and relaxation. At the fourth stage, maintenance, persons often attempt to strengthen their abstinence through stimulus and response generalization. Finally, the relapse stage is characterized by difficulties in maintaining goals at reduction and cessation of substance use.

INTEGRATED CBT INTERVENTIONS FOR PTSD AND SUD

Several clinical demonstration and research efforts have extended the phased treatment approach to programmatic treatment of individuals with co-existing SUD and PTSD (Abueg & Fairbank, 1992; Najavits, 1999; Triffleman, Carroll, & Kellogg, 1999). Abueg and Fairbank (1992) described a clinical demonstration program that used an integrated stage model to treat adult combat veterans with PTSD and SUD. This program consisted of five integrated stages based of the Prochaska and DiClemente model: (1) precommitment, (2) commitment, (3) action, (4) generalization, and (5) relapse. An initial precommitment stage consists of detoxification, initial stabilization, and development of a strong therapeutic alliance. Next, a commitment phase involves motivational interviewing to help the client set reasonable short-term goals, set realistic expectations about therapy in general, and reinforce the client for past successes and cognitions that are consistent with change in therapy (see Maisto, Wolfe, & Jordan, 1999; Miller & Rollnick, 1991). In the commitment stage, education about SUD and PTSD is also provided. The client is encouraged to begin to understand how the disorders have interacted based upon personal experiences highlighted by the therapist.

As learning progresses, the client moves from commitment to the action stages (Stage 3: practice). The substance of the interventions at this stage includes CBT for SUD and PTSD, including coping skills training (e.g., problem-solving training, self-control training) and exposure therapy. Although the client is expected to begin to experience relief from symptoms and other signs of therapeutic progress, monitoring of expectations is important to maintain a realistic view of the need for a long-term commitment to behavior change. The next stage (generalization), reflects the improvement in the skills of the client to anticipate opportunities to use previously learned techniques. The client, family, and therapist collaborate to decide which new challenges to undertake—in the community, school, or work environment, and family. Emphasis is placed on broadening the social support network and deepening existing ties.

The fifth stage, relapse, focuses upon the potential for lapse and relapse, particularly in the area of returning to use of the substance of choice. Intervention through relapse-prevention training includes adaptations that incorporate strategies for coping with trauma cues and PTSD symptoms as high-risk situations for substance use (Marlatt & Gordon, 1985).

Two integrated programs for co-occurring PTSD and SUD have developed manualized CBT interventions: (1) "Substance Dependence Posttraumatic Stress Disorder Therapy" (SDPT; Triffleman, Carroll, & Kellogg, 1999), and (2) "Seeking Safety" (Najavits, 1999; Najavits, Weiss, & Leise, 1996; Najavits et al., 1998). The SDPT program is an outpatient, two-phase, 20-week individual therapy that is an adaptation and integration of the Cognitive-Behavioral Coping Skills Therapy program developed for Project MATCH (Kadden et al., 1992), stress-inoculation training (SIT; Kilpatrick & Veronen , 1983), and *in vivo* exposure (Marks, Lovell, Noshirvani, Livanou, & Thrasher, 1998). SDPT uses a two-phase model: Phase 1 "Trauma-Informed and Addictions Focused Treatment" and Phase 2 "Trauma-Focused, Addictions Informed." The first phase of SDPT emphasizes establishment of abstinence and education on PTSD symptoms and the interactions between PTSD and SUD. The second phase focuses on the treatment of PTSD through SIT and *in vivo* exposure, with continued active monitoring of the client's substance use and abstinence.

"Seeking Safety" (Najavits, 1999; Najavits, Weiss, & Leise, 1996; Najavits et al., 1998) is a manualized 12-week treatment program consisting of 24 sessions (twice weekly) that includes CBT, interpersonal psychotherapy, and case management. The first stage of treatment involves stabilization and safety taught through safe coping skills, setting a safety plan, increasing client's awareness of risk-taking through self-monitoring, and reporting unsafe behaviors at each session. During the first stage of treatment, clients learn about the two disorders and why they frequently co-occur. Later stages of "Seeking Safety" include exposure therapy.

Developing integrated CBT interventions for adolescents with dual PTSD and SUD will require nontrivial modifications to programs such as SDPT and Seeking Safety. For example, integrated interventions for youth with co-occurring PTSD and SUD will likely require (1) extensive involvement of the parent(s), guardian(s), or other family members in treatment-planning and implementation; (2) provision of services in age-specific settings; (3) greater emphasis on peer, family, and school outcomes; and (4) modifications to the content and stagewise timing of psychoeducation, coping skills training, exposure therapy, and other CBT modules to better account for the developmental status of adolescents and associated variability of their PTSD and SUD symptoms picture (Cohen, 1998; Perrin, Smith, & Yule, 2000; van Bilsen & Wilke, 1999).

To begin with the first of these considerations, of the various treatments for adolescent SUD studied to date, family therapy models have the most empirical support (Weinberg et al., 1998). CBT models of family therapy typically include communication training and problem-solving training for adolescents and their parents, but may also include techniques to improve parental monitoring of the adolescent, and contingency contracting. These latter components of treatment can, at least temporarily, increase conflict in families of substance-abusing adolescents. Therapists who deliver such CBT need to be skilled not only in adolescent psychotherapy, but also in family therapy, since they must master the ability to maintain an alliance with the parent(s) and the teenager even when there is considerable conflict between the parties.

It is unlikely, however, that treatment of PTSD would occur optimally within a pure family therapy modality. Components of effective PTSD treatment, such as exposure, or other skills training, are likely to require an individual or group modality as part of the integrated CBT. Therefore, the therapist offering integrated CBT for co-occurring PTSD and SUD is likely to need to integrate treatment modalities as well as treatment targets. Simultaneous family and individual (or group) CBT presents particular challenges, including the need to delineate confidentiality boundaries very carefully, to determine with whom to share urine drug-screen results, and to define clearly how family work is conceptualized and directed toward the goal of overcoming the adolescent's problems.

Regarding treatment settings, adolescent mental health and substance-abuse services have been delivered in clinics, in schools, or in homes. School settings can serve to "normalize" the experience of seeking treatment. Although most school-based services have targeted disruptive behavior disorders or substance-abuse problems, and many have been prevention rather than treatment programs, internalizing disorders such as childhood depression have been addressed in school settings and programs (Stark, Reynolds, & Kaslow, 1987). Family involvement, however, may be enhanced by locating treatment in clinics or in homes, and by meeting in the evenings or on weekends. Thus the therapist delivering integrated CBT for SUD and PTSD will need to determine the location and schedule that make optimal levels of adolescent and parent involvement most likely.

Global assessment of functioning as an index of treatment efficacy with adolescents differs from that with adults. In place of marital satisfaction and occupational functioning, assessment instruments need to address the adolescent's relationships with parents and siblings, the level of overall family conflict and cohesiveness, the quality of peer social support, and involvement in school, athletic, social, and recreational activities.

Modifications to the content of treatment and to its organization or sequence are also required in the treatment of adolescents. The engagement process with adolescents can be more complex and more lengthy than with adults, in part because of developmental conflicts over the meaning of help-seeking and in part because the parents and the adolescent must be engaged. Strategies to enhance engagement have been developed for use with adolescents with SUD (Szapocznik et al., 1988; Szapocznik & Williams, 2000), and these should be considered for inclusion in treatments for dually diagnosed teenagers. Additional diagnoses are likely in adolescents with co-occurring SUD and PTSD, including other anxiety disorders, disruptive behavior disorders, or mood disorders. Although integrated CBT should remain focused on the primary diagnoses of SUD and PTSD, provision needs to be made in the treatment manuals for ancillary treatment of other co-occurring conditions.

Treatment manuals for CBT with adolescents who have co-occurring SUD and psychiatric disorders need to include clear principles pertaining to certain critical issues: the model of parent/family involvement, the limits of confidentiality, and guidelines for selection of ancillary components to address comorbidity. A modular approach to treatment represents one method for organizing integrated CBT. Core and optional skill training sessions are identified, along with guidelines for choosing optional modules. The core modules target those problems most likely to characterize adolescents with SUD and PTSD. Optional modules enable the therapist to address the individualized needs of the particular adolescent and family.

The Evidence Base

To date, CBT is the most rigorously evaluated intervention for PTSD (Friedman, 2000; Rothbaum, Meadows, Resick, & Foy, 2000). CBT has been demonstrated in several recent randomly controlled studies to be effective in treating traumatized children and adolescents (Cohen & Mannarino, 1996; Goenjian et al., 1997; Perrin, Smith, & Yule, 2000). Among CBT modules, exposure is perhaps the most thoroughly evaluated intervention to date (Friedman, 2000). Exposure treatment methods involve confronting fearful stimuli associated with the traumatic memories within the context of a stable therapeutic relationship (Fairbank & Nicholson, 1987). The process of exposure therapy for PTSD involves the client experiencing the arousal associated with the traumatic event through imagery or *in vivo* exposure exercises and intentionally maintaining the arousal until it diminishes.

Exposure therapy has been used to treat PTSD symptoms associated with sexual assault, motor vehicle accidents, and war, and has been applied in the treatment of adults, adolescents, and children who have experienced traumatic events (Berliner & Saunders, 1996). For example, four controlled clinical trials of the efficacy of exposure therapy for war-related PTSD in men have reported generally positive findings (Boudewyns & Hyer, 1990; Cooper & Clum, 1989; Glynn et al., 1999; Keane, Fairbank, Caddell, & Zimering, 1989). Two randomly controlled studies of exposure therapy for female sexual assault survivors also found exposure therapy to be efficacious in reducing PTSD symptoms (Foa, Rothbaum, Riggs, Murdock, 1991; Foa et al., 1999).

Resick and Schnicke (1992) reported improvements in the functioning of rape survivors using a particular form of CBT: cognitive-processing therapy. The authors describe this treatment as including education about PTSD symptoms, exposure, and cognitive therapy. Instead of using *in vivo* imagery presentation, the exposure component involved having participants write and read a detailed account of the rape. Safety, trust, power, esteem, and intimacy were beliefs addressed in cognitive therapy. Treatment was administered in a group format over 12 weekly sessions and compared to a wait list control. Treatment subjects improved significantly from pretreatment to posttreatment on depression and PTSD measures and maintained these gains at the six-month follow-up. The wait list group did not significantly improve.

Another frequently reported behavioral approach to treating PTSD involves teaching clients specific coping skills for reducing or managing PTSD symptoms and/or alternative responses to fear and anxiety. Specific interventions applicable to PTSD and SUD include relaxation training, anger-management training, thought-stopping, assertiveness training, self-dialogue, problem-solving skills training, homework assignments and diary-keeping, and relapse prevention (Friedman, 2000). An example of this approach is Kilpatrick and Veronen's (1983) stress-inoculation training (SIT) procedure for the treatment of rape victims. Directed at the acquisition and application of coping skills, the SIT package includes Jacobsonian relaxation, diaphragmatic breathing, role playing, cognitive modeling, thought-stopping, and guided self-dialogue. Clients are given homework assignments that require them to practice each coping skill.

The effectiveness of SIT has been examined in controlled studies (Foa et al., 1991; Foa et al., 1999; Resnick, Jordan, Girelli, Hutter, & Marhoefer-Dvorak, 1988). In one of these studies, Foa and colleagues (1991) reported findings from a randomized trial of the comparative efficacy of SIT and prolonged exposure (PE) for treating rape-related PTSD. Specifically, these investigators compared the effectiveness of a wait list control group and three interventions: PE, SIT, and supportive counseling (SC). PE consisted of both *in vivo* exposure exercises and imaginal exposure, SIT consisted of a modified version of Kilpatrick and Veronen's (1983) multi-intervention package, and SC consisted of a form of problem-oriented counseling where the counselors played a supportive role in the clients recovery. No instructions for exposure or stress management were included in the SC regimen. Wait list clients were randomly assigned to one of the three treatments following a 5-week period. Treatment consisted of nine twice-weekly individual sessions conducted by a female therapist. Indicators of general psychological distress and PTSD re-experiencing, avoidance, and arousal symptoms were collected at intake, at completion of treatment, and at follow-up (mean = 3.5 months posttreatment). While only SIT produced significantly more improvement than wait list on PTSD symptoms at termination, PE produced superior outcome at follow-up. Clients in the SIT and supportive counseling conditions showed little improvement of symptoms between termination and follow-up, while clients in the PE group, which received *in vivo* and imaginal exposure, continued to improve. The authors interpreted these findings as suggesting that SIT procedures produce immediate relief in PTSD symptoms because they are aimed at the acquisition of anxiety-management skills, but show decreased effectiveness over time as performance compliance erodes, and PE shows less of an effect than SIT in the short term (a function of temporary increased levels of arousal induced by repetitive exposure to traumatic memories) but greater effectiveness over the long term because therapeutic exposure is thought to lead to permanent change in the rape memory, thus producing durable gains.

Future Directions

Application of integrated CBT for adolescents with SUD and PTSD will likely require multimodal intervention models, with commensurate broad-based therapist training. The treatment itself will require developmentally sensitive modifications in treatment setting, assessment domains, treatment organization, and content.

11

An Annotated Review of the Evidence Base for Psychosocial and Psychopharmacological Interventions for Children with Selected Disorders

BARBARA J. BURNS

SCOTT N. COMPTON

HELEN L. EGGER

ELIZABETH M. Z. FARMER

ELIZABETH B. ROBERTSON

Introduction

This chapter presents the evidence base primarily for clinic or school-based interventions focussed on four common childhood disorders or related symptom patterns. These relatively common conditions include attention-deficit/hyperactivity disorder (ADHD), major depressive disorder (MDD), disruptive behavior disorders, and anxiety disorders and related symptoms. They differ from the interventions described in other chapters for youth with severe emotional and behavioral disorders in several ways. These interventions were developed for specific diagnostic conditions, instead of a range of conditions, and thus are targeted to address a more narrow range of clinical presentations. Most of the treatments are short-term and less intensive.

Although youth with severe disorders frequently present with multiple conditions, the interventions described subsequently may be applicable to specific disorders or problems they experience, while not addressing the full range of their clinical needs. Thus, these more discrete interventions can be considered for use in conjunction with other multifocused interventions described elsewhere in this book. Since the primary focus of the book is on more com-

AUTHORS' NOTE: This chapter is in the public domain and may be reproduced without the permission of the authors or the publisher.

prehensive interventions, none of these diagnostic-specific interventions is presented in depth. This chapter is limited to an introduction to the evidence base for conditions common in children ages 6–12. Specific study references are provided and, for the interested reader, textbooks such as Hibbs and Jensen (1996) provide more thorough information about the interventions.

Literature searches were conducted on treatments for each of the above disorders or related symptoms. Eligible studies were identified primarily through searches of the Medline and PsycINFO databases. To be included in this review, a study had to meet the following criteria: (1) it must focus on one of the specified childhood disorders or related symptoms; (2) it must be a controlled study design, either a randomized clinical trial (RCT), a quasi-experimental design, a within-subject crossover design, or a multiple-baseline design; (3) it must target children in the 6–12 age range (studies were included if the mean age of the sample was 6 through 12 years or, in cases where the mean age was not reported, if the majority of the sample [more than 50%] was between the ages of 6 and 12); (4) it must have been published in a referred journal; and (5) it must have been published between 1985 and 2001, although some earlier studies were included if more recent research on a promising intervention had not been conducted. Variations in these inclusion criteria are delineated in the overview section for each disorder. An important caveat is that treatment studies that addressed multiple or unspecified disorders were not included because of the focus on diagnostic-specific interventions. The review focused on outpatient care; therefore, studies of residential or institutional treatment (i.e., treatment foster care, group homes, residential treatment centers, and hospitals) were not included.

Matrices for each disorder (Tables 11.1 to 11.4) include the following topic headings: the study citation, the primary guiding research question, study design and implementation, sample selection and demographic characteristics, primary dependent measures, major findings, and analytic details. Full names for each of the dependent measures listed by acronym are listed in Table 11.5.

In order to compare the efficacy of different types of treatments across studies, a standardized effect size estimate was also calculated. Standardized effect size estimates are reported only for those studies in which the intervention group showed a statistically significant improvement relative to the comparison group. Standardized effect size estimates were calculated using ES, a computer software program developed to calculate effect size estimates from published studies (Shadish, Robinson, & Congxiao, 1999). ES calculates the standardized mean difference statistic, commonly referred to as Cohen's *d* and computed as:

$$d = \frac{Mt - Mc}{SD}$$

where *Mt* is the mean of the treatment group, *Mc* is the mean of the comparison group, and *SD* is the pooled within-group standard deviation. When the means and standard deviations were not reported or when the outcome of interest was dichotomous (e.g., treatment responder vs. nonresponder), other statistics were entered into the ES software in order to compute d (e.g., 2×2 table of cell frequencies, t-tests, results from a one-way ANOVA, etc.).

All effect size estimates are reported such that positive scores indicate that the treatment group improved more than the comparison group. An effect size estimate (sometimes referred to as Cohen's d) has a standard deviation of 1.0 such that, for example, $d = 0.75$ suggests that the treatment group was three-quarters of a standard deviation higher than the comparison group. Effect size estimates can also be translated into percentile rankings to show what proportion of treated children scored better than control subjects. For example, an effect size of 0.80 suggests that the average treated child scored better than 79% of the control group at posttreatment. Cohen (1992) suggests that effect size estimates of 0.20 indicate a small treatment effect (with 58% of the treatment group scoring better than the control group at posttreatment), 0.50 a medium treatment effect (with 69% of the treatment group scoring better than the control group at posttreatment), and 0.80 a large treatment effect (with 79% of the treatment group scoring better than the control group at posttreatment).

A summary of the treatment research for each disorder or related symptoms is presented briefly in subsequent text, and annotated specific studies are presented in the matrices. The evidence base here does not appear to be as strong as what was reported in *Mental Health: A Report of the Surgeon General* (U.S. DHHS, 1999; see also Burns, Hoagwood, & Mrazek, 1999; Weisz & Jensen, 1999). This is understandable because treatment studies of adolescents were included there and not here.

This review shows that within the existing evidence base for each disorder, psychosocial interventions include an array of behavioral approaches. The psychopharmacology evidence base is clearly strongest for ADHD, weaker for other disorders, and virtually nonexistent for anxiety disorders (with the exception of obsessive compulsive disorder). Adjunctive studies examining a combination of psychosocial and psychopharmacological interventions were rare, with the largest and most sophisticated one for ADHD.

This review and bibliography provide a considerable but brief source of information on the status of controlled treatment research for selected disorders. The matrices can be quickly scanned to obtain details about specific studies (e.g., sample size, gender, and racial/ethnic distribution, and outcomes). Therefore, each matrix provides a starting point for determining known benefits of a specified intervention for a given disorder. Moreover, the matrices offer a way to identify successful interventions that have been tested in reasonably large and well-conducted studies.

An additional comment and caveat is related to the question of what constitutes evidence. In preparing this report, careful attention was given to study selection and accurate abstraction. However, it is possible that relevant studies may have been missed. In addition, clarification about what works will require application of standards to the existing evidence base. Standards of evidence such as those developed by the Society of Clinical Psychology (Lonigan, Elbert, & Johnson, 1998) may require, for example, multiple trials of an intervention, findings reported by multiple teams of investigators, and so forth before an intervention can be added to the evidence base. The determination of whether a given intervention meets criteria for "evidence based" was not made, although the information for making such determinations is largely available in the attached tables.

In conclusion, for clinicians, policymakers, and investigators to utilize the information in this report for decision-making about clinical practice, policy, and further research, multiple issues will require attention. In addition to establishing criteria to assess the adequacy of the evidence base for specific disorders, the utility of these studies for specific target populations (e.g., age, gender, racial/ethnic groups) will require consideration. This is particularly an issue where the representation of such groups has not been addressed in the existing literature.

Studies of Childhood Attention-Deficit/Hyperactivity Disorder

A review of the literature was conducted to identify empirical, peer-reviewed studies of psychosocial and pharmacological treatments of children with attention-deficit/hyperactivity disorder (ADHD). Due to the disproportionately large number of treatment outcome studies of childhood ADHD relative to other childhood mental health disorders, a more selective selection process was used to locate studies appropriate for this review. Systematic computerized literature searches were conducted on PsycINFO and Medline databases, with keywords attention deficit disorder (PsycINFO) and attention deficit disorder with hyperactivity (Medline) and then reduced by identification in the electronic databases by one or more of the following study descriptors: treatment outcome study, controlled clinical trial, or randomized clinical trial. This search strategy yielded 132 empirical peer-reviewed studies that focused on the treatment of children with ADHD. Of these 132 studies, 54 studies were excluded for the following reasons: ADHD was a secondary rather than a primary diagnosis ($n = 12$); the study focus was other than treatment outcome (e.g., predictors of treatment adherence, profile of medication side effects, etc.; $n = 24$); and finally the study design did not meet the criteria for inclusion ($n = 18$). The remaining group of 78 studies was reduced further by excluding pharmacological studies in which the sample size was less than 30 children ($n = 47$). The "greater than 30" sample size criterion was not applied to psychosocial or adjunctive treatments due to the limited number of these studies. This process reduced the number to 31 peer-reviewed treatment outcome studies of children with ADHD. These 31 studies are presented and described in Table 11.1.

Pharmacological treatments for ADHD have been well documented over many decades. Psychostimulant medications, including methylphenidate (Ritalin), dextroamphetamine (Dexedrine and Adderal), and pemoline (Cylert), have been found to be quite effective short-term treatments for symptoms of ADHD. Psychostimulant medications have been shown to have their greatest effect on core symptoms (e.g., hyperactivity, impulsivity, and inattention) and associated features (e.g., defiance, aggression, and oppositionality) of ADHD. Small treatment effects have been reported for learning, school achievement,

Table 11.1.1 Psychosocial Studies of Childhood Attention-Deficit/Hyperactivity Disorder

Study Citation(s)	Guiding Research Question	Study Design/Description	Subject Selection Criteria/Demographic Characteristics	Primary Dependent Measures	Outcomes	Analytic Details
Fehlings, Roberts, Humphries, & Dawe, 1991	Does cognitive-behavioral therapy (CBT) improve the home behavior of children with ADHD?	RCT: individual child CBT plus parent CBT (n = 13) vs. child and parent supportive therapy control (n = 13). Setting: outpatient clinic; Format: group; Duration: 6-8 weeks (12 CBT sessions for children, 8 CBT sessions for parents); Therapists: DK; Treatment manual: yes; Treatment integrity: yes; Participants: children and parents; Follow-up intervals: baseline, posttreatment, 5 months posttreatment.	Sample: boys with ADHD who were referred to Child Guidance Clinic by pediatricians or schools; Age: 7-13 Gender: 100% male; Race/Ethnicity: 96% White 4% African American	SCRS, BPC-R, WWA, MFFT, P-HSCS	Significant differences in favor of CBT for parent ratings on Werry Weiss Activity Scale and child self-esteem were found. No between group differences were observed on other outcome measures.	Analysis sample: completer; Attrition: 4%; Effect Size: Werry Weiss Activity Scale = 0.75
Horn, Ialongo, Greenberg, Packard, Smith-Winberry, 1990	Does the combination of behavioral parent training plus cognitive-behavioral self-control therapy with children lead to better outcomes than either treatment alone?	RCT: behavioral parent training (n = 12) vs. child self-control instruction (n = 12) vs. combination (n = 11). Setting: university-based psychology clinic; Format: group; Duration: 12 weeks (weekly sessions); Therapists: graduate students; Treatment manual: yes; Treatment integrity: yes; Participants: parents and children; Follow-up intervals: baseline, posttreatment, 8 months posttreatment.	Sample: youth referred to a university-based clinic for inattentiveness, impulsivity, and over-activity; Age: 7-11; Gender: 81% male; Race/Ethnicity: 86% White 10% African American 4% other	CBCL, CPRS(b) CTRS, TSCRS, CPT, WRAT-R, P-HSCS, PIC-R	Combined treatment produced significantly more responders than either treatment modality alone. The combined group showed significantly more improvement in self-concept scores. All treatment showed significant reductions in classroom behavioral problems, but these gains were not maintained at the 8-month follow-up.	Analysis sample: completer; Attrition:19%; Effect Size: treatment responders (clinically significant decrease on CBCL externalizing) combined vs. individual = 0.74

216

Study	Question	Treatment	Sample	Measures	Results	Analysis
Linden, Habib, & Radojevic, 1996	Is biofeedback effective for improving ADHD symptoms?	RCT: EEG biofeedback training (*n* = 9) vs. wait-list control (*n* = 9). Setting: outpatient clinic; Format: individual, Duration: 6 months (2 sessions per week); Therapists: DK Treatment manual: DK; Treatment integrity: DK; Participants: children; Follow-up intervals: baseline, posttreatment.	Sample: outpatient children with ADHD/ADD; Age: 5–15; Gender: DK; Race/Ethnicity: DK	ICBRS, SNAP, K-BIT IQ	A positive treatment effect was obtained on measures of intellectual functioning, inattention, and hyperactivity. No between group differences were found on measures of aggression/defiance.	Analysis sample: DK; Attrition: DK; Effect Size: DK; Effect Size: IQ = 1.19, inattention = 1.08
Long, Rickert, & Ashcraft, 1993	Do self-help materials for parents (*i.e.,* bibliotherapy) improve outcomes for youth with ADHD?	RCT: bibliotherapy (*n* = 17) vs. treatment as usual (*n* = 15). Setting: outpatient pediatric clinic; Format: self-help materials sent to home; Duration: DK; Therapists: NA; Treatment Manual: NA; Treatment Integrity: DK; Participants: parents; Follow-up intervals: baseline, 2 months.	Sample: Youth with ADHD being seen in an outpatient pediatric clinic. All diagnosed with ADHD and receiving methylphenidate; Age: 6–11; Gender: 81% male; Race/Ethnicity: DK	CPRS (b), ECBI, HSQ, BRPT, KBP	There was significant improvement in parent knowledge of behavioral principles related to child behavior in the group that received bibliotherapy. There was a significant decrease in intensity of behavioral problems at home and school.	Analysis sample: completer; Attrition: treatment group = 24%, control group = 40%; Effect Size: ECBI Intensity = 0.96

(continued)

Table 11.1.1 Psychosocial Studies of Childhood Attention-Deficit/Hyperactivity Disorder (*Continued*)

Study Citation(s)	Guiding Research Question	Study Design/Description	Subject Selection Criteria/Demographic Characteristics	Primary Dependent Measures	Outcomes	Analytic Details
Pfiffner & McBurnett, 1997	What is the effectiveness of social skills training with and without parent-mediated generalization for youth with ADHD?	RCT: social skills training with parent-mediated generalization (SSP-PG) (*n* = 9) vs. child-only social skills training (SST) (*n* = 9) vs. wait-list control (*n* = 9). Setting: university-based pediatric clinic; Format: group; Duration: 8 weeks (weekly sessions); Therapists: DK; Treatment manual: yes; Treatment integrity: yes; Participants: parents and children; Follow-up intervals, 3–4 months posttreatment.	Sample: recruited via newspaper ads and from consecutive referrals to university-based pediatric clinic. Met criteria for ADHD or UADD; Age: 8–10; Gender: 70% boys; Race/Ethnicity: 96% White 4% African American	SSRS, SSS, TSSK, CLAM, SNAP-R, CBCL, TRF, Satisfaction	Relative to wait list controls, both treatment groups showed significant improvement for parent report of social skills and disruptive behavior. No differences were found between two treatment groups. There was minimal generalization of newly acquired social skills to school setting.	Analysis sample: intent to treat; Attrition: DK; Effect Size: parent rated social skills composite = 2.34
Schmidt, Möcks, Lay, Eisert, Fojkar, Fritz-Sigmund, Marcus, & Masaeus, 1997	Is an oligoantigenic diet effective in treating ADHD?	Double-blind, controlled, within-subject crossover design: Oligoantigenic diet vs. methylphenidate (*n* = 49). Setting: inpatient; Format: diet; Duration: 9 days on special diet (total duration = 1 month); Therapists: NA; Treatment manual: no; Treatment integrity: no; Participants: children; Follow-up Intervals: baseline, twice during each diet phase, end of treatment.	Sample: inpatients with diagnosis of ADHD and/or CD; Age: 6–12; Gender: 96% male; Race/Ethnicity: DK	PALT, CPT, CTRS-A, Observations	Oligoantigenic diet showed modest benefit. 24% of children showed improvement in two behavior ratings during oligoantigenic diet relative to control diet. Methylphenidate resulted in more responders (44%) than oligoantigenic diet.	Analysis sample: completer; Attrition: DK; Effect Size: responders (special diet vs. methylphenidate) = −0.50

Table 11.1.2 Psychopharmacological Studies of Childhood Attention-Deficit/Hyperactivity Disorder

Study Citation(s)	Guiding Research Question	Study Design/Description	Subject Selection Criteria/Demographic Characteristics	Primary Dependent Measures	Outcomes	Analytic Details
Biederman, Baldessarini, Wright, Knee, & Harmatz, 1989	What are the short-term effects of the tricyclic antidepressant desipramine (DMI) for treating ADHD?	RCT: double-blind, placebo-controlled; desipramine (n = 31) vs. placebo (n = 31). Setting: outpatient pediatric psychopharmacology clinic; Duration: 6 weeks; Dosing: average daily dose = 4.6 mg/kg; Compliance monitored: yes; Status of blind assessed: DK; Follow-up intervals: baseline, weekly, end of treatment.	Sample: community-referred children with ADHD to outpatient pediatric psychopharmacology clinic; Age: 6–17; Gender: 93% male; Race/Ethnicity: 93% White 7% Other	CTRS-A, CPRS-A, CGI, CPT, PALT, CDI	Significant improvement in symptoms characteristic of ADHD was obtained on clinician, parent, and teacher ratings. There were no between-group differences on cognitive measures.	Analysis sample: completer; Attrition: 15%; Effect Size: Responders = 1.64; Medication response rate: 68%; Placebo response rate: 10%
Buitelaar, van der Gaag, Swaab-Barneveld, & Kuiper, 1995	What are individual response patterns to methylphenidate and what factors predict drug response?	Double-blind, placebo-controlled, within-subject crossover design. Two four-week blocks on methylphenidate, with 2 weeks drug-free between (n = 46). Setting: outpatient; Length: 10 weeks; Dosing: 3 days at 10 mg/day, then fixed-dose of 10 mg b.i.d., tapered at end (10 mg/day for 3 days); Compliance monitored: DK; Status of blind assessed: DK; Follow-up intervals: baseline, end of treatment.	Sample: outpatients with ADHD being seen at a child psychiatric research unit; Age: 6–13; Gender: 89% male; Race/Ethnicity: DK	CPRS(b), CTRS, CGI	Positive treatment effect was obtained on ratings of behavior at school and at home. Predictors of improvement were high IQ, severe inattentiveness, young age, low severity, and low anxiety. There was a positive response to a single dose predicted response at week 4. Treatment normalized behavior at school and home for 17% of the participants.	Analysis sample: completer; Attrition: DK; Effect Size: NA; Medication response rate: 40%; Placebo response rate: DK

(continued)

Table 11.1.2 Psychopharmacological Studies of Childhood Attention-Deficit/Hyperactivity Disorder (*Continued*)

Study Citation(s)	Guiding Research Question	Study Design/Description	Subject Selection Criteria/Demographic Characteristics	Primary Dependent Measures	Outcomes	Analytic Details
Buitelaar, Van der Gaag, Swaab-Barneveld, & Kuiper, 1996	What are the efficacy and side effects of pindolol as an alternative to stimulants in children with ADHD?	Double-blind, placebo-controlled, within-subject cross-over design. 4-week pindolol vs. 4-week methylphenidate vs. 4-week placebo (*n* = 52). Setting: outpatient clinic; Duration: 10 weeks (randomized to pindolol, methylphenidate, or placebo for 4 weeks; 2 weeks drug free; randomized to pindolol or methylphenidate for 4 weeks); Dosing; first 3 days = 10 mg methylphenidate or 20 mg pindolol, fixed 10 mg methylphenidate b.i.d. or 20 mg pindolol b.i.d. ended with 3 day taper as at beginning; Compliance monitored: yes; Status of blind assessed: yes; Follow-up intervals: baseline, week 2 of treatment, week 4 of treatment.	Sample: children referred to outpatient clinic for problems with attention, impulse control, and activity level; Age: 7–13; Gender: 88% male; Race/Ethnicity: DK	CPRS(b), CTRS, CGI	Overall, pindolol was approximately equally effective relative to methylphenidate on measures of hyperactivity and conduct problems at home and hyperactivity problems at school, but less effective on measures of conduct problems at school. Pindolol side effects caused significantly greater distress in children and parents relative to methylphenidate (after the first 32 subjects enrolled, no more children were randomized to pindolol because of concerns about side effects).	Analysis sample: intent to treat; Attrition: DK; Effect Size: Conners TRS (hyperactivity); pindolol vs. methylphenidate = −0.27; CGI = −0.07; Medication response rate: DK; Placebo response rate: DK

Study	Question	Design/Method	Sample	Measures	Results	Analysis
Conners, Casat, Gualtieri, Weller, Reader, Reiss, Weller, Khayrallah, & Ascher, 1996	What is the safety and efficacy of bupropion in treatment of ADHD?	RCT: double-blind, placebo-controlled. 6-week bupropion hydrochloride ($n = 72$) vs. placebo ($n = 37$). Setting: university-based outpatient clinics; Duration: 5 weeks (1 week placebo for all, 4 weeks randomized); Dosing: based on body weight (escalated from 3 mg/kg of body weight from day 1 to day 3 to 6 mg/kg from day 15 to day 28); Compliance monitored: yes; Status of blind assessed: DK; Follow-up intervals: baseline, day 14, 28, 35.	Sample: children who met criteria for ADHD. Recruited primarily from outpatient clinics, but also from inpatient and via newspaper ads; Age: 6–12; Gender: 90% male; Race/Ethnicity: 75% White 25% Other	CPRS(b), CTRS, CGI	Positive treatment effect was obtained on teacher ratings of aggression and hyperactivity at school; parents also reported symptom reduction but of less magnitude. Clinician ratings of global improvement varied greatly by site with no overall treatment effect when averaged.	Analysis sample: completer; Attrition: 12%; Effect Size: Parent ratings = 0.28, Teacher ratings = 0.41; Medication response rate: DK; Placebo response rate: DK
Gadow, Nolan, Sprafkin, & Sverd, 1995; Gadow, Sverd, Sprafkin, Nolan, & Grossman, 1999	What is the effect of methylphenidate for youth with ADHD and tic disorders?	Double-blind, placebo-controlled, within-subject crossover design. 8-weeks methylphenidate. Setting: outpatient; Duration: 8 weeks; Dosing: 2 weeks placebo, 2 weeks 0.1mg/kg, 2 weeks 0.3 mg/kg, 2 weeks 0.5 mg/kg, minimal effective dose (MED) based on calculation of improvement and tic status for follow-up; Compliance monitored: yes; Status of blind assessed: yes; Follow-up intervals: every 2 weeks during trial, every 6 months up to 2 years for follow up.	Sample: Children with ADHD and chronic motor tic disorder or Tourettes; Age: 6–11; Gender: 91% male; Race/Ethnicity: 86% White 10% African American 4% Other	COC, GSS, CTRS, SSEC, videotaped simulated classroom, CPT	Treatment resulted in significant reduction in hyperactive, disruptive, and aggressive behavior in the school setting. Treatment effect was observed across all three doses of methylphenidate (0.1, 0.3, and 0.5 mg/kg). A clinically insignificant but statistically significant exacerbation of motor tics in the classroom setting was observed. Follow-up data at 6-month intervals for 2 years revealed continuing overall improvement in symptoms characteristic of ADHD and no exacerbation of either motor or vocal tics.	Analysis sample: completer; Attrition: 12% by 2 years; Effect Size: Classroom interference (0.1 mg/kg vs. placebo = 0.33, 0.5 mg/kg vs. placebo = 0.82); Medication response rate: DK; Placebo response rate: DK

(continued)

Table 11.1.2 Psychopharmacological Studies of Childhood Attention-Deficit/Hyperactivity Disorder (*Continued*)

Study Citation(s)	Guiding Research Question	Study Design/Description	Subject Selection Criteria/Demographic Characteristics	Primary Dependent Measures	Outcomes	Analytic Details
Gillberg, Melander, von Knorring, Janols, Thernlund, Hägglöf, Eidevall-Wallin, Gustafsson, & Kopp, 1997	What are the longer term effects of amphetamine of symptoms of ADHD?	RCT: Double-blind, placebo-controlled. 15-month amphetamine sulfate (*n* = 32) vs. placebo (*n* = 30). Setting: outpatient; Duration: 18 months; Dosing: titrated to optimal level over 3 months, then randomized for following 12 months double-blind (mean dosage at randomization = 0.52 mg/kg), ended with 3-month single blind placebo; Compliance monitored: yes; Status of blind assessed: DK; Follow-up intervals: baseline, every 3 months.	Sample: Children with ADHD referred for outpatient treatment (42% comorbid with other disorder); Age: 6–11; Gender: 84% male; Race/Ethnicity: 100% White (Swedish)	CPRS(b), CTRS, BDS, MT	Positive outcomes were obtained on measures of behavioral abnormality by parents and teachers. There was a trend for positive outcomes on measures of learning. Adverse side effects were few and mild. Many subjects in placebo condition (71%) stopped treatment or went to open treatment during 12-month double-blind.	Analysis sample: intent to treat; Attrition: Less than 10%; Effect Size: DK; Medication response rate: DK; Placebo response rate: DK
Manos, Short, & Findling, 1999	What is the effectiveness of a single daily dose of adderall compared to 2 daily doses of methyl-phenidate?	Double-blind titration, placebo-controlled quasi-experimental matched design. Methylphenidate (*n* = 42) vs. Adderall (*n* = 42). Setting: outpatient clinic at teaching hospital; Duration: 4 weeks; Dosing: 5 mg, 10 mg, 15 mg in random sequence; Compliance monitored: yes; Status of blind assessed: parents blind to dose, but not drug; Follow-up intervals: baseline, weekly, end of trial.	Sample: Children with ADHD referred to Assessment and Evaluation unit of teaching hospital; Age: 5–17; Gender: 79% male; Race/Ethnicity: 93% White 5% African American 2% Hispanic	ARS, ASQ Composite ratings by clinician, SSQ-R, SEBMS	Although a significant dose effect was observed for both medications, no between-group treatment differences were observed on parent and teacher ratings	Analysis sample: completer; Attrition: DK; Effect Size: ASQ (adderall vs. methyl-phenidate = 0.42) Medication response rate: Adderall = 95%, Placebo response rate: Methylphenidate = 100%

Study	Question	Design/Method	Measures	Results	Analysis/Effect Size
Nolan & Gadow, 1997	Does methylphenidate normalize ADHD in children with chronic tic disorders and, indirectly, influence the behavior of their peers?	Double-blind, placebo-controlled, within-subject crossover design. 8-week methylphenidate ($n = 34$) Setting: outpatient; Duration: 8 weeks; Dosing: counterbalanced doses (0.1 mg/kg, 0.3 mg/kg, 0.5 mg/kg for 2 weeks each); Compliance monitored: DK; Status of blind assessed: DK; Follow-up intervals: During each treatment condition.	Sample: Children referred to outpatient clinic with ADHD and chronic motor tic disorder or Tourettes; Age: 6–11; Gender: 91% male; Race/Ethnicity: 86% White 10% African American 4% Other	ASOC	Treatment resulted in significant behavioral improvement but complete behavioral normalization was not achieved in many of the children. Little evidence showed that peer behavior improved as a function of subject medication dose. The treatment response of subjects with ADHD and tics is similar to samples of children with ADHD alone.	Analysis sample: completer; Attrition: DK; Effect Size: normalized behavior = 1.12; Medication response rate: normalized behavior = 40% at 0.5 mg/kg; Placebo response rate: 8%
Rapport, Denney, DuPaul, & Gardner, 1994	What is the magnitude and clinical significance of methylphenidate effects on classroom behavior and academic performance of children with ADHD?	Double-blind, placebo, controlled, within-subject crossover design. 6-weeks methylphenidate. Setting: outpatient; Duration: 6-weeks; Dosing: 1 week drug-free baseline, 1 week each on placebo and at various doses (5 mg, 10 mg, 15 mg, 20 mg); Compliance monitored: yes; Status of blind assessed: DK; Follow-up intervals: 3 times per week for 6 weeks.	Sample: community-referred children with ADHD. Normal controls selected from classroom rosters in local elementary schools; Age: 6–11; Gender: 86% male; Race/Ethnicity: 100% White	Classroom observations, CTRS-A, academic performance on normally assigned work	The dose-response effect on classroom behavior was predominately linear. A large proportion of children showed normalization of sustained attention (72%) and classroom functioning (78%) and a large proportion showed no improvement in academic functioning (47%).	Analysis sample: completer; Attrition: DK; Effect Size: normalization (ACTRS), at 5 mg = 0.68, at 20 mg = 1.28; Medication response rate: normalization (ACTRS) = at 20 mg approx. 60%; Placebo response rate: approx. 12%

(continued)

Table 11.1.2 Psychopharmacological Studies of Childhood Attention-Deficit/Hyperactivity Disorder (*Continued*)

Study Citation(s)	Guiding Research Question	Study Design/Description	Subject Selection Criteria/Demographic Characteristics	Primary Dependent Measures	Outcomes	Analytic Details
Schachar, Tannock, Cunningham, & Corkum, 1997	What are the behavioral, situational, and temporal effects of 4 months of methylphenidate?	RCT: methylphenidate ($n = 46$) vs. placebo ($n = 45$). Setting: outpatient; Duration: 4 months; Dosing: titrated for 3–4 weeks to reach target dose of 0.7 mg/kg (average dose 0.6 mg/kg, 31.9 mg/day); Compliance monitored: yes; Status of blind assessed: yes; Follow-up intervals: baseline, 4 months.	Sample: outpatient children with ADHD; Age: 6–12; Gender: DK; Race/Ethnicity: DK	Situational and TIP, ICBRS, Side effects	Positive outcomes were obtained on teacher ratings of core symptoms of ADHD (inattention, hyperactivity-impulsiveness). There were no between-group differences on measures of symptom improvement in parent ratings of home behavior. Treatment gains on teacher ratings were maintained over 4 months. 10% of the treatment group discontinued treatment due to negative side effects.	Analysis sample: completer; Attrition: DK; Effect Size: TIP Inattention (Teacher) = 0.77, IOWA-C (Teacher) = 1.14; Medication response rate: DK; Placebo response rate: DK
Swanson, Wigal, Greenhill, Browne, Waslik, Lerner, Williams, Flynn, Agler, Crowley, Fineberg, Baren, & Cantwell, 1998	What are the time course effects for various doses of Adderall?	Double-blind, placebo-controlled, within-subject crossover design ($n = 33$). Setting: outpatient (Child Development Center); Duration: 7 weeks; Dosing: Random order of 6 medication doses (placebo, Adderall: 5mg, 10mg, 15mg, 20mg, methylphenidate [dose determined by subject's clinical history]); Compliance monitored: yes; Status of blind assessed: DK; Follow-up intervals: 90-minute intervals following medication (in laboratory classroom).	Sample: referrals solicited from outpatient specialty clinics; Age: 7–14; Gender: 79% male; Race/Ethnicity: DK	SKAMP, TRI, SSERS	Objective (written school work) and subjective (teacher ratings) measures revealed significant treatment effects. Adderall's effects were noted quickly (about 1.5 hours after administration) and offset was abrupt (duration of action of about 4 hours). No unusual or serious side effects were noted.	Analysis sample: completer; Attrition: 9%; Effect Size: DK; Medication response rate: DK; Placebo response rate: DK

Author/Year	Research Question	Design/Methodology	Sample	Measures	Results	Other
Zeiner, Bryhn, Bjercke, Truyen, & Strand, 1999	What are the effects on behavior and test performance during treatment with methylphenidate and placebo for children with ADHD?	Double-blind, placebo-controlled, within-subject crossover design. 7-week methylphenidate ($n = 36$). Setting: outpatient; Duration: 7 weeks (3-week treatment, 1-week wash-out, 3-week placebo); Dosing: total daily dose of 0.5 mg/kg; Compliance monitored: DK; Status of blind assessed: DK; Follow-up intervals: last week of each trial period (weeks 3 and 7).	Sample: outpatient children with ADHD. Age: 7–11; Gender: 100% male; Race/Ethnicity: DK	PACS, CTRS	Positive treatment effect was obtained on behavioral measures of hyperactivity and defiance at home and school. Neuropsychological tests showed positive treatment effect for sustained attention, the ability to process complex information, and motor coordination.	Analysis sample: completer; Attrition: DK; Effect Size: PACS hyperactivity (home) = 0.49; CTRS hyperactivity (school) = 0.92; Medication response rate: CTRS recovered = 44%; Placebo response rate: DK

Table 11.1.3 Adjunctive Studies of Childhood Attention-Deficit/Hyperactivity Disorder

Study Citation(s)	Guiding Research Question	Study Design/Description	Subject Selection Criteria/Demographic Characteristics	Primary Dependent Measures	Outcomes	Analytic Details
Abikoff & Gittelman, 1985	Among children on maintenance stimulant medication, does cognitive training enhance academic performance and facilitate withdrawal of stimulant while maintaining academic gains?	RCT: Cognitive training plus medication (*n* = 21) vs. attention control plus medication (*n* = 14) vs. medication alone (*n* = 15). Setting: outpatient; Duration: 16-week cognitive training, 24 weeks total (4 week maximum placebo, 16-week maintenance, 4 week follow-up) attention-control and medication alone switched to placebo, cognitive training group randomized to continue medication (*n* = 10) or placebo medication (*n* = 10); Therapists: Masters in Special Education; Dosing: individualized (mean = 39–47 mg/day); Treatment manual: yes; Treatment integrity: yes; Participants: children (with brief interaction and information to parents); Follow-up intervals: baseline, 16 weeks, 20 weeks.	Sample: community-referred children with cross-situational ADHD (via home and school reports); Age: 6–12; Gender: 90% male; Race/Ethnicity: DK	CTRS, BRS, HAS, Achievement Tests, Cognitive Tests	Cognitive training did not result in improved behavioral, academic, or cognitive functioning relative to the other two treatment groups. Cognitive training did not facilitate withdrawal of medication.	Analysis sample: completer; Attrition: DK; Effect Size: NA

| Abikoff, Ganeles, Reiter, Blum, Foley, & Klein, 1988 | What is the effectiveness of intensive cognitive training for boys with ADHD who are academically deficient? | RCT: cognitive training plus medication ($n = 11$) vs. remedial tutoring plus medication ($n = 10$) vs. medication alone ($n = 13$). Setting: outpatient; Format: individual; Duration: 16 weeks for main intervention, booster sessions every 2 weeks during 6-month follow-up period; Therapists: Masters in Special Education; Dosing: methylphenidate (up to 60 mg/d) or dextroamphetamine (up to 35 mg/d); Treatment manual: yes; Treatment integrity: yes; Participants: children; Follow-up intervals: baseline, end of treatment, 6-month follow-up. | Sample: community-referred boys with ADHD, positive treatment response to stimulant medication, and academic deficiency; Age: 7–12; Gender: 100% male; Race/Ethnicity: 76% White 21% African American 3% Hispanic | GORT, SAT, MFFT, DESBRS, HPC, P-HSCS | The results showed no significant improvement in academic performance, self-esteem, or perceptions of academic functioning due to cognitive training. At the 6-month follow-up, children in the cognitive training group were rated as more improved in math and reading by teachers; however, this finding did not coincide with changes in achievement tests. | Analysis sample: completer; Attrition: DK; Effect Size: NA |

(continued)

Table 11.1.3 Adjunctive Studies of Childhood Attention-Deficit/Hyperactivity Disorder (*Continued*)

Study Citation(s)	Guiding Research Question	Study Design/Description	Subject Selection Criteria/Demographic Characteristics	Primary Dependent Measures	Outcomes	Analytic Details
Brown, Borden, Wynne, Schleser, & Clingerman, 1986; Brown, Wynne, Borden, Clingerman, Geniesse, & Spunt, 1986	What are the effects of methyl-phenidate, cognitive therapy, and their combination for children with ADD?	RCT: 2 × 2 double-blind, placebo-controlled. Methylphenidate plus attentional control ($n = 8$) vs. cognitive training plus placebo ($n = 10$) vs. methylphenidate plus cognitive training ($n = 9$) vs. attentional control plus placebo ($n = 8$). Setting: outpatient; Format: individual; Duration: 3 months; Therapists: Masters in Psychology or Special Education; Dosing: individualized (mean = 20.08 mg/day, 0.3 mg/kg); Treatment manual: yes; Treatment integrity: yes; Participants: children; Follow-up intervals: pretest, end of treatment, 3 months posttreatment.	Sample: outpatient children with ADHD or ADD who were at least 1 year behind in at least one subject area; Age: 5–13; Gender: 80% male; Race/Ethnicity: DK	MFFT, CCT, WRAT, CPRS, CTRS, ACTeRS	There was no significant improvement in characteristic symptoms of ADD across the four treatment groups. The adjunctive use of cognitive therapy failed to help maintain treatment gains following discontinuation of medication. Study appears to be underpowered. Effect sizes suggest utility of medication in addition to either cognitive training or attention control.	Analysis sample: completer; Attrition: 5%; Effect Size: vs. attention control/placebo control (CT plus placebo = −0.18, Methylphenidate plus attention control = 0.63, Methylphenidate plus CT = 0.41)

Study	Research Question	Design/Method	Measures	Findings	Analysis
Horn, Ialongo, Pascoe, Greenberg, Packard, Lopez, & Wagner, 1991; Horn, Ialongo, Pascoe, Greenberg, Packard, Lopez, & Wagner, 1993	What are the effects of high and low-doses of methylphenidate, with and without behavioral parent training and child self-control instruction, for youth with ADHD?	RTC: 2×3 double-blind, placebo-controlled. Medication (placebo, low-dose MPH, high-dose MPH) ($n = 96$, 16 in each of 6 treatment conditions). Setting: outpatient; Format: group; Duration: 12 sessions; Therapists: graduate students; Dosing: placebo, low-dose = 0.4 mg/kg, high-dose = 0.8 mg/kg; Treatment manual: yes; Treatment integrity: yes; Participants: parents and children, school consultation; Follow-up intervals: baseline, posttreatment, 9-month follow-up.	Sample: outpatient children with ADHD (50% comorbid with CD or ODD); Age: 7-11; Gender: 77% male; Race/Ethnicity: 85% White 9% African American 4% Hispanic 2% Asian American	CBCL, CPRS, CTRS, CPT, TCCPRSS, WRAT-R, P-HSCS, PIC-R	The combination of medication and behavioral intervention did not improve outcomes over high-dose medication alone. On teacher ratings, low-dose in combination with behavioral intervention was significantly more effective than low-dose alone and as effective as high-dose alone. The 9-month follow-up failed to reveal positive outcomes for combined psychosocial intervention. The results suggest that treatment benefits dissipate when medication is withdrawn.	Analysis sample: completer; Attrition: 18%; Effect Size: NA
Klein & Abikoff, 1997	What is the relative efficacy of methylphenidate, behavior therapy, and their combination?	RCT: behavior therapy plus placebo ($n = 28$) vs. methylphenidate ($n = 29$) vs. behavior therapy plus methylphenidate ($n = 29$). Setting: outpatient; Format: individual; Duration: 12 weeks total, 8 week behavior therapy; Therapists: DK; Dosing: titrated to maximum of 60 mg/day (mean = 40-41 mg/day); Treatment manual: yes; Treatment integrity: DK; Participants: parents, teachers, children; Follow-up intervals: baseline, end of treatment (8 weeks).	Sample: outpatient children with ADHD; Age: 6-12; Gender: 94%; Race/Ethnicity: 83% White 14% African American 2% Hispanic 1% Asian	CTRS, CPRS, CPRS (2), HBS, Classroom Observations, WRAT, WISC-R, MFFT	The combination of behavior therapy and methylphenidate was the most effective treatment. The second most effective treatment was methylphenidate alone, while the least effective was behavior therapy alone.	Analysis sample: completer; Attrition: 15%; Effect Size: CGI Improved (Teachers) (methylphenidate vs. behavior therapy = 0.28, Combined vs. behavior therapy = 1.25)

(continued)

Table 11.1.3 Adjunctive Studies of Childhood Attention-Deficit/Hyperactivity Disorder (*Continued*)

Study Citation(s)	Guiding Research Question	Study Design/Description	Subject Selection Criteria/Demographic Characteristics	Primary Dependent Measures	Outcomes	Analytic Details
Pelham, Carlson, Sams, Vallano, Dixon, & Hoza, 1993	What are the separate and combined effects of behavior modification and methylphenidate on classroom behavior and academic performance?	Within-subjects alternating treatments design. Behavior Modification vs. no Behavior Modification alternated by week. Within this, rotated low-dose MPH, high-dose MPH, placebo on daily basis (n = 31). Setting: summer treatment program (day treatment); Format: classroom; Duration: 8 weeks; Therapists: teacher and aide; Dosing: alternated placebo, low-dose (approx. 0.3 mg/kg), high-dose (approx. 0.6 mg/kg); Treatment manual: DK; Treatment integrity: DK; Participants: children; Follow-up intervals: daily.	Sample: Children with ADHD participating in a summer day treatment program; Age: 5–9; Gender: 100% male; Race/Ethnicity: 94% White 6% African American	Classroom observations, accuracy and productivity on assigned academic tasks, ICBRS.	There was a significant main effect for both interventions alone, with the effect size of methylphenidate twice that of behavior modification. Little was gained by the higher dose of methylphenidate or behavior modification over the effects of the low-dose methylphenidate.	Analysis sample: completer; Attrition: DK; Effect Size: Average across measures, all vs. placebo plus no behavior management (BM = 1.24, low-dose/noBM = 2.54, low-dose+BM = 2.94, high-dose/noBM = 2.71, high-dose/BM = 2.73)

Study	Question	Design	Sample	Measures	Findings	Analysis
The MTA Cooperative Group, 1999. (Multimodal Treatment Study of Children with Attention-Deficit/Hyperactivity Disorder)	What are the effects of medication management, intensive behavioral treatment, a combination of these, or standard community care across a relatively extended period and multiple communities?	RCT: medication management ($n = 144$) vs. behavioral treatment ($n = 144$) vs. combined treatment ($n = 144$) vs. community-based usual care ($n = 146$). Setting: outpatient; Format: group and individual; Duration: 14 months (behavioral treatment = 27 group and 8 individual sessions, child-focused treatment = 8 week summer camp, school-based = teacher consultation and paraprofessional aide); Dosing: titration to best dose on variety of medications; Treatment manual: yes; Treatment integrity: yes; Participants: parents, children, schools; Follow-up intervals: baseline, 14 months.	Sample: community-referred youth with ADHD; Age: 7-9; Gender: 80% male; Race/Ethnicity: 61% White 20% African American 8% Other 11% DK	SNAP, SSRS, MASC, WIAT, classroom observations	This is the largest and best designed study, to date, of treatments for children with ADHD. All treatments showed improvement in ADHD symptoms. Combined treatment showed no added benefit to medication management alone in reducing core symptoms of ADHD. Combined treatment was superior to other treatments in several non-ADHD domains (oppositional/aggressive symptoms) and positive functioning outcomes (parent-child relations).	Analysis sample: intent to treat; Attrition: 3.5%; Effect Size: Teacher reported hyperactivity vs. community treatment (combined treatment = 0.64, medication = 0.56, behavioral = 0.18)

and cognitive tasks. Side effects of stimulant medications are a common concern for children and parents, but findings indicate that most side effects are mild, decrease over time, and are dose-dependent.

Behavioral training for parents and teachers and classroom contingency management are the primary psychosocial treatments investigated with children with ADHD. Individual psychosocial treatments applied to children directly, including cognitive-behavior therapy, cognitive training, and social-skills training, have been less beneficial. While psychosocial treatments do not appear to achieve improvements as substantial as those found with stimulant medication, they have been found useful in changing parenting and teacher practices.

Adjunctive interventions are treatments that include both pharmacological and psychosocial modalities across multiple settings. Studies assessing the combined impact of cognitive training and stimulant medication have found little incremental benefit over medication alone. The most recent and largest adjunctive study to date, the Multimodal Treatment Study of Children with ADHD (the MTA) has shown that combined treatment was not superior to well-delivered and well-monitored psychostimulant medication at reducing the core symptoms of ADHD. However, combined treatment outcomes were achieved with lower medication doses. Combined treatment was also superior at reducing associated features of ADHD, including defiance, aggression, oppositionality, internalizing symptoms, and parent-child relationships.

Studies of Childhood Major Depressive Disorder

This literature review identified empirical studies of psychosocial and pharmacological treatments of children with depression. It was done in two stages. First, systematic computerized literature searches were conducted on PsycINFO and Medline databases with keywords depression and major depression. The resulting list of references was reduced to include only those studies that met inclusion criteria as described in the introduction. Reference lists obtained from review articles and book chapters were also searched to ensure that all of the relevant studies had been identified. This search strategy resulted in 28 potential studies. This list was further reduced by excluding studies for the following reasons: depression was a secondary comorbid diagnosis (e.g., mental retardation, medical illness); the study focus was other than treatment outcome (e.g., effects of extended evaluation on symptoms of depression, factors related to correspondence to teacher and child ratings, information processing in children who had recovered from depression); or the study design did not meet criteria for inclusion. This process identified 11 peer-reviewed controlled studies of children with either depression or depressive symptoms. These studies are presented and described in Table 11.2.

Perhaps the most striking conclusion that can be drawn from the current review of empirical studies of childhood depression is the relative paucity of well-controlled outcome studies with this age group, possibly associated with the relatively low prevalence of depression in middle childhood. Psychosocial and pharmacological interventions are the two primary treatment modalities

Table 11.2.1 Psychosocial Studies of Childhood Depressive Disorder

Study Citation(s)	Guiding Research Question	Study Design/Description	Subject Selection Criteria/Demographic Characteristics	Primary Dependent Measures	Outcomes	Analytic Details
Jaycox, Reivich, Gillham, & Seligman, 1994; Gillham, Reivich, Jaycox, & Seligman, 1995	To evaluate the efficacy of a CBT prevention program for children at risk for depression.	Quasi-experimental design; cognitive-behavior prevention program (CBT-P; $n = 69$) vs. combined wait list and no participation control group (WL; $n = 74$). Setting: school; Format: group; Participant: child; Duration: 12 weeks; Therapists: 3 graduate-level trainees; Treatment manual: yes; Treatment integrity: unspecified; Follow-up interval: 6, 12, 18, and 24 months.	Children who reported elevated depressive symptoms and parental conflict. Age: 10–13 (M = 11.4); Gender: 54% male; Race/Ethnicity: 83% white 11% African American 6% other	CDI, RCDS, CBCL, teacher measure of classroom behavior	CBT-P group reported significantly fewer depressive symptoms at posttreatment, 6-month, and 2-year follow-up; no significant between-group differences on CBCL at posttreatment and 6-month follow-up; teacher's ratings of classroom behavior also improved; results showed that subject's ability to attribute negative events to temporary causes (rather than stable causes) mediated treatment.	Analysis sample: completer; Attrition: CBT-P = 13%, WL = 16%; Effect Size: CDI = 0.27, RCDS = 0.38; Effect Size (at 24-months): CDI = 0.53, RCDS = 0.64
Kahn, Kehle, Jenson, & Clark, 1990	To evaluate the efficacy of an adolescent CBT program for the treatment of depressive symptoms in a middle school population.	RCT; cognitive-behavior therapy (CBT; $n = 17$) vs. relaxation training (RT; $n = 17$) vs. self-modeling treatment (SM; $n = 17$) vs. wait list control (WL; $n = 17$). Setting: school; Format: group and individual; Participant: child; Duration: 12 weeks; Therapists: 1 school psychologist and 1 school counselor; Treatment Manual: yes; Treatment integrity: yes; Follow-up interval: 4 weeks.	Children with moderate to severe depression based on a multi-stage assessment model that included self-report measures and a structured clinical interview. Age: 10–14; Gender: 52% female; Race/Ethnicity: unspecified	RADS, CDI, PH, BID	Compared to WL, all active treatment groups showed a significant decrease in depressive symptoms and an increase in self-esteem; treatment gains maintained at 4-week follow-up for CBT group, 50% of SM group relapsed; subjects in CBT group showed most improvement.	Analysis sample: completer; Attrition: not reported; RADS Effect Size: CBT = 1.89; RT = 1.30; SM = 1.41; CDI Effect Size: CBT = 1.68; RT = 1.06; SM = 1.11

(continued)

Table 11.2.1 Psychosocial Studies of Childhood Depressive Disorder (*Continued*)

Study Citation(s)	Guiding Research Question	Study Design/Description	Subject Selection Criteria/Demographic Characteristics	Primary Dependent Measures	Outcomes	Analytic Details
Liddle & Spence, 1990	To evaluate the efficacy of social competency training for the treatment of primary school children with DSM III-R depression.	RCT; social competence training (SCT; $n = 11$) vs. attention placebo control (APC; $n = 10$) vs. wait list control (WL; $n = 10$). Setting: school; Format: group; Participant: child; Duration: 8 weeks; Therapists: 1 school psychologist and 1 school counselor; Treatment Manual: unspecified; Treatment integrity: yes; Follow-up interval: 8 weeks.	Children who scored above 19 on the CDI and above 40 on the CDRS. Age: 7–11 (M = 9.2); Gender: 68% male; Race/Ethnicity: unspecified.	CDI, CDRS, Child MESSY, Teacher MESSY, LSSP	Subjects in all three groups improved over time on the CDI; at follow-up, all three groups continued to show improvement on the CDI and deteriorate on the Teacher's MESSY; no between-group differences were found on any outcomes at posttreatment or at 8-week follow-up; SCT failed to produce positive changes on self-report and teacher report measures of social competence.	Analysis sample: completer; Attrition: not reported; Effect Size: n/a
Stark, Reynolds, & Kaslow, 1987	To evaluate the efficacy of two interventions (based on treatments with demonstrated efficacy with depressed adults) for the treatment of childhood depression.	RCT; self-control training (SCT; $n = 9$) vs. behavioral problem-solving (BPS; $n = 10$) vs. wait list control (WL; $n = 9$). Setting: school; Format: group; Participant: child; Duration: 12 sessions; Therapists: 1 graduate-level trainee, 1 Ph.D. psychologist; Treatment Manual: yes; Treatment integrity: yes; Follow-up interval: 8 weeks.	Children who scored above 16 on the CDI at T1 and above 12 at T2 and above 40 on the CDRS-R. Age: 9–12; Gender: 57% male; Race/Ethnicity: unspecified	CDI, CDS, CDRS-R, CBCL, CSEI, RCMAS	Compared to the WL group, subjects in both active treatments reported significantly less depressive symptoms at posttreatment and treatment gains were maintained at 8-week follow-up; neither active intervention appeared overall superior; improvements in depressive symptomatology failed to generalize to home environment; both groups reported fewer symptoms of anxiety at posttreatment.	Analysis sample: completer; Attrition: not reported; CDI Effect Size: SCT = 1.25, BPS = 1.05; CDS Effect Size: SCT = 0.82, BPS = 0.41; CDRS Effect Size: SCT = 0.98, BPS = 0.65

Study	Purpose	Design/Intervention	Sample	Measures	Results	Notes
Vostanis, Feehan, Grattan, & Bickerton, 1996a; Vostanis, Feehan, Grattan, & Bickerton, 1996b; Vostanis, Feehan, & Grattan, 1998	To evaluate the efficacy of CBT for clinically depressed outpatient children and adolescents.	RCT; cognitive-behavior therapy (CBT; n = 29) vs. non-focused "supportive" intervention (NFI; n = 28). Setting: clinical outpatient; Format: individual; Participant: child; Duration: average 6 sessions (range 2-9); Therapists: 3 child psychiatrists; Treatment Manual: yes; Treatment integrity: yes; Follow-up interval: 9 and 24 months.	Outpatient children with DSM-III-R major or minor depressive disorder or dysthymia based on K-SADS structured interview. Age: 8-14 (M = 12.7); Gender: 56% female; Race/Ethnicity: 88% White 9% Asian 3% African American	MFQ, RCMAS, SEI, AG, TEC	Both groups improved significantly by posttreatment; no significant between-group differences were found on any clinical measure at posttreatment; 87% of CBT subjects and 75% of NFI subjects no longer met diagnostic criteria for their depressive disorder; treatment gains in both groups were maintained at 9-month follow-up without any significant differential treatment effect; at 2-year follow-up 20% met DSM criteria for depression and 39% reported frequent significant symptoms during previous year; child's pre- and posttreatment self-esteem and co-morbidity at posttreatment were significant predictors of long-term outcome.	Analysis sample: completer; Attrition: 9% withdrew within 2 sessions; only 50% completed the full CBT program; Effect Size: n/a
Weisz, Thurber, Sweeney, Proffitt, & LeGagnoux, 1997	To evaluate the efficacy of a brief CBT group intervention for the treatment of mild-to-moderate depressive symptoms in a middle school population.	RCT; cognitive-behavior therapy (CBT; n = 16) vs. no treatment control (NTC; n = 32). Setting: school; Format: group; Participants: child; Duration: 8 sessions; Therapists: 5 graduate-level trainees, 1 Ph.D. psychologist; Treatment Manual: yes; Treatment integrity: yes; Follow-up interval: 9 months.	Children who scored above 10 on the CDI and above 33 on the CDRS-R. Age: 8-12 (M = 9.6); Gender: 54% male; Race/Ethnicity: 63% White 37% African American	CDI, CDRS-R	Compared to NTC group, CBT group reported significantly fewer depressive symptoms at posttreatment; normative comparisons showed that 50% vs. 16% of subjects in the CBT group moved into the normal range on CDI at posttreatment; treatment gains were maintained at 9-month follow-up.	Analysis sample: completer; Attrition: not reported; Effect Size: CDI = 0.53, CDRS-R = 0.16

Table 11.2.2 Psychopharmacological Studies of Childhood Depressive Disorder

Study Citation(s)	Guiding Research Question	Study Design/Description	Subject Selection Criteria/Demographic Characteristics	Primary Dependent Measures	Outcomes	Analytic Details
Emslie et al., 1997	To evaluate the efficacy, safety, and tolerability of fluoxetine for the treatment of child and adolescent major depressive disorder.	Double-blind, placebo-controlled RCT; fluoxetine (FXT; n = 48) vs. placebo (PBO; n = 48). Setting: outpatient university clinic; Duration: 8 weeks; Dosing: fixed, 20 mg; Compliance monitored: yes; Status of blind assessed: unspecified.	Children with DSM-III-R major depressive disorder based on DICA and CDRS-R score greater than 40. Age: 7–17 (M = 12.3); Gender: 54% male; Race/Ethnicity: 73% White 27% Other	CGI, CDRS-R, CGAS, BPRS-C, CDI/BDI, WSAC	Although both groups improved relative to baseline, improvement was greatest in the FXT group; weekly CDRS-R scores were significantly different by week 5; no significant drug by age or drug by gender interactions were found; only 31% of FXT group and 23% of PBO group reported minimal symptoms at posttreatment (as rated on the CDRS-R); between group differences were less evident on self-report measures (CDI, WSAS), clinician ratings of general psychiatric symptoms (BPRS-C), and global functioning (CGAS); FXT was well-tolerated.	Analysis sample: intent-to-treat; Attrition: FXT = 29%, PBO = 46%; Effect Size: CGI-I = 0.52, CDRS-R = 0.55, CDI/BDI = 0.11; Response rate (based on CGI ratings): FXT = 56%, PBO = 33%
Geller et al., 1992; Geller, Cooper, McCombs, Graham, & Wells, 1989	To evaluate the relationship between steady state nortriptyline (NT) plasma levels and treatment response in depressed children.	Double-blind, placebo-controlled RCT; nortriptyline (NT, n = 26) vs. placebo (PBO, n = 24). Setting: outpatient university clinic; Duration: 8 weeks; Dosing: flexible, to achieve fixed steady state NT plasma level (60–100 ng/ml); Compliance monitored: yes; Status of blind assessed: unspecified.	Children with DSM-III-R major depressive disorder based on K-SADS and CDRS-R score greater than 39. Age: 6–12; Gender: 70% male; Race/Ethnicity: 90% White 10% Other	CDRS, K-SADS MDD, CBCL, CBCL-T, PSS, CDI	No significant difference in rate of response between NT and PBO, nor on any outcome measures; no significant association between mean NT plasma level and rate of response.	Analysis sample: completer; Attrition: 17% (not reported by group); Mean plasma level: 89.9 ng/ml; Effect Size: n/a; Response rate: NT = 31%, PBO = 17%.

236

Study	Purpose	Design/Methods	Sample	Measures	Results	Analysis
Hughes et al., 1990	To evaluate the relationship between comorbidity and response to imipramine (IMI) in depressed children.	Double-blind, placebo-controlled RCT; children with depression alone or concomitant anxiety disorder assigned to imipramine (IMI-DA; $n = 7$) or placebo (PBO-DA; $n = 5$) vs. children with depression and concomitant conduct or oppositional disorder assigned to imipramine (IMI-C/OD; $n = 6$) or placebo (PBO-C/OD; $n = 9$). Setting: inpatient hospital; Duration: 6 weeks; Dosing: unspecified; Compliance monitored: unspecified; Status of blind assessed: unspecified.	Children with DSM-III major depressive disorder based on consensus using data from DICA, CDI, CDRS, and CGI. Age: 6–12; Gender: unspecified; Race/Ethnicity: unspecified	CDRS	Children with depression alone or concomitant anxiety disorder had a higher drug response rate (4/7) and a lower placebo rate (1/5) than children with depression and concomitant conduct or oppositional disorder; the response rate for drug and placebo for the latter group was 2/6 and 6/9, respectively; response rate was defined as a 50% reduction in CDRS scores.	Analysis sample: completer; Attrition: 13% (not reported by group); Mean Dose: unspecified; Effect Size: IMI-DA = 0.92, IMI-C/OD = −0.76; Response rate: IMI-DA = 57%, PBO-DA = 20%, IMI-C/OD = 33%, PBO-C/OD = 67%
Preskorn, Weller, Hughes, Weller, & Bolte, 1987	To evaluate the efficacy of imipramine (IMI) for the treatment of childhood depression.	Double-blind, placebo-controlled RCT; imipramine (IMI; $n = 10$) vs. placebo (PBO; $n = 12$). Setting: inpatient hospital; Duration: 6 weeks; Dosing: flexible, to achieve fixed steady state IMI plasma levels (125–250 ng/m); Compliance monitored: unspecified; Status of blind assessed: unspecified.	Children hospitalized with DSM-III MDD via DICA and CDRS-R score above 20 Sample: inpatient; Age: 6–12; Gender: unspecified; Race/Ethnicity: unspecified	CGI, CDRS-R, CDI	When therapeutic IMI plasma levels were achieved (125 to 250 ng/ml), IMI was superior to PBO; no between group difference was found on CDI at posttreatment; IMI benefit was more pronounced in dexamethasone (DST) nonsuppressors compared to DST suppressors.	Analysis sample: completer; Attrition: not reported; Mean plasma level: unspecified; Effect Size: insufficient information provided; Response rate: insufficient information provided

(continued)

Table 11.2.2 Psychopharmacological Studies of Childhood Depressive Disorder (*Continued*)

Study Citation(s)	Guiding Research Question	Study Design/Description	Subject Selection Criteria/Demographic Characteristics	Primary Dependent Measures	Outcomes	Analytic Details
Puig-Antich et al., 1987	To evaluate the efficacy of imipramine (IMI) for the treatment of childhood depression.	Double-blind, placebo-controlled RCT; imipramine (IMI; $n = 20$) vs. placebo (PBO; $n = 22$). Setting: outpatient; Duration: 5 weeks; Dosing: Fixed dosing schedule; Compliance monitored: yes; Status of blind assessed: unspecified.	Children who met RDC criteria for MDD via the K-SADS Age: M = 9.11; Gender: 61% male; Race/Ethnicity: 42% White 37% African American 21% Hispanic	Nine depression items from K-SADS-P	Based on K-SADS-P, results showed a nonsignificantly higher rate of response to PBO than to IMI; found, retrospectively, a significant positive linear relationship between total maintenance plasma level (IMI plus metabolite desipramine) and clinical response; clinical response rates were 87% for subjects above the median plasma level and 47% for subjects below the median.	Analysis sample: completer; Attrition: IMI = 20% IMI, PBO = 0%; Mean dose: 4.35 mg/kg/d; Effect Size: n/a; Response rate: IMI = 56%, PBO = 68%

that have been studied. The psychosocial interventions investigated include individual and group cognitive-behavior therapy, self-control training, and problem-solving and social-skills training. The pharmacological interventions include tricyclic antidepressants (imipramine, nortriptyline) and selective serotonin reuptake inhibitors (fluoxetine).

Generally, it can be concluded that both cognitive behavior therapy and self-control therapy are efficacious treatments for children with symptoms of depression when compared against a waitlist control group. Studies that utilized an alternative treatment group or an attention placebo group found few significant differences between active treatments. Thus, it appears that children respond positively to virtually any credible intervention. Moreover, with few exceptions, the inclusion criteria for psychosocial treatments were based on depressive symptoms, rather than requiring a diagnosis of depression, and treatments usually occurred in school settings with an average of 12 sessions. Few of these studies reported follow-up data. In the few studies reporting longitudinal data, treatment gains were maintained at follow-up.

Research addressing the efficacy of tricyclic antidepressants for the treatment of childhood depression failed to find superiority for its use over placebo. Thus, there is no evidence to suggest that tricyclic antidepressants should be used in the treatment of children with depression. However, studies investigating the effectiveness of selective serotonin reuptake inhibitors are promising. One recent double-blind, placebo-controlled study of fluoxetine for childhood depression reported significant treatment effects relative to placebo. Well-designed studies regarding the safety, efficacy, and long-term use of antidepressant medication need to be conducted before strong statements can be made regarding their overall efficacy in the treatment of childhood depression.

Studies of Childhood Disruptive Behavior Disorders

The evidence base for non-residential interventions for disruptive behavior disorders is presented in Table 11.3. The review includes prevention and treatment studies. Therefore, interventions that identify youth who are "at risk" for developing conduct problems are included. Studies in which ADHD was the primary diagnostic label were excluded (but are included in the ADHD section of this report). Studies could be included if they focused on youth with a definable psychiatric diagnosis (e.g., conduct disorder, oppositional defiant disorder) or on youth with externalizing behaviors that may contribute to these types of disorders. The review includes a number of interventions designed to be delivered via schools. However, we did not search the education literature for education-specific interventions (e.g., special education was not searched).

Searches were conducted in PsycINFO and Medline electronic databases, beginning with key words behavior disorders, conduct disorder, and disruptive. This net was intended to be broad to prevent omission of relevant articles. This search resulted in 314 articles. The final set was selected by reading abstracts or articles. Articles were excluded if they had a total sample size of less than 30, focused on program descriptions or epidemiologic topics, had in-

Table 11.3.1 Psychosocial Studies of Childhood Disruptive Behavior Disorders: Parent Training

Study Citation(s)	Guiding Research Question	Study Design/Description	Subject Selection Criteria/Demographic Characteristics	Primary Dependent Measures	Outcomes	Analytic Details
Taylor, Schmidt, Peplar, & Hodgins, 1998	Is Webster-Stratton's Parents and Children Series (PACS) effective in a typical service setting?	RCT: Webster-Stratton's PACS (n = 46) vs. eclectic typical treatment (n = 46) vs. wait list controls (n = 18). Setting: mental health center; Format: PACS = group, Eclectic = individual/family therapy; Duration: 11–14 weeks; Therapists: therapists at public MH center (BA, MA, and PhD); Treatment manual: yes; Treatment integrity: yes; Participants: parents; Follow-up intervals: pretreatment and 4 months after start of treatment.	Sample: families of children who were referred to a public community mental health center for assistance related to conduct problems; Age: 3–8; Gender: 73% male; Race/Ethnicity: DK	ECBI, CBCL, PDR, satisfaction.	PACS and eclectic treatment showed improvements compared to wait list controls for total problems. Mothers in PACS group reported significantly fewer problems on the ECBI problem score and higher treatment satisfaction than mothers in eclectic treatment.	Analysis sample: complex (different comparisons for different outcomes) Attrition: DK Effect Size: ECBI (PACS vs. WL = .57; Eclectic vs. WL = .43; PACS vs. Eclectic = .49)
Webster-Stratton, Kolpacoff, & Hollinsworth, 1988; Webster-Stratton, Hollinsworth, & Kolpacoff, 1989	What are the outcomes associated with three cost-effective parent-training treatment programs?	RCT: Individually administered videotape modeling (IVM) (n = 49) vs. Group discussion videotape modeling (GDVM) (n = 48) vs. Group discussion (GD) (n = 47) vs. wait list (n = 50). Setting: clinic; Format: group; Duration: 10–12 weekly sessions; Therapists: experienced clinicians; Treatment manual: yes; Treatment integrity: yes; Participants: parents; Follow-up intervals: baseline, completion of treatment, 1 year posttreatment.	Sample: self-referred or professionally referred families of children with behavior problems; Age: 3–8; Gender: 69% male; Race/Ethnicity: DK	ECBI, CBCL, PDR, PSI, Parent-child interactions.	Significant changes were observed compared to controls, for families in all treatment groups. There were few differences among the three interventions; however, there was a consistent trend for better outcomes associated with GDVM. Follow-ups at 1 year posttreatment showed that gains were maintained.	Analysis sample: DK Attrition: 10% Effect Size: ECBI total (mother's reports) (IVM vs. Control = 1.1; GDVM vs. Control = 0.8; GD vs. Control = 1.1)

| Webster-Stratton & Hammond, 1997 | Can clinical effectiveness and generalization of parent training be increased by also including child training? | RCT: Child training (CT) (n = 22) vs. parent training (PT) (n = 26) vs. PT+CT (n = 22) vs. control (n = 22).

Setting: clinic; Format: group; Duration: 22–24 weeks; Therapists: experienced master's- and PhD-level therapists; Treatment manual: yes; Treatment integrity: yes; Participants: parents and children; Follow-up intervals: baseline, 2 months posttreatment, 1 year later. | Sample: children with ODD or CD; Age: 4–7; Gender: 74% male; Race/Ethnicity: 86% White 14% Other | CBCL, ECBI, PSI, PDR, BPBQ, DPICS-R, WCSPDG | Overall, all three treatment conditions showed greater improvements than controls, and C+T training showed the greatest improvements. All treatment groups showed improved parent reports of child's behavior and improved interactions with peers. CT+PT was superior to CT on improving parenting skills and to PT on improving children's social problem-solving. At posttreatment, 80.8% of PT mothers and 70% of CT+PT mothers reported CBCLs in normal range, compared to 37% of CT mothers and 27.3% of controls. At one year, follow-up effects were maintained, with some increased effectiveness for CT+PT. | Analysis sample: intent to treat; Attrition: 4%; Effect size: CBCL (total by mother) (CT vs. CON = 0.49; PT vs. CON = 1.27; CT+PT vs. CON = 1.25) |

Table 11.3.2 Psychosocial Studies of Childhood Disruptive Behavior Disorders: Clinic-Based Interventions

Study Citation(s)	Guiding Research Question	Study Design/Description	Subject Selection Criteria/Demographic Characteristics	Primary Dependent Measures	Outcomes	Analytic Details
Fonagy & Target, 1994	Which youth with disruptive behavior disorders are most likely to benefit from psychodynamic treatment?	Chart review of youth who received psychoanalysis and psychotherapy at Anna Freud Centre; children with disruptive behavior disorders (n = 135) vs. matched sample of children with emotional disorders (n = 135). Setting: clinic; Format: individual; Duration: varied (1–5 sessions per week up to 3+ years); Therapists: experienced psychoanalysts and trainees; Treatment manual: not specified; Treatment integrity: DK; Participants: children; Follow-up intervals: baseline and end of treatment.	Sample: Closed treatment files for youth who received psychoanalysis; Age: 3–17 (M = 9); Gender: 75% male; Race/Ethnicity: DK	DSM-III-R diagnoses; CBCL; CGAS	33% of disruptive youth were not diagnosable at completion of treatment. Improvement was greater for youth with ODD than with CD. Overall, youth with disruptive disorders improved less than youth with emotional disorders. The article also models other factors associated with improvement during treatment.	Analysis Sample: varies Attrition: DK Effect Size: no longer diagnosable at end of treatment (ext. vs. emot. = –0.46).
Grizenko, Papineau, & Sayegh, 1993; Grizenko, 1997	What are the effects of a multimodal day treatment program for children with disruptive behavior disorders?	Quasi-experiment: day treatment (n = 15) vs. wait list (n = 15) Setting: day treatment; Format: day treatment; Duration: approximately 4 months; Therapists: multidisciplinary team; Treatment manual: DK; Treatment integrity: DK; Participants: children and families (family therapy and liaison); Follow-up intervals: baseline, posttreatment, 6-month follow-up, 5 years.	Sample: Youth with disruptive disorders seeking admission to a day treatment program (referred by school, social worker, or outpatient services due to inability to function at school/home) Age: 5–12; Gender: 77% male; Race/Ethnicity: DK	RCBP, HSES, DSRS, IPR, MESSY, FAM, WRAT-R	The day treatment group showed significantly better improvement than wait list group on all measured outcomes (except academic performance). Follow-up at 5 years showed some deterioration of outcomes, but still was an improvement over baseline.	Analysis Sample: intent to treat Attrition: DK Effect Size: RCBP Total = 2.5

242

| Kazdin, Bass, Siegel, & Thomas, 1989 | To what extent do three alternative treatments produce changes at home and school and does a practice component augment impact of cognitively based treatment? | RCT: problem-solving skills training (PSST) (n = 37) vs. PSST plus in vivo practice (PSST+P) (n = 38) vs. relationship therapy (RT) (n = 37).

Setting: outpatient and inpatient; Format: individual; Duration: 25 sessions; Therapists: master's-level; Treatment manual: yes; Treatment integrity: yes; Participants: children; Follow-up intervals: baseline, posttreatment, 1 year. | Sample: Children seen at a diagnostic triage center with severe antisocial behavior;
Age: 7–13;
Gender: 78% male;
Race/Ethnicity:
55% white
46% African American | CBCL, SBCL, PDR, CATS(b), SEI | All groups improved across time on parent, teacher-, and child-completed measures. For most measures, PSST and PSST+P groups showed less deviant and more prosocial behavior than RT children. The practice component appeared to enhance PSST. PSST+P children did better on nearly all measures, but only 3 were significant (low need achievement, aggression, and total disability—all school-based measures). At 1 year follow-up, PSST and PSST+P children continued to have more positive outcomes than RT group. At this point, there were no significant differences between PSST and PSST+P. | Analysis Sample: completer; Attrition: 13% Effect Size: CBCL non-clinical range (PSST vs. RT = 0.69, PSST+P vs. RT = 0.85) |
| Kazdin, Siegel, & Bass, 1992 | What are the relative effects of parent management training, problem-solving skills training, and a combination of these treatments? | RCT: child-focused problem-solving skills training (PSST) (n = 29) vs. parent management training (PMT) (n = 31) vs. combination (n = 37).

Setting: outpatient clinic of a psychiatric facility; Format: individual; Duration: 6–8 months (PSST = 25 weekly sessions, PMT = 16 sessions); Therapists: master's-level; Treatment manual: yes; Treatment integrity: yes; Participants: parents and children (in each treatment condition); Follow-up intervals: baseline, posttreatment, 1 year posttreatment. | Sample: Children referred to outpatient Child Conduct Clinic;
Age: 7–13;
Gender: 78% male;
Race/Ethnicity:
69% White
31% African American | CBCL, TRF, HRI, IAB, CATS(b), SRD, PDR, PSI | All groups improved over time. The combination group showed greatest improvement in a variety of areas, including antisocial and delinquent behavior, depression, and family functioning. The combined group had largest percentage of the group in normal range (CBCL) by posttreatment. Between posttreatment and 1-year follow-ups, PSST+PMT and PSST both showed further improvements. The combined group showed continuing improvement in child behavior (total CBCL) and parent stress. PSST showed continued improvement in child behavior (PDR). Only PMT showed no further improvements from posttreatment to follow-up. | Analysis Sample: completer; Attrition: 22% Effect Size: CBCL Total (Combined vs. PSST = 0.45, Combined vs. PMT = 0.39) |

(continued)

Table 11.3.2 Psychosocial Studies of Childhood Disruptive Behavior Disorders: Clinic-Based Interventions (*Continued*)

Study Citation(s)	Guiding Research Question	Study Design/Description	Subject Selection Criteria/Demographic Characteristics	Primary Dependent Measures	Outcomes	Analytic Details
Luk, Staiger, Mathai, Field, & Adler, 1998	What are the relative effects of modified cognitive-behavioral therapy vs. conjoint family therapy vs. eclectic therapy?	RCT: modified cognitive-behavioural therapy (MCBT) (*n* = 12) vs. conjoint family therapy (FT) (*n* = 9) vs. eclectic therapy (ET) (*n* = 11). Setting: outpatient clinic; Format: family therapy; Duration: 12 sessions over 24 weeks; Therapists: staff therapists; Treatment manual: guidelines; Treatment integrity: treatment record; Participants: families; Follow-up intervals: baseline, 6 months.	Sample: Children referred to a regional mental health services with symptoms of ODD/CD; Age: (M = 8.5); Gender: 63% male; Race/Ethnicity: DK	CBCL, ECBI, FAD, PSI, DAS, HSES	Outcomes at 6 months after baseline showed no significant differences between groups. There were significant improvements for all groups in parent ratings of internalizing and externalizing behaviors, irritability, and aggressiveness.	Analysis Sample: intent to treat Attrition: DK Effect Size: CBCL Total (MCBT vs. ET = 0.38, FT vs. ET = 0.63)

Table 11.3.3 Psychosocial Studies of Childhood Disruptive Behavior Disorders: Community-Based Interventions

Study Citation(s)	Guiding Research Question	Study Design/Description	Subject Selection Criteria/Demographic Characteristics	Primary Dependent Measures	Outcomes	Analytic Details
Burns, Farmer, Angold, Costello, & Behar, 1996	Does the addition of a case manager to a treatment team affect outcomes for youth and families?	RCT: treatment team led by a case manager ($n = 82$) vs. treatment team without a case manager ($n = 85$). Setting: public mental health center; Format: individualized; Duration: individualized; Therapists: case managers, primarily BA-level; Treatment manual: no; Treatment integrity: yes; Participants: family with focus on target child; Follow-up intervals: baseline, 3, 6, 9, 12 months postbaseline.	Sample: Children with SED who presented for outpatient services at public mental health center Age: 8–17; Gender: 53% boys; Race/Ethnicity: 77% White 13% African American 10% Other	CASA; CAFAS, CAPA, CABA, Parent satisfaction	Youth with case managers remained in services longer, received a wider array of services, had fewer inpatient days, had more community-based services, and had greater parent satisfaction with treatment. Symptoms and functioning did not differ between groups.	Analysis Sample: intent to treat; Attrition: experimental = 10%, control = 13%; Effect size: n/a
Clark, Lee, Prange, & McDonald, 1996	Can a wraparound strategy be used to improve outcomes for youth in the foster care system?	RTC: regular foster care ($n = 78$) vs. Fostering Individualized Assistance Program (FIAP) ($n = 54$). Setting: home/community; Format: individualized; Duration: unclear; Therapists: family specialists (case managers/ counselors), credentials unclear; Treatment manual: no; Treatment integrity: unclear; Participants: families; Follow-up intervals: unclear, final follow-up 2.5 years after randomization.	Sample: Youth in foster care with behavioral/ Emotional disturbance Age: 7–15; Gender: DK; Race/Ethnicity: DK	Placement, runaway, incarceration	During the approximate 2.5 years after program entry, youth in FIAP showed fewer placement changes, less time spent running away, and fewer days incarcerated.	Analysis sample: unclear; Attrition: DK; Effect size: n/a

(continued)

Table 11.3.3 Psychosocial Studies of Childhood Disruptive Behavior Disorders: Community-Based Interventions (*Continued*)

Study Citation(s)	Guiding Research Question	Study Design/Description	Subject Selection Criteria/Demographic Characteristics	Primary Dependent Measures	Outcomes	Analytic Details
Evans, Armstrong, & Kuppinger, 1996	How do outcomes from Family-Centered Intensive Case Management compare to results from Family-based Treatment (a version of Treatment Foster Care)?	RCT: Family-Centered Intensive Case Management (FCICM) (*n* = 27) vs. Family-based Treatment (*n* = 15). Setting: home; Format: individualized; Duration: individualized; Therapists: family specialists, case managers, paraprofessionals; Treatment manual: no; Treatment integrity: yes; Participants: families (treatment foster care families and natural families); Follow-up intervals: every 6 months during treatment and 6 months post-treatment.	Sample: children with SED referred for out of home placement. Age: 5–12; Gender: 91% male; Race/Ethnicity: 67% African American 33% White	CBCL, CAFAS, FACES III, CDF	A significant decrease in symptoms on CDF at 6 months and 1 year for the FCICM group was observed. The FCICM group showed significant improvement in behavior, moods and emotions, and role performance. There were no significant differences between groups or across time for FACES III.	Analysis sample: youth in study for at least one year (*n* = 17); Attrition: n/a (ongoing study); Effect size: n/a
Lochman, Lampron, Gemmer, Harris, & Wyckoff, 1989	Does anger-coping group intervention (with and without adjunctive teacher consultation) improve problem behavior and social competence?	RCT: Anger coping (AC) (*n* = 11) vs. anger coping plus teacher consultation (ACTC) (*n* = 13) vs. no treatment (UC) (*n* = 8). Setting: schools; Format: group; Duration: anger coping = 18 weekly sessions (45–60 minutes each), teacher consultation = 6 contact hours in groups; Therapists: school counselors and public mental health staff or trainees; Treatment manual: DK; Treatment integrity: DK; Participants: child, teachers; Follow-up intervals: posttest.	Sample: Teacher-nominated aggressive/disruptive boys; Age: 9–13; Gender: 100% male; Race/Ethnicity: 69% African American 31% White	BOSPT; MCBC; PCSC	There were posttreatment differences in off-task disruptive–aggressive behavior, perceived social competence, and teacher-reported aggressiveness. Intervention groups, with and without teacher consultation, showed similar improvements. Effect sizes suggest larger effects for ACTC than for AC.	Analysis sample: intent to treat; Attrition: 0%; Effect size: BOSPT (ACTC vs. UC = 0.81; AC vs. UC = .40); MCBC (ACTC vs. UC = 0.60; AC vs. UC = 0.22)

Citation	Research Question	Method	Sample	Measures	Results	Analysis
Lochman, Coie, Underwood, & Terry, 1993	Is a comprehensive social relations intervention effective for improving social status, problem behavior, and prosocial behaviors for aggressive, rejected and nonaggressive, rejected children?	RCT: Social skills and cognitive-behavioral strategies vs. non-intervention control group for aggressive, rejected and nonaggressive, rejected youth (AR intervention $n = 9$; R intervention $n = 17$; AR control = 9; R control = 17). Setting: school; Format: group & individual; Duration: 26 individual sessions, 8 group sessions; Therapists: graduate students and PhD psychologist; Treatment manual: DK; Treatment integrity: DK; Participants: child; Follow-up Intervals: post-intervention and one year.	Sample: Children with high standardized scores for aggression (i.e, starts fights) and/or high "liked least" scores on sociometric nominations; Age: 4th grade; Gender: 52% male; Race/Ethnicity: 100% African American	TBC, peer nominations and ratings; HSES	Significant reductions in aggression and improvement in prosocial behavior were observed at postintervention and 1-year follow-up for aggressive, rejected group only. No effect was found when entire treatment vs. control groups were compared.	Analysis sample: completer; Attrition: Control = 35%, Intervention = 45% postintervention; Effect size: Aggression (ARI vs. ARC = 0.85), Social Preference (ARI vs. ARC = 0.89)
Schoenwald, Ward, Henggeler, & Rowland, 2000; Henggeler, Rowland, Randall, Ward, Pickrel, Cunningham, Miller, Zealberg, Hand, & Santos, 1999	What is the effectiveness of Multisystemic Therapy (MST) vs. hospitalization for youth approved for emergency psychiatric hospitalization?	RCT: MST ($n = 57$) vs. hospitalization ($n = 56$). Setting: community; Format: individualized; Duration: 4 months (mean of 97.1 hours of contact for MST); Therapists: master's-level therapists supervised by child psychiatrist; Treatment manual: yes; Treatment integrity: yes; Participants: youth and families; Follow-up intervals: baseline, 1–2 weeks postbaseline, 4 months postbaseline.	Youth presenting with a psychiatric emergency (62% with disruptive behavior disorders) and deemed eligible for hospitalization prior to randomization Age: 10–17; Gender: 65% male; Race/Ethnicity: 64% African American 34% White 1% Asian American 1% Hispanic	GSI-BSI; CBCL; FACES-III; arrests; Service Utilization Survey	MST was more effective than hospitalization on most domains. Youth in MST spent fewer days in any out of home placement, showed a decrease in externalizing symptoms, improved school attendance, and improved family functioning. MST also had higher consumer satisfaction. Hospitalization was more effective than MST at improving self-esteem.	Analysis sample: completer; Attrition: 2.6% from randomization to T1, no attrition after T1; Effect size: CBCL = 0.48, FACES-III = 0.49

Table 11.3.4 Prevention Studies of Childhood Disruptive Behavior Disorders

Study Citation(s)	Guiding Research Question	Study Design/Description	Subject Selection Criteria/Demographic Characteristics	Primary Dependent Measures	Outcomes	Analytic Details
Conduct Problems Prevention Research Group, 1999a, 1999b	What is the effectiveness of Fast Track, a multisite, multicomponent preventive intervention for young children at high risk for long-term antisocial behavior?	Quasi-experimental: kindergartners were screened for behavioral problems; half of the schools were designated as intervention (child n = 445) and half as control (child n = 446); intervention includes universal (adapted version of Promoting Alternative Thinking Strategies) and selective components (parent groups, child social skills training, academic tutoring). Setting: schools/homes; Format: whole school/group/individual; Duration: school-year; Therapists: teachers/experienced therapists from participating communities; Treatment manual: yes; Treatment integrity: yes; Participants: children and parents; Follow-up intervals: kindergarten, end of Grade 1.	Sample: Kindergartners with early disruptive patterns; Age: kindergarten; Gender: 69% male; Race/Ethnicity: 51% African American 47% White 2% Pacific Islander and Hispanic	CBCL, PDR, TRF, SCR, SPS, SCS, peer nominations	Outcomes were assessed for the 1st grade year. The intervention group showed improvement in reading, positive peer interaction and peer preference scored, more positive parenting, and behavioral improvements. Effects were similar for boys and girls and for African American and white students.	Analytic strategy: all available Attrition: less than 10% Effect size: CBCL Total = 0.01

Citation	Research Question	Design/Method	Sample	Measures	Results	Analysis Sample
Vitaro & Tremblay, 1994; McCord, Tremblay, Vitaro, & Desmarais-Gervais, 1994; Tremblay, Pagani-Kurtz, Masse, Vitaro, & Pihl, 1995	What are the effects of a preventive intervention (The Montreal Prevention Experiment) through early adolescence?	RCT: Montreal Prevention Experiment (n = 46) vs. control (n = 56); intervention includes parent training, social skills training, and cognitive problem-solving. Setting: school, home; Format: group, individual; Duration: 2 years; Therapists: DK; Treatment manual: yes; Treatment integrity: yes; Participants: children and parents; Follow-up intervals: baseline, annual at end of school year (grades 4–6).	Sample: Kindergartners with elevated aggression and risk of later conduct problems (based on teacher report); Age: 7–8 during treatment; Gender: 100% male; Race/Ethnicity: 100% French-speaking, White, Canadians	SBQ, PEI, SRD	At age 12, teachers reported less aggressiveness for treatment group. More boys in the treatment group remained in regular classroom placements and more (30% vs. 14%) were rated as having satisfactory school adjustment. There were nonsignificant trends toward less self-reported delinquency and less disruptive friends by the treatment group.	Analysis sample: all available; Attrition: 24% by age 10; Effect size: SBQ at age 10 (1 year posttreatment) = 0.22; at age 12 = 0.39
Walker, Kavanagh, Stiller, Golly, Severson, & Feil, 1998	What are the effects of a prevention program (First Step to Success) for diverting at-risk kindergartners from an antisocial path?	RCT: First Step to Success (n = 46) vs. wait list controls (n = 46); intervention includes proactive, universal screening, school intervention, and parent training. Setting: school and home; Format: whole-school, group, individual; Duration: 3 months; Therapists: graduate students and school personnel; Treatment manual: yes; Treatment integrity: yes; Participants: teachers, children, parents; Follow-up intervals: baseline, postintervention, 1st grade, 2nd grade.	Sample: Kindergartners who showed early signs of antisocial behavior; Age: kindergartners; Gender: 74% male; Race/Ethnicity: 93% White 7% Minority	TRAB, TRMB; Observations; TRF	Outcomes assessed during 1st and 2nd grade showed improved adaptive behavior, less maladaptive behavior, and less aggression for intervention youth. Results from postintervention remained fairly consistent at longer follow-ups (e.g., through 2nd grade).	Analysis sample: all available; Attrition: 3% postintervention; Effect size: CBCL Aggression at postintervention = 0.99

Table 11.3.5 Psychopharmacological Studies of Childhood Disruptive Behavior Disorders

Study Citation(s)	Guiding Research Question	Study Design/Description	Subject Selection Criteria/Demographic Characteristics	Primary Dependent Measures	Outcomes	Analytic Details
Campbell, Adams, Small, Kafantaris, Silva, Shell, Perry, & Overall, 1995	What is the efficacy and safety of lithium for children with treatment-refractory aggressiveness and explosiveness with CD?	RTC: Double-blind, placebo-controlled, within-subject alternating treatments design. Lithium (n = 25) vs. placebo (n = 25). Setting: inpatient; Duration: 10 weeks (2 week placebo, 6 week random assignment to placebo or lithium, 2 week posttreatment placebo); Dosing: stepwise progression 600–2,100 mg/day using coded schedule; Compliance monitored: yes; Status of blind assessed: DK; Follow-up intervals: baseline, 4 weeks, 6 weeks.	Sample: inpatients with treatment-refractory aggressiveness and explosiveness CD; Age: 5–12; Gender: 92% male; Race/Ethnicity: 48% Hispanic 38% African American 8% White 6% other	GCJS, CPRS(a), CGI, CTRS	During lithium period, children showed moderate or marked improvement [Global Clinical Judgments (Consensus) Scale Ratings—68% vs. 40% for placebo]. Other measures showed trends in favor of lithium. Results replicate earlier findings on superiority of lithium over placebo, but current results show somewhat higher rates of placebo responders than previous.	Analysis sample: completer; Attrition: none after start of treatment Effect size: marked/moderate improvement = 0.64; Medication response rate: 68%; Placebo response rate: 40%

| Cueva, Overall, Small, Armenteros, Perry, & Campbell, 1996 | What is the short-term efficacy and safety of carbamazepine to reduce aggressiveness in children with CD? | RTC: Double-blind, placebo-controlled, parallel-groups design. By end of baseline period, 23 remained eligible: carbamazepine ($n = 12$) vs. placebo ($n = 11$). Setting; inpatient; Duration: 9 weeks (2 week placebo, 6 week treatment, 1 week posttreatment placebo); Dosing; stepwise progression 200–1000 mg/day using coded schedule; Compliance monitored: yes; Status of blind assessed: yes; Follow-up intervals: twice during placebo baseline, 4 weeks, 6 weeks, end of posttreatment placebo. | Sample: inpatients with treatment-resistant aggressiveness and explosiveness CD; Age: 5-12; Gender: 91% male; Race/Ethnicity: 41% African American 46% Hispanic 9% White 4% Asian | GCJS, CGI; CPRS(b) | Carbamazepine was not more successful than placebo in reducing aggressive behavior. The study was underpowered. The effect size estimate suggests positive findings for carbamazepine. Treatment produced a number of side effects (transient leukopenia, rash, dizziness, pilopia). Nine youth were eliminated from the initial sample because of reduction or cessation of aggressive behavior during initial placebo period. | Analysis sample: completer; Attrition: 44% from baseline; 9% after baseline placebo; Effect size: 0.73; Medication response rate: 82%; Placebo response rate: 54% |

(continued)

Table 11.3.5 Psychopharmacological Studies of Childhood Disruptive Behavior Disorders (*Continued*)

Study Citation(s)	Guiding Research Question	Study Design/Description	Subject Selection Criteria/Demographic Characteristics	Primary Dependent Measures	Outcomes	Analytic Details
Greenhill, Solomon, Pleak, & Ambrosini, 1985	Is molindone as effective as thioridazine in treating children with undersocialized conduct disorder, aggressive type?	RCT: double-blind, parallel-groups design. Thioridazine ($n = 16$) vs. molindone ($n = 15$). Setting: inpatient; Duration: 8 weeks (1 week off drug; 1 week placebo; 1 week titration on treatment drug; 3 weeks fixed dose; 2 week posttreatment placebo); Dosing: initial dose equivalent to 125 mg thioridazine or 25 mg molindone. Titrated to sedation, fixed for 3 weeks (overall treatment mean: thioridazine = 169.9 mg/day, molindone = 26.8 mg/day); Compliance monitored: DK; Status of blind assessed: raters knew when active drug given, but not which drug; Follow-up intervals: placebo baseline, treatment week 1, treatment week 4, posttreatment placebo.	Sample: inpatients with undersocialized CD, aggressive type; Age: 6–11; Gender: 100% boys; Race/Ethnicity: 45% African American 36% Hispanic 19% White	CRS, DOTES, IAG, CPRS(b), CGI	Ratings comparing placebo and active treatment periods showed clinical improvement for both groups, but no differential change. Thioridazine was associated with more sedation.	Analysis sample: completer; Effect Size: degree of improvement (CGI) = 0.67; Medication response rate: NA Placebo response rate: NA

| Klein, 1998; Klein, Abikoff, Klass, Ganeles, Seese, & Pollack, 1997 | Would methylphenidate hydrochloride, which is effective in ADHD, be effective for treating CD? | RCT: double-blind, methylphenidate ($n = 41$) vs. placebo ($n = 42$).

Setting: outpatient; Duration: 5 weeks; Dosing: pretest titration up to 60 mg/day in 2 divided doses, adjusted during treatment on basis of adverse effects and clinical response (average treatment dose = 41.3 mg/day); Compliance monitored: DK; Status of blind assessed: DK; Follow-up intervals: baseline, end of treatment. | Sample: Youth with CD (2/3 also had ADHD) recruited from schools and juvenile probation; Age: 6–15; Gender: 89% male; Race/Ethnicity: 65% White 29% African American 6% Hispanic | CTRS, QBC-R, COC | Improved ratings were observed on a range of behavioral outcomes by the parent and teacher report. Effects of methylphenidate are not dependent on severity of co-occurring ADHD symptoms. Significantly more children in the treatment group were rated as improved by all informants. Changes to the research protocol were required to include youth with CD and co-occurring ADHD because of the relative rarity of "pure" CD cases in actual clinical practice. | Analysis sample: completer; Attrition: NA Effect Size: responders (mean report) = 1.47; Medication response rate: by teachers' ratings: 59%, by mothers 78%, by psychiatrists 68%. Placebo response rate: by teachers 9%, mothers 27%, psychiatrists 11% |

sufficient data to examine outcomes at the completion of intervention, or did not meet inclusion criteria described in the introduction. In addition to this search, we also examined older citations from the review by Brestan and Eyberg (1998) of the literature on treating disruptive behavior disorders. This resulted in a total of 30 articles reviewed. Brestan and Eyberg's review summarized research through 1995 and has been cited extensively in many recent publications. The current review extends, rather than duplicates, the Brestan and Eyberg article.

Results from the present review are discussed within five heuristic categories: parent training, community-based interventions, clinic-based treatments, prevention programs, and psychopharmacological treatments. These categories were developed to provide structure in a field with quite diverse approaches to intervention. In contrast to the research literature for other disorders in this review, adjunctive studies examining combined psychosocial and pharmacological interventions were not found.

Parent training is highlighted because it is a generic heading that captures both of the "well-established" treatments identified by Brestan and Eyberg. Support seems to be particularly strong for Webster-Stratton's Parents and Children Series. Most of the research on this intervention has been directed toward parents of youth in the preschool and early school years.

Community-based interventions primarily include treatments that are delivered in the child and family's natural ecology and that focus on meeting the individualized needs of youth and their families. Multisystemic therapy (MST) has the strongest evidence within this section. However, most studies of MST have focused on adolescents, rather than youth under the age of 13. Various approaches to case management appear to have positive effects, particularly on treatment-related outcomes, but large direct effects on symptoms and functioning have not been found.

Clinic-based interventions included a heterogeneous set of individual and family interventions. Overall, this set of interventions showed improvements over time for youth. However, differential improvement between groups was not always significant. This section provides findings that suggest possible effectiveness of several interventions (e.g., day treatment, Problem Solving combined with Parent Management Training, Family Effectiveness Training). However, the research base is not particularly strong.

Preventive interventions are unique for disruptive disorders within this review. This is in part because the risk factors for disruptive disorders have been consistently determined, and therefore, prevention programs have been developed to reduce the probability of later problems in at-risk youth. All interventions in this section include a multifaceted intervention that targets the multiple risk factors for the development of disruptive disorders. An intervention conducted by Tremblay and colleagues (1995) has the longest follow-up data, and results look promising into early adolescence and beyond. Two recent studies included here are Fast Track and LIFT. Initial outcomes from these projects look promising, but more time is needed to assess their long-term effects.

Research on pharmacological interventions is relatively rare for disruptive disorders (except for youth with comorbid ADHD). Recent studies suggest potentially positive benefits of lithium and methylphenidate hydrochloride. In both cases, the evidence is not yet extensive.

Overall, interventions for disruptive disorders tend to focus on the child's behavior and significant others (particularly parents). There is some evidence for the effectiveness of a variety of approaches. There is also growing evidence for the effectiveness of multifaceted prevention programs to prevent development of disorders in at-risk youth. In the treatment of disruptive disorders, children age 6–12 are a relatively understudied population. More attention has been given to youth who are younger (e.g., preschoolers) or older (e.g., adolescents). There is a tremendous need for additional research to build upon the positive interventions described here and to examine long-term effectiveness.

Studies of Childhood Anxiety Disorders

Studies of outpatient interventions for anxiety symptoms and anxiety disorders in school-aged children are presented in Table 11.4. Several approaches were combined to identify relevant published studies. The following key words and synonyms were searched in PsycINFO and Medline: anxiety, worries, fears, anxiety disorder, separation anxiety disorder, generalized anxiety disorder, overanxious disorder, avoidant disorder, panic disorder, agoraphobia, phobia, simple phobia, social phobia, selective mutism, school refusal, and obsessive-compulsive disorder. The results of these searches were then crossed with the appropriate age group (6–12 years old), with treatment modalities (treatment, psychopharmacology, psychotherapy, cognitive-behavior therapy, intervention, behavior modification), then with study design and time frame (1985–2001). Studies investigating school refusal/school phobia and elective mutism were also included because the behavior is so often associated with anxiety and anxiety disorders. Reference lists obtained from review articles and book chapters were searched to ensure that the relevant studies were identified. The initial pool of 75 articles was then reduced using the general inclusion criteria for this project. Forty-four papers were excluded for the following reasons: open-label drug study, single case report, all subjects older than 12 years old, retrospective chart review, or no comparison group. The final anxiety matrix (Table 11.4) includes 31 papers. The matrix divides the treatments into two categories: psychosocial studies and psychopharmacological studies. No adjunctive studies that met our criteria were found.

Four studies evaluated various behavioral treatments for childhood simple phobias, six studies systematically evaluated the efficacy of cognitive-behavioral interventions for a mix of anxiety disorders, and one study systematically evaluated the efficacy of cognitive-behavior therapy when presented in a group format versus the more traditional child-focused individual format. Five studies evaluated the potential benefit of cognitive-behavioral interventions for the treatment of childhood PTSD and related symptoms and two studies evaluated the efficacy of cognitive-behavioral treatments for the treatment of children with comorbid school refusal and anxiety disorders. Cognitive-behavior therapy (CBT), systematic desensitization and exposure have been found to reduce anxiety symptoms and fears. Interestingly, in several of the CBT stud-

Table 11.4.1 Psychosocial Studies of Childhood Anxiety Disorders

Study Citation(s)	Guiding Research Question	Study Design/Description	Subject Selection Criteria/Demographic Characteristics	Primary Dependent Measures	Outcomes	Analytic Details
Barrett, 1998	To evaluate the efficacy of CBT and family management training procedures presented in group format for childhood anxiety disorders	RCT; child-only group CBT (GCBT; n = 19) vs. child and parent group CBT plus family management training (GCBT+; n = 15) vs. wait list control (WL; n = 16). Setting: university outpatient clinic; Format: group; Participants: child and parents; Duration: 12 weekly sessions; Therapists: four registered psychologists; Treatment manual: yes; Treatment integrity: yes; Follow-up interval: 12 months.	Children with DSM-III-R overanxious disorder (n = 30), separation anxiety disorder (n = 26), or social phobia (n = 4) based on ADIS-C/P structured interviews Age: 7–14; Gender: 53% male; Race/Ethnicity: DK (only non-English speaking households reported)	ADIS-C, ADIS-P, clinician ratings of improvement, FSCC-R, CBCL	Both treatment groups showed significant improvements on clinician, child, and parent outcomes at posttreatment and follow-up; 56% of GCBT, 71% of GCBT+, and 25% of WL subjects no longer met diagnostic criteria for any current anxiety disorder; no significant difference between treatment groups on diagnostic status at posttreatment or follow-up; compared to GCBT, GCBT+ was associated with marginally better improvement at posttreatment and follow-up on clinician, child, and parent outcomes.	Analysis sample: completer; Attrition: GCBT = 17%, GCBT+ = 12%, WL = 20%; FSSCR effect size: GCBT = 1.58, GCBT+ = 2.53; CBCL-I (mother) effect size: GCBT = 3.37, GCBT+ = 3.98; CBCL-I (father) effect size: GCBT = 2.11, GCBT+ = 3.27; Response rate: GCBT = 65%, GCBT+ = 85%, WL = 25%

Study	Purpose	Design/Method	Sample	Measures	Results	Analysis
Barrett, Dadds, & Rapee, 1996	To evaluate the efficacy of CBT with and without family management training procedures for the treatment of select childhood anxiety disorders	RCT; cognitive-behavior therapy (CBT; n = 28) vs. cognitive-behavior therapy plus family management (CBT+; n = 25) vs. wait list control (WL; n = 23). Setting: university clinic; Format: individual and family; Participants: child and parent(s); Duration: 12 sessions; Therapists: five registered clinical psychologists; Treatment manual: yes; Treatment integrity: yes; Follow-up interval: 6 and 12 months.	Children with DSM-III-R overanxious disorder (n = 30), separation anxiety disorder (n = 30), or social phobia (n = 19) based on ADIS-C/P structured interviews. Age: 7–14 (M = 9.3); Gender: 57% male; Race/Ethnicity: unspecified	ADIS-C/P, RCMAS, FSSC-R, CBCL, DASS, FEAR	Compared to WL group, both active treatments were associated with clinically significant gains across multiple outcomes, which were maintained over 6- and 12-month follow-up period; RCMAS revealed an overall reduction in self-reported anxiety across time for all three groups; compared to CBT, CBT+ was superior on several outcomes, with differences greatest on clinician ratings; younger children and girls improved most in CBT+ condition; 100% of the younger children in the CBT+ group achieved a no-diagnosis status at posttreatment compared to 56% of the younger children in the CBT group.	Analysis sample: completer; Attrition: CBT = 11%, CBT+ = 8%, WL = 17%; CBCL-I effect size: CBT = 0.96, CBT+ = 1.19; FSSC-R effect size = CBT = 0.49, CBT+ = 0.73; Response rate: CBT = 57%, CBT+ = 84%, WL = 26%
Barrett, Duffy, Dadds, & Rapee, 2001	To evaluate the long-term efficacy of CBT for the treatment of select childhood anxiety disorders	Follow-up study; cognitive-behavior therapy (CBT; n = 31), cognitive-behavior therapy plus family management (CBT+; n = 21). See Barrett et al. (1996) for details on the original study design.	See Barrett et al. (1996). Age at follow-up: 13–21 (M = 16.08); Gender distribution at follow-up: 54% male; Race/Ethnicity: unspecified	ADIS-C, RCMAS, FSSC-R, CBCL, DASS, FEAR	Average length of time since completion of treatment was 6.17 years (5.33 to 7.08); treatment gains were maintained at long-term follow-up, as measured by clinician, parent, and child ratings; 86% achieved a no-diagnosis status at long-term follow-up, compared to 80% at the 12-month follow-up period; 13% had relapsed by long-term follow-up; contrary to previous findings, CBT and CBT+ were found to be equally effective at long-term follow-up.	Analysis sample: completer Attrition: 32% of original total sample did not participate in follow-up study; Effect size: n/a

(continued)

Table 11.4.1 Psychosocial Studies of Childhood Anxiety Disorders (*Continued*)

Study Citation(s)	Guiding Research Question	Study Design/Description	Subject Selection Criteria/Demographic Characteristics	Primary Dependent Measures	Outcomes	Analytic Details
Beidel, Turner, & Morris, 2000	To evaluate the efficacy of social effectiveness therapy for the treatment of childhood social phobia	RCT; social effectiveness therapy for children (SET-C; *n* = 30) vs. nonspecific treatment control (NSTC; *n* = 20). Setting: university clinic; Format: group and individual; Participants: child and parent; Duration: twice weekly for 12 weeks; Therapists: unspecified; Treatment manual: yes; Treatment integrity: unspecified; Follow-up interval: 6 months.	Children with DSM-IV diagnosis of social phobia based on parent and child ADIS-C/P structured interview Age: 8–12 (M = 10.5); Gender: 60% female; Race/Ethnicity: 70% Caucasian 22% African American 4% Hispanic 4% Biracial	CDI, EPI, SPAI-C, STAI-C, CBCL-I, ADIS-C, K-GAS, behavioral measures, daily diary	Compared to NSTC, SET-C was associated with significantly more improvement across multiple domains, including improved social skills, reduced social fear, anxiety and distress, and improved functioning in daily social interactions; improvement was consistent across self-ratings, parent ratings, and independent evaluators; no differential treatment effects were noted based on race, gender, or age; treatment gains were sustained at 6-month follow-up	Analysis sample: completer; Attrition: SET-C = 14%, NTC = 20%; Effect size: SPAI-C = 0.91, CBCL-I = 0.89, K-GAS = 1.46; Response rate: SET-C = 67%, NTC = 5%
Berliner & Saunders, 1996	To evaluate the relative efficacy of adding stress inoculation training and gradual exposure to standard group treatment for sexually abused children.	RCT; conventional sexual abuse group therapy (CGT; *n* = 32) vs. conventional sexual abuse group therapy plus stress inoculation training and gradual exposure (CGT+; *n* = 48). Setting: outpatient specialty clinic; Format: group; Participants: child; Duration: 10 sessions; Therapists: master's-level clinical social workers; Treatment manual: yes; Treatment integrity: yes; Follow-up interval: 1 and 2 years.	Children with a history of child sexual abuse; 81% had a chart diagnosis of PTSD. Age: 4–13 (M = 8.2); Gender: 89% female; Race/Ethnicity: 74% White 11% African American 6% Hispanic 9% Other	FSSC-R, SAFE, RCMAS, CBCL, CDI, CSBI	The addition of stress inoculation training and gradual exposure to standard group treatment did not produce greater improvement on measures of fear and symptoms of anxiety; outcomes for both groups improved over time; depending on outcome, 20% to 40% of children in both groups improved by at least one SD at 2-year follow-up; 5% to 15% of children in both groups deteriorated substantially over time.	Analysis sample: completer; Attrition: 67% completed treatment and of these, 87% and 78% completed the 1- and 2-year follow-up, respectively; Effect size: n/a

Study	Purpose	Design/Method	Sample	Measures	Results	Analysis sample/Effect size
Celano, Hazzard, Webb, & McCall, 1996	To evaluate and compare the efficacy of two interventions for sexually abused girls and their nonoffending female caretakers.	RCT; recovering from sexual abuse program, based on Finkelhor's four-factor model (RAP, $n = 15$) vs. treatment as usual (TAU; $n = 17$). Setting: hospital outpatient clinic; Format: individual and conjoint; Participants: child and caretaker; Duration: 8 sessions; Therapists: licensed clinicians and trainees; Treatment manual: yes; Treatment integrity: unspecified; Follow-up interval: none.	Girls with a documented history of sexual abuse. Age: 8–13 ($M = 10.5$); Gender: 100% female; Race/Ethnicity: 75% African American 22% White 3% Hispanic	CBCL, CITES-R, CGAS, PRIDS, PAS	Both treatments were associated with significant reductions in self-reported PTSD symptomatology and improved overall functioning; compared to TAU, RAP was more effective in increasing abuse-related caretaker support of the child, decreasing caretaker self-blame, and decreasing expectations of negative impact on child.	Analysis sample: completer; Attrition: RAP = 40%; TAU = 23%; Effect size: PRIDS = 0.21, PAS-SB = 0.18, PAS-NI = 0.48, CGAS = 0.38
Cornwall, Spence, & Schotte, 1996	To evaluate the efficacy of emotive imagery for the treatment of childhood simple phobia, specifically darkness fears	RCT; emotive imagery therapy (EIT; $n = 12$) vs. wait list control group (WL; $n = 12$). Setting: university outpatient clinic; Format: individual; Participants: child; Duration: 6 sessions; Therapists: one master's-level psychologist; Treatment manual: yes; Treatment integrity: unspecified; Follow-up interval: 3 months.	Children with DSM-III-R simple phobia (darkness fears) based on ADIS structured interview Age: 7–10 ($M = 8.25$); Gender: unspecified; Race/Ethnicity: unspecified	ADIS-C, ADIS-P, RCMAS, FSSC-R, DFBQ, FT, darkness tolerance test (behavioral measure)	Compared to WL, EIT was associated with significantly greater reductions on all child and parent outcome measures, and behavioral measures; EIT group continued to show greater reductions in symptoms of darkness phobia at 3-month follow-up	Analysis sample: completer; Attrition: 0%; Effect size: FSSC-R = 0.53; RCMAS = 0.52; darkness tolerance test = 1.59

(continued)

Table 11.4.1 Psychosocial Studies of Childhood Anxiety Disorders (*Continued*)

Study Citation(s)	Guiding Research Question	Study Design/Description	Subject Selection Criteria/Demographic Characteristics	Primary Dependent Measures	Outcomes	Analytic Details
Dadds, Spence, Holland, Barrett, & Laurens, 1997	To evaluate a combined child and parent intervention for the prevention and early intervention of anxiety symptoms in children	Multi-site RCT; group child CBT and parent-focused intervention (CBT+; *n* = 61) vs. no treatment control (NTC; *n* = 67). Setting: school; Format: group; Participants: child and parents; Duration: 10 child sessions, 3 parent sessions; Therapists: clinical psychologists and graduate-level trainees; Treatment manual: yes; Treatment integrity: yes; Follow-up interval: 6 months.	Children with DSM-IV anxiety problem (disorder or features) based on child or teacher report and verified by ADIS-P structured interview; 74% of total sample met DSM-IV criteria for anxiety diagnosis Age: 7–14 (M = 9.39); Gender: 73% female; Race/Ethnicity: unspecified	ADIS-P, RCMAS, CBCL, ratings of change by clinician and parent of child and family adjustment	At posttreatment, both groups showed improvement in rates diagnosis, with nonsignificant between-group differences; at 6-month follow-up, the treatment group emerged with lower rates of diagnosis; of the children who had features of anxiety at pretreatment, 54% of the control group developed a diagnosable anxiety disorder, compared with 16% in the treatment group; ratings of change by parents and clinicians also showed that treatment was associated with greater child and family adjustment at posttreatment and follow-up; no between-group differences were found on the CBCL and RCMAS at posttreatment and follow-up; no differential treatment effects for age, gender, or diagnosis were found at posttreatment or 6-month follow-up.	Analysis sample: completer; Attrition: CBT+ = 3%, CTRL = 4%; Effect size: 0.60 (based on differences in rates of diagnosis at 6-month follow-up).

Study	Purpose	Method	Sample	Measures	Results	Notes
Dadds et al., 1999	To evaluate the long-term outcomes (12- and 24-month) of the Dadds et al. (1997) prevention and early intervention of anxiety project	Follow-up study; sample size at 12-month follow-up: CBT+ = 52, NTC = 56; sample size at 24-month follow-up: CBT+ = 52, NTC = 53. See Dadds et al. (1997) for details on the original study design.	See Dadds et al., 1997. At follow-up. Age: unspecified; Gender: unspecified; Race/Ethnicity: unspecified	ADIS-P by telephone, ratings of change by clinician and parent of child and family adjustment	At 12-month follow-up, no significant between-group differences in rates of anxiety diagnosis were found (intervention = 37%, control = 42%); however, significant between-group differences in rates of diagnosis rates emerged at 24-month follow-up (intervention = 20%, control = 39%); factors found to predict poor initial treatment response were: severity of pretreatment diagnosis, being female, parental anxiety, and being in the control group; whereas, pretreatment severity and being in the control group were the only two predictors of chronicity at 24 months	Analysis sample: completer; Attrition: CBT+ = 15%, NTC = 16%; Effect size: 0.43 (based on differences in rates of diagnosis at 24-month follow-up)
Deblinger & Lippman, 1996; Deblinger, Steer, & Lippmann, 1999	To evaluate the differential efficacy of child or nonoffending mother participation in CBT for treatment of PTSD in sexually abused children	RCT; child-only cognitive-behavior therapy (CBT-C; n = 24) vs. parent-only cognitive-behavior therapy (CBT-P; n = 22) vs. combined child and parent cognitive-behavior therapy (CBT-CP; n = 22) vs. standard community care (TAU; n = 22). Setting: outpatient specialty clinic; Format: individual and conjoint; Participants: child and parent; Duration: 12 sessions; Therapists: unspecified; Treatment manual: unspecified; Treatment integrity: yes; Follow-up interval: 3, 6, 12, and 24 months.	Children with documented history of contact sexual abuse and DSM-III-R PTSD or features of PTSD (subsyndromal) based K-SADS-E structural interview. Age: 7–13; Gender: 83% female; Race/Ethnicity: 72% White, 20% African American, 6% Hispanic, 2% Other	K-SADS-E, STAIC, CDI, CBCL, PPQ	Compared to children who did not receive the experimental treatment (CBT-P and TAU), children who did (CBT-C and CBT-CP) reported significantly greater reductions in overall PTSD symptomatology; compared to mothers who did not receive the experimental treatment (CBT-C and TAU), mothers who did (CBT-P and CBT-CP) reported greater use of effective parenting skills, noted significant decreases in their children's externalizing behaviors, and their children also reported significantly fewer symptoms of depression; all treatment gains were maintained at follow-up periods, except gains in parenting skills.	Analysis sample: completer; Attrition: CBT-C = 4%; CBT-P = 12%; CBT-CP = 12%; TAU = 16%; CBCL-E effect size: CBT-C = 0.15, CBT-P = 0.81, CBT-CP = 0.54; CDI effect size: CBT-C = 0.68, CBT-P = 0.47, CBT-CP = 0.74; PTSD effect size: CBT-C = 0.91, CBT-P = 0.54, CBT-CP = 0.88

(continued)

Table 11.4.1 Psychosocial Studies of Childhood Anxiety Disorders (*Continued*)

Study Citation(s)	Guiding Research Question	Study Design/Description	Subject Selection Criteria/Demographic Characteristics	Primary Dependent Measures	Outcomes	Analytic Details
Flannery-Schroeder & Kendall, 2000	To evaluate the efficacy of CBT presented in group format for the treatment of childhood anxiety disorders	RCT; group CBT (GCBT; $n = 12$) vs. individual CBT (ICBT; $n = 13$) vs. wait list control (WL; $n = 12$). Setting: university outpatient clinic; Format: individual and group; Participants: child; Duration: 18 weekly sessions; Therapists: 8 doctoral trainees; Treatment manual: yes; Treatment integrity: yes; Follow-up interval: 3 months.	Children with DSM-III-R generalized anxiety disorder ($n = 21$), separation anxiety disorder ($n = 11$), or social phobia ($n = 5$) based on ADIS-C/P structured interviews Age: 8–14; Gender: 54% male; Race/Ethnicity: 89% non-minority 11% minority	ADIS-C, ADIS-P, RCMAS, STAIC, CQ-C, SASC-R, CDI, SPPC, LS, FM-C, CBCL	Compared to WL, both ICBT and GCBT groups reported significantly lower general anxiety and enhanced coping abilities; 73% of ICBT, 50% of GCBT, and 8% of WL subjects did not meet criteria for their primary diagnosis at posttreatment; only ICBT group showed improvements in self-reported state anxiety (however, pretreatment scores on STAIC were significantly lower for GCBT group and GCBT subjects were proportionally younger); measures of social functioning showed no between-group differences; treatment gains in both groups were maintained at follow-up.	Analysis sample: completer and intent-to-treat; Attrition: GCBT = 0%, ICBT = 31%, WL = 17%; RCMAS effect size: GCBT = 1.11, ICBT = 0.79; CQ-C effect size: GCBT = 1.69, ICBT = 0.74; CBCL-I (mother) effect size: GCBT = 0.84, ICBT = 1.52; Response rate: GCBT = 50%, ICBT = 64%, WL = 0%.

Study	Purpose	Design/Method	Sample	Measures	Results	Analysis
Kendall, 1994	To evaluate the efficacy of CBT for the treatment of select childhood anxiety disorders	RCT; cognitive-behavior therapy (CBT; $n = 27$) vs. wait list (WL; $n = 20$). Setting: university clinic; Format: individual; Participants: children; Duration: average of 17 sessions for CBT (range 16–20), 8 weeks for WL; Therapists: 7 graduate-level trainees; Treatment manual: yes; Treatment integrity: yes; Follow-up interval: 1 year.	Children with DSM-III-R diagnosis of overanxious disorder ($n = 30$), separation anxiety ($n = 8$), or avoidant disorder ($n = 9$) based on ADIS-P structured interview. Age: 9–13; Gender: 60% male; Race/Ethnicity: 75% White 1% African American 24% Other	RCMAS, STAIC, FSSC-R, CDI, CQ-C, NASSQ, CBCL, STAIC-A-Trait-P, CBCL-T, CPTR, behavioral observations	Compared to WL, CBT group reported significantly lower general anxiety and enhanced coping abilities; parent ratings of anxiety/depression and social competence also improved; teacher ratings did not change; total behavioral observational score differentiated the CBT and WL groups; based on the CBCL-I, 60% of subjects were within the nondeviant range at posttreatment; subject's perception of the therapeutic relationship or therapist's perception of parental involvement were not related to outcomes	Analysis sample: completer; Attrition: 22% (not reported by group); Effect size: RCMAS = 0.87, FSSC-R = 0.38, CQ-C = 1.25, CBCL-I = 1.22; Response rate: CBT = 66%, WL = 5%
Kendall & Southam-Gerow, 1996	To determine whether treatment gains found by Kendall (1994) would be sustained 2 years after treatment and examine children's perception of the therapeutic process	Follow-up study; of the eligible subjects ($n = 44$), 36 agreed to participate in follow-up study. see Kendall (1996) for details on the original study design; follow-up interval: 2–5 years ($M = 3.35$).	See Kendall (1994). Age: $M = 15.61$ (range = 11.33–18.25); Gender: 56% male; Race/Ethnicity: unspecified	RCMAS, CQ-C, NASSQ, CDI, CBCL, STAIC-A-Trait-P, CQ-P, ADIS-P	Subjects treated between 2–5 years earlier largely maintained their treatment gains from previous 1-year follow-up; at long-term follow-up 74% of the subjects remained below clinical levels on the CBCL; when subjects were asked to identify what was most important about treatment, the most frequent response was the therapeutic relationship rather than specific treatment components	Analysis sample: completer; Attrition: 18%; Effect size: n/a

(continued)

Table 11.4.1 Psychosocial Studies of Childhood Anxiety Disorders (*Continued*)

Study Citation(s)	Guiding Research Question	Study Design/Description	Subject Selection Criteria/Demographic Characteristics	Primary Dependent Measures	Outcomes	Analytic Details

Kendall et al., 1997	To replicate and extend Kendall (1994) study; to evaluate the influence of comorbidity on outcomes; to compare outcomes by treatment segment (cognitive-educational, enactive exposure)	RCT; cognitive-behavior therapy (CBT; *n* = 60) vs. wait list control (WL; *n* = 34).
		
		Setting: university clinic; Format: individual; Participants: children; Duration: average of 18 sessions for CBT (range 16–20), 8 weeks for WL; Therapists: 11 graduate-level trainees; Treatment integrity: yes; Treatment manual: yes; Follow-up interval: 1 year.
			Children with DSM-III-R diagnosis of overanxious disorder (*n* = 55), separation anxiety disorder (*n* = 22), avoidant disorder (*n* = 17) based on ADIS-C/P structured interviews
			
			Sample: volunteers and referrals;
			Age: 9–13;
			Gender: 62% male;
			Race/Ethnicity:
			  85% Caucasian
			  5% African American
			  2% Hispanic
			  2% Asian
			  6% Other
				ADIS, RCMAS, STAIC, FSSC-R, CDI, CQ-C, NASSQ, CBCL, STAIC-A-Trait-P, CQ-P, CBCL-T, behavioral observations	Results were overall very similar to earlier study; CBT group reported significantly lower general anxiety and enhanced coping abilities; parent ratings of anxiety/depression and social competence also improved; teacher ratings did not change; subjects who were not diagnosis free also experienced significant improvement; total behavioral observational score differentiated the CBT and WL groups; based on the CBCL-I, 56% of subjects were within the nondeviant range at posttreatment; no therapist effects were found; comorbidity was not found to moderate outcome; treatment gains were sustained at follow-up.	Analysis sample: completer; Attrition: CBT = 13%; WL = 21%; Effect size: RCMAS = 0.59, FSSC-R = 0.51, CQ-C = 0.92, CBCL-I (mother) = 0.71; Response rate: CBT = 53%, WL = 6%

King et al., 1998	To evaluate the efficacy of CBT for the treatment of school-refusing children	RCT; cognitive-behavior therapy and parent/teacher behavior management (CBT; *n* = 17) vs. wait list control (WL; *n* = 17). Setting: outpatient clinic; Format: individual; Participants: children, parents, teachers; Duration: 6 sessions; Therapists: 3 registered psychologists; Treatment manual: yes; Treatment integrity: yes; Follow-up interval: 12 weeks.	Children who met Berg and colleagues' (1969) criteria for school refusal Age: 5–15 (M = 11.03); Gender: 53% male; Race/Ethnicity: unspecified	School attendance, FT, FSSC-II, RCMAS, CDI, SEQSS, CBCL, CBCL-T, GAF	Compared to WL, CBT group reported significantly greater level of school attendance, reduced negative affect, and increased confidence in ability to cope with anxiety-provoking situations; parent reports of CBT children also showed significant improvement for internalizing problems; no significant between-group differences were found on teacher reports; treatment gains were maintained at 12-week follow-up	Analysis sample: completer; Attrition: 0% Effect size: School attendance = 1.10, FT = 0.96, FSSC-II = 0.42, RCMAS = 0.47, CBCL-I = 0.58

Study	Purpose	Design/Method	Sample	Measures	Results	Analysis
King et al., 2000	To evaluate the efficacy of CBT, with and without caregiver involvement, for the treatment of sexually abused children suffering from PTSD symptoms	RCT; child cognitive-behavior therapy (CBT-C; n = 12) vs. family cognitive-behavior therapy (CBT-F; n = 12) vs. wait list control (WL; n = 12). Setting: outpatient clinic; Format: individual and family; Participants: child and caregiver; Duration: 20 weeks; Therapists: 4 registered psychologists; Treatment manual: yes; Treatment integrity: yes; Follow-up interval: 12 weeks.	Children with a history of child sexual abuse and DSM-IV PTSD based on ADIS-C or features of PTSD (subsyndromal); 69% met DSM-IV criteria for PTSD. Age: 5–17 (M = 11.5); Gender: 69% female; Race/Ethnicity: unspecified	ADIS-C PTSD, FT, CQ-SAC, RCMAS, CBCL, GAF	Compared to WL group, both active treatments were associated with fewer symptoms of PTSD on the ADIS, lower self-reported emotional distress associated with sexual abuse, lower CBCL PTSD scores, and higher clinician ratings of global functioning; all improvements were sustained at follow-up; no differences between active and WL groups on the RCMAS; with the exception of fear thermometer scores, which favored the F-CBT group at follow-up, there were no significant differences between CBT-C and CBT-F groups on any outcome measure at posttreatment or follow-up; 60% of subjects in both treatments achieved no diagnosis status at posttreatment (vs. 20% in WL); improvements were maintained at follow-up	Analysis sample: intent-to-treat; Attrition: CBT-C = 25%, CBT-F = 25%, WL = 17%; PTSD effect size: CBT-C = 1.09, CBT-F = 1.24; CQ-SAC effect size: CBT-C = 0.44, CBT-F = −0.02; RCMAS effect size: CBT-C = 0.46, CBT-F = 0.32; Response rate: 60% (both treatments), WL = 20%
Last, Hansen, & Franco, 1998	To evaluate the efficacy of CBT to that of a credible attention-placebo control for the treatment of school-refusing children	RCT; 12-week cognitive-behavior therapy (CBT; n = 20) vs. educational-support therapy (EST; n = 21). Setting: university clinic; Format: individual; Participants: child and parent; Duration: 12 sessions; Therapists: unspecified; Treatment manual: unspecified; Treatment integrity: unspecified; Follow-up interval: 4 weeks.	Children with school refusal and DSM-III-R anxiety disorder based on K-SADS-P structure interview. Age: 6–17 years (CBT M = 11.67; EST M = 12.40); Gender: 67% female; Race/Ethnicity: 90% Caucasian 4% African American 6% Hispanic	School attendance, GIS, FSSC-R, STAIC-M, CDI, K-SADS	Few significant differences between CBT and EST treatments were found; children in both groups improved over time on a variety of measures; treatment gains were maintained (or increased) in both groups at follow-up; younger children and children with higher baseline school attendance levels showed the greatest improvement; no significant effects were found for any other sociodemographic or clinical variables	Analysis sample: intent to treat; Attrition: CBT = 38%, EST = 13%; Effect size: n/a

(continued)

Table 11.4.1 Psychosocial Studies of Childhood Anxiety Disorders (*Continued*)

Study Citation(s)	Guiding Research Question	Study Design/Description	Subject Selection Criteria/Demographic Characteristics	Primary Dependent Measures	Outcomes	Analytic Details
March, Amaya-Jackson, Murray, & Schulte, 1998a	To evaluate the efficacy of group CBT for the treatment of pediatric PTSD following a single-incident stressor	Single case multiple baseline across settings design; cognitive-behavioral psychotherapy (CBT; $n = 17$). Setting: school; Format: group; Participants: child; Duration: 18 sessions; Therapists: unspecified; Treatment manual: yes; Treatment integrity: unspecified; Follow-up interval: 6 months.	Children with DSM-IV PTSD following a single-incident stressor; diagnosis made via CAPS-C. Sample: volunteer; Age: 10–15 (M = 12.1); Gender: 67% female; Race/Ethnicity: 49% African American 49% White 1% Asian 1% American Indian	CAPS-C, CATS(a), CGI, CTRS, MASC, CDI, STAEI, LOCS-C	Subjects treated with CBT showed significant improvement on all primary measures at posttreatment; 57% of subjects who completed protocol no longer met criteria for PTSD at posttreatment; 86% were PTSD symptom free at 6-month follow-up; improvement was also observed on measures of depression, anxiety, and anger; teacher ratings (CTRS) did not change.	Analysis sample: intent to treat; Attrition: 18%; Effect size: n/a
Menzies & Clarke, 1993	To evaluate the differential efficacy of *in vivo* exposure, vicarious exposure, and the combination of both in the treatment of childhood water phobia	RCT; *in vivo* exposure plus vicarious exposure (IVVE; $n = 12$) vs. vicarious exposure (VE; $n = 12$) vs. *in vivo* exposure (IVE; $n = 12$) vs. wait list control (WL; $n = 12$). Setting: university pool; Format: individual; Participants: child; Duration: 3 sessions; Therapist: male undergraduate student; Treatment manual: unspecified; Treatment integrity: unspecified; Follow-up interval: 12 weeks.	Children with parent identified water phobia. Age: 3–8 (M = 5.5); Gender: 65% male; Race/Ethnicity: unspecified	BRS, CWP, PCWP	Both IVE and IVVE groups showed significant improvement relative to WL; however, there was no significant difference between IVE and IVVE groups at posttreatment and follow-up; posttreatment scores for VE group were not significantly different than WL; thus, vicarious exposure failed to produce benefits when used alone and failed to enhance benefits achieved through *in vivo* exposure	Analysis sample: completer; Attrition: IVVE = 8%; VE = 8%; IVE = 8%; Effect size: insufficient information provided

266

Study	Purpose	Design/Methods	Sample	Measures	Results	Analysis
Muris, Merckelbach, Holdrinet, & Sijsenaar, 1998	To evaluate the efficacy of eye movement desensitization and reprocessing (EMDR) and exposure (in vivo and computerized) for the treatment of spider phobic children	RCT; eye movement desensitization and reprocessing (EMDR; n = 9) vs. exposure in vivo (EIV; n = 9) vs. exposure computerized (EC; n = 8). Setting: university clinic; Format: individual; Participants: child; Duration: 2 sessions; Therapists: one trained EMDR therapist, one behavioral scientist; Treatment manual: yes; Treatment integrity: unspecified; Follow-up interval: none.	Children with DSM-III-R specific phobia (spider phobia) based on DISC-R structured interview. Age: 8–17 (M = 12.58); Gender: 100% female; Race/Ethnicity: 100% Caucasian	SPQ-C, SAM, BAT, VOC, SUDS	Although EMDR was associated with a significant decrease in SUDS and VOC scores, EIV produced superior treatment effects on all subjective and behavioral outcomes; EMDR did not potentate the efficacy of subsequent exposure in vivo treatment; EMDR produced marginally better effects than computerized exposure	Analysis sample: completer; Attrition: 0%; EIV effect size (relative to EMDR): SPQ-C = 1.12, BAT = 0.82; EMDR effect size (relative to EC): SPQ-C = 0.01, BAT = 0.06
Silverman et al., 1999a	To evaluate the efficacy of group CBT for the treatment of selective childhood anxiety disorders	RCT; child group cognitive-behavior with concurrent parent sessions (GCBT; n = 25) vs. wait list control (WL; n = 16). Setting: university clinic; Format: child group, parent group, brief conjoint group; Participants: child and parent; Duration: unspecified; Therapists: licensed psychologist and graduate-level trainees; Treatment manual: yes; Treatment integrity: yes; Follow-up interval: 3, 6, and 12 months.	Children with a DSM-III-R anxiety disorder (social phobia, over-anxious disorder, or generalized anxiety disorder) based on ADIS. Age: 6–16 (M = 9.96); Gender: 61% male; Race/Ethnicity: 45% White 49% Hispanic 5% Other	ADIS, RCMAS, FSSC-R, CDI, CBCL, RCMAS-P, FSSC-R/P, PGRS	Compared to WL, GCBT children showed significant improvements across all primary outcome measures (child, parent, and clinician ratings); based on CBCL-I score, 82% of children in GCBT group and 9% in the WL group were within the nondeviant range at posttreatment; treatment gains were maintained at follow-up assessments; subjects who had not recovered continued to show improvement at follow-up assessments.	Analysis sample: completer and intent to treat; Attrition: GCBT = 32%, WL = 16%; Effect size: RCMAS = 0.58, FSSC-R = 0.65, CBCL-I = 1.25, PGRS = 1.78; Response rate: GCBT = 64%, WL = 13%

(continued)

Table 11.4.1 Psychosocial Studies of Childhood Anxiety Disorders (*Continued*)

Study Citation(s)	Guiding Research Question	Study Design/Description	Subject Selection Criteria/Demographic Characteristics	Primary Dependent Measures	Outcomes	Analytic Details
Silverman et al., 1999b	To evaluate the relative efficacy of contingency management and self-control treatment procedures for the treatment of childhood phobic disorders	RCT; graduated child *in vivo* exposure plus self-control procedures (SC; n = 41) vs. graduated child *in vivo* exposure plus contingency management (CM; n = 40) vs. nonspecific education support control (ES; n = 23). Setting: university clinic; Format: individual and conjoint; Participants: child and parent; Duration: 10 sessions; Therapists: two postdoctoral fellows, five graduate-level trainees; Treatment manual: yes; Treatment integrity: yes; Follow-up interval: 3, 6, and 12 months.	Children with DSM-III-R phobic disorder (84% simple phobia) based on ADIS-C/P structured interviews Age: 6–16 (M = 9.83); Gender: 52% male; Race/Ethnicity: 62% White 37% Hispanic 2% Other	ADIS, RCMAS, FSSC-R, FT, CDI, CNCEQ, RCMAS-P, FSSC-R/P, CBCL, PGRS	The overall pattern of results showed that all three treatment groups showed significant improvement across all outcome measures and across child, parent, and clinician ratings; treatment gains were maintained at follow-up assessments; based on the CBCL-Anxious/Depressed subject, 75% of ES subjects, 67% of CS subjects, and 56% of CM subjects were within the nondeviant range at posttreatment	Analysis sample: intent-to-treat; Attrition: SC = 22%; CM = 18%, ES = 30%; Effect size: n/a; Response rate: CS = 88%, CM = 55%, ES = 56%

Study	Purpose	Design/Method	Sample	Measures	Results	Notes
Spence, Donovan, & Brechman-Toussaint, 2000	To evaluate the efficacy of an integrated CBT intervention with and without a parental component for the treatment of childhood social phobia	RCT; parent involved CBT (CBT-P; $n = 17$) vs. no parent involved CBT (CBT; $n = 19$) vs. wail list control (WL; $n = 14$). Setting: university; Format: group; Participants: child and parent, treated separately; Duration: 12 sessions, plus 2 booster sessions at 3 and 6 months; Therapists: two psychologists; Treatment manual: yes; Treatment integrity: unspecified; Follow-up interval: 6 and 12 months.	Children with DSM-IV diagnosis of social phobia based on ADIS-P semi-structured interview. Age: 7-14 ($M = 10.68$); Gender: 62% male; Race/Ethnicity: unspecified	ADIS-P, RCMAS, SCAS, SWQ-PU, SSQ-P, SCQ-P, behavioral observation in school setting, BAT-CR	Compared to WL, both treatments were associated with significantly lower child self-report measures of anxiety and social phobia; parents and independent observer ratings of social skill and social competence also improved across both treatments; no significant differences between the two active treatments were found on any of the questionnaire measures; however, a nonsignificant trend emerged showing superior treatment effects for CBT-P in the percentage of children who no longer met diagnostic criteria at posttreatment; treatment gains maintained in both groups at follow-up	Analysis sample: completer; Attrition: CBT-P = 5%, CBT = 17%, WL = 26%; ADIS-P effect size: CBT-P = 1.88, CBT = 1.01; RCMAS effect size: CBT-P = 0.45, CBT = 0.46; BAT-CR effect size: CBT-P = 0.57, CBT = 0.75; Response rate: CBT-P = 88%, CBT = 58%, WL = 7%

Table 11.4.2 Psychopharmacological Studies of Childhood Anxiety Disorders

Study Citation(s)	Guiding Research Question	Study Design/Description	Subject Selection Criteria/Demographic Characteristics	Primary Dependent Measures	Outcomes	Analytic Details
Black and Uhde, 1994	To evaluate the efficacy of fluoxetine for reducing symptoms associated with childhood elective mutism	Double-blind, placebo-controlled RCT; fluoxetine (FXT; n = 6) vs. placebo (PBO; n = 9). Setting: unspecified; Duration: 12 weeks; Dosing: forced upward titration (maximum dose: 0.6 mg/kg/day); Compliance monitored: yes; Status of blind assessed: unspecified.	Children with DSM-III-R diagnosis of elective mutism based on structured interviews with parent (PARIS) and child (designed by authors). Age: 5–16 (M = 8.5); Gender: 60% female; Race/Ethnicity: unspecified	PQ, TRS, parent CGI change scores, clinician CGI change and severity scores, teacher CGI change and severity scores	Although subjects in both groups showed significant improvement across time, most subjects remained very symptomatic at posttreatment; clinician, child, and most teacher ratings failed to show a significant difference between FXT and PBO; subjects treated with FXT were significantly more improved than PBO on only two parent outcomes (parent mutism change scale and global change scale); FXT was generally well tolerated	Analysis sample: n/a; Attrition: FXT = 0%, PBO = 0%; Mean dose: 21.4 mg/day (0.60 to 0.62 mg/kg/day); Effect size: na; Response rate (based on clinician CGI-I): FXT = 50%, PBO = 44%
Graae, Milner, Rizzotto, & Klein, 1994	To evaluate the efficacy of clonazepam for the treatment of childhood anxiety disorders	Double-blind, placebo-controlled, within-subject crossover experimental design (total n = 15); clonazepam (CZP) vs. placebo (PBO). Setting: university outpatient clinic; Duration: 4 weeks; Dosing: fixed, up to 2 mg/day; Compliance monitored: yes; Status of blind assessed: unspecified.	Children with DSM-III-R anxiety disorder (primarily separation anxiety disorder) based on DISC. Age: 7–13 (M = 9.8); Gender: 53% male; Race/Ethnicity: 100% Caucasian	PQ, TRS, CMAS, CGAS, BPRS	Although some children improved on CZP, comparisons on BPRS and CGI at end-phases (when CZP or PBO had been tapered off) or when CZP or PBO was at its maximum (week 3), did not reveal a statistically significant benefit for CZP; problematic side effects of drowsiness, irritability, and oppositional behavior were common; no support for the efficacy of CZP for the treatment of childhood anxiety disorders was found	Analysis sample: completer; Attrition: 20%; Mean dose: unspecified Effect size: n/a; Response rate: unable to calculate

270

Reference	Purpose	Method	Sample	Measures	Findings	Analysis sample/outcomes
Klein, Koplewicz, & Kanner, 1992	To evaluate the efficacy of imipramine for the treatment separation anxiety disorder in children who received concomitant behavior therapy	Two-phase study: open clinical treatment (behavior therapy) followed by double-blind, placebo-controlled RCT; imipramine (IMI; $n = 11$) vs. placebo (PBO; $n = 10$); nonresponders to open clinical treatment were eligible for RCT. Setting: university outpatient clinic; Duration: 6 weeks; Dosing: flexible; Compliance monitored: unspecified; Status of blind assessed: unspecified.	Children with DSM-III separation anxiety based on two clinician interviews. Age: 6–16 (M = 9.5); Gender: 67% male; Race/Ethnicity: 95% Caucasian 5% Hispanic	CTQ-M, CPQ-M, CMAS, CGI	Fifty-three percent of subjects experienced sufficient symptom reduction following 4 weeks of behavior therapy to preclude entry into RCT; none of the child, mother, clinician, or teacher ratings, showed significant improvement for children receiving IMI; rates of improvement for IMI and PBO were approximately 50%; the most frequent side effect was irritability or angry outbursts	Analysis sample: completer; Attrition: IMI = 0%, PBO = 10%; Effect size: n/a; Mean dose: 153 mg/day; Effect size: n/a; Response rate: IMI = 50% (average), PBO = 48% (average)
March et al., 1998b	To evaluate the safety and efficacy of sertraline hydrochloride for the treatment of childhood obsessive-compulsive disorder	RCT; sertraline (SER; $n = 92$) vs. placebo (PBO; $n = 95$). Setting: multisite, 12 university and community clinics; Duration: 12 weeks; Dosing: fixed or forced upward titration; Compliance monitored: unspecified; Status of blind assessed: unspecified.	Children with DSM-III-R obsessive-compulsive disorder based on clinical interview and NIMH GOCS score greater than 6. Age: 6–17 (M = 12.6); Gender: unspecified; Race/Ethnicity: unspecified	CY-BOCS, NIMH GOCS, CGI-S, CGI-I	Compared to PBO, SER group exhibited significantly greater improvement on the CY-BOCS, NIMH GOCS, and CGI-I; statistically and clinically significant differences emerged at week 3 and persisted for the duration to the trial; 13% of SER subjects discontinued treatment because of adverse events compared to 3% of PBO subjects; age, gender, and other demographic characteristics did not predict outcome	Analysis sample: intent-to-treat; Attrition: SER = 20%, PBO = 14%; Mean dose: 167 mg/d; Effect size: CGI-I = 0.40 (rating of 1 or 2 at end point), CY-BOCS = 0.37 (based on 25% decrease in score from baseline); Response rate: SER = 42%, PBO = 26%

(continued)

Table 11.4.2 Psychopharmacological Studies of Childhood Anxiety Disorders (*Continued*)

Study Citation(s)	Guiding Research Question	Study Design/Description	Subject Selection Criteria/Demographic Characteristics	Primary Dependent Measures	Outcomes	Analytic Details
Riddle et al., 1992	To evaluate the safety and efficacy of fluoxetine for the treatment of childhood obsessive-compulsive disorder	Double-blind, placebo-controlled, crossover design; fluoxetine (FLX) vs. placebo (PBO; *n* = 13). Setting: university clinic; Duration: 8 weeks; Dosing: fixed, 20 mg/day; Compliance monitored: yes; Status of blind assessed: unspecified.	Children with DSM-III-R obsessive-compulsive disorder based on clinical interview and CGI-OCD score greater than 3. Age: 8–17 (M = 11.8); Gender: 57% female; Race/Ethnicity: 99% Caucasian 1% other	CY-BOCS, CGI-OCD, LOI-CV, RCMAS, CDI, CGAS	Mean obsessive-compulsive symptoms decreased 30% to 45% following 8 weeks of FLX and 12% to 27% following 8 weeks of PBO; CGI-OCD change scores were significantly greater while taking FLX; CY-BOCS showed no benefit for FLX over PBO; FLX was generally well-tolerated, with mild to moderate side effects, insomnia and fatigue being the most common; one child became suicidal on FLX (resolved when drug was discontinued).	Analysis sample: completer; Attrition: 50% who crossed to PBO terminated due to symptom resurgence; Mean dose: 20 mg/day; Effect size: unable to calculate; Response rate: unable to calculate.
Riddle et al., 2001	To evaluate the safety and efficacy of fluvoxamine for the treatment of childhood obsessive-compulsive disorder	RCT, multicenter; fluvoxamine (FXM; *n* = 57) vs. placebo (PBO; *n* = 63). Setting: varied; Duration: 10 weeks; Dosing: flexible upward titration 50 to 200 mg/day; Compliance monitored: unspecified; Status of blind assessed: unspecified.	Children with DSM-III-R OCD based on clinical interview; CY-BOCS > 15, NIMH-GOCS > 7. Age: 8–17 (49% 8–12); Gender: 53% male; Race/Ethnicity: 96% Caucasian 4% Other	CY-BOCS, NIMH-GOCS, CGI-C, CGI-P, CGI-S, CDRS-R	Compared to PBO, FXM was significantly better in reducing the severity of OCD symptoms on primary (CY-BOCS) and secondary outcomes (NIMH-GOCS, CGI-C, CGI-P, and CGI-S); no significant change in CDRS-R scores were noted; responder analyses were marginally significant; higher rates of clinical response were found in children aged 8–12; significant between-group differences were noted by week 1 and peaked by week 3; medication was generally well tolerated	Analysis sample: intent-to-treat; Attrition: FXM = 33%, PBO = 42%; Mean dose: 165 mg/day; Effect size: CY-BOCS = 0.31, CDRS-R = –0.04, Clinician CGI = 0.54, Parent CGI = 0.43, Subject CGI = 0.35; Response rate: FXM = 42%, PBO = 26% (based on 25% reduction from baseline in CY-BOCS scores).

Study	Purpose	Design/Method	Sample	Measures	Results	Analysis
Simeon et al., 1992	To evaluate the safety and efficacy of alprazolam for the treatment of childhood overanxious and avoidant disorders	Double-blind, placebo-controlled RCT; alprazolam (APZ; $n = 17$) vs. placebo (PBO; $n = 13$). Setting: unspecified; Duration: 4 weeks; Dosing: flexible upward titration at 2-day intervals; Compliance monitored: unspecified; Status of blind assessed: unspecified; Follow-up interval: 6 and 10 weeks.	Children with primary diagnosis of overanxious or avoidant disorder; method of diagnosis unspecified. Age: 8–16 (M = 12.6); Gender: 77% male; Race/Ethnicity: unspecified	BPRS-C, CGI, ARC, STAIC, CMAS, SRQ	Both groups showed significant improvement posttreatment; no significant between-group differences on global ratings of clinical improvement; the small number of significant between-group differences on rating scales that did emerge favored the PBO group; APZ was well tolerated, side effects were few and mild	Analysis sample: completer; Attrition: 0%; Mean dose: 1.57 mg/day; Effect size: n/a; Response rate: insufficient information provided
The Research Unit on Pediatric Psychopharmacology Anxiety Study Group, 2001	To evaluate the safety and efficacy of fluvoxamine in the treatment of childhood anxiety disorders	RCT; fluvoxamine (FXM; $n = 63$) vs. placebo (PBO; $n = 65$). Setting: multisite, university clinics; Duration: 8 weeks; Dosing: flexible upward titration; Compliance monitored: yes; Status of blind assessed: yes; Follow-up interval: none.	Children with DSM-IV separation anxiety disorder ($n = 76$), social phobia ($n = 73$), or generalized anxiety disorder ($n = 84$) based on K-SADS-C/P structured interviews. Age: 6–17 (M = 10.3); Gender: 51% male; Race/Ethnicity: 63% White 19% Hispanic 7% African American 11% Other	PARS, CGI-I	Based on clinician ratings, subjects in the FXM group were rated as having significantly fewer symptoms of anxiety and higher rates of clinical response compared to PBO; significant between-group differences on the PARS was noted by week 3 and peaked by week 6; FXM was generally well tolerated, abdominal discomfort and increased motor activity were the most common side effects; 5 out of 63 children in FXM group discontinued treatment due to adverse events, compared to 1 out of 65 children in PBO group.	Analysis sample: intent-to-treat; Attrition: FXM = 16%, PBO = 21%; Mean dose: 2.9 mg/kg of body weight; Effect size: CGI-I (percent < 4) = 1.13, PARS = 1.11; Response rate: FXM = 76%, PBO = 29% (based on percent CBI-I < 4)

ies nonspecific therapeutic interventions were also effective in reducing anxiety symptoms.

The psychosocial treatment literature for children with PTSD is at a very early stage and pharmacological research is nonexistent. This limited evidence base, considering the small number of studies, is further characterized by relatively small sample sizes (a range of 15–100 subjects) which precludes further analysis by gender or racial/ethnic group, despite diversity in these study samples. The current status of PTSD treatment research suggests both further treatment development and controlled replications of the two well-delineated interventions, identified as cognitive behavior therapy, as next steps.

The majority of the psychopharmacologic studies of childhood anxiety disorders have targeted the treatment of obsessive-compulsive disorder (OCD). Among the eight studies presented in Table 11.4.2, three studies focused on the treatment of OCD. The remaining five studies examined medications for the treatment of separation anxiety disorder, any DSM-III-R anxiety disorder, avoidant or overanxious disorder, and elective mutism.

Psychopharmacologic studies of the treatment of childhood OCD included three studies of selective serotonin re-uptake inhibitors (SSRIs): fluoxetine (Prozac), sertraline (Zoloft), and fluvoxamine (Luvox). The positive results of these three studies have demonstrated the efficacy of SSRIs in the treatment for childhood OCD. Findings from the remaining five studies addressing psychopharmacological treatment of other childhood anxiety disorders have produced mixed results. Three studies found no significant benefit for drug therapy over placebo for treating a variety of childhood anxiety disorders. The studies with nonsignificant findings include one double-blind, placebo-controlled cross-over design of clonazepam for the treatment of mixed anxiety disorders, one double-blind, placebo-controlled randomized design of imipramine for the treatment of childhood separation anxiety, and one double-blind, placebo-controlled randomized trail of alprazolam for the treatment of childhood overanxious and avoidant disorders.

Results from a large multicenter study of fluvoxamine for the treatment of mixed childhood anxiety disorders found that subjects who received active medication were rated by clinicians as having significantly fewer symptoms of anxiety and higher rates of clinical response (76% versus 29% for placebo). Results from this study demonstrate that fluvoxamine is efficacious for the short-term treatment of childhood separation anxiety disorder, generalized anxiety disorder, and social phobia; however, conclusions regarding its long-term efficacy remain unclear.

Elective mutism is often considered by anxiety researchers as a subtype of social phobia (Black & Uhde, 1994) and one study has evaluated the efficacy of fluoxetine in reducing the symptoms associated with this disorder. Results found that children who received active medication were rated by their parents as significantly more improved than children who received placebo. However, clinician, child, and teacher reports did not show a significant benefit in favor of fluoxetine. Moreover, children in both groups remained very symptomatic after treatment.

In conclusion, the effectiveness of behavior therapy and cognitive-behavior therapy for treatment of childhood anxiety disorders has been shown in a number of studies. With the exception of childhood OCD, the evaluation of psychopharmacological agents for the treatment of childhood anxiety disorders is in its early stages of development.

General Conclusions

Across treatments for the four categories of disorders (ADHD, major depression, disruptive behavior, and anxiety), several psychosocial approaches to treatment appear promising for a variety of childhood problems. The strongest findings are for behavioral approaches in the treatment of childhood disruptive disorders and childhood anxiety disorders. The most consistent effects for psychopharmacological treatment are not surprisingly for ADHD. The evidence for treatment of childhood depression remains unclear. This first effort to examine the degree of change associated with specific interventions revealed a wide range of effect size estimates.

For ADHD, the largest effects were found for psychopharmacological interventions. Psychosocial treatment yielded substantial effects when compared to nontreated controls, but the effects were smaller than those found with psychopharmacological approaches. Recent evidence suggests that combinations of psychosocial and psychopharmacological interventions may produce slightly larger effects than either treatment alone.

A variety of treatments have been investigated for the treatment of childhood depression, but none of these treatments has been replicated. Moreover, active psychosocial treatments have been found to be no more effective than attention-placebo, suggesting that the mechanism of change is poorly understood. Effect size estimates for psychosocial studies of childhood depression range from medium to large and small to medium for psychopharmacological treatments.

For disruptive disorders, the largest effects were found for parent training and interventions that included a focus beyond the child (e.g., parent training combined with child training, child problem-solving combined with real-world practice). Tests of treatment efficacy showed larger effect sizes than those in studies of treatment effectiveness. However, interventions delivered in usual practice settings (i.e., home, school, and public clinic) still showed promising medium effect size estimates.

For anxiety disorders, the effect size estimates for psychosocial treatments range from small to very large with parents reporting the largest estimates of treatment effect and children reporting the smallest treatment gains. For psychopharmacological treatments of childhood anxiety disorders, effect sizes range from small to large on clinician-administered outcomes, and small to medium on parent and child measures.

Interventions which appear ready for broad dissemination based on consistency of findings, effect size estimates, and experience in usual care clinical settings include: the parent training model by Webster-Stratton and colleagues, multisystemic therapy, and Kazdin's problem-solving skills approach for disruptive behavior disorders; psychopharmacological treatments for ADHD; and behavioral and cognitive-behavioral interventions (developed by Kendall and colleagues and replicated by others) for childhood anxiety disorders.

The identification of so few interventions for children age 6–12 as ready for the field suggests further treatment development efforts. There is a tremendous need for replication, for larger sample sizes, and longer-term follow-up. Some interventions may be candidates for adaptation to older age children (e.g., Webster-Stratton) while in other cases a downward extension age-wise from adolescence to younger children may be appropriate (e.g., for the treatment of childhood depression). Extending interventions based on classical efficacy studies to effectiveness studies in real-world practice settings represents another obvious further step, while the development of new treatments should actually be initiated in such settings.

Overall, this review suggests a variety of positive directions for effective treatment of the included disorders. It also highlights the vast number of unanswered questions facing research and practice. Additional research is needed to extend current knowledge, to focus on youth in the 6–12 age range, to understand key factors and processes that lead to positive changes, to facilitate treatment development and dissemination, and to examine the effects of treatment for these disorders during childhood on key outcomes in adolescence and young adulthood.

12

Psychopharmacology in the Context of Systems of Care

ANDRES J. PUMARIEGA
AMOR S. DEL MUNDO
BOONEY VANCE

Systems of care for children's mental health have the promise of making child mental health services accessible and effective for the majority of children in this nation. The effectiveness of these systems are not only a result of the co-ordination of agencies and the integration of interventions into the child's natural environment, but are also due to the advances of treatment technologies in child mental health. An important area of advance in treatment technology is that of psychopharmacological treatment (Jensen, Hoagwood, & Petti, 1996; Campbell & Cueva, 1995).

It was only two decades ago that the use of medications to treat children's emotional and psychiatric disorders was considered controversial within child and adolescent psychiatry. Psychoanalytically oriented psychotherapeutic approaches were seen as more natural interventions for children, especially due to their emphasis on dealing with unresolved conflicts and traumas from earlier developmental stages. However, pioneering child and adolescent psychiatrists began to recognize the potential benefits of pharmacological interventions in the treatment of children with serious mental and emotional disorders. As far back as the late 1930s, Bradley (1937) identified that stimulants reduced school refusal, reduced hyperactivity, and improved the school performance of children identified as "hyperkinetic." It was not until the 1960s that investigators proceeded to test the effectiveness of stimulants in treating children with attention-deficit/hyperactivity disorder (ADHD) using double-blind, placebo-controlled research methodology. These trials formally opened the era of psychopharmacology with children, not only through establishing the most commonly used pharmacological agents, but also by using the same standard for efficacy in psychopharmacology for children as for adults (Barkley, 1977).

As other agents were established for the treatment of adults, their use with children closely followed. Pediatric prescribing practices for psychotropic medications have moved further ahead than the available research studies, especially on the long-term effects of these agents (Jensen, et al., 1999a). However, an increasing number of well-designed clinical trials of psychotropic agents with children and adolescents in recent years have led to more formal indications being established for the use of these agents (Campbell & Cueva, 1995). Significant concerns, however, remain around the use of psychopharmacological agents in the treatment of childhood psychiatric and behavioral disorders. Many authors have expressed concern about the excessive and unnecessary use of psychotropic medication with children to compensate for inadequate time available to teachers or parents in dealing with disruptive behaviors, or the inconvenience in addressing them among the needs of other children (Barkley, 1988). Concern about short-term side effects, long-term impact on the growth and development of children, and the potential of addiction are also frequently expressed. One recent study indicates boys with ADHD who used stimulant medications were less likely to abuse substances than boys with ADHD who did not use stimulants (Biederman, Wilens, Mick, Spencer, & Faraone, 1999). A more basic concern of both parents and educators is about the use of diagnoses to guide the selection of appropriate psychotropic agents, resulting in children being labelled and stigmatized. An unspoken fear underlying such concerns is that of "medicalizing" and "pathologizing" childhood behavior, thus taking power/authority away from parents, teachers, and children themselves. Due to the technical nature of decision-making, there is loss of input and control (Gadow, 1997).

Research on the benefits and risks of psychopharmacological treatment for children is still in its early stages but is progressively increasing in numbers and quality. Weisz and Jensen (1999) report more than 80 psychopharmacological trials with children and adolescents for disorders not involving ADHD, and over 200 trials for ADHD. This compares to over 400 published psychotherapy clinical trials. There is approaching comparability in the scientific evidence available for the benefit of psychopharmacological treatments as that available for psychotherapy. Weisz and Jensen (1999) analyze the available evidence for efficacy and effectiveness of both these modalities. They find limitations in the level of evidence available for both modalities, with insufficient sample sizes; lack of longitudinal follow-up; insufficient attention to age, gender, and ethnic differences; and lack of evaluation of functional outcomes being major weaknesses. Very few studies, mostly in the treatment of ADHD, compare the relative benefits of these modalities. Jensen and Payne (1998), in their review of 15 well-controlled studies comparing medication and psychotherapeutic approaches in the treatment of ADHD, found that medication treatment alone was consistently superior to behavioral treatments in treating ADHD symptoms. However, medication treatment was found to be equivalent in addressing non-ADHD domains of behavior or functioning, and combined treatments (medication and behavioral therapies) may allow clinical benefits to be achieved at lower medication doses.

The Multimodal Treatment Study of Children with ADHD (MTA), funded by the National Institute of Mental Health (Greenhill et al., 1996; Greenhill, Halperin, & Abikoff, 1999; MTA Cooperative Group, 1999a, 1999b), was the largest (579 participants) and longest (14 months) comparative study of pharmacological and behavioral treatment for children, randomizing participants to medication alone, behavioral therapy, combination treatment, and community treatment. Medication and combination treatment were found to be more effective than behavioral therapy alone or usual community treatment. The latter is surprising given that over two thirds of community treatment involved medication at some point. Experimental medication treatment may have been more effective since it adhered to a strict protocol that included careful monitoring of adherence, thrice-daily dosing, regular coordination with teachers, and sufficient time during appointments for close communication and education with the child and family, as well as careful adjustment. Though combination therapy was slightly better than medication alone, this difference was significant in focused areas, such as parent-child relations, academic achievement, and in reducing coexisting symptoms of anxiety. Studies such as the MTA may ultimately point to pharmacotherapy and psychotherapy providing different benefits across different domains or parameters of function or symptomatology. This supports the individualization of treatment interventions, which makes inherent sense in the treatment of children with serious emotional or mental disorders.

Approaches to the Selection of Pharmacological Agents

Psychopharmacological treatment is consistent with the demands for greater scientific evidence and accountability in the mental health treatment of children defined by careful assessment and monitoring of diagnostic criteria, symptoms, and untoward effects. The selection of psychopharmacological agents is based on two main criteria: (1) the psychiatric diagnosis for which the agent is used or selected, following the DSM-IV (APA, 1994) criteria; and (2) the response of target symptoms amenable to pharmacological intervention. Treatment efficacy trials of pharmacological agents use either or both of these parameters for the evaluation of these agents. Diagnostic criteria are used to define the population of children or adolescents for which these agents are selected, with basic neurochemical research addressing the biological mechanisms associated with the expression of given disorders. Target symptoms are used as the actual parameters of efficacy of action of these agents. Both of these parameters are measured using objective instruments with established validity and reliability, particularly systematic diagnostic interviews, such as the Diagnostic Interview Schedule for Children (DISC; Shaffer et al., 1996), the Diagnostic Interview for Children and Adolescents (DICA; Reich, Welner, & Herjanic, 1994), the Child and Adolescent Psychiatric Assessment (CAPA; Angold et al., 1995), the child version of the Schedule of Affective Disorders and Schizophrenia (Kiddie SADS; Chambers et al., 1985), and systematic symptom rating scales that measure related symptom domains.

Current psychiatric diagnostic nosology (i.e., DSM-IV) that is descriptive and nontheoretical has facilitated more specific testing of the efficacy of treatment modalities on different clinical populations, including medications. This, in turn, has led to further advances in the development of such treatments (Gittleman-Klein, Spitzen, & Cantwell, 1978). However, these diagnostic systems are far from flawless, and they are in constant evolution depending on advances in epidemiological, biological, and psychological research. There are inherent challenges to the application of such otherwise objective criteria to the evaluation of children with mental and emotional disorders. The application of psychiatric diagnoses to children and adolescents has inherent limitations. The process of emotional and cognitive development is superimposed onto the process of a disease or disorder, often leading to incomplete symptom expression or symptoms being expressed in alternate ways. Epidemiological research linking childhood and adolescent disorders to adult disorders is also limited in its scope, creating uncertainty about similarities between the same disorder presenting in childhood and adulthood. Some studies support the lack of clarity and validity in clinical child diagnosis, especially in relation to the prognosis of the child, with many children with disruptive behavioral disorders having comorbid serious mental illness when evaluated systematically (Caron & Rutter, 1991). As a result, the severity of a child's condition is not necessary related to the diagnostic or formal clinical status, but may be more clearly expressed in functional ability to successfully negotiate his or her roles within the family, with peers, at school, and in other community settings. In fact, some researchers have suspected that the difficulty in demonstrating the efficacy of certain pharmacological agents for certain disorders may be due to the adequacy of the diagnostic assessment of the children or adolescents studied, such as with antidepressant treatment of adolescents (Geller, Reising, Leonard, Riddle, & Walsh, 1999). There are also problems with the reliability and validity of clinician diagnoses, which often do not adhere to the criteria set by the diagnostic nosology and may result in inappropriate prescribing due to the errors in making a diagnosis.

Symptomatically based assessment can overcome some of the limitations presented by the lack of clear diagnostic assessments. The careful selection and measurement of target symptoms using valid and reliable measurements is the basis for establishing treatment efficacy in psychopharmacological research, even when structured, systematic diagnostic assessment is used to determine study inclusion (Conners, 1992). However, there is a small but growing body of research that evaluates the use of psychopharmacological agents in the treatment of focused problem behaviors (such as aggression or self-injurious behaviors) independent of diagnostic determination. Such studies use multiple target behaviors as the main criteria both for treatment selection and for the determination of efficacy (see "Symptomatic Management of Children with SED" section of this chapter). This approach is similar to that used in the selection and application of behavioral interventions, with more recent approaches in behavioral interventions using more broad-based target behavioral assessment as well as contextual and functional assessment (Pelham & Murphy, 1986; Ollendick & Hersen, 1993). This approach can be adapted for the evaluation of pharmacological treatment involving severe emotional disorders (SED), which do not easily fit diagnostic criteria outlined in the DSM-IV but have clear target behaviors that interfere in daily functioning.

Psychopharmacological Interventions

Below, we will briefly review the current state of psychopharmacological treatment with children and adolescents. We will organize our discussion around the two main organizing principles previously discussed: pharmacological agents for the treatment of established psychiatric diagnoses, and psychopharmacological agents selected to control or treat specific behaviors experienced by a child, regardless of the presence of a clear diagnosis.

TREATMENT OF SPECIFIC DISORDERS

Depression

Childhood depression, which interferes with mood, cognition, behavior, socialization, and development, is now recognized as a widespread debilitating and often chronic illness affecting 3–5% of children and youth. In addition, this illness can result in significant numbers of lost school days, lost workdays for parents and other caregivers, and considerable treatment expense and distress for the family (Fleming & Offord, 1990).

Children and adults with depression were initially treated with tricyclic antidepressants (TCAs), such as amitryptiline (Elavil), imipramine (Tofranil), nortryptiline (Pamelor), amoxapine (Doxepin), desipramine (Norpramine), and clomipramine (Anafranil). Although they were effective with adults, double-blind, placebo-controlled trials with tricyclic antidepressants have failed to demonstrate their efficacy with children and adolescents (Geller et al., 1999), except for one study of intravenous clomipramine (Sallee, Vrindavanam, Deas-Nesmith, Carson, & Sethuraman, 1997). Further, tricyclic antidepressants are well known to produce a high incidence of adverse effects, especially with children. Central side effects of TCAs include drowsiness, ataxia, anxiety, insomnia, nightmares, confusion, decreased cognition, and seizures. Dry mouth, blurred vision, and constipation commonly result from blockade of muscarinic, cholinergic receptors. In addition, TCAs can precipitate delusions and worsen psychosis in patients with schizophrenia. TCAs are potentially life-threatening in the case of an overdose. Seizures, coma, respiratory depression, hypotension, cardiac arrhythmia, and acute renal failure commonly occur in TCA overdose in children, with death usually resulting from cardiac arrhythmias secondary to effects on cardiac conduction. Children are more vulnerable than adults to the toxic effects of TCAs because they produce a greater proportion of cardiotoxic or nephrotoxic metabolites (Pumariega, Muller, & Rivers-Buckeley, 1982; Goel & Shanks, 1994; Ryan, 1990; DeVane & Salle, 1996; Geller et al., 1999). The TCAs are now primarily used for depressed children who do not respond to other medications. Although not supported by research, such use also occurs in health plans where restrictive formularies promote their use due to their significantly lower costs.

The newer class of selective serotonin reuptake inhibitors (SSRIs) such as fluoxetine (Prozac), paroxetine (Paxil), sertraline (Zoloft), fluvoxamine (Luvox), and citalopram (Celexa) has been successful in effecting favorable therapeutic outcomes in adults with markedly better side-effect profiles. These agents are currently in the process of undergoing Food and Drug Administration trials for children and adolescents. Double-blind, placebo-controlled trials of SSRIs with children with depression have shown efficacy greater than placebo (Simeon, Dinicola, Ferguson, & Copping, 1990; DeVane & Salle, 1996; Emslie et al., 1997). The SSRIs have a relatively lower side-effect profile and easy once-a-day administration due to longer serum half-life. The most frequent adverse effects are nausea, headache, diarrhea or loose stools, insomnia, dry mouth, and, predominantly in males, sexual dysfunction. Adverse effects appear to decrease in frequency and severity with long-term use (DeVane & Salle, 1996; Grimsley & Iann, 1992; Emslie, Walkup, Plizka, & Ernst, 1999). The SSRIs also appear to be safer than TCAs in case of an overdose. Doogan (1991) reports four cases of sertraline poisoning that resolved with no significant sequelae and without need for intensive monitoring. However, severe sertraline intoxication in a child after accidental ingestion has been reported; prolonged tachycardia, hypertension, hallucinations, coma, and hyperthermia occurred in this patient (Kaminski, Robbins, & Weibley, 1994). The NIMH-supported multisite Treatment of Adolescents with Depression Study (MH80008), which is currently being implemented, will systematically compare fluoxetine treatment of depression with cognitive-behavior therapy, combination therapy, and placebo control (March, 1999).

The monoamine oxidase inhibitors (MAO-Is) are another class of antidepressants that have been primarily reserved for treatment-resistant depression with adults because of their potentially toxic side effects (due to their interaction with foods high in the amino acid tyramine, which appears in many wines, cheeses, and nuts). These side effects make the risk associated with their use in children and adolescents far outweigh any potential benefits. Newer forms of these agents that do not have the same degree of side effects are showing efficacy in treating depressed adults (Emslie et al., 1999).

Newer, primarily adrenergic agents such as bupropion (Wellbutrin), venlafaxine (Effexor), nefazodone (Serzone), and mirtazapine (Remeron) are being increasingly used in treatment-resistant depression as alternatives to the MAO-Is and the TCAs. These have side-effect profiles that are even more favorable than those of the SSRIs. The results of small trials with children and adolescents so far are mixed, with one small double-blind, placebo-controlled study failing to show difference from placebo (Mandoki, Tapia, Tapia, Summer, & Parker, 1997). Larger scale studies are currently underway (Emslie et al., 1999).

The concurrent administration of lithium carbonate, anticonvulsants, and stimulants to augment the efficacy of antidepressants has been used as an additional means of addressing treatment-resistant depression in adults. This practice has shown promise with children in two uncontrolled studies with lithium (Ryan, Meyer, Dachille, Mazzie, & Puig-Antich, 1988; Strober, Freeman, Rigali, Schmidt, & Diamond, 1992), but has not been systematically studied. Severe depression in children and adolescents is often accompanied by symptoms of psychosis (such as hallucinations, delusions, problems with reality testing, or violent behavior), which, in fact, occur more frequently than with adults. The addition of antipsychotic medication in such circumstances can be beneficial (Ryan, 1990; Gadow, 1997), especially the newer antipsychotic medications such as olanzepine and risperidone (Zarate et al., 1998; Frazier et al., 1999).

Anxiety Disorders

Anxiety disorders (panic disorder, obsessive-compulsive disorder, generalized anxiety disorders, social anxiety disorder, separation anxiety disorder, and posttraumatic stress disorder) are the most common psychiatric disorders in either children or adults, affecting approximately 10–15% of children (Shaffer et al., 1996; Verhulst, Van der Ende, Ferdinand, & Kasius, 1997). Although the majority of children with anxiety disorders do not experience serious impairment, a significant percentage of them go on to have significant disruption of their academic, social, and interpersonal function as a result of the severity of their illness. Some of these disorders, such as posttraumatic stress disorder and obsessive-compulsive disorder, used to be considered rare among children and adolescents, but are now known to affect significant percentages within these age groups (Bernstein, Borchardt, & Perwien, 1996).

The SSRIs are being increasingly used to treat children with anxiety disorders. Both fluvoxamine and sertraline are FDA-approved for the treatment of obsessive-compulsive disorder in children, with large multisite placebo-controlled trials supporting efficacy (Riddle et al., 2001; March et al, 1998b) as well as other placebo-controlled studies. A small placebo-controlled study supports the use of fluoxetine in selective mutism, which is often associated with social anxiety disorder in young children (Black, Udhe, & Tancer, 1992). Noncontrolled studies in the treatment of other anxiety disorders with children suggest that these medications not only contribute to the relief of the typical physiological symptoms of anxiety, but are also quite effective in addressing the cognitive aspects of these disorders, such as worrying, rumination, decreased concentration, and repetitive or intrusive thinking or behaviors (Murdoch & McTarish, 1992; Bernstein, Borchardt, & Perwien, 1996). Buspirone, a serotonergic receptor agonist, has also been used for the treatment of anxiety disorders in adults and has some support from noncontrolled studies with children, but no controlled studies with children or adolescents have been reported (Riddle et al., 1999).

The few studies of benzodiazepines, such as alprazolam (Xanax) and clonazepam (Klonopin), in children and adolescents with anxiety disorders show mixed results. Uncontrolled (open trial) studies are supportive of efficacy, but placebo-controlled studies show marginally better efficacy than placebo in sustained anxiety disorders, while showing efficacy with acute anxiety precipitated by medical procedures. Problems such as risks for abuse and dependence, sedation, withdrawal symptoms, and disinhibition of impulsive or aggressive behaviors and psychotic symptoms have been reported (Bernstein, Borchardt, & Perwien, 1996). Their short-term use may be considered in acute situational anxiety such as posttrauma or surgery, or in the short-term management of anxiety disorders prior to the onset of action of other agents (Riddle et al., 1999).

Beta blockers (propranolol) and alpha agonists have been suggested for use in controlling anxiety symptoms. No systematic studies of a beta blocker or alpha agonists have been completed with children and adolescents with anxiety disorders, though uncontrolled studies are promising in the treatment of PTSD and hyperventilation syndrome associated with panic disorder (Famularo, Kinsherff, & Fenton, 1988; Joorabchi, 1977). Clonidine has been suggested for the adjunctive management of affective, cognitive, and physiological symptoms of PTSD (Bernstein, Borchardt, & Perwien, 1996). These medications have associated risks of hypotension, bradycardia, and other significant cardiac side effects, as well as sedation, bronchoconstriction, hypoglycemia, and others (Riddle et al., 1999). Antihistamines, such as diphenhydramine (Benadryl) and hydroxyzine (Atarax or Vistaril), are commonly used in treating anxiety disorder in children, though effects are mostly those of general sedation. They are typically safe to administer, with oversedation and behavioral disinhibition being the most common side effects. (Bernstein, Borchardt, & Perwien, 1996).

Attention-Deficit/Hyperactivity Disorder

Attention-deficit/hyperactivity disorder (ADHD) is one of the most prevalent and persistent psychiatric disorders to affect school-age children, affecting 3–7% of this population. It is a disorder characterized by serious and continuous difficulties in three specific areas: attention span, impulse control, and extraneous motoric activity. ADHD is a chronic disorder that starts in early childhood and can extend through adulthood, having negative effects on a child's life in his or her home, school, and community (APA, 1994). This is a disorder that has significant future consequences in terms of academic achievement or school completion, especially due to the high level of co-occurring learning disorders as well as the impact of ADHD symptoms. It is also associated with other adverse psychiatric disorders and social distress in longitudinal studies, such as co-occurring bipolar disorder and conduct disorder, criminal activity or incarceration, unemployment, and auto accidents (Barkley, Fischer, Edelbrock, & Smallish, 1990; Cantwell, 1996). Data from national surveys showed a 100% increase in diagnoses between 1990 and 1993, from approximately 1 million to 2 million cases. ADHD is probably overdiagnosed because of failure to consider psychiatric conditions that are either co-occurring or have similar presenting symptoms. These include mood disorders (bipolar or depressive disorders), anxiety disorders, intermittent explosive disorder, child abuse/neglect, substance abuse, or chaotic home environment (Cantwell, 1996). There is considerable concern about possible overprescription of stimulants for the treatment of ADHD; however, available data suggests a mixed picture of both over- and underdiagnosis and treatment (Bussing, Zima, & Belin, 1998; Bussing, Zima, Perwien, Belin, & Widawski, 1998; Greenhill, Halperin, & Abikoff, 1999).

ADHD is highly responsive to behavioral and pharmacologic treatment. Stimulant medication continues to be the most effective treatment available. In more than 170 controlled short-term studies involving over 5,000 school-age children with ADHD, 70% of participants responded to a single stimulant medication (Schachar & Tannock, 1993). Short-term studies support response to the most salient symptoms of ADHD. However, few show across-the-board symptom resolution and long-term benefits in academic achievement and social skills. Stimulant medication is superior to placebo, other drug classes, and nonpharmacological treatments. (Greenhill, et al., 1996; Greenhill, Halperin, & Abikoff, 1999; MTA Cooperative Group, 1999a; MTA Cooperative Group, 1999b).

Methylphenidate (Ritalin) and dextroamphetamine (Dexedrine), both of which are shorter-acting agents, are the main stimulant agents used in the treatment of ADHD in children. Pemoline (Cylert) and Adderall (a combination of various amphetamines), both of which are longer-acting types or preparations of stimulants, are also useful alternatives for nonresponders or those children who require more extensive symptom coverage. A longer-acting preparation of methylphenidate (Ritalin SR), which uses a sustained release delivery system, is also available. All forms of stimulants should be tried before moving to nonstimulants (Rosenberg, Holttum, & Gershon, 1994).

Although children significantly differ in age and body weight, contemporary studies generally do not index stimulant doses by body weight (Rapport, DuPaul, & Kelly, 1989). Child patients need to be monitored for drug-adverse effects such as decreased appetite, dizziness, drowsiness, lack of sleep, stomachache, headache, tics/nervous movements, anxiety, disinterest in others, euphoria, nightmares, sadness, and staring into space. Most of these side effects are dose-related and subject to individual differences. Many of these diminish within one to two weeks of beginning the medication and all, except the possibility of tics, disappear upon ceasing pharmacotherapy. These risks can be reduced by giving the child small doses at the beginning of therapy and working up slowly to the smallest dose that achieves meaningful results. Earlier reports of growth retardation with the stimulants have not been proven in controlled studies, with any effect on growth being related to its effect on appetite (DuPaul, Barkley, & McMurray, 1994). Response to the stimulants characterized by mood liability, crying spells, and irritability can be suggestive of misdiagnosis of either primary or co-occurring depression or bipolar disorder. In children where ADHD is accompanied by depressive symptoms, newer antidepressants such as the SSRIs, bupropion (Wellbutrin), and venlafaxine (Effexor) may be beneficial either coadministered with stimulants or instead of them (Emslie et al., 1999).

Clonidine (Catapres), an alpha-two adrenergic agonist, has been used as an adjunctive medication along with stimulants for children who have significant difficulties with impulsivity, aggression, and/or sleep. Two small single-use controlled studies with children suggest efficacy over placebo, but not superiority to stimulants (Hunt, Minderas, & Cohn, 1985; Gunning, 1992). Its use in combination with stimulants for the control of aggression and impulsivity, though widespread, lacks supporting evidence from controlled studies, with only two uncontrolled studies supporting its use as an adjunct (Hunt, 1987; Comings, Comings, Tacket, & Li, 1990). This medication needs to be carefully titrated so as to prevent hypotension or bradycardia as a significant side effect. There are four reported cases of sudden death with the combined use of clonidine and methylphenidate, and about 20 emergency room reports of significant cardiac side effects, all thought to be related to a rare adverse interaction between these agents (Swanson et al., 1995). Guanfacine, another alpha agonist, has been shown to have potential benefits in ADHD in some uncontrolled trials. It has some potential advantages over clonidine in terms of longer half-life and greater selectiveness of action on attention, but controlled studies are needed (Riddle et al., 1999).

Bupropion (Wellbutrin), one of the newer primarily adrenergic antidepressants, has demonstrated efficacy in the treatment of ADHD in double-blind, controlled studies, though its effect is somewhat less robust than that of stimulants. It is being rapidly considered as a second-line agent in the treatment of ADHD (Casat, Pleasants, Schroeder, & Parler, 1989; Clay, Gualtieri, Evans, & Guillion, 1988; Emslie et al., 1999). The tricyclic antidepressants, particularly imipramine and desipramine, have demonstrated efficacy over placebo in the treatment of ADHD, but side-effect profiles described previously and the development of tolerance limit their use (Geller et al., 1999). Antipsychotic major tranquilizers such as thioridazine (Mellaril) have been used to manage children with ADHD and high levels of aggression and impulsivity by older practitioners. Their significant short-term and long-term side effects make them unacceptable for this purpose (see following section on schizophrenia). New agents are currently being tested for ADHD, such as the newer MAO-Is, and in the future, clinicians will have a broader spectrum of medical therapeutic options (DuPaul, Barkley, & McMurray, 1994; Emslie et al., 1999).

The National Institutes of Health sponsored a Consensus Conference on the Diagnosis and Treatment of ADHD in November of 1998, summarizing the results of the MTA Study and bringing together the state-of-the-art in the diagnosis and treatment of this disorder (NIH, 1998). The Consensus Conference concluded that, despite the controversy surrounding various aspects of ADHD, evidence exists supporting its validity, and effective treatments have been established primarily for short-term treatment, particularly using stimulant medications, with lack of consistent improvement beyond the core symptoms leading to the need for combined treatment strategies. It recommended further research on the long-term efficacy, effectiveness, and safety of treatment, more consistent diagnostic procedures and practice guidelines, and research on causal factors and prevention. However, the conference concluded that diagnosis and treatment were sufficiently established to call for improved awareness of this disorder by the health service sector and work on reducing barriers to evaluation and intervention, including health coverage and integration of services with educational services.

Bipolar Disorder

Childhood-onset bipolar disorder (otherwise known as manic-depressive illness) is now thought to have a chronic course into adulthood, with serious consequences. Children and adolescents with this disorder have a high rate of suicide. Violent behavior can occur during severe manic episodes. Children with rapid mood cycling show a poorer response to treatment. The effective diagnosis of this disorder can often be life-saving and significantly change the short- and long-term outcome for children (Geller & Luby, 1997).

Although lithium carbonate has been considered the first-line agent for the treatment of bipolar disorder and is known to improve its course and prognosis, only 50–60% of individuals with bipolar disorder achieve significant control of their symptoms with lithium alone (Geller & Luby, 1997). There are some small controlled studies supporting the use of lithium in the treatment of juvenile bipolar disorder, including one that demonstrated efficacy in combined bipolar disorder and secondary drug dependence in adolescents (Geller et al., 1998; Ryan, Bhatara, & Perel, 1999). Lithium has multiple potential side effects, including gastrointestinal, neurological, renal, endocrine, and cardiovascular effects, as well as a high overdose lethality (Ryan, Bhatara, & Perel, 1999).

Mood stabilizing agents like valproate (Depakote), carbamazepine (Tegretol), or clonazepam are alternatives frequently used with adults, in combination with lithium or as efficacious alternatives for rapid-cycling mood disorders. Given the frequency of rapid-cycling symptoms with children and adolescents and the need for safer alternatives to lithium, these agents are being frequently used with younger populations. However, there are no controlled studies and few anecdotal data on carbamazepine in children. There are some promising uncontrolled studies of valproate as a mood stabilizer (Ryan, Bhatara, & Perel, 1999). Valproate and carbamazepine have the added beneficial feature that blood levels can be measured, with established norms for therapeutic ranges and toxic levels. However, there are concerns about a report associating the use of valproate with a metabolic syndrome characterized by obesity, hyperinsulinemia, lipid abnormalities, polycystic ovaries, and hyperandrogenism, particularly in younger women being treated for seizures (Isovarji, Laatikainen, Pakarinen, Juntunen, & Myllyla 1993), though its generalizability to psychiatric populations is still unknown. Since bipolar disorder can be accompanied by psychotic symptoms, such as hallucinations and delusional thinking, which can be additionally dangerous, the concomitant use of antipsychotic medication is often necessary (Geller & Luby, 1997; also see next section).

Schizophrenia and Other Psychotic Disorders

Schizophrenia is a chronic mental and cognitive disorder marked by characteristic psychotic symptoms, such as hallucinations and delusions, disorders in affect and form of thought, and markedly impaired cognitive function. Early onset of schizophrenia is often associated with negative symptoms (such as the blunting of emotional expressiveness and lack of volition to pursue interests).

It has a very poor prognosis that is associated with cognitive deterioration and even documented brain morphological changes (Remschmidt, Schulz, Martin, Warnke, & Trott, 1994). Psychotic symptoms can also accompany severe presentations of other psychiatric disorders such as depression, bipolar disorder, and anxiety disorders.

Antipsychotic medications have been shown clearly to be effective in treatment of psychotic symptoms. The older antipsychotics such as chlorpromazine (Thorazine), thioridazine (Mellaril), haloperidol (Haldol), fluphenazine (Prolixin), and thiothixene (Navane) have been proven efficacious in the treatment of the psychotic symptoms associated with schizophrenia in a number of controlled studies with children (Campbell, Rapoport, & Simpson, 1999). However, these agents have significant short-term side effects, such as oversedation, Parkinsonian-like extrapyramidal symptoms (EPS), and anticholinergic-like side effects (e.g., dry mouth, blurred vision, difficulty with urination). They are also not particularly efficacious in addressing negative symptoms in schizophrenia. Chronic and/or high dosage use is also associated with tardive dyskinesia, an involuntary movement disorder especially involving buccofacial and fine motor movement, which can become irreversible. Children and adolescents may be at particularly high risk for developing extrapyramidal side effects as well as tardive dyskinesia. Another serious risk associated with the use of antipsychotics is neuroleptic malignant syndrome, which involves the acute onset of muscle rigidity, fever, severe extrapyramidal symptoms, tachycardia, tachypnea, diaphoresis, altered consciousness, and altered blood chemistries. This condition is rare, usually associated with the initiation of antipsychotic medication, and, although it can be fatal, it is usually reversible with early detection and management (Silva, Munoz, Alpert, Perlmutter, & Diaz, 1999). These medications continue to have a role in the management of acute psychosis, especially in their injectable form, and as second-line agents (Grcevich, Findling, Rowane, Friedman, & Schulz, 1996).

The newer atypical antipsychotics such as risperidone, olanzepine, quetiapine, and clozapine may prove more useful in the treatment of schizophrenia and psychotic symptoms in general, given both their relatively lower side effects and better efficacy in treating negative symptoms (Werry & Aman, 1993). Clozapine has already been demonstrated superior to haloperidol in one controlled study of children across all measures of psychosis, though neutropenia and seizures were significant problems for one third of participants (Kumra et al., 1996). In open trials, risperidone is also showing similar promise, but is associated with high rates of EPS and weight gain, a problem particularly for adolescent girls (Armenteros, Whitaker, Welikson, Stedge, & Gorman, 1997).

Autism and Other Pervasive Developmental Disorders

Pervasive developmental disorders involve severe, pervasive impairment in multiple areas of socioemotional and cognitive development. These include social interaction, communication, and stereotyped repetitive behavior, interests, or activities (APA, 1994). The impairments in these most severe childhood psychiatric disorders are significant when compared to a person's chronological and expected developmental level. The best known of these disorders is autistic disorder, though other forms such as Asperger's disorder, Rhett's disorder, and childhood disintegrative disorder have been recently defined.

Pharmacotherapy is a valuable adjunct in comprehensive treatment and habilitation programs to improve a variety of associated symptoms and to enhance developmental progression. Antipsychotics are the most frequently used agents for the reduction of target symptoms such as stereotypies, aggression, self-injurious behavior, and hyperactivity. Haloperidol has demonstrated efficacy in addressing these symptoms in a number of controlled studies, and thiothixene, pimozide, and risperidone have demonstrated promise in uncontrolled trials (Perry, Pataki, Munoz-Silva, Armenteros, & Silva, 1997; Campbell, Rapoport, & Simpson, 1999). The SSRIs have been demonstrated to diminish obsessive-compulsive and stereotypical behaviors and to improve social reciprocity and learning in uncontrolled as well as a few controlled studies (McDougle, 1998; Emslie et al., 1999). Sedative hypnotics can be used for the management of agitation in this disorder, but they are not good treatment options in the presence of self-injurious behaviors given their propensity to cause disinhibition (Werry & Aman, 1993). Naltrexone, an opiate antagonist, was at first thought to be promising as a treatment for autism in noncontrolled studies, but in subsequent controlled studies it was not found effective in autistic symptoms other than hyperactivity, with no effect on self-injurious behavior (Riddle et al., 1999). Secretin, a hormonal substance that regulates pancreatic secretions, has been recently touted as a possible treatment for autistic disorder, but no controlled studies exist supporting its efficacy (Perry & Bangaru, 1998; Lightdale & Heyman, 1999).

Eating Disorders

Anorexia nervosa and bulimia affect a high percentage of adolescents (a total of 3–5%), with significant psychosocial and medical morbidity and even mortality (both from starvation effects and· suicide). Antidepressant medications have been used in the treatment of eating disorders, with the few studies so far involving only young women. There is conflicting evidence of the benefits for anorexia nervosa from antidepressants, though there is some indication of reduced frequency of binging and purging resulting from treatment with the tricyclic antidepressants, the SSRIs, and the monoamine oxidase inhibitors (Jimerson, Herzog, & Brotman, 1993; Thiel, 1997; Jacobi, Dahme, & Rustenbach, 1997). Bupropion is contraindicated in the treatment of bulimia due to the risk of seizures (Steiner & Lock, 1998). Cyproheptadine (Periactin), a drug with antihistaminic and antiserotonergic properties, is an effective adjunct in the treatment of patients with the restricting type of anorexia nervosa, either as an appetite stimulant or through reduction of gastrointestinal malaise (Steiner & Lock, 1998).

Tourette's Disorder and Other Tic Disorders

Children and adolescents with tic disorders, including Tourette's disorder, suffer from spontaneous involuntary motor and verbal behaviors as well as associated problems with hyperactivity and impulsivity. Some psychotropic medications have demonstrated efficacy in controlled studies of the treatment of tic disorders, including antipsychotics, such as haloperidol and pimozide (Campbell, Rapoport, & Simpson, 1999) and desipramine (Singer et al., 1995a). Clonidine has been suggested as another treatment and has support from uncontrolled studies, but mixed results were found in controlled studies (Riddle et al., 1999).

Symptomatic Management of Children with SED

AGGRESSION AND VIOLENT BEHAVIOR

The majority of children who present for psychiatric treatment are brought in by family members concerned about their child's aggressive behavior. Mood stabilizers such as lithium, valproic acid, and carbamazepine have been used in the management of unpredictable rage or intermittent explosive behavior. The results of uncontrolled and controlled studies with these agents show mixed results, though mostly supporting their efficacy in managing aggressive symptoms (Ryan, Bhatara, & Perel, 1999). However, carbamazepine and valproic acid are anticonvulsants used in the treatment of complex partial seizures, or psychomotor seizures, another condition that should be suspected in children with unprovoked aggression with no recall of the episodes. Beta blockers, such as propranolol, and alpha agonists, such as clonidine, are also used to control aggression in children, with uncontrolled studies supporting their use but no controlled studies (Riddle et al., 1999). In cases of severe aggression or agitation, short-acting benzodiazepines such as lorazepam (Ativan) can be administered intramuscularly for acute management. Some children with ADHD have been shown to benefit from SSRIs for the management of co-occurring mood and behavioral symptoms in a couple of open trials, but these studies need to be followed up with controlled studies (Barrickman, Noyes, Kuperman, Schumacher, & Verda, 1991; Gammon & Brown, 1993). Antipsychotic agents have been used to manage severe aggressiveness, with haloperidol, molindone, and thioridazine demonstrating efficacy in controlled studies (Campbell, Rapoport, & Simpson, 1999). However, antipsychotic medications should be used rarely in the management of aggressive disorder given their significant short- and long-term side effects, and then only in acute situations when other treatments have failed (Arredondo & Butler, 1994; Popper & Zimnitzky, 1995).

ENURESIS

Enuresis consists of repeated urination into clothes or bed twice weekly for at least three consecutive months. According to DSM-IV (APA, 1994), the diagnosis is not made until the child is at least 5 years old. Children with enuresis are at higher risk for developmental delays. TCAs, particularly imipramine, can be effective in controlling enuresis on a short-term basis (Rapoport et al., 1980); however, tolerance often develops after six weeks of therapy. Desmopressin acetate, an antidiuretic administered intranasally, has been shown to be effective in reducing enuresis. Electrolyte levels should be checked early in treatment (Thompson & Rey, 1995).

COMPULSIVE BEHAVIORS AND SELF-INJURIOUS BEHAVIOR

Children who exhibit compulsive and self-injurious behaviors include children with severe emotional disorders and a history of traumatization, children with variants of anxiety disorders (such as trichotillomania, or compulsive hair-pulling), and youth with incipient serious personality disorders. All of these children and youth typically fail to respond to other treatments. Children and adolescents presenting with mood lability and compulsive, stereotypical, and self-injurious behaviors (SIBs) can potentially benefit from the use of SSRIs (Emslie et al., 1999). Naltrexone also appears to be a treatment option for some children with SIBs (Riddle et al., 1999). The opiate hypothesis maintains that patients engage in self-injurious behavior either because they are partially analgesic or because SIB supplies a "fix" for an additional endogenous opiate system. Learning, memory, and compliance are also improved with opiate blockers (Sandman, 1991). However, formal evaluation of chronic treatment and long-term effects have not been reported (Emslie et al., 1999; Riddle et al., 1999).

SLEEP DISORDER

Sleep disorder can accompany a variety of emotional and psychiatric disorders in children. The type of sleep disorder and the associated symptoms often dictate the type of pharmacological intervention to be used. Children with initial insomnia can be treated with mild antihistamines such as diphenhydramine (Benadryl) or hydroxyzine (Vistaril, see Popper & Zimnitzky, 1995). Clonidine has also been used for sleep disorders in children with ADHD, including those being treated with methylphenidate (Riddle et al., 1999). Treatment with sedative hypnotics is sometimes used, though the concern about tolerance, dependence, and addiction also applies for this application, so their use should only be for short duration. Trazodone, with its longer-acting profile, may be used as a sleep aid in children who have problems with both initial insomnia and intermittent insomnia. Adjunctive agents for disrupted sleep may be useful when a child's sleep needs to be regularized so that it provides them sufficient rest to allow for normal function at school on the following day. They are typically not needed over the long term unless levels of stressors in the environment are not addressed, or the child suffers from one of the above disorders, which may require more definitive treatment (Popper & Zimnitzky, 1995).

Other types of sleep disorder require different interventions. The tricyclic antidepressants have a role in the treatment of sleep walking or night terrors. These conditions (along with some forms of enuresis) can be considered disorders of initial stages of sleep—namely when the child transitions from deep to shallower sleep—and resolve themselves with nervous system maturation, usually by adolescence, but may cause nighttime safety concerns in the meantime (Balon, 1994). Narcolepsy, a rare sleep disorder that involves continual involuntary transition into sleep at all hours of the day, is another condition for which stimulants are efficacious agents. Narcolepsy should be suspected when a child continually falls asleep during the day in the face of adequate night-time sleep and no other emotional problems (Dahl, Holttum, & Trubnick, 1994).

Context of Pharmacotherapy in Systems of Care

A number of practical issues need to be addressed within systems of care in order to ensure the success and effectiveness of pharmacological interventions. Addressing these issues ensures that pharmacotherapy can be integrated with other therapeutic modalities in a community-based systems approach.

PARENTAL AND CHILD EDUCATION, CONSENT, AND ALLIANCE

True informed consent is the cornerstone of decision-making about pharmacological interventions. The parents (and the child, where appropriate) need to be fully informed of the risk and benefits of any medication in an interactive discussion using appropriate language that is understandable and allows for questions and responses. Side effects of medications and what the parents and child can do in the event side effects occur should be carefully discussed. Parents should also understand the importance of regular follow-ups to monitor response to medication and side effects. Collaboration with parents is essential in making dose adjustments and in ensuring adherence with medication treatment. This involves helping parents feel empowered to make the ultimate decisions around medication and to feel an equalization of the power differential associated with dealing with medical professionals (Werry & Aman, 1993).

It is also extremely important to educate parents as well as child services professionals (e.g., teachers, counselors, caseworkers, and probation officers) about emotional and psychiatric disorders and the use of pharmacological agents as a means of empowerment and of demystifying psychopharmacology, with a resultant increase in comfort with such treatment. In the age of consumerism, there is ready information access on the Internet and through advocacy groups, lay-oriented books, and educational materials. Parents and child service professionals should be suspicious of clinicians who hide behind technical language and incomprehensible terminology.

An issue that often arises in pharmacological treatment is the reluctance on the part of parents to allow school personnel or other human-services professionals to know whether a child is on a psychotropic medication. Parents in such situations often fear discrimination and stigma from the resultant labeling of their child if this information is disclosed publically. However, lack of information by such professionals can result in serious problems if the child experiences adverse effects without their knowledge, or inappropriate expectations if the child's condition is poorly understood. The achievement of a stigma-free environment in communities and schools needs to be a high priority among child services and mental health professionals. This should involve education of child service professionals and children, as well as the development of appropriate procedures for medication administration or side-effect management that do not single out children adversely in public (e.g., educational or recreational) settings.

The importance of addressing medication treatment directly with the child cannot be overlooked. The clinician(s) involved should evaluate and address the child's self-concept, self-esteem, and perceived stigma due to taking medications. They should also address fears of side effects as well as the realities of such. Children and teens can at times shift the responsibility and locus of control for their symptoms or problems; their active involvement and control needs to be encouraged. Clinicians need to actively enlist treatment adherence by the child, including honest reporting of side effects and developmentally appropriate responsibility for taking and keeping track of medications (Werry & Aman, 1993).

VALUE VERSUS LIMITATIONS OF DIAGNOSIS

The limitations of psychiatric diagnosis have been previously outlined. However, the benefits of diagnostic assessment can outweigh its limitations for children and adolescents who clearly meet diagnostic criteria for one of multiple disorders, since these can guide clinicians to the pharmacological interventions that should be considered. Ultimately, the combination of diagnostic assessment and the determination of target symptoms is most useful. The lack of clarity around diagnostic assessment should serve as a cautionary note in the use and selection of agents given the relatively few double-blind placebo-controlled trials of purely symptomatic/behavioral indications for the psycho-pharmacotherapy of children. However, a lack of diagnostic clarity should not serve as an absolute contraindication to pharmacological treatment, especially when behavioral, psychotherapeutic, and environmental interventions have been given adequate trials without sufficient results.

SYMPTOMATIC ASSESSMENT AND MONITORING/REASSESSMENT

The use of target symptoms to evaluate the effectiveness of a pharmacological agent for a given child or adolescent should parallel the assessment of the effectiveness of other treatment modalities. These should be identified in the child's individualized treatment plan, with adequate assessment of baseline symptom/behavioral levels to allow for effective assessment of treatment response. The model that is most useful in this process is that of a single-case design commonly used to evaluate behavioral interventions. Ideally, different interventions should be introduced sequentially, allowing for multiple baselines to be measured as interventions are added, though the exigencies of real-life needs and urgencies may preclude this approach at times.

Assessment in child mental health requires information from multiple observers in the evaluation of symptomatology, given the incomplete nature of the report of any single observer (parents, teachers, friends, or the child). A number of instruments have been designed to collect multi-informant data and score it in an integrative manner for diagnostic assessment and treatment outcome monitoring. Empirically derived instruments, which measure behavioral symptoms and social functioning, have been developed as means of identifying children with significant emotional or behavioral disorders and assessing them across different settings and environments. They offer a complementary alternative to diagnostically driven identification. Additionally, they can serve as efficient means of screening populations of children, since many are directly self-administered by key informants (such as the child, parent, and teacher) without needing significant interviewer assistance. The Child Behavior Checklist/Teacher Report Form/Youth Self Report (Achenbach, 1991b) is a prime example of this type of instrument. Additionally, instruments that evaluate a child's global level of functioning or functioning across different life domains has been found to be invaluable in assessing the effectiveness of treatment modalities. The Child and Adolescent Functional Assessment Scale (Hodges & Wong, 1996) and the Children's Global Assessment Scale (Shaffer et al., 1983) are examples of such functional instruments.

Multiple informants are also needed to evaluate specific types of behaviors or symptoms in response to pharmacological intervention across different settings and environments. The Conners' Scales (for ADHD; Conners, 1969, Conners & Wells, 1997), the Child Depression Inventory (Kovacs, 1981), the State-Trait Anxiety Inventory for Children (STAIC; Spielberger, 1973), the Multidimensional Anxiety Scale for Children (MASC; March, Parker, Sullivan, Stallings, & Conners, 1997), and the Yale-Brown Obsessive Compulsive Scale for Children (Y-BOCS-C; Goodman & Price, 1992) are examples of instruments that measure specific areas of symptomatology. To determine effectiveness and adjunct dosages, these rating scales should be obtained from parents, teachers, other child service professionals, and youth. This information benefits the clinician, child services professionals, and parents by organizing information about drug response in ways that are most direct and usable. Functional data from the school environment is invaluable in making rational decisions about the usefulness of a given pharmacological agent or dose for a given child. The informants across child-serving systems can offer different perspectives about the child's symptoms and level of functioning. Continuities or disparities in observations of a child's behavior across settings or contexts are invaluable for determining whether the dosing of a medication should be changed or whether a behavioral intervention should be implemented instead of adding a medication.

When using antidepressant or mood-stabilizing agents, the need for an adequate period to allow for build-up of serum levels should be considered. It often takes two to three weeks, or even longer, before adequate response can be seen. This is in contrast to shorter-acting agents such as the stimulants and short-acting benzodiazepines, whose effects are seen in hours or days. Therefore, adequate treatment periods should be considered before discontinuation of medication. Another complicating factor is the differential time course and dosage required by different agents to effect on different symptoms. For example, in ADHD a complicating phenomenon in evaluating medication-dose efficacy is the reported findings of a curvilinear relationship between dose and attentional improvement, resulting in a "therapeutic window" effect, as compared to a more linear relationship between dose and efficacy in reducing hyperactivity and impulsivity (Rosenberg, Holttum, & Gershon, 1994). This latter finding may complicate the validity and reliability of different observers. For example, teachers may be torn between identifying the effect on attention and learning versus the effects on disruptive behavior and classroom disruptions. Dosage levels and schedules need to be carefully assessed and adjusted to fit the child's educational needs and function/activity levels (e.g., timing for peak action, reduction of side effects, improvement of sleep hygiene, etc.).

The use of pharmacological agents also requires baseline and reassessment monitoring of common or more serious medication side effects, as well as biochemical or physiological measures of various bodily functions to prevent adverse events, such as cardiac monitoring through electrocardiograms and the monitoring of liver enzymes or blood counts for hematological effects. Physiological factors that may contribute to dose adjustment and drug interactions need to be considered and reassessed periodically, such as interactions with other medications or medical conditions, the child's physical size, weight, and nutritional patterns, and other maturational and hormonal factors, which clearly change over time.

The use of pharmacological agents with children requires closer monitoring than is common with adults, so this requires some adjustment in the expectations and practices of mental health services within systems of care. This needs to be considered by case managers in systems of care as well as in the plans for resource availability for such systems.

INTEGRATION WITH OTHER TREATMENT MODALITIES

Pharmacotherapy is never a sole modality in treating children and adolescents with severe emotional disorders. A multimodal treatment approach guided by a multidisciplinary team is the most effective approach. Pharmacotherapy is being increasingly used for rapid symptom relief and return to functioning, while cognitive, behavioral, and psychosocial therapies are being seen as most effective in relapse prevention and the development of long-term adaptive skills (Cantwell, 1996). A well-integrated, multimodal treatment approach requires the education of and close communication among clinicians, other child services professionals, and parents. Joint definition of intervention/treatment goals, tracking of target symptoms, evaluation of level of function, close monitoring of medication side effects, and fidelity/adherence to treatment modality techniques and dosage need to be achieved for such an approach to be successful.

Ideally, such an integrated treatment plan should be coordinated across agencies or settings in which the child or adolescent is involved. Unfortunately, such integration may not be encouraged due to fears by agencies of incurring significant portions of the total costs of treatment, including medical treatment. This is most often seen in the lack of coordination across school, community, and home settings around behavioral and pharmacological management, or the lack of coordination and continuity of care plans when a child is transferred across different care settings or levels of care. Interagency systems of care with clear interagency agreements can set the stage for such treatment integration (Pumariega et al., 1997).

CULTURAL COMPETENCE IN PSYCHOPHARMACOTHERAPY

A common assumption about psychopharmacotherapy is that, since this is an area of intervention that is biologically based, cultural competence principles are not important in its implementation. However, research is emerging that challenges this assumption and makes cultural competence a critical principle in psychopharmacotherapy as well as in other areas of mental health treatment and services. The interpretation, expression, measure, and threshold of behavioral and emotional symptoms can also vary across cultures, making the establishment of baselines and outcomes more challenging. Significant cultural bias found in clinical psychiatric diagnostic assessment of children and adolescents (Kilgus, Pumariega, & Cuffe, 1995; Fabrega, Ulrich, & Mezzich, 1993) can readily lead to the inappropriate use or withholding of psychopharmacotherapy for culturally diverse children. For example, Zito and colleagues (1997) found that African American children were less likely to receive stimulant medications than White children in treatment settings. The perception by ethnic and racial minorities of psychopharmacological agents as means for social control adversely influences the acceptability of these agents among such populations. Cultural and ethnic norms around family medical decision-making and consent need to be considered in (1) presenting the recommendations to use such agents; and (2) soliciting informed consent, where elders may assume a greater role than in traditional White middle-class families.

Additionally, there are cross-racial and cultural biological considerations that need to be attended to in psychopharmacological treatment. A new science of ethnopsychopharmacology is developing its own body of literature pointing to genetic and nutritional factors that can contribute to differential pharmacological response across ethnic and racial groups (Ling, Poland, & Nakasaki, 1993). A case in point relates to the metabolism of most pharmacological agents, especially the selective serotonin reuptake inhibitor antidepressants. These agents are metabolized by a series of liver enzymes called cytochrome P450 enzymes, with various of these enzymes responsible for the metabolism of different agents. Genetic polymorphisms have been described for many drug metabolizing enzymes in White, Asian, and African-origin populations (Smith & Mendoza, 1996; Masimirembwa & Hasler, 1997). Additionally, nutritional factors such as citrus and corn content in the diet, which vary in different ethnic groups, inhibit the action of some of these enzymes. The level of action of the cytochrome P450 enzymes can determine the level of dosage needed to achieve therapeutic action as well as the emergence of side effects (Smith & Mendoza, 1996; Sramek & Pi, 1996; Rudorfer & Potter, 1999).

Role of Professionals in Pharmacotherapy

The close and effective collaboration among professionals of different disciplines can ensure the success of pharmacotherapy within the context of a system of care. The roles of various provider groups related to psychopharmacology is described in this section.

CASE MANAGERS AND THERAPISTS

In different systems of care, the case manager role may be defined separately or may be integrated into other roles, such as therapists or even psychiatrists. Case managers have critical roles to play in the implementation of pharmacotherapy. They can provide objective assessment of the child's baseline symptoms/behaviors and functions and reassessment of his/her response and of side effects, at times also using observer rating versions of many of the instruments described above. They can also facilitate the communication of observations and concerns from the child and family relating to the use of medications. The maintenance of adherence with medication regimens can also become a major focus of their work, both by supporting the child and family in this endeavor and by providing valuable feedback to the psychiatrist or other medical professionals about the practicality of the regimen prescribed. Therapists who are not case managers can also provide important input and feedback about the effectiveness of pharmacotherapy through their evaluation of the child, both clinically and through the use of systematic measures, as well as supporting the child and family in pursuing pharmacotherapy and ensuring their active participation in treatment through bringing up questions and concerns and accessing information about the medication.

PSYCHIATRISTS

Child and adolescent psychiatrists (or general psychiatrists in workforce-shortage areas) have critical roles in the treatment of children with severe emotional and behavioral disorders. They can provide effective diagnostic evaluation for children suspected of severe disorders and can serve as clinical consultants to other professionals in interdisciplinary treatment teams in the construction, implementation, and reevaluation of treatment plans. They can initiate pharmacotherapeutic treatment and, upon stabilizing the child's condition, transition care to other medical professionals. They can consult with other mental health professionals on the implementation of a wide range of therapeutic modalities, including psychotherapeutic, behavioral, group, and family interventions. Child and adolescent psychiatrists can be involved in program consultation and community education around emotional and psychiatric disorders, and can provide systems of care consultation. Child and adolescent psychiatrists, with their combined medical and psychiatric training, can serve as effective liaisons between medical and nonmedical professionals. In these days of more systematic treatment approaches, child and adolescent psychiatrists can also help design protocols as well as policy and procedures for pharmacological treatment within school settings (Pumariega et al., 1997).

OTHER MEDICAL PROFESSIONALS

Pediatricians are actively involved in monitoring the physical and cognitive development of children. They can provide screening assessment and first-line treatment for children with uncomplicated emotional and behavioral disorders, as well as assume care for children with more serious disorders, in consultation with child psychiatrists. They also care for concomitant physical illnesses in children with behavioral and emotional disorders. Family physicians can serve some of the roles defined above, but their more limited training in childhood development and psychopathology may limit their involvement in assessment. They can work closely with families on the child's overall physical and emotional health. Nurse practitioners and school nurses can also play important roles in providing screening evaluation, monitoring the efficacy of pharmacotherapy in consultation with child psychiatrists, and in outreach to the home and the community.

TEACHERS AND OTHER EDUCATIONAL PROFESSIONALS

Educational professionals can serve important roles in effective pharmacotherapy within a school context. They can readily provide objective observations on a child's behavior, either naturalistically or with the aid of rating tools. This is due to their ready access to other children for comparative assessment, which can be invaluable in diagnosis and in monitoring medication efficacy/outcomes. They can help destigmatize emotional and psychiatric disorders and treatment with pharmacotherapy among other students and their families. They are in excellent positions to observe and report side effects, especially those affecting learning or cognition. Educational professionals can also reassure children and parents as they face the decisions about initiating pharmacotherapy and adhering to it.

School psychologists can serve important roles in psychopharmacological treatment through their performance of psychoeducational testing, which can help to refine the selection of target symptoms and evaluation of the efficacy of treatment on educational function. They can also develop behavioral interventions to compliment pharmacological treatment and improve the child's overall functioning.

Conclusions

Psychopharmacological treatments are becoming important treatment modalities within systems of care for children's mental health. The strength of the psychopharmacology evidence base is further summarized in the Report of the Surgeon General on Mental Health (U.S. DHHS Surgeon General's Report, 1999; also see Table 12.1.). The efforts of clinicians, child psychiatrists, and other researchers should be fully integrated across the array of interventions available to children, so that treatment can be truly individualized. Researchers should increasingly move beyond simple efficacy studies towards studies of the effectiveness of these treatments within community-based, interagency treatment settings, including the evaluation of multimodal treatments and their impact on the child's functioning and the family's burden of care (Weisz & Jensen, 1999). Clinicians in interagency systems of care need to attend to the state of

Table 12.1 Grading the Level of Evidence for Efficacy of Psychotropic Drugs in Children

| Category | Indication | Efficacy | | Safety | | Estimated Frequency of Use |
		Short-Term	Long-Term	Short-Term	Long-Term	Rank
Stimulants	ADHD	A	B	A	A	1
Selective Serotonin Reuptake Inhibitors	Major Depression	B		A	C	
	OCD	A	C	A	C	
	Anxiety Disorders	C	C	C	C	2
Central Adrenegic Agonists	Tourette's syndrome	B	C	B	C	
	ADHD	C	C	C	C	3
Valproate and Carbamazepine	Bipolar disorders	C	C	A	A	
	Aggressive conduct	C	C	A	A	4
Tricyclic Antidepressants	Major depression	C	C	B	B	
	ADHD	B	C	B	B	5
Benzodiazepines	Anxiety disorders	C	C	C	C	6
Antipsychotics	Childhood schizophrenia and psychoses	B	C	C	B	
	Tourette's syndrome	A	C	B	B	7
Lithium	Bipolar disorders	B	C	B	C	
	Aggressive conduct	B	C	C	C	8

Key: A = >2 randomized controlled trials (RCTs).
B = At least 1 RCT
C = Clinical opinion, case reports, and uncontrolled trials

Source: Jensen et al., 1999

the art in medication treatments given the rapidly changing knowledge base about these agents. The knowledge base incorporated into systems of care should include not only the indications, contraindications, side effects, and dosing of these agents, but also the state of the art in assessment and reassessment tools and instruments that improve decision-making about treatment modalities. Knowledge and skills in the effective implementation of nonpharmacological interventions by clinicians also need to be stressed within such systems. It is the lack of these alternatives within systems of care that often lead to premature or inappropriate implementation of pharmacotherapy.

Systems of care for children's mental health must also institute structural changes to effectively incorporate the use of pharmacotherapy. Practice guidelines for the treatment of various disorders need to be institutionalized within systems of care that provide direction about the initiation of medication treatment. Increasingly, professional organizations and federal agencies are developing and promoting such practice guidelines, which are regularly updated to account for new research findings (American Academy of Child and Adolescent Psychiatry, 1998a, 1998b, 1998c). These guidelines can direct appropriate referral practices to either pediatricians or child and adolescent psychiatrists for evaluation of pharmacotherapy when other less invasive interventions, such as cognitive-behavior therapies and parent training, have failed or have proven insufficient. Such practice guidelines are best implemented within systems that are adequately staffed with well-trained clinicians working within interdisciplinary teams and where families are integral members and collaborators on behalf of the child. The goal for children's mental health in the new millennium should be for all communities to achieve this level of access and quality of care for all their children.

Part IV

Conclusion and Commentary

13

Policy Implications Relevant to Implementing Evidence-Based Treatment

MICHAEL J. ENGLISH

There is a sense of urgency in America about the health and welfare of the nation's children. Policymakers are under pressure to act quickly and on the basis of reliable evidence. As this volume demonstrates, more is known about the effective treatment of children with severe emotional disorders (SED) than ever before. The magnitude of the need is immense. About one in five children has a diagnosable mental disorder. Nearly half of these children suffer sufficient functional/emotional impairment to be considered severely emotional disturbed. It appears that such disorders are affecting more and younger children, and 80% of these children receive no specialty mental health services at all, let alone the services that are most effective (Bazelon Center for Mental Health Law, 1999). The key policy question for this chapter is, how strong are the incentives to change this disturbing picture?

Mental Health: A Report of the Surgeon General, the recent publication (U.S. DHHS Surgeon General's Report, 1999), supplies a context for this chapter and for the author's perspective on key policy implications. The report contains four messages: (1) mental illness is real, (2) mental health treatment is effective, (3) persons with the symptoms of mental illness should seek help, and (4) stigma is a barrier to help-seeking. With respect to services for children and adolescents, the Surgeon General concludes that:

- preventive interventions have been shown to be effective;
- efficacious psychosocial and pharmacologic treatments exist for many mental disorders in children;
- primary care and the schools are major settings for dealing with mental disorders in children and adolescents;
- the multiple problems associated with "severe emotional disorder" in children and adolescents are best addressed with a "systems" approach;

AUTHOR'S NOTE: This chapter is in the public domain and may be reproduced without the permission of the author or the publisher.

- families have become essential partners in the delivery of mental health services for children and adolescents; and,

- cultural differences exacerbate the general problems of access to appropriate mental health services.

The interventions and mechanisms described in this volume are among those referenced by the Surgeon General. Each presents its own unique opportunities for children and families coping with the burden of emotional disorders. Each raises both special and overarching policy questions that must be addressed before the service delivery systems envisioned by the Surgeon General can become a reality.

Further context is provided by the author's experience with implementation of the federal Comprehensive Community Mental Health Services for Children and their Families Program (Children's Services Grant Program, P.L. 102-321). Under the Children's Services Grant Program, 67 communities have implemented systems of care for children with SED and their families. These communities range from a neighborhood in the South Bronx to the Navajo Nation in Arizona and New Mexico. This experience includes hard-learned lessons about the difficulties of creating successful partnerships among child serving agencies, the sea change of giving power to parents, and the disappointment of losing children to their hopelessness and the deceits of self-centered bureaucracies. Fortunately, this experience also includes many stories of success and some very important data on the changes that do occur for the benefit of children in these communities.

This chapter suggests possible policy implications of emerging community-based interventions, highlighting their theories of change, the changing roles of key participants, and their potential impact on the environments within which these practices are evolving. These implications affect many policy-related activities, ranging from articulation of community values in legislation to regulating service access and quality. Public financing of the right services for children is key but establishing the framework within which services shall be rendered is equally important. Thankfully, this book addresses both service and context very well. The following sections in this chapter address important policy implications on the following topics: (1) systematic service delivery, (2) community-based care, (3) prevention and early intervention, (4) families, (5) payers, (6) providers, (7) child-serving agencies, (8) research, and (9) training.

Taking a Systematic Approach to Service Delivery

A central theme of this volume is that children and adolescents deserve and benefit from services that are well coordinated, comprehensive, and delivered in natural environments. The more severe a child's emotional difficulties, the more likely it is that these difficulties will interfere with a broad range of activities at home, in school, and in the community. Contributions to a child's healthy development need to come from home, school, and other community agencies, such as child welfare and juvenile justice. The role of systems of care, described in chapter 2, provides a framework for making these contributions. The genesis of systems of care for children with SED lies in the federal Child and Adolescent Service Systems Program, begun in the mid-1980s (Stroul & Friedman, 1986). Systems of care target children and adolescents with SED in typical public service settings. Federal Children's Services Grants fund development of systems of care in a wide variety of communities. The Children's Services Grant Program has been operating since 1993; subject to appropriations, it is an indefinite program that could provide service capacity development opportunities for innumerable communities during the foreseeable future. As Duchnowski and colleagues correctly point out (see chapter 2), evolution of the system of care model has effected three key shifts in the way services are delivered: (1) change in the location of services from institutions to family-based care, (2) changes in the manner of service delivery from office-based to community care; and (3) change from a "pathological family" perspective to a strengths-based approach that capitalizes on the resilience of children and the supportive capacities of their families. Each of these shifts has dramatic policy implications.

Each of the chapters on clinical interventions—essentially chapters 3 through 12—contains a related message: Children with SED have many challenges that require multiple interventions to be successful. The message is consistent with that of other observers (e.g., Hoagwood, Jensen, Petti, & Burns, 1996). No one intervention provides the silver bullet; rather, it is the combination of interventions and the artfulness of their coordination that holds the greatest opportunity for success (Hibbs & Jensen, 1996; Abikoff & Hechtman, 1996). The Surgeon General's Report reaches a similar conclusion even from the perspective of treating a single disorder: "To be fully effective, treatment for ADHD needs to be conducted across settings (school, home, community) and by different people (e.g., parents, teachers, therapists)—a consistency and comprehensiveness that can be hard to achieve" (p. 148). The systematic approach to service delivery described in the chapters on wraparound and case management is crucial to ensuring the efficient delivery of the right combination of treatment interventions. If policymakers understand that multiple interventions are most often required for children and adolescents with SED, the vehicle for delivering each intervention with the proper coordination, sequencing, and individualization becomes even more important.

The chapters on individual interventions provide further examples of the critical need for implementing multimodal treatment strategies. In chapter 12, Pumariega and colleagues insist that pharmacological interventions are adjunctive to psychosocial therapies within a system of care. By stating unequivocally that medication should *never* be the sole modality, the authors land squarely within the framework of multimodal treatment within a system of care framework. This conclusion would oppose the evolution of a "medication only" service strategy, found in some managed care models. Rather, many of the specific recommendations—such as information-sharing on response to medication and monitoring side effects by case managers, families, teachers, and other members of the treatment team—argue strongly for adoption of a systematic, integrated approach to planning and service delivery.

Multisystemic therapy, described in chapter 5, is based on the careful co-ordination of a host of discrete interventions that range from medication to par-ent behavioral training, with room for great flexibility in developing a treat-ment plan that meets the unique needs of the youth being served. Similarly, the First Step to Success intervention described in chapter 9 is multimodal, in-cluding skill development and behavior management components coupled with a parent training and caregiving element, called homeBase. Treatment fos-ter care is also multimodal, including a wide range of interventions that in-clude monitoring and supervision, skill building using behavioral techniques, family therapy, and crisis and respite services, as well as traditional psychiatric consultation (see chapter 6).

The policy implications of these and other multimodal approaches to treat-ment for SED are many-faceted. Multidisciplinary treatment planning is in-creasingly important as a vehicle for assuring that providers use complemen-tary interventions and avoid conflicting treatment objectives. Practitioners need to collaborate on both service scheduling and timing as well as on sharing in-formation on treatment outcomes and complications, making formal commu-nication among providers a policy objective. Payers should consider funding bundled services rather than paying piecemeal for specific interventions. Prac-tice guidelines should explicitly address the appropriate service combinations that are known to be effective for certain diagnoses or co-occurring conditions. Inasmuch as emotional and behavioral disorders and substance abuse co-occur in a high percentage of treated adolescents, integration, or at least care-ful coordination, of mental health and substance abuse services should be pro-moted. Services researchers should focus on the effectiveness of particular ser-vice combinations as well as on individual interventions administered alone.

Also at the service system level, many observers emphasize the significance of the system of care approach in managing services and service providers. In-deed, many argue that the primary benefit of services integration through sys-tems of care is the elimination of fragmentation and duplication existing in many systems functioning today. Multiple public agencies have an obligation to collaborate in delivering services to common clients, both for the conven-ience of the client and for the efficient use of public resources. The lack of cross-agency communication, turf battles, intragovernment competition for re-sources, dumping clients from one system to another, and finger-pointing rather than problem-solving when failures occur are all characteristics of poor public programming, the elimination of which is valuable in itself. The systematic ap-proach to service delivery addresses both improved services and improved management within a single framework, making development and mainte-nance of effective program management within a multiagency collaborative en-vironment a critical goal.

Effective service delivery mechanisms are not a substitute for effective clin-ical treatment. Systems of care provide a service delivery vehicle for clinical treatment and for support services. Absent effectiveness data for the treatment components of systems of care, there is less-than-compelling evidence, and much controversy, about the extent to which systems of care affect clinical outcomes for children directly (Bickman et al., 1995). Implementing systems of care that utilize ineffective clinical interventions is unlikely to yield improved clinical outcomes, even if such systems have a critical bearing on access to service, child and family engagement, and the integration of services in ways that improve the efficiency of other service systems. Clinical improvement in systems of care, measured by symptom and functional scales, has not exceeded clinical improvements found among children served in usual-care systems. However, recent data collected on demonstration programs through the national multisite evaluation of CMHS's Comprehensive Community Mental Health Services for Children and Their Families Program show notable improvements in functional outcomes for children served in systems of care. Based on information obtained through April 1999 on the initial 22 grant communities funded in 1993 and 1994, functional outcomes were available on samples of between 962 and 2,885 children assessed at enrollment time, at 6 months, and at 12 months while the children remained in services. Findings indicated notable improvements for children after 1 year in services, including (1) reductions in law enforcement contacts, (2) improved grades and fewer absences from school, (3) improved behavioral functioning, and (4) more stable living arrangements achieved. Furthermore, after 1 year in services, 71% of the children's caregivers were "satisfied" or "very satisfied" with their children's progress (U.S. DHHS, 1997).

The policy implications of these findings are twofold. First, all of those with a stake in improving service delivery—children, families, providers, payers, program administrators, researchers, and policymakers—need to be clear about what they expect from which component of the service delivery system. Conflicting expectations need to be eliminated through public dialogue. Clinical outcomes such as remission of symptoms and improvement in functioning should be expected of clinical interventions. Improved living conditions for children and their families should be expected of support services such as housing, day care, transportation, and income support. Expectations of the service delivery mechanism should be related to service-system-level outcomes, including access, service utilization, efficiency of delivery, satisfaction, and retention of clients in mainstream community environments. Second, policy must address both selection and funding of the most effective services *and* how those services can be best delivered to target populations. One cannot decide to adopt a particular service delivery mechanism without reference to the specific clinical and supportive interventions that will be provided. Otherwise one cannot reasonably expect positive clinical outcomes—or, conversely, expect that availability of a specific intervention automatically makes it accessible alone or in combination with other needed interventions. In many respects, it is the lack of clarity regarding the program theory underlying the system of care approach that contributes to differences in expectations about what benefits will derive from its implementation. The lesson is that the provision of both clinical interventions and the organization of services delivery mechanisms must be promoted by policy; neither addressed alone is likely to yield positive results for children.

Implementing systems of care provides a context for the development of critically important service partnerships and for the organization of clinical treatments that are deliverable in a systematic versus serendipitous manner. The organizing principles of systems of care—comprehensive, individualized treatment planning, reduction of service fragmentation, expansion of service options, and improved service accessibility—should contribute to improved efficiency and quality. To date, proof of reasonably expected efficiencies has been lacking. Clear articulation of expectations of service system efficiency and rigorous evaluation of efficiencies actually achieved should be a policy priority.

Finally, the system of care framework provides a convenient vehicle for articulating the overall values a community associates with serving children with SED and their families. Many argue that establishing firm, jointly held values is critical to building effective service delivery systems. Legislative strategies should include an infrastructure of values and expectations that guide the way children, families, providers, and public administrators relate to one another and how they establish and preserve a common vision for an effective service delivery system. Creation of governing boards and/or examples of legislative frameworks for systems of care in the Children's Services Grant Program include gubernatorial councils to oversee the evolution of the service system. This provides continuity and a forum for preserving a common vision that all stakeholders support.

The wraparound approach described in chapter 4 is deeply embedded in the systems of care service delivery model (Burns & Goldman, 1999). One important contribution of chapter 4 is to articulate the similarities and differences between wraparound and a system of care. Policymakers need to understand that adoption of systems of care does not necessarily mean that the wraparound approach will be used, and vice versa. With respect to wraparound itself, there are two aspects of the approach that have special policy significance:

- *Flexibility:* No process of mandating or funding a specific intervention model would conform to the wraparound approach; the need to tailor specific responses to individual needs is at the core of wraparound. Rather, legislating or regulating the degree of permissible flexibility in selecting the most appropriate service mix would best reflect conformance with the wraparound approach. Legislating and/or regulating flexibility is a difficult concept and hard to translate into concrete policy recommendations. The wraparound chapter provides principles, explanation, and language that helps make the approach much more acceptable to policymakers.
- *Fidelity:* Absent a specific method for measuring fidelity, measuring conformance to effective wraparound practice becomes difficult using traditional approaches. An acceptable balance between flexibility and accountability needs to be established for wraparound to be attractive from a policy perspective. Development of uniform practice standards is a critical policy objective because they can provide measurable structure to providers.

Finding a feasible utilization review mechanism is also needed. Determinations of medical necessity seem to have little relevance to the wraparound approach. Peer-reviewed "contribution to treatment plan" could be an alternative criterion.

Community-Based Care: Keeping Children at Home

With some exceptions, the promising interventions collected in this volume do not all achieve the highest level of evidence for their effectiveness. But, when making policy now, one must compare the evidence base for these interventions against that for interventions commonly employed in our mental health systems. The record for many of these latter interventions is not strong. Inpatient hospitalization has the weakest research support of all the traditional treatment interventions (U.S. DHHS Surgeon General's Report, 1999). All three of the controlled studies of the effectiveness of inpatient hospitalization compared to community care found that community care was at least as effective as inpatient treatment (Flomenhaft, 1974; Winsberg, Bialer, Kupietz, Botti, & Balka, 1980; Schoenwald, Ward, Henggeler, Rowland, & Brondino, 2000). Residential treatment centers also have only weak evidence for their effectiveness (U.S. DHHS Surgeon General's Report, 1999). Indeed, there appear to be severe risks associated with residential treatment, including the learning of antisocial or bizarre behavior from exposure to deviant peers, failure to learn behavior needed in the community, possibility of trauma associated with separation from the family, difficulty returning to the family, and victimization in residential treatment centers (Barker, 1998). Similar risks exist in inpatient hospital settings, particularly with longer-term hospitalizations. Even outpatient psychotherapy, which has a relatively strong evidence base for efficacy in clinical research settings, has evidence that its positive effects diminish greatly in typical public clinic settings (Weisz, Donenberg, Han, & Weiss, 1995; Weisz & Weiss, 1993). Given that the vast majority of today's public mental health dollars are spent on these traditional interventions, important questions exist about the wisdom of continuing the level of investment in these interventions at the expense of introducing one or more of the newer evidence-based interventions described in this volume and elsewhere (see U.S. DHHS Surgeon General's Report, 1999).

CREATING COMMUNITY ALTERNATIVES

Feasible alternatives to inpatient hospital and residential treatment permit mainstream living for children with emotional problems. By contributing to effective community-based service delivery systems, the clinical interventions and service delivery mechanisms described in this volume decrease the need for out-of-home placement and increase the probability that a child can continue living with his or her family, remain in school, and maintain social relationships with healthy, prosocial peers. The value of preserving in-home living alone justifies strong policy support for community-based interventions.

Moreover, removing children from their "normal" environments of home, school, and community creates its own risk of exacerbating emotional problems (Rosenblatt, 1998). Adoption of interventions that are delivered in these normal environments offer the opportunity to avoid these pitfalls. In addition, community supports, (i.e., family, friends, classmates, teachers, and mentors) carry the responsibility for youth and have value over the long haul. They provide continuous relationships that offer meaning beyond "therapy." They are the converse of institutional relationships that need to terminate in order to be successful. Institutionalization breaks relationships and creates isolation for children. Home and family values, preservation from doing harm, and maintenance of community relationships constitute a sound foundation for good policy. With evidence of cost savings and a lot of community reinvestment opportunities, policymakers have a solid chance to make good decisions about the future of mental health treatment for children and adolescents.

A system of care operationalizes the values of keeping children at home under the care and supervision of their parents. They give parents as much of a role in guiding and delivering care as they wish to take and reward communities by reducing demands for institutions of all kinds. Therefore, systems of care have intrinsic value for a wide range of public policy objectives. System of care principles, such as personal responsibility and integrity of the family, are compatible with those underlying welfare reform. These values also underlie preferences for adoption and permanency over foster care and for reuniting parents with their children wherever possible within the child welfare system. A system of care values partnerships with schools and juvenile justice. They envision communities that "take care of their own" rather than look for places to keep children with troubles out of sight and mind. Treatment services are to be provided on an individualized basis, and when they are needed—not always identical with managed care practices. The values of systems of care are attractive to conservative and liberal policymakers alike because they balance individual and family responsibility with effective caregiving for persons with high needs and vulnerabilities.

. . . EVEN THOSE WHO ARE MOST DIFFICULT

Both multisystemic therapy and treatment foster care target youth engaged in aggressive, antisocial behavior who most often have already encountered the juvenile justice system. These interventions have demonstrated effectiveness in both reducing symptoms of emotional disorder and decreasing the amount and severity of delinquent behavior (see chapters 5 and 6). They address the needs of the most challenging, feared, and expensive youth in the public system. There are many incentives for policymakers to support adoption of these models.

Multisystemic therapy is extremely attractive to anyone who seeks discipline and consistency in the delivery of clinical mental health services. A strong evidence base, standardization, well-conceived training, supervision, and a clear quality assurance plan are hallmarks of the therapy. In chapter 5, Schoenwald and Rowland report that replication of MST without quality monitoring has been somewhat disappointing. Further, high-quality pursuit of the feasibility of implementation of interventions is crucial because the CMHS experience with systems of care implementation is that a very high percentage (29%) of children referred for treatment in the system of care sites have a conduct disorder diagnosis. In addition, 14% of children in the CMHS program have been referred from juvenile justice agencies.

Chamberlain points out that by targeting aggressive, antisocial youth for the treatment foster care intervention, such programs may address up to half of the children and adolescents that are brought to mental health clinics (chapter 6). Evaluation of treatment foster care has demonstrated that association with delinquent peers and consistency of discipline have the greatest correlation with the amount and severity of further delinquent behavior (chapter 6). Since both juvenile detention and placement in group homes for delinquent youth actually increase association with delinquent peers, these data suggest that current policies favoring detention and management of delinquent youth in group settings actually increase the likelihood of future criminal behavior. Conversely, maintenance of youth in normal community settings not only discourages delinquent peer associations but increases opportunities for associations with prosocial peers who can act as role models for positive behaviors.

Including Prevention and Early Intervention as Critical Elements of a System of Care

Traditional conceptions of community-based mental health care for youth suffering from SED unfortunately begin with the existence of a full-blown disorder. The diagnosis is a threshold criteria for entry into the mental health system. Early intervention and prevention primarily have been the province of education, substance abuse, and violence prevention experts, not the mental health system. Policymakers should be reinforced in their resolve to include prevention in any formulation of an effective mental health services delivery system.

Inasmuch as there are known risk factors for SED and substance abuse (Hawkins & Catalano, 1992) and there are effective interventions (such as First Step to Success) that can offset these risk factors and may change a child's developmental trajectory, it makes sense to include prevention and early intervention within the public mental health mission. Such a change in mission, however, would constitute a sea change for most state public mental health systems as they are generally limited to serving only those suffering from a diagnosed severe illness. By focusing on at-risk youth in general, employing preventive and healthy development technologies, valuing health promotion and encouraging early intervention, communities can contribute to reducing the prevalence of SED among children and adolescents. Stated differently, the success of prevention interventions like First Step argues convincingly for adoption of the public health model in developing and improving mental health service delivery systems. The Surgeon General's Report on Mental Health makes this point persuasively (1999).

The discussion in chapter 7 on the role that mentoring can play in promoting resilience among high-risk youth also highlights the importance of the public health model. Mentoring embodies many key elements of the public health approach. By addressing risk and protective factors, it acquires a prevention orientation. In fact, the mentoring model described for treating youth with SED is based on the underlying theory and effective model employed by the Big Brothers Big Sisters of America program and is preventive in nature (see chapter 7). By focusing on developing resilience, the intervention is premised on health promotion. Use of professional mentors who are recruited from the community, as well as employment of mentoring within a youngster's natural environment, underscore community-wide involvement in the therapeutic and preventive enterprise.

Recognizing That Families Are the Key to a Successful System of Care

Systems and service-level policy are affected by the major shift in the roles key stakeholders play in both delivering and being the customers of services. Within the broad framework of changing roles, the most central and abiding shift is that of families. Family providers can be effective. For example, family support (see Chapter 8) is basically a parent-provided service. The originators of this intervention adopted a program theory that capitalized on the unique experiences of mothers who have raised children with SED to deliver critical social supports as well as training to mothers in similar circumstances. In chapter 2, Duchnowski and colleagues describe the role of family providers as presenting the hope for increased services effectiveness, especially given the tremendous discrepancy between need and available services in the country. Transitioning of service coordination responsibilities to a family member is reported as an important result of the wraparound approach in chapter 4.

There is little doubt that family members currently bear the yeoman's share of care for children with SED. If family-delivered services increase as a proportion of the interventions delivered within a system of care, as they probably should, important policy questions are posed. Will family providers be appropriately compensated for delivering services? What credentials should family providers be required to possess? How should their services be supervised, and by whom? How does one reconcile the potentially conflicting roles family members play as providers and recipients of service? The answers to these policy questions will determine the extent to which the nation is ready to support a changing vision of effective mental health care. If families are encouraged to take increasing responsibility for behavioral health care, the above policy questions could create incentives—e.g., fair compensation, recognition of life experiences to meet education and training requirements; provision of supports such as respite, child care, and transportation in aid of service delivery—then service delivery would shift from provider-centered to family-provided, a revolutionary change in policy. Answers that do not provide incentives—little or no compensation, etc.—may relegate families to their traditional roles as passive subjects of the treatment process who often stand on the sidelines. Additional research is needed to determine how effective family (and other "peer" providers) can be (Osher, deFur, Spencer, & Toth-Dennis, 1999).

The value of supporting families with direct services is emphasized throughout the book. Because the interventions are mostly directed toward parents and not children, and the intervention must be reimbursable to be feasible, the parent must be eligible to receive the service under private medical insurance or one of the public benefits programs. Under traditional rules, this is not likely to be the case because only services delivered directly to the "patient" are typically reimbursed. Changes in reimbursement policy are, therefore, critical to improving family involvement in the therapeutic process. Because of this problem, the CMHS Children's Services Grant Program allows reimbursement for services to families and encourages states to provide matching funds for this purpose.

The evaluation of family support services, another important test of the value and effectiveness of peer support mechanisms, is under investigation in the behavioral health field. For example, the use of peer counselors as key clinical providers within the substance abuse treatment arena has been long established. The Center for Mental Health Services is currently in the earliest stages of testing the effectiveness of adult consumer-provided human services as an adjunct to traditional community-based mental health treatment for adults with severe mental illness in its Consumer-Operated Human Services Study. As discussed in chapter 4, the theory that a number of different types of peers—parents, youth, teachers, caseworkers—can provide effective services based on their unique experience holds great promise as a strategy in any system of care. Also, engagement of peer providers is a vehicle for expanding the provider base, especially in areas of the country such as rural and frontier districts, where there are shortages of professionally trained traditional providers. Assuming that peer providers can be demonstrably effective, critical policy questions arise, similar to those raised with family providers: credentialing, required education and training, reasonable compensation, expectations about routine workload and performance, and how peers will relate to their professional colleagues. More questions than answers exist at present. In this instance, there is great risk that policy considerations directed at preserving existing relationships, as well as limiting compensation to traditional providers, could prevent an important and effective intervention from entering mainstream mental health.

As noted in chapter 2, family advocacy has evolved from case-centered advocacy to systems-level advocacy during the past several years. Indeed, federal policy codifies family involvement in state mental health planning as a prerequisite for receiving the Federal Mental Health Block Grant. Implications arise from the fact that families are emerging as a potent political force that, when organized, can have a significant effect on state and federal policymaking. The success of the Federation of Families for Children's Mental Health in organizing families and strengthening the family voice has and will likely continue to expedite family influence on policymaking. Families play an increasingly critical role in policymaking for several important reasons: because they are locally based, they can tell very compelling personal stories of both need and benefits; because they vote, family members may be the most effective advocates for service system improvement and service capacity expansion; and because their vested interest in treatment outcomes encourages both persistence and the desire to learn about state-of-the-art services. These characteristics make families an especially important target audience for sponsors of evidence-based exemplary practices. Undoubtedly, policymakers will have to listen and respond to family advocates more and more in the future.

Payor of Services

Information about the number of children who need treatment and increasing the number severed, coupled with knowledge about and use of treatments that work, increases the potential cost of delivering services. Debates among the states about the size of the population with mental problems are reflective of the extent to which large rises in estimated prevalence rates change the resource equation in the states dramatically. The extent to which emotional problems are identified as risk factors for other problems, such as substance abuse and criminal justice involvement, ups the ante for the risks and costs of failing to serve these children and adolescents as well. All of the interventions and delivery mechanisms described herein are expensive, some more so than others. Most policymakers will ask the same question when encouraged to support new or expanded programming: Who will pay for it? A few reminders are helpful.

For at least 20 years, advocates for development of community-based service delivery systems for children and adolescents have offered that the resources to fund new services can be derived from reinvesting funds diverted from institutional care. This argument for funding systems of care was especially focused on eliminating out-of-state placements in residential treatment programs and reinvesting the savings in local communities. The argument still has merit. Until 1985, more than 75% of public mental health funds for treatment of children and adolescents with SED was invested in institutional care (Burns, 1991). The Children's Services Grant Program has documented cost savings derived from reductions in out-of-state as well as in-state placements in residential treatment facilities. For example, during a study conducted in a county-based system of care on the west coast, services provided to children with severe impairment as assessed with the Child and Adolescent Functional Assessment Scale (Hodges & Wong, 1996) cost an average of $13,106. However, the average cost of care in a residential treatment center for children at the severe impairment level was estimated to be almost twice as much at $26,100 (Rosenblatt, 1998; Substance Abuse and Mental Health Services Administration, 1999). Also, staff from the wraparound program in Milwaukee, Wisconsin, reported that the average monthly cost to care for a child in its publicly financed managed system of care was $2,800, which was 37% less than the average monthly cost of $4,449 for serving a child in a typical out-of-home residential placement (Goldman & Faw, 1999).

MEDICAID

The Medicaid program—Title XXI of the Social Security Act—authorizes federal funds for supporting assessment and treatment of physical and mental illnesses among low-income and disabled families. Federal funds are dependent on the state match, often at a 50-50 ratio. Medicaid funds, a broad array of loosely defined services, include categories covering all the types of services described in this volume. The Early Periodic Screening, Diagnosis, and Treatment (EPSDT) provisions in Medicaid require that all states screen eligible children for emotional disorder, diagnose any conditions found through the screen, and then furnish appropriate treatment for these conditions [42 U.S.C., Section 1396d(a)]. This provision alone creates a funding strategy under Medicaid, although minimally utilized, for treating eligible children with SED. Additionally, a wide variety of home- and community-based mental health services can be funded on approval of 1115 or 1915b waivers. Most observers agree that the federal definitions of these service categories are broad enough to accommodate all of the promising treatments for children with emotional problems.

Thus, in theory, all of the interventions and service delivery mechanisms described in this volume could be funded under Medicaid. There are examples of Medicaid funding in at least one state for each of these interventions (Bazelon Center for Mental Health Law, 1999). So, why don't all the states fund the most effective, least restrictive services for their children who have emotional problems? While there is no single definitive answer, there are many likely explanations. States choose not to bear even 50% of the costs of care wherever it can be avoided, disturbed children are seen as bad children rather than sick children, mental disorders are not viewed as "severe" like physical disorders, and the unfounded view still persists that children can be helped best in the hospital. This list goes on and on. In any event, the policy-relevant fact is clear: A state can fund the services described in this volume under the Medicaid program if it chooses to do so. In fact, the Bazelon Center Report referenced above contains a great many examples of states that are currently funding some or most of the services under discussion. Interestingly, there is considerable evidence that large amounts of federal and state dollars are being spent under Medicaid to pay for services that are both more restrictive and less effective.

MANAGED CARE

No policy discussion of Medicaid or of funding treatment service capacity is complete without addressing managed care. Theoretically, the combination of tools and techniques that make up managed care should promote the development of integrated service systems like those characterized in this volume. Use of capitation and case-rate financing mechanisms should be ideal for blending the different categorical funding sources needed to finance multisystemic, multicomponent, community-based interventions that would be delivered within a system of care model. But theory does not match reality.

There are three nonexclusive rationalizations for the lack of success in improving services under managed care. First, managed care has been adopted primarily as a cost-containment mechanism, eschewing service expansion for assuring that only "medically necessary" services are consumed by public beneficiaries. Second, because it specifies limits on annual and lifetime use, the managed care model is less effective for persons with severe, chronic conditions that require long-term care rather than acute care. Third, proprietary managed care organizations tend to do only what they are explicitly authorized and paid to do. They alone will not create cross-agency networks for the public benefit. They cannot offer a wide variety of services if their contract limits benefits to specific interventions, often only traditional medical interventions. Private, contract-managed care organizations cannot create integrated systems that include services for which many public agencies are responsible; they can only manage the system once it is designed by a public authority.

The policy implication is that no one has yet taken advantage of the potential for managed care to contribute to development of improved service systems or to adopt less traditional forms of effective treatment. By taking advantage of capitation and other case rate mechanisms to control utilization while using flexibility in organizing services at the individual client level, managed care organizations hold the promise of combining the best of both worlds. A less explored option is public sector managed care. The results of public sector managed versus fee-for-service are promising in respect to access, intensity of services, and reduction of institutional care (Burns, Teagle, Schwartz, Angold, & Holtzman, 1999).

THE CHILDREN'S HEALTH INSURANCE PROGRAM

The Children's Health Insurance Program (CHIP), part of the Balanced Budget Act of 1997, authorizes federal expenditures of up to $24 billion over 5 years to assist states to extend health care coverage to children in low-income families whose income is less than 200% of the federal poverty level (P.L.105-33). States can offer coverage in one of three ways: (1) expand Medicaid, (2) create a state-run program, or (3) combine Medicaid with a state-run program. CHIP is significant because it extends federal support to a larger number of children and adolescents and provides greater flexibility for creating benefit programs that can take advantage of the most effective interventions and service delivery mechanisms available (see SAMHSA, 1999). Every state has the option to offer a wide variety of covered services, including all of the services described in this volume. Service categories include inpatient and outpatient mental health, inpatient and outpatient substance abuse treatment, home- and community-based services, and case management/care coordination. In Medicaid expansion programs, covered children have all the same entitlements as categorically eligible children, including screening and medically necessary services under EPSDT (Bazelon Center for Mental Health Law, 1999).

POOLED FUNDING

The practice of pooling funds offers the prospect of increasing the financial soundness of systems of care to deliver effective treatment with funding from multiple child service systems. Conceptually, pooled funding allows programs to leverage resources from many different sources and use the resulting pool to pay for the range of services that constitute the system in a particular community. An advantage of implementing pooled funding strategies is that it allows greater flexibility to adapt services to the unique needs of individual children and their families, eliminating the prospect that unneeded services will be imposed simply because that is what the system is capable of paying for.

Once policymakers are willing to support the funding of expanded services to obtain the best clinical and societal results, the potential savings associated with long-term cost offsets in extended treatment and costs of other public systems can become a reality. The experience of Wraparound Milwaukee is informative. Wraparound Milwaukee is a public sector managed care organization that serves children at risk for residential placement. It has acted as both Milwaukee's system integrator and its integrated service provider. Children are referred from child welfare and juvenile justice; funding is pooled from Medicaid, mental health, and the justice and child welfare agencies. There is a provider network of over 150 agencies. Since 1994, 650 children have been served. In that time, residential placements have been reduced from 360 to 190, inpatient days from 24,000 to 10,000 for Medicaid-eligible children, and improvements in functional levels have been achieved.

Changing Provider Roles

Traditionally, providers—especially those in the core clinical disciplines of psychiatry, psychology, social work, and nursing—have had a primary influence on treatment decision-making at the case, program, and system levels. Under the medical model, clinicians are seen as the experts whose judgment must be given the most credence at both the caregiving and the policy level. This position is rapidly changing vis-à-vis behavioral health care in general and child mental health in particular, as evident in almost all the chapters of this volume. Parent involvement in treatment planning and delivery is emphasized in all the interventions. Key roles are envisioned for lay persons, such as mentors, caseworkers from other child serving agencies, and a variety of client and family peers. In some respects, traditional clinicians have been seen as impediments to the adoption of cutting-edge interventions because of perceived ideological differences and lack of appropriate training. Potential policy pitfalls abound.

First and foremost, the potential exists for traditional providers to become adversaries of emerging new treatment technologies. Many reasons for such a dilemma can be imagined: the threat of lost jobs, loss of prestige, ideological conflict, loss of control over clinical decision-making, creation of treatment expectations that exceed providers' capacities or competencies, and the simple fear of change. Policymakers should remind themselves that the causes for opposition may be unrelated to the utility of the proposed changes. But, unless traditional providers become willing and hearty supporters of emerging evidence-based interventions and service delivery mechanisms, real systems change will be difficult, if not impossible, to accomplish. Explicit strategies to achieve the support of clinicians are needed, ranging from simply determining how they can benefit from proposed changes to making sure that they are provided every opportunity to receive training in evidence-based interventions and to participate in managing service and system change processes.

Almost all of the service interventions described in this volume are delivered by persons other than clinicians trained in the core clinical disciplines. Clinicians could also be trained to deliver any of these interventions; alternatively, their roles are more likely to become those of trainer, consultant, or supervisor. Treatment foster care is delivered by foster parents; mentoring by nonprofessional or volunteer mentors; family support by experienced parent peers; the home-based element of First Step to Success by specially trained parents. Other interventions have at least one component provided by a nonclinician, usually a family member, as with multisystemic therapy, family-centered case management, and wraparound. Broadening the provider network creates more opportunity to increase service availability, provides for greater family and community engagement in the therapeutic process, opens doors for new employment opportunities and their attendant economic benefits to the community, and improves prospects for improved outcomes in a larger number of life domains.

With respect to outcomes, the domains most often influenced by traditional service models involve normalizing events such as stabilization of the home and reduction of out-of-home placements, mainstreaming in schools, decreases in juvenile justice involvement, improvements in family and peer relationships, and development of coping skills and resilience. All of these outcomes reflect societal values, as well as individual quality of life. But, broad expansion of services beyond the traditional services can cause tremendous upheaval across many community processes. Current health care reimbursement mechanisms are not well suited to this expanded framework. Neither fee-for-service nor managed care models have quality assurance mechanisms suitable for monitoring nontraditional behavioral health care providers. Traditional roles are turned upside down, creating anxiety and blurred lines of accountability. The resulting policy conundrum is that rapid change brings the promise of substantially improved child and family outcomes and yet, puts enormous pressures on traditional providers and service systems.

One special concern is the potential for conflict among family members and providers as the balance of power in therapeutic roles shifts. For many reasons, traditional providers can be threatened by the emergence of demanding and very vocal family members who see themselves as entitled to direct the therapeutic process for their children as full partners in that process (Simpson et al., 1999). Conversely, a family's closeness to the challenges of SED and their lack of formal training in the course of treatment can create unreasonable expectations about the results that can be obtained. Policymakers can help by assuring that families and providers are encouraged to participate jointly in policy formulation to achieve common objectives.

Policymakers need to understand that each of the cutting-edge interventions and service delivery mechanisms that hold the most promise depend heavily on traditional clinical services as essential components (e.g., diagnostic-specific psychosocial interventions and psychopharmacology). It is the strength of the partnership among clinicians, families, other providers, and program managers that will determine the success or failure of efforts to implement change. For this and other related reasons, policymakers need to recognize that partnership-building tools, including agent-of-change negotiation and facilitation skills, need to be supported to assist communities trying to improve services for children with SED. Programs designed to build partnerships and to support consensus-building among diverse stakeholders are critical priorities in developing community-based systems of care. The CMHS Community Action Grant Program is designed for this purpose. Support is provided to engage key stakeholders in consensus-building activities that yield a decision to adopt the evidence-based practice. A second phase grant is also available to support overcoming actual implementation barriers, such as lack of training in the service system.

Ultimately, the changing roles of traditional providers and emerging new provider groups affect the balance among constituencies in the policy-making process. There can be no doubt that the expansion of service roles beyond traditional disciplines has democratized the deliberative process at the federal, state, and local level, and will continue to do so. Policymakers must be increasingly attuned to the views and needs of consumers and their families and must balance these perspectives with those of traditional providers much more carefully. Thankfully, the bottom line is that all stakeholders agree that children and adolescents deserve the most effective treatment possible, consistent with their individual rights, prerogatives, and liberties. Perhaps the best strategy for achieving consensus and for balancing different interests is to always get to that bottom line as fast as possible.

Changing Relationships among Child-Serving Agencies

Traditionally, mental health policy has been introverted, focused primarily on how specialty mental health programs can gain resources, develop capacity, and improve learning about service provision. At the same time, the evidence mounts that isolation of children and adolescents (and adults as well) in specialty mental health programs outside their normal family and community can cause an exacerbation of the very problems that treatment is intended to ameliorate (Barker, 1998). Thus, there is increasing pressure to deliver mental health services in the environments where clients are found rather than by removing them from those environments. This pressure is already causing major changes in the way mental health and other agencies relate to one another. The policy ramifications of an integrated approach to service programming are staggering.

SCHOOLS

Historically, schools and mental health providers have not enjoyed productive partnerships, largely due to each seeing the other as either a place to unburden oneself of problem kids or as the unfair source of burden on the other (see chapter 2). But, opportunities do exist. The Individuals with Disabilities Education Act (IDEA; P.L. 94-142 as amended) requires schools to provide special education services to children and adolescents whose disabilities interfere with their education. For children with SED, services include assessment, counseling, and behavior management as well as special classes and schools. IDEA presents special opportunities to promote integration of mental health services in school settings. Systems of care offer the opportunity to make specialty mental health care available to children while they remain in school. Still, many barriers need to be overcome before mental health services are routinely integrated into school settings.

The recent federal interdepartmental Safe Schools/Healthy Students Grant Program is an example of future directions for public policy. Under this program, the Departments of Education, Justice, and Health and Human Services voluntarily pooled their resources designated for school violence prevention to offer localities (in this case, school districts) a single source of revenue with which to implement a comprehensive, integrated plan for reducing youth violence and improving healthy child development. Comprehensive, coordinated problem-solving; provision of multiple interventions; and concrete action-oriented partnerships among key child-serving agencies characterize the new approach.

The results of the LaGrange Area Department of Special Education experiment offers a promising example, demonstrating the feasibility of the school system as the lead agency in delivering wraparound services to children with emotional disabilities. Inasmuch as wraparound services are not classically "clinical" in the sense that providers all must be credentialed mental health professionals, it makes sense that providers in other settings and disciplines could be at least equally suitable for delivering a coordinated system of community care (see chapter 4). Such an approach taken in a school system takes advantage of the critical fact that kids are in school and don't have to be recruited into another setting for services to be provided. As noted in chapter 2, the evaluation of the Vanderbilt School-Based Counseling Program found that 96% of the children and families offered school-based services began them, compared to only 13% of those offered off-site (Catron, Harris, & Weiss, 1998).

Furthermore, delivery of services within the school setting promotes more continuity and stability for children and their families and avoids the relative isolation encountered in specialty mental health settings. Placing system-level coordination in the hands of a primary service sector other than mental health could go far toward eliminating the stigma associated with participation in mental health programs and encourage more families to take advantage of the services being offered. Policymakers and mental health program managers need to be willing to sacrifice some control if this results in less stigma and more opportunity for children and adolescents to receive the services they need.

JUVENILE JUSTICE

Estimates are that two thirds of the 100,000 youth detained in juvenile justice settings have a diagnosable emotional disorder other than or in addition to conduct disorder (Teplin, 2000). The literature is overrun with evidence that mental health services in the juvenile justice system, if any, are fragmented and severely inadequate. The later observations were confirmed in a survey of 24 sites in 9 states jointly conducted by the National GAINS Center and the National Mental Health Association as part of their federally sponsored Justice for Juveniles Initiative (Cocozza, Stainbrook, Faenza, & Siegfried, 1999). A key finding of the survey was that most communities deliver services in a piecemeal fashion, that few programs specifically target the needs of juvenile justice youth, and that even fewer communities have programming for co-occurring mental health and substance abuse disorders, which are common in this population.

Two interventions contained in this volume specifically target delinquent youth for treatment: multisystemic therapy and treatment foster care. With a proven record of effectiveness and demonstrably decreased recidivism rates among treated youth, these interventions hold great promise for reducing the pressure on juvenile justice authorities running overcrowded facilities for difficult-to-manage youth. Additionally, both the principles and practice of systems of care provide potential solutions for problems of service fragmentation and lack of continuity encountered by youth in the juvenile justice system who are suffering from an emotional disorder. These prospects create tremendous incentives for juvenile justice authorities to seek out partnerships with mental health providers who can deliver these effective interventions. The incentives for mental health providers are less clear. In order to create incentives for mental health agencies to welcome juvenile justice referrals, resources likely must be added to existing programs. Pooling of juvenile justice and mental health resources to fund interventions directed at juvenile justice clients is an attractive option.

In many respects, the time appears right for improved relations between mental health and juvenile justice authorities. Effective services can be delivered, and the mechanisms for coordinating services and for plugging system gaps are available. Increasingly, both mental health and juvenile justice officials acknowledge the value of using partnerships to achieve their goals. For example, in OJJDP Fact Sheet #82, published in July, 1998, Shay Bilchik, administrator of OJJDP observes, "We must increase the number of quality treatment programs in the community and in juvenile institutions." In support of this goal, OJJDP has transferred funds to the Center for Mental Health Services to strengthen the capacity of 31 of its Child Services Grant Program sites to serve youth in the juvenile justice system. Policymakers have to challenge these officials to overcome some final barriers. The partners need to create a common vision that sets the right balance between assuring community protection and providing youth with the treatment they need. Mental health officials need to acknowledge responsibility for juvenile justice populations at the same time juvenile justice relinquishes some control over these youth. Everyone needs to pay attention to the problem by providing appropriate screening and assessment, welcoming youth and their families to services, and helping these youngsters as they attempt to transition from antisocial to prosocial living. This would seem to be preferable to anticipating the transition of youth from the juvenile to the adult criminal justice systems.

CHILD WELFARE

More than a quarter million youth who need mental health care are now in foster care, where only a small fraction receive mental health care at all. In fact, based on a number of studies of youth entering foster care, the rates of behavior problems, developmental delays, and need for psychological intervention ranges from 39% to 80%, resulting in an estimated 195,000 to 400,000 youth (Clausen, Landsverk, Granger, Chadwick, & Litrownik, 1998; Garland & Besinger, 1997; Halfon, Medonca, & Berkowitz, 1995; Hochstadt, Jaudes, Zimo, & Schachter, 1987; Landsverk & Garland, 1999; Simms, 1989). The traditional child welfare/mental health relationship has been duplicative and competitive. Mental health services have commonly been delivered by child welfare systems as an adjunct to foster care or by paying extensively for residential care, independent of the community mental health system. As noted in chapter 6, treatment foster care has been frequently available through the foster care system in addition to the traditional therapies, particularly the residential treatment often provided in out-of-state programs. Indeed, the sometimes greater availability of mental health care to children and adolescents in foster care gives rise to the unfathomable circumstance of parents having to give up custody of their children so they can get the treatment they need—a tragedy for our society. A recent study found that this problem exists in approximately half the states. Nearly one fourth of the parents interviewed in another survey reported that they had been advised by public officials that they needed to relinquish custody to get needed mental health services for their children (Bazelon Center for Mental Health Law, 1999).

A growing body of effective clinical interventions deliverable within a system of care provides hope and specific techniques for reducing or eliminating the custody-for-treatment conundrum. If child welfare can tap effective services from a service delivery system under the overall responsibility of mental health authorities, major benefits can result. This point of view is reflected in existing agreements among the American Public Welfare Association, The National Association of State Mental Health Program Directors, and the Federation of Families for Children's Mental Health. These agreements address the same fundamental policy implications explicit in the services and mechanisms described in this volume: providing better service coordination, keeping children at home, providing multimodal treatment, emphasizing prevention and early intervention, and engaging families in service delivery. They are all necessary prerequisites for accomplishing the fundamental goals of the child welfare system—that is, providing for the health and welfare of children under conditions of safety, stability, and permanency.

Research Policy: Expecting More

Without a doubt, much more rigorous research will be needed before anyone can conclusively decide what is the best treatment approach for children and adolescents with or at risk of mental problems and their sequelae (Burns, 1999;

Institute of Medicine, 1989). It is easy to assume that more public funds need to be invested in basic, clinical, and services research. Perhaps the only important dictum is that all three enterprises merit support. In determining the best formula for delivering clinical and related support services, the challenge will be to merge the best research findings into a coherent body of knowledge that can be applied in systems of care for populations who exist in varying circumstances across the country. This goal has been achieved for a number of disorders and interventions (National Advisory Mental Health Council, 2001).

Other, more complicated questions remain. Where do providers and families fit into the research enterprise? Who are the intended beneficiaries of publicly funded clinical and services research? What gaps in research methods need to be filled? How does one define the success of the research enterprise?

With respect to family and provider roles in research, this book supports the notion that families and providers should play a more significant role in formulating research questions, conducting research, and analyzing results. Both CMHS and NIMH have embarked on approaches that would achieve this result. CMHS supports training family members in evaluation theory and practice. Its multisite effectiveness study protocol calls for consumer and family involvement in all phases of evaluation activity, including formulation of questions, study design, study execution and analysis of results. In a report entitled "Bridging Science and Service," the National Advisory Mental Health Council (1999) recommended several important directions NIMH can take to improve consumer, family, and provider involvement. Key proposed changes to current practice include involving consumers, families, and providers in:

- setting research priorities;
- incorporating clinician and consumer decision-making, implementation, and adherence processes into interventions research; and,
- conducting reviews of NIMH research applications.

Each of these moves gives consumers, families, and providers a more meaningful role in establishing research priorities, defining the expected outcomes of effective services, evaluating their own roles in the delivery of effective services, interpreting research data, and determining the significance of particular findings. These contributions should influence the relevance of mental health services research resulting in service provision that is responsive to the needs of children and families. Policymakers will benefit from the insights provided from these perspectives and from the higher return on investment from publicly funded services research.

It is especially important to heed the call for improving research methods that bridge the gap between determining efficacy in laboratory settings and effectiveness in naturalistic clinical settings (see Special Section on Efficacy and Effectiveness in Volume 63, *Journal of Consulting and Clinical Psychology*, 1995). Current efficacy research does not accommodate to determining effectiveness in messy real-world settings. New methods need to be employed that allow consideration of moderating and mediating influences in typical clinical settings. Factors such as cultural differences, the effects of multiple simultaneously delivered treatment interventions, and the influence of environment on outcomes need to be better addressed. The impact on outcomes by the evolving nature of treatment programs, frequent changes in providers, the lack of comprehensive training in new interventions, and the extent of compliance have to be routinely assessed before a clear picture can emerge from effectiveness research. Program and client goals need to take precedence in formulating research questions and setting research priorities.

Making Training and Education Responsive to Today's Treatment Technology

The observation in chapter 2 that there are significant barriers to multidisciplinary training on the principles and methods for community-based systems of care is symptomatic of the distance between training and practice discussed in chapter 1. There is increasing concern that training, especially at the preservice level, bears little relation to the changing trends in service delivery and the demands on providers, and even less to the needs of the children and families being served by child-serving agencies (Meyers, Kaufman, & Goldman, 1999).

Postgraduate education for the core mental health disciplines is in need of updating to include the most recent knowledge about treatments that work. But the need does not stop there. Curricula for new disciplines like those described for families, peers, and lay providers in this volume need to be formally recognized, and tailored training made available. For example, East Carolina University in Greenville, North Carolina, created a partnership among faculty from six schools and departments to develop and use state-of-the-art curricula for providers, family members, community representatives, and university graduate students to train all participants in their roles in developing and implementing community-based treatment and support services within a system of care for children and adolescents with SED. Similarly, in-service and continuing education programs need to be oriented to these emerging best practices. Traditionally trained clinicians have neither the specific training nor a general orientation to the theory or practice that underlies the newer community-based interventions. They need an opportunity to acquire new perspective and the skills to implement new interventions. Nontraditional providers need the same ongoing training in order to continue developing their skills and keep abreast of the newest techniques. From the public perspective, it makes little sense to invest in the development of new, more effective treatments and then fail to support the training to deliver them. Public funding for training, especially mental health services training, makes sense and should be part of an overall strategy for improving services to children and adolescents.

It is becoming more and more apparent that effective training for the management of clinical service programs must also include development of the skills needed to achieve productive partnerships among multiple providers, consumers, and families. The CMHS programs of technical assistance to grantees of the Children's Services Grant Program (as well as generalized technical assistance to a wide variety of state and local providers, managers, and policy-makers) is increasingly focused on developing partnering, leadership, and communication skills that enable individuals to engage in collaborations that are easy to talk about but very difficult to achieve.

Conclusions

The emergence of effective service delivery mechanisms and effective clinical treatments have many policy implications indeed:

- Public resources can be invested with reasonable expectations that they will yield human and societal returns well worth the investment.
- Service delivery mechanisms exist that enable effective treatments to be delivered efficiently to those who need them.
- Children and adolescents with emotional problems can remain in their homes and communities if provided effective community-based treatment.
- Families can and should play the crucial role in the treatment of their children with emotional disorders.
- Traditional clinical practice holds less prospect for improved child and community outcomes than the practices described within this volume, creating challenges and tremendous opportunities for clinicians.
- Productive partnerships with schools, juvenile justice, and child welfare will be necessary if the goal of effective mental health care is to be achieved.
- Researchers need support to pursue the work of determining the efficacy and effectiveness of the practices described herein, to push the envelope further in finding both promising new interventions and service delivery mechanisms, and to help with translating this learning into information that families and providers can use to improve outcomes for youth with emotional problems.
- Colleges and universities can contribute to better mental health care for youth by reforming traditional curricula and offering training and education to providers outside the traditional disciplines, including parents, teachers, mentors, foster care parents, and others who want to support healthy childhood development and the mental health and happiness of future generations.

While not the subject of this volume, its lessons must be learned within the context of the stigma that those with severe emotional problems and mental illness bear. By creating the fear of discovery, stigma often bars children, adolescents, and adults from the treatment they need. Policymakers must address stigma and its elimination in order to take advantage of the many opportunities improved treatments and service delivery mechanisms provide.

Hopefully, the policymakers who read this chapter will ultimately agree with the Surgeon General (U.S. DHHS, 1999) when he says:

Promoting mental health for all Americans will require scientific know-how but, even more importantly, a societal resolve that we will make the needed investment. The investment does not call for massive budgets; rather, it calls for the willingness of each of us to educate ourselves and others about mental health and mental illness, and thus to confront the attitudes, fear, and misunderstanding that remain as barriers before us. It is my intent that this report will usher in a healthy new millennium of mind and body for the Nation (p.v.).

Acknowledgments

Thanks to Rolando L. Santiago, Ph.D., who provided descriptive, outcome, and cost data from the national multisite evaluation of the Comprehensive Community Mental Health Services for Children and Their Families Program. Dr. Santiago is the federal project officer who oversees CMHS contracts to conduct the national evaluation.

14

A Profitable Conjunction: From Science to Service in Children's Mental Health

KIMBERLY HOAGWOOD

BARBARA J. BURNS

JOHN R. WEISZ

Perhaps it was the dysphoria that accompanies the ends of centuries, but it was not uncommon in the last two decades of the 20th century to hear concerns expressed about the lack of evidence on treatments or services for children with mental health problems. The science base, insofar as it existed, was seen as largely irrelevant and esoteric. It sat for the most part on academic shelves. It was not able to answer questions that were important to families, clinicians, or administrators responsible for delivery of services to children and adolescents with serious mental health needs.

Perhaps it is the optimism that accompanies the beginning of a new century, but in fact, as this book attests, much is now known about the effectiveness, impact, and outcomes of a range of treatments and services for children with severe emotional and behavioral disorders. And the picture is *not* bleak. Between 1998 and the present, there have been at least six major reviews summarizing evidence for the effectiveness of treatments (pharmacological, psychosocial, or their combination), services, and preventive interventions for children with or at risk for clinical disorders (Burns, Hoagwood, & Mrazek, 1999; Jensen et al., 1999a; Weisz & Jensen, 1999; Loeber & Farrington, 1998; U.S. DHHS Surgeon General's Report, 1999; Rones & Hoagwood, 2000). There have been two major reviews of science and policy on social and emotional factors in young children: one, a scientific review of longitudinal studies that has identified causal, fixed, and malleable risks for social or behavioral problems among young children (Loeber & Farrington, 1997); the second a review of federal programs and policies that could map onto, but in many cases ignores, the science base (Foundations and Agencies Network Monograph, 2000). All of these reviews build upon a long history of meta-analyses examining the impact of psy-

AUTHORS' NOTE: This chapter is in the public domain and may be reproduced without the permission of the author or the publisher.

chosocial treatments and cognitive behavioral strategies for children and adolescents (Casey & Berman, 1985; Kazdin, Bass, Ayers, & Rodgers, 1990; Weisz, Weiss, Alicke, & Klotz, 1987; Weisz, Weiss, Han, Granger, & Morton, 1995).

As is attested to by the chapters in this book, evidence for the effectiveness of specific community-based services does exist. A range of services has been studied scientifically, building on a body of theory, to examine whether and under what conditions specific services do or do not lead to improvements in the functioning of children and their families. Because it is far too easy for there to be service drift—i.e., loose adaptation of a service to fit within the constraints of a particular service system—and because such drift is associated with poorer outcomes (Henggeler, Pickrel, & Brondino, 2000), training materials have been developed for the services described in this book to enable new users to adopt and deliver them with fidelity to the principles of the therapy or the service.

This book also makes clear that, as is true in any developing field, the evidence for the effectiveness of mental health services for youth is still uneven. There is a stronger evidence base for some services than for others. For example, multisystemic therapy (MST), treatment foster care (TFC), and some forms of intensive case management (ICM) have had a decade-long history of randomized trials to develop, refine, and test their impact. Some services described in this book, such as wraparound, special education services (First Step to Success), and mentoring, are in earlier stages of development, but at this time are demonstrating promising results in their potential to effect positive outcomes among children and adolescents. The chapters in this book highlight both the solidity of findings for some services and the promise of others.

This book is an attempt to bring the research base on effective services for children and adolescents closer to service implementation—to create, in essence, an islet that will connect the shorelines of research and practice. Such a connection places demands upon the science, revealing questions that have not yet been sufficiently answered by ongoing research programs and highlighting new areas of inquiry regarding the uptake, dissemination, and implementation of the evidence base that need amplification. Because science is self-correctional—that is, it is the nature of science to change direction as new knowledge accumulates and methods improve—a close linkage between science and services is needed to maximize the chance that services will be based on the best evidence available at any time. In order to achieve this linkage, however, it is necessary to develop new research to practice translational models that will accelerate the pace by which evidence-based services will be used in what Weisz, Weiss, and Donenberg (1992) called "the crucible of real life."

Burns (1999) argued that the continuing problems of well-documented and persistent unmet need for mental health care among children and adolescents in this country necessitate timely response by both the scientific and practitioner fields. She proposed the creation of a research agenda on clinical interventions for youth which would accomplish four tasks: (1) synthesize (through reviews of the evidence base) the status of science on promising interventions, (2) assess quality indicators of outcomes to improve standards of clinical practice, (3) evaluate outcome measures, and (4) develop a new research phase model for connecting research to practice. This book, along with the important other reviews referred to earlier (Burns, Hoagwood, & Mrazek, 1999; Foundations and Agencies Network Monograph, 2000; Jensen et al., 1999a; Weisz & Jensen, 1999; Kazdin, 1996; Loeber & Farrington, 1998; U.S. DHHS Surgeon General's Report, 1999; Rones & Hoagwood, 2000; Weisz, Weiss, & Donenberg, 1992) takes an important step not only in identifying the evidence base on service effectiveness but in describing it in sufficient detail to enable it to be used in clinical practice.

In this chapter we build on the Burns' agenda. We first describe what is meant by evidence-based practice and discuss why it matters. We then identify six categories of research in which studies are needed to amplify, strengthen, and extend the science on evidence-based services for children and adolescents. Finally, we argue that developing a science that will be serviceable for children requires a different and more iterative model of the relationship between research and practice. We then describe one such model.

What Does "Evidence Based" Mean?

In the field of children's mental health science and service delivery, the term "evidence based" refers to a body of knowledge, obtained through carefully implemented scientific methods, about the prevalence, incidence, or risks for mental disorders, or about the impact of treatments or services on mental health problems. It is a shorthand term denoting the quality, robustness, and validity of the scientific evidence that can be brought to bear on questions of etiology, distribution or risk for disorders, and outcomes of care for children with mental health problems. Criteria for assessing what constitutes an evidence base have been offered. Kazdin (1996) describes four domains that constitute such criteria: a theory to relate a hypothesized mechanism to the clinical problem; basic research to assess the validity of the mechanisms; preliminary outcome evidence to demonstrate that a therapeutic approach changes the relevant outcomes; and process-outcome connections, which display the relationships between process change and clinical outcomes (p. 78). More specific and operational criteria have been proposed by the Society of Clinical Psychology of the American Psychological Association (Lonigan, Elbert, & Johnson, 1998) and applied to studies of specific childhood syndromes (e.g., depression, anxiety, conduct, and attention-deficit/hyperactivity disorders). The criteria for "well-established" therapies requires at least two scientifically defensible group-design studies conducted by different investigative teams, or more than nine single-case studies with strong experimental designs, and treatment manuals. Therapies designated as "probably efficacious" generally require at least two studies demonstrating the intervention to be more effective than a no-treatment control group, or several single-case design studies demonstrating its impact, as well as manuals that prescribe therapy.

WHY IS USING THE EVIDENCE BASE IMPORTANT?

One might say that it is *not* a service if it is untested. Delivery of untested services, whose long-term impact on families and children is entirely unknown, can cause harm. This is not a trivial problem. A recent article (Dishion, Mc-Cord, & Poulin, 1999) reported that peer group interventions (including group counseling sessions run and supervised by clinicians and summer camps) significantly *increased* problem behavior among high-risk adolescents, including substance abuse, delinquency, and violence. They referred to this as "deviancy training," to suggest that the positive reinforcement occurring in teen groups (via laughter, social attention, and interest in deviant behavior) promotes further socially maladaptive behaviors.

NEW RESEARCH DIRECTIONS

As this book indicates, a solid and growing body of evidence for the impact of a range of community-based mental health services exists. Some of the evidence-based services described in this book have followed the principles identified by Kazdin (1996) in developing a theory of the relationship between the service and clinical improvement, testing this relationship. In some cases, the evidence base has been extended to the generalizabilty of efficacy-based treatments (by studying transportability into standard service settings). Yet it is increasingly clear that the public health goal of a public health science (and child services research *is* a public health science) is to ensure that science-based services can be embedded into everyday practice. This necessitates new areas of investigation—what might be called dissemination and implementation science—to understand how best to position and sustain effective services in communities and to identify factors that impede this positioning. Achieving this goal requires both a new genre of study and persistent attention to questions about *why* services are effective.

Changing Practitioner Behaviors

As knowledge about treatments and services with known outcomes becomes more widely available (e.g., combination or medication therapies for children with ADHD), it will be important to understand how best to change practitioner behaviors such that this knowledge will be used. Different strategies are likely to be needed for changing the behaviors of practitioners from different disciplines. While practice guidelines have been developed by professional associations such as the American Academy of Child and Adolescent Psychiatry or the American Academy of Pediatrics, adoption of these into everyday practice may necessitate studies of characteristics of the practice environment, disciplinary history, or credentialing traditions that impede or facilitate such adoption. Approaches such as academic detailing (widely used by pharmaceutical industry) or use of key opinion leaders within communities (Kelly et al., 1991) may be valuable approaches for changing practice. For example, theories of social diffusion (Winett et al., 1995) suggest that adoption of new strategies or behaviors (such as cessation of smoking, or eating a healthier diet) depends in part on the social value attached to the opinions of leaders who encourage such changes. The impact of opinion leadership with reference to children's mental health treatments or services could be examined for its applicability to a range of services, providers, and service environments.

Changing Organizational Behaviors

As work by Glisson and Himmelgarn has shown (1998), the organizational culture and context within which mental health providers work have a direct influence on the attitudes, motivations, and behaviors of providers, and consequently have an indirect influence on child outcomes. Studies of the impact of organizational culture and climate for sustaining the fidelity of the therapeutic process and outcomes need to be conducted if science-based services are to be maintained within community-based agencies, schools, or health care settings. Studies are also needed to identify aspects of the practice environment that facilitate therapists' fidelity to treatment. In addition, it will be important to examine those proximal features of the practice environment that influence the clinician/patient relationship and assess why some clinicians are motivated to change and adopt new strategies and others are not.

Amplification of Interventions to Increase Organizational or Community Fit

Several hundred studies of school mental health services have been published since 1985 (Rones & Hoagwood, 2000) and several hundred studies of psychosocial treatments for children similarly exist in the literature (Durlak, Wells, Cotton, & Johnson, 1995; Kazdin & Weisz, 1998). Yet, for the most part, these services have no sustaining power within the schools, clinics, or agencies beyond the tenure of their creators. They come and go as grant support, academic hirings, and faculty interests come and go. Studies of the augmentations that will help to maintain scientifically driven services within a range of agencies and organizations are needed. Augmented models, such as additions of wraparound services to core prevention programs, neighborhood resource centers, or additions of case management to after-school programs may increase the likelihood that these services will be sustained.

Adaptation of Treatments to Increase Organizational or Community Fit

Because there now exists a knowledge base of hundreds of treatment studies demonstrating improved outcomes for children with a range of behavioral, emotional, or psychiatric problems, extension of this knowledge into a range of community settings would be valuable. However, to date, attention to the kinds of adaptations necessary in order to make these treatments practical and feasible for use in community settings has occurred rarely. Because much of the knowledge about treatment efficacy has been developed in academic settings, a new generation of research is needed to address questions such as how far to adapt a manualized therapy for use within a mental health clinic (given that most children will only attend four to five sessions), what kinds of outcomes to assess when a treatment is embedded in a new service setting, or how to engage families in the tailoring of a treatment to enable it to match familial values or experiences. It will also be important to develop research-based triage standards to determine when children's mental health needs can best be managed by persons with different levels of training in mental health issues. In addition, issues about whether to treat co-occurring disorders sequentially or simultaneously will need to be addressed for children with mental health and substance abuse problems.

Deconstruction of Interventions to Identify Core Potencies

In the past five years, there has been a concerted effort by the clinical treatment research field to move beyond small-scale efficacy trials to broader based effectiveness studies (Hoagwood, Jensen, Petti, & Burns, 1996). This emphasis on the translation from efficacy to effectiveness studies has resulted in an increase in studies that focus on more heterogeneous populations, more real-world settings (for example, pediatric health offices), and a wider range of outcomes with which to investigate the applicability of the treatment under consideration. However, important as this direction has been—and it remains critically important—it would appear that some reverse engineering is also needed. Buyers of services are willing to pay only for those core elements of interventions that potentiate the outcomes of interest. Studies are needed to answer, for example, questions about those components of cognitive-behavior therapies, family therapies, home visitation programs, or parent-training programs that are core to obtaining certain outcomes. Studies are sorely needed that deconstruct or dismantle therapies into elements that eventuate in certain outcomes and are practically amenable to being taught to (for example) nurse practitioners, teachers, and health care paraprofessionals. At the same time, therapies that are not amenable to such deconstruction should be identified. If outcomes suffer, then no deconstruction is valuable.

Related to this is the issue of identifying the dosage of a given service that is needed in order to obtain a particular outcome. In part, this interest in dose is being urged forward by the exigencies of health care accountability. At the present time, the notion of service dose cannot be made meaningful until (1) the services themselves are well specified, (2) the active ingredients comprising the service can be specified, and (3) appropriate statistical scaling methods of dosage are used (Hoagwood, 1997).

Measurement Development: Functioning and Impairments

Measurement of child mental health outcomes has been dominated by attention to syndromes, presenting problems, and diagnoses. Yet of most importance to most health care administrators, teachers, parents, or front-line clinicians are problems related to a child's functioning. Unfortunately, the measures that are currently available for assessing functional impairments or competencies are quite limited and reflect outdated notions of what functioning is. The most widely used measures are either global, thus inadequately reflecting cultural variations, or confound functioning with diagnosis (Canino, Costello, & Angold, 1999). Conceptual problems also plague the area of measurement of functioning. The basic concept of it originated from Vineland's notion of "social usefulness," a concept that was pertinent in its applicability to adults with mental retardation in the 1930s but is hardly sufficient for understanding children's mental health needs today. Further, the theoretical notions of "functioning" are conceptualized, measured, and used in different ways across the major service systems in which children are seen. "Functioning," as the word is used in health settings, refers to events and consequences such as losing a limb and requiring prosthetic devices. In education, it is used to refer to skills such as social or communication abilities, as well as poor handwriting. In mental health settings, a child's functioning may refer to a clinician's global rating of whether the child completes tasks in school or at home. Thus, measurement approaches that will not confound functioning with clinical syndromes, that will reflect culturally specific attitudes (rather than global ratings), and that can flexibly assess core elements of functioning are needed to cross health, education, and mental health settings.

THE RESEARCH TO PRACTICE PROBLEM

These new research directions will help to connect the research base to clinical practice. However, it should be acknowledged that one impediment to the efficiency and usefulness of the research base has been the scientific model that has driven the development of a usable science. That is, one reason that efficacy studies have not been readily deployed into service settings may be that the research model used to drive the development, refinement, and testing of those treatments does not mesh well with the exigencies of clinic or community-based care (Weisz, 2000a).

The culture of psychological science as brought to bear on questions of the efficacy of treatments for children has typically involved conducting such studies within controlled and somewhat rarefied environments, such as university laboratories. Over the past 40 years, a large number of controlled clinical trials and within-group studies have been published on the impact of psychosocial treatments, and have demonstrated that specific treatments are efficacious for about two dozen clinical conditions in children. These studies have typically been conducted in or in close connection to university laboratories. Studies of conventional treatments delivered in clinics and clinical programs have demonstrated much weaker effects (Weisz & Weiss, 1993). There has been an implicit assumption that once the laboratory studies of the efficacy of treatments have been completed, the results will be usable and relevant outside of these laboratories. But, as Weisz and colleagues have noted (Weisz & Weiss, 1993; Kazdin & Weisz, 1998; Weisz, 2000b), there are numerous differences between the conditions of most research and the conditions in which everyday treatment is delivered. These differences may mean that treatments developed through efficacy trials may need adaptation to fit into many clinics and other service settings. The challenge of addressing the discrepancy between treatments as tested within controlled environments and treatments or services as tested within real-world clinics or community settings has been identified as a major impediment to closing the gap between science and practice (Burns, 1999; Burns, Hoagwood, & Mrazek, 1999; Hoagwood, 1997; Jensen, Hoagwood, & Petti, 1996; Jensen, Hoagwood, & Trickett, 1999b; Weisz & Weiss, 1993; Kazdin & Weisz, 1998).

Weisz refers to the older model as the Medical-Pharmaceutical (MP) Model. The model entails a series of controlled laboratory trials, with dissemination, implementation, and deployment occurring at the end of the testing process (Weisz, 2000a). This model may not be well suited to ultimate use in clinics or community settings because, as Weisz points out, many of the real-world factors that MP researchers might consider "nuisance" variables and therefore rule out or control experimentally are precisely those variables that need to be understood and addressed if treatments are to work well in real clinical practice. These variables or real-world exigencies (e.g., co-occurring disorders, parent substance abuse or pathology, life stresses that lead to early termination or no-shows for therapy visits, or therapists too overwhelmed to learn a new treatment protocol) may need to be directly addressed within the development, refinement, and testing of treatments and services if these interventions are to be maximally effective.

As the field of services research expands, it will be important to take advantage of opportunities to study new services as they arise, and to do so in a timely manner. Judging by past performance, when treatments are developed and tested via the MP model, 10–20 years may be required to advance to the point at which the treatment can be understood with respect to its effects within a practice setting. This time frame is impractical and inefficient if the goal of a public health science of children's services is to improve practice. Instead, a new model is needed that will encourage studies of the real-world effectiveness of new treatments or services within the context of the practice setting where the service is ultimately to be placed.

A NEW MODEL FOR CONNECTING RESEARCH TO PRACTICE: THE CLINIC/COMMUNITY INTERVENTION DEVELOPMENT MODEL (CID)

To provide a framework for conceptualizing how treatments and services can be developed, tested, and deployed within practice settings, the authors have developed the Clinic/Community Intervention Development Model (CID), as an extension of Weisz's Clinic-Based Treatment Development (CBTD) Model. The CID model is designed to accelerate the pace at which the science base for mental health services can be developed, adapted, refined, and taken to scale in a variety of practice settings or communities. The model outlines a series of steps that begin and end with the practice setting (e.g., clinic, school, health center, etc.) where the treatment or service will ultimately be delivered. The scientific phases for developing treatments or services for children's mental health problems are described, from manual development to wide-scale dissemination, with the goal of ensuring that the end product—a scientifically valid treatment or service—will be grounded, useable, and relevant to the practice context for which it is ultimately intended. Steps 1–6 are described thoroughly by Weisz (2000a) and are summarized here, with minor modifications, to make them adaptable to a range of interventions involving treatment, service, or prevention. Steps 7–8 extend the model to the dissemination and implementation of the intervention into a variety of practice settings or communities.

Step 1: Theoretically and clinically informed construction, refinement, and manualizing of the protocol within the context of the practice setting where it is ultimately to be delivered

Step 2: Initial efficacy trial under controlled conditions to establish potential for benefit

Step 3: Single-case applications in practice setting, with progressive adaptations to the protocol

Step 4: Initial effectiveness test, modest in scope and cost

Step 5: Full test of the effectiveness under everyday practice conditions, including cost-effectiveness

Step 6: Effectiveness of treatment variations, effective ingredients, core potencies, moderators, mediators, and costs

Step 7: Assessment of goodness-of-fit within the host organization, practice setting, or community

Step 8: Dissemination, quality, and long-term sustainability within new organizations, practice settings, or communities

Step 1: Development and Manualizing of Protocol

As with any new therapy or service, the first step is to develop, pilot test, and refine a manual for the protocol. The scientific and theoretical literature is useful in identifying the constructs and the rationale for the intervention and the hypothesized explanation for intended outcomes, but the experiences of clinicians, practitioners, or other mental health providers within the setting in which the treatment or service is to be developed are essential for ensuring that the protocol reflects the needs and capacities of those who will ultimately deliver it.

Step 2: Efficacy Trial

An initial test of the protocol occurs in this step under controlled conditions and with children who have significant problems but not severe pathology. Typically these children will be recruited for the study and will not have been referred for treatment in service settings. This step is intended to assess whether the service compared to a control condition results in positive outcomes among children, who are usually volunteers. The purpose of this step is to ensure that the protocol does no harm, and has the potential to be beneficial. The controlled conditions also enable the investigator to test whether the hypothesized relationship between the intervention and the consequences is supported.

Step 3: Single Case Applications

This step involves a series of pilot tests with cases referred from the practice setting to research-trained practitioners or clinicians who are familiar with the protocol. Across the series of individual cases, adaptations will be made to the protocol to reflect what is learned about individual variations. The object is to keep the development and refinement of the protocol closely connected to practice, with increasing involvement of real-world cases in real-world prac-

tice settings. At the same time, an equally important goal is to maintain sufficient scientific control over the testing of the new protocol such that the intervention is developed in an ethical and scientific manner, and no harm is done
to the participants. This third step therefore should involve supervision from
both the research team that has developed the manualized protocol and from
the practitioner or clinical staff, to ensure confidence that the protocol is appropriate for the needs of the clients, of the clinical staff, and of the practice
setting.

Step 4: Initial Effectiveness Trial

This step involves a trial of the newly adapted protocol within the practice setting itself. Clients who are typically seen in the practice are randomly
assigned to either receive the new protocol or to receive services as usual. The
protocol is delivered by research-trained staff, generally not yet by actual practice staff, in order to assess the impact of the new protocol under slightly more
controlled conditions than are normal in practice settings.

Step 5: Full Effectiveness Trial

This step entails a randomized field trial in which the protocol is tested
within the practice setting itself. Clients are randomly assigned to receive either the protocol or services as usual; the actual clinic or practice-setting staff
members are randomly assigned to either deliver the new protocol or to deliver services as usual. Outcomes are tracked for their long-term (i.e., at least
12-month) impact, and a range of outcomes is assessed, including cost-effectiveness. Embedded within this trial can be tests of those moderators or mediators hypothesized to be related to outcome variations.

Step 6: Effectiveness of Moderators and Mediators

A variety of studies can be launched in this step to address factors that im-
pinge upon outcomes—for example, tests of outcome moderators and tests of
variations in the treatment or service, such as differential impact of treatment
for children alone versus children plus parents. Also included here would be
tests of the mediators of child improvement (i.e., the change processes that potentiate outcomes). Tests of treatment variations and mediators are especially
important in our efforts to keep treatments streamlined and efficient. Findings
will be very relevant circumstances where pared-down versions of the treatment and service may be requested. Outcomes attained or not attainable
through such minimized versions need to be understood. Tests of augmented
models of the protocol can fit within this step as well.

Step 7: Goodness-of-Fit Within the Organizational or Practice Context

This step involves a series of studies to assess organizational characteristics that may influence the willingness of practitioners to adopt or to use the
protocol or the ability of the institution, agency, or practice setting to sustain
the service with fidelity to improved outcomes. Studies in this step would in-

clude examination of features of the organizational culture or context that impede or facilitate the uptake or adoption of the new protocol. Variables such as workplace flexibility, practitioner autonomy, leadership style, productivity requirements, incentive structure, workplace staff turnover, practitioner motivation, or attitudes towards change may influence both the ability of clinicians or providers to use the new service and the ability of the organization or practice environment to sustain it.

Step 8: Dissemination and Quality in a Variety of Organizational or Practice Contexts

The difference between this final step and the previous one is that this involves a series of studies about the disseminability of the effective treatment or service to multiple agencies, organizations, clinics, or communities. The purpose of this step is to examine the range of variations in organizational culture or context across multiple practice settings that facilitate the uptake of the effective service, generate long-term outcomes, and sustain the service within the sociology of improved practice. Improvements in practice depend upon knowledge of those structural elements of agencies, clinics, schools, or other practice environments that interfere with or support the quality of care and the delivery of quality services (e.g., fiscal structure; extent to which families are engaged in treatment development, selection, or delivery; clinician autonomy or motivation; workplace flexibility). Studies of variations in practice environments that enable providers to deliver the service with fidelity to the protocol will lead to improvements in the quality of care across a range of delivery agencies.

The CID is presented here as a model for speeding up the process of developing scientifically valid and effective services within the crucible of practice settings. Because the gap between need for mental health care and its delivery to children and families continues to be painfully large, because the majority of services delivered are untested, and because empirical studies have demonstrated that most real-world services are ineffective (Bickman, 1996b; Weisz, Weiss, & Donenberg, 1992), it is crucial that a more accelerated model for development and testing of effective services be made available to guide the field.

An additional potential benefit of the CID model is external validity. Findings on component effects, service variations, moderators, and mediators that emerge from research in service settings are likely to have greater external validity—greater relevance to the functioning of interventions with referred children—than findings emerging from studies conducted under less clinically representative conditions.

Conclusion

The growth of evidence-based science on children's services in the past 10 years has been phenomenal. Not only can results be synthesized, meta-analyzed, and reviewed, but the practical step of embedding science-based practices into a range of communities can become a reality. But complacency is not an option. Creating a usable science of children's mental health services requires constant attention to the factors that may undercut or diminish their impact, and persistent focus on understanding why and under what conditions such services can *attain* their intended outcomes and can be *sustained* within communities. Factors that may adversely influence the effectiveness of services may come from within or without: They may arise from within the developing child and family contexts, which place new demands for flexible adaptation of the service; they may arise from policy changes, organizational restructuring, or even social change, such as political elections that remove or put in place new programs that may support or erode service delivery.

The theoretical and practical stumbling blocks identified above are not intransigent. However, they require the application of new paradigms of science and practice (Jensen & Hoagwood, 1997; Jensen, Hoagwood, & Trickett, 1999b) that move scientific investigations away from ivory towers and into the trenches of real-world practice.

References

Abikoff, H., & Gittelman, R. (1985). Hyperactive children treated with stimulants: Is cognitive training a useful adjunct? *Archives of General Psychiatry, 42,* 953–961.

Abikoff, H., Ganeles, D., Reiter, G., Blum, C., Foley, C., & Klein, R. (1988). Cognitive training in academically deficient ADD-H boys receiving stimulant medication. *Journal of Abnormal Child Psychology, 16,* 411–432.

Abikoff, H.B., & Hechtman, L. (1996). Multimodal therapy and stimulants in the treatment of children with attention deficit hyperactivity disorder. In E.D. Hibbs & P.S. Jensen (Eds.), *Psychosocial treatments for child and adolescent disorders: Empirically based strategies for clinical practice* (pp. 341–369). Washington, DC: American Psychological Association.

Abueg, F.R., & Fairbank, J.A. (1992). Behavioral treatment of the PTSD-substance abuser: A multidimensional stage model. In P. Saigh (Ed.), *Posttraumatic stress disorder: A behavioral approach to assessment and treatment* (pp. 111–146). New York: Pergamon Press.

Achenbach, T.M. (1991a). The Child Behavior Checklist: Manual for teacher's report form. Burlington, VT: University of Vermont, Department of Psychiatry.

Achenbach, T.M. (1991b). *Integrative Guide for the CBCL 4-18, YSR, and TRF Profiles.* Burlington, VT: University of Vermont, Department of Psychiatry.

Achenbach, T.M. (1991c). *Manual for the child behavior checklist and 1991 profile.* Burlington, VT: University of Vermont, Department of Psychiatry.

Adelman, H.S., Taylor, L., Weist, M.D., Adelsheim, S., Freeman, B., Kapp, L., Lahti, M., & Mawn, D. (1999). Mental health in schools: A federal initiative. *Children's Services: Social Policy, Research, and Practice, 2,* 95–115.

Ajzen, I. (1988). *Attitudes, personality and behavior.* Chicago: Dorsey Press.

Albano, A.M., Chorpita, B.F., & Barlow, D.H. (1996). Childhood anxiety disorders. In E.J. Mash & R.A. Barkley (Eds.), *Child psychopathology* (pp. 196–241). New York: The Guilford Press.

American Academy of Child and Adolescent Psychiatry. (1991). Practice parameters for the assessment and treatment of attention deficit/hyperactivity disorders. *Journal of the American Academy of Child and Adolescent Psychiatry, 30,* 1–3.

American Academy of Child and Adolescent Psychiatry. (1992). Practice parameters for the assessment and treatment of conduct disorders. *Journal of the American Academy of Child and Adolescent Psychiatry, 31,* IV–VII.

American Academy of Child and Adolescent Psychiatry. (1993). Practice parameters for the assessment and treatment of anxiety disorders. *Journal of the American Academy of Child and Adolescent Psychiatry, 32,* 1089–1098.

American Academy of Child and Adolescent Psychiatry. (1996). *Level of care placement criteria for psychiatric illness.* Washington, DC: Author.

American Academy of Child and Adolescent Psychiatry. (1997a). Practice parameters for the assessment and treatment of children and adolescents with bipolar disorder. *Journal of the American Academy of Child and Adolescent Psychiatry, 36,* 157–176.

American Academy of Child and Adolescent Psychiatry. (1997b). Practice parameters for the assessment and treatment of children and adolescents with substance use disorders. *Journal of the American Academy of Child and Adolescent Psychiatry, 36,* 140S–156S.

American Academy of Child and Adolescent Psychiatry. (1998a). Practice parameters for the assessment and treatment of children and adolescents with posttraumatic stress disorder. *Journal of the American Academy of Child and Adolescent Psychiatry, 37 (10 Supp),* 4S–26S.

American Academy of Child and Adolescent Psychiatry. (1998b). Practice parameters for the assessment and treatment of children and adolescents with obsessive-compulsive disorder. *Journal of the American Academy of Child and Adolescent Psychiatry, 37 (10 Supp),* 27S–45S.

American Academy of Child and Adolescent Psychiatry. (1998c). Practice parameters for the assessment and treatment of children and adolescents with depressive disorders. *Journal of the American Academy of Child and Adolescent Psychiatry, 37 (10 Supp)*, 63S–86S.

American Academy of Child and Adolescent Psychiatry. (1999). Practice parameters for the assessment and treatment of children, adolescents, and adults with mental retardation and comorbid mental disorders. *Journal of the American Academy of Child and Adolescent Psychiatry, 38, (12 Supp)*, 5S–31S.

American Psychiatric Association. (1994). *Diagnostic & statistical manual of mental disorders*, 4th Edition. Washington, DC: American Psychiatric Press.

Anderson, J.C., & McGee, R. (1994). Comorbidity of depression in children and adolescents. In W.M. Reynolds & H.F. Johnston (Eds.), *Handbook of depression in children and adolescents: Issues in clinical child psychology* (pp. 581–601). New York: Plenum Press.

Angold, A., & Costello, E.J. (2001). The epidemiology of depression in children and adolescents. In I.M. Goodyer (Ed.), *The depressed child and adolescent* (2nd ed.) (pp. 143–178). New York: Cambridge University Press.

Angold, A., Costello, E.J., Farmer, E.M.Z., Burns, B.J., & Erkanli, A. (1999). Impaired but undiagnosed. *Journal of the Academy of Child and Adolescent Psychiatry, 2*, 129–137.

Angold, A., Prendergast, M., Cox, A., Harrington, R., Simonoff, E., & Rutter, M. (1995). The Child and Adolescent Psychiatric Assessment (CAPA). *Psychological Medicine, 25*, 739–753.

Aos, S., Phipps, P., Barnoski, R., & Leib, R. (1999). *The comparative costs and benefits of programs to reduce crime: A review of national research findings with implications for Washington state*. Olympia, WA: Washington State Institute for Public Policy.

Armenteros, J., Whitaker, A., Welikson, M., Stedge, D., & Gorman, J. (1997). Risperidone in adolescents with schizophrenia: An open pilot study. *Journal of the American Academy of Child and Adolescent Psychiatry, 36*, 694–700.

Armstrong, L.K. (1995). Transitional case management. In B.J. Friesen & J. Poertner (Eds.), *From case management to service coordination for children with emotional, behavioral, or mental disorders* (pp. 317–326). Baltimore: Paul H. Brookes.

Arredondo, D., & Butler, S. (1994). Affective co-morbidity in psychiatrically hospitalized adolescents with conduct disorder or oppositional defiant disorder: Should conduct disorder be treated with mood stabilizers? *Journal of Child and Adolescent Psychopharmacology, 4*, 151–158.

Asarnow, J.R., & Asarnow, R.F. (1996). Childhood-onset schizophrenia. In E.J. Mash & R.A. Barkley (Eds.), *Child Psychopathology* (pp. 340–361). New York: Guilford Press.

Asher, S.R., & Coie, J.D. (Eds.). (1990). *Peer rejection in childhood*. New York: Cambridge University Press.

Attkisson, C., Rosenblatt, A.B., Dressser, K.L., Baize, H.R., Clausen, J.M., & Lind, S.L. (1997). Effectiveness of the California system of care model for children and youth with severe emotional disorders. In C.T. Nixon & C.A. Northrup (Eds.), *Evaluating mental health services: How do programs for children work in the real world?* (pp. 146–208). Thousand Oaks, CA: Sage.

Austin, C. (1983). Case management in long-term care: Options and opportunities. *Health and Social Work, 8*, 16–30.

Backer, T., Liberman, R., & Kuehnel,T. (1986). Dissemination and adoption of innovative psychosocial interventions. *Journal of Consulting and Clinical Psychology, 54*, 111–118.

Balon, R. (1994). Sleep terror disorder and insomnia treated with trazodone: A case report. *Annals of Clinical Psychiatry, 6*, 161–163.

Bandura, A. (1971). *Psychological modeling: Conflicting theories*. Chicago: Aldine-Atherton.

Bandura, A. (1977). *Social learning theory*. Englewood Cliffs, NJ: Prentice Hall.

Bandura, A. (1982). Self-efficacy: Toward a unifying theory of behavioral change. *Psychological Review, 84*, 191–215.

Barabasz, A.F. (1973). Group desensitization of test anxiety in elementary school. *The Journal of Psychology, 83*, 295–301.

Barker, P. (1998). The future of residential treatment for children. In C. Schaefer & A. Swanson (Eds.), *Children in residential care: Critical issues in treatment* (pp. 1–16). New York: Van Nostrand Reinhold.

Barkley, R. (1977). A review of stimulant drug research with hyperactive children. *Journal of Child Psychology and Psychiatry, 18*, 137–165.

Barkley, R. (1988). The effects of methylphenidate on the interactions of preschool ADHD children with their mothers. *Journal of the American Academy of Child and Adolescent Psychiatry, 27*, 336–341.

Barkley, R., Fischer, M., Edelbrock, C., & Smallish, L. (1990). The adolescent outcome of hyperactive children diagnosed by research criteria: An eight year prospective follow-up study. *Journal of the American Academy of Child and Adolescent Psychiatry, 29*, 546–555.

Barkley, R.A. (1981). *Hyperactive children: A handbook for diagnosis and treatment*. New York: Guilford Press.

Barkley, R.A. (1987). *Defiant children: A clinician's manual for assessment and parent training*. New York: Guilford Press.

Barkley, R.A., (1990). *Attention deficit hyperactivity disorder: A handbook for diagnosis and treatment*. New York: Guilford Press.

Barkley, R.A., Shelton, T.L., Crosswait, C., Moorehouse, M., Fletcher, K., Barrett, S., Jenkins, L., & Metevia, L. (2000). Multi-method psycho-educational intervention for preschool children with disruptive behavior: Preliminary results at post-treatment. *Journal of Child Psychology and Psychiatry and Allied Disciplines, 41*, 319–332.

Barrett, P.M. (1998). Evaluation of cognitive-behavioral group treatments for childhood anxiety disorders. *Journal of Clinical Child Psychology, 27*, 459–468.

Barrett, P.M., Dadds, M.R., & Rapee, R.M. (1996). Family treatment of childhood anxiety: A controlled trial. *Journal of Consulting and Clinical Psychology, 64*, 333–342.

Barrett, P.M., Duffy, A.L., Dadds, M.R., & Rapee, R.M. (2001). Cognitive-behavioral treatment of anxiety disorders in children: Long-term (6-year) follow-up. *Journal of Consulting and Clinical Psychology, 69*, 135–141.

Barrickman, L., Noyes, R., Kuperman, S., Schumacher, E., & Verda, M. (1991). Treatment of ADHD with fluoxetine: A preliminary trial. *Journal of the American Academy of Child and Adolescent Psychiatry, 30*, 762–767.

Bateman, B.D., & Herr, C.L. (1981). Law and special education. In J.M. Kauffman & D.P. Hallahan (Eds.), *Handbook of Special Education* (pp. 330–360). Englewood Cliffs, NJ: Prentice Hall.

Bauman, L., Stein, R., & Ireys, H. (1991). A framework for conceptualizing interventions. *Sociological Practice Review, 2*, 241–251.

Bazelon Center for Mental Health Law. (1999). *Making sense of Medicaid for children with serious emotional disturbance*. Washington DC: Author.

Beck, J.S. (1995). *Cognitive therapy: Basics and beyond*. New York: Guilford Press.

Becker, J.V. (1998). What we know about the characteristics and treatment of adolescents who have committed sexual offenses. *Child Maltreatment, 3*, 317–329.

Beckstead, J.W., & Evans, M.E. (2000). Child and family outcomes: A comparison under two systems of care in New York State. *Journal of Social Services, 4*, 143–151.

Behar, L.B. (1997). The Fort Bragg evaluation: A snapshot in time. *American Psychologist, 52*, 557–559.

Beidel, D.C., Turner, S.M., & Morris, T.L. (1999). Psychopathology of childhood social phobia. *Journal of the American Academy of Child and Adolescent Psychiatry, 38*, 643–650.

Bell, C.B., & Jenkins, E. (1993). Community violence and children on Chicago's south side. *Psychiatry, 56*, 46–54.

Bergman, L.R., & Magnusson, D. (1997). A person-oriented approach in research on developmental psychopathology. *Developmental Psychopathology, 9*, 291–319.

Berliner, L., & Saunders, B. (1996). Treating fear and anxiety in sexually abused children: Results of a controlled 2-year follow-up study. *Child Maltreatment, 1*, 294–310.

Berney, T.P., Kolvin, I., Bhate, S.R., Garside, R.F., Jeans, J., Kay, B., & Scarth, L. (1981). School phobia: A therapeutic trial with clomipramine and short-term outcome. *British Journal of Psychiatry, 138*, 110–118.

Bernstein, G.A., & Borchardt, C.M. (1991). Anxiety disorders of childhood and adolescence: A critical review. *Journal of the American Academy of Child and Adolescent Psychiatry, 30*, 519–532.

Bernstein, G.A., Borchardt, C., & Perwien, A. (1996). Anxiety disorders: A review of the past 10 years. *Journal of the American Academy of Child and Adolescent Psychiatry, 35*, 1110–1119.

Bernstein, G.A., Garfinkel, B.D., & Borchardt, C.M. (1990). Comparative studies of pharmacotherapy for school refusal. *Journal of the American Academy of Child and Adolescent Psychiatry, 29*, 773–781.

Bickman, L. (1990). *Advances in program theory. New Directions for Program Evaluation*, No 47. San Francisco: Jossey-Bass.

Bickman, L. (1996a). Implications of a children's mental health managed care demonstration project. *Journal of Mental Health Administration, 23*, 107–117.

Bickman, L. (1996b). A continuum of care: More is not always better. *American Psychologist, 31*, 689–701.

Bickman, L., Foster, E.M., & Lambert, W. (1996). Who gets hospitalized in a continuum of care? *Journal of the American Academy of Child and Adolescent Psychiatry, 35*, 74–80.

Bickman, L., Guthrie, P.R., Foster, E.M., Lambert, E.W., Summerfelt, W.T., Breda, C.S., & Heflinger, C.A. (1995). *Evaluating managed mental health services: The Fort Bragg experiment*. New York: Plenum Press.

Bickman, L., & Heflinger, C.A. (1995). Seeking success by reducing implementation and evaluation failures. In L. Bickman & D.G. Rogs (Eds.), *Children's mental health services: Research, policy, and evaluation.* Thousand Oaks, CA: Sage.

Bickman, L., Heflinger, C.A., Northrup, D., Sonnichsen, S., & Schilling, S. (1998). Long term outcomes to family caregiver empowerment. *Journal of Child and Family Studies, 7,* 269–282.

Bickman, L., Noser, K., & Summerfelt, W.T. (1999). Long-term effects of a system of care on children and adolescents. *Journal of Behavioral Health Services and Research, 26,* 185–202.

Bickman, L., Summerfelt, W.T., & Noser, K. (1997). Comparative outcomes of emotionally disturbed children and adolescents in a system of services and usual care. *Psychiatric Services, 48,* 1543–1548.

Biederman, J., Baldessarini, R.J., Wright, V., Knee, D., & Harmatz, J.S. (1989). A double-blind placebo controlled study of desipramine in the treatment of ADD: I. Efficacy. *Journal of the American Academy of Child and Adolescent Psychiatry, 28,* 777–784.

Biederman, J., Rosenbaum, J.F., Bolduc-Murphy, E.A., Farone, S.V., Chaloff, J., Hirshfeld, D.R., & Kagan, J.J. (1993). A 3-year follow-up of children with and without behavioral inhibition. *Journal of the American Academy of Child and Adolescent Psychiatry, 32,* 814–821.

Biederman, J., Wilens, T., Mick, E., Spencer, E., & Faraone, S.V. (1999). Pharmacotherapy of attention-deficit/hyperactivity disorder reduces risk for substance abuse disorder. *Pediatrics, 104,* 20.

Birmaher, B., Ryan, N.D., Williamson, D.E., Brent, D.A., Kaufman, J., Dahl, R.E., Perel, J., & Nelson, B. (1996). Childhood and adolescent depression: A review of the past 10 years. Part I. *Journal of the American Academy of Child and Adolescent Psychiatry, 35,* 1427–1439.

Black, B. (1995). Separation anxiety disorder and panic disorder. In J.S. March (Ed.), *Anxiety disorders in children and adolescents* (pp. 212–234). New York: The Guilford Press.

Black, B., & Uhde, T.W. (1994). Treatment of elective mutism with fluoxetine: A double-blind, placebo-controlled study. *Journal of the American Academy of Child and Adolescent Psychiatry, 33,* 1000–1006.

Black, B., Udhe, T.W., & Tancer, M. (1992). Fluoxetine for the treatment of social phobia. *Journal of the American Academy of Child and Adolescent Psychiatry, 29,* 36–44.

Blagg, N.R., & Yule, W. (1984). The behavioural treatment of school refusal: A comparative study. *Behaviour Research and Therapy, 22,* 119–127.

Blum, R. (1987). Contemporary threats to adolescent health in the United States. *Journal of the American Medical Association, 257,* 3390–3395.

Boney-McCoy, S., & Finkelhor, D. (1995). Psychosocial sequelae of violent victimization in a national youth sample. *Journal of Consulting and Clinical Psychology, 63,* 726–736.

Borduin, C.M., Henggeler, S.W., Blaske, D.M., & Stein, T. (1990). Multisystemic treatment of adolescent sexual offenders. *International Journal of Offender Therapy and Comparative Criminology, 35,* 105–114.

Borduin, C.M., Mann, B.J., Cone, L.T., Henggeler, S.W., Fucci, B.R., Blaske, D.M., & Wilson, R.A. (1995). Multisystemic treatment of serious juvenile offenders: Long-term prevention of criminology and violence. *Journal of Consulting and Clinical Psychology, 63,* 569–578.

Borkman, T. (1976). Experiential knowledge: A new concept for the analysis of self-help groups. *Social Service Review, 50,* 445–456.

Boudewyns, P.A., & Hyer, L. (1990). Physiological response to combat memories and preliminary treatment outcome in Vietnam veteran PTSD patients with direct therapeutic exposure. *Behavior Therapy, 21,* 63–87.

Bowen, N. (1999). *Profiles of success: Characteristics of Willie M participants and services associated with high behavioral functioning, Part 1: Comparison of time 1 profiles of Willie M participants with high and low behavioral functioning at time 2.* Raleigh, NC: Willie M Program Evaluation Branch, Division of Mental Health, Department of Health and Human Services.

Bradley, C. (1937). The behavior of children receiving benzadrine. *American Journal of Psychiatry, 94,* 577–585.

Bratter, T.E., Cameron, A., & Radda, H.T. (1987). Mentoring: Extending the psychotherapeutic and pedagogical relationship with adolescents. Revised from keynote address: 4th Conference of the European Federation of Therapeutic Communities; Dublin, Ireland.

Brent, D.A., Perper, J.A., Goldstein, C.E., Kolko, D.J., Allan, M.J., Allman, C.J., & Zelenak, J.P. (1988). Risk factors for adolescent suicide: A comparison of adolescent suicide victims with suicidal inpatients. *Archives of General Psychiatry, 45,* 581–588.

Breslau, N., Kessler, R.C., Chilcoat, H.D., Schultz, L.R., Davis, G.C., & Andreski, P. (1998) Traumatic and posttraumatic stress disorder in the community: The 1996 Detroit Area Survey of Trauma. *Archives of General Psychiatry, 55,* 626–631.

Brestan, E.V., & Eyberg, S.M. (1998). Effective psychosocial treatments of conduct-disordered children and adolescents: 29 years, 82 studies, and 5,272 kids. *Journal of Clinical Child Psychology, 27,* 180–189.

Brewin, C.R., Dalgleish, T., & Joseph, S.A. (1996). A dual representation theory of posttraumatic stress disorder. *Psychological Review, 103,* 670–686.

Brinson, T., & Treanor, V. (1988). Alcoholism and posttramatic stress disorder among combat Vietnam veterans. *Alcoholism Treatment Quarterly, 593/4,* 65–83.

Briones, D.P., Heller, P., & Chalfant, H. (1990). Socioeconomic status, ethnicity, psychological distress, and readiness to utilize a mental health facility. *American Journal of Psychiatry, 147,* 1333–1340.

Bromet, E., Sonnega, A., & Kessler, R.C. (1998). Risk factors for DSM-III-R posttraumatic stress disorder: Findings from the National Comorbidity Study. *American Journal of Epidemiology, 147,* 353–361.

Bronfenbrenner, U. (1979). *The ecology of human development.* Cambridge, MA: Harvard University Press.

Brook, J.S., Cohen, P., & Brook, D.W. (1998). Longitudinal study of co-occurring psychiatric disorders and substance use. *Journal of the American Academy of Child and Adolescent Psychiatry, 37,* 322–330.

Brown, P.J., & Ouimette, P.G. (1999). Introduction to the special section on substance use disorder and posttraumatic stress disorder comorbidity. *Psychology of Addictive Behaviors, 13,* 75–77.

Brown, P.J., Stout, R.L., & Mueller, T. (1999). Substance use disorder and posttraumatic stress disorder comorbidity: Addiction and psychiatric treatment rates. *Psychology of Addictive Behaviors, 13,* 115–122.

Brown, R.T., Borden, K.A., Wynne, M.E., Schleser, R., & Clingerman, S.R. (1986). Methylphenidate and cognitive therapy with ADD children: A methodological reconsideration. *Journal of Abnormal Child Psychology, 14,* 481–497.

Brown, R.T., Wynne, M. A., Borden, K. A., Clingerman, S. R., Geniesse, R., & Spunt, A. L. (1986). Methylphenidate and cognitive therapy in children with attention deficit disorder: A double-blind trial. *Journal of Developmental and Behavioral Pediatrics, 7,* 163–170.

Brunk, M., Henggeler, S.W., & Whelan, J.P. (1987). A comparison of multisystemic therapy and parent training in the brief treatment of child abuse and neglect. *Journal of Consulting and Clinical Psychology, 55,* 311–318.

Bruns, E.J., Burchard, J.D., & Yoe, J.T. (1995). Evaluating the Vermont system of care: Outcomes associated with community-based wraparound services. *Journal of Child and Family Studies, 4,* 321–339.

Bruns, E.J., & Burchard, J.D. (2000). Impact of respite care services for families with children experiencing emotional and behavioral problems. *Children's Services: Social Policy, Research, and Practice, 3,* 39–61.

Bruns, E.J., Ermold, J., & Burchard, J.D. (2001). The wraparound fidelity index: Results from an initial pilot test. In C.C. Newman, C.J. Liberton, K. Kutash, & R. Friedman (Eds.), *The 13th annual research conference proceedings, a system of care for children's mental health: Expanding the research base* (pp. 339–342). Tampa, FL: University of South Florida, The Louis de la Parte Florida Mental Health Institute, Research and Training Center for Children's Mental Health.

Bryant, B. (1981). Special foster care. *Journal of Clinical Child Psychology, 10,* 8–20.

Budney, A.J., & Higgins, S.T. (1998). *A community reinforcement plus vouchers approach: Treating cocaine addiction.* Rockville, MD: National Institute on Drug Abuse, NIH Pub. No. 98–4309.

Buitelaar, J.K., Van der Gaag, R.J., Swaab-Barneveld, H., & Kuiper, M. (1995). Prediction of clinical response to methylphenidate in children with attention-deficit hyperactivity disorder. *Journal of the American Academy of Child and Adolescent Psychiatry, 34,* 1025–1032.

Buitelaar, J.K., Van der Gaag, R.J., Swaab-Barneveld, H., & Kuiper, M. (1996). Pindolol and methylphenidate in children with attention-deficit hyperactivity disorder: Clinical efficacy and side-effects. *Journal of Child Psychology and Psychiatry and Allied Disciplines, 37,* 587–595.

Burchard, J.D., & Bruns, E.J. (1998). The role of the case study in the evlauation of individualized services. In M.H. Epstein, K. Kutash, & A.J. Duchnowski (Eds.), *Outcomes for children and youth with behavioral and emotional disorders and their families: Programs and evaluation best practices* (pp. 363–384). Austin, TX: Pro-Ed.

Burchard, J.D., Burchard, S.N., Sewell, R., & VanDenBerg, J. (1993). *One kid at a time: Evaluative case studies and description of the Alaska Youth Initiative Demonstration Project.* Juneau, AK: State of Alaska, Division of Mental Health and Mental Retardation.

Burns, B.J. (1991). Mental health service use by adolescents in the 1970s and 1980s. *Journal of the American Academy of Child and Adolescent Psychiatry, 30,* 144–150.

Burns, B.J. (1994). The challenges of child mental health services research. *Journal of Emotional and Behavioral Disorders, 2,* 254–259.

Burns, B.J. (1999). A call for a mental health services research agenda for youth with serious emotional disturbance. *Mental Health Services Research, 1,* 5–20.

Burns, B.J., Costello, E.J., Angold, A., Tweed, D., Stangl, D., Farmer, E.M.Z., & Erkanli, A. (1997). Children's mental health service use across service sectors. *Health Affairs, 14,* 148–159.

Burns, B.J., Farmer, E.M.Z., Angold, A., Costello, E.J., & Behar, L. (1996). A randomized trial of case management for youths with serious emotional disturbance. *Journal of Clinical Child Psychology, 25,* 476–486.

Burns, B.J., & Friedman, R.M. (1990). Examining the research base for child mental health services and policy. *Journal of Mental Health Administration, 17,* 87–98.

Burns, B.J., & Goldman, S.K. (1999). *Promising practices in wraparound for children with serious emotional disturbance and their families. Systems of care: Promising practices in children's mental health,* 1998 series, Volume IV. Washington DC: Center for Effective Collaboration and Practice, American Institutes for Research.

Burns, B.J, Goldman, S.K., Faw, L., & Burchard, J.D. (1999). The wraparound evidence base. In B.J. Burns & S.K. Goldman (Eds.), *Promising practices in wraparound for children with serious emotional disturbance and their families. Systems of care: Promising practices in children's mental health, 1998 series, Vol. IV.* (pp. 77–100).Washington DC: Center for Effective Collaboration and Practice, American Institutes for Research.

Burns, B.J., Gwaltney, E.A., & Bishop, G.K. (1995). Case management research: Issues and directions. In B.J. Friesen, & J. Poertner, (Eds.), *From case management to service coordination for children with emotional, behavioral, or mental disorders: Building on family strengths* (pp. 353–372). Baltimore: Paul H. Brookes Publishing.

Burns, B.J., Hoagwood, K., & Maultsby, L.T. (1998). Improving outcomes for children and adolescents with serious emotional and behavioral disorders: Current and future directions. In M.H. Epstein, K. Kutash, & A.J. Duchnowski (Eds.), *Outcomes for children and youth with behavioral and emotional disorders and their families: Programs and evaluation best practices* (pp. 685–707). Austin, TX: Pro-Ed.

Burns, B.J., Hoagwood, K., & Mrazek, P.J. (1999). Effective treatment for mental disorders in children and adolescents. *Clinical Child and Family Psychology Review, 2,* 199–254.

Burns B.J., Teagle S.E., Schwartz M., Angold A., & Holtzman A. (1999). Public sector–managed behavioral health care: A Medicaid carve-out for children and adolescents. *Health Affairs, 18,* 214–225.

Bussing, R., Zima, B., & Belin, T. (1998). Variations in ADHD treatment among special education students. *Journal of the American Academy of Child and Adolescent Psychiatry, 37,* 968–976.

Bussing, R., Zima, B., Perwien, A., Belin, T., & Widawski, M. (1998). Children in special education programs: Attention deficit disorder, use of services, and unmet needs. *American Journal of Public Health, 88,* 880–886.

Butler, L., Miezitis, S., Friedman, R., & Cole, E. (1980). The effect of two school-based intervention programs on depressive symptoms in preadolescents. *American Educational Research Journal, 17,* 111–119.

Cairns, R.B., & Cairns, B.D. (1994). *Lifelines and risks: Pathways of youth in our time.* New York: Harvester Wheatsheaf.

Cairns, R.B., Mahoney, J., Xie, H., & Cadwallader, T.W. (1999). Middle childhood. In W.K. Silverman & T.H. Ollendick (Eds.), *Developmental issues in the clinical treatment of children* (pp. 108–124). Boston: Allyn & Bacon.

Campbell, M., Adams, P.B., Small, A.M., Kafantaris, V., Silva, R.R., Shell, J., Perry, R., & Overall, J.E. (1995). Lithium in hospitalized aggressive children with conduct disorder: A double blind and placebo controlled study. *Journal of the American Academy of Child and Adolescent Psychiatry, 34,* 445–453.

Campbell, M., & Cueva, J. (1995). Psychopharmacology in child and adolescent psychiatry: A review of the past seven years. Part II. *Journal of the American Academy of Child and Adolescent Psychiatry, 34,* 1262–1272.

Campbell, M., Rapoport, J., & Simpson, G. (1999). Antipsychotics in children. *Journal of the American Academy of Child and Adolescent Psychiatry, 38,* 537–545.

Cañino, G., Costello, E.J., & Angold, A. (1999). Assessing functional impairment and social adaptation for child mental health services research. *Mental Health Services Research, 1,* 93–108.

Cantwell, D. (1996). Attention deficit disorder: A review of the past 10 years. *Journal of the American Academy of Child and Adolescent Psychiatry, 35,* 978–987.

Carlberg, C., & Kavale, K. (1980). The efficacy of special versus regular class placement for exceptional children: A meta-analysis. *Journal of Special Education, 14,* 295–309.

Carter, C.S. (1998). Neuroendocrine perspectives on social attachment and love. *Psychoneuroen-docrinology, 23,* 779–818.

Caron C.S., & Rutter, M. (1991). Co-morbidity in child psychopathology: Concept, issues, and research strategies. *Journal of Child Psychology and Psychiatry, 32,* 1063–1080.

Casat, C., Pleasants, D., Schroeder, D., & Parler, D. (1989). Buproprion in children with attention deficit disorder. *Psychopharmacological Bulletin, 25,* 198–201.

Casey R.J., & Berman J.S. (1985). The outcome of psychotherapy with children. *Psychological Bulletin, 98,* 388–400.

Caspi, A., Elder, G.H., & Herbener, E.S. (1990). Childhood personality and the prediction of life-course patterns. In L.N. Robins & M. Rutter (Eds.), *Straight and devious pathways from childhood to adulthood* (pp. 13–35). Cambridge: Cambridge University Press.

Catron, T., Harris, V.S., & Weiss, B. (1998). Posttreatment results after 2 years of services in the Vanderbilt School-Based Counseling project. In M.H. Epstein, K. Kutash, & A.J. Duchnowski (Eds.), *Outcomes for children and youth with behavioral and emotional disorders and their families: Programs and evaluation best practices* (pp. 633–656). Austin, TX: Pro-Ed.

Cauce, A.M., Morgan, C.J., Wagner, V., Moore, E., Sy, J., Wurzbacher, K., Weeden, K., Tomlin, S., & Blanchard, T. (1994). Effectiveness of intensive case management for homeless adolescents: Results of a 3-month follow-up. *Journal of Emotional and Behavioral Disorders, 2,* 219–227.

Cauce, A.M., Paradise, M., Embry, L., Morgan, C.J., Lohr, Y., Theofelis, J., Heger, J., & Wagner, V. (1998). Homeless youth in Seattle: Youth characteristics, mental health needs, and intensive case management. In M.H. Epstein, K. Kutash, & A. Duchnowski (Eds.), *Outcomes for children and youth with behavioral and emotional disorders and their families: Programs and evaluation best practices* (pp. 611–632). Austin, TX: Pro-Ed.

Cavanaugh, D.A., Lippitt, J., & Moyo, O. (2000). Resource guide to selected federal policies affecting children's emotional and social development and their readiness for school. In *Off to a good start: Research on the risk factors for early school problems and selected federal policies affecting children's social and emotional development and their readiness for school.* Chapel Hill: University of North Carolina, Frank Porter Graham Child Development Center.

Celano, M., Hazzard, A., Webb, C., & McCall, C. (1996). Treatment of traumagenic beliefs among sexually abused girls and their mothers: An evaluation study. *Journal of Abnormal Child Psychology, 24,* 1–17.

Chamberlain, P. (1990a). Comparative evaluation of specialized foster care for seriously delinquent youths: A first step. *Community Alternatives: International Journal of Family Care, 2,* 21–36.

Chamberlain, P. (1990b). *Mediators of male delinquency: A clinical trial.* Grant No. R01-MH47458, Bethesda, MD: Center for Studies of Violent Behavior and Traumatic Stress, National Institute of Mental Health, U.S. Public Health Service.

Chamberlain, P. (1994). *Family connections: Treatment foster care for adolescents with delinquency.* Eugene, OR: Northwest Media.

Chamberlain, P. (1997). *Female delinquency: Treatment processes and outcomes.* Grant No. R01 MH54257, Child and Adolescent Treatment and Preventive Intervention Research Branch, National Institute of Mental Health, U.S. Public Health Service.

Chamberlain, P., & Mihalic, S.F. (1998). Multidimensional Treatment Foster Care. In D.S. Elliott (Ed.), *Book eight: Blueprints for violence prevention.* Boulder, CO: Institute of Behavioral Science, University of Colorado at Boulder.

Chamberlain, P., Moreland, S., & Reid, K. (1992). Enhanced services and stipends for foster parents: Effects on retention rates and outcomes for children. *Child Welfare, 71,* 387–401.

Chamberlain, P., Ray, J., & Moore, K.J. (1996). Characteristics of residential care for adolescent offenders: A comparison of assumptions and practices in two models. *Journal of Child and Family Studies, 5,* 259–271.

Chamberlain, P., & Reid, J.B. (1987). Parent observation and report of child symptoms. *Behavioral Assessment, 9,* 97–109.

Chamberlain, P., & Reid, J.B. (1991). Using a specialized foster care treatment model for children and adolescents leaving the state mental hospital. *Journal of Community Psychology, 19,* 266–276.

Chamberlain, P., & Reid, J.B. (1998). Comparison of two community alternatives to incarceration for chronic juvenile offenders. *Journal of Consulting and Clinical Psychology, 66,* 624–33.

Chambers, W., Puig-Antich, J., Hirsch, M., Paez, P., Ambrosini, P., Tabrizi, M., & Davies, M. (1985). The assessment of affective disorders in children and adolescents by semistructured interview: Test-retest reliability of the schedule for affective disorders and schizophrenia for school-age children, present episode. *Archives of General Psychiatry, 42,* 696–702.

Chambless, D.L., & Hollon, S.D. (1998). Defining empirically supported therapies. *Journal of Consulting and Clinical Psychology, 66,* 7–18.

Chambless, D.L., Sanderson, W.C., Shoham, V., Bennett Johnson, S., Pope, K.S., Crits-Christoph, P.,

Baker, M., Johnson, B., Woody, S.R., Sue, S., Beutler, L., Williams, D.A., & McMurry, S. (1996). An update on empirically validated therapies. *The Clinical Psychologist, 49,* 5–18.

Chemtob, C., Roitblatt, H.L., Hamada, R.S., Carlson, J.G., & Twentyman, C.T. (1988). A cognitive action theory of post-traumatic stress disorder. *Journal of Anxiety Disorders, 2,* 253–275.

Cicchetti, D., & Rogosch, F.A. (Eds.). (1999). *Conceptual and methodological issues in developmental psychopathology research* (2nd ed.). New York: John Wiley & Sons.

Clark, D.B., & Neighbors, B. (1996). Adolescent substance abuse and internalizing disorders. *Child and Adolescent Psychiatric Clinics of North America, 5,* 45–57.

Clark, D.B., Parker, A., & Lynch, K. (1999). Psychopathology and substance-related problems during early adolescence: A survival analysis. *Journal of Clinical Child Psychology, 28,* 333–341.

Clark, H.B., & Hieneman, M. (1999). Comparing the wraparound process to positive behavioral support: What we can learn. *Journal of Positive Behavior Interventions, 1,* 183–186.

Clark, H.B., Lee, B., Prange, M.E., & McDonald, B.A. (1996). Children lost within the foster care system: Can wraparound service strategies improve placement outcomes? *Journal of Child and Family Studies, 5,* 39–54.

Clark, H.B., Prange, M.E., Lee, B., Boyd, L.A., McDonald, B.A., & Stewart, E.S. (1994). Improving adjustment outcomes for foster children with emotional and behavioral disorders: Early findings from a controlled study on individualized services. *Journal of Emotional and Behavioral Disorders, 2,* 207–218.

Clark, H.B., Prange, M.E., Lee, B., Stewart, E.S., McDonald, B.A., & Boyd, L.A. (1998). An individualized wraparound process for children in foster care with emotional/behavioral disturbances: Follow-up findings and implications from a controlled study. In M. Epstein, K. Kutash, & A. Duchnowski (Eds.), *Outcomes for children and youth with behavioral and emotional disorders and their families: Programs and evaluation best practices* (pp. 513–542). Austin, TX: Pro-Ed.

Clarke, G.N., Hawkins, W., Murphy, M., & Sheeber, L. (1993). School-based primary prevention of depressive symptomatology in adolescents: Findings from two studies. *Journal of Adolescent Research, 8,* 183–204.

Clarke, G.N., & Lewinsohn, P.M. (1984). *The coping with depression course adolescent version: A psychoeducational intervention for unipolar depression in high school students.* Eugene: University of Oregon Press.

Clarke, R.T., Schaefer, M., Burchard, J.D., & Welkowitz, J.W. (1992). Wrapping community-based mental health services around children with a severe behavioral disorder: An evaluation of Project Wraparound. *Journal of Child and Family Studies, 1,* 241–61.

Clausen, J.M., Landsverk, J., Granger, W., Chadwick, D., & Litrownik, A. (1998). Mental health problems of children in foster care. *Journal of Child and Family Studies, 7,* 283–296.

Clay, T., Gualtieri, C., Evans, R., & Guillion, C. (1988). Clinical and neuropsychological effects of the novel antidepressant bupropion. *Psychopharmacological Bulletin, 24,* 143–148.

Cobb, S. (1976). Social support as a modifier of life stress. *Psychosomatic Medicine, 38,* 300–314.

Cocozza, J.J., Stainbrook, K.A., Faenza, M., Siegfried, C. (1999). Justice for juveniles: Community perspectives on the mental health and substance abuse needs of youth involved in the juvenile justice system. Alexandria, VA: The National Mental Health Association and Delmar, NY: The National GAINS Center.

Cohen, J. (1988). *Statistical power analysis for the behavioral sciences.* Hillsdale, NJ: Lawrence Erlbaum Associates.

Cohen, J. (1992). A power primer. *Psychological Bulletin, 112,* 155–159.

Cohen, J.A. & American Academy of Child and Adolescent Psychiatry Work Group on Quality Issues. (1998). Summary of the practice parameters for the assessment and treatment of children and adolescents with posttraumatic stress disorder. *Journal of the American Academy of Child and Adolescent Psychiatry, 37,* 997–1001.

Cohen, J.A., & Mannarino, A.P. (1996). A treatment outcome study for sexually abused preschool children: Initial findings. *Journal of the American Academy of Child and Adolescent Psychiatry, 35,* 42–50.

Cohen, S., & Wills, T.A. (1985). Stress, social support, and the buffering hypothesis. *Psychological Bulletin, 98,* 310–357.

Cole, P.M., & Putnam, F.W. (1992). Effect of incest on self and social functioning: A developmental psychopathology perspective. *Journal of Consulting and Clinical Psychology, 60,* 174–184.

Comings, D., Comings, B., Tacket, T., & Li, S. (1990). The clonidine patch and behavior problems. *Journal of the American Academy of Child and Adolescent Psychiatry, 29,* 667–668.

Conduct Problems Prevention Research Group. (1999a). Initial impact of the Fast Track Prevention Trial for Conduct Problems: I. The high-risk sample. *Journal of Consulting and Clinical Psychology, 67,* 631–647.

Conduct Problems Prevention Research Group. (1999b). Initial impact of the Fast Track Prevention Trial for Conduct Problems: II. Classroom effects. *Journal of Consulting and Clinical Psychology, 67,* 648–657.

Connell, J.P., & Kubisch, A.C. (1998). Applying a theory of change approach to the evaluation of comprehensive community initiatives: Progress, prospects, and problems. In K. Fullbright-Anderson, A.C. Kubisch, & J. P. Connell (Eds.), *New approaches to evaluating community initiatives, Vol. 2: Theory, measurement and analysis* (pp. 15–44). Washington, DC: Aspen Institute.

Conners, C. (1969). A teacher rating scale for use in drug studies with children. *American Journal of Psychiatry, 126,* 884–888.

Conners, C. (1992). Methodology of antidepressant trials for treating depression in adolescents. *Journal of Child and Adolescent Psychopharmacology, 2,* 11–22.

Conners, C., & Wells, K. (1997). *Conners-Wells Self-Report Scale.* North Tonawanda, NY: Multi-Health Systems.

Conners, C.K., Casat, C.D., Gualtieri, C.T., Weller, E., Reader, M., Reiss, A., Weller, R.A., Khayrallah, M., & Ascher, J. (1996). Bupropion hydrochloride in attention deficit disorder with hyperactivity. *Journal of the American Academy of Child and Adolescent Psychiatry, 35,* 1314–1321.

Conrad, K.J., & Conrad, K.M. (1994). Reassessing validity threats in experiments: Focus on construct validity. In K.J. Conrad (Ed.), *Critically evaluating the role of experiments. New Directions for Program Evaluation,* No. 63. San Francisco: Jossey-Bass.

Cooper, N.A., & Clum, G.A. (1989). Imaginal flooding as a supplementary treatment for PTSD in combat veterans: A controlled study. *Behavior Therapy, 3,* 381–91.

Corder, B.F., Ball, B.C., Haizlip, T.M., Rollins, R., & Beaumont, R. (1976). Adolescent parricide: A comparison with other adolescent murder. *American Journal of Psychiatry, 133,* 957–961.

Cornell, D.G., Benedek, E.P., & Benedek, D.M. (1987). Juvenile homicide: Prior adjustment and proposed typology. *American Journal of Orthopsychiatry, 57,* 383–393.

Cornwall, E., Spence, S.H., & Schotte, D. (1996). The effectiveness of emotive imagery in the treatment of darkness phobia in children. *Behaviour Change, 13,* 223–229.

Costello, E.J., Angold, A., Burns, B.J., Stangl, D.K., Tweed, D.L., Erkanli, A., & Worthman, C.M. (1996). The Great Smoky Mountains Study of Youth: Goals, design, methods, and the prevalence of DSM-III-R disorders. *Archives of General Psychiatry, 53,* 1129–1136.

Costello, E.J., Angold, A., & Keeler, G.P. (1999). Adolescent outcomes of childhood disorders: The consequences of severity and impairment. *Journal of the American Academy of Child and Adolescent Psychiatry, 38,* 121–128.

Costello, E.J., Costello, A.J., Edelbrock, C., Burns, B.J., Dulcan, M., Brent, D., & Janiszewski, S. (1988). Psychiatric disorders in pediatric primary care: Prevalence and risk factors. *Archives of General Psychiatry, 45,* 1107–1116.

Costello, E.J., Erkanli, A., Fairbank, J.A., & Angold, A. (in press). The prevalence of potentially traumatic events in childhood and adolescence. *Journal of Traumatic Stress Studies.*

Costello, E.J., Messer, S.C., Bird, H.R., Cohen, P., & Reinherz, H.Z. (1998). The prevalence of serious emotional disturbance: A re-analysis of community studies. *Journal of Child and Family Studies, 7,* 411–432.

Cottrell, N., & Epley, S. (1977). Affiliation, social comparison, and socially mediated stress reduction. In J. Suls & R.L. Miller (Eds.), *Social comparison processes: Theoretical and empirical perspectives.* Washington, DC: Hemisphere.

Council of Scientific Affairs. (1991). Hispanic health in the United States. *Journal of the American Medical Association, 265,* 248–252.

Cowan, E.L. (1994). The enhancement of psychological wellness: Challenges and opportunities. *American Journal of Community Psychology, 22,* 149–179.

Crespi, T.D., & Rigazio-DiGilio, S.A. (1996). Adolescent homicide and family pathology: Implications for research and treatment with adolescents. *Adolescence, 31,* 353–367.

Cross, T., Bazron, B., Dennis, K., & Isaacs, M. (1989). *Towards a culturally competent system of care: A monograph on effective services for minority children who are severely emotionally disturbed.* Washington, DC: Georgetown University Child Development Center.

Cueva, J.E., Overall, J.E., Small, A.M., Armenteros, J.L., Perry, R., & Campbell, M. (1996). Carbamazepine in aggressive children with conduct disorder: A double-blind and placebo-controlled study. *Journal of the American Academy of Child and Adolescent Psychiatry, 35,* 480–490.

Cumblad, C. (1996). *The pathways children and families follow prior to, during, and after contact with an intensive, family-based, social service intervention in urban settings.* Unpublished doctoral dissertation, Department of Educational Psychology, Counseling, and Special Education, Northern Illinois University.

Dahl, R., Holttum, J., & Trubnick, L. (1994). A clinical picture of child and adolescent narcolepsy. *Journal of the American Academy of Child and Adolescent Psychiatry, 33,* 834–841.

Dalgleish, T. (1993). *The judgment of risk in traumatised and non-traumatised disaster survivors.* Unpublished master's thesis. London: University of London.

Dane, A.V., & Schneider, B.H. (1998). Educational environments for students with E/BD. In D.A. Sabatino & B.L. Brooks (Eds.), *Contemporary interdisciplinary interventions for children with emotional/behavioral disorders* (pp. 113–142). Durham, NC: Carolina Academic Press.

Davis, D.A., Thomson, M.A., Oxman, A.D., & Haynes, R.B. (1995). Changing physician performance: A systematic review of the effect of continuing medical education strategies. *Journal of the American Medical Association, 274,* 700–705.

Day, C., & Roberts, M. (1991). Activities of the Child and Adolescent Service System Program for improving mental health services for children and families. *Journal of Clinical Child Psychology, 20,* 340–350.

Deas, D., & Thomas, S.E. (2001). An overview of controlled studies of adolescent substance abuse treatment. *American Journal on Addictions, 10,* 178–189.

Deblinger, E., & Lippman, J. (1996). Sexually abused children suffering posttraumatic stress symptoms: Initial treatment outcome findings. *Child Maltreatment, 1,* 310–322.

Deblinger, E., Steer, R.A., & Lippman, J. (1999). Two year follow-up study of cognitive behavioral therapy for sexually abused children suffering post-traumatic stress symptoms. *Child Abuse and Neglect, 23,* 1371–1378.

de Haan, E., Hoogduin, K.A.L., Buitelaar, J.K., & Keijsers, G.P.J. (1998). Behavior therapy versus clomipramine for the treatment of obsessive-compulsive disorder in children and adolescents. *Journal of the American Academy of Child and Adolescent Psychiatry, 37,* 1022–1029.

De Man, A. (1999). Correlates of suicide ideation in high school students: The importance of depression. *Journal of Genetic Psychology, 160,* 105–114.

Deno, S.L. (1985). Curriculum-based measurement: The emerging alternative. *Exceptional Children, 52,* 219–232.

Derogatis, L.R., & Spencer, P.M. (1982). *The Brief Symptom Inventory (BSI): Administration, scoring, & procedures manual—I.* Baltimore: Clinical Psychometric Research.

DeVane, C., & Salle F. (1996). Serotonin selective reuptake inhibitor in child and adolescent psychopharmacology: A review of published experience. *Journal of Clinical Psychiatry, 57,* 56–66.

DeVeaugh-Geiss, J., Moroz, G., Biederman, J., Cantwell, D., Fontaine, R., Greist, J.H., Reichler, R., Katz, R., & Landau, P. (1992). Clomipramine hydrochloride in childhood and adolescent obsessive-compulsive disorder: A multicenter trial. *Journal of the American Academy of Child and Adolescent Psychiatry, 31,* 45–49.

Deykin, E.Y., & Buka, S.L. (1997). Prevalence and risk factors for posttraumatic stress disorder among chemically dependent adolescents. *American Journal of Psychiatry, 154,* 752–757.

Diggle, E., Liang, K., & Zeger, S. (1994). *Analysis of longitudinal data.* New York: Oxford University Press.

Dishion, T.J., French, D.C., & Patterson, G.R. (1995). The development and ecology of antisocial behavior. In D. Cicchetti & D.J. Cohen (Eds.), *Developmental psychopathology, Vol. 2: Risk, disorder, and adaptation,* (pp. 421–471). New York: John Wiley & Sons.

Dishion, T.J., McCord, J., & Poulin, F. (1999). When interventions harm: Peer groups and problem behavior. *American Psychologist, 54,* 755-765.

Dishion, T.J., & Patterson, G.R. (1997). The timing and severity of antisocial behavior: Three hypotheses within an ecological framework. In D.M. Stoff, J. Breiling, & J.D. Maser (Eds.), *Handbook of antisocial behavior* (pp. 205–217). New York: John Wiley & Sons.

Disney, E.R., Elkins, I.J., McGue, M., & Iacono, W.G. (1999). Effects of ADHD, conduct disorder, and gender on substance use and abuse in adolescence. *American Journal of Psychiatry, 156,* 1515–1521.

Donnelly, J. (1994). *A comparison of youth involvement and a sense of unconditional care with wraparound versus traditional services.* Unpublished master's thesis. Psychology Department, University of Vermont, Burlington, Vermont.

Donovan, W., Leavitt, L., & Walsh, R. (1990). Maternal self-efficacy: Illusory control and its effect on susceptibility to learned helplessness. *Child Development, 61,* 1638–1647.

Doogan, D. (1991). Toleration of safety of sertraline: Experience worldwide. *International Journal of Clinical Psychopharmacology, 6 (Supp.),* 47–56.

Dreir, M., & Lewis, M. (1991). Support and psychoeducation for parents of hospitalized mentally ill children. *Health and Social Work, 16,* 11–21.

Duchnowski, A.J. (1994). Innovative service models. *Journal of Clinical Child Psychology, 23 (Supp.),* 13–18.

Duchnowski, A.J., & Friedman, R.M. (1990). Children's mental health: Challenges for the nineties. *Journal of Mental Health Administration, 17,* 3–12.

Duchnowski, A.J., Hall, K.S., Kutash, K., & Friedman, R.M. (1998). The alternatives to Residential

Treatment Study. In M.H. Epstein, K. Kutash, & A.J. Duchnowski (Eds.), *Outcomes for children and youth with behavioral and emotional disorders and their families: Programs and evaluation best practices* (pp. 55–80). Austin, TX: Pro-Ed.

Dunlap, G., & Childs, K. (1996). Intervention research in emotional and behavioral disorders: An analysis of studies from 1980–1993. *Behavioral Disorders, 21*, 125–136.

Dunst, C.J., Trivette, C.M., & Deal, A.G. (1988). *Enabling and empowering families: Principles and guidelines for practice.* Cambridge, MA: Brookline Books.

Dunst, C.J., Trivette, C.M., & Deal, A.G. (1994). *Supporting and strengthening families, Vol. 1: Methods, strategies, and practices.* Cambridge, MA: Brookline Books.

DuPaul, G., Barkley R., & McMurray, M. (1994). Response of children with ADHD to methylphenidate: Interaction with internalizing symptoms. *Journal of the American Academy of Child and Adolescent Psychiatry, 33*, 894–903.

Durlak, J.A., Wells, A.M., Cotten, J.K., & Johnson, S. (1995). Analysis of selected methodological issues in child psychotherapy research. *Journal of Clinical Child Psychology, 24*, 141–148.

Eber, L., & Osuch, R. (1995). Bringing the wraparound approach to school: A model for inclusion. In C.J. Liberton, K. Kutash, & R.M. Friedman (Eds.), *The 7th annual research conference proceedings, a system of care for children's mental health: Expanding the Research Base* (pp. 143–152). Tampa, FL: University of South Florida, Florida Mental Health Institute, Research and Training Center for Children's Mental Health.

Eber, L., Osuch, R., & Redditt, C.A. (1996). School-based applications of the wraparound process: Early results on service provision and student outcomes. *Journal of Child and Family Studies, 5*, 83–99.

Eber, L., Osuch, R., & Rolf, K. (1996). School-based wraparound: How implementation and evaluation can lead to system change. In C.J. Liberton, K. Kutash, & R.M. Friedman (Eds.), *The 8th annual research conference proceedings, a system of care for children's mental health: Expanding the Research Base* (pp. 143–147). Tampa, FL: University of South Florida, Florida Mental Health Institute, Research and Training Center for Children's Mental Health.

Eddy, J.M., & Chamberlain, P. (2000). Family management and deviant peer association as mediators of the impact of treatment condition on youth antisocial behavior. *Journal of Consulting and Clinical Psychology, 68*, 857–863.

Eddy, M., Reid, J., & Fetrow, B. (2000). An elementary-school based prevention program targeting modifiable antecedents of youth delinquency and violence: Linking the Interests of Families and Teachers (LIFT). *Journal of Emotional and Behavioral Disorders, 8*, 165–176.

Education of the Handicapped Act Amendments of 1986, P.L. 99–457. (October 8, 1986). Title 20, U.S.C. 1400 et seq. *U.S. Statutes at Large, 100*, 1145–1177.

Elliott, D., Koroloff, N., Koren, P., Friesen, B. (1998). Improving access to children's mental health services: The family associate approach. In M.H. Epstein, K. Kutash, & A. Duchnowski (Eds.), *Outcomes for children and youth with emotional and behavioral disorders and their families: Program and evaluation best practices.* Austin, TX: Pro-Ed.

Elliott, D.S. (1994). Serious violent offenders: Onset, developmental course, and termination—The American Society of Criminology 1993 Presidential Address. *Criminology, 32*, 1–21.

Elliott, D.S., Huizinga, D., & Ageton, S.S. (1985). *Explaining delinquency and drug use.* Beverly Hills, CA: Sage.

Emslie, G.J., Rush, A.J., Weinberg, W.A., Kowatch, R.A., Carmody, T., & Mayes, T.L. (1998). Fluoxetine in child and adolescent depression: Acute and maintenance treatment. *Depression and Anxiety, 7*, 32–39.

Emslie, G.J., Rush, A.J., Weinberg, W.A., Kowatch, R.A., Hughes, C.W., Carmody, T., & Rintelmann, J. (1997). A double-blind, randomized, placebo-controlled trial of fluoxetine in children and adolescents with depression. *Archives of General Psychiatry, 54*, 1031–1037.

Emslie, G.J., Walkup, J., Plizka, S., & Ernst, M. (1999). Nontricyclic antidepressants: Current trends in children and adolescents. *Journal of the American Academy of Child and Adolescent Psychiatry, 38*, 517–528.

England, M.J., & Cole, R.F. (1992). Building systems of care for youth with serious mental illness. *Hospital and Community Psychiatry, 43*, 630–633.

Epanchin, B.C. (1998). Education as treatment: Forty years of Project Re-EDucation. In D.A. Sabatino & B.L. Brooks (Eds.), *Contemporary interdisciplinary interventions for children with emotional/behavioral disorders* (pp. 199–222). Durham, NC: Carolina Academic Press.

Epstein, M.H., & Cullinan, D. (1998). *Scale assessing emotional disturbance.* Austin, TX: Pro-Ed.

Epstein, M.H., Jayanthi, M., McKelvey, J., Frankenberry, E., Hardy, R., Dennis, K., & Dennis, K. (1998). Reliability of the wraparound observation form: An instrument to measure the wraparound process. *Journal of Child and Family Studies, 7*, 161–170.

Epstein, M.H., Kutash, K., & Duchnowski, A. (Eds.) (1998). *Outcomes for children and youth with emo-*

tional and behavioral disorders and their families: Programs and evaluation best practices. Austin, TX: Pro-Ed.

Evans, M.E., Armstrong, M.I., Dollard, N., Kuppinger, A.D., Huz, S., & Wood, V.M. (1994). Development of an evaluation of treatment foster care and family-centered intensive case management in New York. *Journal of Emotional and Behavioral Disorders, 2,* 228–239.

Evans, M.E., Armstrong, M.I., & Kuppinger, A.D. (1996). Family-centered intensive case management: A step toward understanding individualized care. *Journal of Child and Family Studies, 5,* 55–65.

Evans, M.E., Armstrong, M.I., Kuppinger, A.D., Huz, S., & Johnson, S. (1998a). *A randomized trial of family-centered intensive case management and family-based treatment: outcomes of two community-based programs for children with serious emotional disturbance.* Tampa, FL: University of South Florida.

Evans, M.E., Armstrong, M.I., Kuppinger, A.D., Huz, S., Johnson, S. (1998b). *A randomized trial of family-centered intensive case management and family based treatment: Final report.* Tampa, FL: University of South Florida.

Evans, M.E., Armstrong, M.I., Kuppinger, A.D., Huz, S., & McNulty, T.L. (1998c). Preliminary outcomes of an experimental study comparing treatment foster care and family-centered intensive case management. In M.H. Epstein, K. Kutash, & A. Duchnowski (Eds.), *Outcomes for children and youth with behavioral and emotional problems and their families: Programs and evaluation best practices* (pp. 543–580). Austin, TX: Pro-Ed.

Evans, M.E., Banks, S.M., Huz, S., & McNulty, T.L. (1994). Initial hospitalization and community tenure outcomes of intensive case management for children and youth with serious emotional and behavioral disabilities. *Journal of Child and Family Studies, 3,* 225–234.

Evans, M.E., Boothroyd, R.A., & Armstrong, M.I. (1997). Development and implementation of an experimental study of the effectiveness of intensive in-home crisis services for children and their families. *Journal of Emotional and Behavioral Disorders, 5,* 93–105.

Evans, M.E., Dollard, N., & McNulty, T.L. (1992). Characteristics of seriously emotionally disturbed youth with and without substance abuse in intensive case management. *Journal of Child and Family Studies, 1,* 305–314.

Fabrega, H., Ulrich, R., & Mezzich, J. (1993). Do Caucasian and Black adolescents differ at psychiatric intake? *Journal of the Academy of Child and Adolescent Psychiatry, 32,* 407–413.

Fairbank, J.A., Ebert, L., & Costello, E.J. (2000). Epidemiology of traumatic events and post-traumatic stress disorder. In D. Nutt, J.R.T. Davidson, & J. Zohar (Eds.), *Post-traumatic stress disorder: Diagnosis, management and treatment* (pp. 17–27). London: Martin Dunitz.

Fairbank, J.A., Friedman, M.J., & Basoglu, M. (2001). Psychosocial models. In E. Gerrity, T. M. Keane, & F. Tuma (Eds.), *The mental health consequences of torture* (pp. 65–72). New York: Kluwer Academic/Plenum.

Fairbank, J.A., & Keane, T.M. (1982). Flooding for combat-related stress disorders: Assessment of anxiety reduction across traumatic memories. *Behavior Therapy, 13,* 499–510.

Fairbank, J.A., & Nicholson, R.A. (1987). Theoretical and empirical issues in the treatment of post-traumatic stress disorder in Vietnam veterans. *Journal of Clinical Psychology, 43,* 44–55.

Famularo, R., Kinsherff, R., & Fenton, T. (1988). Propranolol treatment for childhood posttraumatic stress disorder, acute type: A pilot study. *American Journal of Diseases of Children, 142,* 1244–1247.

Fanshel, D., Finch, S., & Grundy, J. (1990). *Foster children in a life course perspective.* New York: Columbia University Press.

Farmer, E.M.Z. (1993). Externalizing behavior in the life course: The transition from school to work. *Journal of Emotional and Behavioral Disorders, 1,* 179–188.

Farmer, E.M.Z., Burns, B.J., Chamberlain, P., & Dubs, M.S. (2001). Assessing implementation of therapeutic foster care: Issues, approaches, and findings. Manuscript submitted for publication.

Farmer, E.M.Z., Burns, B.J., Guiles, H.B., Behar, L., & Gerber, D.I. (1997). Conducting randomized clinical trials in children's mental health: Experiences from one venture. In C.T. Nixon, & D.A. Northrup, (Eds.), *Evaluating mental health services* (pp. 209–230). Thousand Oaks, CA: Sage.

Farmer, E.M.Z., Stangl, D.K., Burns, B.J., Costello, E.J., & Angold, A. (1999). Use, persistence, and intensity: Patterns of care for children's mental health across one year. *Community Mental Health Journal, 35,* 31–46.

Farmer, T.W., Pearl, R., & Van Acker, R. (1996). Expanding the social skills deficit framework: A developmental synthesis perspective, classroom social networks, and implications for the social growth of students with disabilities. *Journal of Special Education, 30,* 232–256.

Farrington, D.P. (1983). Offending from 10 to 25 years of age. In K.T. Van Dusen & S.A. Mednick (Eds.), *Prospective studies of crime and delinquency* (pp. 17–37). Boston: Kluwer-Nijhoff.

Farrington, D.P. (1991). Childhood aggresssion and adult violence: Early precursors and later-life outcomes. In D.J. Pepler & K.H. Rubin (Eds.), *The development and treatment of childhood aggression* (pp. 5–29). Hillsdale, NJ: Lawrence Erlbaum.

Farrington, D.P. (1994). Early developmental prevention of juvenile delinquency. *Criminal Behavior and Mental Health, 4,* 209–227.

Farrington, D.P. (1997). A critical analysis of research on the development of antisocial behavior from birth to adulthood. In D.M. Stoff, J. Breiling, & J.D. Maser (Eds.), *Handbook of Antisocial Behavior* (pp. 234–240). New York: John Wiley & Sons.

Faw, L. (1999). The state wraparound survey. In B.J. Burns & S.K. Goldman (Eds.), *Promising practices in wraparound for children with serious emotional disturbance and their families. Systems of care: Promising practices in children's mental health,* 1998 Series, Vol. IV (pp. 61–66). Washington DC: Center for Effective Collaboration and Practice, American Institutes for Research.

Faw, L., Grealish, E.M., & Lourie, I.S. (1999). Training and quality monitoring. In B.J. Burns & S.K. Goldman (Eds.), *Promising practices in wraparound for children with serious emotional disturbance and their families. Systems of care: Promising practices in children's mental health,* 1998 Series, Vol. IV (pp. 67–76). Washington DC: Center for Effective Collaboration and Practice, American Institutes for Research.

Federal Register. (1977). 42, 42478.

Federal Register. (1981). 46, 3866.

Federal Register. (1993). 58, 29425.

Fehlings, D.L., Roberts, W., Humphries, T., & Dawe, G. (1991). Attention deficit hyperactivity disorder: Does cognitive behavioral therapy improve home behavior? *Journal of Developmental and Behavioral Pediatrics, 12,* 223–228.

Feldman, S. (1997). The Fort Bragg demonstration and evaluation. *American Psychologist, 52,* 560–561.

Festinger, L. (1954). A theory of social comparison processes. *Human Relations, 7,* 117–140.

Field, T., Morrow, C.J., Valdeon, C., Larson, S., Kuhn, S., & Schanberg, S. (1992). Massage reduces anxiety in child and adolescent psychiatric patients. *Journal of the American Academy of Child and Adolescent Psychiatry, 31,* 125–131.

Fine, G., & Borden, J.R. (1992). Parents Involved Network (PIN): Outcomes of parent involvement in support group and advocacy activities. In A. Algarin & R. Freidman (Eds.), *The 4th annual research conference proceedings, a system of care for children's mental health: Expanding the research base* (pp. 25–29). Tampa, FL: University of South Florida, Florida Mental Health Institute, Research and Training Center for Children's Mental Health.

Fishbein, M., & Ajzen, I. (1975). *Belief, attitude, intention and behavior: An introduction to theory and research.* Reading, MA: Addison-Wesley.

Fishbein, M., Bandura, A., Triandis, H.C., Kanfer, F.H., Becer, M.H., Middlestadt, S.E., & Eichler, A. (1992). *Factors influencing behavior and behavior change: Final report—theorist's workshop.* Rockville, MD: National Institute of Mental Health.

Fisher, J., & Nadler, A. (1974). The effect of similarity between donor and recipient on reactions to aid. *Journal of Applied Social Psychology, 4,* 230–243.

Fisher, J., Nadler, A., & Whitcher-Alagna, S. (1983). Four theoretical approaches for conceptualizing reactions to aid. In A. Nadler, J. Fisher, & B. DePaulo (Eds.), *New directions in helping, Vol. 1: Recipient reactions to aid.* New York: Academic Press.

Fisher, P. A., Ellis, B. H., & Chamberlain, P. (1999). Early intervention foster care: A model for preventing risk in young children who have been maltreated. *Children Services: Social Policy, Research, and Practice, 2,* 159–182.

Flament, M.F., Koby, E., Rapoport, J.L., Berg, C.J., Zahn, T., Cox, C., Denckla, M., & Lenane, M. (1990). Childhood obsessive-compulsive disorder: A prospective follow-up study. *Journal of Child Psychology and Psychiatry, 31,* 363–380.

Flament, M.F., Rapoport, J.L., Berg, C.J., Sceery, W., Kilts, C., Mellström, B., & Linnoila, M. (1985). Clomipramine treatment of childhood obsessive-compulsive disorder: A double-blind controlled study. *Archives of General Psychiatry, 42,* 977–983.

Flannery-Schroeder, E.C., & Kendall, P.C. (2000). Group and individual cognitive-behavioral treatments for youth with anxiety disorders: A randomized clinical trial. *Cognitive Therapy and Research, 24,* 251–278.

Fleming, S., & Offord, D. (1990). Epidemiology of childhood depressive disorders: A critical review. *Journal of the American Academy of Child and Adolescent Psychiatry, 29,* 571–580.

Flomenhaft, K. (1974). Outcome of treatment for adolescents. *Adolescence, 9,* 57–66.

Foa, E.B., Dancu, C.V., Hembree, E.A., Jaycox, L.H., Meadows, E.A., & Street, G.P. (1999). A comparison of exposure therapy, stress inoculation training and their combination for reducing posttraumatic stress disorder in female assault victims. *Journal of Consulting and Clinical Psychology, 67,* 194–200.

Foa, E.B., Keane, T.M., & Friedman, M.J. (2000). Introduction to the practice guidelines for the treatment of PTSD. In E.B. Foa, T. M. Keane, & M. J. Friedman (Eds.), *Effective treatments for PTSD: Practice guidelines from the International Society for Traumatic Stress Studies.* New York: Guilford Press.

Foa, E.B., & Kozak, M.J. (1986). Emotional processing of fear: Exposure to corrective information. *Psychological Bulletin, 99,* 20–35.

Foa, E.B., Rothbaum, B.O., & Molnar, C. (1995). Cognitive-behavioral therapy of post-traumatic stress disorder. *Journal of Traumatic Stress, 8,* 675–690.

Foa, E.B., Rothbaum, B.O., Riggs, D.S., & Murdock, T.B. (1991). Treatment of posttraumatic stress disoder in rape victims: A comparison between cognitive behavioral procedures and counseling. *Journal of Consulting and Clinical Psychology, 59,* 715–723.

Foa, E.B., Steketee, G., & Rothbaum, B.O. (1989). Behavioral/cognitive conceptualizations of posttraumatic stress disorder. *Behavior Therapy, 20,* 155–176.

Fonagy, P., & Target, M. (1994). The efficacy of psychoanalysis for children with disruptive disorders. *Journal of the American Academy of Child and Adolescent Psychiatry, 33,* 45–55.

Foster Family–Based Treatment Association. (1995). *Program standards for Treatment Foster Care.* New York: Author.

Foundations and Agencies Network Monograph. (2000). *Off to a good start: Research on risk factors for early school problems and selected federal policies affecting children's social and emotional development and their readiness for school.* Chapel Hill, NC: University of North Carolina, Frank Porter Graham Child Development Center.

Fraser, M.W., Nelson, K.E., & Rivard, J.C. (1997). The effectiveness of family preservation services. *Social Work Research, 21,* 138–153.

Frazier, J., Meyer, M., Biederman, J., Wozniak, J., Wilens, T., Spencer, T., Kim, G., & Shapiro, S. (1999). Risperidone treatment for juvenile bipolar disorder: A retrospective chart review. *Journal of the American Academy of Child and Adolescent Psychiatry, 38,* 960–965.

Friedman, M.J. (2000). *Post traumatic stress disorder: The latest assessment and treatment strategies.* Kansas City, MO: Compact Clinicals.

Friedman, M.J., Davidson, J.R.T., Mellman, T.A., & Southwick, S.M. (2000). Pharmacotherapy for PTSD. In E.B. Foa, T.M. Keane, & M.J. Friedman (Eds.), *Effective treatments for PTSD: Practice guidelines from the International Society for Traumatic Stress Studies.* New York: Guilford Press.

Friedman, R.M. (1997). Services and service delivery systems for children with serious emotional disorders: Issues in assessing effectiveness. In C.T. Nixon & D.A. Northrup (Eds.), *Evaluating mental health services: How do programs for children work in the real world?* (pp. 16–44). Thousand Oaks, CA: Sage.

Friedman, R.M., & Burns, B.J. (1996). The evaluation of the Fort Bragg demonstration project: An alternative interpretation of the findings. *Journal of Mental Health Administration,* (1996, 23), 128–136.

Friedman, R.M., Katz-Leavy, J.W., Manderscheid, R.W., & Sondheimer, D.L. (1996). Prevalance of serious emotional disturbance in children and adolescents. In R.W. Manderscheid & M.A. Sonnenschein (Eds.), *Mental Health, United States, 1996* (pp. 71–88). Rockville, MD: Center for Mental Health Services.

Friedman, R.M., Kutash, K., & Duchnowski, A.J. (1996). The population of concern: Defining the issues. In B.A. Stroul (Ed.), *Children's mental health: Creating systems of care in a changing society* (pp. 69–96). Baltimore: Paul H. Brookes.

Friend, M., & Bursuck, W.D. (1999). *Including students with special needs.* Boston: Allyn & Bacon.

Friesen, B.J. (1996). Redefining family support: Innovations in public-private partnership. In G. Singer, L. Powers, & A. Olson (Eds.), *Family, community, and disability* (pp. 259–286). Baltimore: Paul H. Brookes.

Friesen, B.J., & Briggs, H.E. (1995). The organization and structure of service coordination mechanisms. In B.J. Friesen & J. Poertner (Eds.), *From case management to service coordination for children with emotional, behavioral, or mental disorders* (pp. 63–94). Baltimore: Paul H. Brookes.

Friesen, B.J., & Huff, B. (1996). Family perspectives on systems of care. In B.A. Stroul (Ed.), *Children's mental health: Creating systems of care in a changing society* (pp. 41–67). Baltimore: Paul H. Brookes.

Friesen, B.J., & Koroloff, N.M. (1990). Family centered services: Implications for mental health administration and research. *Journal of Mental Health Administration, 17,* 13–25.

Friesen, B.J., & Stephens, B. (1998). Expanding family roles in the system of care: Research and practice. In M.H. Epstein, K. Kutash, & A.J. Duchnowski (Eds.), *Outcomes for children and youth with behavioral and emotional disorders: Programs and evaluation best practices* (pp. 231–253). Austin, TX: Pro-Ed.

Fromm, E. (1956). *The Art of Loving.* New York: Harper & Brothers.

Gadow, K.D. (1997). An overview of three decades of research in pediatric psychopharmacology. *Journal of Child and Adolescent Psychopharmacology, 7,* 219–236.

Gadow, K.D., Nolan, E., Sprafkin, J., & Sverd, J. (1995). School observations of children with attention-deficit hyperactivity disorder and comorbid tic disorder: Effects of methylphenidate treatment. *Journal of Developmental and Behavioral Pediatrics, 16,* 167–176.

Gadow, K.D., Sverd, J., Sprafkin, J., Nolan, E.E., & Grossman, S. (1999). Long-term methylphenidate therapy in children with comorbid attention-deficit hyperactivity disorder and chronic multiple tic disorder. *Archives of General Psychiatry, 56,* 330–336.

Galbicka, G. (1994). Shaping in the 21st century: Moving percentile schedules into applied settings. *Journal of Applied Behavior Analysis, 27,* 739–760.

Gammon, G., & Brown, T. (1993). Fluoxetine and methylphenidate in combination for treatment of attention deficit disorder and co-morbid depression. *Journal of Child and Adolescent Psychopharmacology, 3,* 1–10.

Garber, A.M. (2001). Evidence-based coverage policy. *Health Affairs, 20,* 62–82.

Garland, A.F., & Besinger, B.A. (1997). Racial and ethnic differences in court referred pathways to mental health services for children in foster care. *Youth and Youth Services Review, 19,* 651–666.

Garmezy, N., Masten, A., & Tellegen, A. (1984). The study of stress and competence in children. *Child Development, 55,* 97–111.

Gecas, V. (1989). The social psychology of self-efficacy. *Annual Review of Sociology, 15,* 291–316.

Geller, B., Cooper, T.B., McCombs, H.G., Graham, D., & Wells, J. (1989). Double-blind, placebo-controlled study of nortriptyline in depressed children using a "fixed plasma level" design. *Psychopharmacology Bulletin, 25,* 101–108.

Geller, B., Cooper, T.B., Sun, K., Zimerman, B., Frazier, J., Williams, M., & Heath, J. (1998). Double-blind and placebo controlled study of lithium for adolescent bipolar disorders with secondary substance dependency. *Journal of the American Academy of Child and Adolescent Psychiatry, 37,* 171–178.

Geller, B., & Luby, S. (1997). Child and adolescent bipolar disorder: A review of the past 10 years. *Journal of the American Academy of Child and Adolescent Psychiatry, 36,* 1168–1176.

Geller, B., Reising, D., Leonard, H., Riddle, M., & Walsh, T. (1999). Critical review of tricyclic antidepressant use in children and adolescents. *Journal of the American Academy of Child and Adolescent Psychiatry, 38,* 513–516.

Giaconia, R.M., Reinherz, H.Z., Hauf, A.C., Paradis, A.D., Wasserman, M.S., & Langhammer, D.M. (2000). Comorbidity of substance use and post-traumatic stress disorder in a community sample of adolescents. *American Journal of Orthopsychiatry, 70,* 253–262.

Giaconia, R.M., Reinherz, H.Z., Silverman, A.B., Pakiz, B., Frost, A.K., & Cohen, E. (1994). Age of onset of psychiatric disorders in a community population of older adolescents. *Journal of the American Academy of Child and Adolescent Psychiatry, 33,* 706–717.

Gillberg, C., Melander, H., von Knorring, A.L., Janols, L.O., Thernlund, G., Hägglöf, B., Eidevall-Wallin, L., Gustafsson, P., & Kopp, S. (1997). Long-term stimulant treatment of children with attention-deficit hyperactivity disorder symptoms: A randomized, double-blind, placebo-controlled trial. *Archives of General Psychiatry, 54,* 857–864.

Gillham, J.E., Reivich, K.J., Jaycox, L.H., & Seligman, M.E. (1995). Prevention of depressive symptoms in schoolchildren: Two-year follow-up. *Psychological Science, 6,* 343–351.

Gittelman, R., Mannuzza, S., Shenker, R., & Bonagura, N. (1985). Hyperactive boys almost grown up: I. Psychiatric status. *Archives of General Psychiatry, 42,* 937–947.

Gittelman-Klein, R., & Klein, D.F. (1973). School phobia: Diagnostic considerations in the light of imipramine effects. *Journal of Nervous and Mental Disease, 156,* 199–215.

Gittleman-Klein, R., Spitzen, R., & Cantwell, D. (1978). Diagnostic classification and psychopharmacologic indications. In Werry, J. (Ed.), *Pediatric psychopharmacology: The use of behavior modifying drugs in children.* New York: Brunner/Mazel.

Glantz, M.D., & Leshner, A.I. (2000). Drug abuse and developmental psychopathology. *Development and Psychopathology, 12,* 795–814.

Glasser, W. (1965). *Reality therapy: A new approach to psychiatry.* New York: Harper & Row.

Glisson, C., & Hemmelgarn, A. (1998). The effects of organizational climate and interorganizational coordination on the quality and outcomes of children's service systems. *Child Abuse and Neglect, 22,* 401–421.

Glover, S.H., & Pumariega, A.J. (1998). The importance of children's mental health epidemiologi-cal research with culturally diverse populations. In M. Hernandez & M.R. Isaacs (Eds.), *Promoting cultural competence in children's mental health services* (pp. 271–303). Baltimore: Paul H. Brookes.

Glynn, S.M., Eth, S., Randolph, E.T., Foy, D.W., Urbatis, M., Boxer, L., Paz, G.B., Leong, G.B., Firman, G., Salk, J.D., Katzman, J.W., & Crothers, J. (1999). A test of behavioral family therapy to augment exposure for combat-related PTSD. *Journal of Consulting and Clinical Psychology, 67,* 243–51.

Godin, G., & Kok, G. (1996). The theory of planned behavior: A review of its applications to health-related behaviors. *American Journal of Health Promotion, 11,* 87–97.

Goel, K., & Shanks, R. (1994). Amitriptyline and imipramine poisoning in children. *British Medical Journal, 1,* 261–263.

Goenjian, A.K., Karayan, I., Pynoos, R.S., Minassian, D., Najarian, L.M., Steinberg, A.M., & Fairbanks, L.A. (1997). Outcome of psychotherapy among early adolescents after trauma. *American Journal of Psychiatry, 154,* 536–542.

Goldman, S. K., & Faw, L. (1999). Three wraparound models as promising approaches. In B.J. Burns & S.K. Goldman (Eds.), *Promising practices in wraparound for children with severe emotional disturbance and their families. Systems of care: Promising practices in children's mental health,* 1998 Series, Vol. IV (pp. 17–59). Washington, DC: Center for Effective Collaboration and Practice, American Institutes for Research.

Golly, A., Sprague, J., Walker, H., Beard, K., & Gorham, G. (2000). The First Step to Success program: An analysis of outcomes with identical twins across multiple baselines. *Behavioral Disorders, 25,* 170–182.

Golly, A., Stiller, B., & Walker, H.M. (1997). *First Step training guide.* Longmont, CO: Sopris West, Inc.

Golly, A., Stiller, B., & Walker, H.M. (1998). Replication and social validation of an early intervention program. *Journal of Emotional and Behavioral Disorders, 6,* 243–250.

Gonzalez, J., Field, T., Yando, R., Gonzalez, R., Lasko, D., & Bendell. D. (1994). Adolescents' perceptions of their risk-taking behavior. *Adolescence, 29,* 701–709.

Goodman, W., & Price, L. (1992). Assessment of severity and change in obsessive-compulsive disorder. *Psychiatric Clinics of North America, 15,* 861–869.

Gottfredson, D.C. (1997). School-based crime prevention. In L. Sherman, D. Gottfredson, D. Mackenzie, J. Eck, P. Reuter, & S. Bushway (Eds.), *Preventing crime: What works, what doesn't, what's promising.* College Park, MD: Department of Criminology and Criminal Justice.

Gottlieb, B. (1988). Marshaling social support: The state of the art in research and practice. In B.H. Gottlieb (Ed.), *Marshaling social support.* Newbury Park, CA: Sage.

Graae, F., Milner, J., Rizzotto, L., & Klein, R.G. (1994). Clonazepam in childhood anxiety disorders. *Journal of the American Academy of Child and Adolescent Psychiatry, 33,* 372–376.

Graham, P., & Rutter, M. (1985). Adolescent disorders. In M. Rutter & K. Hersov (Eds.), *Child and adolescent psychiatry, modern approaches.* Oxford: Blackwell Scientific.

Granovetter, M. (1973). The strength of weak ties. *American Journal of Sociology, 78,* 1360–1380.

Graziano, A.M., & Mooney, K.C. (1980). Family self-control instruction for children's nighttime fear reduction. *Journal of Consulting and Clinical Psychology, 48,* 206–213.

Graziano, A.M., & Mooney, K.C. (1982). Behavioral treatment of "nightfears" in children: Maintenance of improvement at 2 1/2- to 3-year follow-up. *Journal of Consulting and Clinical Psychology, 50,* 598–599.

Grcevich, S., Findling, R., Rowane, W., Friedman, L., & Schulz, C. (1996). Risperidone in the treatment of children and adolescents with schizophrenia: A retrospective study. *Journal of Child and Adolescent Psychopharmacology, 6,* 251–257.

Green, B.L. (1994). Psychosocial research in traumatic stress: An update. *Journal of Traumatic Stress, 7,* 341–362.

Greenbaum, P.E., Dedrick, R.F., Friedman, R.M., Kutash, K., Brown, E.C., Lardieri, S.P., & Pugh, A.M. (1998). National Adolescent and Child Treatment Study (NACTS): Outcomes for children with serious emotional and behavioral disturbance. In M.H. Epstein, K. Kutash, & A.J. Duchnowski (Eds.), *Outcomes for children and youth with behavioral and emotional disorders and their families: Programs and evaluation best practices* (pp. 21–54). Austin, TX: Pro-Ed.

Greenbaum, P.E., Dedrick, R.F., Friedman, R.M., Kutash, K., Brown, E.C., Lardieri, S.P., & Pugh, A.M. (1996). National Adolescent and Child Treatment Study (NACTS): Outcomes for children with serious emotional and behavioral disturbance. *Journal of Emotional and Behavioral Disorders, 4,* 130–146.

Greenbaum, P.E., Prange, M.E., Friedman, R.M., & Silver, S.E. (1991). Substance abuse prevalence and comorbidity with other psychiatric disorders among adolescents with severe emotional disturbances. *Journal of the American Academy of Child and Adolescent Psychiatry, 30,* 575–583.

Greenberg, M. (1980). A theory of indebtedness. In K. Gergen, M. Greenberg, & R. Willis (Eds.), *Social exchange: Advances in theory and research.* New York: Plenum Press.

Greenberg, M., Domitrovich, C., & Bumbarger, B. (1999). *Preventing mental disorders in school-age children: A review of the effectiveness of prevention programs.* State College, PA: Prevention Research Center for the Promotion of Human Development, Pennsylvania State University.

Greenhill, L.L., Abikoff, H., Arnold, L., Cantwell, D., Conners, C., Elliott, G., Hechtman, L., Hinsaw, S., Hoza, B., Jensen, P., March, J., Newcorn, J., Pelham, W., Severe, J., Swanson, J., Vitiello, B., & Wells, K. (1996). Medication treatment strategies in the MTA: Relevance to clinicians and researchers. *Journal of the American Academy of Child and Adolescent Psychiatry, 35,* 1304–1313.

Greenhill, L.L., Halperin, J., & Abikoff, H. (1999). Stimulant medications. *Journal of the American Academy of Child and Adolescent Psychiatry, 38,* 503–512.

Greenhill, L.L., Solomon, M., Pleak, R., & Ambrosini, P. (1985). Molindone hydrochloride treatment of hospitalized children with conduct disorder. *Journal of Clinical Psychiatry, 46 (Section 2),* 20–25.

Grimsley, S., & Iann, M. (1992). Paroxetine, sertraline & fluvoxamine: New selective serotonin reuptake inhibitors. *Clinical Pharmacy, 11,* 930–957.

Grizenko, N. (1997). Outcome of multimodal day treatment for children with severe behavior problems: A five year follow-up. *Journal of the American Academy of Child and Adolescent Psychiatry, 36,* 989–997.

Grizenko, N., Papineau, D., & Sayegh, L. (1993). A comparison of day treatment and outpatient treatment for children with disruptive behaviour problems. *Canadian Journal of Psychiatry, 38,* 432–435.

Gunnar, M. (1992). Reactivity of the hypothalamic-pituitary-adrenocortical system to stressors in normal infants and children. *Pediatrics, 90, (3 supp. 2),* 491–497.

Gunning, B. (1992) *A controlled trial of clonidine in hyperactive children.* Dissertation, Department of Child and Adolescent Psychiatry, Academic Hospital, Rotterdam, The Netherlands.

Gutterman, E.M., Markowitz, J.S., LoConte, J.S., & Beier, J. (1993). Determinants for hospitalization from an emergency mental health service. *Journal of the American Academy of Child and Adolescent Psychiatry 32,* 114–122.

Haley, J. (1976). *Problem solving therapy.* San Francisco: Jossey-Bass.

Halfon, N., Medonca, A., & Berkowitz, G. (1995). Health status of children in foster care: The experience of the Center for the Vulnerable Child. *Archives of Pediatric and Adolescent Medicine, 149,* 386–392.

Halpern, R., & Larner, M. (1988). The design of family support programs in high-risk communities: Lessons from the Child Survival/Fair Start Initiative. In D. Powell (Ed.), *Parent education as early childhood education.* Norwood, NJ: Ablex.

Hammer, K.M., Lambert, E.W., & Bickman, L. (1997). Children's mental health in a continuum of care: Clinical outcomes at 18 months for the Fort Bragg demonstration. *Journal of Mental Health Administration, 24,* 465–471.

Hansen, C., Sanders, S.L., Massaro, S., & Last, C.G. (1998). Predictors of severity of absenteeism in children with anxiety-based school refusal. *Journal of Clinical Child Psychology, 27,* 246–254.

Hawkins, J.D., & Catalano, R.F. (1992). *Communities that care: Action for drug abuse prevention.* San Francisco: Jossey-Bass.

Hawkins, J.D., Catalano, R.F., Gillmore, M.R., & Wells, E.A. (1989). Skills training for drug abusers: Generalization, maintenance, and effects on drug use. *Journal of Consulting and Clinical Psychology, 57,* 559–563.

Hawkins, J.D., Catalano, R.F., & Miller, J.Y. (1992). Risk and protective factors for alcohol and other drug problems in adolescence and early adulthood. *Psychological Bulletin, 112,* 64–105.

Hazell, P., O'Connell, D., Heathcote, D., & Henry, D. (2000). Tricyclic drugs for depression in children and adolescents. *Cochrane Database of Systematic Reviews* [computer file](3), CD002317.

Helfinger, C.A. & Bickman, L. (1996). Family empowerment: A conceptual model for promoting parent-professional partnership. In C.A. Heflinger & C. Nixon (Eds.), *Families and mental health services for children and adolescents* (pp. 92–116). Thousand Oaks, CA: Sage.

Heflinger, C.A., Bickman, L., Northrup, D., & Shonnichsen, S. (1997). A theory-driven intervention and evaluation to explore family caregiver empowerment. *Journal of Emotional and Behavioral Disorders, 5,* 184–191.

Henggeler, S.W. (1997). The development of effective drug abuse services for youth. In J.A. Egertson, D.M. Fox, & A.I. Leshner (Eds.), *Treating drug abusers effectively* (pp. 253–279). New York: Blackwell.

Henggeler, S.W., & Borduin, C.M. (1995). Multisystemic treatment of serious juvenile offenders and their families. In I.M. Schwartz & P. AuClaire (Eds.), *Home-based services for troubled children* (pp. 113–130). Lincoln, NE: University of Nebraska Press.

Henggeler, S.W., Borduin, C.M., Melton, G.B., Mann, B.J., Smith, L., Hall, J.A., Cone, L., & Fucci, B.R. (1991). Effects of multisystemic therapy on drug use and abuse in serious juvenile offenders: A progress report from two outcome studies. *Family Dynamics of Addiction Quarterly, 1*, 40–51.

Henggeler, S.W., Melton, G.B., Brondino, M.J., Scherer, DG., & Hanley, J.H. (1997a). Multisystemic therapy with violent and chronic juvenile offenders and their families: The role of treatment fidelity in successful dissemination. *Journal of Consulting and Clinical Psychology, 65*, 821–833.

Henggeler, S.W., Melton, G.B., & Smith, L.A. (1992). Family preservation using multisystemic therapy: An effective alternative to incarcerating serious juvenile offenders. *Journal of Consulting and Clinical Psychology, 60*, 953–961.

Henggeler, S.W., Melton, G.B., Smith, L.A., Schoenwald, S.K., & Hanley, J.H. (1993). Family preservation using multisystemic treatment: Long-term follow-up to a clinical trial with serious juvenile offenders. *Journal of Child and Family Studies, 2*, 283–293.

Henggeler, S.W., Pickrel, S.G., & Brondino, M.J. (2000). Multisystemic treatment of substance-abusing and -dependent delinquents: Outcomes, treatment fidelity, and transportability. *Mental Health Services Research, 1*, 171–184.

Henggeler, S.W., Rodick, J.D., Borduin, C.M., Hanson, C.L., Watson, S.M., & Urey, J.R. (1986). Multisystemic treatment of juvenile offenders: Effects on adolescent behavior and family interactions. *Developmental Psychology, 22*, 132–141.

Henggeler, S.W., Rone, L., Thomas, C., & Timmons-Mitchell, J. (1998a). *Multisystemic therapy.* In D.S. Elliott (Series Ed.), *Blueprints for violence prevention.* University of Colorado, Center for the Study and Prevention of Violence, Boulder, CO: Institute for Behavioral Sciences.

Henggeler, S.W., Rowland, M.D., Pickrel, S.G., Miller, S.L., Cunningham, P.B., Santos, A.B., Schoenwald, S.K., Randall, J., & Edwards, J.E. (1997b). Investigating family-based alternatives to institution-based mental health services for youth: Lessons learned from the pilot study of a randomized field trial. *Journal of Clinical Child Psychology, 26*, 226–233.

Henggeler, S.W., Rowland, M.D., Randall, J., Ward, D.M., Pickrel, S.G., Cunningham, P.B., Miller, S.L., Edwards, J., Zealberg, J.J., Hand, L.D., & Santos, A.B. (1999). Home-based multisystemic therapy as an alternative to the hospitalization of youths in psychiatric crisis: Clinical outcomes. *Journal of the American Academy of Child and Adolescent Psychiatry, 38*, 1331–1339.

Henggeler, S.W., & Schoenwald, S.K. (1998). *The MST supervisory manual: Promoting quality assurance at the clinical level.* Charleston, SC: MST Institute.

Henggeler, S.W., Schoenwald, S.K., Borduin, C.M., Rowland, M.D., & Cunningham, P.B. (1998b). *Multisystemic treatment of antisocial behavior in children and adolescents.* New York: Guilford Press.

Henggeler, S.W., Schoenwald, S.K., & Pickrel, S.G. (1995). Multisystemic therapy: Bridging the gap between university- and community-based treatment. *Journal of Consulting and Clinical Psychology, 63*, 709–717.

Hernandez, J., & DiClemente, R.J. (1992). Self-control and ego identity development as predictors of unprotected sex in late adolescent males. *Journal of Adolescence, 15*, 437–447.

Hernandez, M., Hodges, S., & Cascardi, M. (1998a). The ecology of outcomes: System accountability in children's mental health. *The Journal of Behavioral Health Services and Research, 25*, 136–150.

Hernandez, M., Isaacs, M.R., Nesman, T., & Burns, D. (1998b). Perspectives on culturally competent systems of care. In M. Hernandez & M.R. Isaacs (Eds.), *Promoting cultural competence in children's mental health services* (pp. 1–25). Baltimore: Paul H. Brookes.

Hibbs, E.D., & Jensen, P.S. (Eds.). (1996). *Psychosocial treatments for child and adolescent disorders: Empirically based strategies for clinical practice.* Washington, DC: American Psychological Association.

Hill, C.E., Nutt, E.A., & Jackson, S. (1994). Trends in psychotherapy process research: Samples, measures, researchers, and classic publications. *Journal of Counseling Psychology, 41*, 364–377.

Hillard, J.R., Slomowitz, M., & Deddens, J. (1988). Determinants of emergency psychiatric admission for adolescents and adults. *American Journal of Psychiatry, 145*, 1416–1419.

Hoagwood, K. (1997). Interpreting nullity: The Fort Bragg experiment—a comparative success or failure. *American Psychologist, 52*, 546–550.

Hoagwood, K., & Cunningham, M. (1992). Outcomes of children with emotional disturbance in residential treatment for educational purposes. *Journal of Child and Family Studies, 1*, 129–140.

Hoagwood, K., & Erwin, H.D. (1997). Effectiveness of school-based mental health services for children: A 10-year research review. *Journal of Child and Family Studies, 6*, 435–451.

Hoagwood, K., Jensen, P.S., Petti, T., & Burns, B.J. (1996). Outcomes of mental health care for children and adolescents: I. A comprehensive conceptual model. *Journal of the American Academy of Child and Adolescent Psychiatry, 35,* 1055–1063.

Hobbs, N. (1964). Mental health's third revolution. *American Journal of Orthopsychiatry, 34,* 822–833.

Hoberman, H.M. (1992). Ethnic and minority status and adolescents mental health services utilization. *Journal of Mental Health Administration, 19,* 246–267.

Hochstadt, N.J., Jaudes, P.K., Zimo, D.A., & Schachter, J. (1987). Medical and psychosocial needs of children entering foster care. *Child Abuse and Neglect, 11,* 53–62.

Hodges, K. (1990). *Child and Adolescent Functional Assessment Scale.* Nashville, TN: Vanderbilt Child Mental Health Services Evaluation Project.

Hodges, K. (1994). *Child and Adolescent Functional Assessment Scale.* Ypsilanti, MI: Department of Psychology, Eastern Michigan University.

Hodges, K., & Wong, M. (1996). Psychometric characteristics of a multidimensional measure to assess impairment: The Child and Adolescent Functional Assessment Scale. *Journal of Child and Family Studies, 5,* 445–467.

Hodges, K., & Wong, M.M. (1997). Use of the Child and Adolescent Functional Assessment Scale to predict service utilization and cost. *Journal of Mental Health Administration, 24,* 278–290.

Hofer, M.A. (1984). Relationships as regulators: A psychobiologic perspective on bereavement. *Psychosomatic Medicine, 46,* 183–197.

Hogue, A., Liddle, H.A., & Rowe, C. (1996). Treatment adherence process research in family therapy: A rationale and some practical guidelines. *Psychotherapy, 33,* 332–345.

Holahan, C.J., & Moos, R.H. (1981). Social support and psychological distress: A longitudinal analysis. *Journal of Abnormal Psychology, 90,* 365–370.

Hollister, R.G., & Hill, J. (1995). Problems in the evaluation of community-wide initiatives. In J. P. Connell, A.C. Kubisch, L.B. Schorr, & C.H. Weiss (Eds.), *New approaches to evaluating community initiatives: Concepts, methods, and contexts* (pp.127–172). Washington, DC: Aspen Institute.

Hops, H., & Walker, H.M. (1988). *CLASS (Contingencies for Learning Academic and Social Skills).* Seattle: Educational Achievement Systems.

Horn, W.F., Ialongo, N.S., Greenberg, G., Packard, T., & Smith-Winberry, C. (1990). Additive effects of behavioral parent training and self-control therapy with attention deficit hyperactivity disordered children. *Journal of Clinical Child Psychology, 19,* 98–110.

Horn, W.F., Ialongo, N.S., Pascoe, J.M., Greenberg, G., Packard, T., Lopez, M., Wagner, A., & Puttler, L. (1991). Additive effects of psychostimulants, parent training, and self-control therapy with ADHD children. *Journal of the American Academy of Child and Adolescent Psychiatry, 30,* 233–240.

Horvath, A.O. (1995). The therapeutic relationship: From transference to alliance. *In Session—Psychotherapy in Practice, 1,* 7–17.

Hudson, J., Nutter, R., & Galaway, B. (1990). Specialist foster family–based care: North American developments. In B. Galaway, D. Maglajlic, J. Hudson, P. Harmon, & J. McLagan (Eds.), *International perspectives on specialist foster family care* (pp. 17–24). St. Paul, MN: Human Service Associates.

Huffman, L.C., Mehlinger, S.L., & Kerivan, A.S. (2000). Risk factors for academic and behavioral problems at the beginning of school. In *Off to a good start: Research on the risk factors for early school problems and selected federal policies affecting children's social and emotional development and their readiness for school.* Chapel Hill, NC: University of North Carolina, Frank Porter Graham Child Development Center.

Hughes, C.W., Preskorn, S.H., Weller, E., Weller, R., Hassanein, R., & Tucker, S. (1990). The effect of concomitant disorders in childhood depression on predicting treatment response. *Psychopharmacology Bulletin, 26,* 235–238.

Huizinga, D. (1995). Developmental sequences in delinquency: Dynamic typologies. In L.J. Crockett & A.C. Crouter (Eds.), *Pathways through adolescence* (pp. 15–34). Mahwah, NJ: Lawrence Erlbaum.

Hunt, R. (1987). Treatment effects of oral and transdermal clonidine in relation to methylphenidate: An open pilot study in ADD-H. *Psychopharmacological Bulletin, 23,* 111–114.

Hunt, R., Minderas, R., & Cohn, D. (1985). Clonidine benefits children with attention deficit disorder and hyperactivity: Report of a double blind, placebo-crossover therapeutic trial. *Journal of the American Academy of Child and Adolescent Psychiatry, 24,* 617–629.

Hunter, R.W. (1993). Parents as policy-makers: A handbook for effective participation. Portland, OR: Research & Training Center on Family Support and Children's Mental Health, Portland State University.

Hyde, K.L., Burchard, J.D., & Woodworth, K. (1996). Wrapping services in an urban setting. *Journal of Child and Family Studies, 5,* 67–82.

Hyde, K.L., Woodworth, K., Jordan, K., & Burchard, J.D. (1995). Wrapping services in an urban setting: Outcomes of service reform in Baltimore. In C. Liberton, K. Kutash, & R. Friedman (Eds.), *The 7th annual research conference proceedings, a system of care for children's mental health: Expanding the research base* (pp. 255–260). Tampa, FL: University of South Florida, Florida Mental Health Institute, Research and Training Center for Children's Mental Health.

Ialongo, N., Edelsohn, G., Werthamer-Larsson, L., Crockett, L., & Kellam, S. (1995). The significance of self-reported anxious symptoms in first grade children: Prediction to anxious symptoms and adaptive functioning in fifth grade. *Journal of Child Psychology and Psychiatry and Allied Disciplines, 36*, 427–437.

Ialongo, N.S., Horn, W.F., Pascoe, J.M., Greenberg, G., Packard, T., Lopez, M., Wagner, A., & Puttler, L. (1993). The effects of a multimodal intervention with attention-deficit hyperactivity disorder children: A 9-month follow-up. *Journal of the American Academy of Child and Adolescent Psychiatry, 32*, 182–189.

Ignelzi, S., & Dague, B. (1995). Parents as case managers. In B.J. Friesen & J. Poertner (Eds.), *From case management to service coordination: Building on family strengths* (pp. 327–336). Baltimore: Paul H. Brookes.

Illback, R.J., Neill, T.K., Call, J., & Andis, P. (1993). Description and formative evaluation of the Kentucky IMPACT Program for children with serious emotional disturbance. *Special Services in the Schools, 7*, 87–109.

Illback, R.J., Nelson, C.M., & Sanders, D. (1998). Community-based services in Kentucky: Description and 5-year evaluation of Kentucky IMPACT. In M.H. Epstein, K. Kutash, & A.J. Duchnowski (Eds.), *Outcomes for children and youth with behavioral and emotional disorders and their families: Programs and evaluation best practices* (pp. 55–80). Austin, TX: Pro-Ed.

Insel, T.R. (1997). A neurobiological basis of social attachment. *American Journal of Psychiatry, 6*, 726–735.

Institute of Medicine. (1989). *Research on children and adolescents with mental, behavioral, and developmental disorders*. Washington, DC: National Academy of Sciences.

Intagliata, J. (1992). Improving the quality of community care for the chronically mentally disabled: The role of case management. In S.M. Rose (Ed.), *Case management and social work practice* (pp. 25–55). New York: Longman.

Ireys, H., Sills, E., Kolodner, K., & Walsh, B. (1996). Social support intervention for parents of children with juvenile rheumatoid arthritis: Results of a randomized trial. *Journal of Pediatric Psychology, 21*, 633–641.

Isovarji, J., Laatikainen, T., Pakarinen, A., Juntunen, K., & Myllyla, V. (1993). Polycystic ovaries and hyperandrogenism in women taking valproate for epilepsy. *New England Journal of Medicine, 329*, 1383–1388.

Jacobi, C., Dahme, B., & Rustenbach, S. (1997). Comparison of controlled psycho- and pharmacotherapy studies in bulimia and anorexia nervosa. *Psychotherapy and Psychosomatic Medical Psychology, 47*, 346–364.

Jaycox, L.H., Reivich, K.J., Gillham, J., & Seligman, M.E. (1994). Prevention of depressive symptoms in school children. *Behaviour Research and Therapy, 32*, 801–816.

Jensen, P.S., Bhatara, V., Vitiello, B., Hoagwood, K., Feil, M., & Burke, L. (1999a). Psychoactive medication prescribing practices for U.S. children: Gaps between research and clinical practice. *Journal of the American Academy of Child and Adolescent Psychiatry, 38*, 557–565.

Jensen, P.S., & Hoagwood, K. (1997). The book of names: DSM-IV in context. *Development and Psychopathology, 9*, 231–249.

Jensen, P.S., Hoagwood. K., & Petti T. (1996). Outcomes of mental health care for children and adolescents: II. Literature review and application of a comprehensive model. *Journal of the American Academy of Child and Adolescent Psychiatry, 35*, 1064–77.

Jensen, P.S., Hoagwood, K., & Trickett, E.J. (1999b). Ivory towers or earthen trenches? Community collaborations to foster real-world research. *Applied Developmental Science, 3*, 206–212.

Jensen, P.S., & Payne, J. (1998). Behavioral and medical treatments for attention deficit hyperactivity disorder: Comparisons and combinations. In *NIMH Consensus Development Conference: Diagnosis and treatment of attention deficit hyperactivity disorder* (pp. 143–155). Bethesda, MD: National Institutes of Health, Office of the Director.

Jimerson, D., Herzog, D., & Brotman, A. (1993). Pharmacological approaches in the treatment of eating disorders. *Harvard Review of Psychiatry, 1*, 82–93.

Jivanjee, P.R., Moore, K.R., Schultze, K.H., & Friesen, B.J. (1995). *Interprofessional education for family-centered services: A survey of interprofessional/interdisciplinary training programs*. Portland, OR: Portland State University.

Johnson, S. (1998). Cost study. In M.E. Evans, M.I. Armstrong, A.D., Kuppinger, S. Huz, & S. Johnson, (Eds.), *A randomized trial of family-centered intensive case management and family-based treatment: Final report* (pp. 75–109). Tampa, FL: University of South Florida.

Johnston, L.D., O'Malley, P.M., & Bachman, J.G. (1999). National survey results on drug use from the Monitoring the Future study, 1975–1998. Volume I: Secondary school students (NIH Publication No. 99-4660). Rockville, MD: National Institute on Drug Abuse.

Joint Commission on Mental Health of Children. (1969). *Crisis in child mental health: Challenge for the 1970s.* New York: Harper & Row.

Joorabchi, B. (1977). Expressions of the hyperventilation syndrome in childhood: Studies in the management, including an evaluation of the effectiveness of propranolol. *Clinical Pediatrics, 16,* 1110–1115.

Kadden, R.M. (1999). Cognitive behavior therapy. In P.J. Ott, R.E. Tarter, & R.T. Ammerman (Eds.), *Sourcebook on substance abuse: Etiology, epidemiology, and treatment.* Boston: Allyn & Bacon.

Kadden, R.M., Carroll, K., Donovan, D., Cooney, N., Monti, P., Abrams, D., Litt, M., & Hester, R. (Eds.). (1992). *Cognitive-behavioral coping skills therapy manual: A clinical research guide for therapists treating individuals with alcohol and dependence.* Rockville, MD: National Institute on Alcohol Abuse and Alcoholism.

Kahn, J.S., Kehle, T.J., Jenson, W.R., & Clark, E. (1990). Comparison of cognitive-behavioral, relaxation, and self-modeling interventions for depression among middle-school students. *School Psychology Review, 19,* 196–211.

Kaminer, Y., Burleson, J.A., Blitz, C., Sussman, J., & Rounsaville, B.J. (1998). Psychotherapies for adolescent substance abusers: A pilot study. *Journal of Nervous and Mental Disease, 186,* 684–690.

Kaminski, C., Robbins, M., & Weibley, R. (1994). Sertraline intoxication in a child. *Annals of Emergency Medicine, 23,* 1371–1374.

Kamradt, B. (1996). *The 25 Kid Project: How Milwaukee utilized a pilot project to achieve buy-in among stakeholders in changing the system of care for children with severe emotional problems.* Paper presented to the Washington Business Group on Health.

Kanfer, F.H., Karoly, P., & Newman, A. (1975). Reduction of children's fear of the dark by competence related and situational threat–related verbal cues. *Journal of Consulting and Clinical Psychology, 43,* 251–258.

Kaplan, H.B. (1996). Toward an understanding of resilience: A critical review of definitions and models. In M.D. Glantz, J.L. Johnson, & L. Huffman (Eds.), *Resiliency and development: Positive life adaptations* (pp. 17–83). New York: Plenum.

Kashani, J.H., & Cantwell, D.P. (1983). Characteristics of children admitted to inpatient community mental health center. *Archives of General Psychiatry, 40,* 397–400.

Kashani, J.H., Jones, M., Bumby, B., & Thomas, L. (1999). Youth violence: Psychological risk factors, treatment, prevention, and recommendations. *Journal of Emotional and Behavioral Disorders, 7,* 200–210.

Kaslow, N.J., Deering, C.G., & Racusin, G.R. (1994). Depressed children and their families. *Clinical Psychology Review, 14,* 39–59.

Kaslow, N.J., & Thompson, M.P. (1998). Applying the criteria for empirically supported treatments to studies of psychosocial interventions for child and adolescent depression. *Journal of Clinical Child Psychology, 27,* 146–55.

Katon, W., Robinson, P., Von Korff, M., Lin, E., Bush, T., Ludman, E., Simon, G., & Walker, E. (1996). A multifaceted intervention to improve treatment of depression in primary care. *Archives of General Psychiatry, 53,* 924–932.

Katz-Leavy, J., Lourie, I., Stroul, B., & Zeigler-Dendy, C. (1992). *Individualized services in a system of care.* Washington, DC: Georgetown University, CASSP Technical Assistance Center.

Kauffman, J.M. (1997). *Characteristics of emotional and behavioral disorders of children and youth* (6th Ed.). Columbus, OH: Merrill.

Kauffman, J.M., Lloyd, J.W., Baker, J., & Reidel, T. (1995). Inclusion of all students with emotional or behavioral disorders? Let's think again. *Phi Delta Kappa, 76,* 542–546.

Kazdin, A.E. (1987). *Conduct disorders in childhood and adolescence.* London: Sage.

Kazdin, A.E. (1994). Interventions for aggressive and antisocial children. In L.D. Eron, J.H. Gentry, & P. Schlegel (Eds.), *Reason to hope: A psychological perspective on violence and youth* (pp. 341–382). Washington, DC: American Psychological Association.

Kazdin, A.E. (1996). Problem solving and parent management in treating aggressive and antisocial behavior. In E.D. Hibbs & P.S. Jensen (Eds.), *Psychosocial treatments for child and adolescent disorders: Empirically based strategies for clinical practice* (pp. 377–408). Washington, DC: American Psychological Association.

Kazdin, A.E. (1997). A model for developing effective treatments: Progression and interplay of theory, research, and practice. *Journal of Clinical Child Psychology, 26,* 114–129.

Kazdin, A.E. (2000). Developing a research agenda for child and adolescent psychotherapy research. *Archives of General Psychiatry, 57,* 829–835.

Kazdin, A.E., Bass, D., Ayers, W.A., & Rodgers, A. (1990). Empirical and clinical focus of child and adolescent psychotherapy research. *Journal of Consulting and Clinical Psychology, 58,* 729–740.

Kazdin, A.E., Bass, D., Siegel, T., & Thomas, C. (1989). Cognitive-behavioral therapy and relationship therapy in the treatment of children referred for antisocial behavior. *Journal of Consulting and Clinical Psychology, 57,* 522–535.

Kazdin, A.E., Siegel, T.C., & Bass, D. (1992). Cognitive problem solving skills therapy and parent management training in the treatment of antisocial behavior in children. *Journal of Consulting and Clinical Psychology, 60,* 733–747.

Kazdin, A.E., & Weisz, J.R. (1998). Identifying and developing empirically supported child and adolescent treatments. *Journal of Consulting and Clinical Psychology, 66,* 19–36.

Keane, T.M., Fairbank, J.A., Caddell, J.M., & Zimering, R.T. (1989). Implosive (flooding) therapy reduces symptoms of PTSD in Vietnam combat veterans. *Behavior Therapy, 20,* 245–260.

Keane, T.M., Fairbank, J.A., Caddell, J.M., Zimering, R.T., & Bender, M.E. (1985). A behavioral approach to assessing and treating posttraumatic stress disorder in Vietnam veterans. In C.R. Figley (Ed.), *Trauma and its wake: The study and treatment of posttraumatic stress disorder* (pp. 257–294). New York: Brunner/Mazel.

Keane, T.M., & Kaloupek, D.G. (1982). Imaginal flooding in the treatment of a posttraumatic disorder. *Journal of Consulting and Clinical Psychology, 50,* 138–140.

Keane, T.M., Zimering, R.T., & Caddell, J.M. (1985). A behavioral formulation of posttraumatic stress disorder in Vietnam veterans. *Behavior Therapist, 8,* 9–12.

Kelly, J.A., St. Lawrence, J.S., Diaz, Y.E., Stevenson, L.Y., Hauth, A.C., Brasfield, T.L., Kalichman, S.C., Smith, J.E., & Andrew, M.E. (1991). HIV risk behavior reduction following intervention with key opinion leaders of population: An experimental analysis. *American Journal of Public Health, 81,* 168–171.

Kendall, P.C. (1994). Treating anxiety disorders in children: Results of a randomized clinical trial. *Journal of Consulting and Clinical Psychology, 62,* 100–110.

Kendall, P.C., & Braswell, L. (1993). *Cognitive-behavioral therapy for impulsive children.* New York: Guilford Press.

Kendall, P.C., Flannery-Schroeder, E., Panichelli-Mindel, S.M., Southam-Gerow, M., Henin, A., & Warman, M. (1997). Therapy for youths with anxiety disorders: A second randomized clinical trial. *Journal of Consulting and Clinical Psychology, 65,* 366–380.

Kendall, P.C., & Southam-Gerow, M.A. (1996). Long-term follow-up of a cognitive-behavioral therapy for anxiety-disordered youth. *Journal of Consulting and Clinical Psychology, 64,* 724–730.

Kendziora, K., Bruns, E., Osher, D., Pacchiano, D., & Mejia, B. (2001). *Wraparound: Stories from the field. Systems of care: Promising practices in children's mental health,* Vol. I. Washington, DC: Center for Effective Collaboration and Practice, American Institutes for Research.

Kerr, M.M., & Nelson, C.M. (1989). *Strategies for managing behavior problems in the classroom* (2nd Ed.). Columbus, OH: Merrill.

Kilgus, M., Pumariega, A., & Cuffe, S. (1995). Influence of race on diagnosis in adolescent psychiatric inpatients. *Journal of American Academy of Child and Adolescent Psychiatry, 35,* 167–172.

Kilpatrick, D.G., Acierno, R., Resnick, H.S., Saunders, B.E., & Best, C.L. (1997). A 2-year longitudinal analysis of the relationships between violent assault and substance use in women. *Journal of Consulting and Clinical Psychology, 65,* 834–847.

Kilpatrick, D.G., Acierno, R., Schnurr, P.P., Saunders, B., Resnick, H.S., & Best, C.L. (2000). Risk factors for adolescent substance abuse and dependence: Data from a national sample. *Journal of Consulting and Clinical Psychology, 68,* 19–30.

Kilpatrick, D.G., Resnick, H.S., Saunders, B.E., & Best, C.L. (1998). Rape, other violence against women, and posttraumatic stress disorder: Critical issues in assessing the adversity-stress-psychopathology relationship. In B.P. Dohrenwend (Ed.), *Adversity, stress, and psychopathology* (pp. 161–176). New York: Oxford University Press.

Kilpatrick, D.G., Saunders, B.E., Amick-Mullan, A., Best, C., Veronen, L.J., & Resnick, H.S. (1989). Victim and crime factors associated with the development of crime-related post-traumatic stress disorder. *Behavior Therapy, 20,* 199–214.

Kilpatrick, D.G., Saunders, B.E., & Resnick, H.S. (1998). Violence history and comorbidity among a national sample of adolescents. Lake George Research Conference on Posttraumatic Stress Disorder Program, Bolton Landing, New York.

Kilpatrick, D.G., Saunders, B.E., Veronen, L.J., Best, C.L., & Von, J.M. (1987). Criminal victimization lifetime prevalence, reporting to police, and psychological impact. *Crime and Delinquency, 33,* 479–489.

Kilpatrick, D.G., & Veronen, L.J. (1983). Treatment for rape-related problems: Crisis intervention is not enough. In L.H. Cohen, W.L. Claiborn, & G.A. Specter (Eds.), *Crisis intervention*. New York: Human Sciences Press.

King, L.A., King, D., Fairbank, J.A., Keane, T.M., & Adams, G.A. (1998). Resilience/recovery factors in posttraumatic stress disorder among female and male Vietnam veterans: Hardiness, postwar social support, and additional stressful life events. *Journal of Personality and Social Psychology, 74*, 420–434.

King, N.J., Tonge, B. J., Heyne, D., Pritchard, M., Rollings, S., Young, D., Myerson, N., & Ollendick, T.H. (1998). Cognitive-behavioral treatment of school-refusing children: A controlled evaluation. *Journal of the American Academy of Child and Adolescent Psychiatry, 37*, 395–403.

King, N.J., Tonge, B.J., Mullen, P., Myerson, N., Heyne, D., Rollings, S., Martin, R., & Ollendick, T.H. (2000). Treating sexually abused children with posttraumatic stress symptoms: A randomized clinical trial. *Journal of the American Academy of Child and Adolescent Psychiatry, 39*, 1347–1355.

Kiresuk, T.J., Smith, A., & Cardillo, J.E. (Eds.) (1994). *Goal attainment scaling: Applications, theory and measurement*. Hillsdale, NJ: Lawrence Erlbaum.

Kisthardt, W.E., & Rapp, C.A. (1992). Bridging the gap between principles and practice: Implementing a strengths perspective in case management. In S.M. Rose (Ed.), *Case management and social work practice* (pp. 112–125). New York: Longman.

Klein, R.G. (1998). Clinical efficacy of methylphenidate in conduct disorder with and without attention-deficit/hyperactivity disorder. *Journal of the American Medical Association, 279*, 1073–1080.

Klein, R.G., & Abikoff, H. (1997). Behavior therapy and methylphenidate in the treatment of children with ADHD. *Journal of Attention Disorders, 2*, 89–114.

Klein, R.G., Abikoff, H., Klass, E., Ganeles, D., Seese, L.M., & Pollack, S. (1997). Clinical efficacy of methylphenidate in conduct disorder with and without attention deficit hyperactivity disorder. *Archives of General Psychiatry, 54*, 1073–1080.

Klein, R.G., Koplewicz, H.S., & Kanner, A. (1992). Imipramine treatment of children with separation anxiety disorder. *Journal of the American Academy of Child and Adolescent Psychiatry, 31*, 21–28.

Knitzer, J. (1982). *Unclaimed children: The failure of public responsibility to children and adolescents in need of mental health services*. Washington, DC: The Children's Defense Fund.

Knitzer, J. (1993). Children's mental health policy: Challenging the future. *Journal of Emotional and Behavioral Disorders, 1*, 8–16.

Knitzer, J., Steinberg, Z., & Fleisch, B. (1990). *At the schoolhouse door: An examination of programs and policies for children with behavioral and emotional problems*. New York: Bank Street College of Education.

Kondas, O. (1967). Reduction of examination anxiety and stage-fright by group desenitization and relaxation. *Behavior Research and Therapy, 5*, 275–281.

Koren, P.E., DeChilo, N., & Friesen, B.J. (1992). Measuring empowerment in families whose children have emotional disabilities: A brief questionnaire. *Rehabilitation Psychology, 37*, 305–321.

Koroloff, N.M., Elliott, D.J., Koren, P.E., & Friesen, B.J. (1990). Connecting low income families to mental health services: The role of the family associate. *Journal of Emotional and Behavioral Disorders, 2*, 240–246.

Koroloff, N.M., & Friesen, B. (1991). Support groups for parents of children with emotional disorders: A comparison of members and non-members. *Community Mental Health Journal, 27*, 265–279.

Koroloff, N.M., McManus, M.C., Pfohl, L., & Sturtevant, J. (1996). *How family members participate in policy-making: Legal advocacy models that work*. Presentation at Building on Family Strengths Conference, Research and Training Center on Family Support and Children's Mental Health, Portland, OR, April 11–13, 1996.

Koroloff, N.M., Stuntzner-Gibson, D., & Friesen, B.J. (1990). Statewide parent organization demonstration project. Final report: Portland, OR: Research & Training Center on Family Support and Children's Mental Health, Portland State University.

Kovacs, M. (1981). Rating scales to assess depression in school-aged children. *Acta Paedopsychiatrica, 46*, 305–315.

Kovacs, M. (1996). Presentation and course of major depressive disorder during childhood and later years of the life span. *Journal of the American Academy of Child and Adolescent Psychiatry, 35*, 705–715.

Kovacs, M., & Devlin, B. (1998). Internalizing disorders in childhood. *Journal of Child Psychology and Psychiatry and Allied Disciplines, 39*, 47–63.

Kumra, S., Frazier, J., Jacobsen, L., McKenna, K., Gordon, C., Lenane, M., Hamburger, S., Smith,

A., Albus, K., Alghband-Rad, J., & Rapaport J. (1996). Childhood onset schizophrenia: A double blind clozapine-haloperidol comparison. *Archives of General Psychiatry, 53,* 1090–1097.

Kutash, K., & Duchnowski, A.J. (1997). Create comprehensive and collaborative systems. *Journal of Emotional and Behavioral Disorders, 5,* 66–75.

Kutash, K., & Rivera, V.R. (1996a). Therapeutic foster care. *What works in children's mental health services? Uncovering answers to critical questions* (pp.69–87). Baltimore: Paul H. Brooks.

Kutash, K., & Rivera, V.R. (1996b). *What works in children's mental health services? Uncovering answers to critical questions.* Baltimore: Paul H. Brookes.

Laird, N., & Ware, J. (1982). Random effects models for longitudinal data. *Biometrics, 38,* 963–974.

Landrum, T.J., Singh, N.N., Nemil, M.S., Ellis, C.R., & Best, A.M. (1995). Characteristics of children and adolescents with serious emotional disturbance in systems of care. Part II: Community-based services. *Journal of Emotional and Behavioral Disorders, 3,* 141–149.

Landsverk, J., & Garland, A.F. (1999). Foster care and pathways to mental health services. In P.A. Curtis, G. Dale, & J.C. Kendall (Eds.), *The foster care crisis: Translating research into policy and practice. Child, youth and family services* (pp. 193–210). Lincoln: University of Nebraska Press.

Lang, P.J. (1977a). Imagery in therapy: An information processing analysis of fear. *Behavior therapy, 8,* 862–886.

Lang, P.J. (1977b). The psychophysiology of anxiety. In H. Akiskal (Ed.), *Psychiatric diagnosis: Exploration of biological criteria.* New York: Spectrum.

Larner, M., & Halpern, R. (1987). Lay home visiting programs: Strengths, tensions, and challenges. *Zero to three: Bulletin of the National Center for Clinical Infant Programs, 8,* 1–7.

Last, C.G., Hansen, C., & Franco, N. (1998). Cognitive-behavioral treatment of school phobia. *Journal of the American Academy of Child and Adolescent Psychiatry, 37,* 404–411.

Lazarus, R., & Folkman, S. (1984). *Stress, appraisal, and coping.* New York: Springer.

Leaf, P.J., Alegria, M., Cohen, P., Goodman, S.H., Horwitz, S.M., Hoven, C.W., Narrow, W.E., Vaden-Kiernan, M., & Regier, D.A. (1996). Mental health service use in the community and schools: Results from the four-community MECA study. *Journal of the American Academy of Child and Adolescent Psychiatry, 35,* 889–897.

Leginski, W., Randolph, F., & Rog, D.J. (1999). How well are we evaluating system change? *Psychiatric Services, 50,* 1257.

Leonard, H.L., Swedo, S.E., Lenane, M.C., Rettew, D.C., Cheslow, D.L., Hamburger, S.D., & Rapoport, J.L. (1991). A double-blind desipramine substitution during long-term clomipramine treatment in children and adolescents with obsessive-compulsive disorder. *Archives of General Psychiatry, 48,* 922–927.

Leonard, H.L., Swedo, S.E., Lenane, M.C., Rettew, D.C., Hamburger, S.D., Bartko, J.J., & Rapoport, J.L. (1993). A 2- to 7-year follow-up study of 54 obsessive-compulsive children and adolescents. *Archives of General Psychiatry, 50,* 429–439.

Leonard, H.L., Swedo, S.E., Rapoport, J.L., Koby, E.V., Lenane, M.C., Cheslow, D.L., & Hamburger, S.D. (1989). Treatment of obsessive-compulsive disorder with clomipramine and desipramine in children and adolescents. *Archives of General Psychiatry, 46,* 1088–1092.

Lewinsohn, P.M., Hops, H., Roberts, R.E., Seeley, J.R., & Andrews, J.A. (1993). Adolescent psychopathology: I. Prevalence and incidence of depression and other DSM-III-R disorders in high school students. *Journal of Abnormal Psychology, 102,* 133–144.

Lewis, D.O., Pincus, J.H., Bard, B., Richardson, E., Prichep, L.S., Feldman, M., & Yeager, C. (1988). Neuropsychiatric, psychoeducational, and family characteristics of 14 juveniles condemned to death in the United States. *American Journal of Psychiatry, 145,* 584–589.

Lewis, S. (1974). A comparison of behavior therapy techniques in the reduction of fearful avoidance behavior. *Behavior Therapy, 5,* 648–655.

Liddle, B., & Spence, S.H. (1990). Cognitive-behaviour therapy with depressed primary school children: A cautionary note. *Behavioural Psychotherapy, 18,* 85–102.

Liddle, H.A. (1996). Family-based treatment for adolescent problem behaviors: Overview of contemporary developments and introduction to the special section. *Journal of Family Psychology, 10,* 3–11.

Lightdale, J., & Heyman, M. (1999). Secretin: Cure or snake oil for autism in the new millennium? *Journal of Pediatric Gastroenterology and Nutrition, 29,* 114–115.

Linden, M., Habib, T., & Radojevic, V. (1996). A controlled study of the effects of EEG biofeedback on cognition and behavior of children with attention deficit disorder and learning disabilities. *Biofeedback and Self Regulation, 21,* 35–49.

Lin, K., Poland, R., & Nakasaki, G. (Eds.). (1993). *Psychopharmacology and psychobiology of ethnicity.* Washington, DC: American Psychiatric Press.

Lipsey, M.W. (1988). Juvenile delinquency intervention. In H.S. Bloom, D.S. Cordray, & R.J. Light

(Eds.), *Lessons from selected program and policy areas: New directions for program evaluation*, No. 37, (pp. 83–127). San Francisco, Jossey-Bass.

Lochman, J.E., Coie, J.D., Underwood, M.K., & Terry, R. (1993). Effectiveness of a social relations intervention program for aggressive and nonaggressive, rejected children. *Journal of Consulting and Clinical Psychology, 61,* 1053–1058.

Lochman, J.E., Lampron, L.B., Gemmer, T.C., Harris, S.R., & Wyckoff, G.M. (1989). Teacher consultation and cognitive-behavioral interventions with aggressive boys. *Psychology in the Schools, 26,* 179–188.

Loeber, R. (1982). The stability of antisocial and delinquent child behavior: A review. *Child Development, 53,* 1431–1446.

Loeber, R., & Farrington, D.P. (1997). Stratagies and yields of longitudinal studies on antisocial behavior. In D.M. Stoff, J. Breiling, & J.D. Maser (Eds.), *Handbook of antisocial behavior* (pp. 125–139). New York: John Wiley & Sons.

Loeber, R., & Farrington, D.P. (Eds.). (1998). *Serious and violent juvenile offenders: Risk factors and successful interventions.* Thousand Oaks, CA: Sage.

Loeber, R., Keenan, K., & Zhang, Q. (1997). Boys' experimentation and persistence in developmental pathways toward serious delinquency. *Journal of Child and Family Studies, 6,* 321–357.

Loeber, R., & Stouthamer-Loeber, M. (1998). Development of juvenile aggression and violence: Some common misconceptions and controversies. *American Psychologist, 53,* 242–259.

Loney, J. (1988). *Adolescent drug abuse: Analyses of treatment research.* Rockville, MD: National Institute on Drug Abuse.

Long, N., Rickert, V.I., & Ashcraft, E.W. (1993). Bibliotherapy as an adjunct to stimulant medication in the treatment of attention-deficit hyperactivity disorder. *Journal of Pediatric Health Care, 7,* 82–88.

Lonigan, C.J., Elbert, J.C., & Johnson, S.B. (1998). Empirically supported psychosocial interventions for children: An overview. *Journal of Clinical Child Psychology, 27,* 138–145.

Lourie, I.S., Stroul, B.A., & Friedman, R.M. (1998). Community-based systems of care: From advocacy to outcomes. In M.H. Epstein, K. Kutash, and A.J. Duchnowski (Eds.), *Outcomes for children and youth with behavioral and emotional disorders and their families: Programs and evaluation best practices.* (pp. 3–19). Austin, TX: Pro-Ed.

Luk, E.S., Staiger, P., Mathai, J., Field, D., & Adler, R. (1998). Comparison of treatments of persistent conduct problems in primary school children: A preliminary evaluation of a modified cognitive-behavioural approach. *Australian and New Zealand Journal of Psychiatry, 32,* 379–386.

Lutzer, V.D. (1987). An educational and peer support group for mothers of pre-schoolers at risk for behavior disorders. *Journal of Primary Prevention, 14,* 1–16.

MacMillan, D., Gresham, F., & Forness, S. (1996). Full inclusion: An empirical perspective. *Behavioral Disorders, 21,* 145–159.

Maercker, A., Schutzwohl, M., & Solomon, Z. (Eds.) (1999). *Posttraumatic stress disorder: Lifespan developmental perspective.* Seattle: Hogrefe & Huber.

Mailick Seltzer, M., Ivry, J., & Litchfield, L.C. (1992). Family members as case managers: Partnership between the formal and infomal support networks. In S.M. Rose (Ed.), *Case management and social work practice* (pp. 229–242). New York: Longman.

Maisto, A.A., Wolfe, W., & Jordan, J. (1999) Short-term motivational therapy. In P.J. Ott, R.E. Tarter, & R.T. Ammerman (Eds.), *Sourcebook on substance abuse: Etiology, epidemiology, and treatment.* Boston: Allyn & Bacon.

Malouf, D.B., & Schiller, E.P. (1995). Practice and research in special education. *Exceptional Children, 61,* 414–424.

Mandoki, M., Tapia, M.R., Tapia, M.A., Summer, G., & Parker, J.L. (1997). Venlafaxine in the treatment of children and adolescents with major depression. *Psychopharmacological Bulletin, 33,* 149–154.

Manos, M.J., Short, E.J., & Findling, R.L. (1999). Differential effectiveness of methylphenidate and Adderall in school-age youths with attention-deficit/hyperactivity disorder. *Journal of the American Academy of Child and Adolescent Psychiatry, 38,* 813–819.

March, J. (1999). Multi-site trial in adolescent depression: Purpose, design, and methods. In B. Vitiello, E. Hibbs, & K. Hoagwood (Co-Chairs), *New NIMH-sponsored studies: How to address public health needs.* Symposium conducted at the annual meeting of the New Clinical Drug Evaluation Unit, Boca Raton, FL.

March, J., Amaya-Jackson, L., Murray, M.C., & Schulte, A. (1998a). Cognitive-behavioral psychotherapy for children and adolescents with posttraumatic stress disorder after a single-incident stressor. *Journal of the American Academy of Child and Adolescent Psychiatry, 37,* 585–593.

March, J., Biederman, J., Wolkow, R., Safferman, A., Mardekian, J., Cook, E., Cutler, N., Dominguez,

R., Ferguson, J., Muller, B., Riesenberg, R., Rosenthal, M., Sallee, F., & Wagner, K. (1998b). Sertraline in children and adolescents with obsessive-compulsive disorder: A multicenter randomized controlled trial. *Journal of the American Medical Association, 280,* 1752–1756.

March, J., Parker, J., Sullivan, K., Stallings, P., & Conners, C. (1997). The Multidimensional Anxiety Scale for Children (MASC): Factor structure, reliability, and validity. *Journal of the American Academy of Child and Adolescent Psychiatry, 36,* 554–565.

Marks, I.M., Lovell, K., Noshirvani, H., Livanou, M., & Thrasher, S. (1998). Treatment of posttraumatic stress disorder by exposure and/or cognitive restructuring: A controlled study. *Archives of General Psychiatry, 55,* 317–325.

Marlatt, G.A., & Gordon, J.R. (Eds.). (1985). *Relapse prevention.* New York: Guilford Press.

Masi, G., Sbrana, B., Poli, P., Tomaiuolo, F., Favilla, L., & Marcheschi, M. (2000). Depression and school functioning in non-referred adolescents: A pilot study. *Child Psychiatry and Human Development, 30,* 161–171.

Masimirembwa, C., & Hasler, J. (1997). Genetic polymorphism of drug metabolizing enzymes in African populations: Implications for the use of neuroleptics and antidepressants. *Brain Research Bulletin, 44,* 561–571.

Maslow, A. (1970). *Motivation in personality.* New York: Harper & Row.

Masten, A.S. (1986). Humor and competence in school-age children. *Child Development, 57,* 461–73.

McCabe, K., Yeh, M., Hough, R.L., Landsverk, J., Hurlburt, M.S., Culver, S.W., & Reynolds, B. (1999). Racial/ethnic representation across five public sectors of care for youth. *Journal of Emotional and Behavioral Disorders, 7,* 72–82.

McCaffrey, R.J., & Fomeris, C.A. (1997). Adolescent substance abuse: A biopsychosocial perspective. In H.W. Reese & M.D. Franzen (Eds.), *Biological and neuropsychological mechanisms* (pp. 199–214). Mahwah, NJ: Lawrence Erlbaum.

McClellan, J.M., & Werry, J.S. (1994). Practice parameters for the assessment and treatment of children and adolescents with schizophrenia. *Journal of the American Academy of Child and Adolescent Psychiatry, 33,* 616–635.

McCord, J., Tremblay, R., Vitaro, F., & Desmarais-Gervais, L. (1994). Boys' disruptive behaviour, school adjustment, and delinquency: The Montreal prevention experiment. *International Journal of Behavioral Development, 17,* 739–752.

McDougle, C. (1998). Psychopharmacology. In D. Cohen & F. Volkmar (Eds.), *Handbook of autism and pervasive developmental disorders* (pp. 707–729). New York: John Wiley & Sons.

McFarlane, A.C. (1998). Epidemiological evidence about the relationship between PTSD and alcohol abuse: The nature of the association. *Addictive Behaviors, 6,* 813–825.

McFarlane, A.C., & Potts, N. (1999). Posttraumatic stress disorder: Prevalence and risk factors relative to disasters. In P.A. Saigh & J.D. Bremner (Eds.), *Posttraumatic stress disorder: A comprehensive text* (pp. 92–102). Boston: Allyn & Bacon.

McFarlane, W. (1990). Multiple family groups and the treatment of schizophrenia. In H. Nasrallah (Ed.), *Handbook of schizophrenia.* Amsterdam: Elsevier.

McManus, M.C., Reilly, L.M., Rinkin, J.L., & Wrigley, J.A. (1993). *An advocate's approach to abolishing custody relinquishment requirements for families whose children have disabilities: The Oregon experience.* Salem, OR: Oregon Family Support Network.

McMiller, W.P., & Weisz, J.R. (1996). Help-seeking preceding mental health clinic intake among African-American, Latino, and Caucasian youths. *Journal of American Academy of Child and Adolescent Psychiatry, 35,* 1086–1094.

McQuaide, S., & Ehrenreich, J.H. (1997). Assessing client strengths. *Families in Society: The Journal of Contemporary Human Services,* Mar/Apr, 201–212.

Meadowcroft, P., Thomlison, B., & Chamberlain, P. (1994). Treatment foster care services: A research agenda for child welfare. *Child Welfare, 33,* 565–581.

Menzies, R.G., & Clarke, J.C. (1993). A comparison of in vivo and vicarious exposure in the treatment of childhood water phobia. *Behavior Research and Therapy, 31,* 9–15.

Meyers, J., Kaufman, M., & Goldman, S. (1999). *Promising practices: Training strategies for serving children with serious emotional disturbance and their families in a system of care. Systems of Care: Promising Practices in Children's Mental Health, 1998 Series,* Vol. V. Washington DC: Center for Effective Collaboration and Practice, American Institutes for Research.

Miller, L.C., Barrett, C.L., Hampe, E., & Noble, H. (1972). Comparison of reciprocal inhibition, psychotherapy, and waiting list control for phobic children. *Journal of Abnormal Psychology, 79,* 269–279.

Miller, M., & Diao, J. (1987). Family friends: New resources for psychosocial care of chronically ill children in families. *Children's Health Care, 15,* 259–264.

Miller, W.R., & Rollnick, S. (1991). *Motivational interviewing: Preparing people to change addictive behavior.* New York: Guilford Press.

Minuchin, P.P. (1985). Families and individual development: Provocations from the field of family therapy. *Child Development, 56,* 289–302.

Minuchin, S. (1974). *Families and family therapy.* Cambridge, MA: Harvard University Press.

Moreau, D.L., Weissman, M., & Warner, V. (1989). Panic disorder in children at high risk for depression. *American Journal of Psychiatry, 146,* 1059–1060.

Morgan, D.P., & Jenson, W.R. (1988). *Teaching behaviorally disordered students: Preferred practices.* Columbus, OH: Merrill.

Morrissey, J.P., Johnsen, M.C., & Calloway, M.O. (1998). Methods for system-level evaluations of child mental health service networks. In M.H. Epstein, K. Kutash, & A.J. Duchnowski (Eds.), *Outcomes for children and youth with behavioral and emotional disorders and their families: Programs and evaluation best practices* (pp. 297–324). Austin, TX: Pro-Ed.

MTA Cooperative Group. (1999a). A fourteen-month randomized clinical trial of treatment strategies for attention deficit hyperactivity disorder. *Archives of General Psychiatry, 56,* 1073–1086.

MTA Cooperative Group. (1999b). Moderators and mediators of treatement response for children with attention deficit/hyperactivity disorder. *Archives of General Psychiatry, 56,* 1088–1096.

Mueser, K.T., Drake, R.E., & Noordsy, D.L. (1998). Integrated mental health and substance abuse treatment for severe psychiatric disorders. *Journal of the Practice of Psychiatry and Behavioral Health, 4,* 129–139.

Munger, R.L. (1993). *Changing children's behavior quickly.* Lanham, MD: Madison Books.

Munger, R.L. (1998). *The ecology of troubled children.* Cambridge, MA: Brookline Books.

Murdoch, D., & McTavish, D. (1992). Sertraline: A review of its psychodynamic and pharmacokinetic properties, and therapeutic potential in depression and obsessive-compulsive disorders. *Drugs, 44,* 604–624.

Muris, P., Merckelbach, H., Holdrinet, I., & Sijsenaar, M. (1998). Treating phobic children: Effects of EMDR versus exposure. *Journal of Consulting and Clinical Psychology, 66,* 193–198.

Murphy, C.M., & Bootzin, R.R. (1973). Active and passive participation in the contact desensitization of snake fear in children. *Behavior Therapy, 4,* 203–211.

Myaard, M.J., Crawford, C., Jackson, M., & Alessi, G. (2000). Applying behavior analysis within the wraparound process: A multiple baseline study. *Journal of Emotional and Behavioral Disorders, 8,* 216–229.

Najavits, L.M. (1999). Seeking safety: A new cognitive-behavioral therapy for PTSD and substance abuse. *NC-PTSD Clinical Quarterly, 8,* 40–45.

Najavits, L.M., Weiss, R.D., & Liese, B.S. (1996). Group cognitive-behavioral therapy for women with PTSD and substance use disorder. *Journal of Substance Abuse Treatment, 13,* 13–22.

Najavits, L.M., Weiss, R.D., Shaw, S.R., & Muenz, L.R. (1998). "Seeking Safety": Outcome of a new cognitive-behavioral therapy for women with post-traumatic stress disorder and substance dependence. *Journal of Traumatic Stress, 11,* 437–456.

National Advisory Mental Health Council. (1999). *Bridging science and service: A report by the National Advisory Mental Health Council Clinical Treatment and Services Workgroup.* Bethesda, MD: National Institute of Mental Health.

National Advisory Mental Health Council. (2001). *Blueprint for change: Research on child and adolescent mental health: Workgroup on Child and Adolescent Mental Health Intervention Development and Deployment.* Washington, DC.

National Institutes of Health Consensus Statement. (1998). Diagnosis and treatment of attention deficit hyperactivity disorder (ADHD) [on-line]. Available: http://odp.od.nih.gov/consensus/cons/110/110_statement.htm.

Nelson, C.M., & Pearson, C.A. (1991). *Integrating services for children and youth with behavioral disorders.* Reston, VA: Council for Exceptional Children.

Newman, E., Riggs, D.S., & Roth, S. (1997). Thematic resolution, PTSD, and complex PTSD: The relationship between meaning and trauma-related diagnoses. *Journal of Traumatic Stress, 10,* 197–213.

Nolan, E.E., & Gadow, K.D. (1997). Children with ADHD and tic disorder and their classmates: Behavioral normalization with methylphenidate. *Journal of the American Academy of Child and Adolescent Psychiatry, 36,* 597–604.

Norris, F.H., & Murrell, S.A. (1990). Social support, life events, and stress as modifiers of adjustment to bereavement by older adults. *Psychology and Aging, 5,* 429–436.

Obler, M., & Terwilliger, R.F. (1970). Pilot study on the effectiveness of systematic desensitization with neurologically impaired children with phobic disorders. *Journal of Consulting and Clinical Psychology, 34,* 314–318.

Olds, D.L., Eckenrode, J., Henderson, C.R., Kitzman, H., Powers, J., Cole, R., & Sidora, K. (1997). Long-term effects of home visitation on maternal life course and child abuse and neglect: Fifteen-year follow-up of a randomized trial. *Journal of the American Medical Association, 278,* 637–643.

Ollendick, T.H., & Hersen, M. (1993). Child behavioral assessment. In T. Ollendick & M. Hersen (Eds.), *Handbook of child and adolescent assessment* (pp. 3–14). Needham Heights, MA: Allyn & Bacon.

Ollendick, T.H., & King, N.J. (1998). Empirically supported treatments for children with phobic and anxiety disorders. *Journal of Clinical Child Psychology, 27,* 56–167.

Ollendick, T.H., Lease, C.A., & Cooper, C. (1993). Separation anxiety in young adults: A preliminary examination. *Journal of Anxiety Disorders, 7,* 293–305.

Olson, D.H., Portner, J., & Lavee, Y. (1985). *Family Adaptability and Cohesion Scales III.* St. Paul, MN: University of Minnesota, Family Social Science Department.

O'Malley, P.M., Johnston, L.D., & Bachman, J.G. (1999). Epidemiology of substance abuse in adolescence. In P.J. Ott, R.E. Tarter, & R.Y. Ammerman (Eds.), *Sourcebook on substance abuse: Etiology, epidemiology, assessment, and treatment.* Boston: Allyn & Bacon.

Osher, T., deFur, E., Nava, C., Spencer, S., & Toth-Dennis, D. (1999). New roles for families in systems of care. *Systems of Care: Promising Practices in Children's Mental Health, 1998 Series,* Vol. I. Washington, D.C.: Center for Effective Collaboration and Practice, American Institutes for Research.

Ouimette, P.C., Moos, R.F., & Finney, J.W. (2000). Two-year mental health service use and course of remission in patients with substance use and posttraumatic stress disorders. *Journal of Studies on Alcohol, 61,* 247–253.

Oxman, A.D., Thomson, M.A., Davis, D.A., & Haynes, R.B. (1995). No magic bullets: A systematic review of 102 trials of interventions to improve professional practice. *Canadian Medical Association Journal, 153,* 1423–1431.

Patterson, G.R. (1982). A social learning approach to family intervention: III. *Coercive family process.* Eugene, OR: Castalia.

Patterson, G.R., Dishion, T.J., & Chamberlain, P. (1993). Outcomes and methodological issues relating to the treatment of antisocial children. In T.R.Giles (Ed.), *Handbook of effective psychotherapy* (pp. 43–88). New York: Plenum.

Patterson, G.R., & Guillion, M.E. (1968). *Living with children: New methods for parents and teachers.* Champaign, IL: Research Press.

Patterson, G.R., Reid, J.B., & Dishion, T.J. (1992). *A Social Learning Approach: IV. Antisocial Boys.* Eugene, OR: Castalia.

Peacock Hill Working Group. (1991). Problems and promises in special education and related services for children and youth with emotional or behavioral disorders. *Behavioral Disorders, 16,* 299–313.

Pearce, C.M., Martin, G., & Wood, K. (1995). Significance of touch for perceptions of parenting and psychological adjustment among adolescents. *Journal of the American Academy of Child and Adolescent Psychiatry, 34,* 160–167.

Pelham, W.E., Carlson, C.L., Sams, S.E., Vallano, G., Dixon, M.J., & Hoza, B. (1993). Separate and combined effects of methylphenidate and behavior modification on boys with attention deficit–hyperactivity disorder in the classroom. *Journal of Consulting and Clinical Psychology, 61,* 506–515.

Pelham, W.E., & Murphy, H. (1986). Attention deficit and conduct disorders. In M. Hersen (Ed.), *Pharmacological and behavioral treatment: An integrated approach* (pp. 108–148). New York: John Wiley & Sons.

Pelham, W.E., Wheeler, T., & Chronis, A. (1998). Empirically supported psychosocial treatments for attention-deficit hyperactivity disorder. *Journal of Clinical Child Psychology, 27,* 190–205.

Penk, W.E., Peck, R.F., Robinowitz, R., Bell, W.E., & Little, D. (1988). Coping and defending styles among Vietnam combat veterans seeking treatment for posttraumatic stress disorder and substance use disorder. *Recent Developments in Alcoholism, 6,* 69–88.

Perkonigg, A., & Wittchen H. (1999). Prevalence and comorbidity of traumatic stress events and posttraumatic stress disorder in adolescents and young adults. In A. Maercker, M. Schutzwohl, & Z. Solomon (Eds.), *Posttraumatic stress disorder: A lifespan developmental perspective.* Seattle: Hogrefe & Huber.

Perrin, S., Smith, P., & Yule, W. (2000). Practitioner review: The assessment and treatment of posttraumatic stress disorder in children and adolescents. *Journal of Child Psychology and Psychiatry, 41,* 277–289.

Perry, R., & Bangaru, B. (1998). Secretin in autism. *Journal of Child and Adolescent Psychopharmacology, 8,* 247–248.

Perry, R., Pataki, C., Munoz-Silva, D., Armenteros, J., & Silva, R. (1997). Risperidone in children and adolescents with pervasive developmental disorder: Pilot trial and follow-up. *Journal of Child and Adolescent Psychopharmacology, 7,* 167–179.

Pfiffner, L.J., & McBurnett, K. (1997). Social skills training with parent generalization: Treatment effects for children with attention deficit disorder. *Journal of Consulting and Clinical Psychology, 65,* 749–57.

Pickrel, S.G., & Henggeler, S.W. (1999). *Village Early Intervention Project (VEIP) executive summary.* Unpublished document, Charleston, SC: Family Services Research Center, Medical University of South Carolina.

Pine, D.S. (1997). Childhood anxiety disorders. *Current Opinion in Pediatrics, 9,* 329–38.

Pine, D.S., Cohen, P., Gurley, D., Brook, J., & Ma, Y. (1998). The risk for early-adulthood anxiety and depressive disorders in adolescents with anxiety and depressive disorders. *Archives of General Psychiatry, 55,* 56–64.

Pisterman, S., McGrath, P., Firestone, P., Goodman, J.T., Webster, I., & Mallory, R. (1989). Outcome of parent-mediated treatment of preschoolers with attention deficit disorder with hyperactivity. *Journal of Consulting and Clinical Psychology, 57,* 628–635.

Popper, C., & Zimnitzky, B. (1995). Child and adolescent psychopharmacology update: January, 1994–December, 1994. *Journal of Child and Adolescent Psychopharmacology, 5,* 1–40.

Porges, S.W. (1997). Emotion: An evolutionary by-product of the neural regulation of the autonomic nervous system. In C.S. Carter, B. Kirkpatrick, & I.I. Lederhendler (Eds.), *The integrative neurobiology of affiliation* (pp. 62–77). New York: New York Academy of Sciences.

Poznanski, E.O., Grossman, J.A., Buchsbaum, Y., Banegas, M., Freeman, L., & Gibbons, R. (1984). Preliminary studies of the reliability and validity of the Children's Depression Rating Scale. *Journal of the American Academy of Child and Adolescent Psychiatry, 23,* 191–197.

Preskorn, S.H., Weller, E.B., Hughes, C.W., Weller, R.A., & Bolte, K. (1987). Depression in prepubertal children: Dexamethasone nonsuppression predicts differential response to imipramine vs. placebo. *Psychopharmacology Bulletin, 23,* 128–133.

Prochaska, J.O., & DiClemente, C.C. (1982). *The transtheoretical approach: Crossing traditional boundaries of change.* Homewood, IL: Dorsey Press.

Prochaska, J.O., & DiClemente, C.C. (1983). Stages and processes of self-change of smoking: Toward an integrated model of change. *Journal of Consulting and Clinical Psychology, 51,* 390–395.

Prochaska, J.O., DiClemente, C.C., & Norcross, J.C. (1992). In search of how people change: Applications to addictive behaviors. *American Psychologist, 47,* 1102–1114.

Project MATCH Research Group. (1997). Matching alcoholism treatments to client heterogeneity: Project MATCH posttreatment drinking outcomes. *Journal of Studies on Alcohol, 58,* 7–29.

Puig-Antich, J., Perel, J.M., Lupatkin, W., Chambers, W.J., Tabrizi, M.A., King, J., Goetz, R., Davies, M., & Stiller, R.L. (1987). Imipramine in prepubertal major depressive disorders. *Archives of General Psychiatry, 44,* 81–89.

Pumariega, A., Muller, B., & Rivers-Buckeley, N. (1982). Acute renal failure secondary to amoxapine overdose. *Journal of the American Medical Association, 282,* 3141–3142.

Pumariega, A., Nace, D., England, M., Diamond, J., Mattson, A., Fallon, T., Hansen, G., Lourie, I., Marx, L., Thurber, D., Winters, N., Graham, M., & Weigand, D. (1997). Community-based systems approach to children's managed mental health services. *Journal of Child and Family Studies, 6,* 149–164.

Quinn, K.P., & Epstein, M.H. (1998). Characteristics of children, youth and families served by local interagency systems of care. In M.H. Epstein, K. Kutash, & A.J. Duchnowski (Eds.), *Outcomes for children and youth with behavioral and emotional disorders and their families: Programs and evaluation best practices* (pp. 81–114). Austin, TX: Pro-Ed.

Quinn, M.M., Kavale, K.A., Mathur, S.R., Rutherford, R.B., & Forness, S.R. (1999). A meta-analysis of social skill interventions for students with emotional or behavioral disorders. *Journal of Emotional and Behavioral Disorders, 7,* 54–64.

Rao, U., Ryan, N.D., Birmaher, B., Dahl, R.E., Williamson, D.E., Kaufman, J., Rao, R., & Nelson, B. (1995). Unipolar depression in adolescents: Clinical outcome in adulthood. *Journal of the American Academy of Child and Adolescent Psychiatry, 34,* 566–578.

Rapoport, J., Buchsbaum, M., Weingartner, H., Zahn, P., Ludlow, C., & Mikkelsen, E. (1980). Dextroamphetamine: Cognitive and behavioral effects in normal and hyperactive boys and normal men. *Archives of General Psychiatry, 37,* 933–943.

Rapoport, J., Mikkelsen, E., Zavadil, A., Nee, L., Gruenau, C., Mendelson, W., & Gillin, J. (1980). Childhood enuresis, II: Psychopathology, tricyclic concentration in plasma, and antienuretic effect. *Archives of General Psychiatry, 37,* 1146–1152.

Rappaport, J. (1981). In praise of paradox: A social policy of empowerment over prevention. *American Journal of Community Psychology, 9,* 1–25.

Rappaport, J. (1987). Terms of empowerment/exemplars of prevention: Toward a theory for community psychology. *American Journal of Community Psychology, 15,* 121–148.

Rapport, M.D., Denney, C., DuPaul, G.J., & Gardner, M.J. (1994). Attention deficit disorder and methylphenidate: Normalization rates, clinical effectiveness, and response prediction in 76 children. *Journal of the American Academy of Child and Adolescent Psychiatry, 33,* 882–893.

Rapport, M.D., DuPaul, G., & Kelly, K. (1989). Attention deficit hyperactivity disorder and methylphenidate: The relationship between gross body weight and drug responses in children. *Psychopharmacology Bulletin, 25,* 285–290.

Reich, W., Welner, Z., & Herjanic, B. (1994). *Diagnostic Interview for Children and Adolescents, Revised (for DSM-IV) Computer Program: Child/Adolescent Version and Parent Version.* North Tonawanda, NY: Multi-Health Systems.

Reid, J.B., & Eddy, J.M. (1997). The prevention of antisocial behavior: Some considerations in the search for effective interventions. In D.M. Stoff, J. Breiling, & J.D. Maser (Eds.), *Handbook of antisocial behavior* (pp. 343–356). New York: John Wiley & Sons.

Remschmidt, H., Schulz, E., Martin, M., Warnke, A., & Trott, G. (1994). Childhood onset schizophrenia: History of the concept and recent studies. *Psychopharmacology Bulletin, 20,* 713–725.

The Research Unit on Pediatric Psychopharmacology Anxiety Study Group. (2001). Fluvoxamine for the treatment of anxiety disorders in children and adolescents. *New England Journal of Medicine, 344,* 1279–1285.

Resnick, H.S., Kilpatrick, D.G., & Lipovsky, J.A. (1991). Assessment of rape-related posttraumatic stress disorder: Stressor and symptom dimensions. *Psychological Assessment, 3,* 561–572.

Resick, P.A., Jordan, C.G., Girelli, S.A., Hutter, C.K., & Marhoefer-Dvorak, S. (1988). A comparative outcome study of behavioral group therapy for sexual assault victims. *Behavior Therapy, 19,* 385–401.

Resick, P.A., & Schnicke, M.K. (1992). Cognitive processing therapy for sexual assault victims. *Journal of Consulting and Clinical Psychology, 60,* 748–56.

Resick, P.A., & Schnicke, M.K. (Eds.) (1993). *Cognitive processing therapy for rape victims.* Newbury Park, CA: Sage.

Rhodes, J.E., Contreras, J.M., & Mangelsdorf, S.C. (1994). Natural mentor relationships among Latina adolescent mothers: Psychological adjustment, moderating processes, and the role of early parental acceptance. *American Journal of Community Psychology, 22,* 211–227.

Rhodes, J.E., & Jason, L.A. (1990). A social stress model of substance abuse. *Journal of Consulting and Clinical Psychology, 58,* 395–401.

Riddle, M.A., Bernstein, G., Cook, E., Leonard, H., March, J., & Swanson, J. (1999). Anxiolytics, adrenergic agents, and naltrexone. *Journal of the American Academy of Child and Adolescent Psychiatry, 38,* 546–556.

Riddle, M.A., Reeve, E.A., Yaryura-Tobias, J.A., Yang, H.M., Claghorn, J.L., Gaffney, G., Greist, J.H., Holland, D., McConville, B.J., Pigott, T., & Walkup, J.T. (2001). Fluvoxamine for children and adolescents with obsessive-compulsive disorder: A randomized, controlled, multicenter trial. *Journal of the American Academy of Child and Adolescent Psychiatry, 40,* 222–229.

Riddle, M.A., Scahill, L., King, R.A., Hardin, M.T., Anderson, G.M., Ort, S.I., Smith, J.C., Leckman, J.F., & Cohen, D.J. (1992). Double-blind, crossover trial of fluoxetine and placebo in children and adolescents with obsessive-compulsive disorder. *Journal of the American Academy of Child and Adolescent Psychiatry, 31,* 1062–1069.

Ritter, B. (1968). The group desensitization of children's snake phobias using vicarious and contact desensitization procedures. *Behavior Research and Therapy, 6,* 1–6.

Robins, L.N., & Radcliff, K.S. (1980). Childhood conduct disorders and later arrest. In L.N. Robins, P.J. Clayton, & J.K. Wing (Eds.), *The social consequences of psychiatric illness* (pp. 248–263). New York: Brunner/Mazel.

Rogers, T., Bauman, L., & Metzger, L. (1985). An assessment of the Reach-to-Recovery Program. *CA—A cancer journal for clinicians, 35,* 116–124.

Rogers, S.J. (1998). Empirically supported comprehensive treatments for young children with autism. *Journal of Clinical Child Psychology, 27,* 168–179.

Rohde, P., Lewinsohn, P.M., & Seeley, J.R. (1996). Psychiatric comorbidity with problematic alcohol use in high school students. *Journal of the American Academy of Child and Adolescent Psychiatry, 35,* 101–109.

Rones M., & Hoagwood, K. (2000). School-based mental health services: A research review. *Clinical Child and Family Psychology Review, 3,* 223–241.

Rose, S.M. (1992). *Case management and social work practice.* New York: Longman.

Rosen, L., Heckman, M., Carro, M., & Burchard, J. (1994). Satisfaction, involvement and unconditional care: The perceptions of children and adolescents receiving wraparound services. *Jour-*

nal of Child and Family Studies, 3, 55–67.

Rosenberg, D., Holttum, S., & Gershon, S. (1994). *Psychostimulant textbook of pharmacotherapy for child and adolescent psychiatric disorders* (pp. 19–50). New York: Brunner/Mazel.

Rosenblatt, A. (1998). Assessing the child and family outcomes of systems of care for youth with serious emotional disturbance. In M.H. Epstein, K. Kutash, & A.J. Duchnowski (Eds.), *Outcomes for children and youth with behavioral and emotional disorders and their families* (pp. 329–362). Austin, TX: Pro-Ed.

Rosenblatt, A., & Attkisson, C.C. (1992). Integrating systems of care in California for youth with severe emotional disturbance. I: A descriptive overview of the California AB377 evaluation project. *Journal of Child and Family Studies, 1,* 93–113.

Rosenblatt, A., & Attkisson, C.C. (1993). Assessing outcomes for sufferers of severe mental disorder: A review and conceptual framework. *Evaluation and Program Planning, 16,* 347–363.

Rossi, P., & Freeman, H. (1993). *Evaluation: A systematic approach.* Newbury Park, CA: Sage.

Rothbaum, B.O., Foa, E.B., Riggs, D.S., Murdock, T., & Walsh, W. (1992). A prospective examination of posttraumatic stress disorder in rape victims. *Journal of Traumatic Stress, 5,* 455–475.

Rothbaum, B.O., Meadows, E.A., Resick, R., & Foy, D.W. (2000). Cognitive-behavioral treatment. In E.B. Foa, T.M. Keane, & M.J. Friedman (Eds.), *Effective treatments for PTSD: Practice guidelines from the International Society for Traumatic Stress Studies.* New York: Guilford Press.

Rubin, A. (1992). Case management. In S.M. Rose (Ed.), *Case management and social work practice* (pp. 5–20). New York: Longman.

Rudorfer, M., & Potter, W. (1999). Metabolism of tricyclic antidepressants. *Cell and Molecular Biology, 19,* 373–409.

Ruffolo, M.C. (1994). Evaluating a MFGPI program for parents of a child with SED. Grant proposal submitted to the National Institute of Mental Health.

Ruffolo, M.C. (1999). Preliminary data analysis for the R29 grant. Unpublished report. Ann Arbor, MI: University of Michigan: Author.

Ruiz, P. (1993). Access to health care for uninsured Hispanics: Policy recommendations. *Hospital and Community Psychiatry, 44,* 958–962.

Russell, L., Rotto, K., & Matthews, B. (1999). Preliminary evaluation findings from Indiana's DAWN Project. In J. Willis, C. Liberton, K. Kutash, & R. Friedman (Eds.), *The 11th annual research conference proceedings, a system of care for children's mental health: Expanding the research base* (pp. 55–58). Tampa, FL: University of South Florida, The Louis de la Parte Florida Mental Health Institute, Research and Training Center for Children's Mental Health.

Rutter, M. (1979). Protective factors in children's responses to stress and disadvantage. In M.W. Kent & J.E. Rolf (Eds.), *Primary prevention of psychopathology: Social competence in children,* Vol. 3 (pp. 49–74). Hanover, NH: University of New England.

Rutter, M. (1985a). Family and school influences on behavioral development. *Journal of Child Psychology and Psychiatry, 26,* 349–368.

Rutter, M. (1985b). Resilience in the face of adversity: Protective factors and resistance to psychiatric disorders. *British Journal of Psychiatry, 147,* 598–611.

Rutter, M., Cox, A., Tupling, C., Berger, M., & Yule, W. (1975). Attainment and adjustment in two geographical areas. *British Journal of Psychiatry, 126,* 493–509.

Rutter, M., Giller, H., & Hagell, A. (1998). *Antisocial behavior by young people.* New York: Cambridge University Press.

Ryan, N. (1990). Heterocyclic antidepressants in children and adolescents. *Journal of Child and Adolescent Psychopharmacology, 1,* 21–31.

Ryan, N., Bhatara, V., & Perel, J. (1999). Mood stabilizers in children and adolescents. *Journal of the American Academy of Child and Adolescent Psychiatry, 38,* 529–536.

Ryan, N., Meyer, V., Dachille, S., Mazzie, D., & Puig-Antich, J. (1988). Lithium antidepressant augmentation in TCA-refractory depression in adolescents. *Journal of the America Academy of Child and Adolescent Psychiatry, 27,* 371–376.

Sallee, F., Vrindavanam, N., Deas-Nesmith, D., Carson, S., & Sethuraman, G. (1997). Pulse intravenous clomipramine for depressed adolescents: Double blind, controlled trial. *American Journal of Psychiatry, 154,* 668–673.

Sameroff, A.J., & Seifer, R. (1983). Familial risk and child competence. *Child Development, 54,* 1254–1268.

Sampson, R.J., & Laub, J.H. (1993). *Crime in the making: Pathways and turning points through life.* Cambridge, MA: Harvard University Press.

Sandman, C. (1991). The opiate hypothesis in autism and self injury. *Journal of Child and Adolescent Psychopharmacology, 1,* 237–248.

Santarcangelo, S., Bruns, E.J., & Yoe, J.T. (1998). New directions: Evaluating Vermont's statewide model of individualized care. In M.H. Epstein, K. Kutash, & A.J. Duchnowski (Eds.), *Outcomes for children and youth with behavioral and emotional disorders and their families: Programs and evaluation best practices* (pp. 55–80). Austin, TX: Pro-Ed.

Saunders, B.E., Kilpatrick, D.G., Hanson, R.F., Resnick, H.S., & Walker, E. (1999). Prevalence, case characteristics, and long-term psychological correlates of child rape among women: A national survey. *Child Maltreatment, 4,* 187–200.

Saxe, L., & Cross, T. (1997). Interpreting the Fort Bragg Children's Mental Health Demonstration Project: The cup is half full. *American Psychologist, 52,* 553–556.

Schachar, R.J., & Tannock, R. (1993). Childhood hyperactivity and psychostimulants: A review of extended treatment studies. *Journal of Child and Adolescent Psychopharmacology, 3,* 81–97.

Schachar, R.J., Tannock, R., Cunningham, C., & Corkum, P.V. (1997). Behavioral, situational, and temporal effects of treatment of ADHD with methylphenidate. *Journal of the American Academy of Child and Adolescent Psychiatry, 36,* 754–763.

Schachter, S. (1959). *The psychology of affiliation.* Palo Alto, CA: Stanford University Press.

Schmidt, M.H., Moecks, P., Lay, B., Eisert, H.G., Fojkar, R., Fritz-Sigmund, D., Marcus, A., & Musaeus, B. (1997). Does oligoantigenic diet influence hyperactive/conduct-disordered children?: A controlled trial. *European Child and Adolescent Psychiatry, 6,* 88–95.

Schoenwald, S.K. (1998). *Multisystemic therapy consultation guidelines.* Charleston, SC: MST Institute.

Schoenwald, S.K., Borduin, C.M., & Henggeler, S.W. (1998). Multisystemic therapy: Changing the natural and service ecologies of adolescents and families. In M.H. Epstein, K. Kutash, & A.J. Duchnowski (Eds.), *Outcomes for children and youth with behavioral and emotional disorders and their families: Programs and evaluation best practices* (pp. 485–511). Austin, TX: Pro-Ed.

Schoenwald, S.K., Brown, T.L., & Henggeler, S.W. (2000). Inside multisystemic therapy: Therapist, supervisory, and program practices. *Journal of Emotional and Behavioral Disorders, 8,* 113–127.

Schoenwald, S.K., & Henggeler, S.W. (1997). Combining effective treatment strategies with family preservation models of service delivery: A challenge for mental health. In R. J. Illback, H. Joseph, Jr., & C. Cobb (Eds.), *Integrated services for children and families: Opportunities for psychological practice* (pp. 121–136). Washington, D.C.: American Psychological Association.

Schoenwald, S.K., Thomas, C.R., & Henggeler, S.W. (1994). Treatment of serious antisocial behavior. In T.E. Scruggs & M.A. Mastropieri (Eds.), *Advances in learning and behavioral disabilities,* Vol. 10B (pp. 1–21). Greenwich, CN: JAI Press.

Schoenwald, S.K., Ward, D.M., Henggeler, S.W., Pickrel, S.G., & Patel, H. (1996). Multisystemic therapy treatment of substance abusing or dependent adolescent offenders: Costs of reducing incarceration, inpatient, and residential placement. *Journal of Child and Family Studies, 5,* 431–444.

Schoenwald, S.K., Ward, D.M., Henggeler, S.W., Rowland, M.D., & Brondino, M.J. (2000). Multisystemic therapy versus hospitalization for crisis stabilization of youth: Out-of-home placement four months post-referral. *Mental Health Services Research, 2,* 3–12.

Scholle, S.H., & Kelleher, K.J. (1998). Managed care: Opportunities and threats for children with serious emotional disturbance and their families. In M.H. Epstein, K. Kutash, & A.J. Duchnowski (Eds.), *Outcomes for children and youth with behavioral and emotional disorders and their families: Programs and evaluation best practices* (pp. 659–684). Austin, TX: Pro-Ed.

Schopler, E. (1971). Parents of psychotic children as scapegoats. *Journal of Contemporary Psychotherapy, 4,* 17–22.

Schriebman, L. (1988). *Autism.* Newbury Park, CA: Sage.

Schulz, A.J., Israel, B.A., Zimmerman, M.A., & Checkoway, B.N. (1995). Empowerment as a multilevel construct: Perceived control at the individual, organizational, and community levels. *Health Education Research, 10,* 309–327.

Schwab-Stone, M.E., Ayers, T.S., Kasprow, W., Voyce, C., Barone, C., Shriver, T., & Weissberg, R.P. (1995). No safe haven: A study of violence exposure in an urban community. *Journal of the American Academy of Child and Adolescent Psychiatry, 34,* 1343–1352.

Scott, D., Scott, L.M., & Goldwater, B. (1997). A performance improvement program for an international-level track and field athlete. *Journal of Applied Behavior Analysis, 30,* 573–575.

Sechrest, L., & Walsh, M. (1997). Dogma or data: Bragging rights. *American Psychologist, 52,* 536–540.

Shadish, W.R., Robinson, L., & Congxiao, L. (1999). ES: A computer program for effect size calculation (Version 1.0). St. Paul, MN: Assessment Systems Corporation.

Shaffer, D., Fisher, P., Dulcan, M., Davies, M., Piacentini, J., Schwab-Stone, M., Lahey, B., Bourdon, K., Jensen, P., Bird, H., Canino, G., & Regier, D. (1996). The NIMH Diagnostic Interview Schedule for Children Version 2.3 (DISC 2.3): Description, acceptability, prevalence rates, and performance in the MECA study. *Journal of the American Academy of Child and Adolescent Psychiatry, 35,* 865–877.

Shaffer, D., Gould, M., Brasic, J., Ambrosini, P., Fisher, P., Bird, H., & Aluwahlia, S. (1983). A children's global assessment scale (CGAS). *Archives of General Psychiatry, 40,* 1228–1231.

Silva, R., Munoz, D., Alpert, M., Perlmutter, I., & Diaz, J. (1999). Neuroleptic malignant syndrome in children and adolescents. *Journal of the American Academy of Child and Adolescent Psychiatry, 38,* 187–194.

Silver, E., Ireys, H., Bauman, L., & Stein, R. (1997). Psychological outcomes of a support intervention for mothers of children with ongoing health conditions: The Parent-to-Parent Network. *Journal of Community Psychology, 25,* 249–264.

Silverman, W.K., Kurtines, W.M., Ginsburg, G.S., Weems, C.F., Lumpkin, P.W., & Carmichael, D.H. (1999a). Treating anxiety disorders in children with group cognitive-behaviorial therapy: A randomized clinical trial. *Journal of Consulting and Clinical Psychology, 67,* 995–1003.

Silverman, W.K., Kurtines, W.M., Ginsburg, G.S., Weems, C.F., Rabian, B., & Serafini, L.T. (1999b). Contingency management, self-control, and education support in the treatment of childhood phobic disorders: A randomized clinical trial. *Journal of Consulting and Clinical Psychology, 67,* 675–687.

Simeon, J.G., Dinicola, V., Ferguson, H., & Copping, W. (1990). Adolescent depression: A placebo controlled fluoxetine study and follow-up. *Progress in Neuropharmacology and Biological Psychiatry, 14,* 791–795.

Simeon, J.G., Ferguson, H.B., Knott, V., Roberts, N., Gauthier, B., Dubois, C., & Wiggins, D. (1992). Clinical, cognitive, and neurophysiological effects of alprazolam in children and adolescents with overanxious and avoidant disorders. *Journal of the American Academy of Child and Adolescent Psychiatry, 31,* 29–33.

Simms, M.D. (1989). The foster care clinic: A community program to identify treatment needs of children in foster care. *Journal of Developmental and Behavioral Pediatrics, 10,* 121–128.

Simpson, J.S., Koroloff, N., Friesen, B.F., & Gac, J. (1999). Promising practices in family-provider collaboration. *Systems of care: Promising practices in children's mental health,* 1998 Series, Vol. I. Washington, D.C.: Center for Effective Collaboration and Practice, American Institutes for Research.

Singer, H., Brown, J., Quaskey, S., Rosenberg, L., Mellits, E., & Denckla, M. (1995a). The treatment of attention deficit disorder in Tourette's syndrome: A double-blind, placebo-controlled study with clonidine and desipramine. *Pediatrics, 95,* 74–81.

Singer, M.I., Anglin, T.M., Song, L.Y., & Lunghofer, L. (1995b). Adolescents' exposure to violence and associated symptoms of psychological trauma. *Journal of the American Medical Association, 273,* 477–482.

Singh, N.N., Landrum, T.J., Donatelli, L.S., Hampton, C., & Ellis, C.R. (1994). Characteristics of children and adolescents with serious emotional disturbance in systems of care. Part I: Partial hospitalization and inpatient services. *Journal of Emotional and Behavioral Disorders, 2,* 13–20.

Smith, M., & Mendoza, R. (1996). Ethnicity and pharmacogenetics. *The Mount Sinai Journal of Medicine, 63,* 285–290.

Snowen, L.R., & Hu, T.W. (1997). Ethnic differences in mental health services use among the severely mentally ill. *Journal of Community Psychology, 25,* 235–247.

Solomon, P. (1992). The efficacy of case management services for severely mentally disabled adults. *Community Mental Health Journal, 28,* 163–180.

Spence, S.H., Donovan, C., & Brechman-Toussaint, M. (2000). The treatment of childhood social phobia: The effectiveness of a social skills training-based, cognitive-behavioural intervention, with and without parental involvement. *Journal of Child Psychology and Psychiatry and Allied Disciplines, 41,* 713–726.

Spielberger, C. (1973). *Preliminary test manual for the State-Trait Anxiety Inventory for Children.* Palo Alto, CA: Consulting Psychologists Press.

Sprafkin, J., & Gadow, K.D. (1996). Double-blind versus open evaluations of stimulant drug response in children with attention-deficit hyperactivity disorder. *Journal of Child and Adolescent Psychopharmacology, 6,* 215–28.

Sramek, J., & Pi, E. (1996). Ethnicity and antidepressant response. *Mount Sinai Journal of Medicine, 63,* 320–325.

Stark, K.D., Reynolds, W.M., & Kaslow, N.J. (1987). A comparison of the relative efficacy of self-control therapy and a behavioral problem-solving therapy for depression in children. *Journal of Abnormal Child Psychology, 15,* 91–113.

Stark, K.D., Rouse, L.W., & Livingston, R. (1991). Treatment of depression during childhood and adolescence: Cognitive-behavioral procedures for the individual and family. In P.C. Kendall (Ed.), *Child and adolescent therapy: Cognitive-behavioral procedures* (pp. 165–206). New York: Guilford Press.

State of North Carolina, Department of Human Resources and Department of Public Instruction. (1999). *Blue Ridge Mentor Project*. Raleigh, NC: Author.

Stein, R., & Jessop, D. (1984). Does pediatric home care make a difference for children with chronic illness? Findings from the Pediatric Ambulatory Care Treatment Study. *Pediatrics, 73,* 845–853.

Steinberg, Z., & Knitzer, J. (1992). Classrooms for emotionally and behaviorally disturbed students: Facing the challenge. *Behavioral Disorders, 17,* 145–156.

Steiner, H., & Dunne, J.E. (1997). Summary of the practice parameters for the assessment and treatment of children and adolescents with conduct disorder. *Journal of the American Academy of Child and Adolescent Psychiatry, 36,* 1482–1485.

Steiner, H., & Lock, J. (1998). Anorexia nervosa and bulimia nervosa in children and adolescents: A review of the past 10 years. *Journal of the American Academy of Child and Adolescent Psychiatry, 37,* 352–359.

Strober, M., Freeman, R., Rigali, J., Schmidt, S., & Diamond, R. (1992). The pharmacotherapy of depressive illness in adolescence. II. Effects of lithium augmentation in non-responders to imipramine. *Journal of the American Academy of Child and Adolescent Psychiatry, 31,* 16–20.

Strober, M., Lampert, C., Schmidt, S., & Morrell, W. (1993). The course of major depressive disorder in adolescents: I. Recovery and risk of manic switching in a follow-up of psychotic and nonpsychotic subtypes. *Journal of the American Academy of Child and Adolescent Psychiatry, 32,* 34–42.

Stroul, B.A. (1989). *Community-based services for children and adolescents who are severely emotionally disturbed: Therapeutic foster care*. Washington, DC: CASSP Technical Assistance Center, Georgetown University Child Development Center.

Stroul, B.A. (1993) *Children's mental health: Creating systems of care in a changing society*. Baltimore: Paul H. Brookes.

Stroul, B.A. (1995). Case management in a system of care. In B.J. Friesen & J. Poertner (Eds.), *From case management to service coordination for children with emotional, behavioral, or mental disorders: Building on family strengths* (pp. 3–25). Baltimore: Paul H. Brookes.

Stroul, B.A. (1996). *Children's mental health: Creating systems of care in a changing society*. Baltimore: Paul H. Brookes.

Stroul, B.A., & Friedman, R.M. (1986). *A system of care for seriously emotionally disturbed children and youth*. Washington, DC: CASSP Technical Assistance Center, Georgetown University Child Development Center.

Stroul, B.A., Pires, S.A., Roebuck, L., Friedman, R.M., Barrett, B., Chambers, K.L., & Kershaw, M.A. (1997). State health care reforms: How they affect children and adolescents with emotional disorders and their families. *Journal of Mental Health Administration, 24,* 386–399.

Sturm, R., Ringel, J., Bao, C., Stein, B., Kapur, K., Zhang, W., & Zeng, F. (2000). *National estimates of mental health utilization and expenditures for children in 1998* (Working Paper 205). Los Angeles, CA: Research Center on Managed Care for Psychiatric Disorders.

Substance Abuse and Mental Health Services Administration. (1999). *A summary of planned mental health and substance abuse services and activities in the state children's health insurance program (CHIP)*. Rockville, MD: Author.

Suls, J., & Miller, R. (Eds.). (1977). *Social comparison processes: Theoretical and empirical perspectives*. Washington, DC: Hemisphere.

Swanson, J.M., Flockhart, D., Udea, D., Cantwell, D., Connor, D., & Williams, L. (1995). Clonidine in the treatment of ADHD: Questions about safety and efficacy. *Journal of Child and Adolescent Psychopharmacology, 5,* 301–304.

Swanson, J.M., Wigal, S., Greenhill, L.L., Browne, R., Waslik, B., Lerner, M., Williams, L., Flynn, D., Agler, D., Crowley, K., Fineberg, E., Baren, M., & Cantwell, D.P. (1998). Analog classroom assessment of Adderall in children with ADHD. *Journal of the American Academy of Child and Adolescent Psychiatry, 37,* 519–26.

Swedo, S.E., Leonard, H.L., & Allen, A.J. (1994). New developments in childhood affective and anxiety disorders. *Current Problems in Pediatrics, 24,* 12–38.

Szapocznik, J., Perez-Vidal, A., Brickman, A., Foote, F., Santisteban, D., Hervis, O., & Kurtines, W. (1988). Engaging adolescent drug abusers and their families in treatment. *Journal of Consulting and Clinical Psychology, 56,* 552–557.

Szapocznik, J., Santisteban, D., Rio, A., Perez-Vidal, A., Santisteban, D., & Kurtines, W.M. (1989). Family effectivenesss training: An intervention to prevent drug abuse and problem behaviors in Hispanic adolescents. *Hispanic Journal of Behavioral Sciences, 11,* 4–27.

Szapocznik, J., & Williams, R.A. (2000). Brief strategic family therapy: Twenty five years of interplay among theory, research and practice in adolescent behavior problems and drug abuse. *Clinical Child and Family Psychology Review, 3,* 117–134.

Takeuchi, D.T., Sue, S., & Yeh, M. (1995). Return rates and outcomes from ethnicity-specific mental health programs in Los Angeles. *American Journal of Public Health, 85,* 638–643.

Tannen, N. (1996). A family-designed system of care: Families First in Essex County, New York. In B.A. Stroul (Ed.), *Children's mental health: Creating systems of care in a changing society* (pp. 375–388). Baltimore: Paul H. Brookes.

Tarico, V., Low, B., Trupin, E., & Forsyth-Stephens, A. (1989). Children's mental health services: A parent perspective. *Community Mental Health Journal, 25,* 313–326.

Taylor, T.K., Schmidt, F., Pepler, D., & Hodgins, C. (1998). A comparison of eclectic treatment with Webster-Stratton's Parents and Children Series in a children's mental health center: A randomized controlled trial. *Behavior Therapy, 29,* 221–240.

Teplin, L. (2000). Juvenile justice and identification of mental health needs. In U.S. Public Health Service, Report of the Surgeon General's Conference on Children's Mental Health: A National Action Agenda. Washington, DC.

Thiel, A. (1997). Are psychotropic drugs necessary for the treatment of anorexia and bulimia nervosa? *Psychotherapy and Psychosomatic Medical Psychology, 47,* 332–345.

Thoits, P.A. (1986). Social support as coping assistance. *Journal of Consulting and Clinical Psychology, 54,* 416–423.

Thomas, A., & Chess, S. (1984). Genesis and evolution of behavioral disorders: From infancy to early adult life. *American Journal of Psychiatry, 141,* 1–9.

Thompson. S., & Rey, J. (1995). Functional enuresis: Is desmopressin the answer? *Journal of the American Academy of Child and Adolescent Psychiatry, 34,* 266–271.

Thornberry, T.P., & Krohn, M.D. (1997). Peers, drug use, and delinquency. In D.M. Stoff, J. Breiling, & J. D. Maser (Eds.), *Handbook of antisocial behavior* (pp. 218–233). New York: John Wiley & Sons.

Tierney, J.P., Grossman, J.B., & Resch, N.L. (1995). *Making a difference: An impact study of Big Brothers/Big Sisters.* Philadelphia: Public/Private Ventures.

Tolbert, H.A. (1996). Psychosis in children and adolescents: A review. *Journal of Clinical Psychiatry, 57,* 4–8.

Torrey, W.C., Drake, R.E., Dixon, L., Burns, B.J., Flynn, L., Rush, A.J., Clark, R.E., & Klatzker, D. (2001). Implementing evidence-based practices for persons with severe mental illnesses. *Psychiatric Services, 52,* 45–50.

Tremblay, R.E., Pagani-Kurtz, L., Masse, L.C., Vitaro, F., & Pihl, R.O. (1995). A bimodal preventive intervention for disruptive kindergarten boys: Its impact through mid-adolescence. *Journal of Consulting and Clinical Psychology, 63,* 560–568.

Triffleman, E., Carroll, K., & Kellogg, S. (1999). Substance dependence posttraumatic stress disorder therapy: An integrated cognitive-behavioral approach. *Journal of Substance Abuse Treatment, 17,* 1–2.

Trivette, C.M., Dunst, C.J., & Hamby, D. (1996). Characteristics and consequences of help-giving practices in contrasting human services programs. *American Journal of Community Psychology, 24,* 273–293.

U.S. Department of Education. (1998). *Twentieth annual report to Congress on implementation of the Individuals with Disabilities Education Act.* Washington, DC: Author.

U.S. Department of Health and Human Services. (1997). *Annual report to Congress on the evaluation of the Comprehensive Community Mental Health Services for Children and Their Families Program, 1997.* Atlanta, GA: Macro International.

U.S. Department of Health and Human Services. (1999). *Mental health: A report of the Surgeon General.* Rockville, MD: U.S. Department of Health and Human Services, Substance Abuse and Mental Health Services Administration, Center for Mental Health Services, National Institutes of Health, National Institute of Mental Health.

U.S. Public Health Service. (2000). *Report of the Surgeon General's conference on children's mental health: A national action agenda.* Washington, DC: Author.

Uvnas-Moberg, K. (1997). Physiological and endocrine effects of social contact. In C.S. Carter, B. Kirkpatrick, & I.I. Lederhendler (Eds.), *The Integrative neurobiology of affiliation.* (pp. 146–163). New York: The New York Academy of Sciences.

Van Bilsen, H., & Wilke, M. (1999). Drug and alcohol abuse in young people. In P. Graham (Ed.), *Cognitive-behaviour therapy for children and families* (pp. 246–261). Cambridge, MA: Cambridge University Press.

Vance, J.E., Fernandez, G., & Biber, M. (1998). Educational progress in a population of youth with aggression and emotional disturbance: The role of risk and protective factors. *Journal of Emotional and Behavioral Disorders, 6,* 214–221.

VanDenBerg, J.E., & Grealish, M.E. (1996). Individualized services and supports through the wrap-around process: Philosophy and procedures. *Journal of Child and Family Studies, 5,* 7–21.

VanDenBerg, J.E., & Grealish, M.E. (1998). *The wraparound process training manual.* Pittsburgh, PA: The Community Partnerships Group.

Vander Stoep, A., Williams, M., Jones, R., Green, L., & Trupin, E. (1999). Families as full research partners: What's in it for us? *Journal of Behavioral Health Services and Research, 26,* 329–344.

Verhulst, F., Van der Ende, J., Ferdinand, R., & Kasius, M. (1997). The prevalence of DSM-III-R diagnoses in a national sample of Dutch adolescents. *Archives of General Psychiatry, 54,* 329–336.

Veronen, L.J., & Kilpatrick, D.G. (1983). Stress management for rape victims. In D. Meichenbaum & M.E. Jaremko (Eds.), *Stress reduction and prevention* (pp. 341–374). New York: Plenum.

Vitaro, F., & Dobkin, P.L. (1996). Prevention of substance use/abuse in early adolescents with behavior problems. *Journal of Alcohol and Drug Education, 41,* 11–38.

Vitaro, F., & Tremblay, R.E. (1994). Impact of a prevention program on aggressive children's friendships and social adjustment. *Journal of Abnormal Child Psychology, 22,* 457–475.

Volkmar, F.R. (1996). Child and adolescent psychosis: A review of the past 10 years. *Journal of the American Academy of Child and Adolescent Psychiatry, 35,* 843–851.

Von Bertalanffy, L. (1968). *General systems theory.* New York: Braziller.

Vostanis, P., Feehan, C., & Grattan, E. (1998). Two-year outcome of children treated for depression. *European Child and Adolescent Psychiatry, 7,* 12–18.

Vostanis, P., Feehan, C., Grattan, E., & Bickerton, W.L. (1996a). Treatment for children and adolescents with depression: Lessons from a controlled trial. *Clinical Child Psychology and Psychiatry, 1,* 199–212.

Vostanis, P., Feehan, C., Grattan, E., & Bickerton, W.L. (1996b). A randomized controlled out-patient trial of cognitive-behavioural treatment for children and adolescents with depression: 9-month follow-up. *Journal of Affective Disorders, 40,* 105–116.

Wagner, B.M. (1997). Family risk factors for child and adolescent suicidal behavior. *Psychological Bulletin, 121,* 246–298.

Walker, H.M. (1998). First step to prevent antisocial behavior. *Teaching Exceptional Children, 30,* 16–19.

Walker, H.M., Colvin, G., & Ramsey, E. (1995). *Antisocial behavior in school: Strategies and best practices.* Pacific Grove, CA: Brooks/Cole.

Walker, H.M., Forness, S., Kauffman, J., Epstein, M., Gresham, F., Nelson, M., & Strain, P. (1998a). Macro-social validation: Referencing outcomes in behavioral disorders to societal issues and problems. *Behavioral Disorders, 24,* 7–18.

Walker, H.M., Kavanagh, K., Stiller, B., Golly, A., Severson, H., & Feil, E.G. (1998b). First Step to Success: An early intervention approach for preventing school antisocial behavior. *Journal of Emotional and Behavioral Disorders, 6,* 66–80.

Walker, H.M., & Severson, H. (1990). *Systematic screening for behavior disorders.* Longmont, CO: Sopris West.

Walker, H.M., Severson, H., & Feil, E. (1995). *The Early Screening Project.* Longmont, CO: Sopris West.

Walker, H.M., Stiller, B., & Golly, A. (1998). First Step to Success: A collaborative home-school intervention for preventing antisocial behavior at the point of school entry. *Young Exceptional Children, 1,* 1–6.

Walker, H.M., Stiller, B., Golly, A., Kavanagh, K., Severson, H., & Feil, E. (1997). *First Step to Success: Helping young children overcome antisocial behavior.* Longmont, CO: Sopris West.

Walsh, B., Ireys, H., & Sills, E. (1996). Implementing a family-to-family network for children with JRA: Challenges and opportunities. *ACCH Advocate, 2,* 20–26.

Waltz, J., Addis, M.E., Koerner, K., & Jacobson, N.S. (1993). Testing the integrity of a psychotherapy protocol: Assessment of adherence and competence. *Journal of Consulting and Clinical Psychology, 61,* 620–630.

Wandersman, L.P. (1987). New directions for parent education. In S. Kagan, D. Powell, B. Weissbourd, & E. Zigler (Eds.), *America's family support programs: Perspectives and prospects* (pp. 207–228). New Haven, CT: Yale University Press.

Washington State Institute for Public Policy. (1998). *Watching the botton line: Cost-effective interventions for reducing crime in Washington.* Olympia, WA: The Evergreen State College.

Webster-Stratton, C., & Hammond, M. (1997). Treating children with early-onset conduct problems: A comparison of child and parent training interventions. *Journal of Consulting and Clinical Psychology, 65,* 93–109.

Webster-Stratton, C., Hollinsworth, T., & Kolpacoff, M. (1989). The long-term effectiveness and clinical significance of three cost-effective training programs for families with conduct-problem children. *Journal of Consulting and Clinical Psychology, 57,* 550–553.

Webster-Stratton, C., Kolpacoff, M., & Hollinsworth, T. (1988). Self-administered videotape therapy for families with conduct-problem children: Comparison with two cost effective treatments and a control group. *Journal of Consulting and Clinical Psychology, 56,* 558–566.

Weil, M.O. (1985). Key components in providing efficient and effective services. In M.D. Weil & J. Karls (Eds.) *Case management in human service practice: A systematic approach to mobilizing resources for clients* (pp. 29–71). San Francisco: Jossey-Bass.

Weil, M.O., & Karls, J. (Eds.). (1985). *Case management in human service practice: A systematic approach to mobilizing resources for clients.* San Francisco: Jossey-Bass.

Weil, M.O., Zipper, I.N., & Dedmon, S.R. (1995). Issues and principles of training for case management in child mental health. In B.J. Friesen & J. Poertner (Eds.), *From case management to service coordination for children with emotional, behavioral, or mental disorders: Building on family strengths* (pp. 211–238). Baltimore: Paul H. Brookes.

Weinberg, N.Z., & Glantz, M.D. (1999). Child psychopathology risk factors for drug abuse: Overview. *Journal of Clinical Child Psychology, 28,* 290–297.

Weinberg, N.Z., Rahdert, E., Colliver, J.D., & Glantz, M.D. (1998). Adolescent substance abuse: A review of the past 10 years. *Journal of the American Academy of Child and Adolescent Psychiatry, 37,* 252–261.

Weiss, B., Catron, T., Harris, V., & Phung, T.M. (1999). The effectiveness of traditional child psychotherapy. *Journal of Consulting and Clinical Psychology, 67,* 82–94.

Weiss, C.H. (1995). Nothing as practical as good theory: Exploring theory-based evaluation for comprehensive community initiatives for children and families. In J.P. Connell, A.C. Kubishch, L.B. Schorr, & C.H. Weiss (Eds.), *New approaches to evaluating community initiatives: Volume 1, Concepts, methods, and contexts* (pp. 37–49). Washington, DC: Aspen Institute.

Weisz, J.R. (Spring, 2000a). Lab-clinic differences and what we can do about them. I. The clinic-based treatment development model. *Clinical Child Psychology Newsletter, 15,* No. 1.

Weisz, J.R. (Summer, 2000b). Lab-clinic differences and what we can do about them. II. Linking research and practice to enhance our public impact. *Clinical Child Psychology Newsletter, 15,* No. 2.

Weisz, J.R. (Fall, 2000c). Lab-clinic differences and what we can do about them. III. National policy matters. *Clinical Child Psychology Newsletter,15,* No. 3.

Weisz, J.R., Donenberg, G.R., Han, S.S., & Weiss, B. (1995). Bridging the gap between lab and clinic in child and adolescent psychotherapy. *Journal of Consulting and Clinical Psychology, 63,* 688-701.

Weisz, J.R., Han, S.S., & Valeri, S.M. (1997). More of what? Issues raised by the Fort Bragg study. *American Psychologist, 52,* 266–273.

Weisz, J.R., & Jensen, P.S. (1999). Efficacy and effectiveness of child and adolescent psychotherapy and pharmacotherapy. *Mental Health Services Research, 1,* 125–157.

Weisz, J.R., Thurber, C.A., Sweeney, L., Proffitt, V.D., & LeGagnoux, G.L. (1997). Brief treatment of mild-to-moderate child depression using primary and secondary control enhancement training. *Journal of Consulting and Clinical Psychology, 65,* 703–707.

Weisz, J.R., & Weiss, B. (1993). *Effects of psychotherapy with children and adolescents.* Newbury Park, CA: Sage.

Weisz, J.R., Weiss, B., Alicke, M.D., & Klotz, M.L. (1987). Effectiveness of psychotherapy with children and adolescents. A meta-analysis for clinicians. *Journal of Consulting and Clinical Psychology, 55,* 542–549.

Weisz, J.R., Weiss, B., & Donenberg, G.R. (1992). The lab versus the clinic: Effects of child and adolescent psychotherapy. *American Psychologist, 47,* 1578-1585.

Weisz, J.R., Weiss, B., Han, S., Granger, D.A., & Morton, T. (1995). Effects of psychotherapy with children and adolescents revisited: A meta-analysis of treatment outcome studies. *Psychological Bulletin, 117,* 450–468.

Wellman, B. (1981). Applying network analysis to the study of support. In B.H. Gottlieb (Ed.), *Social networks and social support* (pp. 171–200). London: Sage.

Werner, E.E. (1989). High-risk children in young adulthood: A longitudinal study from birth to 32 years. *American Journal of Orthopsychiatry, 59,* 72–81.

Werner, E.E., & Smith, R. (1982). *Vulnerable but invincible: A longitudinal study of resilient children and youth.* New York: Adams, Bannister, Cox.

Werner, E.E., & Smith, R.S. (1992). *Overcoming the odds: High risk children from birth to adulthood.* Ithaca, NY: Cornell University Press.

Werry, J., & Aman, M. (1993) *Practitioners guide to psychoactive drugs for children and adolescents.* New York: Plenum.

Willenbring, M., Ridgely, M.S., Stinchfield, R., & Rose, M. (1991). *Application of case management in alcohol and drug dependence: Matching techniques and populations.* Rockville, MD: National Institute on Alcohol Abuse and Alcoholism, Homeless Demonstration and Evaluation Branch.

Williamson, D.E., Ryan, N.D., Birmaher, B., Dahl, R.E., Kaufman, J., Rao, U., & Puig-Antich, J. (1995). A case-control family history study of depression in adolescents. *Journal of the American Academy of Child and Adolescent Psychiatry, 34,* 1596–1607.

Willis, J., Liberton, C., Kutash, K., & Friedman, R.M. (Eds.). (1999). *The 11th Annual Research Conference Proceedings, A System of Care for Children's Mental Health: Expanding the Research Base* (March 8 to March 11, 1998). Tampa, FL: University of South Florida, The Louis de la Parte Florida Mental Health Institute, Research and Training Center for Children's Mental Health.

Wiltz, N.A., & Patterson, G.R. (1974). An evaluation of parent training procedures designed to alter inappropriate aggressive behavior of boys. *Behavior Therapy, 5,* 215–221.

Winett, R.A., Anderson, E.S., Desiderato, L.L., Soloman, L.J., Perry, M., Kelly, J.A., Sikkema, K.J., Roffman, R.A., Norman, A.D., Lombard, D.N., & Lombard, T.N. (1995). Enhancing social diffusion theory as a basis for prevention intervention: A conceptual and strategic framework. *Applied and Preventive Psychology, 4,* 233–245.

Winsberg, B.G., Bialer, I., Kupietz, S., Botti, E., & Balka, E.B. (1980). Home vs. hospital care of children with behavioral disorders: A controlled investigation. *Archives of General Psychiatry, 37,* 413–418.

Winters, K.C., Latimer, W.L., & Stinchfield, R.D. (1999). Adolescent treatment. In P.J. Ott, R.E. Tarter, & R.T. Ammerman (Eds.), *Sourcebook on substance abuse: Etiology, epidemiology, and treatment.* Boston: Allyn & Bacon.

Wood, A., Harrington, R., & Moore, A. (1996). Controlled trial of a brief cognitive-behavioural intervention in adolescent patients with depressive disorders. *Journal of Child Psychology and Psychiatry and Allied Disciplines, 37,* 737–46.

Woodruff, D.W., Osher, D., Hoffman, C.C., Grunes, A., King, M.A., Snow, S.T., & McIntire, J.C. (1999). *The role of education in a system of care: Effectively serving children with emotional or behavioral disorders. Systems of care: Promising practices in children's mental health,* 1998 Series, Vol. I. Washington, DC: Center for Effective Collaboration and Practice, American Institutes for Research.

Yates, A., Beutler, L.E., & Crago, M. (1984). Characteristics of young, violent offenders. *Journal of Psychiatry and the Law, 40,* 41–47.

Yates, B. (1995). Cost-effectiveness analysis, cost-benefit analysis, and beyond: Evolving models for the scientist-practitioner. *Clinical Psychology: Science and Practice, 2,* 385–398.

Yates, B. (1996). *Analyzing costs, procedures, processes, and outcomes in human services: An introduction.* Thousand Oaks, CA: Sage.

Yell, M.L., & Shriner, J.G. (1997). The IDEA amendments of 1997: Implications for special and general education teachers, administrators, and teacher trainers. *Focus on exceptional children, 30,* 1–19.

Yoe, J.T., Santarcangelo, S., Atkins, M., & Burchard, J.D. (1996). Wraparound care in Vermont: Program development, implementation, and evaluation of a statewide system of individualized services. *Journal of Child and Family Studies, 5,* 23–39.

Zarate, C., Narendran, R., Tohen, M., Greaney, J., Berman, A., Pike, S., & Madrid, A. (1998). Clinical predictors of acute response with olanzepine in psychotic mood disorders. *Journal of Clinical Psychiatry, 59,* 24–28.

Zeiner, P., Bryhn, G., Bjercke, C., Truyen, K., & Strand, G. (1999). Response to methylphenidate in boys with attention-deficit hyperactivity disorder. *Acta Paediatrica, 88,* 298–303.

Zigler, E., Taussig, C., & Black, K. (1992). Early intervention: A promising preventative for juvenile delinquency. *American Psychologist, 47,* 997–1006.

Zimmerman, M.A., Israel, B.A., Schulz, A., & Checkoway, B. (1992). Further explorations in empowerment theory: An empirical analysis of psychological empowerment. *American Journal of Community Psychology, 20,* 707–727.

Zimrin, H. (1986). A profile of survival. *Child Abuse and Neglect, 10,* 339–349.

Zito, J., Safer, D., dosReis, S., Magder, L., & Riddle, M. (1997). Methylphenidate patterns among Medicaid youths. *Psychopharmacological Bulletin, 33,* 143–147.

Contributors

Mary I. Armstrong, MSW, MBA, is Director of the Division of State and Local Support, Department of Child and Family Studies, Louis de la Parte Florida Mental Health Institute at the University of South Florida. She is also responsible for the administration and direction of the Division of State and Local Support, a job which includes the evaluation of specialized consultation, training, and technical assistance throughout Florida and other states, as well as the development and management of grants and contracts which focus on system reform, leadership development, systems of care, technical assistance, and evaluation. She is an active member of the National Association of Social Workers and has many publications in both professional journals and textbooks. She is currently a doctoral student in Social Work at Memorial University in St. Johns, Newfoundland.

Sharon R. Booth, Ed.D., currently serves as Coordinating Teacher for the Wake County Public School System in Raleigh, North Carolina. She earned her doctoral degree in Administration and Supervision of Special Education from Virginia Polytechnic Institute and State University in 1991. Her research interests include students with mental health issues that affect learning.

Eric J. Bruns, Ph.D., is Assistant Professor in the Division of Child and Adolescent Psychiatry at the University of Maryland School of Medicine, and also serves as Director of Research and Evaluation at the Family League of Baltimore City. He completed his Ph.D. in clinical psychology at the University of Vermont in 1998, and is part of the Wraparound Vermont Research Team, which is delineating and pursuing a purposeful research agenda on this intervention nationally. In Baltimore, he is a member of the Johns Hopkins Violence Prevention Center and directs several collaborative research initiatives, including one dedicated to studying neighborhood effects on the well-being of urban children, another examining outcomes related to school mental health services, and a third evaluating the implementation and impact of after-school services in Baltimore.

John D. Burchard, Ph.D., is Professor of Clinical Psychology at the University of Vermont. The primary focus of his professional activities has been the evaluation of community-based services for families with children who are experiencing severe emotional and behavioral disorders. Dr. Burchard has been the Commissioner of the Vermont Department of Social and Rehabilitation Services and he was one of the founders of wraparound. He is on the Board of the Vermont Conference on the Primary Prevention of Psychopathology and is on the Editorial Boards of the *Journal of Emotional and Behavioral Disorders* and the *Journal of Child and Family Studies.*

Sara N. Burchard, Ph.D., is Associate Professor of Psychology at the University of Vermont. The focus of her professional activities has been serving individuals with cognitive and emotional challenges and their families in their home communities and schools, and preparing students to do similar work. Dr. Burchard's research has included concurrent and longitudinal investigations of community adjustment of individuals with multiple challenges. She was a founding member of Parent to Parent of Vermont and serves on the board of Vermont Protection and Advocacy and Vermont Defender General's Advisory Board for accommodations for individuals with cognitive challenges involved with the criminal justice system.

Barbara J. Burns, Ph.D., is Professor of Medical Psychology at Duke University Medical Center, and also holds academic appointments at the Uni-versity of North Carolina at Chapel Hill, the University of Arkansas for Medical Sciences, and the Medical University of South Carolina. Dr. Burns directs the Services Effectiveness Research Program at Duke and codirects the

Postdoctoral Research Training Program in Mental Health Services and Systems at Duke and UNC. She is a nationally recognized mental health services researcher with over 190 publications in this area. Her interest in health services research emerged from clinical experience in a model neighborhood health center in Boston, Massachusetts, with integrated health/mental health services. Subsequently, and then for nearly a decade at the National Institute of Mental Health, she pursued a range of topics directed toward improving mental health care for all age groups, from primary care to tertiary care, and eventually focused on community-based services. Throughout her research, teaching, clinical practice, and policy career, Dr. Burns has studied and advocated for responsive and innovative treatment. She recently completed a review of effective treatment for mental disorders in children and adolescents for the U.S. Surgeon General's Report on Mental Health.

Patricia Chamberlain, Ph.D., is a senior researcher at the Oregon Social Learning Center (OSLC) and Executive Director of Community Programs at OSLC. Her interest in interventions for children and adolescents with conduct problems emerged from her early work as a special education teacher. She specializes in helping parents and other adults implement effective methods for working with youth with severe emotional and behavioral problems. She has published numerous journal articles and book chapters in the areas of childhood aggression, delinquency, family treatment, therapy process, research methods, and treatment foster care. She has first-authored two books on treatment foster care and has recently completed a third on treating adolescents in community-based settings.

Scott N. Compton, Ph.D., is Assistant Professor in the Department of Psychiatry and Behavioral Sciences at Duke University Medical Center. He completed his Ph.D. in clinical psychology at the University of Nevada in 1998. His professional interests include pediatric and adolescent mental health epidemiologic and services research, as well as psychosocial and psychopharmacological treatment efficacy and effectiveness research.

John F. Curry, Ph.D., is Associate Professor of Medical Psychology in the Department of Psychiatry and Behavioral Sciences at Duke University Medical Center, and Associate Professor and Director of Clinical Training, Department of Psychology: Social and Health Sciences at Duke University. He earned his Ph.D. in clinical psychology from the Catholic University of America in 1978. Dr. Curry is also a Diplomate in Clinical Psychology of the American Board of Professional Psychology, and has published over fifty articles and chapters. His research interests focus on the psychopathology and treatment of adolescent depression and comorbid disorders, including substance abuse and anxiety disorders. He is interested in the integration of cognitive-behavioral and family approaches to intervention.

Amor S. Del Mundo, M.D., is in private practice of child and adolescent psychiatry in Los Angeles, California. She was previously Director of Child and Adolescent Psychiatry at Louisiana State University in Shreveport where she was also a coinvestigator in pediatric pharmacology funded by the Center for Maternal and Child Health. Her most recent academic position was Director of Child and Adolescent Psychiatry in the Department of Psychiatry and Behavioral Sciences of the James H. Quillen College of Medicine at East Tennessee State University in Johnson City.

Katherine A. DeVet, Ph.D., is Assistant Scientist in the Department of Population and Family Health Sciences at the Bloomberg School of Public Health at the Johns Hopkins University, where she completed a Postdoctoral Fellowship in Prevention Science. In 1999, she received the Early Career Award from the Society of Prevention Research. Her research interests involve prevention of mental health problems in families of children with special needs.

Albert J. Duchnowski, Ph.D., is Professor of Child and Family Studies and Special Education (jointly appointed) at the University of South Florida. He serves as Deputy Director of the Research and Training Center for Children's Mental Health at the Louis de la Parte Florida Mental Health Institute. Dr. Duchnowski received his doctorate in clinical child psychology from Vanderbilt University. He has been Principal Investigator on grants focusing on children with disabilities and training professionals from a multidisciplinary perspective to work with these children and their families. He has numerous publications and has coedited three books on children's mental health services. In addition to academic experience, Dr. Duchnowski was the Director of Pupil Personnel Services and Special Education for 11 years in Gettysburg, Pennsylvania. He has also been a consultant to state directors of special education and children's mental health in 30 states. This consultation has been in the area of collaborative, community-based systems of care for children with disabilities and their families. He is a founding member of the Federation of Families for Children's Mental Health, and served two terms as vice president of the organization. He is also a member of the national Coalition for Mental Health and Special Education, and local advocacy groups.

Helen L. Egger, M.D., is Assistant Professor in the Developmental Epidemiology Program, Department of Psychiatry and Behavioral Sciences, Duke University Medical Center. She attended Yale College and Yale Medical School and completed her adult and child psychiatry residency training at Duke. Her research has been focused on somatic complaints and psychopathology, the presentation of and course of anxiety disorders, and school refusal based on data from longitudinal, population-based data sets gathered on children and adolescents in rural and urban North Carolina. Most recently, Dr. Egger has been developing a new psychiatric interview for parents of preschool children, the Preschool Age Psychiatric Assessment (PAPA). The PAPA is the first comprehensive, developmentally appropriate structured psychiatric interview to examine the presentation of symptoms, disorders, functioning, and impairment in preschoolers.

Michael J. English, J.D., is Director of the Division of Knowledge Development Systems Change in the federal Center for Mental Health Services (CMHS). Mr. English administers CMHS's Programs of Regional and National Significance, which are discretionary grant programs devoted to identifying evidence-based mental health services for children, youth, and adults and supporting their adoption in communities throughout the nation. He also is responsible for the Comprehensive Community Mental Health Services for Children and Their Families Program, and the Projects for Assistance and Transition from Homelessness (PATH) Program. Until 1992, Mr. English served for many years in the public mental health system in the District of Columbia as a litigating attorney and administrator, culminating in his holding the position of Chief Administrator of the D.C. Commission on Mental Health Services for more than four years. In May 1998, Mr. English received the DHHS Secretary's Award for Distinguished Service "for visionary and dynamic leadership in managing the new knowledge development and application initiative to improve services for adults with serious mental illnesses and children with serious emotional disturbances." A graduate of Georgetown Law School, Mr. English has devoted more than twenty years to delivering mental health services effectively to those persons who need it most.

Michael H. Epstein, Ed.D., is Director of the Center for At-Risk Children's Services and William E. Barkley Professor of Special Education at the University of Nebraska. Dr. Epstein has published over 180 professional papers, has served as a consultant to various state and federal agencies and foundations, and is the founding editor of the *Journal of Emotional and Behavioral Disorders*. He is the author of the *Behavioral and Emotional Rating Scale: A Strength Based Approach to Assessment* and the *Scale Assessing Emotional Disturbance*. His research interests include strengths-based assessment, interventions to enhance academic skills of students with severe emotional disturbance, and implementation and fidelity of wraparound services.

Mary E. Evans, R.N., Ph.D., FAAN, is Professor, Director of Research, and Director of the Doctoral Program at the College of Nursing, University of South Florida. Her previous position was Senior Research Scientist for the New York State Office of Mental Health. She has directed controlled studies of case management, published extensively in the child mental health field, and served as a consultant on multiple federal government panels. Her research interests focus on the development, implementation, and evaluation of community-based interventions for children with emotional or behavioral disorders and their families.

John A. Fairbank, Ph.D., is Associate Professor of Medical Psychology in the Department of Psychiatry and Behavioral Sciences at Duke University Medical Center, and Associate Professor in the Department of Psychology: Social and Health Sciences at Duke University. He is Co-Director of the National Center for Child Traumatic Stress sponsored by the Substance Abuse and Mental Health Services Administration (SAMHSA). His professional interests include mental health epidemiologic and services research, particularly in areas related to traumatic stress and to substance abuse and dependence in adults and youth. He is the author of over eighty professional papers and book chapters, and currently serves as president of the International Society for Traumatic Stress Studies.

Elizabeth M.Z. Farmer, Ph.D., is Assistant Professor in the Department of Psychiatry and Behavioral Sciences at Duke University Medical Center. She is a sociologist and mental health services researcher with interests in community-based care for children with severe emotional and behavioral disorders. Her recent and current research focuses on patterns of care for children's mental health services, the role of schools in providing mental health treatment to youth, and effectiveness of community-based residential care (particularly treatment foster care and group homes).

Robert M. Friedman, Ph.D., is Professor and Chair of the Department of Child and Family Studies at the Louis de la Parte Florida Mental Health Institute, University of South Florida. Dr. Friedman is a clinical psychologist who received his B.A. from Brooklyn College, and his M.S.

and Ph.D. from Florida State University. Since 1984 Dr. Friedman has served as Director of the Research and Training Center for Children's Mental Health. He is a researcher, author, policy analyst, and consultant on issues such as the development and evaluation of community-based systems of care, prevalence of emotional disorders in children, new developments in service delivery, and the relationship between the mental health system and other systems. Dr. Friedman has published and presented more than 140 papers and articles. Dr. Friedman is coauthor with Beth Stroul of "A System of Care for Children and Youth with Severe Emotional Disturbances," a monograph on systems of care which has been widely used across the country to plan service delivery systems. He is also coeditor of a Paul H. Brookes book series on systems of care, coeditor of several special journals on children's mental health, and coeditor of *Advocacy on Behalf of Children with Serious Emotional Problems.*

Kimberly Hoagwood, Ph.D., is Associate Director of Child and Adolescent Mental Health Research with the National Institute of Mental Health. She is the leader of the Child and Adolescent Research Consortium, a forum for interdisciplinary scientists across National Institute of Health, whose mission is to set research priorities for the advancement of science in child and adolescent mental health. Dr. Hoagwood directs two research programs at NIMH, and has had a long-standing commitment to mental health services and treatment research. Prior to her appointment at NIMH, Dr. Hoagwood was Research Director at the Texas Education Agency, where she supervised a statewide, multidisciplinary program of research on community-based services for children with serious emotional, behavioral, and psychiatric disorders. Dr. Hoagwood earned her doctorate in school psychology in 1987, and practiced clinically for 9 years. She has held academic appointments at the Pennsylvania State University and the University of Maryland. She has received numerous grants and awards, including the American Psychological Association's Distinguished Contribution award. Among her many publications are articles and books examining the clinical effectiveness of children's services, national psychotropic medication prescribing practices, research ethics, and genetic epistemology in the work of Gabriel Garcia Marquez.

Henry T. Ireys, Ph.D., is Senior Researcher at Mathematica Policy Research in Washington, D.C., and Adjunct Associate Professor in the Department of Population and Family Health Sciences at the Bloomberg School of Public Health at the Johns Hopkins University. Dr. Ireys has authored numerous reports on the outcomes of randomized trials of community-based support programs for families of children with chronic illnesses. In addition, he has been active in policy research pertaining to systems of care for children with special needs.

Peter S. Jensen, M.D., is Director of the Center for the Advancement of Children's Mental Health and Ruane Professor of Psychiatry, College of Physicians and Surgeons at Columbia University. Formerly NIMH Associate Director for Child & Adolescent Research, Dr. Jensen is the author of over 150 scientific papers and book chapters, and has served as the lead NIMH investigator on the multisite Multimodal Treatment of ADHD study (the MTA).

Krista Kutash, Ph.D., is Associate Professor in the Department of Child and Family Studies, Louis de la Parte Florida Mental Health Institute, University of South Florida, and serves as the Deputy Director of the Research and Training Center for Children's Mental Health. Her academic background includes a B.S. degree in Social Work, a MBA with a specialty in Econometrics, and a Ph.D. in Measurement and Evaluation. Her research, training, and consultation activities have made her a nationally recognized authority on improving services for youth with emotional disorders and their families. She has authored two books and has numerous publications and presentations on the topic of services research and evaluation. Her areas of interest include mental health services research and policy analysis for youth with emotional or behavioral disorders, research on school reform and restructuring, and research on treatment fidelity.

Andres J. Pumariega, M.D., is Professor and Director of Child and Adolescent Psychiatry in the Department of Psychiatry and Behavioral Sciences of the James H. Quillen College of Medicine of East Tennessee State University. He has previously served as Director of Child and Adolescent Psychiatry at the University of Texas Medical Branch and the University of South Carolina, as well as Chair of Psychiatry at ETSU. He has been a leader in community child and adolescent psychiatry and community-based systems of care for children's mental health, serving as founding Chair of the Work Group on Community-Based Systems of Care of the American Academy of Child and Adolescent Psychiatry and Chair of the Child Psychiatry Committee of the American Association of Community Psychiatry. His areas of research have included cultural competence in children's mental health, children's mental health services research, and psychopharmacology.

Elizabeth B. Robertson, Ph.D., has been the Chief of the Prevention Research Branch at the National Institute on Drug Abuse since 1997. In that capacity she has broadened the focus of the drug abuse and drug-related HIV infection to include a developmental focus from early childhood through adulthood. In addition, other prevention intervention contexts such as the family, clinical settings, and the media have been targeted for growth. High priority areas for continued portfolio development include the integration of basic prevention research (understanding the underlying biological, social, emotional, and cognitive processes that account for intervention success or failure), and prevention services research. Prior to coming to NIDA, Dr. Robertson led an intramural research program on rural substance abuse for the United States Department of Agriculture's Agricultural Research Service. She has published articles on the contributions of social support and economic stress to family dysfunction and poor adolescent outcomes, the effects of social and biological transitions on adolescent problem behavior, substance abuse among rural children, adolescents, and adults, and the availability and utilization of drug abuse treatment services in rural areas.

Melisa D. Rowland, M.D., is Assistant Professor of Psychiatry and Behavioral Sciences in the Family Services Research Center of the Medical University of South Carolina. Much of Dr. Rowland's research involves developing, implementing, and evaluating clinically effective family-based interventions for youth presenting with severe emotional and behavioral problems. Currently, she has a NIDA-funded K12 award focusing on the development of empirically-grounded, community-based treatments for youth presenting with substance use disorders. She also serves as co-investigator for an Annie E. Casey funded research evaluation of the clinical and cost effectiveness of a multisystemic therapy (MST)-based continuum of services and she served as project coordinator of the large NIMH-funded clinical trial in which youth in psychiatric crisis were randomly assigned to MST family preservation or psychiatric hospitalization.

Diane Sakwa, MBA, founded Families Involved Together (FIT), a parent-led advocacy organization in Baltimore, Maryland. She has been its Director since its beginning in 1991, and has served on numerous councils and commissions to help improve child mental health services. As a parent of a child with a severe emotional disorder, Ms. Sakwa understands the challenges and desperation of raising a child with special needs. Under her leadership, FIT aims to create and sustain a community of families who help each other to recognize the role that families must play in the mental health service system for children.

Sonja K. Schoenwald, Ph.D., is Associate Professor of Psychiatry and Behavioral Sciences and Associate Director of the Family Services Research Center at the Medical University of South Carolina. She received her undergraduate degree in psychology from Stanford University and her doctoral degree in clinical psychology from Duke University. Her research focuses on the development, empirical validation, and dissemination of clinically and cost-effective mental health services for youth with complex clinical problems and their families. Dr. Schoenwald has taken a leadership role in developing the clinical training and consultation protocols used to transport multisystemic therapy (MST) to communities in 25 states, Canada, and Norway, and in the development of research to investigate the transportability and dissemination of evidence-based practices for children and families.

Booney Vance, Ph.D., is Associate Professor and Director of Research, Division of Child and Adolescent Psychiatry, Department of Child and Adolescent Psychiatry and Behavioral Sciences of The Quillen College of Medicine at East Tennessee State University. Dr. Vance has previously served as Chairperson of the Department of Psychology and Education at the University of Maryland, Eastern Shore; Special Assistant to the President, East Tennessee State University; and Director of James Madison University's Child Development Clinic. He has been a consultant to numerous countries in the Middle East and Gulf Region. His areas of research have included psychometric qualities of the WISC-11 and WISC-111, the learning disabled child, and behavior interventions for the elderly in nursing homes.

J. Eric Vance, M.D., was Chief Clinical Consultant for the Willie M. Program for Aggressive Youth in the State of North Carolina. He is currently Associate Medical Director for Children's Services at Seacoast Mental Health Center, Inc. in New Hampshire, where he provides clinical supervision for mental health professionals and paraprofessionals, focused on building protective factors into the lives of youths with severe emotional disorders. He continues to be involved in the development of several mentoring programs for high-risk youth, including a current program in evolution in Portsmouth, New Hampshire, training off-duty police officers to serve as mentors for court-involved high-risk youth. Dr. Vance frequently provides consultation to schools, social service agencies, and state legislative study committees in relation to interventions for vulnerable youth populations, especially implementing the use of mentors and interventions to build resiliency.

Hill M. Walker, Ph.D., is Professor of Special Education, Co-Director of the Institute on Violence and Destructive Behavior, and Director of the Center on Human Development at the University of Oregon. He has a long standing interest in behavioral assessment and in the development of effective intervention procedures for use in school settings with a range of behavior disorders. He is the developer of *First Step for Success*; coauthor, along with Herbert Severson, of *Systematic Screening for Behavior Disorders*; author of *The Acting Out Child: Coping with Classroom Disruption*; and coauthor, along with Geoffrey Colvin and Elizabeth Ramsey, of *Antisocial Behavior in School: Strategies and Best Practices*.

John R. Weisz, Ph.D., is Professor in the Departments of Psychology, Psychiatry, and Biobehavioral Sciences at the University of California, Los Angeles. He received his B.A. from Mississippi College, and his M.S. and Ph.D. from Yale University. He has held faculty positions at Cornell and the University of North Carolina at Chapel Hill. His work focuses on psychological treatments for youth. He is immediate Past-President of the Society of Clinical Child and Adolescent Psychology, and current President of the International Society for the Study of Child and Adolescent Psychopathology.

Index